Medieval London Houses

Medieval London Houses

JOHN SCHOFIELD

PUBLISHED FOR
THE PAUL MELLON CENTRE FOR STUDIES IN BRITISH ART BY
YALE UNIVERSITY PRESS · NEW HAVEN AND LONDON · 1994

Set in Ehrhardt by Best-set Typesetter Ltd., Hong Kong
Printed in Hong Kong through World Print Ltd.

Library of Congress Cataloging-in-Publication Data

Schofield, John, 1948–
    Medieval London houses/John Schofield.
        p.   cm.
    Includes bibliographical references and index.
    1. Architecture, Domestic—Expertising—England—
London.   2. Architecture, Medieval—England—London.
3. London (England)—Buildings, structures, etc.   I. Paul
Mellon Centre for Studies in British Art.   II. Title.
NA7332.S36   1995
728′.09421′0902—dc20   94-36805
                                        CIP

A catalogue record for this book is available from the British
Library.

Title pages illustration: Low-level panorama of the London
waterfront from the south, *c.* 1550. It shows medieval St Paul's
and the western half of the City. Artist unknown.

Contents

Preface and Acknowledgements

This research grew out of my work on archaeological sites in the City of London from 1974. I am grateful to the Museum of London for financial support during research for the PhD on which this study is based, and for access to many Museum facilities. I am also conscious of a great debt to many colleagues in the former Department of Urban Archaeology, and later of the Museum of London Archaeology Service: Tony Dyson, Charlotte Harding, Richard Lea, Gustav Milne and Andrew Westman.

I would like to thank the staff of all the libraries in which I have worked; in particular I wish to thank Ralph Hyde, John Fisher and Jeremy Smith at Guildhall Library Print Room, but also staff of the Ashmolean Museum, the Greater London Record Office, and David Wickham the archivist of the Clothworkers' Company. The Central Research Fund of the University of London supported study tours in Europe in 1982 and 1983. The Leverhulme Foundation and the Paul Mellon Centre for Studies in British Art supported work on the illustrations for this book.

The drawings in this book are by Alison Hawkins, who redrew all the Treswell plans, Alison Balfour-Lynn, Susan Banks, David Bentley, Julie Carr, Sal Garfi, Jenny Hill, Richard Lea, Susan Mitford and Tracy Wellman. The photographs are mainly the work of Andy Chopping, Maggie Cox, Trevor Hurst, Godfrey New and Jan Scrivener. Other photographs are credited below. The text has been prepared at various times by Janet Taylor and Diana Twells. My thanks also to John Nicoll, Stephanie Hallin and Faith Hart at Yale University Press.

Finally, my grateful thanks to individuals who have guided my research at many important points: Caroline Barron, Derek Keene and especially Tony Dyson.

An earlier version of Chapter 6 appeared in the journal *Construction History*, **7**, in 1991.

The author and publishers are grateful to the following for permission to reproduce illustrations: Ashmolean Museum, panorama on title pages, 7–9, 17–18, 20, 23, 38, 41–2, 107, 119–20, 168, 227, 252–3, 257; Caroline Barron and Terry Ball, 10–11; Bildarchiv Preussischer Kulturbesitz, 152; Board of the British Library, 46–7; Trustees of the British Museum, 19; Worshipful Company of Carpenters, 143–6; Guildhall Library, 6, 13, 34, 36, 39, 44, 52–3, 71, 72a, 73, 79, 89, 94–6, 99, 109–13, 117, 140–2, 149, 169, 174, 176, 178–9, 181, 186–7, 189–90, 195, 211, 215, 221–2, 224, 226, 230–2, 240; Worshipful Company of Merchant Taylors, 77; Museum of London, 2, 3, 5, 12, 14–16, 21, 25–33, 35, 37, 40, 43b, 45, 55–6, 63, 66–9, 72b, 74a, 78, 82a, 83–5, 88, 90c, 92–3, 97, 103–5, 114–16, 118, 121–39, 144–6, 151, 153–67, 170–3, 182–4, 196–7, 199–201, 206–7, 237–9, 244–7, 250–1, 254, 264; Royal Commission on Historical Monuments (England) (National Monuments Record), 51, 81, 87, 119, 148, 175, 177, 180, 208, 223; Sir John Soane Museum, 64, 108; Society of Antiquaries, 82b–c, 90a–b; Society of Lincoln's Inn, 102; Yale Center for British Art, Paul Mellon Collection, 261.

Note

Numbers that appear in **bold** in the text refer to Gazetteer entries, which are listed in the latter half of this book.

Square brackets in the captions indicate bibliographic references.

KEY to functions of rooms and open spaces on the plans:

B	Buttery	H	Hall	Sh	Pantry
C	Cellar	K	Kitchen	St	Study
Ch	Chamber	P	Parlour	W	Warehouse
Co	Counting house	Pa	Pantry	Wa	Washhouse
E	Entry	Sb	Stable	Wh	Waterhouse
G	Garden	Sd	Shed	Y	Yard

CHAPTER I

Introduction and Survey of Sources

The evidence addressed in this study is drawn from six main sources: surviving buildings; archaeological excavation; documentary records; panoramas, drawn surveys and plans; contemporary descriptions; and later engravings, photographs and other illustrations. These have combined to produce a selective gazetteer of 201 sites or groups of buildings which are in one way or another illustrative of the various kinds of house-form, construction and decoration present in London in the 400 years from the beginning of the thirteenth century to the opening years of the seventeenth.

The seventeen surviving fragments of secular buildings of this period in the City of London (this study does not include those within the Tower of London) are a peculiar group, the product of chance survival after the Great Fire of London in 1666 and three subsequent centuries of commercial re-development.[1] At Guildhall, traces of three successive stone buildings (two of which can be examined today) have been recorded;[2] elsewhere in the city are fragments of four smaller undercrofts, including one below Merchant Taylors' Hall (**148**, **177**, **186**, cf. **172**), two timber buildings above gateways in Fleet Street and at Smithfield (**77**, **188**), and fifteenth- or sixteenth-century halls and other buildings at five inns of lawyers, nearly all restored after considerable war damage (**47**, **78**, **94**, **103**, **105**). In Southwark the west gable of the hall of the Bishop of Winchester's town-house (**193**) can be seen, and to the north-west of the city a large part of a late sixteenth-century noble residence is preserved in the Charterhouse (**48**). To this group of *in situ* remains should be added the hall of Crosby Place (**22**), removed to Chelsea, and the façade of Paul Pindar's house in Bishopsgate (**28**), now in the Victoria and Albert Museum.

These are almost all fragments of well-built, prestigious buildings, and though a small number of London undercrofts date from the thirteenth century (most notably, the west undercroft of Guildhall), the majority of the standing remains date from the fifteenth or sixteenth century. It is axiomatic that only the better sort of building would have survived into early modern times even if the Great Fire of London had not taken place. The buildings which were recorded by eighteenth- and nineteenth-century antiquaries were also generally the more remarkable or durable structures, such as stone undercrofts, or the buildings of the late medieval and post-medieval period; a similar pattern can be found both in the region and in other medieval English towns where more has survived.[3]

The fragments of buildings of the period in London are notable for including a large number of halls and their roofs, constituting a major source of information. The physical bulk of Guildhall's walls has preserved enough evidence to make possible a reconstruction of its original roof.[4] Smaller fifteenth-century roofs survive at Barnard's Hall and Lincoln's Inn; the ornamented ceiling of Crosby Hall, now at

Chelsea, appears to be in a class of its own as a domestic construction. The halls at Gray's Inn (1560), Middle Temple (1572) and Staple Inn (1581) show the progressive introduction of Renaissance details into the woodwork of the medieval assembly-hall.[5] Two Tudor gatehouses, both too large to be used in a study of domestic buildings except by way of analogy, survive at Lambeth Palace (1490) and Lincoln's Inn (1519);[6] but Merchant Taylors' Hall still retains its fourteenth-century kitchen, serving as an example of a building type which was probably widespread among larger medieval residences and company halls.

Four fairly complete examples and several fragments of undercrofts survive inside modern buildings. Guildhall's two undercrofts, of *c.* 1270 and 1410–30, are both of three aisles, as befits a structure below a large public building (see Chapter 2, below); the domestic undercrofts, where known, were smaller structures of two aisles or, more commonly, one row of vaulted bays. These one-row undercrofts ran either at right angles to the street down the side of a property or under the street-range of a larger complex. In several prominent tenements of courtyard plan, the hall was also raised on an undercroft which might be vaulted in stone; this practice continued into the second half of the fifteenth century, when brick was employed to form vaulted cellars beneath the halls at Crosby Place (1466–75) and Lincoln's Inn (1489). The surviving buildings also provide examples of windows, doors, stairs and fireplaces.

Though all these buildings have suffered great damage and undergone much restoration, they remain a small corpus of construction techniques in stone, brick and timber. Guildhall, in its various successive forms, provides datable examples of stonework and mouldings from the fifteenth-century hall, undercroft and porch. The introduction of brick during the fifteenth century can be traced in the surviving undercrofts and other structures, for instance the hall, chambers and gatehouse at Lincoln's Inn (1489–1520). By contrast, the timbers now seen in medieval and Tudor buildings in the city are heavily restored. The frontage of Staple Inn to Holborn of 1586 was probably not originally built to look as Waterhouse restored it in 1894; it seems to have had small panels and not close studding. Similarly the restorations of Prince Henry's Room, Fleet Street, and at West Smithfield cannot be guaranteed, though both structures incorporate original material. The notable screen of 1574 at Middle Temple was restored from hundreds of pieces after war damage.

Secondly, pre-Fire domestic buildings have been excavated on a number of sites in the city, all since the Second World War. The sites lie in two zones of differing potential: the waterfront area south of Thames Street, where the deposits are exceptionally deep due to the frequent raising of the ground level against the Thames, and the rest of the city

inland, where medieval remains have been destroyed by later building (especially nineteenth-century cellars) to a far greater degree.[7]

Excavation on the known sites of three great residences have produced partial plans: Neville's Inn (**153**), Warwick Inn (**185**) and the Inn of the Bishop of Bath in the Strand (**157**), where Hollar's engravings of 1646 and map evidence place an excavated undercroft and other walls in a recognisable context. At Warwick Inn and Bath Inn, courtyard houses of the fourteenth century are indicated. Fragments of more ordinary domestic buildings are commonly found on sites throughout the city, but on inland sites, apart from fortuitous survivals such as the undercroft supporting a post-Fire building at 7–8 Philpot Lane (**148**, cf. **186**), the remains which survive to be recorded are only the deeper foundations, cesspits and wells. The waterfront zone provides fuller evidence, in the form of building and property plans from the twelfth to the sixteenth centuries, constructional details and internal or external features.[8] These include parts of undercrofts with vaulting arrangements, doors and windows, cellars, wells and cesspits (e.g. **31–2, 71, 117**). Destruction debris can include fragments of tile floors, door and window mouldings, timbers and rooftiles. Archaeological investigations, particularly the large-scale exercises since 1973, have also produced two further major sources of evidence: a series of well-preserved wooden riverside revetments (e.g. **164, 171–2**), with a corpus of timber carpentry which is otherwise largely absent from the city or its records;[9] and many objects, currently under study, which include house fittings such as locks, window and door fittings, candlesticks, window cames and glass, and perhaps fragments of furniture.[10]

A third main source is reconstruction from documentary records. For direct comparison with the surviving or archaeological evidence this depends on density of information over a long period, and sufficient information of the right type (e.g. measured dimensions).

Before 1250, historical sources such as charters, deeds, rentals and chronicles are available almost by accident, surviving in the records of a small number of large religious institutions – St Paul's, Westminster Abbey, the priory of Holy Trinity Aldgate, for example. After 1250 the city government attempted to record changes of property ownership and the wills of citizens more systematically. From these it is usually possible to reconstruct the ownership and layout of properties on archaeological sites. Occasionally, but rarely, measurements are supplied. One can normally tell how many properties existed in the medieval period; occasionally details of buildings upon them; and sometimes personal details about their owners and their families. More tends to be forthcoming from properties along the waterfront, which seem to have changed hands more often; or from sites which were additionally a matter of royal or civic concern, such as properties near the defences or close to public buildings.[11]

The problem, at the outset, was how to choose a sample of these records in the time available for the thesis on which this book is based; documentary records were only one of six main types of evidence to be investigated. Since the object of the study was to describe buildings, records of property ownership and land tenure were not necessarily the main focus of attention. It was decided to concentrate on those records

which illuminated either contemporary building-plans (most notably, the series by Ralph Treswell in 1607–14) or archaeological sites. In addition, a small number of bodies of archival information were deliberately chosen as medium-sized, 'typical' institutions of the kind which between them can reasonably be taken to offer a fair idea of standard practice, procedures and attitudes to the construction and maintenance of buildings in medieval and Tudor London, and which could be amplified at appropriate points from a necessarily more selective reference to the archives of other institutions. These chosen archives, in descending order of frequency of use, have been (a) a livery company, the Clothworkers' Company; (b) a post-monastic hospital, Christ's Hospital (founded 1552); and, to a lesser extent, (c) a monastic archive, that of Holy Trinity Priory, Aldgate (*HTA Cartulary*). What follows is a review of the wider spectrum of documentary sources, with notes on their use in this study.

A prime documentary source has been the records of livery companies. Eighty-three companies existed in or before 1666. Only a small number of companies owned property by 1500, but many preserved records which trace their acquired properties back to the fourteenth and occasionally to the twelfth centuries. Company records proper are numerous in the fifteenth and sixteenth centuries; they consist of deeds and wills, rentals and accounts, court minute books, plans and views.[12] Livery company records have provided information on three topics in particular: the appearance of the company halls and their associated buildings; accounts of company property in the city; and details of property management by the companies, though these have only been noted incidentally.

Stow mentions the sites of forty-six company halls; a further seven are shown on Hollar's map of the fire-damaged area in 1667, and a further five on the map produced by Ogilby and Morgan in 1677 (surveyed in 1676). These fifty-eight halls are noted in the gazetteer, along with a number of other properties which functioned as halls before the companies moved to the sites noted by Stow. The records of these sixty hall-complexes (building and repair accounts, and a small number of plans) are a prime source of information about the appearance of the main rooms in the medieval domestic complex; the hall, parlour and kitchen (**52, 96, 128, 139, 144, 147, 149, 162, 166, 173, 177–8**). Details of medieval gardens (**128, 139, 178**) and of almshouses (**1, 34, 60, 131, 147, 177, 183**) are also substantially from this source.

Before the Great Fire of 1666 there were fifty-four companies who had records of property-ownership in the city.[13] The more prominent companies such as the Goldsmiths, Grocers and Merchant Taylors began to acquire property in the fourteenth century. Many lost a proportion of those lands held for chantry purposes in 1548, but in the following half-century there was a spate of bequests of lands to companies, or of funds from which lands were bought. The Goldsmiths had so much property that by 1478 they had what was in effect a clerk of works to supervise craftsmen carrying out repairs; the company had its own builder's yard for materials and in 1496 appointed an official carpenter, with a house rent-free. They and other companies put marks on their property as an aid to definition of boundaries.[14] Until about 1560, rebuilding of a secular property in London generally fell to

the landlord, and thus building accounts are especially full until that date; thereafter responsibility for rebuilding generally passed to the tenant, and repairs can only be perceived in company records via the view, a usually annual perambulation of the company's properties.[15]

The company estate chosen for special scrutiny has been that of the Clothworkers' Company in the city, which was surveyed and delineated in 1612 by Ralph Treswell (**14–15, 33, 46, 55–7, 61–2, 69–70, 72, 74, 76, 86, 101, 133, 139–40, 142, 168–9, 176, 179, 183–4, 189–90**).[16] The conjunction of surveyed plans (whose character is outlined below) with a good survival of other documentation (chiefly the Company's Court Orders (CCO), Book of Deeds and Wills (CDW), boxes of deeds (CD), and Renter Wardens' Accounts (CRW)) makes possible the most detailed reconstructions of individual properties during the later sixteenth century. Building accounts are available for several houses of 1537–65 which were surveyed, perhaps not much altered, in 1612 (**14, 72, 133, 139**). Properties (apart from their halls) of other companies appear in the gazetteer only if there is a pre-Fire plan (**67**) or a notable body of information (**49, 123**).

A second major documentary source has been the records of a corporate institution, Christ's Hospital (founded 1552; records in the Guildhall Library); extensive documentation and a second series of surveys (of 1607–14) by Ralph Treswell survive, providing histories of a wide range of houses whose plans and extent are known (**3, 7, 10, 12, 26, 35, 88, 109, 145, 147, 150, 154, 181, 194, 196**).[17] Whereas a portion of the Clothworkers' estate was assembled by 1530, all the Christ's Hospital estate resulted from bequests or purchases in the period *c.* 1570–1610, and thus there is a higher proportion of property which was formerly in religious hands (monastic or chantry) within the Christ's Hospital portfolio.

In medieval London, religious houses and bishoprics were the most numerous type of landowner and landlord – over 170 English religious houses and bishoprics held property or advowsons in London.[18] These records have been sampled via printed calendars: notably, the cartulary of Holy Trinity Priory, Aldgate (*HTA Cartulary*), which has been useful for charting the early tenurial histories of several properties. Other religious bodies in medieval London whose records have been consulted include St Paul's, the priory of St Mary Clerkenwell, and St Bartholomew's Hospital.[19] The upheaval of the Dissolution transferred many London properties of the religious houses into secular ownership, and often into the guardianship of secular institutions, particularly the livery companies and Christ's Hospital; and thus the surveys of Ralph Treswell in 1607–14 include plans of properties belonging or paying quit-rents, seventy years previously, to religious houses such as Holy Trinity Priory, Aldgate (**10, 139, 154**), St Mary Overey Priory, Southwark (**194, 196**) and St Mary Spital (**26, 72**). The former Hermitage of St James's in Monkwell Street (**140**) had previously belonged to Garendon Abbey in Leicestershire. Many of the other properties in the gazetteer had probably belonged to religious houses at some time during their history.

The records (churchwardens' accounts, vestry minutes, cartularies, views, assessments and other records) of thirteen parishes which had comparatively good pre-Fire documentation have also been examined.[20] As with the property of religious houses, the large-scale transfer of parish lands, particularly chantry property, at the Reformation had the consequence that ex-parish property figures significantly in the surveys of Ralph Treswell at the opening of the seventeenth century: parts of the former estate of the Fraternity of Holy Trinity of St Botolph Aldersgate (**7**), St Andrew Baynard Castle (**13**) and ex-chantry property in Pudding Lane (**150**). Though recent work[21] on the records of the Fraternity of Holy Trinity has been valuable, parish records as a group seem to be comparatively unfruitful. Apart from a contract with the parish of St Swithun (**44**), only one further gazetteer entry was derived mainly from parish records alone: a large house in Botolph Lane bequeathed to the parish of St Mary at Hill in 1472 (**30**). Otherwise parish records have been useful for details concerning repairs and materials for parish properties; for charting the pressure on certain churchyards by adjacent secular building, and later by the parishes themselves in building on strips adjacent to the church, especially shops; and for information on the use of taverns by parish councils from the second half of the fifteenth century (for these last two processes, see Chapter 3).

A third class of relevant documents has been building contracts or detailed building leases, arranged for a variety of landlords or clients. Sixteen examples dating from 1308 to 1532 relate to domestic buildings in the City of London or Southwark; they deal mainly with the erection of blocks of shops, but also include a tavern, a garden gallery and two complete domestic complexes (**2, 11, 40, 44, 87, 89–90, 114, 141, 146, 175, 191–2, 199**).[22] These contracts provide accurately dated examples of room sizes, plan form and constructional details of many kinds. They supply the earliest documented examples of developments, perhaps peculiar to London, of the first-floor kitchen by 1308, and second-floor privies by 1310. Later, by contrast, the declining occurrence of the term *solar* in contracts after 1373 may indicate that the term itself fell out of use in the city, as buildings with more than two storeys became the norm in London streets. The contracts give dated examples of major rooms in better houses, and the size and position of a hall, parlour or kitchen can be reconstructed in outline. Six of the sixteen contracts are for blocks of shops, varying from three to twenty shops in size; and four of these six are from the period 1369–83. This might be an accident of survival, but it might also reflect a resurgence of construction as the city recovered from the Black Death. As a group also the contracts provide evidence, complementary to the archaeological record, for the disposition of privies and sizes of timbers used in construction, though generally the contracts are more concerned with the forms of future buildings than with building materials.

Other records of land-owners and occupiers have been used to fill out the picture. Wills of London citizens could be enrolled in other courts besides, or in addition to, the Husting; the choice 'being determined principally by the nature and extent of the testator's estate and his place of residence'.[23] The decision, on practical grounds, not to investigate wills thoroughly means that inventories have not been systematically sought or collected, though an extension to the present study could profitably do this.[24]

Members of the royal family held properties in the city at various times, but there was no extensive long-term Crown

holding in London and the topic is not addressed here. Some houses in the gazetteer had intervals of royal ownership (e.g. Coldharbour II in Thames Street, **170**). Records of royal interest or jurisdiction, largely concerning the more substantial town-houses of nobles and prominent citizens, have been sampled by means of printed calendars and summaries.[25] In particular, inquisitions post-mortem relating to London have been found useful in reconstructing some property histories (*Inq. PM*, 1485–1603). Details of the town-houses and wardrobe accounts of nobles or distant members of the royal family are accessible in printed sources, notably in studies by C. L. Kingsford in *London Topographical Record* (*LTR*, x–xiii).[26]

The City itself owned comparatively few domestic properties at this period, although in the course of the fourteenth and fifteenth centuries lands were left to the City for charitable purposes and areas of 'common soil' were taken more firmly into the City's care. In addition the City managed the Bridge House Estates, which produced an income to maintain London Bridge. The properties forming this estate were largely acquired by the mid fourteenth century. For the present study only the building accounts have been examined, but it is clear that further information could be abstracted from records of the Bridge House and other City Lands; study of the early eighteenth-century plans in the City Lands Plan Books (CLRO), for example, would provide information on literally dozens of sixteenth-century buildings, especially those built over the city ditch.[27]

The administrative and judicial records of the City are especially full after 1300.[28] The main administrative records used in this study have been the Letter Books (*Cal. LB*, *A* etc., 1275–1498), the Repertories of the Court of Aldermen (CLRO, 1495–1600) and Journals of the Court of Common Council (CLRO, 1416–1600), the last two often by means of the card index in CLRO (CCPR). The main judicial records are the calendars of the Mayor's Court Rolls (*Cal. EMCR*, 1298–1307), and of the Plea and Memoranda Rolls (*Cal. Plea & Mem. R.*, 1323–1482). The deeds entered on the Husting Rolls (CLRO, 1258–1600) have been sampled with specific questions or sites in mind.

Building regulations form an important sub-group of city records. According to tradition, regulations encouraging the use of stone in building for settling boundary disputes between neighbours were drawn up in the mayoralty of Henry Fitzailwin in 1189.[29] This *Assisa de Edificiis* was frequently copied by compilers of the city's custumals, and the cleanest text survives in *Letter Book C*, dating to the early fourteenth century. A further series of regulation was drawn up under Fitzailwin after a fire in 1212; these cover roof materials and other fire-prevention measures. This body of regulation was the basis of procedure in cases of *Assize of Nuisance* (surviving records for 1301–1427), in which the mayor and aldermen, informed in many cases by the specialist advice of the Viewers (appointed masons and carpenters), decided in cases of complaint about building operations brought by one neighbour against another. The Viewers' certificates survive for the period 1509–53. These court cases, and the later reports, are extremely valuable evidence for the problems of day-to-day maintenance of medieval buildings which were very often constructed of timber, lath and plaster, and constantly sus-

ceptible to penetration by rainwater or leaking sewage. The disputes are full of illustrative anecdotes concerning drains, gutters and cesspits, but also boundaries, fences, chimneys, overhanging buildings, encroachments, access, doors and windows.

Apart from a very few crude sketches, the pictorial evidence for London begins in the period 1480–3 with the view of London, including the Tower, in the poems of Charles, Duke of Orleans,[30] and, two generations later, the panorama by van Wyngaerde of *c.* 1540.[31] Wyngaerde's drawing is especially useful for details of house-construction, since he offers a close-up of the borough in Southwark and its surrounding buildings (Figs. 7–9, 17–18, 20, 23; for Southwark, Figs. 42, 110, 119, 167–8). Despite the dating of the watermark on sheets of the panorama to 1544–6, a date of *c.* 1540 for the drawing of the London view is preferred here. The main pieces of evidence for dating are the changing of the dedication of the chapel on the bridge from St Thomas Becket to (as on Wyngaerde) St Thomas Apostle (after 1538); the tower of Holy Trinity Priory is shown before its radical semi-demolition by Audley before his death in 1544 (site 8); Holywell Priory (destroyed by 1544) is shown; and Somerset House (1549) is not shown. The copperplate map, and the derivative wood-cut 'Agas' map (*c.* 1559, amended for the surviving impressions *c.* 1570),[32] occasionally give significant information but are most useful for showing the relative density of the built-up areas both within and outside the city walls in the mid sixteenth century.

Several further panoramas or map-views, all from the south, were drawn and engraved in subsequent years. The most useful are the anonymous 'low-level' view of the London waterfront *c.* 1550 attributed (probably wrongly) to Wyngaerde (Fig. 41); the woodcut map-view of *c.* 1550 in the Pepysian collection, Magdalen College, Cambridge; the map by Braun and Hogenberg in *Civitates Orbis Terrarum* (1572–1618); the panorama of *c.* 1600 by Norden, and that of about the same time by Visscher, which was based on Norden.[33] The engravings of Hollar are also extremely useful: his panorama of 1647 features the city waterfront and Southwark (Figs. 24, 261) and other drawings include a plan of the Steelyard (used in Fig. 22), views of the Royal Exchange (e.g. Fig. 25), Bath or Arundel House (Figs. 35, 45) and the remarkable bird's-eye view of the Strand in 1656 (Figs. 46–7).[34]

Pre-Fire London appears in the background of a number of paintings, but contemporary paintings of individual secular buildings are few. Those used in this study include the painting, later engraved, of the Coronation Procession of Edward VI which shows Cheapside (Figs. 63, 131),[35] and the interior of an office at the Steelyard (Fig. 152).

Ground-plans of houses in London before the end of the sixteenth century are both very few and generally restricted to the outline of the site only.[36] During the second half of the sixteenth century, however, probably due to the great increase in the land market consequent upon both the Dissolution and the Reformation, the land surveyor became an established profession. Especially useful are two collections of house-plans by Ralph Treswell the elder, who surveyed property for the Clothworkers' Company and for Christ's Hospital in 1607–14 (the majority of plans are dated 1610–

12).[37] Together, the two collections feature fifty-three blocks of London property. The majority are ground-plans of individual buildings, or groups of contiguous buildings, with doorways, stairs and chimneys shown, along with yards and gardens. Timber-framed walls are ubiquitous, with brick walls shown in red and occasional stone walls identifiable by their width. In the majority of cases the plans are accompanied by a text of reference describing, with measurements, the upper chambers of each building. Thus the buildings can be reconstructed in three dimensions – though the height of each storey is lacking – and statistics concerning the size of rooms, the number of rooms in each tenancy, the proportion that were heated, and the proportions of groundspace covered by buildings or cellared can be calculated. The plans also furnish examples of more specialised buildings: there are taverns (**181**, **194**), inns with extensive stables (**10**, **12**), a row of cookshops (**88**), company halls (**139**, **147**, cf. **127**) and almshouses (**147**, **183**). These surveys provide much of the information otherwise lacking in the archaeological record, which generally produces only the lower parts of foundations, cellars and wells. Valuable information is provided for plans of rooms, especially halls, parlours, kitchens, butteries and other service rooms, shops and warehouses, studies and closets; dimensions of rooms and above the ground floor and upper chambers such as galleries; and outside the houses, the extent of their gardens, and the position of wells and privies. Treswell's work provides a sample or snap-shot view of contemporary housing in the opening years of the seventeenth century, a picture of a townscape made up from many elements of different dates. It has proved difficult to identify the medieval cores, if they existed, of the buildings shown in the surveys. They do however provide a detailed picture of houses in the opening years of the seventeenth century without the centuries of subsequent alteration suffered by contemporary houses in other historic towns.

The two best-known descriptions of medieval London are William Fitzstephen's *Description of the Noble City of London*, written about 1174 as a prelude to a biography of St Thomas Becket, and which is largely too general for use here, and John Stow's *Survey of London* of 1598, published in 1603 (cited in this book simply as 'Stow'). Stow mentions over 200 secular buildings of interest in London and its immediate environs; 128 of these sites within the city and Southwark are included in the present gazetteer. They are almost all houses of nobles, or religious or civic dignitaries, though Stow also inspected excavations where he noted previous medieval buildings, along with Roman remains and finds. In 1586, during the rebuilding of Ludgate, he noted that the fabric produced a Hebrew inscription probably taken from one of the Jews' houses in 1215; in Leadenhall Street (then Aldgate Street) in 1590 he recorded remains of a possible early medieval undercroft.[38] Stow lamented the speed and brutality of the changes to buildings and to the urban landscape in his lifetime, changes which derived as he knew from the Reformation and from the massive influx of immigrants into late sixteenth-century London. He recorded with regret the breaking up of old buildings, though he also took pride in the increased prosperity of the Elizabethan city and the newer buildings which reflected that wealth. In one respect this present study begins with Stow's account of London, and

attempts to delve behind it into the buildings he passes over with little or no comment.

Accounts of London by contemporary foreign visitors have added significant perspectives at various points. In about 1500, a Venetian diplomat called London 'truly the metropolis (*metropoli*) of England'.[39] Comparison with the buildings, whether existing or now destroyed, of other European towns has been instructive throughout this study. Though this topic has not been addressed in great detail, one of the major conclusions of this study has been that we can now assemble for medieval and Tudor London a large body of information about its domestic buildings, sufficient in quantity and quality to compare with contemporary houses, shops and inns in places such as Venice, Siena, Florence, Budapest, Cologne, Bruges, Paris, Edinburgh, Goslar, Munich, Hamburg and Lübeck.

Many old buildings outside the area of the Great Fire were the subjects of engravings, sketches or watercolours in the eighteenth and nineteenth centuries, often on the eve of demolition. Engravings of notable individual London buildings were appearing by 1720[40] but the earliest significant body of work on pre-Fire secular buildings in London is Carter's *Views of Ancient Buildings* of 1786–93, which includes engravings of Ely Place (**106**) and Bermondsey Abbey gatehouse.[41] Crosby Place (**22**) appears in an engraving by Carter in the 1790 edition of Pennant's *History of London*, and J. T. Smith's celebrated *Antiquities of London*, drawn in 1791–1800, includes the earliest representations of the Gerard's Hall undercroft (**13**) and of timber framing in the London area – the rector's house at Newington Butts.[42] Engravings are useful not only for interior views of houses, halls and undercrofts, but especially for exterior views showing timber framing and detail such as exuberant carved timber-work. Even more valuable, because they were drawn on the spot, are the original antiquaries' sketches, only some of which were later engraved; the earliest original drawings used here, work by John Carter and Jacob Schnebbelie, date from the 1770s and 1780s. From the mid nineteenth century, photographs fill out the picture to a lesser but equally welcome extent, though archaeological draughtsmanship still preferred the watercolour and the pencil, as shown in the work of Thomas Shepherd, Henry Hodge and others.

The main types of evidence for the houses of medieval and Tudor London – surviving fragments, archaeological excavations, documentary records, panoramas, engravings and contemporary surveys (particularly those of John Stow and Ralph Treswell) – are largely complementary. Each type of evidence has both merits and shortcomings. The archaeological evidence is rich only in certain areas, such as along the waterfront or increasingly (as shown by the most recent discoveries) in the area in the north-east of the city, unaffected by the Great Fire. Deeds and wills tell of property owners and occupiers, but rarely give thorough descriptions of individual buildings. Panoramas and engravings are useful for details, and the former for providing overviews of the city, but both types of drawing may be selective in what they portray. Nevertheless, when used to illuminate each other, these various sources supply information for as detailed a picture of a medieval city as can be found anywhere in Europe.

CHAPTER 2

The Topographical Setting

The Site

The City of London today is virtually flat, except for a slight drop down to the river. Although it was never as hilly as Siena or Edinburgh, London's early stages of growth were moulded to contours, and only later were the inclines smoothed out in all directions (Fig. 1). The Roman city was founded on two low hills which formed plateaux on the north bank of the Thames, at the upstream edge of estuarine marshes. The topography of hills, streams and the initially steep slope down to the river conditioned the shape of the city and the position of its gates and of its major streets.[1] Natural features of the topography continued to influence boundaries, even of the city itself, throughout the medieval period; from perhaps the late twelfth century the city boundary at Charterhouse Lane was marked approximately by a length of Faggeswell Brook, and in 1422 the boundary between Middlesex and London near Holborn Bars was marked by a water-course, either a ditch or a stream.[2]

The two hills of London were divided by the Walbrook stream, and the western hill was bordered on its other, western, side by the larger Fleet. In both cases the mouth of the stream as it met the Thames, fairly wide in Roman times, was gradually constricted during the medieval period and the intramural course of the Walbrook was largely covered over by 1500.

The Walbrook was formed by a confluence of several streams in the northern part of the intramural city, with its main tributaries flowing in from north of the wall; the building of the Roman city wall across this area in the early third century may have contributed to the formation of the marsh later called the Moor, but this area was probably always boggy. In the medieval period the stream was a distinct topographical feature: in 1263 it was used to divide the wards into two groups, east and west.[3] Around 1300 the main course of the stream flowed past the chancel of St Stephen Walbrook, and the upkeep of a nearby bridge over the Walbrook was traditionally the responsibility of four adjacent tenements, indicated by posts fixed before them.[4] The tributaries were used as property boundaries,[5] and during the thirteenth and fourteenth centuries there were efforts to clear obstructions in or over the stream caused by buildings, firewood, beams, privies and pigsties.[6] By 1415, however, the banks of the stream near the Thames were being walled on the City's instruction, and the process of constriction accelerated.[7] By Stow's time the stream had been largely vaulted over with brick (shown in Treswell's plan of site **127**, below, Fig. 233) and paved level with the streets.[8] Even so, the area of the confluence of streams within the city wall was not densely built up until the seventeenth century.

North of the city wall lay the Common Moor, which was sufficiently waterlogged in 1301 to make inspection by boat necessary;[9] grates, occasionally cleaned, allowed the Walbrook through the wall.[10] Efforts were made to drain this area and dry it out by dumping soil in 1498, 1512 and 1527[11] which cumulatively raised the ground level by as much as 12 ft over a large area to form Moorfields.

The Fleet river cut a deep valley along the western side of the walled city. Roman bridges carried roads across the river at Fleet Street, where the bridge has recently been located in excavations, and presumably at Holborn. In 1307 the Earl of Lincoln complained that whereas boats could previously come under Fleet bridge and reach Holborn bridge, they were now prevented by the refuse of tanners, raising of the quay and diverting of the water to the Templars' mill below Castle Baynard (i.e. Baynard's Castle I).[12] Concern throughout the fourteenth century[13] may have had some effect, since two vessels of twenty tons were able to bring stones up to Holborn bridge for the paving of Holborn in 1417.[14] In 1502 the Fleet was scoured so that oyster and herring boats could row up to Holborn bridge and keep their markets there as they had before.[15] Concern with the state of the Fleet, and attempts to deepen it and remove wharves and privies, continued throughout the sixteenth century;[16] a property tax of a fifteenth granted for this purpose in 1589 raised much money but little practical success.[17] Another of Treswell's plans of 1612 (**76**; Fig. 49) vividly illustrates the problem.

Thus the occupied area of the city was gradually, but continually, changing its physical shape throughout these centuries, around the constraint of the medieval defences. The greatest change was the increase in area of the intramural city by as much as one sixth along the riverfront between the twelfth century and the end of the sixteenth, which is described further below. That extension, and the smaller reclamations into the Fleet valley, had consequences for the contours of the original ground surface beneath the rest of the city. After the Great Fire in 1666 much thought was given to the improvement of the city, and Thames Street was raised by between 2 and 8 ft along its whole length by using fire rubble; the usual heightening, measured at the foot of the many lanes reaching Thames Street from the north, was between 4 and 7 ft. The rubble was carefully graded to reduce the slope of these lanes, and a depth of between 1 and 3 ft removed from the streets such as Eastcheap which they met at their northern ends, and which marked the top of the original plateau. At Fleet Bridge, Ludgate Hill was raised by 6 ft.[18] The map of the medieval city onto which the contours of *c.* 1840 have been drawn (Fig. 1) does not therefore take account of these modifications; the hills and valleys of the medieval city were even more pronounced.

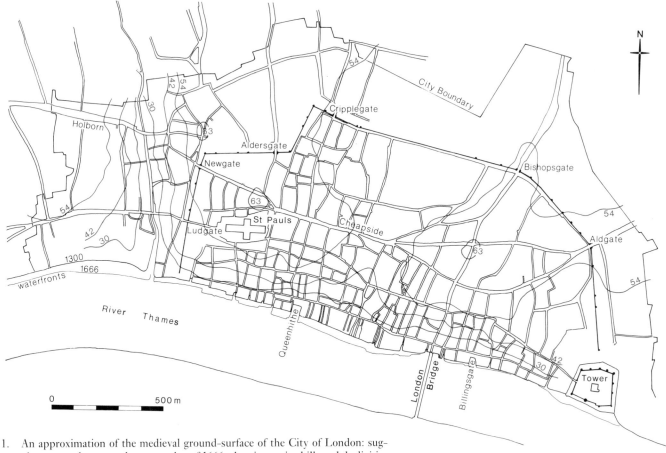

1. An approximation of the medieval ground-surface of the City of London: suggested contours drawn on the street-plan of 1666, showing major hills and declivities (after D. Bentley). The contours are in feet.

The Suburbs and Westminster

The land immediately surrounding the city was predominantly under cultivation until the spread of building which so horrified Stow and his contemporaries in the late sixteenth century. At the opening of the fourteenth century, for instance, the land immediately north of Holborn, outside one of the west gates of the city, included both arable and meadow.[19] The meadows were sometimes sold or leased to be dug for the extraction of sand or clay, both west of the city[20] and perhaps also to the east, outside Aldgate; archaeological investigation in this area often reveals shallow backfilled quarries.[21]

Beyond each of the five main gates stretched the suburbs, originally ribbon developments along major roads which, as in other towns, would have encouraged a concentration of the rural population into service industries, especially in respect to the transport of goods or persons (i.e. inns).[22] The city gates acted as funnels for the main intramural markets, and charged tolls; outside the gates at Aldersgate, Bishopsgate and Aldgate the greater width of the road, like the large open space of St Giles at the north gate of Oxford, may reflect the pressure of carts queueing to enter the city, and also have encouraged an unofficial market in goods before tolls were paid. In the suburbs blacksmiths and their forges were common in the late thirteenth century.[23]

Trades which produced smoke, noise, stench or much industrial waste were generally to be found towards the periphery of the intramural settlement or beyond the walls. Potters (*ollarii*) are recorded south of Fleet Street (Crocker Lane, Whitefriars, 1278),[24] and, with (or as) bell-founders, around Billiter Lane and Aldgate.[25] Documentary references indicate that tanners were to be found on the banks of the Fleet from the thirteenth century;[26] their debris and waste filled the moat of the Fleet Prison in 1355, and their weirs obstructed streams. In 1422 tanners were indicted by the wardmote of Farringdon Without throughout the length of the Fleet in the parishes of St Andrew and St Sepulchre;[27] in 1477 they were forbidden to cast their rubbish in the city ditch. Many of the monastic houses lay in the suburbs and their consumption of meat would have contributed to the market in hides; St Bartholomew's Hospital contained a tannery, mentioned in 1330, and in 1456 *le Tannehows* gate was in Dokelane, which ran along the east side of the precinct.[28] Tanning and skinning were also early suburban industries in Southwark, distanced by the width of the river and yet near the markets by virtue of the bridge.[29] Tilers are known in East Smithfield and in the parish of St Sepulchre from 1230: a tilery was functioning in the latter parish in 1376. A medieval tile kiln was found in Farringdon Street, in this district, in 1870, where a *Lymebrynnerslane* is mentioned in 1407.[30] The suburbs of Holborn, Smithfield and Fleet Street were particularly used by butchers for the dumping of offal in the fourteenth and fifteenth centuries.[31]

One type of building found in the immediate suburbs, but

2. Elevation of the city wall (west side) at Tower Hill, in 1980

century, were common in southern England by 1300; a wind-mill was noted on the land comprising Grey's (Gray's) Inn, west of the city, in 1323.[40] The sites of two mills are shown north of the city on the plan of the waterworks for Charterhouse in *c.* 1430, and on the copperplate and 'Agas' maps of *c.* 1559.

Though many of the watermills, and the post-mills shown in the panoramas, were used for the grinding of corn, the use of mills for the fulling of cloth had spread from Normandy in the twelfth century. Fulling-mills are known on royal or ecclesiastical estates in the late twelfth and early thirteenth centuries, and outside the City at places such as Wandsworth, Old Ford, Stratford and Enfield. In London itself the mechanisation of fulling seems to have been resisted and the actual extent of fulling-mills in and around the city is so far unknown.[41]

Westminster was a separate settlement around the abbey and royal palace of Edward the Confessor (and possibly a site of royal habitation before); another study has recently been made of its urban character and development. In the thirteenth century, stimulated by royal building works and the settling of many government functions around the palace, Westminster enjoyed a period of growth which was possibly already coming to an end before the general crisis around 1350. After 1360, monastic landlords (in this case, predominantly the Abbey) invested in much new building; but this ceased to be profitable in the decade after 1410. During the half century which followed, falling rents and empty houses bear witness to demographic recession, which was gradually reversed by improving fortunes after about 1475.[42] It is a sequence of trends which accurately mirrored the fortunes of the City itself.

Defences

The city wall, John Stow calculated,[43] was 2 miles 608 feet long; apart from an extension in the south-west corner resulting from the arrival of the Blackfriars in the late thirteenth century, it was based upon the Roman wall of the early third century (Fig. 2). Although earlier phases of the Tower were contained within the south-eastern angle of the wall, later circuits of the castle broke through its line so that by 1300 the city wall proper began on the north side of the Tower moat. From there it stretched north and westwards in an arc punctuated by six gates and a number of posterns. None of the suburbs, including Southwark, was ever walled, though a ditch and pale around the suburbs was once proposed, during a period of unrest in 1385.[44]

The characteristic Roman construction of squared ragstone with string courses of triple layers of red building tiles must have been visible above ground along many stretches of wall in the medieval period (Fig. 2). The walls were formidable enough to discourage William I from a protracted siege in 1066. In the reign of John concern about the defences led to the taking of stone from Jews' houses for repair work;[45] in addition, murage, first granted in 1233,[46] was granted sporadically until the early fourteenth century. The medieval work, albeit much repaired especially in modern times, is visible at Tower Hill, Cooper's Row and St Alphege

more so in surrounding villages, was the mill. The Bishop of London had four mills in his manor of East London in 1086 and at least three others were in the vicinity; one private mill probably lay at Old Ford.[32] In the twelfth century there were several mills in the immediate periphery of the city, one of which had to be moved so that the defences of the Tower could be expanded.[33] Another stood on the southern river bank east of the Paris Garden Manor, fed by a contributory stream.[34] The Templars built a mill on the east bank of the Fleet below the first Baynard's Castle in 1159; it was removed in 1307, having caused serious floods and silting at the Fleet mouth.[35] Mills are mentioned at Wapping and Stepney in the thirteenth century, and another lay in the Holborn valley in the 1230s, when the third spurgel of the Greyfriars' conduit lay near the mill of Thomas de Basynge.[36] In 1303 there were twenty-eight mills near the city, owned mostly by wholesalers in the grain trade or fishmongers,[37] and mills continued to be seen in the outskirts of the city in the fourteenth and fifteenth centuries.[38] In 1559 mills were erected on sheds in front of the piers over the southern two arches of London Bridge, alongside the Bridge House storehouse, with ten ovens and later a brewhouse.[39]

Many of these examples were watermills, using the many streams which flowed into the Thames, and the great majority of mills may also have been driven by water. Windmills, known in other European countries from the early thirteenth

Churchyard. The Cooper's Row section includes round-headed embrasures, possibly of the twelfth century, and traces of a stair to the walkway. In the section at St Alphege Churchyard traces of rebuildings attributed to the early medieval period and to the mid fourteenth century have been observed, though this is complicated by the various periods of building of the church of St Alphege which lay on the wall at this point.[47]

In 1278 Edward I licenced the Archbishop of Canterbury to extend the line of the city wall south of Ludgate westwards to the Fleet and then southwards to the Thames, within which extension the Blackfriars were granted their second site, which included the former Baynard's Castle I.[48] This extension has been recorded at several points. The northern section of wall was built of 'firestone', brick or tile fragments, flint and ragstone; two small yellow bricks of late thirteenth-century type were also recovered in one sighting in 1925. Part of the western arm along the Fleet was recorded in 1984 and 1990; its west face was seen to change character along its length, from large well-dressed rectangular ashlar blocks to small, irregular and crudely worked ragstone with flint, confirming the spasmodic construction suggested by the documentary record.[49]

The most substantial rebuilding of the city wall in the medieval period was in 1477, when Mayor Ralph Jocelyn ordered large-scale repairs, including the enlarging of an existing postern to form Moorgate and the cleansing of the ditch. Brickearth for bricks was dug in Moorfields, and chalk was brought from Kent and burned there for lime; patches of burnt chalk containing finds of late fifteenth-century date found at 4–6 Finsbury Circus in 1920 were perhaps traces of this activity.[50] The Skinners' Company repaired the wall between Aldgate and Bishopsgate;[51] the mayor and his company, the Drapers, between Bishopsgate and Moorgate; other companies, and the executors of Sir John Crosby, contributed to the work as far as Cripplegate postern; and finally the Goldsmiths from Cripplegate to Aldersgate.

Traces of this rebuilding have been found in a number of places. The parapet of the wall incorporated bricks in diaper work, seen in engravings of sections now destroyed (Fig. 3) and in the surviving section in St Alphege Garden. Brick arches built against the back of the wall have been noted in three locations, and may well have been continuous over a long distance.[52] This strengthening of the wall with arches at its base may in part have been against cannon. Gunports in the upper fabric of the wall might be expected, by analogy with late medieval defences of other towns, e.g. Canterbury, but they have not been recorded. A gunport is shown on the city wall in the earliest woodcut view, admittedly symbolic and impressionistic, by Wynkyn de Worde (working from St Paul's Churchyard) in 1510.

Inside the wall lay the bank, originally of Roman date, but evidently still occasionally to be seen (in one case as a hazard) in the medieval period.[53] Outside the wall ran the ditch, recut on a substantial scale in 1212–13 and 1477,[54] which formed a series of moated arms divided by causeways leading to the gates. The width of the ditch and the open land beside it was probably 80–90 ft, at which distance extramural streets such as Old Bailey and Houndsditch grew up along the outer edge. The ditch was wider along the north side where it merged in

3. The north side of the city wall in the churchyard of St Giles Cripplegate (J. T. Smith 1793)

parts with the Moor; along this stretch there was no extra-mural street.[55]

By the middle of the fourteenth century, perhaps aided by the gradual devolvement of ownership of streets and lanes in the city, in the civic mind, from the king to the commonalty, a space of 16 ft around the walls and gates was regarded as common soil.[56] It is however clear that encroachment up to the walls and around gates along the ditch edges was a recurring problem; by about 1340, for instance, the ditch north of Ludgate had been filled in and built on for at least a short distance along Old Bailey.[57] The cleansing of 1477 must have re-established a viable ditch defence, but from the mid sixteenth century the ditch began to disappear for good. The length between Newgate and Aldersgate was vaulted over and the land given to Christ's Hospital.[58] Despite some efforts to keep other parts of the ditch open, the space between the wall and the extramural streets became the site of gardens and tentergrounds (shown in the copperplate map of c. 1559) and eventually of houses.[59]

Whether the six Roman gates of London survived into the early medieval period or whether their sites were merely gaps in the wall is not known, but the coincidence of all six major medieval gates upon the sites of their Roman predecessors argues for some continuity of fabric. A Uuestgetum (presumably singular, though the form could be plural) is mentioned in 857, and either Newgate or Ludgate is a candidate; Cripplegate, Aldersgate and Aldgate are mentioned in the first half of the eleventh century.[60]

All the main gates were rebuilt in some fashion during the medieval period (Fig. 4). The succession of gates at Aldgate

has been briefly revealed by excavation. On the north-west (exterior) side, fragmentary traces of a second gate above the foundations of the Roman structure may be the gate rebuilt by Norman, prior of the adjacent Holy Trinity Priory at the opening of the twelfth century. Above this was found the north edge of a tower of a third gate which overlay the filled-in end of the Norman ditch; nearby lay a ditch attributed to 1215.[61] The gate must have been defensible in 1471, when Kentish rebels attacked the city at Aldgate but were repulsed, and in this late medieval form is presumably shown on the Wyngaerde and later panoramas as a low squarish structure with two semi-circular towers flanking the outer entrance. Stow saw evidence of two pairs of gates and two portcullises, but only one set was by then in place. John Symonds' plan of Holy Trinity Priory, probably of about 1586, includes a plan of the western tower. The gate was rebuilt in 1607–9.[62]

Bishopsgate, rebuilt according to Stow by the Hanse merchants in 1479,[63] is shown in the copperplate map of *c.* 1559. Its inner side comprised an arch and portcullis with a pedestrian arch to the west. Above the main gateway lay a chamber and two turrets apparently with machicolations. Two weatherbeaten statues of bishops, one on each side, were noted by Strype in 1720; in 1813 Pennant described four statues, two of bishops and two others conjectured to be Alfred and Aethelred of Mercia, but the copperplate map shows only one niche for a statue on the south side (unless this represents an oriel window).[64]

Cripplegate, according to Fabian, was rebuilt by the brewers in 1244, and in 1336–7 timbers from Guildhall were used in its repair; it was again rebuilt in 1491 through a bequest of 400 marks by Edmund Shaa, goldsmith and mayor in 1483.[65] Aldersgate was covered in lead and a house added for the gate-keeper in 1335; it was presented to the Aldersgate wardmoot in 1510 as 'in jeopardy of falling down, it sinks so sore'. In 1922–3 excavations on the east side of Aldersgate on the site of the gate revealed a polygonal turret probably of the north-east corner, 36–37 ft in advance of the city wall, 'but [it] contained no work of a date recognisably anterior to the fifteenth century'.[66] The gate is crudely shown on the Agas map, and appears smaller than the other gates, including Moorgate. It was rebuilt in 1617.

The succession of Roman and medieval structures at Newgate has been observed several times but no detailed structural history has yet been attempted. In the medieval

4. Plans of the seven city gates (William Leybourn 1676). The outside of each gate is towards the top.

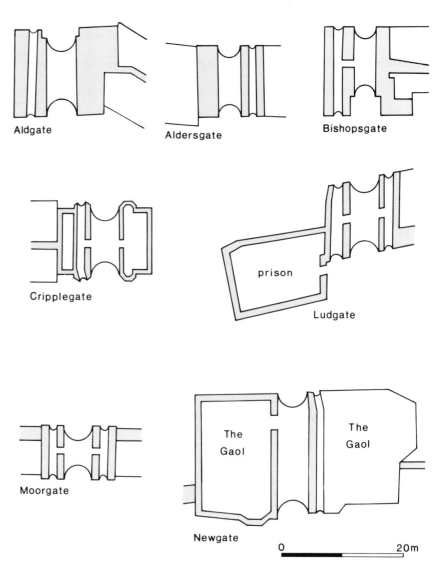

period two large angular towers with faces of ragstone ashlar straddled the road. A new stone tower at Newgate is mentioned in 1406. The gate was rebuilt in 1423–31 by Whittington's executors; its representation in *c.* 1617 (on one of a series of plans which seem to be copies of plans of perhaps thirty years earlier) shows chequerwork over both arches of the main gate on the eastern, inner side.[67]

Ludgate was rebuilt in 1215 and again in 1586; the latter included the addition of a clock, a 'double dial', and erection of statues of Queen Elizabeth and three men in Roman costume, taken by Stow to be of King Lud and his two sons.[68] These statues have survived and now stand in the porch of the church of St Dunstan in the West, Fleet Street.

Two of the gates had specific secondary functions: permanent prisons were to be found at Newgate and Ludgate. At the latter, which had been a prison since 1378, a rectangular building (called a 'quadrant' by Stow) was built on the south side in 1463, with lodgings over it and a leaded roof to walk on above (shown in Fig. 4); what may be the east wall of this structure still survives to a height of about 30 ft above street level in the east wall of 37 Ludgate Hill.[69] In addition the rooms over each gate and the larger posterns were customarily let to city or royal officials on condition that the fabric was kept in good repair and the premises would be vacated in time of emergency. In this way, for example, Cripplegate was let to Thomas de Kent, serjeant to the mayor, in 1307; Geoffrey Chaucer lived above Aldgate for fourteen years from 1374. Details of many lettings of these and the other gates survive for the fourteenth to sixteenth centuries.[70]

The two most important postern or minor gates built in the medieval period were the Tower postern (pre-1190, rebuilt in the late thirteenth century, slipped into the Tower moat 1440)[71] and Moorgate, enlarged from a postern into a gate in 1415, when the Moor outside was to be laid out in gardens.[72] In addition, archaeological excavation at Duke's Place in 1977 found a door in the city wall, adjacent to the end of the dorter of Holy Trinity Priory, suggesting communication between the monastery and its extramural garden. Such a privilege was presumably unusual, the result of the enclosure of that stretch of defences which lay within the precinct, which had been allowed by Henry I; in this case the postern was closed up by Jocelyn's brick arches in 1477.[73] During the later sixteenth century, as the importance of the defences declined, at least one other postern was forced through by the City itself, at Greyfriars in 1552.[74]

London was also defended by D-shaped interval towers (traditionally, but incorrectly, called bastions) along the wall. The eastern series of towers, from the site of the Tower to the headwaters of the Walbrook, is probably fourth-century in date. Up to eighteen towers have been discovered or inferred, though not all were necessarily in use in the Middle Ages; Bastion 4A, south of Aldgate, (discovered in 1979) was demolished by the thirteenth century.[75] The western series, which resumed west of Cripplegate (cf. **140**; Fig. 66), are likely to be of medieval date.[76] A possible d⟶ some is 1257, when Henry III caused the wall of the city, ⟶ch was decayed and destitute of towers, to be repaired ⟶ more seemely wise' at the charge of the City.[77] The extension to the city wall around the Blackfriars was also towered; a ⟶wer found beneath Pilgrim Street on the northern sector of the

PUBLIC ARCHITECTURE.
INSIDE VIEW OF THE WATCH-TOWER DISCOVERED NEAR LUDGATE HILL, MAY 1, 1792.

5.   View from the south of an interval tower in the city wall extension around the Blackfriars (J. T. Smith 1792)

extension in 1792 was square rather than round (Fig. 5). In 1276 Edward I urged the City to build a tower where the wall met the Thames,[78] and a further tower is shown in this position in some of the sixteenth-century panoramas.

Like the gates, the interval towers were also often leased or converted to special purposes during peace time. In 1235, for instance, Henry III made a life grant to Alexander Swereford, treasurer of St Paul's, for the use of a turret north of Ludgate (probably B21), enabling him to erect in it such buildings as he pleased, to have full use of it in time of peace for storage of goods, but to surrender it in time of war so that it could resume its military function.[79] In 1305 and 1314 there are references to towers near Bishopsgate which suggest they were occupied by chaplains of the adjoining churches – All Hallows London Wall and St Augustine Papey.[80] From the thirteenth century certain of the northern towers were regularly inhabited by anchorites or hermits;[81] the Hermitage of St James (**140**) lay on the wall adjacent to tower B12 near the north-west corner of the city. In the next century there is evidence of at least two aristocratic owners of houses adjacent to the defences on the inner side making building encroachments, in one case apparently a watch-tower on the wall itself (**11**, **153**). During the later sixteenth century encroachments into the towers by adjacent occupiers had an increasingly permanent character, as the defences became obsolete.[82]

The City boundaries were marked, on the principal approach roads, by markers called the Bars. These are known

from the late twelfth century; that at Holborn is mentioned in 1183, and at Smithfield and Aldersgate in 1197. Presumably these were obstructions of some kind with token defensive purposes, and, as at Canterbury, there was a tendency for rural roads to meet immediately outside them.[83] By 1554 Temple Bar comprised a gate, since in that year a new gate at Temple Bar is mentioned; the Chamberlain was to commit the key to the City's tenant and arrange the opening times for the gate. In 1584 a tenement lay over and on both sides of the gate. In this context a large and remarkable medieval stone cellar on the south side of the Bar which survived into the nineteenth century (Fig. 6) could perhaps be the base of a gate tower rather than, as is usually supposed, a domestic undercroft.[84]

The Waterfront

During the medieval period the city literally expanded into the River Thames. The reclaimed waterfront zone is comparatively rich in documentary, cartographic and archaeological information, and thus the strip of land south of Thames Street and the buildings upon it will figure frequently in this study.

The development of the land south of Thames Street probably radiated out from three centres of early activity: the two Saxon landing-points for merchandise at *Etheredshithe* (later Queenhithe), first documented in 899, and Billingsgate, recorded *c.* 1000;[85] and the pre-Conquest foreign settlement at Dowgate, later the Steelyard. By the twelfth century churches were established south of Thames Street at Dowgate (All Hallows the Great), the bridge (St Magnus) and probably at Botolph Wharf, just above Billingsgate and perhaps originally part of that landing area (St Botolph). With the sole addition of All Hallows the Less, these remained the only churches south of the street, indicating that by the time of formation of parishes in the twelfth century these locations were already areas of substantial reclamation and river-based activity. Lanes leading down to the Fleet also prompted areas of development along its eastern bank: private wharves used by ecclesiastical institutions are recorded here in the twelfth and early thirteenth centuries.[86]

The chief topographical result of the constant, if irregular, process of land reclamation from the twelfth century to the sixteenth was that by the latter date, parts of the quayside lay up to 80 m (260 ft) south of Thames Street which marked the tenth-century river bank.[87] In the later medieval period, as in the eleventh and twelfth centuries, Queenhithe and

6. A medieval vault under Child's Bank, Fleet Street (J. Emslie 1878), possibly part of the substructure of the medieval Temple Bar

7. Three Cranes Wharf, Thames Street, from Wyngaerde's panorama of *c.* 1540. The line of Thames Street is marked by St Martin Vintry church beyond.

Billingsgate (along with Botolph Wharf) were the main official points of entry for general riverborne cargoes, while Dowgate became the quarters of the Hanseatic League. In addition, there were prominent wharves serving the wine trade at Vintry. Some wharves served as major access points for human traffic, rather like the landing-places for *traghetti* in modern Venice; in 1540, for instance, Three Cranes Wharf had a landing-stage embellished with flags on posts (Fig. 7).

Castles, Religious Houses and Parish Churches

Behind the waterfront stretched the city's network of streets and lanes. These went through and around larger complexes of royal and religious buildings, which by their number, scale and quality of construction were dominant features in the topography of their neighbourhoods. In addition the high number of parish churches, which were largely in stone, formed points of reference in the immediate surroundings of the secular buildings which are the prime concern here. This section can only list the main known building types.

London had three Norman castles: the White Tower (finished 1097) in the east, and two smaller fortifications in the west, the sites of which are only approximately known, Baynard's Castle I (possibly finished by 1087) and Montfichet's Tower (finished by 1136). The main building periods at the Tower of London were under William I and William II (the White Tower), Richard I (the Bell and Wardrobe Towers and a curtain wall, by 1190), Henry III (the inner circuit of towers, Coldharbour Gate and Great Hall, 1220–50), Edward I (the enlarged landward entrance, the creation of the outer ward, the watergate of St Thomas's Tower, 1277–85), Edward III (heightening of the outer river wall and other works, 1336–9), Edward IV (the 'bulwark', 1480) and Henry VIII (Brass Mount, rebuilding of St Peter ad Vincula, the Brick Tower, Queen's House).[88] At the other end of the city, the building of Baynard's Castle II by Henry VII in 1497–1501 and Bridewell Palace by Henry VIII in 1515–23[89] are similarly useful for dated examples of a number of innovations in residential planning and construction techniques.

St Paul's Cathedral was rebuilt from 1087, though engravings indicate that much of the nave probably dated from after a serious fire of 1136. The tower was rebuilt by 1221, the choir extended by 1255, and the Chapter House was under construction in 1332. In chronological order of foundation,

the earliest monastic houses were St Mary Overey Southwark (founded 1106; destroyed by fire *c.* 1212; rebuilt by the end of the fourteenth century; nave rebuilt 1469), Holy Trinity Priory Aldgate (1108; choir first half of twelfth century) and St Bartholomew's Hospital and Priory (1123; in the priory, twelfth-century choir, west front of thirteenth century, Lady Chapel *c.* 1330, cloister rebuilt fifteenth century). Further hospitals, nunneries and houses of the crusading orders followed: the Knights Templar (*c.* 1128 in Holborn; moved to New Temple, Fleet Street, 1161; round nave and porch of church, *c.* 1160–85, chancel *c.* 1220), Knights Hospitallers, Priory of St John of Jerusalem, Clerkenwell (*c.* 1144; crypt of *c.* 1140 and *c.* 1180, south gatehouse 1504), the nunnery of St Mary, Clerkenwell (*c.* 1145), Hospital of St Katharine by the Tower (1148), the Hospital of St Mary without Bishopsgate (St Mary Spital; 1197), St Helen's Bishopsgate (Benedictine nunnery, before 1216; thirteenth-century church and cloister, fourteenth-century chapels, church rebuilt 1475), the Hospital of St Thomas of Acre, Cheapside (early thirteenth century), the Hospital of St Mary of Bethlehem (1247) and the Hospital of Elsyng Spital, founded in 1329 (the fourteenth-century crossing of the nave survives).[90]

All the main mendicant orders had large houses in London: the Blackfriars (1221, moved site 1275; church finished 1288, other parts datable to the late thirteenth and fourteenth centuries), Greyfriars (1222; church finished 1337), Whitefriars (1247), Austin Friars (1253; church 1354–60), Crutched Friars (before 1269); and several minor orders (e.g. Minoresses *c.* 1293–4). The London Charterhouse was founded in 1371, and it retains the largest proportion of medieval and Tudor religious building (fifteenth-century gatehouse and precinct wall, fragments of cells and other conventual buildings, early sixteenth-century domestic ranges).[91] The sites chosen for religious communities tended to lie in out-of-the-way, under-occupied fringes of the intramural city or in the suburbs, and thus their locations serve as a rough guide to the relative density of population in various areas at the time of their foundation.

Throughout the medieval city, local points of topographical and architectural significance were provided by about 110 parish churches; the total number fluctuated slightly due to reorganisation and the aftermath of the dissolution of religious houses.[92] Eighty-nine churches were destroyed or badly damaged in the Great Fire of 1666; substantial remains of the period 1200–1600 survive today in only ten churches, and several of these were bombed in the Second World War (All Hallows Barking; All Hallows Staining (tower only); St Andrew Undershaft; St Ethelburga; St Giles; St Helen; St Katharine Cree (tower of 1504 only); St Mary le Bow (crypt); St Olave Hart Street; St Sepulchre). Few have had their architectural histories written; a review of the main trends in the building history of London's medieval parish churches will be found elsewhere.[93]

Public Buildings and Works

A detailed examination of all the public buildings and civic works in medieval London is beyond the scope of this survey, and apart from their influence, if any, on the character of

houses, the whole second rank of public buildings and services – prisons, the water system and public latrines, and all but one of the inland markets – will not be dealt with here.[94] What follows is a summary of the building history of London Bridge and the two largest public buildings, Guildhall and Leadenhall; and as a selection of the other public buildings, the two waterfront landing installations at Queenhithe and Billingsgate, together with the Custom House and, as a trading establishment of some size, the Steelyard. The last four lay south of Thames Street and bordered on the river.

The combination of civic works and conspicuous piety, often through private sponsorship, was a strong tradition by the late twelfth century when work began on London Bridge (1176–1207), comprising nineteen arches and 906 ft in length. The long-held view that a Saxon bridge lay just downstream has been rejected[95] and it now seems likely that the Saxon and medieval bridges were on the same alignment as their Roman predecessor. A chapel on the bridge, possibly dating from the early thirteenth century, was rebuilt in 1384–97 by Henry Yevele, and is shown in Wyngaerde's panorama of *c.* 1540 (Fig. 9). Towards the south end of the bridge were two gatehouses (Fig. 8), the inner and larger of 1426 guarding a drawbridge which allowed the passage of shipping upstream to Queenhithe. Other buildings on the bridge are implied in accounts of a fire in Southwark in 1212, and some of them were shops in 1244; by 1358 there were 138 shops on the bridge, the rents of which went towards the upkeep of the fabric. The City maintained a works department known as the Bridge House for this purpose; it kept large stocks of stone, timber (including building frames for other Bridge property in the city) and ironwork in a yard on the bank near the south end of the bridge.[96]

The building which most embodied and projected the City's civic pride was Guildhall itself. The archaeological and architectural history of this complex up to 1600 can be divided into four parts: (1) before the late thirteenth century, (2) rebuildings of *c.* 1280 – *c.* 1340, (3) the major rebuilding of 1411–40 and (4) additions in the late fifteenth and early sixteenth centuries.[97]

In the second quarter of the twelfth century *terra Gialle* measured 132 ft long and 52 ft wide, and was held of St Paul's; the location is not specified. In 1232–46 *Gildhalla* can be placed in the parish of St Lawrence Jewry, and deeds of the later thirteenth century fix it on or about the present site. The earliest comprehensive remains date to the late thirteenth century, but at two places works preceding this phase have been noted. In the north wall of the west crypt a pilaster of the crypt blocked a recess with a carefully prepared white plaster surface, suggesting that the crypt was a modification of an earlier stone building, at least along its northern side. The lower of two different wall fragments below the fifteenth-century porch to the south-east, of ragstone on a mortared ragstone foundation, is also probably of a building two phases before the fifteenth century. This wall had a dressed rag face on the west, 1.2 m (4 ft) below the floor-level of the fifteenth-century porch. Together these two fragments suggest a stone building preceded the late thirteenth-century rebuilding, but there is no further indication of date. Excavations of 1988 and 1993 beneath and east of Guildhall Yard have uncovered a Roman amphitheatre and eleventh- or

8. Detail of the south end of London Bridge from Wyngaerde's panorama of *c.* 1540, showing the outer gateway with statues

9. Detail of London Bridge from Wyngaerde's panorama of *c.* 1540, showing the drawbridge and the main gate (1426) and the chapel of St Thomas as rebuilt by Henry Yevele (1381–4)

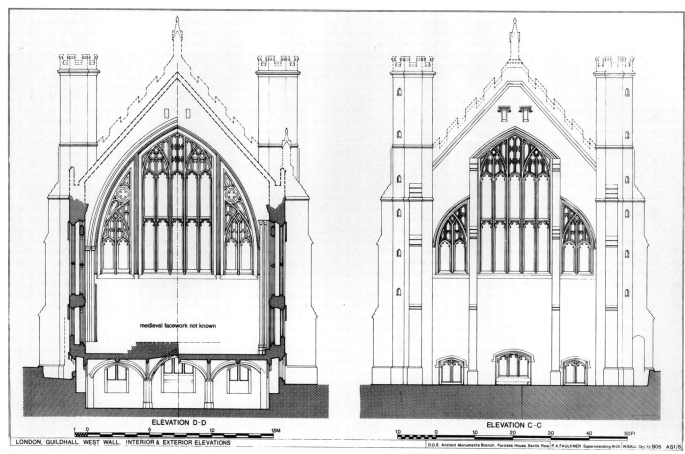

medieval facework not known

ELEVATION D-D

LONDON, GUILDHALL, WEST WALL, INTERIOR & EXTERIOR ELEVATIONS

ELEVATION C-C

D.O.E. Ancient Monuments Branch, Fortress House, Saville Row   P. A. FAULKNER Superintending Arch. W. BALL Oct. 72 905   AS1/8

10. Elevations of the west end of Guildhall: interior (left) and exterior (right) [Barron, *Guildhall*]

11. Plan of Guildhall, after rebuilding of 1411–40 [Barron, *Guildhall*]

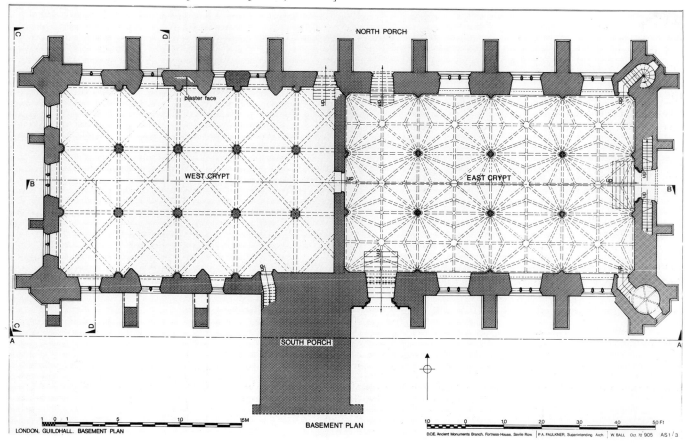

NORTH PORCH

plaster face

WEST CRYPT

EAST CRYPT

SOUTH PORCH

BASEMENT PLAN

LONDON, GUILDHALL, BASEMENT PLAN

D.O.E. Ancient Monuments Branch, Fortress House, Saville Row   P. A. FAULKNER, Superintending Arch.   W. BALL Oct. 72 905   AS1/3

12. East crypt of Guildhall looking west, in *c*. 1895

twelfth-century timber buildings above it, and no doubt the early history of Guildhall will be greatly clarified in due course by these discoveries.

The surviving west undercroft, now much restored, is of three aisles which were five bays long, the easternmost bays truncated by the west wall of the later east undercroft (Fig. 10). The windows of the west undercroft in their present form probably date from alterations in the late fifteenth century, and the vaulting alone can be dated, though only roughly, to 1200–1340. Documentary evidence would suggest dates of either the 1280s, since work on the adjacent chapel began in the 1290s, or 1333–5, when repairs are recorded; the closest architectural analogy, an undercroft of *c*. 1290 at Penshurst Place, Kent, suggests the former date.

To the east and south-east of the main building were other structures. The repairs of 1333–5 may have included the construction of additional rooms, since references to other chambers then occur with greater precision. The Upper or Council Chamber (where the Court of Common Council met by 1370) implies a two-storeyed structure, which may have been in a north-south wing at the east end of the hall. Archaeological observation during post-Second World War rebuilding recorded a length of walling, of ragstone and bands of knapped flint, beneath the west wall of the fifteenth-century porch which may be part of this wing; the use of knapped flint in this way would suggest a date in the fourteenth century. A chapel to the south of the hall and on the east side of Guildhall Yard was under construction in the 1290s, and a garden of Guildhall, at its east end, is mentioned in 1311.

Guildhall was rebuilt in 1411–30 by John Croxton, mason, whose previous work is not known. Work on the roof was in progress in 1418, and in 1423 Richard Whittington left money to pave the hall with Purbeck marble; construction may have been finished by 1430. Croxton inserted buttresses in the west undercroft (necessary support for the new unaisled hall if the previous hall had been aisled), cut off the easternmost bay of the undercroft and built a new east undercroft of three aisles, four bays long (Figs. 11–12). The columns in the new undercroft were of Purbeck, and the masonry of the walls was at least partly executed in a chequerwork pattern of light and dark stone. The hall above, 151½ ft by 48 ft, was the largest open span in medieval England apart from Westminster Hall (1394–1402), which it resembled (Fig. 10). The original roof was of seven transverse stone arches. On both sides of the hall a higher rank of windows were seen through an internal stone screen; one of the lower windows, of two lights under a four-centred arch, survives on the south side. The two-bay porch, rebuilt several times, has tierceron vaulting and blank arcading on its interior walls. The porch façade to Guildhall Yard originally contained statues of Christ in Majesty above Law and Learning, with the lowest row of statues representing Discipline, Justice, Fortitude and Temperance (Figs. 13–14); the last four are now in the Museum of London. Two glazed louvres were provided for the Guildhall roof from a bequest in 1481–2, and a kitchen, buttery, pantry and other offices were added at the north-west corner of the hall in 1501–5.

North of the main hall lay a two-storey complex of rooms

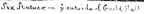

Six Statues on y outside of Guild Hall

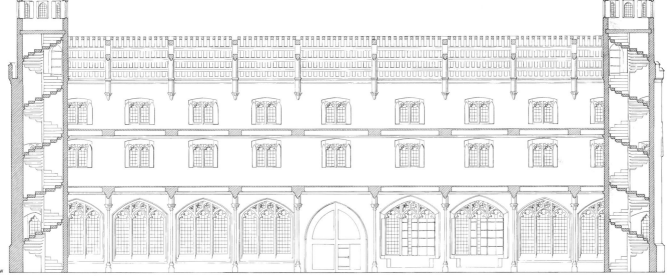

13. (*far left*) Statues from Guildhall porch (J. Carter 1783)

14. (*above left*) South elevation of Guildhall porch, after the fire of 1785 (J. Schnebbelie)

15. (*left*) Leadenhall chapel and the east quadrant of Leadenhall during demolition (J. T. Smith 1812)

16. (*above*) Reconstructed elevation and section through north range of Leadenhall (M. Samuel 1989)

including the Mayor's Court (begun 1424) and a room used by the Court of Aldermen, linked to the hall by a northern porch. These rooms were built on a series of undercrofts which were used as civic markets in the fifteenth century.

A library was built south of the chapel in 1423–5 and the chapel itself rebuilt, apparently to the south of its former position by the porch, from about 1434 to 1455; arched foundations survived beneath later buildings until 1987, and details of the internal arcades, doors and windows (presumably repaired after the Great Fire) were drawn by Buckler and others in the early nineteenth century.[98]

The building history of Leadenhall is by contrast the product of a shorter campaign of impressive enthusiasm in the mid fifteenth century. The site had been used as a market for 'foreign' (from outside the city) poultry by 1321, and for cheese by 1377. The site was conveyed to the City in 1411,

17. Queenhithe (right foreground) from Wyngaerde's panorama of *c.* 1540. In the upper right is the Eleanor Cross in Cheapside.

18. Billingsgate from Wyngaerde's panorama of *c.* 1540. The waterfront properties on the right probably include Pakemann's Wharf (**175**).

and in 1440 work started on the 'garner to be made at Ledynhall' under Croxton. In 1443 lead was bought for the roof and in 1444 land bought to make an entrance into Leadenhall Street. Simon Eyre, mayor in 1445, made a substantial contribution to the work and especially to a chapel on the east of the new quadrangular building (Fig. 15). An assessment of 1477 mentions eight houses on each of the east and west sides, and a seld or market hall on the ground floor with two storeys above it. By Stow's time the market functions had declined, apart from the storage of wool sacks, and most of the rooms were used for storing or repainting decking and scenery used in street pageants.[99]

A study of Leadenhall, based upon excavation of part of the site in 1984–6, shows that the impressive quadrangle and chapel were built in one operation, all in stone and with stylistic similarities to Guildhall, which was nearing completion. The main ranges, comprising open arcades on the ground floor with two floors of large rooms above, were battlemented and had octagonal corner turrets (Fig. 16). On the Leadenhall Street frontage was a gate, without architectural emphasis, flanked by traceried unglazed windows along the street-side which were barred with iron. The chapel resembled Guildhall in its windows with cinquefoiled heads and the evidence of blank arcading similar to that in the Guildhall porch.[100] As a granary and market building Leadenhall would seem to be a fifteenth-century construction of international importance, to be compared to the large public market buildings of Ypres, Bruges and Ghent; its quadrangle of arcades resembled the larger market squares in certain bastide towns (both French and English) of late thirteenth-century and fourteenth-century Gascony. It should also be understood in the context of the concern in several large European cities over the supply of grain, as shown by the building of Or San Michele in Florence in the fourteenth century, or the extensive warehouses called the Granai in fifteenth-century Venice. Perhaps the building of Leadenhall in 1440 was partly in response to the famine of 1437–8, the second most severe famine of the medieval period in northern Europe after that of 1315–18.[101]

Other London buildings, this time on the waterfront, had arcades which may have had similar market functions to Leadenhall. Queenhithe, above the bridge, and Billingsgate, below it, were both pre-Conquest landing places which evolved during the medieval period as inlets, as reclamation on private properties pushed out alongside them. Queenhithe handled up-river traffic (especially corn from Berkshire and Oxfordshire), and connected with the western market street of Cheapside by means of a grid of streets; though there was some blurring of distinctions, Billingsgate generally handled the down-river trade. Ordinances relating to St Botolph's Wharf in 1368–9 direct most of the downstream trade there, and say nothing of Billingsgate. Regulations of 1463 divided cargoes, especially of victuals, between Billingsgate and Queenhithe.[102]

Queenhithe was handling corn in the twelfth century, and a range of commodities landed are recorded from the mid thirteenth century. The custom of 1302 shows that bakers, brewers and others bought corn there, and rates for porterage were worked out. In 1307 granaries and a brewhouse are recorded at the north-east corner, and two granaries with

garrets in 1310. Wyngaerde shows the dock as surrounded by a wharf on three sides, with stairs down to the shore at the south-east corner (Fig. 17). An open space on the north side, as at Billingsgate, was known as the *Romeland*; development of surrounding properties would suggest that the sides of the inlet were forming by 1237. The panorama by Visscher (1616, but derived from earlier drawings) shows that the range on the west of the dock had an open arcade on the ground floor. In 1525 a cornmill was set up on barges by the dock, but did not last long. In 1566 a new granary was erected under the terms of the will of Sir John Lyon, grocer and mayor in 1554; this building was probably near the wharf as cranage would be direct from barges.[103]

Billingsgate is also shown in Wyngaerde's panorama of *c*. 1540 (Fig. 18). Despite the apparently close-set buildings there was also a *Romeland* to the north of the inlet. On the west side Wyngaerde shows another arcaded range three bays wide. This is likely to be the range shown in the background of an illuminated manuscript illustration of the Tower of the late fifteenth century (Fig. 19). It might have been one of the results of the extension of Billingsgate carried out in 1449 with £1,000 from the lands of Sir Thomas Haseley.[104]

19. Billingsgate and London Bridge shown in the background of an illustration from the poems of the Duke of Orleans, 1460–80 (BM MS Royal 16.F.2, f. 73). The view looks west along the waterfront.

20.   Custom House (with the double arcade) from Wyngaerde's panorama of *c.* 1540

21.   The Elizabethan Custom House, from an engraving of 1663 by Bartholomew Howlett (re-engraved 1815 and published in Wilkinson, *Londina Illustrata*, 1825)

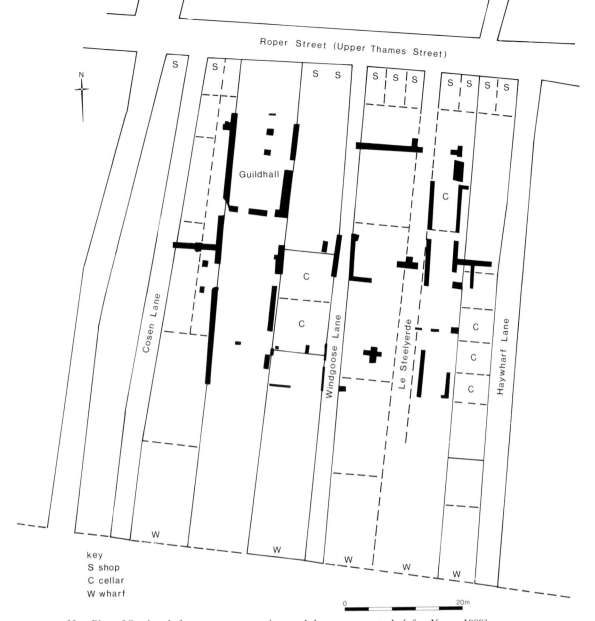

Roper Street (Upper Thames Street)

Guildhall

Cosen Lane

Windgoose Lane

Le Steelyerde

Haywharf Lane

key
S shop
C cellar
W wharf

0   20m

22.   Plan of Steelyard, from recent excavations and documentary study [after Keene 1989]

Two further waterfront complexes, neither of them built by the City, may also be described at this point. The siting of the Custom House at the east end of the waterfront presumably related to the need to bring goods, or samples of them, from ships to be certified. This was easier downstream of the bridge. In 1326 the City petitioned the king not to remove the tron for wool to the New Temple, which not only lay outside the city, but was a difficult place to bring wool to by river, especially in time of frost – i.e. when the river above the bridge was prone to icing over. The first known Custom House, built by John Churchman in 1382–3 'to serve for tronage, or weighing of wools in the Port of London', lay on the waterfront at the east end of Thames Street, and originally comprised a range parallel to the river. In 1383 a small chamber for a latrine and a solar over the counting house were added; in front lay a stone quay. A western wing at right angles was added by *c.* 1540, when its southern end, with an open ground-floor arcade in two bays, was drawn by Wyngaerde (Fig. 20). Parts of the medieval building were retained when the main block was rebuilt in brick in the reign of Elizabeth I (Fig. 21).[105]

Upstream of the bridge, near Dowgate, the house of the Cologne merchants was established by 1170; by 1244 they had a Guildhall of their own. A *gildhallae Teutonicorum* is mentioned in 1260; together with the merchants of Lübeck and Hamburg, the men of Cologne specialised in wool and the cloth trade. The elements of the Steelyard can be seen in a plan which combines archaeological and documentary evidence (Fig. 22). They comprised three blocks from Thames Street to the river, trisected by Windgoose and Steelyard Lanes. At the north-west corner stood the hall, perhaps the oldest part, with its gable to Thames Street and a tower at its southern end (Fig. 23). The complex included a council chamber, a wine tavern on the street, houses and offices for the merchants – one of which provided the setting for a portrait of a Hanse merchant by Holbein (Fig. 152) – and rows of warehouses running to a quay on which there was a crane, misdrawn by Hollar (Fig. 24). On certain panoramas (Norden *c.* 1600; Visscher, 1616) the western warehouse range is shown with an open arcade on the ground floor.[106]

Thus each of the four waterfront establishments probably had an arcaded range on the western, upstream side. These

23. The Steelyard (right foreground) from Wyngaerde's panorama of *c.* 1540

24. Steelyard (left foreground) and its surroundings, including Clothworkers' Stairs (**168**) and Coldharbour II (**170**) (Hollar 1647)

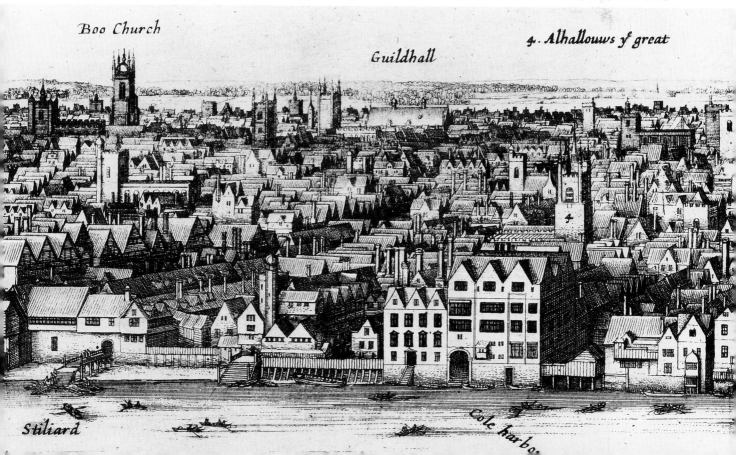

25. The Royal Exchange: interior of courtyard (Hollar 1647)

ranges presumably served the same function as open-sided markets, such as Leadenhall, or market halls in other medieval towns; but at King's Lynn, where arcades have been noted in the ground floor of the Hanseatic warehouse (*c.* 1300) and the warehouse of the private house known as Hampton Court (fifteenth century), it has also been suggested that such porticos on the riverside were to minimise flood damage: the rising river and freak tides did less damage if allowed to flow through the range.[107]

A courtyard surrounded by an open arcade was again the main feature of the most important new public building of the sixteenth century in London – Thomas Gresham's Royal Exchange. In 1567–9 Gresham and the City built the Royal Exchange in Cornhill (Fig. 25), modelled on the bourse built in Antwerp in 1531. It was designed by Hendrick van Paesschen of Antwerp; the timber came from Gresham's manor of Battisford in Suffolk, but the stone came at least partly from Flanders. Statues for the inner façades were carved in England, but a statue of Queen Elizabeth was made in Antwerp.[108]

Medieval and Tudor London thus had a series of public and semi-public buildings of architectural note, even distinction, to match those of its European trading partners.[109]

The Dissolution and Its Effects

In the sixteenth century, and especially during its second half, there were violent changes to the medieval topography of the city. Many religious precincts, which had previously formed large quasi-permanent features of the landscape, were claimed for secular use and drastically altered, resulting in the sudden appearance of a group of large mansions carved out of the monastic buildings.

The first suppression at Holy Trinity Priory, Aldgate, took place in 1532, fully three years before the general Dissolution. Although the churches within two precincts (St Bartholomew's Priory, Smithfield; St Helen's Nunnery, Bishopsgate) and within three friaries (the Austin Friars, Blackfriars and Greyfriars) re-emerged as parish churches, the majority of the monastic precincts had by the end of the reign of Henry VIII been transferred to courtiers or officials of the Court of Augmentations. Thus Austin Friars passed to Sir William Paulet, Lord Treasurer; St Bartholomew's Priory to Sir Richard Rich, Lord Chancellor; and to the south-east of the city, the rural Bermondsey Abbey to Sir Thomas Pope, treasurer of the Court of Augmentations.[110]

Three main changes to the topography and built fabric of the city can be discerned in the period 1530–1600. During the comparatively short span of 1532–70 several of the monastic complexes were rebuilt, often in drastic and bizarre manner, into urban palaces by royal officials and courtiers; three of these noble residences are described here (see Chapter 3 and sites **8**, **48**, **54**). Secondly, in the later part of the century, beginning perhaps around 1560, the same precincts were subject to increased fragmentation and gradual conversion into either industrial premises and areas of small-scale housing (**8**) or housing speculations of quality, perhaps attempting to profit from the cachet of the noble houses which formed the topographical and social focuses of the precincts (**54**; Fig. 43a–b). Significantly, the precincts exhibiting fragmentation

into industrial premises lay on the east side of the city, thus forming nuclei for the formation of the East End of London in the following century.

Thirdly, the numerous urban properties of the monasteries and former chantries were released onto the market and created a great scope for land transference and probably rebuilding by new owners, particularly those who wished to let out properties for rent to the expanding population; in certain areas of the city as much as 60 per cent of the property may have been in ecclesiastical ownership before the Dissolution, and thus now released.[111] In the precincts houses of all sizes and qualities were going up very fast; along the sides of suburban roads, fields were disappearing under housing. The scattered evidence gives the impression that this was the greatest intensity of secular building since the good times of the early fourteenth century.

A Great Rebuilding was originally identified in better (i.e. those of yeomen or higher) houses outside London by Hoskins and dated to the period 1570–1640.[112] More recent work has suggested two periods of increased activity, 1570–80 and 1620–40, with a national slump in building in the 1590s due to the dislocation of the economy after seven bad harvests.[113] The national picture is one of great disturbance at the Dissolution, three decades of slow growth thereafter and a burst of building activity in 1570–80. In London, however, although some central land values dipped in the 1590s,[114] large and attractive houses were being built in the same decade in the outer parts of the city, particularly along the main suburban streets (and at St Bartholomew's priory, **54**). In general, as reflected in the repeated civic and royal proclamations against them, new buildings and subdivision of older buildings continued almost without check. The surveys of Ralph Treswell in 1607–14 describe, in part, the new generation of buildings about which his contemporary John Stow complained so bitterly. By 1600 London was divided into three parts: the old mercantile city within the walls; Westminster, already geared to the professions, government and conspicuous consumption; and the rising suburbs on the north, east and especially south sides, where manufacturing was the main economic activity.

Domestic building in London in the thirteenth to sixteenth centuries should therefore be seen against a background of almost continuous royal, religious and civic construction in and around the city. The enquiry which occupies the following chapters seeks to establish, among other things, whether any high and low peaks of domestic building activity mirrored the periods of intense construction on larger sites or had their own pattern, and what styles, techniques and materials employed on domestic house sites may have been influenced by or borrowed (or bought) from public projects.

We can also attempt to outline how the physical growth of the city, horizontally or vertically, coped with its fluctuating level of population at various times. Some of the larger features which determined or influenced the topography of the City of London in 1200 had a long history: the Roman wall, forum, fort and a small number of major street alignments, and an early Saxon cathedral. Of more recent date were substantial late Saxon realignments of streets and expansions into the River Thames at designated points. During the medieval period many religious houses were established, helping to crystallise further local topography. Between about 1100 and about 1450 the waterfront continued its expansion and enlarged the area of intramural city by almost one-sixth. From the eleventh century, suburbs developed to the west, to the east (to a lesser extent) and across the river to the south in Southwark. A recent estimate of London's population at various points in the period suggests that 25,000 people lived in London (the intramural city and the immediate suburbs) in 1100; 40,000 in 1200; 100,000 in 1300; perhaps 60,000 by 1500, and 80,000 by 1560 (with a further 20,000 inhabitants of the expanding suburbs north of the river).[115]

In the middle of the sixteenth century, circumstances changed rapidly. The opening up of the religious precincts, previously restricted areas, coincided with a massive increase in population. It has been suggested that in 1560–80, the population of the city within and without the walls rose by 31 per cent, but in 1600 had fallen slightly to 125 per cent of the 1560 figure; whereas in the suburbs north of the river the population increase in 1560–80 was probably 100 per cent, rising to 275 per cent of the 1560 figure by 1600 (and 550 per cent of that figure by 1620).[116] This increase resulted in further development of the suburbs and widespread subdivision of existing buildings, including the former religious buildings within the precincts themselves. The circumstances of house building in London can therefore be initially divided into two periods: one from 1200 to about 1550, which may have had its own internal peaks and troughs, and a great surge of rebuilding and subdivision in 1550–1600.

If the mean household size remained constant throughout the period, then many houses must have lain empty during the main period of decrease in population, from 1350 to about 1560. Recent work on the area at the west end of Cheapside suggests that a trend of net losses in the number of houses (in that they became vacant plots) began shortly after 1300; land values declined, though not in a regular slide, as they appear to recover in 1360–70, only to decline again.[117] Perhaps some of the remaining houses became larger, because there were fewer people to house (a process also observed in other towns, for instance Gloucester)[118] but this has yet to be adequately documented. The population, according to the model given above, began to rise dramatically after 1500, and so would have overtaken the capacity of the available housing stock by about 1560. Then, as we know from Stow, Treswell and the City's own concern, the building-boom began, especially in the suburbs.

To a lesser degree, this is the building history of many medieval towns in Britain. However London, by its sheer size, was in a different category. Such an intensity of prestigious buildings and constructions within a single urban area was not present anywhere else in the country, and there were no towns of remotely comparable grandeur in the vicinity. The nearest town to London with more than one religious house was Guildford. Other ancient cities such as Canterbury, Winchester and York had numerous parish churches, but the largest of them, York, only had 42 churches against London's figure of 110. Only York had a comparable number of religious houses in total. Bristol, Norwich and York had imposing stone defences; but the area of settlement within these boundaries was never as extensive, or as densely occupied, as in the capital.

CHAPTER 3

Properties and Buildings

Streets, Properties and Buildings, 900–1200

Although this study is concerned mainly with secular building in London in the period 1200–1600, a short preparatory section is required to outline some of the most important processes which had helped form the townscape as it appeared at the beginning of the thirteenth century. Some of these influences, such as that of the larger Roman ruins which inhibited or affected movement, have not yet been studied in detail and perhaps will remain so until there has been much more archaeological excavation in the city; but the degree of work since 1973 has now made it possible to suggest the way in which many of the streets of medieval London were laid out, or began forming, from the late ninth century; and to reveal something of the nature of the buildings which lay along those streets. Much is still debated and the following summary is based largely upon two recently investigated areas: streets leading off both sides of Cheapside, and streets leading south from Eastcheap to the adjacent waterfront area between London Bridge and Billingsgate. These zones were, however, perhaps the two most important commercial areas in Saxon London, and both incorporated a grid of streets which indicates a measure of civic or royal planning.[1]

The early development of buildings and property plots in the post-Roman city can be described in three chronological stages: the establishment of the street-system and the shape and size of the earliest property plots in the late ninth or tenth century; timber cellars and the buildings of which they may have formed part in the eleventh century; and the appearance of stone buildings in the late eleventh or twelfth century. At the beginning of the period considered in detail here, the *Assize of Building* of 1189–1212 demanded a certain standard in construction of all buildings, and laid down regulations concerning boundary walls, cesspits and gutters, and roofing materials.

Suggestions about the character of London's earliest post-Roman streets have arisen from recent archaeological work in the streets leading north and south from Cheapside.[2] In the late ninth and tenth centuries Bow Lane was already established, as indicated by street surfaces and a building recorded at Well Court (32) on the east side of the Lane. At Watling Court (31), on the west side of Bow Lane and south of Watling Street, only 'dark earth' (the widespread and largely featureless soil of the Saxon centuries) was recorded for this period, but the alignment of rubbish pits or cesspits on the Bow Lane frontage suggests that properties had been formed along the lane; areas devoid of pits suggest the sites of ground-level buildings along the street. At sites north of Cheapside in Milk Street (138) and Ironmonger Lane, sunken-floored buildings were to be found, in both cases entered from or on a Roman street apparently still in use. In both cases a new street on a different alignment (in the case of Ironmonger Lane, north to

south rather than east to west) was to be the focus of boundaries by the opening of the eleventh century or shortly after.

Most of the medieval streets around Cheapside can be identified on documentary grounds by the thirteenth century. A possible historical context for the establishment of at least one of the grid-squares near the river and Queenhithe has been suggested.[3] Land grants of 889 and 898 or 899 can be identified with an area bounded by Bread Street Hill, Trinity Lane, Little Trinity Lane and Thames Street, together occupying one of the major grid squares. Measurements only are used in the earlier grant, but lanes bounding the property are mentioned in the later grant. Bread Street, leading direct from Queenhithe to Cheapside, would clearly have been a vital element in such a scheme, as might Bow Lane/Garlick Hill on the east side of Queenhithe. The suggested late ninth-century date of the first post-Roman street at Well Court, establishing the line of the later Bow Lane, would seem to point to a large-scale replanning of the area south of Cheapside at this period. The establishment of the first Milk Street, to the north of Cheapside, can only be inferred with certainty during or by the late tenth or more probably early eleventh century; but, as demonstrated archaeologically at Well Court, the laying out of the street may well have preceded building along its edges by some years.

Detailed study arising out of recent comprehensive excavation is also currently under way for the waterfront area around the bridge.[4] Lanes leading from the major street axis of Cannon Street – Eastcheap down to the riverfront can be dated to the late ninth or tenth century, in the cases of Botolph Lane[5] and Miles Lane.[6] In both cases timber buildings were soon erected along the new streets, within the tenth century. At the foot of the slope and on the southern, riverbank, side of Thames Street (which as a thoroughfare seems to have grown from a track running along the line of the ruins of the late Roman riverside city wall), the construction of an embankment between the bridge and Billingsgate (both first mentioned by the mid eleventh century) is dated at the New Fresh Wharf site (174) to sometime during the last three decades of the tenth century. This embankment, which may have been in public use, was later heightened and divided by fences into plots in the first quarter of the eleventh century. These plots correspond with properties mentioned in documents by the mid twelfth century and occasionally delineated by measurements in the fourteenth century, and thus it seems likely that they were laid out as private properties in the early eleventh. Similar contemporary material has been recorded in other English towns such as Lincoln and Northampton, though rarely on major streets.[7]

Suggestions about the size and shape of individual plots elsewhere in the city cannot be made until the eleventh century due to the imperfect survival of strata of this period. Buildings lining the streets, and perhaps in form aligned side-

26. (31) Watling Court: timber buildings and pits of the eleventh century, with the superimposed outline of the twelfth-century stone Building 6, from excavations in 1978

on to the street, are indicated at Bow Lane, Milk Street and Botolph Lane in the tenth century, but there is no clear indication of plot shape. On the west side of Botolph Lane near its junction with Thames Street (or perhaps, at this period, only with the foreshore and the dilapidated Roman riverside city wall) up to three small buildings with similar internal plans were standing in a row;[8] but it is not known if they were individual buildings or parts of a unitary construction, nor is the depth back from the street of any of them known.

Archaeological evidence suggests a gradual increase in density of buildings both along street frontages and in the spaces behind them during the eleventh century. In the mid to late eleventh century at a site in Ironmonger Lane, for instance, areas devoid of pit-digging strongly suggest a building had been constructed along the Lane frontage. At Well Court, two successive timber buildings encroached onto Bow Lane and in effect established its present eastern side. At Watling Court to the south-west, three large timber buildings with sunken or cellar floors were erected, including the first on Basing Lane (the medieval lane now represented by the north part of Cannon Street, west of its junction with Bow Lane) to the south (Fig. 26). Areas devoid of contemporary pit-digging again suggest that ground-level buildings occupied the frontage to Bow Lane, and perhaps also to Basing Lane. Since

the cellars cannot be linked with any particular trade (unless, like their fourteenth-century successors, they were associated with the distribution of wine), they must be relics of townhouses with larger than normal storage capabilities.[9]

So far archaeological study has not elucidated the origins of the tradition of long and narrow properties found in medieval towns, including parts of London, by the twelfth century, though there are examples in York of long narrow properties dating from the tenth century. Presumably economic or commercial pressures would place a higher premium on street and river frontages, and this would be reflected in the layout of properties. At the same time, in Cheapside, and in other towns such as Worcester or Lübeck, some parts at least of the street-frontages were made up of large territorial units, which subdivided over time to produce, by the seventeenth century, the characteristic narrow tenements.[10]

The largest urban estates or compounds are known only fragmentarily through documentary references. There are references from the mid ninth century to individual *hagas* and *burhs* in London, some with specific names such as *Ceolmundingachaga*, near the 'Westgate', given to Worcester cathedral in 857 or the *burh* of St Paul's mentioned *c*. 975. These apparently record the residences or estates of prominent individuals or of communities, some based outside the city.[11] A significant residence called Aldermanbury seems

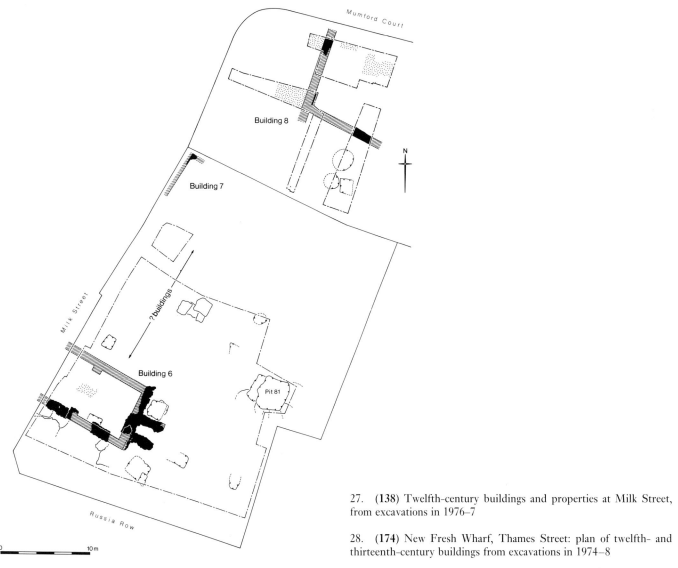

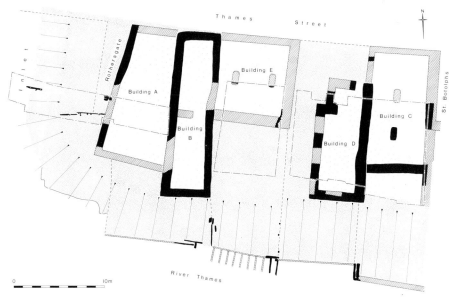

27. (138) Twelfth-century buildings and properties at Milk Street, from excavations in 1976–7

28. (174) New Fresh Wharf, Thames Street: plan of twelfth- and thirteenth-century buildings from excavations in 1974–8

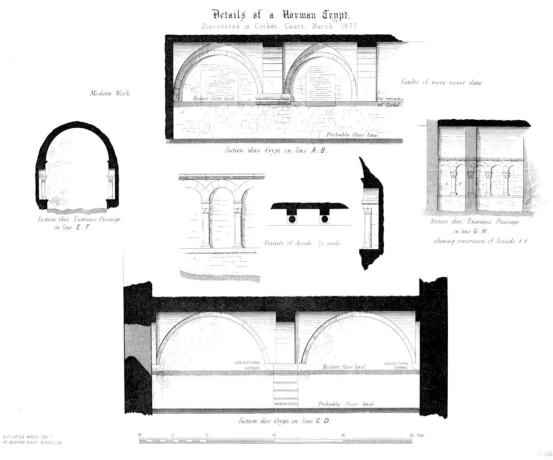

29. **(91)** Norman house at Corbet Court, Gracechurch Street: sections and elevations [Loftus-Brock 1872]

30. **(91)** Norman house at Corbet Court, Gracechurch Street: plan [Loftus-Brook 1872]

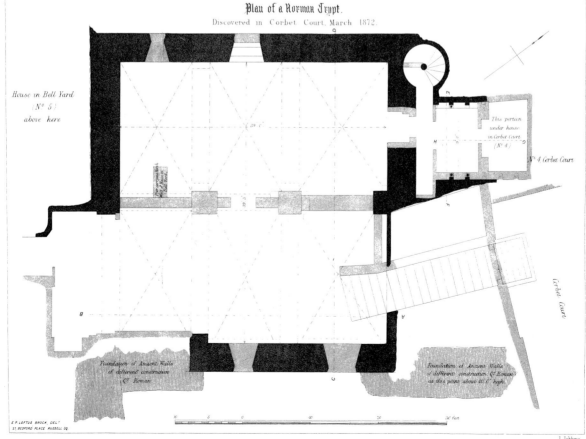

to have been based around the east gate of the Roman Cripplegate fort, which was presumably of stone and still a defensible structure. In *c.* 1127 Aldermanbury was called a soke (an area of private jurisdiction); it also had rights in the adjacent church of St Mary. There were no doubt numerous sokes in the eleventh-century city, but their study makes little contribution to an understanding of contemporary buildings. It is however reasonable to suppose that by 1000, the king's palace and the town-houses of many great men lay within the city walls.[12]

Beginning around 1100, but increasingly during the first half of the twelfth century, stone buildings can be traced on the recently excavated sites, both in the streets around Cheapside and in the waterfront zone between London Bridge and Billingsgate. There are three main types: (i) a rectangular stone building of one or two chambers at basement level, at right angles to the street and adjacent to the street (**32**, Building 8; **138**, Building 6); (ii) a large stone building away from the street, either square or rectangular (**91, 198**) and (iii) a smaller, square undercroft which may have supported a small stone building, or which may have been a subterranean part of a larger ground-level structure (**31**, Building 6; **199**).[13]

The stone buildings of the twelfth century with gables to the street, as at Milk Street (Fig. 27) or New Fresh Wharf (Fig. 28), must be seen as the successors to the cellared timber buildings of the eleventh century, with the development that the ground floor of the stone structures communicated directly with the street. This new siting provided storage at the street frontage rather than, as formerly, deep within the property; the latter position continued to be provided, when required, by additional cellars along the side of the property (as at New Fresh Wharf) or beneath a major building away from the frontage.

Stone buildings were also erected away from street frontages; two were recorded in the nineteenth century. A Romanesque town-house recorded in 1870 at Corbet Court, off Gracechurch Street, was square in plan; the ground floor was entered by a short porch with blank arcading along its walls (**91**; Figs. 29–30). Similar buildings of square plan have been recorded in Southampton and Stamford.[14] A building revealed in 1829 in Southwark, perhaps of mid to late twelfth-century date, comprised an undercroft of four barrel-vaulted bays, thinner but about a quarter longer than the Milk Street building. From one end an arch led to a further building of at least two bays which may have been the undercroft for a porch to the door of the hall, which survived above (**198**; Figs. 32a–b). This second example is notable for having basement windows down one side only, the opposite side from both the range at right angles and a first-floor doorway. This leads to the suggestion that the stone range, for a long time erroneously believed to be part of the Inn of the prior of Lewes (which was actually adjacent), may be a solar block to a vanished ground-floor timber hall; the door on the first floor would be at the top of stairs from the hall.[15] Stone houses in other towns were often away from the frontage: for instance, three of the seven recorded early medieval stone houses in Colchester[16] and two twelfth-century houses at Winchester, in *Tannerestret* and *Calpestret.*[17]

The third form of stone building, the smaller square or near-square undercroft, is best represented by the twelfth-century undercroft within the Inn of the prior of Lewes (**199**; Fig. 33). The undercroft was of four quadripartite vaulted bays with a central column with a scalloped capital; a doorway led east from the north-east bay, and windows were recorded in the north, east and south walls, implying that the structure, if part of a larger building, would have lain at the latter's east end. There are continental parallels for this form of square stone building, in Cologne, Viterbo (north of Rome) and Prague; the less prestigious examples need not have been vaulted, but might have been ceiled with beams.[18] These parallels help to explain foundations of similar size excavated at the Watling Court site (**31**) in 1978. A building with stone foundations measured about 6 m (19 ft 9 in) north to south by at least 6.4 m (21 ft) east to west internally. The construction is intrinsically undated, but it cut pits of the early twelfth century and was in turn stratigraphically earlier than a fourteenth-century well which was dug against its northern side. It may have been a small almost square stone building like that in Southwark, though it need not have been vaulted.

Though small in area, Building 6 lay adjacent to Basing Lane and on the site of a large timber-cellared building (the largest excavated example in the city to date; Fig. 26). It is possible that as little as fifty years separated the demolition of the timber cellar (Building 3) from the construction of Building 6. The coincidence of siting of a prestigious building of timber in the second half of the eleventh century and one of stone in the second half of the twelfth century, is probably significant. It suggests that the property, on the corner of Bow Lane and Basing Lane, was a superior residence in both the eleventh and twelfth centuries.

During the twelfth century, stone buildings could therefore be seen on several major London streets, sometimes set back from those streets within their own grounds. The term 'stone house' is often used as a term of distinction in cartularies of monastic establishments with property in London, the deeds there recorded being generally of the last decade of the twelfth century and the opening of the thirteenth century, mostly in central parishes.

Apart from the cathedral close,[19] the parts of the city in which stone houses might predominate would be the Jewry, commercial centres and the waterfront, where there would be a need for secure storage. In London as elsewhere, Jews were among the occupiers of stone houses. The spreading of Jewish communities in medieval English cities has been attributed to the immediately post-Conquest period, the main source possibly being the community at Rouen.[20] Although at their greatest extent they may not have exceeded 2 per cent of the population even in large cities such as London or Norwich,[21] the Jews were a distinct element in early medieval urban society. In London the main Jewry was a large area to the north of Cheapside, including the street now known as Old Jewry (*Vicus Judaiorum*, 1128) but extending to Milk Street and the parishes of St Lawrence Jewry and St Mary Aldermanbury in the west (see **17, 46**).[22] There are in addition references which suggest another Jewish area may have lain near the protection of the Tower, perhaps in or at the south end of Jewry Street, Aldgate,[23] but no Jewish house-sites have yet been identified there.

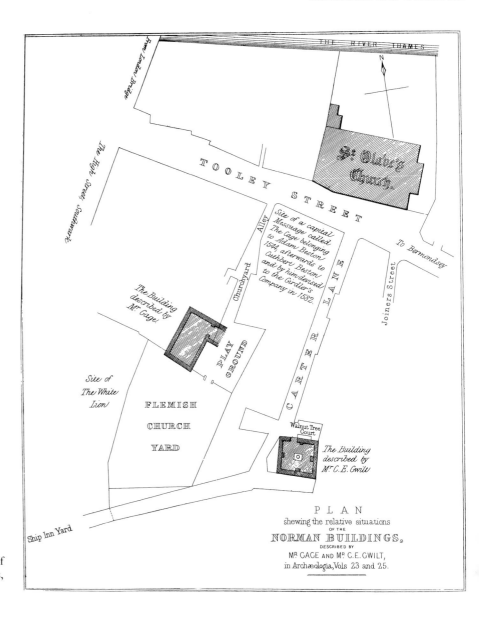

31. **(198–9)** Site plan of the town-houses of
the Earl of Warenne and of the prior of Lewes,
Tooley Street, Southwark (J. Basire 1859)

The areas where twelfth-century stone houses appear first within London, the central commercial areas (Cheapside and Gracechurch Street) and the central part of the waterfront (i.e. near to those commercial zones), are similar to those occupied by stone houses in other towns. In Colchester the known fragments of substantial early medieval stone buildings are found within two blocks of the High Street, an area now thought to have been occupied by Jewish houses.[24] In Canterbury, the twenty-seven known stone houses are almost all to be found in the central area (i.e. the High Street and streets to north and south of it). One house (Burgate) is first mentioned *c.* 1180 and all the others *c.* 1200 or in the early thirteenth century.[25] In Norwich the excavation of a notable late twelfth-century stone building on the waterfront at St Martin at Palace Plain, probably a warehouse for the nearby cathedral, has occasioned a survey of early secular stone buildings in that city. Only two are physically extant, but records principally of the fourteenth century speak of at least sixteen probable examples. Unlike Colchester and Canterbury, early medieval Norwich was a port with continental connections; and an apparent concentration of stone structures on King Street, bordering the Wensum on the southern approach to the town, invites comparison with both London (New Fresh Wharf) and King's Lynn.[26]

The evidence for Milk Street Building 6, and possibly for two further stone buildings on properties to the north along Milk Street **(138)** suggests that secular stone buildings were being built on London streets at the comparatively early date of around 1100. Stone buildings of the earlier part of the twelfth century have also been recorded in the larger cities which were London's early medieval trading partners, such as Cologne and Ghent, and slightly further afield at Regensburg and Prague.[27] It is to these larger cities that we should look to understand the context of the development of more important secular buildings in London at this time.

A fire of 1136 began at London Bridge and allegedly reached St Clement Danes by way of St Paul's. According to a City tradition preserved in the fifteenth-century compilation of charters and procedural notes called *Liber Albus*,[28] the memory of the fire helped to bring about the first surviving civic building regulations issued under Henry Fitzailwin's mayoralty in 1189 (traditionally; now dated to the period

1192/3–1212).[29] A further set of regulations were drawn up by Fitzailwin after another serious fire in 1212.[30]

These regulations cover dimensions of walls, provision of gutters, and arrangements for the siting of privies. Stone walls on property boundaries, whether supporting buildings or not, were to be 3 ft wide and usually constructed jointly by the adjoining owners, each giving half the land and bearing half the cost, to a height of 16 ft. Alternatively one party donated the land and the other built on it, the donor receiving half ownership, and therefore building rights, in the wall. It was also possible, if desired, to build two walls back-to-back along the boundary (cf. **181**, though by 1600 the survival of such stone walls, as demonstrated by archaeological and plan evidence, was a great rarity). If 'arches' (usually interpreted to mean aumbries, but possibly including the blank arcading fashionable in twelfth-century houses; e.g. **91**) were required, each neighbour could excavate to a depth of 1 ft, leaving a thickness of 1 ft of wall between the properties. Gutters (horizontal drains) were required to draw water on to the land of the owner whose building they served, unless it could be directed on to the highway. If a person had vacant land on which he wished to build, but a neighbour's house had a gutter which spilled water on to his land, he could take down the neighbour's gutter during rebuilding but had to make provision for it in the new construction.

Cesspits ('necessary chambers') were of stone or timber by *c.* 1200; a privy of stone had to be 2½ ft and a timber cesspit 3½ ft (sometimes in subsequent cases in the *Assize* called '3½ feet of earth') from a property boundary. Since in a common wall 3 ft wide the boundary would run down the middle, this meant that the edge of the stone pit could be as close as 1 ft from the interior face of the wall. This was probably the usual practice, together with the use of wall-chutes from upper chambers. Cesspits attached to houses, and therefore probably using intramural chutes, are known in London from the early thirteenth century, though archaeologically recorded examples date usually from the fourteenth;[31] there are earlier examples outside London in merchants' houses at Southampton.[32] The relationship between the siting of privies and property boundaries is explored further below (see p. 86–7).

Rules about roofing were formalised further after the fire of

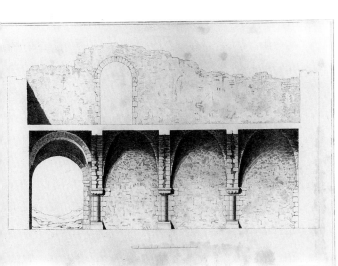

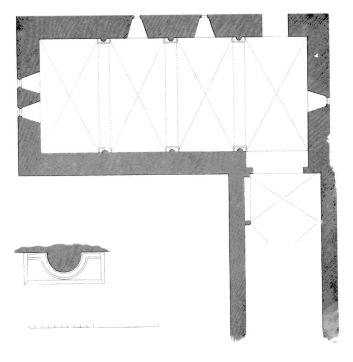

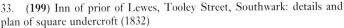

32. (**198**) Town-house of the Earl of Warenne, Tooley Street, Southwark: (a) (*left*) section

(b) (*below left*)   Plan (both J. C. Buckler 1831)

33. (**199**) Inn of prior of Lewes, Tooley Street, Southwark: details and plan of square undercroft (1832)

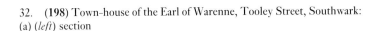

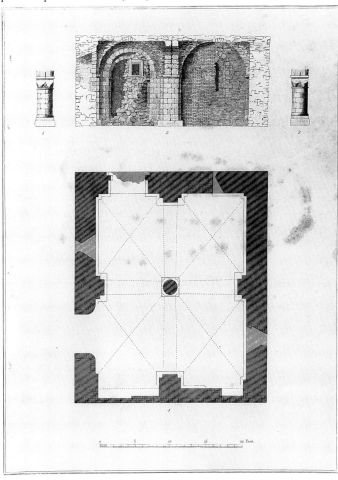

34.   (193) Bishop of Winchester's Inn, Southwark: view of interior of hall looking west after fire of 1819 (F. Coltman)

1212. Reeds, straw, rushes or stubble were banned and roofs were to be covered with tiles, shingles or boards. Buildings roofed with reeds or rushes were to be plastered over within eight days, and wooden buildings in Cheap which endangered their stone neighbours were to be removed. The earliest occurrence of clay roof tiles in archaeological deposits, however, dates to the first half of the twelfth century, anticipating the regulations by a large margin.[33]

Thus the topography of streets, properties and building alignments was already fixed by 1200; custom had been influencing the setting of the house for over 200 years, and now civic regulation codified aspects of its construction and features.

Larger Private Houses, 1200–1600

London was, by 1200, capital of England, and the major port of the whole kingdom. Religious and secular leaders came to attend, or officiate in, legal actions at the courts or the Exchequer, as well as to attend royal councils; here they also sent their servants for luxuries. From at least the eleventh century, if not before, some had built town-houses in the city, though their form is not known in detail until the twelfth and thirteenth centuries.

In the vast majority of cases where their plans can be ascertained, the houses of religious and noble leaders, company halls and the inns of court were of courtyard plan. The hall of the property normally lay at the rear of a yard, though occasionally to the side on more restricted sites, with a range of buildings (often separately let) fronting the street. This courtyard type has been called Type 4 in a London typology of house-plans shown in the Treswell surveys of 1607–14.[34]

Both archbishops, eighteen bishops, at least twenty-two abbots and at least six priors each established a town-house in London or its suburbs during the medieval period. There were two purposes for such a house: the provision of accommodation for those engaged in the everyday affairs of the house or the see, such as the selling of produce or the buying of goods; and as the town-house of the bishop or abbot himself when in London. As Henry of Blois, Bishop of Winchester, is reported to have said *c.* 1147–50, '[because of] many inconveniences and losses that I and my predecessors have sustained through the lack of a house to use for royal business and other affairs in the neighbourhood of London . . . I have procured the house and land that were of Orgar the Rich and many other lands lying around them of the soke of the church and monks of Bermondsey' (**193**).

The first function, to provide an urban base, can be seen to have a longer history than the second, to be near the king;

until the second decade of the thirteenth century, when meetings of parliament began to crystallise at Westminster, the documented twelfth-century town-houses of the religious are to be found in the City or in Southwark, close to the port and markets and emphasising their interest in commerce (**20, 135**). The Archbishop of Canterbury may have been in possession of a seat in Southwark before the Conquest, and a number of houses were erected in the suburb by the middle of the twelfth century. John Stow, knowledgeable in architectural matters, described the Inn of the abbot of St Augustine's, Canterbury (acquired 1215), as 'a great house of stone and timber . . . which was an ancient piece of work, and seemeth to be one of the first builded houses on that side the river' (**201**). Several other monastic houses in southern England made urban bases in Southwark, the suburb through which a traveller from the distant house would pass on his way into the city (**197, 199, 200**).[35]

The first half of the thirteenth century however saw a marked swing towards Westminster and the road to it (the Strand outside the city boundary, Fleet Street within it); first to settle here, before 1225, was probably Ralph Neville, Bishop of Chichester and (of special interest here) Chancellor (**47**). By 1294 five other bishops and the Archbishop of York had houses in the area: the Bishops of Bath (by 1231–8), Durham (by 1237), Norwich (by 1237), Carlisle (by 1238) and the Archbishop of York (in 1240–5) (**158–61**).[36] The Archbishop of Canterbury had settled on Lambeth in the last decade of the twelfth century. During the late thirteenth and fourteenth centuries further bishops, abbots and priors established London houses in Fleet Street and around Holborn; and on both sides of the mouth of the Fleet by taking advantage of the suppression of the Templars (**36–7, 151, 159**; the Inn of the abbot of Faversham – not in the gazetteer – lay next to the Templars' property by 1246).[37]

Engravings and surviving buildings or fragments provide glimpses of three episcopal residences: those of the Bishop of Winchester in Southwark (**193**; Figs. 34, 103, 122a, 261–2), of the Bishop of Bath in the Strand (**157**; Figs. 35, 45–6, 243) and of the Bishop of Ely in Holborn (**107**; Figs. 36–7, 227). Dating largely from 1285–90, this included a private chapel

on two floors (now St Etheldreda, Ely Place) (Fig. 37), the design of which resembled that of royal chapels such as St Stephen's (with which it may have shared the same architect, Michael of Canterbury) and the Ste Chapelle in Paris.[38] These religious residences were generally laid out on a grand scale, with courtyard in front and private garden behind (Fig. 36). They also included subsidiary buildings to accommodate large entourages. The Inn of the abbot of Waltham, at the Dissolution, incorporated a dormitory; at least several Inns (and probably all of them) had stables (**135; 200, 199, 158, 197, 104**)[39] – when site-numbers in parentheses are out of numeric order, they are listed in chronological order of first reference to the particular feature under discussion.

A larger group of houses of secular lords, knights and prominent public servants in the thirteenth and fourteenth centuries is more difficult to characterise. Though often long in extent, the immediately available documentary information on them is sketchy, being confined in the main to successions of title established by diligent searching through many kinds of records by modern scholars. Unlike religious owners, secular lords rarely compiled cartularies, and they bought and sold property like any other asset. Often the owner of the property had a rural seat and used his London town-house only when on business in the capital or as an outstation for the procuring of necessaries and luxuries. Some nobles rented houses when in town on this seasonal business. The royal household and the extraordinarily rich, especially in the second half of the thirteenth and early fourteenth centuries, had an establishment called a wardrobe, a special place for storage of luxuries, which did not necessarily function as a residence. The expenses of the wardrobe of Bogo de Clare in 1284–5, for instance, include payments for robes, furs, drapery, carpets and banquaria (rugs for seats or benches), spices, plate (especially silver or silver-gilt cups), horses and lawsuits.[40] These wardrobes were evidently primarily storehouses, but the lord and his family would occasionally lodge in them, so presumably they contained some domestic facilities. Like the religious residences, the noble houses contained stables for housing the horses and equipment of a large retinue in transit (**67**).

(**157**) Bishop of Bath's Inn (Arundel House), Fleet Street: south side of main court (Hollar 1646)

The three diagnostic chambers of the fourteenth-century secular noble residence were the hall, undercroft and tower. The large hall of stone (and later of brick) was a durable feature, but no examples from secular noble residences of the thirteenth or fourteenth centuries are known in detail, though they are occasionally mentioned (**14, 28**); undercrofts, often sited below the hall or other principal buildings, have survived slightly better (**198, 18, 51, 37, 114, 22, 47**). Towers are known at several fourteenth-century houses, in documentary record or in the panoramas (**42, 11**; probably of this date at **114**; Fig. 38), though none has yet been excavated. It seems that lords, despite the comparative absence of clan-fighting which governed the domestic architecture of cities such as Siena or Genoa, still had sufficient influence and apparent need to build or maintain such towers. Crenellations, presumably largely on the hall, were infrequently licenced during the fourteenth century (see Chapter 5) and were primarily decorative and symbolic; although most large houses had gateways, they were only made of stone in exceptional cases, as at Berkeley's Inn, Thames Street, or that of the abbot of Stratford Langthorne, Clement's Lane[41] (for gates, see also **11, 200, 199, 158, 22, 30, 47, 197, 165** and Chapter 4). These were not truly fortified complexes, but their layout bears comparison with contemporary forms of accommodation such as Stokesay Castle or, within the Tower of London, the suite of rooms connected to the Bloody Tower which was built in 1360–6.[42]

36. (*right*) (**106**) Bishop of Ely's Inn, Holborn: plan in 1776

37. (**106**) Bishop of Ely's Inn, Holborn: view of chapel and cloister from north-east (J. Carter 1776)

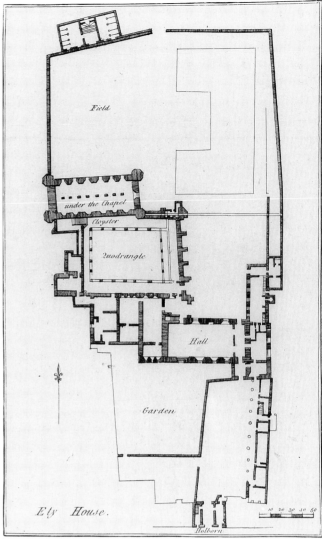

38. (**114**) Pulteney's Inn (with tower, middle) and (**170**) Coldharbour II, Thames Street (left foreground), from Wyngaerde's panorama of *c*. 1540

Parallels for these houses may be found in the Home Counties around London, for example in Kent, where there are three examples of mid and late thirteenth-century rural houses of status: Nettlestead Place (*c*. 1250–60), Old Soar, Plaxtol (*c*. 1290), and Penshurst Place (late thirteenth century in parts); or further afield, a good parallel is found at Little Wenham Hall, Suffolk (1270–90).[43]

Large thirteenth-century houses were to be found throughout the city, but two particular concentrations, both on the west side, are noteworthy. Some suburban mansions around Fleet Street and Holborn became the legal inns during the thirteenth and early fourteenth centuries (see below); and, nearby, the settling of the Blackfriars in the south-west corner of the city after 1275 seems to have encouraged high status residences to colonise the waterfront below and next to the precinct, in the area later to accommodate the second Baynard's Castle (**3**, **163**; Salisbury Inn, Fécamp Inn – later Burley Inn, Scrope's Inn and Berkeley's Inn, all in Thames Street).[44]

These mansions may have been influenced by the court styles of Henry III and Edward I, being perhaps scaled-down versions of royal palaces, but equally, the court may have shared a style with other prominent residences in the city. Alexander the Carpenter, for example, master carpenter at the royal palace in 1234–40 and 1259–60 and at Westminster Abbey in 1239–56, also repaired the London houses of the Bishop of Durham in 1237.[45] The hall of the Bishop of Durham in the Strand (**161**) had lofty marble pillars, perhaps similar to those in the king's hall at Winchester; across the Thames, the Archbishop of Canterbury's palace at Lambeth included a substantial chapel on its own undercroft, no doubt part of a complex as rich as those surviving at Wells or Lincoln.[46] It has been argued that although there were periods when royal building initiatives have characteristics idiosyncratic enough to be called a style (e.g. during the reigns of Henry III and Henry VIII), such coherence is lacking at other times, and the majority of royal mansions were never owned by the Crown for long periods.[47] The idea of a court style can only be sought at Westminster, and thus possibly in the City of London also. The Eleanor crosses may represent the taste

of Edward I's court, but they may equally be said to represent the decorative style favoured by the leading London masons of the day.[48] Further archaeological work may throw light on this question by unearthing fragments of mouldings or coats of arms, such as were noted by Stow on stone gates or other buildings of these houses (e.g. **17, 124**).

Rich foreigners also had houses or establishments within the city, and they might have had distinctive residences. There might also have been more general continental influences on the architecture of well-appointed homes.

So far French influence on the domestic architecture of London has been little researched; in the thirteenth century stone buildings may well have looked similar in London, Paris or Le Puy,[49] but by the fifteenth century the timber-framed traditions of the two countries were rather different. Similarly with German and Low Countries affiliations; the Romanesque style in stone buildings was pervasive throughout Europe, but timber-framing was specialised. In addition, there is no clear suggestion that merchant depots in cities away from the mother-country were blatantly nationalist in tone; rather, establishments of merchants abroad are more likely to have accepted the architectural style of the host country. The English in Bruges had a house in local style[50] and the Hanse in London do not seem to have had anything distinctively German about their Steelyard (see Chapter 2). One potentially significant group, however, were the Italians.

40. (*right*) (**22**) Crosby Place, Bishopsgate: interior of hall, now in Chelsea

North Italian cities such as Siena, Florence, San Gimignano and Lucca may already have sprung to mind when considering the occurrence of towers on fourteenth-century domestic sites. Italian banking families were firmly established in London during the early part of the reign of Henry III.[51] Sienese merchants were used to further the king's business in the papal court; in 1239 a Burgundio Bacarelli is mentioned in this context.[52] In 1251 Matthew Paris noted that the merchants bought *nobilissima palatia Londini* for themselves, and set up house in the manner of native citizens; so much so that during one of the periodic persecutions they decided to remain in England because of the losses, especially in their property, they would suffer if they escaped. In Edward I's reign a list of the home-towns of the bankers can be drawn up from his payments to them: Lucca, Siena, Pistoia and several families from Florence. At a later period, returns of 1440 show that of 250 foreign merchants then in the city, 185 were Italian. Apart from the house of the Bardi of Florence in Lombard Street, however, first mentioned in 1318 and which later became the Pope's Head tavern (**124**), and parts of an Italian merchant's house which survived rebuilding by John Crosby in 1466 (**22**), very little is known of the appearance of the Italians' houses (cf. **42**).[53]

39. (**22**) Crosby Place, Bishopsgate: exterior of hall in the early nineteenth century (T. Shepherd)

41. **(169)** Coldharbour I, Thames Street (left), in the low-level panorama of *c.* 1550

42. **(195)** Suffolk House, Southwark, from Wyngaerde's panorama of *c.* 1540

During the fifteenth century, two processes affected these superior residences: the proliferation of company halls, some based on former noble residences, and the transformation of others, particularly many of the ecclesiastical residences, wholly or partially into taverns.

Several noble houses, or parts of them, were conveyed to livery companies to form their halls (e.g. **11, 139, 162**; for the livery halls as a group, see pp. 44–50) or became part of company estates (e.g. **122**). In this way prominent houses of secular lords were subject, like any others, to the property market; but residences belonging to religious bodies tended to stay in the institutions' possession and thus these changed character more slowly.

The religious mansions were particularly prone to being let out on an increasingly regular basis, and some at least were taverns. By Chaucer's time part of the Inn of the abbot of Hyde in Southwark had become the Tabard Inn; parts of the second town-house of the prior of Christchurch, Canterbury, in Tooley Street, Southwark (**200**), was let out to dyers, fullers and masons in the fifteenth century. By the time of the Dissolution the Inn of St John Colchester in Mincing Lane was called the Bell, and that of the prior of Lewes in Southwark (**199**) the Walnut Tree.[54]

Crosby Place (**22**) of 1466–75, the hall of which has survived, stands out from these processes of gradually changing functions; it was probably, as Stow thought, exceptional for its age (Figs. 39–40, 67, 74a, 105, 116, 122b, 124, 128c, 136, 194–6). The house of John Crosby, a grocer and Member of Parliament who was knighted for his services to Edward IV, was removed to Chelsea in 1907. It illustrates the narrow gap between the house of a merchant who moved in royal circles and a royal palace itself. Crosby retained (at least at basement level) one wing of an already large mansion, which had once been occupied by a distinguished Italian merchant, to form the southern range of a courtyard entered from Bishopsgate via a passage under six tenements. The hall and parlour block were of ashlar-fronted brick on brick undercrofts. A semi-octagonal oriel window at the dais end of the hall incorporated Crosby's crest in its stone vault. The hall (Fig. 40) and upper parlour (Fig. 74a) had richly gilded and ornamented timber ceilings, and behind the main house lay gardens and a private gate to St Helen's church where Crosby and his wife lie in one of the chapels, his merchant's mark featuring (until the bomb-blast of 1992) in the stained glass of the windows. The hall resembles that of Eltham Palace (1479) and may have been built, like Eltham, by the king's mason, Thomas Jurdan.[55] The roof was designed by Edmund Graveley, a warden of the Carpenters' Company.[56] Presumably Crosby Place was exceptional only in quality, and there were others like it; we do not know anything about the houses of magnates of the immediately previous generation such as Richard Whittington or Simon Eyre. It might be suggested that the houses of the wealthy merchants of the fifteenth century were one means of diffusing architectural standards and styles from the milieu of royal palaces, just as those of the religious leaders may have been in the thirteenth century; but this cannot be pursued until we have more and better records of buildings in both centuries.

The undoubted magnificence of Crosby Place is matched by details of the interior of a royal residence within the city a few years later, from accounts concerned with extensive repairs to Coldharbour II in Thames Street in 1485 (**170**). The house was firmly in the royal class; since its rebuilding by Alice Perrers in the 1370s it had entertained Richard II in 1397, had been used by Henry IV for receiving ambassadors and perhaps by the Prince of Wales when briefly ruling the country in 1410–11. Up to twenty-two rooms used by the noble occupants and their attendants are mentioned: the hall, great chamber and chapel, a parlour next to the garden, individual wardrobes for the lord and lady, separate lodgings for members of the family and the chaplain. The house had a second, Little Hall with its own buttery. The great chamber overlooked the river, and may be shown in the anonymous panorama of *c.* 1550 (Fig. 41; see **169–70** for comment). The rest of the complex included a large gatehouse with a porter's lodge, stable, wine cellar, kitchen and numerous service rooms and houses, the whole served by perhaps seven separate stairs, one a watergate to the Thames. The privies were in Sege Alley, evidently to one side of the building and probably connecting with the river. At this mansion the principal servants had individual chambers: the steward's chamber had a bay window and a chimney, while that of the clerk of the kitchen had a flat lead roof. Other servants with chambers were the cook, the cater (purveyor), and the controller. The palatial luxury is expressed most of all in the details and variety of the glass inserted, some of it for the first time (see Chapter 5).

The refurbished Coldharbour II represents a royal mansion at the very beginning of the Tudor period; fitted out by order of the king's mother, it was one of the settings for celebrations at the marriage of Prince Arthur in 1501. In this year, according to Stow, Henry VII finished rebuilding Baynard's Castle, which now comprised the varied river-front façade known from the panoramas (e.g. Fig. 227). The site was excavated in 1972 and details are awaited.

The next style or fashion which might have had an influence on the larger secular houses in London was that associated with Henry VIII (1509–46). Henry rarely left south-east England during his reign, and it is here that the Italian and French aspects of his palace culture were disseminated among the houses of his followers, from Norfolk to Hampshire. This was more French than Italian; the details of the roof of Hampton Court hall, for example, resemble those in contemporary French churches.[57] Two major buildings in this style are recorded in London, both outside the walled city: Bridewell Palace (1515–23)[58] and Suffolk House (**195**) in Southwark (1518–20), the latter shown in Wyngaerde's panorama of *c.* 1540 (Fig. 42).[59] These grand examples do not however appear to have been followed by the prominent citizens or other occupiers of note in London. The first thirty years of the sixteenth century saw instead the more modest reappearance of the tower, this time in timber or brick as a stair-turret or as free-standing in a garden (see p. 84), and the erection of garden galleries and other garden houses (see p. 89–90) along with innovations in decoration, for instance in brick (diapering and moulded bricks for chimneys) and woodwork.

Far greater changes to the character of the grand house in London followed the Dissolution of the monastic houses. A considerable number of noble urban residences were constructed within religious precincts, adapting the monastic

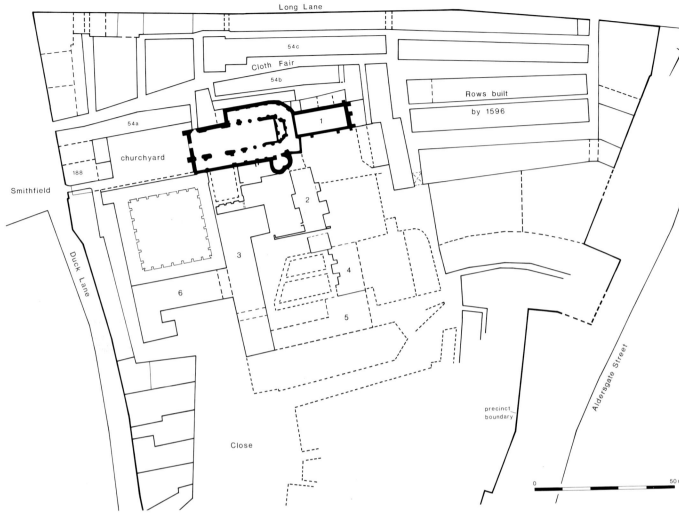

43.   Post-Dissolution houses: (a) the breaking-up of St Bartholomew
Smithfield into high-status residences (numbered 1–6), from a survey
of 1616, showing the Cloth Fair development 54 and other sites

(b)   (8) Duke's Place, Aldgate: the Ivy Chamber, from plans by
J. Symonds surveyed about 1586 (R. Lea)

buildings and clothing them in timberwork and glazing and
inserting newly fashionable interiors.

The constraints of developing a restricted urban site, already fairly full of substantial stone buildings, must have
severely hampered any attempt to emulate contemporary rural grand houses. At the Charterhouse (48) two courts were
contrived on the Bridewell and Hampton Court model, with
the hall on one side of the inner court (Fig. 44). By the end of
the century galleries are found in several of the apartments
into which the London houses had been divided (e.g. the two
galleries at Duke's Place (8) and a house in the former
Ladychapel at St Bartholomew Smithfield, with an adjacent
gallery) (Fig. 43a).[60] It is however difficult to identify suites of
rooms – the great chamber, withdrawing chamber, bedchamber and closet, and long gallery – which are a feature of large
houses of this period elsewhere. If the Audley mansion at
Duke's Place originally extended to and included the Ivy
Chamber in the crossing of the priory church, as seems possible, then the high end of the hall would have led via a gallery
to a kind of prospect house, the Ivy Chamber (Fig. 43b). The
copperplate engraving of London of *c*. 1559 shows details

44.   (48) Charterhouse: exterior of the hall (J. Crowther 1885)

of the garden of Winchester Place, transformed out of the Austin Friars by Paulet, containing a fountain.

Details concerning the accommodation for the lord's often substantial household and entourage are extremely sketchy. Lodgings had been a distinct form of accommodation in castles and manor-houses since the fifteenth century; those at Lincoln's Inn and Staple Inn have had their internal details rebuilt. Hollar's view of the north side of the court at Arundel House (Fig. 45) shows what may be timber-framed lodgings for the nobleman's entourage.

This and the other views of the Strand in 1646 and 1656 (Figs. 46–7) show a group of prestigious sixteenth-century town-houses in the area around Somerset House (1549): the houses of the Earl of Leicester (rebuilt 1549 and 1563, in 1656 known as Essex House), Arundel House (gallery, 1604–20), Russell or Bedford House, and especially Salisbury House, rebuilt by Simon Basil for the Earl of Salisbury (Sir Robert Cecil) in 1599. Here was the earliest recorded example in London of the seventeenth-century fashion of a courtyard bordered on the streetside not by buildings, but by a railing and an ornamented metal gate; the medieval preference for privacy in placing the main buildings away from the public gaze was being replaced by the desire to display to all comers.

By the time of Stow and Treswell at the end of the sixteenth century, many older noble houses in the city were no longer to be seen above ground, or were hardly recognisable (111, 165, 169). The gardens of Northumberland Inn in Fenchurch Street, Aldgate (71), had been converted into bowling-alleys; Pulteney's house in Lawrence Pountney Lane (114) was sold by the Earl of Sussex in 1561 and split into two halves, one of which became Merchant Taylors' School. The Inn of the Earl of Oxford had been let to poulterers for the stabling of horses and stowing of poultry.[62] The hall of the Bigods of Norfolk at Brokenwharf (165) was a brewery; several religious town-houses had become taverns, as noted above. Apart from livery company halls (which are discussed next), houses which retained their courtyards were comparatively rare (72, 76, 142–3, 179). Yards had often been built over (145) or were encroached upon (72; Figs. 48–50).

Though they were individually often under pressure, a certain zoning of the better residences was becoming apparent by this time. Stow and his near-contemporary the playwright Dekker both noticed that certain streets were favoured by the 'worthiest citizens' for their large houses: St Mary Axe (cf. 137; Fig. 179) and Lime Street on the one hand, but also Milk Street and Bread Street, apparently quiet enclaves near

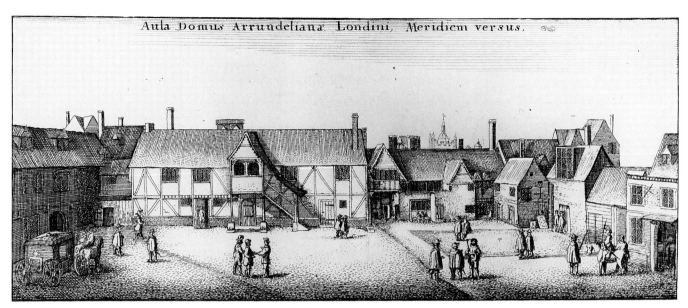

45.   (157) Arundel House, Fleet Street: view of north side (Hollar 1646)

to but sufficiently secluded from Cheapside.[62] Nor were the few remaining large houses inhabited only by prominent citizens; in 1595 a list was made of 121 gentlemen who had seats in the country and who maintained a London residence. These were mostly to be found in the peripheral wards: nearly half (forty-eight) were in the northern and peripheral wards of Farringdon Without, Aldersgate, Cripplegate and Bishopsgate (cf. **25**).[63] The particular cachet of certain districts in the late sixteenth-century city seems to have presaged the move to more exclusive squares of the second quarter of the seventeenth century at Lincoln's Inn Fields and Covent Garden, out to the west and towards Westminster.

Among larger mansions, the livery company halls formed a distinct and ancient group. Although certain crafts formed recognised groups during the twelfth century, the advance in powers and social position of the guilds came in the late thirteenth and early fourteenth centuries. In the 1270s and 1280s the apprentice system, if not already established, was greatly developed; the first recorded pageant in which every citizen took part according to his craft dates from 1300, when 600 citizens accompanied their new queen Margaret to Westminster 'with the cognisances of their misteries embroidered on their sleeves'.[64] It is likely that early medieval groups of craftsmen had meeting halls, but details are vague: the tanners, for instance, had a hall in the parish of St Peter le Poor in the twelfth century.[65] Four or five crafts may have possessed halls around 1400: the Goldsmiths, Merchant Taylors, and possibly the Skinners, Cordwainers and Saddlers.

Merchant Taylors' Hall (**177**; Figs. 51, 77, 86) survives to illustrate both the form and the problems of analysis. A large mansion with gates to Cornhill and Threadneedle Street (then called Broad Street) passed in 1347 from John Yakeslee, tent-maker to the king, to a group of his fellow merchant tailors and linen-drapers. The existing hall can be dated only roughly to the fourteenth century, so that it is unclear whether Yakeslee or the company built it; at the east end of the building, two surviving bays of an undercroft, which extended at least one further bay to the north, may well be a

relic of the private house and precede the walls of the hall. The medieval kitchen, on its present site by 1388 and rebuilt in 1432–3, could also incorporate fragments of the previous mansion. This mixture of elements from both before and after acquisition by the company illustrates two common features of the adaptation of private houses as company halls by the crafts. A prominent member of the craft would bequeath a house, nearly always a courtyard house with a large hall suitable for the ceremonies and convivial meetings of the brethren, to a group of trustees, including members of the guild. Once in possession the company would generally adapt and expand the buildings, but not fundamentally alter their arrangement. Typical additions were a parlour or the laying-out of a formal garden, two developments which were also taking place in larger houses in private hands. The need for a central hall for feasting, working meetings and ceremony helped to prolong the life of the large, open-roofed hall as a building form into the early years of the seventeenth century. The courtyard form persisted after the Great Fire, as Ogilby and Morgan's map of 1677 (Fig. 52) shows; though the buildings were now of brick with stone dressings, the site plan of the livery company hall remained traditional until the twentieth century.

The early fifteenth-century halls, with the possible exception of the Merchant Taylors', were in or near areas associated with their trades from 1300, as attested by the street-name evidence which seems to indicate trade groupings of or before the late thirteenth century. After 1400, however, the siting of new halls, being dependent largely on individual bequest, was more random. By the time an unknown hand listed prominent halls in the city in the later fifteenth century there were twenty-seven halls belonging to twenty-five companies (the Fishmongers had three separate halls); eight of these are mentioned for the first time. The list, which can be dated to around and quite possibly precisely 1475, may reflect the emergence of several halls in the favourable circumstances of the reign of Edward IV, during which nine guilds were officially recognised.[66]

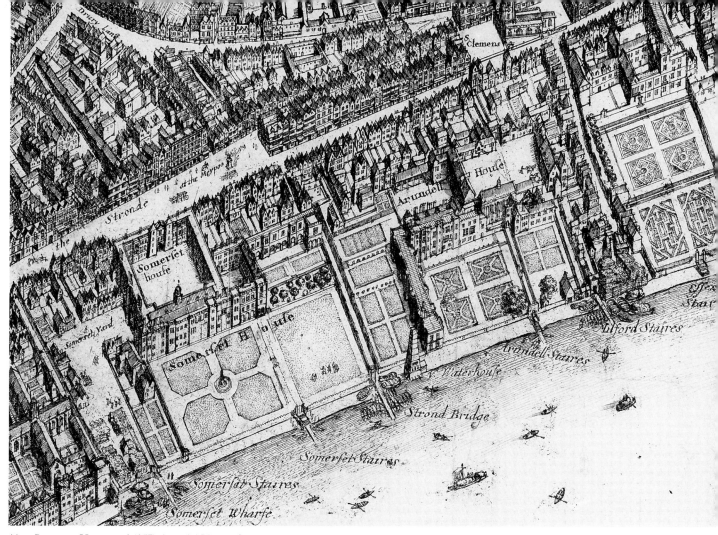

46.   Somerset House and (**157**) Arundel House, Strand (Hollar 1656)

47.   (**159**) Salisbury House, Worcester House, Bedford House and Exeter House, Strand (Hollar 1656)

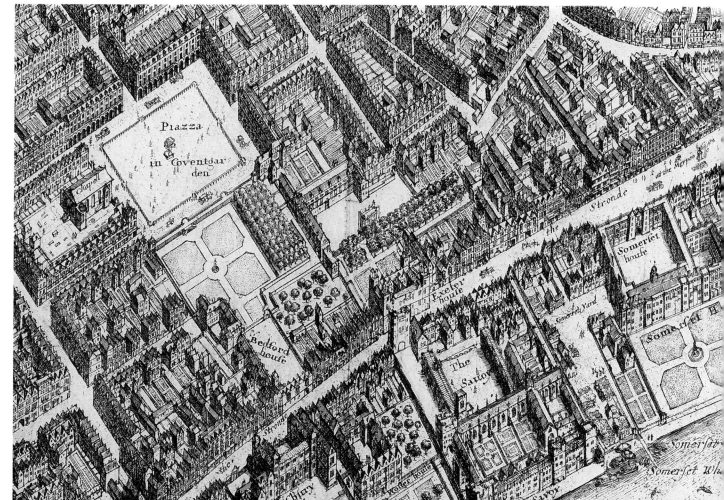

48. (*above left*)   (**143**) Lady Lucy's house, Dean's Court, Old Ba[
(Treswell 1612)

49. (*above*)   (**75**) 1–6 Fleet Lane, 16–21 Farringdon Street, Mod[
Court (Treswell 1612)

50. (*left*)   (**142**) Foxe's Court, [St] Nicholas Lane (Treswell 16[

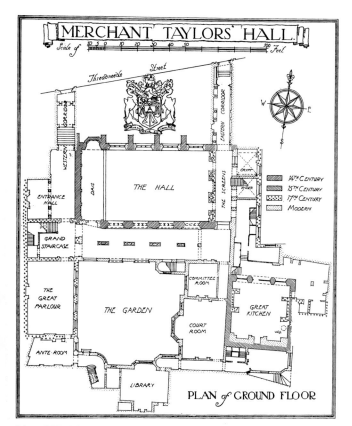

51. **(177)** Merchant Taylors' Hall, Threadneedle Street: plan, 1929 [RCHM, *City*]

The halls listed and with known dates of establishment or first mention in the period 1400–75 were those of the Brewers (after 1404, by 1423), Grocers (1411), Cutlers (1420), Drapers (1425), Carpenters (1429), Fishmongers in Thames Street (1433), Barber-Surgeons (1440–5), Vintners (1446), Salters (1454), Shearmen (1456), Haberdashers (1460) and Tallow-Chandlers (site II, 1475). In addition the Mercers had had rooms in the Hospital of St Thomas of Acon since 1391. Halls mentioned for the first time in Harley MS 541 are those of the Bakers, Bowyers, Curriers, Dyers, Fishmongers' second and third halls, Fullers and Tilers. The manuscript lists all the company halls which are independently dated up to the Tallow-Chandlers' (site II, in Dowgate) in 1475, with three exceptions: the Parish Clerks (1448), the Ironmongers (1457) and the Tallow-Chandlers' first hall in Broad Street (mentioned in 1465). The list does not include the halls of the Pewterers (1475), Pinners (1480), Coopers (1490), Blacksmiths (1494–5) or Joiners (1497), and is therefore dated here to around, and quite possibly in, 1475.

The type of building thought suitable for a company hall at this period is illustrated by two which were newly built in the fifteenth century: the Grocers' **(149)** in 1427 and the Carpenters' **(128)** in 1429. The Grocers constructed a stone hall with an impressive bay window which survived the Great Fire (Fig. 53). A parlour and chapel were integral parts of the scheme. The Carpenters levelled five cottages in London Wall to make room for their new hall, which also had a bay window by 1442; lively carved corbels (Figs. 143–4) supported arch-coupled roof trusses of a quality equal to those of the new hall of a legal school at Barnard's Inn in Holborn **(105)**.

Of the sixty companies who had places at the mayor's feast at Guildhall in 1532, forty-five had halls.[67] Since 1475 there had been a constant trickle of existing halls acquired for companies or heard of for the first time: the Pewterers (1475), Coopers (1480), Blacksmiths (1494–5), Joiners (1497), Weavers (1498), Cooks (1500), Waxchandlers (1501), Leathersellers I (early sixteenth century), Embroiderers (*c.* 1519), Innholders (1522), Founders (1531) and Painter-Stainers (1532). In addition the Bakers moved across the city to a second hall in 1506 and the Fullers took up temporary residence at site **72** (Fig. 54) in Fenchurch Street in 1520–8, thereafter combining with the Shearmen to become the Clothworkers' Company.

The wealth of surviving company accounts and deeds of this period means that the company hall complex, so often repeated throughout the city, is one of the main sources of information about secular medieval building history in London. It resembled both the grander residence (several company halls were formerly noble residences), and the private houses of the more prominent citizens who formed the livery. The company hall was also an estate office, and a centre for charitable functions. From the second decade of the fifteenth century some of the companies built almshouses by the hall,

52. Detail of Ogilby and Morgan's map (1677) showing Dowgate Hill and Cloak Lane, with sites **(53)** Cutlers' Hall (C21), **(65)** Tallow-Chandlers' Hall (C22), and **(66)** Skinners' Hall (C33)

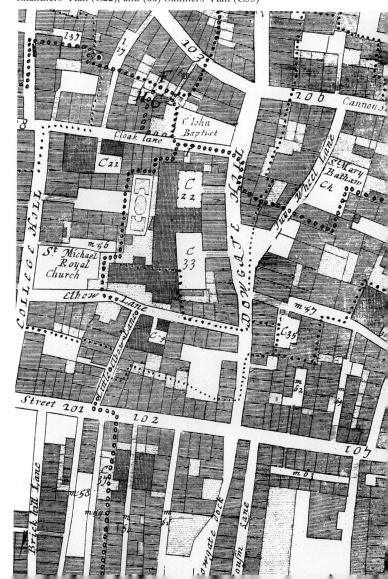

or nearby. The Merchant Taylors, the Brewers, and the Carpenters (**177, 1, 128**) were among the earliest; unfortunately
no plans of these earliest almshouses have survived, the
known plans being of sixteenth-century date (see below).

Many smaller companies never had a hall of their own;
some hired a hall from a company that did, or a fraternity hall
(**7**), while others met in taverns. Groups of foreign weavers
were segregated and made to meet in different churchyards,
so they would not fall out and fight.[69]

In the decades after 1530, livery companies, like individuals, took advantage of the increased availability of suitable
properties. In 1548 the Butchers moved from Beech Lane,
outside the walls, to the former parsonage of St Nicholas
Shambles (**155**), made available by the post-Reformation re-
structuring of parishes in the vicinity of the Greyfriars and
the redundancy of two parish churches. Parts of recently
dissolved monastic houses were also adapted or rebuilt as
company halls: the Leathersellers moved to the former dorter
and chapter house of St Helen's Bishopsgate nunnery (**96**),
which they rebuilt as a first-floor hall and parlour respectively
(Figs. 55–6), and in 1612 the Woodmongers, having for some
reason left the hall bearing their name in Peter's Hill (**147**),
were probably meeting in the hall in Duke's Place (**8**). In 1568
the Tilers and Bricklayers, now a united company, built or
acquired a hall occupying the rear of two properties in
Leadenhall Street (**118**) which came to them via Thomas
Audley and which may thus also have been the property of
Holy Trinity Priory. The Mercers succeeded in retaining
hold of their hall within the former hospital of St Thomas of
Acon in Cheapside, and the Apothecaries acquired part of
Blackfriars.[69]

Several companies rebuilt their halls during the period

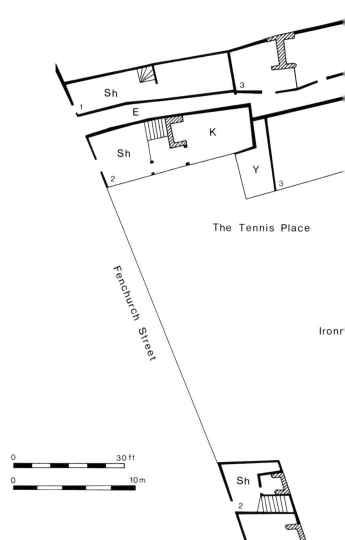

54. (*right*)   (**71–3**) 115 and 118 Fenchurch Street, 12–14 Billiter Street
(Treswell 1612)

53.   (**149**) Grocers' Hall, Poultry (undated, *c.* 1750)

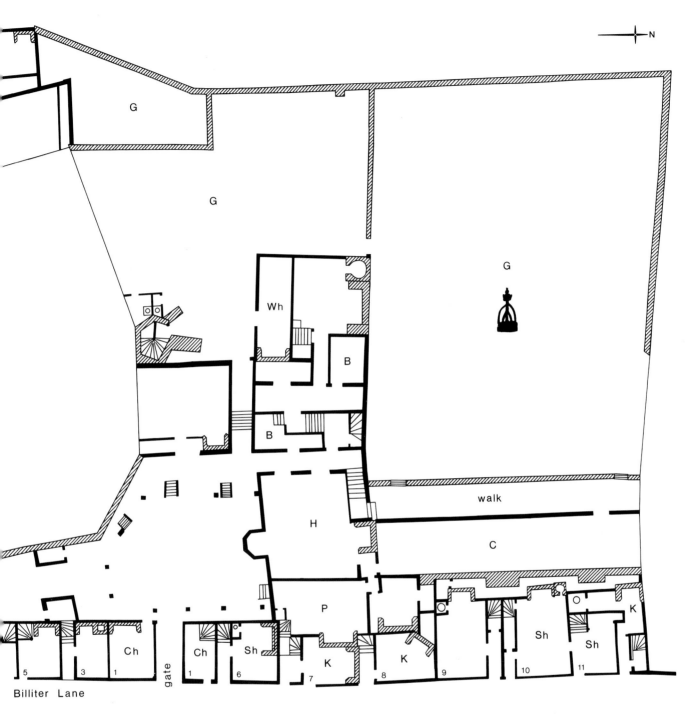

1540–1600, though the fortunes of others declined. The Clothworkers rebuilt their hall in 1549, the Cordwainers between 1559 and 1577, and the Ironmongers in 1578. In addition Stow's *Survey* of 1598 provides the first mention of four halls which could either be of recent origin or older sites without documentation.[70] The Pinners, on the other hand, had decayed as a company and in 1545 their hall passed to the Plaisterers;[71] the hall of the Woodmongers at Peter's Hill, as noted, was in private possession by 1581.

The hall complex of a successful livery company in 1612 is illustrated by Clothworkers' Hall in Mincing Lane (**139**; Fig. 57). The hall had been rebuilt in 1549 and the parlour in 1594; both were of brick, on undercrofts and with canted bay windows. The parlour lay on the south side of the complex to

form part of a three-storey range at right angles to the hall. The upper chambers of this range included a plate chamber, dry larder, gallery, counting house, armoury, and Ladies' Chamber.

A further specialised use of the large mansion was to be turned into a collegiate establishment for legal training; this happened to several houses in the extramural area to the west. The concentration of legal inns here, between the City and Westminster, has been traced in origin to a writ of 1234 by Henry III which ordered schools of law within the City to be closed; this may have encouraged a drift towards Westminster and the land between the two cities, which we have already noted in the case of ecclesiastical inns.[72] The medieval and Tudor form of the legal inns, which would have had

55. (**96**) Leathersellers' Hall, Great St Helen's, before demolition in 1799, from a drawing in the Gardiner Collection [Black 1871]

56. (**96**) Leathersellers' Hall, Great St Helen's: section through thirteenth-century undercroft of nuns' dorter with Leathersellers' Hall on first floor (W. Capon before 1799)

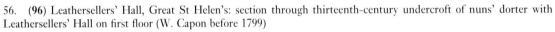

specialised characteristics stemming from their collegiate nature, has not been pursued in detail here; their secular origins and fabric details (some of significance for building history) are briefly noted in the gazetteer (**47, 78, 82, 94, 103, 105–6, 108**). Lincoln's Inn (**47**), for instance, was based on the Inn of the Bishop of Chichester in Chancery Lane. The Society of Lincoln's Inn augmented the premises with eleven new chambers in 1450–1, and rebuilt the hall of the property in 1489–92; between the hall and Chancery Lane, around a large courtyard, they erected two arms of a quadrangle of brick buildings and a prominent gatehouse in 1518–20, digging the clay for the bricks from their own land, at the same time as Henry VIII's workmen were erecting similar buildings at Bridewell Palace a short distance to the south-east, south of Fleet Street. These two modern local developments may have brought a new tone to the area between Westminster and the City before the creation of Somerset House (1549) and other courtiers' mansions among the old bishops' palaces of the Strand.

To summarise, the courtyard house had appeared in London by the twelfth century, when prominent stone buildings were constructed back from the street frontage; possibly some notable pre-Conquest timber buildings were laid out at the rear of courtyards (see above, p. 28) but this is as yet uncertain. A prominent ground-floor hall at the back of a court was evidently the sign of wealth and status in the thirteenth century; religious and secular leaders both favoured the form. A similar placing of buildings back from the street has been noticed for the urban residences of rural religious houses in York and Edinburgh.[73] Despite the incomplete nature of the record, it can be suggested that London had a greater number of such buildings than other British towns, at least in the thirteenth and fourteenth centuries. Thereafter the large house was particularly prone to subdivision, change in use and quite often demolition. Here our records are particularly deficient, for Stow mentions many large old houses which apparently survived or could be fragmentarily observed within living memory; we therefore cannot assess how exceptional Crosby Place was, though it was clearly of high quality. More certainly, by the end of the sixteenth century few large medieval houses remained intact for John Stow to muse over or Ralph Treswell to survey.

Medium-sized and Narrow Properties

The corpus of house-plans by Treswell in 1607–14 shows a variety of forms of medium-sized and smaller houses, but two main types (Types 3 and 2) may be discerned. These can also be traced back into the medieval period.

The Type 3 house (filling a whole property, and of three to six rooms in ground-floor plan) did not have a true courtyard with a formal gate to the street, though it might have a yard with buildings along one side (Fig. 58), or an alley running the length of a long, narrow property. The latter arrangement is illustrated most clearly by properties on the waterfront south of Thames Street, before they were subject to widescale subdivision (Figs. 254–5).

The great majority of waterfront properties were between 3 m (10 ft) and 11 m (37 ft) wide. Many had an alley down one

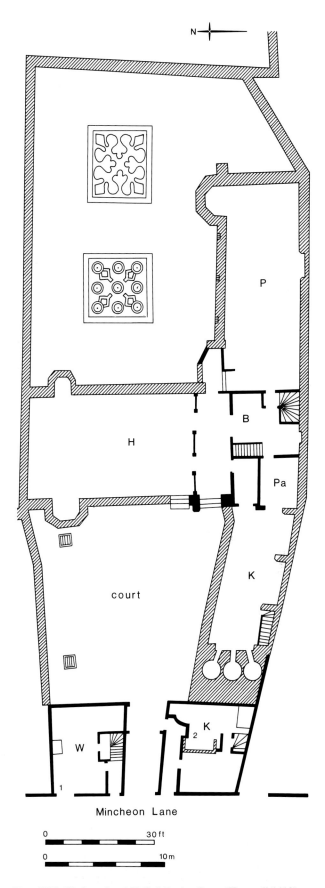

57. (**139**) Clothworkers' Hall, Mincing Lane (Treswell 1612)

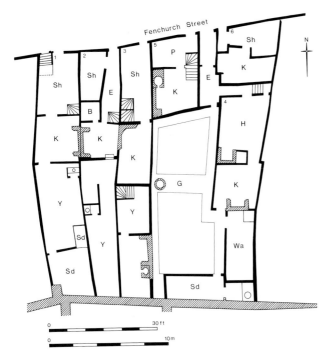

58. **(70)** 47–48 Fenchurch Street (Treswell 1612)

59. Lobby entrance houses: (a) (*below*) **(189)** West Smithfield
(Pheasant Court)

(b) (*below right*)   **(55)** Swan Alley, house on west of plot

(c) (*bottom right*)   House on east of plot (all Treswell 1612)

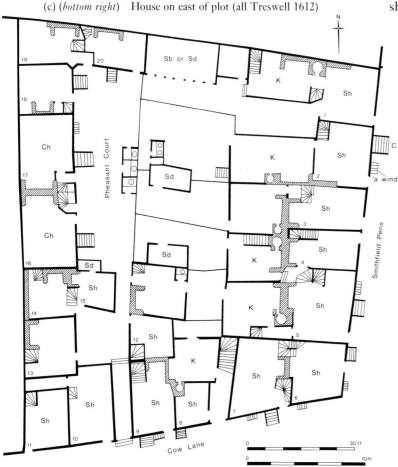

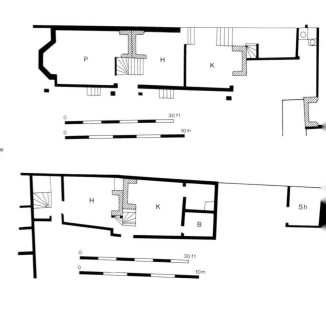

side, and in consequence buildings were usually arranged down the side of the plot behind the street range. Such an arrangement can be inferred from a building lease of 1384 for a property at Pakemann's Wharf, downstream of Billingsgate (**175**; Fig. 256). A street range was to be three storeys high, and behind would be the main living rooms including a hall and parlour, kitchen and buttery, all on vaults 7 ft high expressly for merchandise. The wharf, which was to be enlarged, was to be faced with stone.

The street range of the property commonly comprised shops, sometimes let separately. A property to the west of Billingsgate was described in 1334 as having three shops in the front of the tenement; in 1436–7 the same tenement, now called *Le lyon on the hoop*, comprised two shops and a solar above on the street side, with two further solars lying above the gate which gave entrance to the tenement, and a hall and cellar behind.[74] This arrangement is very similar to that at Pakemann's Wharf. In neither case is it known whether the street range was one or two rooms deep.

Along, usually at the side of, most waterfront properties ran the access alley from the street to the river and the main water supply. This originated for the most part as a private thoroughfare, in some cases becoming public through time and custom. In 1343 some fifty alleys were regarded as public, and the fact that the names of about half of them were suffixed by *-gate* or *-wharf* suggests a public origin, probably by the eleventh and twelfth centuries.[75] One of the properties excavated at New Fresh Wharf (**174**) was known as *le Brodegate* by 1349, and the alley was just over 2 m (6 ft 7 in) wide. The surfaces within the street range were of mortar and oyster shells, but cobbled to the south where the alley was exposed.

The lanes were the occasion of some litigation between neighbours, or when an allegedly common lane was obstructed. In 1346, for instance, William Trig was accused of blocking Trig Lane, then called Fissingwharf Lane, to the west of his tenement with wooden stalls, wood and other things so that access, formerly allowed to all citizens conveying their goods and merchandise to and from the river by horse and cart, was denied. In this case the defendant could prove that the lane, though common, has never been wide enough for use by carts, which could not turn in it.[76]

Smaller, and more uniform in its characteristics, was a house with two rooms on three or more floors (Type 2), such as those surveyed in Abchurch Lane (Fig. 50). This type is known from documentary and archaeological evidence in London from the early fourteenth century (141, 174); the five houses of this type at Abchurch Lane may have been those built on the site shortly before 1390. In Type 2 houses the ground floor was a shop and warehouse, sometimes with the two rooms thrown together to form one, or a tavern (194). The hall lay usually on the first floor at the front, overlooking the street. In the Abchurch Lane examples, the kitchen was a separate building reached across a small yard, but in the majority of the type as surveyed by Treswell the kitchen occupied a back room on the first floor.

The Type 2 house was particularly common in situations where no adjacent private open space was available, and was especially notable for forming frontages of larger houses behind it; from the middle of the thirteenth century in the case of central streets (32) and by the opening of the fourteenth century along the waterfront (174).

Two further types of medium-sized house have been recognised in the area of London and might be expected in the city: the Wealden house and the lobby-entrance house. The Wealden house, always timber-framed, normally comprised an open hall with two-storeyed jettied wings at each end; the eaves of the roof were carried over the recess in the middle on prominent braces. The basic distribution is in Kent and Sussex, though the type has now been found in all the Home Counties, Bedfordshire and Cambridgeshire, and in towns such as Coventry and York.[78] The form dates from the late fourteenth century to perhaps the 1530s, and a London origin for the design has been suggested.[79] If, as noted below in Chapter 6, jetties were found first in London during the second quarter of the thirteenth century, the Wealden form could well have been present in the city by 1250, and been a forerunner of the fourteenth-century fashion for jettied cross-wings. Unfortunately no definite example has yet been identified.

In contrast the lobby-entrance house, a common form in south-east England by 1600,[80] is present in several of the Treswell surveys, in open locations or as a subdivision of a range along a yard where the entrance could not or need not be in the end against a street (55–6, 189; Fig. 59a–c). The lobby-entrance house should be classified by its number of ground-floor rooms, usually as Type 2; the entrance lay in the side of the building rather than in one end, and opened into a small lobby against the side of the axial stack.

The Smallest Houses

Though buildings of a single storey and of one room in plan have been recorded in Saxon London, with examples from the tenth and eleventh centuries, no archaeological examples of small houses of the Middle Ages have yet been recorded in detail in London as they have, for instance, in Winchester.[81] These humble dwellings did not survive into the era of the engraving, and as they commonly lay along street-frontages, excavation has not uncovered them because of later street-widening and the digging of cellars, especially in the nineteenth century. Sometimes the existence of buildings, probably forming continuous façades and one room deep, are inferred from the absence of rubbish pits near the line of the street, as at Bow Lane and Milk Street in the eleventh and twelfth centuries (31, 138). As noted above, some of the frontages of both larger and middle-sized tenements may have been only one room deep. Many one-room plan houses are however shown by Treswell in the surveys of 1607–14 (e.g. Figs. 49–50, 54, 66). Houses with only one room on each floor, or at most one room and an entry or passage (Type 1) were to be found both on principal streets, where they formed a screen for the larger houses behind (72, 76), and in courtyards where they could assume awkward, angular shapes to take up the available space (88, 140, 154). On principal streets such as Fish Street Hill a one-room plan house could reach five and a half storeys.[82]

Alehouses, Taverns and Inns; Cookshops

In medieval London, as in the rest of England, there were three main types of victualling house: in ascending order of size and status, the alehouse, the tavern and the inn, though the distinctions were often blurred. In addition, London had shops, often run by bakers, which dealt in cooked food. A similar extensive range of establishments could be found at Westminster.[83]

In 1309 the author of a chronicle guessed that there were 1,334 brewers in London; this probably included many part-timers.[84] The industry developed during the fourteenth century and prominent brewers could maintain one of the earliest recorded company halls, bequeathed to them in 1408 (1). In 1418 the Brewers' Company had 234 paid-up members. Alehouses had a pole outside the door, its length regulated in 1292;[85] alebrewers used a hoop, presumably of metal, as a sign. In general alehouses would not require much space for storage, as ale would not keep. The introduction of hops into London, from at least 1420 (perhaps for the large Flemish population), made it necessary to incorporate storage areas into brewhouses, since beer made with hops could be stored and transported. *Brewhouses* were evidently considerable establishments: the Saracen's Head in Aldersgate in 1463, for example, included a well-furnished brewhouse, a hall with two glazed windows, two privies and three refurbished stables.[86] The largest examples contained horse-mills, to grind the malt; but otherwise brewhouses were evidently similar to dyehouses in the character of their installations, since there are cases of dyers and brewers using the same lead troughs and vats.[87]

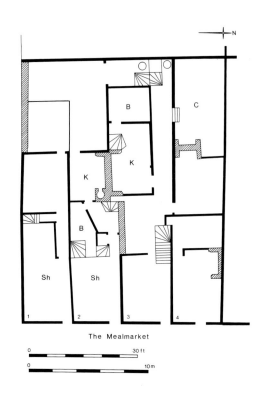

The Mealmarket

60.   Two taverns: (a) (*left*) (**181**) The White Hart, Knightrider Street

(b) (*above*)   (**194**) The Mealmarket, Southwark (Treswell 1610–11)

The chronicler of 1309 also noted 354 taverns in the city. Taverns were drinking houses where wine was available; and as such they became the virtual monopoly of the Vintners' Company in 1364. A tavern would have a pole not more than 7 ft in length bearing a sign of leaves.[88]

Taverns in undercrofts are recorded by the early fourteenth century (**51**).[89] Some undercrofts were evidently built as drinking-places from the start. The Peter and Paul tavern in Paternoster Row, rebuilt in 1342, comprised an undercroft provided with fireplaces and therefore presumably suitable for social drinking, and drinking rooms or partitioned areas on both ground and first floors (**146**). During the fifteenth century the main drinking areas seem to have concentrated on the ground floor of buildings, and then the cellar was abandoned; three small taverns surveyed by Treswell in 1610–12 had drinking rooms on the ground floor only, with cellars no different from those of private houses (Fig. 60a).[90] In larger taverns, rooms were given individual names as an aid to serving drink; an inventory of the Mouth tavern, outside Bishopsgate, in 1612 mentions rooms called the Percullis, the Pomgrannatt, the Three Tuns, the Crosse Keys and the King's Head, whereas the domestic chambers (identified by their furnishings and linen) are not named.[91] Presumably such special names referred to decorative devices on the walls of the rooms.

Taverns were used by companies as an alternative to their halls, perhaps partly for the convenience of having wine and food ready to hand. The Weavers, for instance, had a hall but dined in taverns: in one year, 1552–3, the company used the Gote in Cheap six times, the Red Bull in Thames Street and

the Horse Head in Cheap five times each, and went once to the White Horse and the Bishop's Head in Lombard Street, and to the Rose in Fenchurch Street. The Pewterers used the Pope's Head tavern (**124**) for co-ordination meetings for their search activities throughout the country.[92] The Cheapside area was thick with taverns which must have had a frequent trade in company meetings and feasts, possibly in special chambers. Taverns were also used by parish councils conducting their business: to seal contracts on new building ventures, to settle local arbitrations, or for dinners for lawyers conducting litigation on the parish's behalf.[93] Such establishments could be large: in 1585 at Westminster, an area with a similar clientele requiring meeting places, the Bear had twenty-one rooms.[94] On the other hand small taverns closely resembled private houses (e.g. **194**; Fig. 60b) and modifications from one function to the other were probably minimal; in 1595, for instance, the Vintners complained that several houses in Hosier Lane (Bow Lane), Fenchurch Street, Thames Street, Aldersgate and Smithfield had been converted into taverns.[95]

Inns or hostels were inspected by aldermen in 1282,[96] and in 1384 a total of 197 inns were listed by ward.[97] The main concentration was in Farringdon Without, with 50 inns in Fleet Street, 25 in Holborn and 20 in Smithfield. By comparison Bread Street ward, which contained Cheapside, had 22, and Castle Baynard ward only 9. No figures are given for Bishopsgate ward, but several in Bishopsgate Street are mentioned during the fifteenth century, and some may have been there during the previous century.[98]

By 1345 a guest could obtain a single room;[99] in 1380 the

custom of the realm, it was noted, was that the keeper of a hostelry was responsible for the goods left by the guest, who should also receive a key to a single room.[100] It was also possible to have a set of rooms; in 1390 a suite at an inn in the parish of St Benet Paul's Wharf comprised a hall, chamber, buttery and kitchen.[101] Inns naturally would have a large number of windows, for which they were prosecuted by neighbours; in 1422 their lattices and pentices commonly encroached on the highway, especially in Bishopsgate. The inn would have stabling for horses, even when in a central position such as Friday Street.[102]

Predictably inns were to be found in numbers immediately outside London's gates, where custom concentrated and where long properties could incorporate stable yards, and in Southwark. One such was the Crowne, Aldgate, surveyed by Treswell in 1610 (**10**; Fig. 61). This was constructed round two yards: the front yard with the main buildings and, reached through a second gateway with storeys over it, the stable yard with haylofts. Illustrations of other inns show that they sometimes had galleries at first-floor level looking down into the courtyard, in the manner of surviving examples in other towns (Fig. 96).[103]

A final form of victualling house in the metropolis was the eating-house and the shop which sold baked food. In *c.* 1174 Fitzstephen described a public eating-house 'among the wineshops which are kept in ships and cellars' on the bank of the river, evidently at Vintry.[104] Inns and later taverns provided meals, and in the Treswell surveys several buildings, especially on street-corners or adjacent to market areas such as Smithfield, had large ovens and may have sold hot food (e.g. **33**, **69**, **88**, **189**; Fig. 62).

Blocks of Shops; Selds

Shops were constructed in blocks of three or more from the early fourteenth century, and the street-name *Row* occurs in London from the opening of the fourteenth century. A row in London presumably resembled surviving examples elsewhere such as Lady Row in York of 1314; two storeys high, jettied on the first floor, and with simple living accommodation above a ground-floor shop.[105] Three London contracts indicate the nature of unitary blocks of shops in the later fourteenth century, and these also appear to have contained living accommodation in the form of halls or solars. In 1369 St Paul's contracted with Roger Fraunkeleyn and John Page, carpenters, to build an L-shaped range of twenty shops at the corner of Godliman and Knightrider Streets, totalling 86 yards in length and probably of two-room plan (**89**). In 1370 St Paul's had Piers de Webenham, mason, construct cellars for a row of eighteen shops north of St Paul's brewery; these shops were 25 ft deep and therefore probably of two chambers in ground-floor plan. Each shop evidently had a chimney and a privy (**90**). Thirdly, in 1373 the prior of Lewes leased to William de Wyngtryngham, carpenter, land inside the gate of his Inn in Tooley Street, Southwark, to build two opposing rows of shops, five on one side and six on the other; they were to be 12 ft deep, i.e. probably containing one room on the ground floor, and with a first-floor jetty (**199**).

Unitary designs for blocks of shops are not heard of after

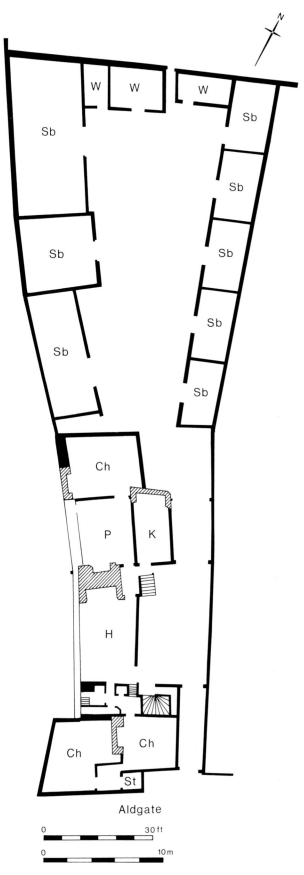

61. (**10**) The Crowne, Aldgate (Treswell 1610)

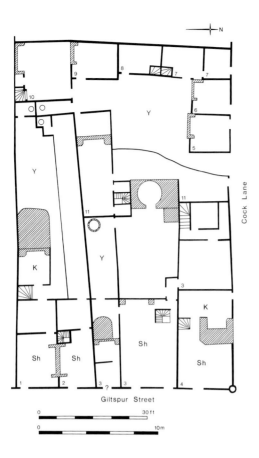

Giltspur Street

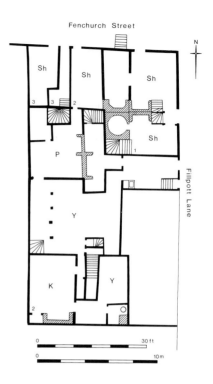

Fenchurch Street

62.   Examples of shops with large hearths: (a) (*left*) (**88**) Pie Corner, Giltspur Street (Treswell 1610–11)

(b) (*above*)   (**69**) 11–12 Fenchurch Street (Treswell 1612)

the late fourteenth century until the end of the fifteenth century, and then only in a form which seems exceptionally extravagant: Goldsmiths' Row, Cheapside, built by goldsmith Thomas Wood in 1491 (**49**). This too included houses, but now on a more substantial scale (Fig. 63). The interior plan of this row is not known before the Great Fire, but presumably the ground floors resembled those later surveyed by Treswell on major streets, and a stair would lead up into the domestic rooms. A slightly different design was employed in a unitary frame of five units, but only a single room deep, which was erected as the frontage of Staple Inn to Holborn in 1586 (Figs. 170–1); rooms above must always have been reached by stairs from the court behind, and were presumably built as lodgings for the inmates of the Inn. The structural similarities between shops and houses, and the frequent occurrence of a shop within an otherwise domestic structure, are examined further in Chapter 4.

The word *seld* described, in the late thirteenth century, specialised buildings which congregated in Cheapside, though occasionally found elsewhere, for instance near Vintry on the waterfront. They appear to have been long spaces aligned at right angles to the street, enclosed by stone walls, containing booths or chests for individual sellers, rather like a Middle Eastern bazaar or souk. It seems likely that these places were roofed, though the plan of at least one is apparently trapezoidal, and rather wide for normal spans.[106] The term *seld* was also used later of the covered arcade forming the ground floor at Leadenhall, which probably had a similar character of weather-proof area for display of goods on a large scale by a number of traders or craftsmen.

Almshouses and St James's Hermitage

Several of the livery companies – not necessarily the richer or major companies – founded almshouses near their halls in the early fifteenth century; a similar date, or slightly later, is suggested for the building of almshouses in Bruges and other Flemish cities. The earliest recorded in London are the Merchant Taylors (1414), followed by the Cutlers (1420–40), Brewers (1423) and Salters (1454). No plan of these early foundations survives. The executors of Richard Whittington bought properties in College Hill and founded there an almshouse to be supervised by the Mercers' Company in 1423–5; the almshouses lay along one side of an internal yard, with an unknown number of rooms or cells and a communal hall for eating.[107]

The foundation of almshouses was particularly a feature of the immediately post-Dissolution years: those of the Drapers (1535; Fig. 64), Haberdashers (1539), Clothworkers (1540) and Parish Clerks (1543). Treswell surveyed two sets of almshouses: those at Whitefriars bequeathed to the Cloth-workers' Company by the Countess of Kent in 1540 (**183**; Fig. 65a) and those built at St Peter's Hill by David Smith, embroiderer to Elizabeth I, in 1576 and bequeathed to Christ's Hospital (**147**; Fig. 65b). Both were variants of the courtyard plan, but with the difference that in 1610–12 the Whitefriars almshouses contained one resident on each floor with a single room each, whereas the residents of the St Peter's Hill almshouses had a ground-floor chamber, a chamber above and a garret.

Here we should also consider the Hermitage of St James in Monkwell Street (**140**), though its plan is known only in 1612,

63. (49) Goldsmiths'
Row, Cheapside: detail
from the engraving by
Grimm after painting of
c. 1547

64. (60) Drapers'
Almshouses, Crutched
Friars: front view in about
1800 by J. Whichelo (Sir
John Soane Museum)

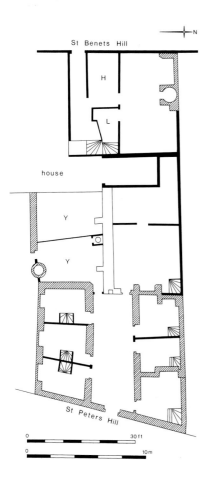

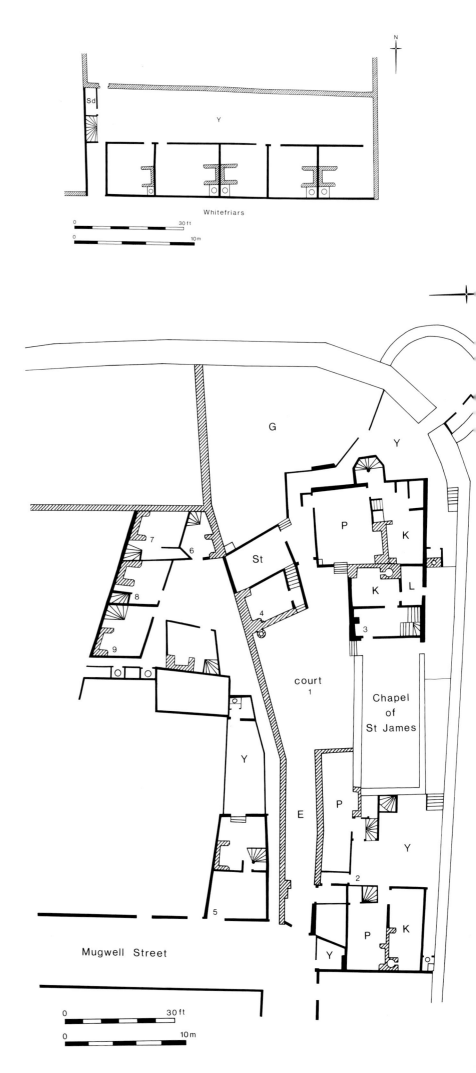

St Benets Hill

H

L

house

Y

Y

St Peters Hill

0   30 ft
0   10 m

Sd

Y

Whitefriars

0   30 ft
0   10 m

65.   Plans of two sets of almshouses: (a) (*above*) (147) Woodmongers' Hall and Smith's almshouses, [St] Peter's Hill (Treswell 1611)

(b) (*above right*)   (183) Countess of Kent's almshouses, later 28–30 Tudor Street (Treswell 1612)

66. (*right*)   (140) St James's Hermitage, Monkwell Street (Treswell 1612)

G

Y

7

6

St

P

K

8

K

L

3

9

4

court
1

Chapel
of
St James

Y

E

P

5

P

Y

2

Y

P

K

Mugwell Street

0   30 ft
0   10 m

when it was in secular ownership (Fig. 66). The hermitage was said to be granted to Richard I's chaplain Warin in 1189, but the chief medieval building evident in 1612 was the chapel with its basement vaulting dated to around 1140. It is notable that the chapel lies against the Roman and medieval city wall, being inserted into the bank behind the wall. On the one hand, this must have been a privilege granted to the original builder, whether Warin or somebody else in previous decades. On the other hand, we might also ask why the builder of the chapel wanted it to back onto the city wall. In a similar position on the wall, almost exactly the same distance to the east of Cripplegate as the Hermitage was to the west of the gate, lay the church of St Alphege; the significance of these positions, if any, is not known.

Accretion and Subdivision

Detailed documentary study, at least of central properties round Cheapside, is beginning to show that properties could change their shape and area over time; part of the next door tenement such as a cellar or larder might be annexed and then claimed back; a garden leased out and then sold, or the frontage might become a row of smaller dwellings.[108] Although amalgamations to form larger properties did occur, the more noticeable tendency over the medieval period was for properties to be subdivided and their open spaces built over. Subdivision of properties, often as the result of a will, was common by the fourteenth century.[109] By custom, the widow's 'chamber' consisted of the hall, the principal chamber, and the cellar; she was further allowed the use of the oven, the stable, the privy and the yard, together with other necessaries, as long as she remained unmarried.[110] A property was usually subdivided along existing partitions between rooms, but there are also cases where a tenement was taken down and rebuilt into several smaller plots.[111]

Subdivision of property after the death of the owner was not the only indication of the pressure on space. Since at least the opening of the fourteenth century, the City had used the mechanism of the *Assize of Nuisance* to handle disputes between neighbours where building works compromised the safety and privacy of adjacent properties. At least 574 specific complaints were made under the *Assize* in 1301–1437. The largest group of complaints concerned drains, gutters and water disposal (138, or 24 per cent), followed by building operations (94, 16 per cent), windows, apertures and resulting impairment of privacy (79, 14 per cent), obstruction of public or common amenities, or failure to observe the land-owner's obligations (from 1301, the Walbrook; 1305, land near the city wall; 1306, a lane to the Thames and a bridge (jetty) into the river; 1307, a path giving access to a tenement across what was claimed to be church land; 1309, interference with street drains; 1311, the obligation to pave the roadway outside one's tenement: 49 cases, 8.5 per cent). Ruin or decay of a tenement, with the consequences for adjacent properties, was cited in 41 cases (7 per cent), fences and earthen walls in 36 cases (6 per cent), privies in 34 cases (6 per cent), and overhanging buildings (whether leaning or as a result of jetty construction is not clear) in 33 cases (6 per cent). The remaining 70 cases (12 per cent) are complaints about miscellaneous

damage, obscured lights, industrial premises, chimneys or ovens, animals, pentices and partitions. City regulation, then, was concerned with construction along property boundaries, drains and privacy – the ways in which one occupier ran into another. The City authorities were concerned with standards along the outer margins of private properties, not, as the District Surveyors of today are, with standards of construction both inside and outside the property. This concern is especially noticeable in the nature of the complaints from the later surviving series of 1505–58 (*Viewers' Certificates*). They concern delineation of boundaries, the fair division of responsibility for joint privies, and the ejection of rubbish – the murmurings of citizens who increasingly had to rub shoulders with each other.

The contemporary Dissolution of the monasteries released much new land onto the property market, and from the 1570s wills show that many citizens held often substantial amounts of former monastic or chantry property.[112] Though the detailed processes are not yet researched, it seems likely that in the main the new landlords developed their sites for rent from housing, rather than laying out new and larger residences for themselves. This was of course easy at a time when many immigrants were flooding into the city. Thus it seemed to observers that new building and subdivision of existing properties were equal evils. Stow reacted strongly against 'pestering' of new tenements;[113] the City had been concerned with the problem since 1550, and in 1580 they sent a letter to the Privy Council, complaining 'of the vast increase of new buildings and number of inhabitants within the City and suburbs of London, chiefly occasioned by the great resort of people from all parts of the Kingdom to settle here . . .'[114] A royal proclamation followed, banning new buildings within three miles of the city gates.[115] Further reminders or proclamations followed, presumably because of slack observance, in 1583, 1593 and 1602.[116]

Colonisation of former religious precincts, especially by aliens or foreigners, was particularly rife. When in about 1586 John Symonds surveyed the transformed shell of the church of Holy Trinity Priory, Aldgate, once the town-house of the Duke of Norfolk, he found houses sprouting from above the Romanesque arches of the roofless choir, in front of the great window of the Ivy Chamber (Fig. 36); they were both one- and two-room dwellings, i.e. Type 1 and Type 2 houses (very probably with attic storeys, though these were not surveyed). This precinct was inhabited by a number of Dutchmen, probably refugees (8). Two decades later the surveys of Treswell show many instances of small houses packed together or larger houses subdivided (**57, 69, 76, 142, 145, 150, 181, 189**).

The houses at Holy Trinity Priory were of a peculiar form because of their situation; they had no ground floors, but were approached by narrow stairs from the former aisle below. This first-floor emphasis would however have been unremarkable at the time, when many houses in the city were comprised of living accommodation above ground-floor shops, an arrangement first evident in the early fourteenth century. What is at present not clear is when, and in what circumstances, several different tenancies occupied separate floors of a house in the manner of modern flats.[117] Widows commonly occupied single chambers, from cellars to garrets, as shown by Treswell's surveys (sites in Fleet Lane, **75**, and

West Smithfield, **189**; see **169** for a household of widows in Thames Street). Almshouses could have residents with single rooms on different floors (**183**), and by 1483–5 a parish property seems to have had a similar charitable purpose, being let out in a number of portions and with seven tenants having only a single chamber each.[118] But evidence for 'flats' in the modern sense is largely lacking up to and including the time of Treswell's surveys. In 1607–14 a small number of tenants in alleys lived on the first floor or higher with no rooms on the ground floor (**76, 179**). In the surveys it is much more common for a tenancy to have one or two rooms on the ground which comprised its street or ground-floor entrance, even if the tenancy spread out over several rooms in the storeys above (e.g. **181/3**).

Conclusions

So far, the combined efforts of archaeological excavation and documentary study have only succeeded in painting a broad outline of the ways in which streets, properties and buildings were laid out in the tenth to twelfth centuries in London.[119] There seems to have been a period, during the twelfth century and perhaps during the late eleventh century, when increasing business promoted a new emphasis of buildings towards the street in the central areas and along parts of the waterfront. We are still ignorant of the social or economic focus of buildings on the sites before this came about, or how the transition happened in detail.

A second and related question concerns the emergence, on substantial residences, of the courtyard plan with a main building, often of stone, at the rear of a yard (with a further yard or garden behind it) or at the rear of a whole plot. Leaders of the church, of aristocratic society and of the merchant community aspired to a common style of house with a courtyard and an open hall of lofty proportions. The siting of the main building away from the street can be traced back to certain larger stone houses of the twelfth century, and may have been presaged by the large timber buildings with cellars of the eleventh century; by about 1250, prominent merchants lived in houses of this type. The courtyard house has been called Type 4 in London. Though some noble houses were turned to other uses during the fifteenth and sixteenth centuries, livery company halls shared the form and helped to keep active the gradually obsolescent medieval assembly hall into the seventeenth century. Thus status was linked to plan-form and house type.

Any typology of medieval urban house-plans must build on the work of W. A. Pantin, who studied forty medieval houses from seventeen English towns.[120] He saw the Type 4 houses as one species of 'parallel' house, in which the hall lay parallel to the street, and described fourteenth- to sixteenth-century examples from Exeter, Norwich and Oxford, as well as his own reconstruction of the 1405 Bucklersbury contract (**40**).[121]

Pantin was concerned with the hall as the central feature of the tenement and the problems of adaptation on restricted urban sites; he therefore deliberately omitted both the smallest houses, in which development was only vertical, and the largest ('such as Arundel House in the Strand, or the Bishop's Palace or the Old Deanery at Salisbury') where space allowed full introduction of the manor-house plan. The London typology is wider, dealing with these extremities of the continuum, and Pantin's types fit within the middle range.

The wide range of houses of smaller dimensions in London can be gathered into three main types: of three to six rooms in ground-floor plan (Type 3), of two rooms in plan (sometimes with a separate kitchen) (Type 2) and of one room in plan (Type 1). We have virtually no complete plans of these houses in London before 1607–14. Pantin's typology of 'right-angle' type houses of either 'narrow' (i.e. filling the tenement) or 'broad' (i.e. leaving space for an alley) plan and its replication in other studies[122] show the variety of arrangement within the Type 3 band. The criterion of grouping together all houses with the hall at right angles to the street, whether the hall lay in the middle or at the side of the property, is however confusing: Pantin thus places courtyard houses such as Hampton Court, King's Lynn, and the Bridewell, Norwich, in the same 'broad' category as much smaller houses.

In another study, Pantin traces the Type 2 form in the post-medieval period in Oxford;[123] it is also found in other towns such as Exeter from about 1500.[124] The Type 1 house, with one room on each floor (occasionally augmented on the ground floor by an entry), was not considered by Pantin. It is found in the seventeenth century in King's Lynn, Norwich and Yarmouth. In Norwich such 'cottages' were on the one hand created out of the subdivision of larger properties in the seventeenth century, but are now seen to have been a late medieval form also.[125]

Although Treswell surveyed a comparatively small proportion of the houses then standing, it is striking that there is no example in his work of a house presenting its long side to a street, as found in other medieval towns. Even the Type 1 houses, which were generally rectangular rather than square in plan, presented their narrower sides to the street. In suburban streets such as Bishopsgate Without, Houndsditch and in Southwark, houses generally had their gables to the street. Some houses with the long side to the street are shown by Wyngaerde in Southwark in *c.* 1540 (Fig. 120), and one or two have been noted in plans and drawings of pre-Fire houses in streets such as Crutched Friars, but they must be considered atypical of the intramural capital. Some lobby-entrance houses existed, but they were away from the street frontage.

Finally, though the present study has only briefly surveyed other related types of domestic building, it is notable that, with the exception of almshouses, all the types considered – alehouses, taverns, inns, and blocks of shops – had similarities with houses in their plan and general size of rooms, and houses frequently changed into one or other of these more specialised places with little trouble. The same is true of those buildings or parts of houses where industrial processes were carried out. Rooms in medieval buildings were easily and frequently adapted for a variety of purposes.

CHAPTER 4

Development of Rooms and Open Spaces, 1200–1600

Some of the general house types to be found in medieval and Tudor London having been outlined in the previous chapter, the focus of enquiry can now be tightened further. This chapter is concerned with a description of the development of the rooms and spaces of which the medieval domestic property in London was composed, how those spaces were used and how they related to each other. From this may emerge significant patterns which might either be a consequence of outside influences, for example fashion in building design, or be a result of the pressures of urban living which would find particular expression in a large city.

Courtyard, Gate and Porch

By 1300 many larger houses comprised buildings around a courtyard, entered through a range of buildings fronting the street. It is possible that some eleventh-century timber buildings in the area south of Cheapside lay at the back of yards (see Chapter 3 and **31**) and the position of known or probably twelfth-century stone buildings (e.g. on the site of Blackwell Hall, **18**) suggests that in London, as in Winchester, some early stone houses were found at the back of courtyards. Properties with courtyards are mentioned, for instance, in 1202–3 in St Alban's parish and in *c.* 1225–45 in the parish of St Martin Outwich.[1] By the middle of the thirteenth century, houses of prominent citizens were of courtyard plan (**32**); and the form was shared with livery company halls, which often first appear in records as citizens' residences.

By the time of the Treswell surveys, courtyards within larger house-complexes were surrounded by buildings, and were sometimes bordered on several sides by a gallery which would have further encroached into the court with its pillars (**72**); smaller courts, surrounded by buildings, were often angular, restricted and can hardly have seen the light (e.g. **76**, Blacksmith's Court; **140**, yard to the south of the main complex). At the same time a more substantial place such as Robert Lee's house (formerly Zouche's Inn) in Leadenhall Street in 1607, formerly the residence of a Lord Mayor, had a courtyard, though constricted, laid with Purbeck marble slabs (**115**).

The courtyard was entered by a gate, either of wooden leaves hanging simply between two buildings of the street range or given special architectural emphasis by means of stone or brick jambs. Two gates were singled out by the justices of the 1246 Eyre (judges' report) for encroaching on the highway,[2] and presumably this indicates structures of some prominence. References to stone gates before the fourteenth century are rare, but examples can be cited in other large towns,[3] and it is likely that in London any early medieval examples were eventually rebuilt or replaced after centuries of abrasive use. John Stow saw 'arched gates' at several

former noble residences (e.g. **165**). Some properties had buildings called 'the great gate' or 'gatehouse'[4] but such references carry no further information. The name *le Brodegate* is attached to several houses in London, and may have signified either a prominent gatehouse or simply a wider than usual timber gate.[5] Gatehouses of brick with stone dressings became fashionable throughout the south-east of England during the fifteenth century,[6] and in London were built at larger establishments such as Lambeth Palace (1490) and Lincoln's Inn (1519). No domestic examples are yet known in the city, though the quality of some larger houses and many company halls was such as to have made their presence likely. Two surviving gatehouses, those at Charterhouse (*c.* 1440) and Lincoln's Inn, retain their wooden gate leaves and ironwork.[7]

Information about entrances to ordinary yards is not plentiful until the Treswell surveys, which show a variety of gates and passageways (called *entries*) to private or common courtyards. Comparatively few gateways, only those at the grander houses (e.g. **76/1**, Lady Wood) or inns (**10**) were wide enough for carts or coaches, then coming into fashion. One house in the Old Bailey (**143**) was approached by a long pedestrian alley, and had its coach-house and yard at the back, behind the garden and entered from the adjacent street. Even a large gateway such as that into Foxe's Court in Nicholas Lane (**142**), though 9 ft wide, was simply a passage beneath the street range. At Robert Lee's house (**115**) such a passage, between an outer and inner gate, had on one side a porter's lodge and on the other side a cistern and urinal. Here also the ladders and fire-buckets were stored.

Large houses had backgates (**22**, **115**; Figs. 67, 201) or gates to several streets (**42**, **67**). Houses south of Thames Street which directly bordered on the river sometimes had watergates; these were a feature of larger establishments such as Coldharbour (**169–70**), Fishmongers' Hall (**173**) and the houses along the Strand as shown in the sixteenth-century panoramas. The riverside range of Bridewell Palace (1523) was meant to provide access to the palace which had a cramped landward entrance. London's medieval and Tudor riverside, as shown in the panoramas, resembled Venice in several respects, and this accent on communication and display on the river affected the design of the major buildings on the water's edge.

The gate to a tenement does not seem to have been a place for embellishment or show, except in the case of almshouses where a tablet above an archway might commemorate the sponsor (Fig. 68). The door to the main house, by contrast, was often given prominence with a pentice or, later, a porch. Simple porches were present in pre-Conquest timber buildings excavated on several sites.[8] A grander forebuilding of stone, containing a stair to a first-floor door, is likely to have formed part of the stone houses at Corbet Court and perhaps Southwark, as is suggested in such houses elsewhere.[9]

67. (**22**) Crosby Place, Bishopsgate: the back gate into Priory Close, from an engraving before 1908 by E. L. Blackburn [Goss 1930]

68. Entrance to Milbourne's almshouses, Coopers' Row, Crutched Friars (J. W. Archer 1853)

Porticus, translated *porches*, were a regular problem to the itinerant judges in the 1246 Eyre; as their express concern was encroachment on the highway, this indicates that the porches in question (which may have been built of timber or stone) were for doors opening directly onto the street.[10] In 1252–3 a seld in Cheapside possessed an *atrium* through which access was gained to two solars.[11] Porches (perhaps here simply pentices) are also criticised for being too low in the wardmote of 1421.[12] More substantial porches of medieval or Tudor date, and probably of stone, are seen in later illustrations of the Inns of the Bishops of Bath and Ely (**157**, **107**; Figs. 36–7); the most ornate example was no doubt at Guildhall, of *c.* 1440.[13] The name *Ledenporche* is used of several tenements in the city from the late fourteenth century,[14] and presumably signifies a porch with a low-pitched lead roof; though as pentices could be covered with lead, this need not have meant a grand structure. Overall porches were probably a rarity in medieval domestic buildings. Though not at all evident in the Treswell surveys, porches are a feature of fashionable houses of the time (e.g. Charterhouse, **48**, Fig. 44; **67**) and are common in the designs (largely of 1596–1603) in Thorpe's *Book of Drawings*. At Robert Lee's house in 1607 the main porch contained two wainscotted seats; a second porch at the foot of the stairs, adjacent to the parlour, led into the garden (**115**).

Hall

Twelfth-century stone houses such as the one at Corbet Court (**91**) and the house of the Warennes in Southwark (**199**) presumably incorporated first-floor halls, though in the latter case the building could have been a solar or chamber block to an adjacent, lost, ground-floor hall. Well-documented examples of halls of the thirteenth century are largely those within religious residences, for example the enormous first-floor hall of the Bishop of Winchester in Southwark (**193**), built by 1220–1, and the hall of the Bishop of Ely's house in Holborn (**107**; Fig. 69), built in 1290.

Halls in the houses of secular or religious leaders were often of stone, sometimes raised on basements which might be either vaulted (undercrofts) or horizontally ceiled with beams. Where undercrofts have been recorded within other larger complexes, a stone hall above the undercroft can sometimes be presumed, e.g. at Gerard's Hall (1290) or Neville's Inn (fourteenth century) (**18**, **153**).

During the fifteenth century brick began to be used behind stone facing, for example at Crosby Place (1466); slightly later, brick with stone dressings became fashionable, as seen in the halls of the Inns of Court (e.g. hall of Lincoln's Inn, 1492; Middle Temple, 1572; Staple Inn, 1581; **47**, **78**, **103**).

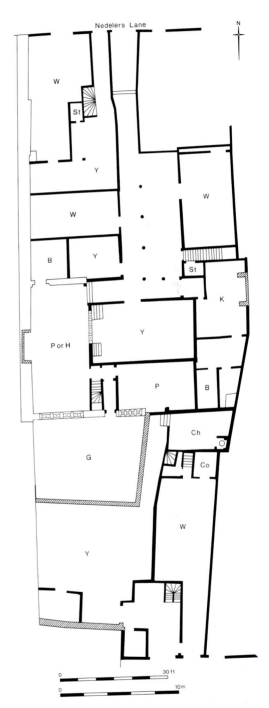

69. (**107**) Bishop of Ely's Inn, Holborn: south view of hall (S. Hooper *c.* 1776)

Treswell shows one hall apparently built completely of brick at Clothworkers' Hall (rebuilt 1548) (Fig. 57), but this building probably also had stone dressings. By this time only a small number of halls built partly of stone, probably of some antiquity, were to be seen (**10**, Fig. 61; **145**, Fig. 70).

Medieval halls of timber-framed construction were of two general types: aisled and unaisled (i.e. without posts supporting the roof). The aisled hall can be traced in manorial centres in the counties around London from the late eleventh century. In some respects London sokes were similar organisational units and very possibly the lord of the soke would have a hall where business was transacted; similarly and more certainly, the sheriffs held their courts in their own houses during the greater part of the thirteenth century, and it is therefore likely that halls of manorial size were to be found in the early medieval city. Some religious courts continued to be held in houses in London in the later medieval period, and this may have influenced the architecture of certain prominent houses. The archdeacon of London, for instance, held court in a house (otherwise unidentified) on the west side of Milk Street in 1456; in a house (presumably the same) in the same parish his predecessors heard divorce cases in the fourteenth century.[15] The form of these halls, however, is unknown. References to *aisled* halls in London are confined to the late thirteenth and early fourteenth centuries, and then only to possible rather than probable examples. In 1292 a *Stapeledehall* is mentioned in the parish of All Hallows Barking, followed by a Stapled Hall in the parish of St Botolph Bishopsgate in 1330 and Stapled Hall, later Staple Inn, Holborn (**103**), in 1333–4;[16] it is possible that the name derives from OE *stapel* or post, and signifies a hall with posts.[17]

Aisled halls continued to be built in surrounding counties during the fourteenth century.[18] The form was however declining in popularity by this time due to the development of new kinds of roof, the hammerbeam (from *c.* 1290)[19] and especially the crown-post roof (possibly from as early as *c.* 1250)[20] neither of which required the support of aisle-posts. The city probably reflected, and possibly led, the change to

70. (**145**) 3–4 Pancras Lane (Treswell 1610–11)

71. (**105**) Barnard's Hall, Holborn: interior looking west (J. P. Emslie 1875)

72. Halls of the legal inns: (a) (*below*) (**108**) Furnival's Inn, Holborn: interior looking west (R. B. Schnebbelie 1819)

(b) (*right*) (**78**) Inner Temple Hall in the nineteenth century

crown-post roofs, and therefore to unaisled halls, during the fourteenth century (see Chapter 6).[21] The earliest private halls of which detailed records survive, Merchant Taylors' Hall (177) in the fourteenth century and those of the legal inns at Barnard's Inn (105; Fig. 71) and Furnival's Inn (108; Fig. 72a; cf. 72b) in the fifteenth century, are unaisled.

On wider plots, the hall, whether standing on an undercroft or directly on the ground, normally lay across the tenement, either at the rear (40) or towards the middle of the depth and dividing the front courtyard from the garden behind (22, 105, 139, 177; Fig. 73); on narrower plots, the hall lay to one side behind the street range, but was entered from the internal yard (10, 70, 172, 175; probably at 18). During the thirteenth century, properties along streets (especially those which formed frontages to larger complexes) developed separately from the property behind, producing building-forms of increased compactness. From the early fourteenth century occur references to halls on the first floor of timber-framed buildings which fronted onto streets, notably in three contracts of 1310, 1383 and 1410 for houses with shops in the central area (Cheapside, Addle Lane and Friday Street respectively; 141, 2, 87). At the Peter and Paul Tavern, Paternoster Row (146), in 1342, the hall was constructed on the second floor, since drinking rooms occupied the ground and first floors. Here one might compare York, where two of the four examples of first-floor halls were within buildings which were inns for considerable periods.[22] Late medieval assembly rooms were likewise on the first and higher floors; Mercers' Hall (52) lay on the first floor from the late fourteenth century, and in the last decade of the fifteenth century the hall of the Fraternity of Holy Trinity attached to St Botolph, Aldersgate, was rebuilt also on the first floor (7). Woodmongers' Hall, according to a view of 1628, was a fine chamber of unknown but possibly sixteenth-century date on the second floor (147). Domestic first-floor halls are common in the Treswell surveys, in houses of one-room (Type 1) and two-room (Type 2) plan form; in the two-room plan the hall always occupied the front room over the street when the position is specified (e.g. 14, 86, 133, 139, 176, 179/2, 190/2). A hall on the first floor was also found in larger complexes, including, in rebuilt form, the former fourteenth-century mansion Coldharbour I in Thames Street, in 1612 a brewery (169). The first-floor hall is found in houses in other towns such as Bristol, Exeter, Rye and Watford from about 1450,[23] and was clearly a form necessitated by the use of the whole ground-floor area for commercial purposes.

73. Holborn from Ogilby and Morgan's map of 1677, showing sites of (109) Brooke House, (108) Furnival's Inn, (103) Staple Inn and (105) Barnard's Inn

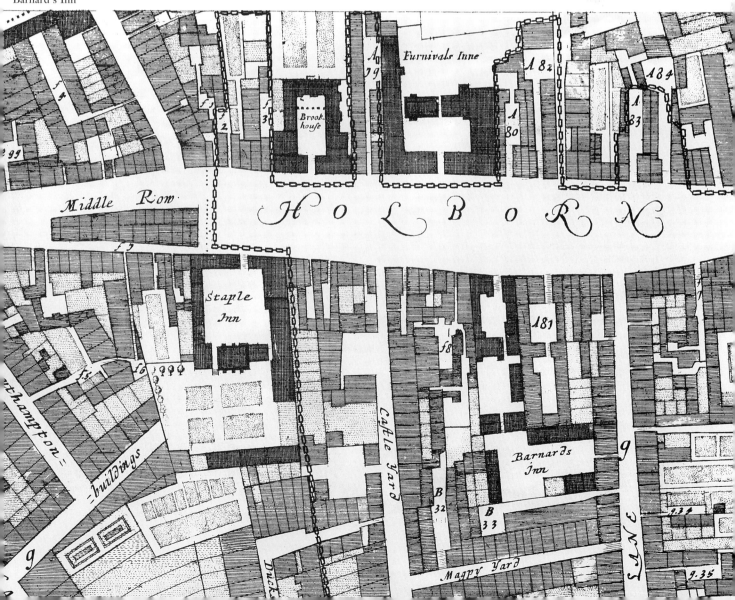

During the later medieval period open halls were no doubt ceiled over to create chambers on an upper floor, but details are lacking in London. Archaeological investigation, recording the lowest parts of walls, cannot usually determine whether a ground-floor hall was open to the roof or was ceiled over from the start (e.g. **172**). It is noteworthy that the majority of the surviving building contracts suggest that halls were on upper floors; the large house at Bucklersbury of 1405 (**40**) is a rare exception. The open hall had been abandoned in up-to-date houses in the region, such as Paycocke's house at Coggeshall (Essex) of *c.* 1500, and generally in smaller towns;[24] this development must have been shared by London houses, though evidence is sparse (see pp. 146–7). Ground-floor rooms which are called halls, and which may originally have been open structures ceiled over by 1600, can be seen in the Treswell surveys (e.g. **56, 70**).

Solar

The solar (from French *sol* 'floor' and *solive* 'beam') was a private room on an upper floor. Stone solars are mentioned in the mid thirteenth century, and earlier examples (cf. **198**) are known elsewhere.[25] In the smallest units, they may well have comprised the only withdrawing-room or bedchamber. By 1246, as the justices of the Eyre noted, solars were a frequent nuisance to the highway, because they jettied out into it;[26] by 1276 there were complaints about solars which fell down and crushed people or which were in a dangerous state of repair.[27]

The position of the solar within the tenement varied depending upon the size of the property, but it always lay on an upper (usually the first) floor. A building contract of 1308 describes how a skinner intended to add a two-storey range to his hall, with a larder and chamber below, and a solar above (**191**). The solar could lie over a shop, a gate, or a stable.[28] It was mainly a private room. In 1322 a man retired to his solar to hang himself; in 1324 a man, having been wounded, was carried to a solar to receive the last rites.[29] The solar could however also be used as a workplace: in 1300, in Cheapside near Milk Street, a man was shearing cloths in a solar when a piece of wood fastened to the outside of the room, used for drying saddles, fell on a passer-by and killed him.[30] By the later fourteenth century the term seems to have been used of any large upper room: one solar in the house of Thomas Mockyng, fishmonger, was called *prentissechaumbre* (presumably where the apprentices slept), and lay above the workmen's room; another great solar in the parish of St Katherine Cree was called *le Wynsoler*.[31] Solars were also to be found in taverns.

The term *solar* seems to have largely died out by 1400, and the wider term *chamber* is used.[32] This may be related in part to the spread of buildings of more than two storeys at this time, with several chambers rather than a single retiring-room.

Parlour and Great Chamber

Documentary references to 'a locutorium called parlour' or an 'interloquitorium' in better houses (i.e. those which figure in wills) begin in the second quarter of the fourteenth century in London. The term *parlorium* is used in 1330.[33] These words denoted a reception room, for conversation and entertainment, separate from the hall but usually not a bedchamber, and usually on the ground floor. In the 1370s William Langland complained that 'now hath each rich man a rule to eaten by himself in a privy parlour . . . or in a chamber with a chimney, and leave the chief hall, that was made for meals, and men to eaten in',[34] showing that parlours were widespread in grand houses by the third quarter of the century. Smaller houses had parlours, but they were sometimes placed on the first floor, when shops occupied the ground storey (e.g. **141, 2**). During the late fourteenth and fifteenth centuries several livery company halls were provided, either by addition or refurbishment, with a parlour as a standard element (e.g. those of the Goldsmiths, 1382; Drapers I, 1425; Carpenters, 1442; Cutlers, 1465; **85, 162, 128, 54**). In the grander halls the parlour formed its own block at one end and at right angles to the hall, the parlour on the ground floor, often with its own bay window (**22**; Fig. 74a; **139**). The parlours at Fishmongers' and Clothworkers' Halls had two storeys above them. From 1485 references occur to Summer Parlours (**30, 98**); evidently some houses and company halls had two parlours, as at the exceptional house of Thomas Dudley in Cannon Street in 1509 (**45**).[35] Treswell shows several houses with two parlours (**3, 140, 143**).

In the Treswell surveys the parlour was found mostly in the larger or well-appointed houses. It could be found in two main positions, and in a number of further, exceptional locations:

(i) In the largest houses, the parlour could be found at the upper end of the hall, in its medieval position (**72/1**). This was the normal position in livery company halls, though the parlour of 1594 at Clothworkers' Hall (**139**) lay at the other end of the hall and could be reached through the screens passage. This was because the hall was open to the roof and the storeyed elements were placed together at the screens end, so that both kitchen and parlour supported two further storeys, forming a range at right angles to the hall.

(ii) In both medium-sized and large houses, the parlour overlooked, and occasionally had access into, the garden of the house. Where no hall is mentioned, proximity to the garden (or at least away from the street) seems to have been influential in the placing of a parlour (**76/1, 179/1, 154/3**; Fig. 75a–b). This proximity was often emphasised by a prominent window overlooking the garden; in certain houses, a quasi-octagonal window took up much of the gable end of the room (**55**). The parlour at Clothworkers' Hall had a canted window at the garden end which was carried up through the storey above.

(iii) In small to medium-sized properties the parlour was rare but not completely absent (**3/2** had two; Fig. 76). It could be found on the first floor, next to a hall (**169, 184**); rarely, it comprised the front room in a small tenancy and was entered directly from the street (three examples at Hart Street, Crutched Friars; **101**) or entered from a side passage (**70/5**).

74. Great Chambers: (a) (22) Crosby Place, Bishopsgate: interior of great parlour and chamber above with floor removed (J. Schnebbelie 1816)

(b) (48) Charterhouse: the Great Chamber

Normally the parlour was buried deep within the property, whether on the ground floor or on an upper storey. Even within a tavern it was a secluded withdrawing room; Treswell's plan of the Sun at Westminster shows that a parlour lay behind the normal drinking rooms.[36]

The parlour had further special characteristics. Its proportions were generally rectangular: thirty examples measured by Treswell had an average length to breadth ratio of 1.35:1, not counting the exceptional parlour of Clothworkers' Hall which was 53 ft × 18 ft (2.9:1). Where the plan is known, there was normally only one entrance and that lay in one of the shorter sides or ends; occasionally, but rarely, a newel stair ascended from a corner opposite the door. Such an arrangement would allow for large windows along one of the longer sides, and often the fireplace lay at the far end. The parlour was also an intentionally comfortable room; the livery company parlour was often wainscotted, at least from the opening of the sixteenth century.[37]

In grander residences, from the third quarter of the fifteenth century, a chamber above the parlour on the first floor began to be called the Great Chamber. This chamber, sumptuously decorated, was used both as a reception room and for dining; it was sometimes called the Dining Chamber.

The earliest instance in London is at Crosby Place (1466; 22; Fig. 74a); others in the present gazetteer are at Charterhouse (48; Fig. 74b) in the mid sixteenth century and at a Lord Mayor's house in Leadenhall Street by 1607 ('the Great Dining Chamber', 153, see Appendix). Some of the grandest of the clothworkers' houses in 1612 had their largest chamber in a similar position, probably at the head of the stair on the first floor (142, 169). At two of these larger properties, the parlour below was now called the Great Parlour, as opposed to the Great Chamber above (115, 169). Charterhouse shows that the Great Chamber was conventionally approached by a richly carved staircase; but this is the only example we know of in London (and the stair itself was destroyed in the Second World War). At Foxe's Court in Nicholas Lane, rebuilt in the 1580s by a clothworker, the staircase which led from the ground floor was in a space 11 ft 6 in × 8 ft, and this was probably another example of the stately approach to a Great Chamber (142).

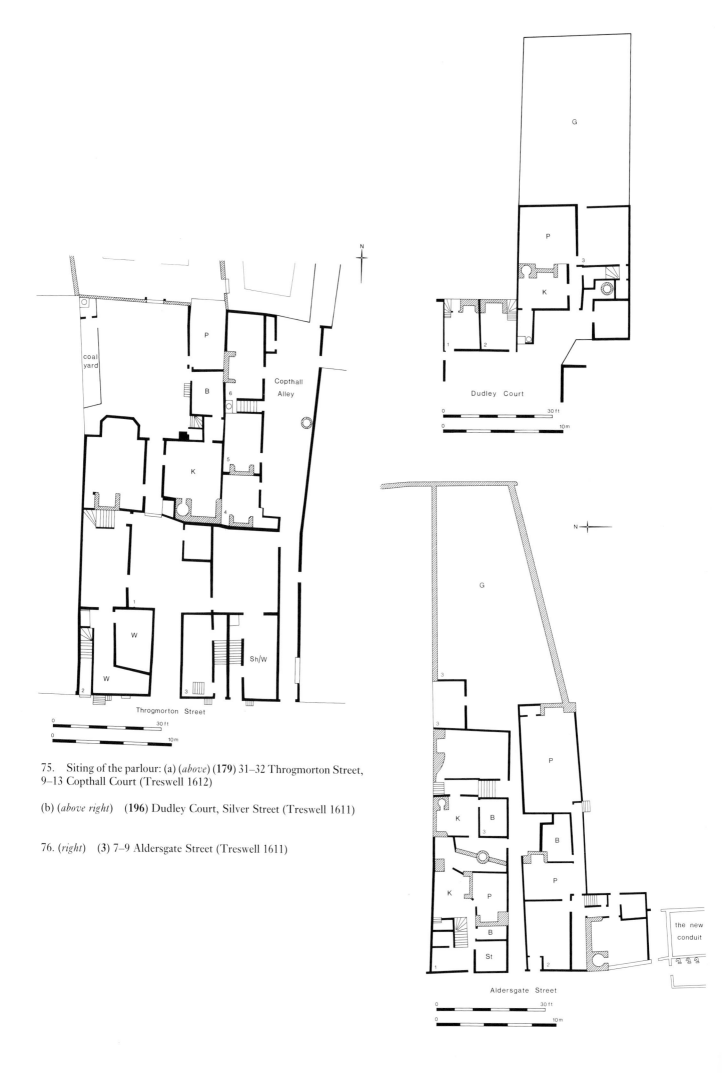

75.   Siting of the parlour: (a) (*above*) (**179**) 31–32 Throgmorton Street, 9–13 Copthall Court (Treswell 1612)

(b) (*above right*)   (**196**) Dudley Court, Silver Street (Treswell 1611)

76. (*right*)   (**3**) 7–9 Aldersgate Street (Treswell 1611)

Chapel

Chapels were naturally to be found in the town-houses of bishops, abbots and priors (**5, 106, 117, 135, 161, 193, 197–8, 200**); the two largest surviving examples, those of the Archbishop of Canterbury at Lambeth[39] and the Bishop of Ely at Holborn (**106**), stood on undercrofts and bore comparison with royal chapels throughout the rest of Europe. Those of the abbot of Waltham and of the Bishop of Durham (**135, 161**) also lay on the first floor, the latter probably on a vault.

The presence of a chapel within a secular noble residence was also traditional, since in the eleventh century the possession of a private church and a belfry was regarded as one of the attributes of thegnly rank. There are some references to chapels in London houses of the nobility, and examples survive in castles and rural manor-houses (**22?, 28, 94, 114, 152, 170, 175**).[40] From the mid thirteenth century until the third decade of the sixteenth century there are glimpses of chapels also in the houses of citizens, usually the richer and more prominent;[41] archaeological excavation on the site of the tenement called *la Rouge Sale* off Watling Street found a small vault which may have supported the fourteenth-century chapel (**31**). The major livery companies such as the Mercers (**52**; by 1391), the Merchant Taylors (**177**; by 1403–4) and Grocers (**149**; 1411) also had chapels within their halls. The Merchant Taylors' chapel, which may have stood over the surviving undercroft at the east end of the hall, had its roof painted with stars of gold, a large window of white glass, and stained altar cloths and other hangings.[42]

The more modest domestic chapel would if possible have had a lead roof and special window glass; sometimes also panelling. It occasionally contained works of art, such as the table (picture) of alabaster of the Passion and images of Our Lady and of St John which stood in the chapel of Lady Colet's house at Stepney, left behind by Richard Gresham in 1523; but otherwise was simply furnished, even in a wealthy household such as that of Thomas Kytson in Milk Street (**138**) in 1527, where the chapel contained an old painted hanging, two sarsenet curtains, a table of Our Lord, a cross of timber, a linen altar-cloth, a pair of latten candlesticks, six short forms and a chest.[43] The bequest of sacred equipment such as the portifory (breviary) or missal may indicate the existence of a chapel in a house, but equally a portable altar may have been used within a chamber.[44]

Tower

Some of the larger houses had towers, and they fall into two main groups: stone towers largely of the thirteenth and fourteenth centuries, and stair turrets of brick or timber in the sixteenth century. The latter are therefore considered below with other forms of stair.

Stone solar towers were features of unfortified building complexes such as episcopal palaces during the twelfth and thirteenth centuries.[45] In Europe such towers were also present in noble town-houses and within religious complexes, and this range of settings would fit the London examples. A possible twelfth-century example from an ordinary, if prominent, tenement has been excavated in Bow Lane (**31**; Fig. 26).

Towers are known at the house called Servat's Tower in Bucklersbury (**42**) in 1305, and at Britanny Inn (**11**) in 1352; the crenellated tower at Pulteney's Inn (**114**), shown in Wyngaerde's panorama of *c.* 1540, is probably also of thirteenth- or fourteenth-century date (licences to crenellate private houses in the city are considered in Chapter 6). A fourteenth-century tower formed part of the buildings of the Middle Temple (**78**), and a tower of unknown but medieval date formed part of the Steelyard complex in Thames Street (Figs. 23–4).[46] The social significance of the tower in an aristocratic household has already been considered above (see pp. 36–8).

Kitchen and Bakehouse

Though medieval kitchens have been excavated on several archaeological sites (e.g. **166, 172**), the results have been meagre and the detailed evidence for their form and use (for instance by analysis of deposits which might contain food debris) has not yet been brought together. As with some of the other rooms and spaces which formed the medieval and Tudor house, we have to start with the comparative abundance of information in the Treswell surveys of 1607–14; but some inferences may be taken back into the medieval period.

The surveys are particularly informative about the positions and character of the kitchen, since it lay on the ground floor in the majority of tenancies. At least seven different positions within houses of varying types can be perceived in London by the opening of the seventeenth century, and it is likely that several were developments of the medieval period.

(i) In a sequence hall – service rooms – kitchen on the ground floor, the usual arrangement of rooms in a medieval house of consequence. This could still be found in 1612, no doubt partly a result of the inhibition to radical alteration imposed by a large kitchen chimney-stack (e.g. **142**). In some cases the kitchen would be in line with the hall (**70/4, 72, 142**); in others, where space was restricted, the kitchen lay at right angles to the hall, sometimes along one side of the entrance court (**76/1, 139**) or, as at Merchant Taylors' Hall, on the private side of the hall (**177**).

(ii) A variant of the previous sequence, when in a substantial property the hall lay on the first floor, as at Bucklersbury in 1405 (**40**): here the kitchen lay at one end of the hall, also on the first floor.

(iii) On the ground floor, in a separate building, usually across a small yard. Evidence is not available in quantity in London (for example, **177, 191**) before Treswell's surveys, when the form is a comparative rarity (**142, 150**). Certainly separate kitchens, whether of stone or timber, are recorded in the region (as at Braxted Hall, Essex) and are presumed to have existed in numbers in other towns, e.g. York.[47] In London they are sometimes implied by records of a tresaunce or cloister which led from the kitchen to the hall, as at Brewers' Hall (**1**) in 1423, and perhaps the arches at Merchant Taylors' Hall are remnants of a tresaunce. The Abchurch Lane examples (**142**) may have been constructed as part of a documented rebuilding shortly before 1390. Although such kitchens may have been of a single storey when built, they were not so by 1612; all the separate kitchens

had chambers above, some reached by a gallery crossing from the main house at first-floor level (see below, galleries). The separate kitchen had been incorporated into the house complex, a process which could well also be of medieval date.

(iv) On the ground floor, behind the shop; especially in Type 2 (two-room plan) houses, forming the back room of the ground floor (**70/1, 70/3, 110, 194**).

(v) A similar position was that in which a kitchen formed half of a two-room ground floor, the other room being a hall or parlour. This was found in the outskirts of the built-up area (**56**).

(vi) On the first floor, behind the front room. Where the shop took up all the ground-floor space in smaller houses, particularly those of Type 2, the kitchen had joined the hall on the first floor from at least the beginning of the fourteenth century (**191**). By 1612 this was a common arrangement in London, not only in central, congested properties but also in peripheral areas where space was no problem (**34, 46, 57/2, 57/3, 179/2, 190**). In several cases the room to the front of the house is called the hall, and it is clear that the hall and kitchen functioned together as related rooms (**34**).

(vii) On the first floor, but in a separate building reached by a gallery. This rare form is known from a plan and survey of Eton College property in Bread Street in 1617 (**61**), and still survives at the mid-seventeenth-century Hoop and Grapes, Aldgate.

In major houses and the company halls the kitchen had specialised adjoining rooms besides the larder and buttery: a pastry, contrived in the thickness of a large kitchen stack to enable dough to rise (**139**), a stillhouse (**115**) and a scouring house, where pewter was cleaned (**115**). In several of the houses surveyed by Treswell the ground-floor privy was also found within or adjacent to the kitchen block. In some cases the privy was part of the structure, but entered by a separate door from the yard (**142**); in other cases, the privy was approached through or off the kitchen (**72, 154/3**; see also **142**, houses along Abchurch Lane). This proximity aided, and was perhaps intended for, the disposal of food waste from the kitchen; larger pieces of food waste and kitchen utensils are often found in medieval cesspits on archaeological sites in the city.

The kitchen, in houses of all social levels, tended to be

77. (**177**) Merchant Taylors' Hall, Threadneedle Street: arches by the kitchen, perhaps part of a tresaunce

square in shape in comparison to the usually more rectangular hall or parlour. This may have been related in part to the functions carried out in it and the size and position of some of the fittings, including the fireplace, oven, pastry board, well and drains, which are considered in the next chapter. The octagonal form, known in monastic contexts outside London and at Sir John de Pulteney's Penshurst Place (1341), has not yet been recorded in London.[48]

Buttery, Pantry and Larder

Like the kitchen, the service rooms in London houses are imperfectly known before surveys of the end of the sixteenth century. Two rooms functioning as buttery and larder, usually flanking a through-passage to a separate kitchen, are rare in rural manors before the end of the thirteenth century;[49] doors in the end of the great hall of the Bishop of Winchester in Southwark (193) in its fourteenth-century rebuilding show that the form was observed in London, though rarely documented. The arches now built into one side of the fifteenth-century kitchen at Merchant Taylors' Hall (177; Fig. 77) may also be a relic of previous service arrangements. Traditionally the *larder* was the store for meat;[50] in a contract of 1308 (191) it lay next to the hall. The terms *pantry* and *buttery* both appear to denote a room in which plates, pots, salts and probably napery were stored.[51] Although the pantry and larder are shown or mentioned in the Treswell surveys (3, 139, 143, 147, 169; cf. a 'dry larder' on the first floor at Clothworkers' Hall), the principal service room was called the buttery, and it was present in many houses of all sizes. Its usual medieval position in larger houses is shown at Clothworkers' Hall and at 118 Fenchurch Street (139, 72); in the latter two, butteries are found between the hall and main kitchen. One was a simple small room with one entrance; but the other, depending upon interpretation of the plan, may be a kind of through-passage with two doors. The buttery was a small chamber, as the measurements show; and it could be attached to either kitchen or hall. Whether on ground floor or at first floor, the kitchen often had an adjacent buttery (3/3, 62, 194/2). Alternatively the buttery was attached to the hall (189/1); or was a small, presumably partitioned area within a hall (70/5).

In larger houses at the end of the sixteenth century, the buttery often contained within it the stair down to the cellars (150; cf. plan of buttery at 72/1), again a feature of houses (mostly surveyed or designed in 1593–1607) in Thorpe's *Book of Drawings*.

Bedroom

Rooms on upper floors which can be identified as bedrooms because they contained beds occur in inventories from the late fourteenth century. Multiplication of bedrooms, from the few references available, seems to be a feature of the fifteenth century. In 1390, for instance, one bedroom sufficed for a grocer and his wife and their five children, two of whom were daughters; in 1485, and in different circumstances, the Conterini and their associates, hiring a large house (30) in St

Botolph Lane from the parish of St Mary at Hill, had ten individual bedrooms. Such luxury may still have been exceptional in normal houses: in 1499 an inventory of a haberdasher's house shows only two bedrooms in use, one containing two beds and the other five.[52] By the time of the Treswell surveys every house had a number of upper chambers, which are not given specific functions. In one case the survey shows that a recent inventory was only partial: the survey, in 1611, of a house at the Woolstaple, Westminster, mentioned fifteen chambers and outhouses, whereas an inventory of 1588 mentioned only nine.[53] Despite this the inventory mentions beds in five chambers.

References to the sleeping-places of apprentices or journeymen and servants are meagre. As noted above, a fishmonger's house in 1390 contained a *prentissechaumbre*; but by the opening of the seventeenth century, it has been argued, only a minority of London's workers lived with their masters.[54] In 1607 the extensive house formerly of Robert Lee in Leadenhall Street (115) had a men's chamber and two chambers for maids, placed in different wings of the house.

Shop, Warehouse and Counting House

This section considers shops and warehouses as parts of the domestic complex, or when it seems likely that blocks of shops included residential accommodation.

By 1300 there were many shops along the main streets of London, but they were usually small in size. A study of the east end of Cheapside, for instance, has shown that at the opening of the thirteenth century small shops lined the Poultry (*Ferronaria*); by the middle of the century shops are known to have formed the frontages of properties west along Cheapside, with up to eight shops crammed into a single (though major) property-width; and by the end of the century similar shops had spread down one side of Soper Lane, at right angles to Cheapside.[55] During the later thirteenth century the shop with solar over became common as a separate unit; several might form parts of the urban estate of a landlord who lived elsewhere. When described, these units were usually two storeys high, commonly two or three shops with a single solar above.[56] In the reign of Henry III Peter Frowyk left thirteen shops, one upper chamber and a cellar, which may have been an early example of a unified row of shops; in 1322 a bequest included a whole private lane, containing about twenty shops on either side.[57] It is likely that rows, either custom-built or formed by gradual accretion, were a feature of early fourteenth-century London, like the surviving Lady Row in York. In 1350 the Bridge wardens had in their yard timber for fourteen shops, framed for immediate building.[58] In the later fourteenth century long blocks of shops were constructed, in one case 86 yards in length (89, 1369); this was part of a general expansion in the number of trading premises, which included public markets such as the Stocks with seventy-one stalls in 1358[59] and private ventures such as the construction of two facing rows of shops within the gatehouse of the prior of Lewes on his property (199) off Tooley Street in suburban Southwark, based on a similar Rent at the east end of the Austin Friars' church in Broad Street. At the same time, the almost continuous rows of small

78.   Shops against
west end of St
Ethelburga,
Bishopsgate (R. West
and W. H. Thoms
1736)

79.   Houses on the
south side of Aldgate
High Street (R. B.
Schnebbelie 1817)

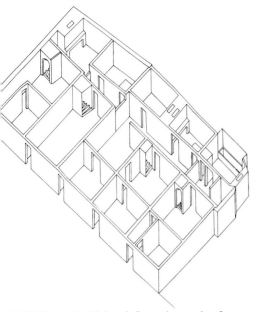

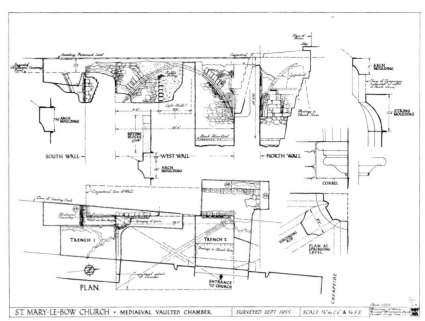

(142) Houses in Abchurch Lane: isometric of ground rs in 1612 (R. Lea)

81. (51) Cheapside house of prior of Christ Church, Canterbury: elevation and plan of undercroft discovered in 1955

shops were disappearing from Cheapside, though the larger properties behind kept their own boundaries.[60]

During the second half of the sixteenth century, several churchyards were bordered by small shops, the rents going to the relief of the parish; the boundaries of these properties, which sometimes survive to the present day, show that these structures were thin rows along street frontages, as narrow as 3½ft wide.[61] Shops built against the west end of St Ethelburga Bishopsgate in about 1570 and 1614 survived until the second quarter of the twentieth century (Fig. 78).

In size the shop was governed by its position within a house-frame or, if specially built, by the availability of timber which was prepared with domestic structures in mind. The shops in a block contracted to be built in 1370 (90) were each 11ft wide and 25ft long. Such a size was common thereafter up to and including the time of the Treswell surveys. At the same time many smaller shops had stalls out in the street, which appear to have been collapsible structures giving temporary extensions. Butchers' houses in Eastcheap, for instance, had stalls in front;[62] such stalls, including those of butchers, were still a feature of suburban London streets in the early nineteenth century (Fig. 79).

By 1612 the great majority of small and medium-sized properties with street frontages had a shop as the ground-floor front room. In some Type 1 houses this was the function of the single ground-floor room. Most of the variation in layout of shops, and their relationship with warehouses behind, is shown in Treswell's plan of Abchurch Lane (142; Fig. 80). Here were three different types of one-room shop: a squarish room between 8ft and 10ft square entered directly from the street; and same, but entered from a passage (cf. 101); and a double-sized shop in which the partition between two ground-floor rooms had been removed. Where the partition had not been removed, the rear room might be a warehouse.

The surveys of 1607–18 also provide examples of lock-up

shops, either of a tenant who lived elsewhere or of one of the tenants in the house above; such shops had no internal stairs upwards (e.g. 50, 69/3; cf. 70/6).

The 1405 Bucklersbury contract, in which a 'great shop' was to be 22ft 4in × 18ft, provides an early example of a larger shop-and-warehouse complex, found in the later sixteenth century on the main commercial thoroughfares such as Cheapside and Cornhill (40, 62). A schedule of The Kaye in Westcheap in 1562 describes a 'great shoppe' with ware benches, a nether warehouse and counting-house; above the wainscoted hall, two parlours and chambers, the garrets had iron fittings and poles attached to their windows for the drying of cloths.[63] A survey in 1617 of a property in Cheapside rebuilt in 1595 (50) shows a similar arrangement; the extensive ground floor was divided into an upper and lower shop by steps, with the rearwards, upper shop possibly top-lit since there were no storeys above it.

The term *warehouse* was used in the sixteenth century and by Treswell in 1612 to signify something different from a storehouse. It may have been in particular a room required by drapers and other people of the cloth trade, literally to house their wares. Further similar facilities were provided by Blackwell Hall, rebuilt in 1588; it had private warehouses, dealing with provincial and foreign customers in the cloth trade.[64] Treswell surveyed a block of property south of Thames Street including warehouses of imposing dimensions on the first and second floors; the ground floor contained several storehouses (169). On properties away from the river, warehouses were to be found across small yards (14; 133/4) or, in the largest houses, around a courtyard (142). On inland sites, warehouses were always on the ground floor, and where space allowed could be independent structures of one or two storeys (142); but they were usually built into the congested building complex as one of many rooms. They were naturally a feature of houses on the principal streets, though also in new houses on the periphery of the market centres (133/4, built

82. **(16)** Gerard's Hall, Basing Lane: undercroft, (a) (*top*) interior looking north, *c*. 1850
(b) (*middle*) Sections
(c) (*bottom*) Plan (both T. Willson 1852; Society of Antiquaries Library, Red Portfolio)

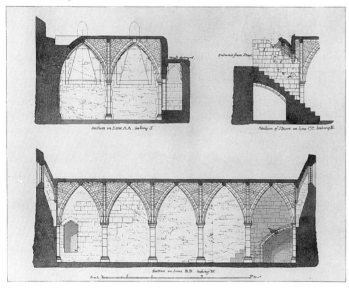

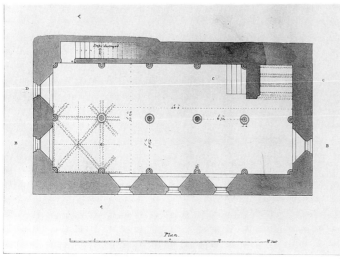

1562). On the northern periphery of the built-up area, and in certain larger houses, they were absent; presumably in the latter cases there was sufficient cellarage (e.g. **72/1**, in Fenchurch Street).

In the fourteenth century, in other towns such as Southampton and King's Lynn, a room within a medieval house might function specifically as a counting house.[65] Such facilities might be expected also in medieval London houses of consequence, but medieval evidence is lacking. In the later sixteenth century the City ruled that the building of counting houses, along with studies, jetties, penthouses and other purprestures, could only be undertaken under licence;[66] evidently many were being built, presumably on the outsides of buildings. One larger house (**115**) had five examples, one on the ground and four on the first floor. In the Treswell surveys the counting house could be found in a variety of positions. The first lay at the back of a warehouse (**145/2**) or at the back of a shop (**46**), both on the ground floor, in the medieval tradition; in these cases it was a small chamber about 6 ft wide and 7 ft or 9 ft long. At 16 Cornhill (**61**) it was probably smaller, apparently part of a gallery leading at first floor from the house to a chamber over the separate kitchen. At Clothworkers' Hall in Mincing Lane (**139**) were two counting houses; on the first floor was a large chamber, 41 ft × 16½ ft, called the Dry Larder, within which at one end was a Plate Chamber, and at the other end a Little Countinghouse. On the second floor another counting house lay in or alongside a gallery, next to two gunpowder houses. Here presumably the counting house had special functions related to the storage of plate or arms common in Elizabethan and Jacobean livery company halls.

Cellar and Undercroft

Along with the shop, the cellar or undercroft is a building feature which is found most commonly in towns. The study of cellars beneath London houses therefore deserves special attention.

Timber-lined cellars of eleventh-century date have been recorded in several parts of the city, notably in the Cheapside and Eastcheap areas (see Chapter 3). Early twelfth-century stone buildings, most probably of two storeys, have been excavated at Bow Lane and in Milk Street at Well Court (**32, 138**), and on the waterfront (**174**). Suggested reconstructions of these buildings assume that the basement storey, at or near ground level, was used for storage. Vaulted undercrofts are recorded below the two known Norman town-houses at Corbet Court and Southwark (**91, 198**) but elsewhere basement storeys ceiled with beams were probably more common; a similar distinction has also been noticed in Lübeck.[67] Both the Corbet Court and Southwark vaults were entered by porch-like chambers, in the former case decorated with blind arcading; evidently the undercroft was worthy of embellishment. Presumably undercrofts throughout the medieval period had brightly painted interiors, in the same manner as vaults and other stonework in churches (the undercroft of the chapel at Lambeth Palace still has areas of plaster lined to look like ashlar on its walls). As in late twelfth-century Canterbury,[68] some of these cellars must have lain next to streets;

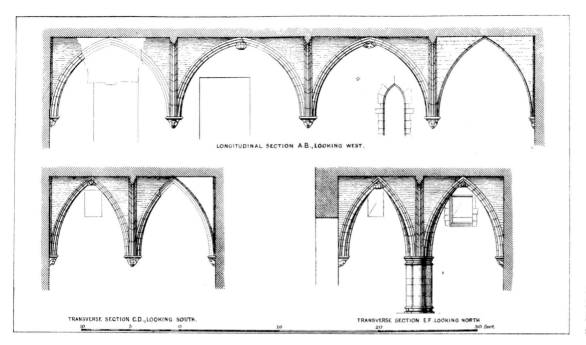

LONGITUDINAL SECTION A.B., LOOKING WEST.

TRANSVERSE SECTION C.D., LOOKING SOUTH.

TRANSVERSE SECTION E.F., LOOKING NORTH.

83. **(119)** Leadenhall Street/Fenchurch Street: undercroft, (a) sections

(b) Plan (both J. Emslie after J. Burt *c.* 1860)

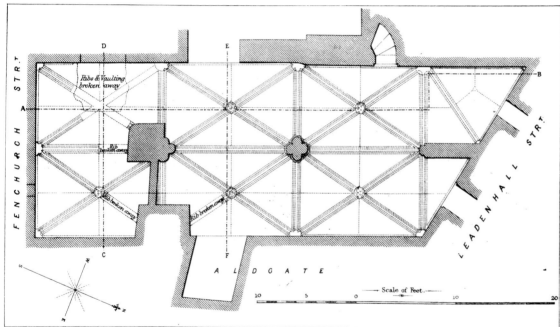

84. **(9)** (*below*) Aldgate/Jewry Street: plan of undercroft [Loftus-Brock 1880]

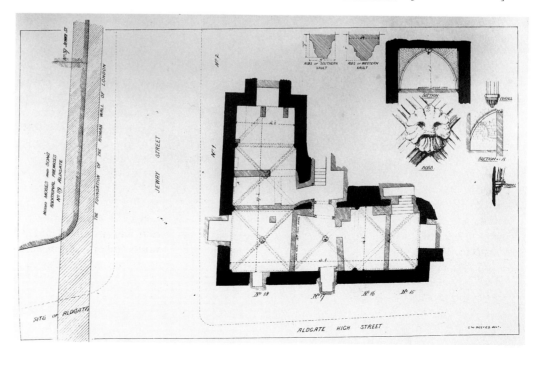

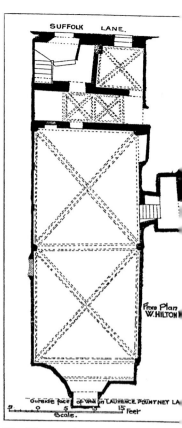

85. (114) Pulteney's Inn, Lawrence Pountney Lane: undercroft, (a) interior, *c.* 1890

(b) Plan, north to right (W. Hilton [?] *c.* 1890)

one 'underground house' mentioned in 1098–1108 may have been near the riverfront.[69] According to Fitzstephen, writing before 1183, there were wine-cellars on the river bank, probably at Vintry.[70] The encroachment of cellars on the highway, not only in central streets but around the extramural market-place space of Smithfield, was a problem dealt with by the justices in the Eyre of 1246, though it was by no means as frequent an offence as the building of solars, pentices or porches.[71] The cellars were indicted because they had steps in the street; presumably this meant steps down from the street rather than up, and indicates that cellars were partly underground by the mid thirteenth century.

Three better-known undercrofts date from the latter part of the thirteenth century: that below the Cheapside residence of the prior of Christchurch, Canterbury (1272–9; **51**; Fig. 81), the western undercroft of Guildhall (*c.* 1280) and the undercroft at Gerard's (Gisor's) Inn, Basing Lane (*c.* 1290; **18**; Fig. 82). Two other undercrofts immediately inside Aldgate, at the junction of Leadenhall Street and Fenchurch Street (**119**; Fig. 83a–b) and at the corner of Aldgate with Jewry Street (**9**; Fig. 84), probably date from around 1300. The four domestic examples were all composed of ribbed quadripartite bays, but were of differing sizes. The Cheapside undercroft was one bay or aisle wide, as was the Jewry Street undercroft which formed an L-shaped street corner; the Aldgate pump and Gerard's Hall undercrofts were of two aisles, and the west undercroft of Guildhall has three aisles (this and its extension of 1411–30, the eastern undercroft, are the only known examples of three-aisled undercrofts in London). During the fourteenth century two-aisled undercrofts with their columns were no longer constructed, and three styles are known: quadripartite vaulting forming one bay over the whole undercroft (i.e. which might in the pre-

vious century have been vaulted with columns: **114**, **129**; Fig. 85), single rows of ribbed quadripartite bays (Merchant Taylors' Hall, **177**; Figs. 86–7) and single rows of bays separated by low transverse stone arches either on simple corbels or dying into the walls (**24**; Figs. 88–9).

The position of the undercroft within the property may have influenced its function, and therefore its decoration. The single-aisled Cheapside and Jewry Street undercrofts lay along street frontages, presumably beneath small shops. A second group of undercrofts, including the two-aisled Gerard's Hall example and the longest private example at Watling Street (**186**; Fig. 90a–c) lay along one side of a property and often communicated directly with the street through one end. A third site was beneath the hall of the property, usually towards the rear of a wide tenement, but cellars in this position seem to have been only rarely vaulted.[72] The vaulted undercroft was definitely tied to the street; and cellars generally were often let separately from the buildings above and around them. Such lettings are known in the waterfront area by *c.* 1180–1200; a separate cellar on St Botolph's Quay is mentioned in 1294.[73]

Cellars involved in the wine trade are known in the Vintry from the late twelfth century, and at Dowgate in 1236.[74] They were required by Gascon wine merchants, who came at the beginning of a vintage season for a few weeks each year. In 1299 they complained to the king about the lack of cellars around the Vintry, and according to Stow several stone houses in the locality were built shortly thereafter.[75] The undercroft at Gerard's (Gisor's) Hall in Basing Lane, datable to *c.* 1290, was probably built by a wine merchant, and cellars

86. (177) Merchant Taylors' Hall, Threadneedle Street: undercroft, looking north

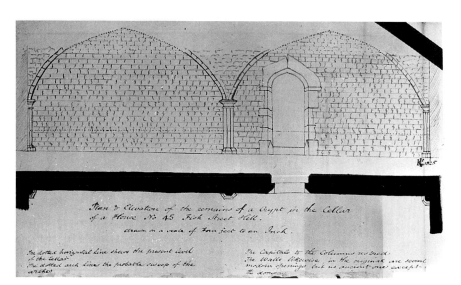

87. (75) 45 Fish
Street Hill: drawing of
side of an undercroft
(unknown artist 1825)

88. (24) 66
Bishopsgate:
undercroft (before
1860)

89. (43) Unknown
site, south of Cannon
Street opposite
London Stone: vaulted
undercroft (T. Dibdin
1851)

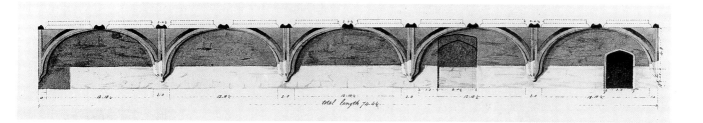

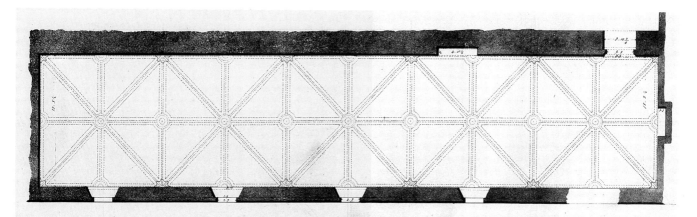

90. (186) 34 Watling Street: undercroft, (a) (*top*) section

(b) (*middle*) Plan (both C. A. Busby 1809; Society of Antiquaries Library, Red Portfolio)

(c) (*below*) Remaining fragment of vaulting at north-west corner, in 1987

in Cheapside itself, including at least one undercroft, that by St Mary-le-Bow already noted, were in use as taverns in the early fourteenth century. A cellar beneath the Peter and Paul tavern in Paternoster Row in 1342 was provided with fire-places and four windows at street-level (**146**); by the mid fourteenth century taverns in cellars were common in London as in other towns. According to the ordinances of the Taverners in 1370, the doors of cellars of a tavern where wines were laid down for sale were to be kept open, without hindrance by bars, cloths, or other obstacles, so that one member of a drinking party could enter to see the wine drawn from the barrels.[76]

Vaulted undercrofts can therefore be associated with the storage and distribution of wine, though this was clearly not their only purpose. Alehouses were also found in cellars from at least the second quarter of the fourteenth century.[77] Cellars also lay below shops, and were used with them; when the shops were built as rows, each shop either had a separate cellar beneath – e.g. a row belonging to the Bridge on the south side of Fenchurch Street in 1358, of seven shops with solars and below the shops seven 'small dwellings' (*parvae mansiones*) – or shared a common cellar.[78] Undercrofts recorded beneath street-ranges, such as on the prominent corner site at Aldgate/Jewry Street (**9**), may have supported shops.

Cellars were still being dug in the opening years of the fifteenth century, as building contracts show (**40, 87**). In 1422 the entrances to many cellars in central or major streets were indicted either for protruding too far into the street or for unsafe doors; some must have been trap-doors.[79] Very few vaulted undercrofts in the city can however be dated to the fifteenth or sixteenth century. Undercrofts vaulted in brick date from as early as 1300 in Bruges and from *c.* 1350 at

91. **(148)** 7–8 Philpot Lane: undercroft in 1981, looking north

Clifton House, King's Lynn, but the earliest dated example in the London area is the undercroft of 1431 below part of the Bridgettine nunnery at Syon, Middlesex. Two may be cited here: the vault of brick beneath the hall of Crosby Place (1466; **22**) and the cellar beneath 7–8 Philpot Lane (**148**; Fig. 91), a brick vault on low stone arches, forming four bays of a street-range undercroft in the traditional manner. Presumably the cellar arched with brick surveyed in Aldersgate by Treswell in 1611 was no newer, and may have been slightly older, than the late fifteenth-century rebuilding of the fraternity hall two floors above it (**7**).[80] Many more buildings had cellars covered by beams, and along the waterfront this would eventually include most of the buildings down the crowded, much sub-divided plot. Excavation of sixteenth-century buildings in Thames Street next to St Botolph Billingsgate church has revealed such cellars, one example reached from the side alley by its own stair (**174**; Fig. 92).

The Treswell surveys of 1607–14 chart the functions of buildings possibly several hundred years old. Active functions for the cellar or undercroft such as taverns or separate lettings for purposes such as shops are generally absent. Only at West Smithfield were cellars lived in (**189**), or in one case used as a kitchen for the house above (**189/6**). The purpose of the cellars in the surveyed houses was clearly for storage, and the capacity of some was considerable. The 'Longe Seller' at

92. **(174)** New Fresh Wharf, Lower Thames Street: cellar down side alley, excavated 1974

118 Fenchurch Street (**72/1**) which lay at or near ground level and supported a range of buildings at right angles to the hall, was 70 ft long and 14 ft wide. In the same block the tenant of the four-and-a-half storey range fronting Fenchurch Street, Arthur Harrison, had a long vault or cellar $83\frac{1}{2}$ ft $\times$ 12 ft under his own and several other tenancies, stretching along Billiter Lane as far as the secondary gate into the large house, besides a second vault 25 ft long under the entry from Fenchurch Street (**72**). Others had cellars which went partly under adjacent tenancies; the Clothworkers' tenant in front of the hall (**139**) leased the great cellar beneath the hall itself.

Many of the cellars had trapdoors or short stairs to the street, which are shown in the ground plans studied here; only in one case was the outside entrance to a cellar into a semi-private yard behind the house (**76/19**). The jutting of these trapdoors into the street was a concern of the Carpenters' Company, who (at least at this later period) issued licences for such works;[81] occasionally the Corporation itself allowed the encroachment of a new vault into the street on payment of a yearly sum.[82] There was therefore still a strong connection between the cellar and the street; though whereas the street-side cellar was rarely, if ever, let out separately, cellars in courts or alleys were regularly sublet.

About a third of Type 1 houses in the Treswell surveys had a cellar, but as much as three-quarters of the plot would be taken up by it. Since the cellar, like the upper rooms, would be measured internally, it is likely that much of the remainder of the small plot below ground would be taken up by thick cellar walls, especially if the cellar were old. Between a half and two-thirds of the Type 2 houses had cellars, but the cellar usually took up only half the ground area; a cellar under the front half of the building was common. About half the Type 3 houses had cellars, but the proportion of ground cellared was highest of all three groups, at just under two-thirds. These figures suggest that the occupiers of all three types or sizes of house fell into two groups: those who had and presumably used cellars, and those who did not, and that this did not bear much relation to the size of house.

The main period for building undercrofts – the ornate, probably exceptional form of cellar – in London appears therefore to be 1270–1400, a period when undercrofts were being built in other towns such as Chester, Southampton, Gloucester, Stamford and Canterbury, and especially the decades 1270–1300. The range of forms (single-, double- or triple-aisled) shown in London is not however evident in these smaller towns. Comparisons must be sought with the larger medieval cities of Europe. A larger number of extant examples, dating from the mid thirteenth century and comprising a comparable richness of variety, have been recorded in Lübeck, where there are several examples of not only double-aisled but triple-aisled vaulted undercrofts.[83]

The recorded vaulted structures, of considerable character and elegance, may be the reduced remnant of a much larger number of original instances. Here the appropriate analogy might be with a place such as Chester, where the Rows, whole streets of undercrofts of the late thirteenth century, are one result of a period of great prosperity as one of the provision bases for Edward I's campaigns into Wales.[84] London's central position in the wine trade, which required cool semi-underground storage for large barrels, may have prompted

the spread of such premises. These undercrofts also adapted easily to become taverns, though with the increasing construction of parlours they would in time have lost out to other more acceptable drinking rooms. During the late fifteenth century vaulting in brick became plainer, and the vaulted cellar became simply a relatively secure or fire-proof form of storage room.

Closet

The term *closet* is first mentioned, in a London context, in the inventory of Edmund Dudley's house in Cannon Street in 1509 (**45**); the closet was also a feature of royal palaces (e.g. Wolsey's Closet, Hampton Court). In fashionable European houses of the late sixteenth and seventeenth centuries any small room might be called a closet (*un cabinet*), but the main purpose of the closet was to be a small chamber off the bedroom, where the occupant could retire for privacy or rest.[85] A closet is mentioned twenty-one times in the two Treswell surveys, in a variety of contexts; it could be found on any floor except the ground floor, even in a garret (**194/4**). It could be found in all types of house, from 'a chamber with a chimney and a little closet over into Fleet Lane' at a Type 1 tenancy of three-and-a-half storeys in Fleet Lane (**76/8**), to the courtyard house at Foxe's Court, Nicholas Lane (**142**), which had two closets among its many rooms.

Treswell often lumped the closet together with other rooms on the same floor, so that it is difficult to determine whether the closet was in every case a separate chamber or merely part of a larger room. In most cases it was probably part of a larger chamber or considered to be an appendage of one (**150/4**); for instance, at the end of a gallery.[86] The closet was not associated with the hall; presumably a small room off the hall was called either a study or a buttery.

The dimensions of the closet, when they are specified, indicate a small chamber along the lines recommended by Sir Roger Pratt in 1660: 'nine feet upon three and a half feet is the least you can allow to the closet'.[87] A 'little closet' at Pudding Lane (**150/4**) was $7\frac{1}{2}$ft × $3\frac{1}{2}$ft, and another in a modest suburban house at Bishopsgate 13 ft × 4 ft (**26/1**). Like its counterpart in Parisian houses, the closet was never heated.[88]

Study

A room called a study is mentioned at the London house of the abbot of Battle in Southwark (**197**) in 1528, and in inventories of parts of Whitehall Palace in 1542 and 1549–50.[89] By the end of the sixteenth century some larger houses outside London might have a small room called a study which, at least in noble households, served as a depository for rarities of all kinds, curiosities and collections.[90] Studies are mentioned sixteen times in the Treswell surveys; and although there are no clues as to what they were used for, several suggestions can be made about their general position within the house, their size and character.

The study could be found on all floors, from the ground (**3/1, 140/1**) to a garret on the third floor (**69/2**). If on the first floor, it was sometimes entered from the hall (**70/5**) or even

stood within it. A study could also be found within a larger chamber on other floors, on the third at the Talbot, Wood Street (**190**), a second-floor garret at Swan Alley (**57/2**), and a third-floor garret at Fenchurch Street (**69/2**). It was usually on the outside of the building, presumably to give the maximum of natural light; if on the ground floor, the study was often placed either jutting into a court (**142**) or next to the street (**3, 10**), where presumably the increase in light was thought more important than the increase in noise, a position sometimes repeated in the upper floors ('the study hanging over the street' on the first floor at 20 Basing Lane, **14** a second-floor chamber with a study situated over the gate to the tenement, **179**). It is notable that a position overlooking the relative quiet of the garden does not seem to have been favoured, and was only present in one house which was in any case surrounded by open spaces (**56**; Fig. 59c). In this house there were two studies, one on top of the other.

In dimensions and shape the study assumed a limited number of forms. The smallest, and quite common, form was a very small squarish room about 3 ft or 4 ft square (**3**). Larger sizes were presumably a result of having a spare room available for this purpose. The two studies in one house at Swan Alley (**56**) were $10\frac{1}{2}$ft × 10ft; what might have been Treswell's own study in Aldersgate Street (**3/1**) was $8\frac{1}{2}$ft square. The largest was a ground-floor room at St James's Hermitage (**140/1**), where the main tenant had a spare room across the entry from his house, 19 ft × 10 ft. This large study was not, however, heated, and in general studies were not provided with a chimney. All the studies shown in the ground-floor plans shared one characteristic – they had only one entrance.

Both closet and study seem to be developments in taste and arrangement of the sixteenth century. The study may well have developed into the private library during the seventeenth century; books did not merit a special room in medieval or Tudor London houses, though they did by the end of the seventeenth century.[91]

Garret

The term *garret* (ME *garite*) originally signified a watchtower, the word being related to OF *guarir*, to preserve (*OED*). Its first recorded use to signify simply an attic room, according to *OED*, is in 1483. As noted above, the word *garrita* might signify a staircase tower or other elevated space. As outlined in Chapter 5, dormer windows probably appeared in London during the fifteenth century, at the same time as the development of the side-purlin roof which allowed freer use of the roof space, unencumbered by the branching and awkward timbers of a crown-post roof. By the time of Treswell, a sizeable minority of garrets were lived in, since they were heated; at least one was used as a workhouse (**70**; de Bees). Garrets could be large, e.g. 30 ft × 22 ft 3 in (**69/1**) or 30 ft × 30 ft (**142/2**), and sometimes partitioned (**72/3, 76/18**). But generally the garret was probably still used for storage. The garret of a tenancy in front of Clothworkers' Hall (**139/1**), for instance, had a 'roof to lay faggots in',[92] and waterside garrets with hoists are shown in the panoramas.

93.   House in Sweedon's Passage, Grub Street (J. T. Smith *c.* 1800; cf. Fig. 169)

Stairs

Evidence for stairs in London houses is rare before the fifteenth century. Solars had steps (*gradus*) in the thirteenth century, but it is not clear if these were ladders or, as seems possible, simple stairs with treads (i.e. of boards) or of blocks of wood, triangular in section; an example of the former has recently been found reused in a thirteenth-century revetment at Sunlight Wharf, Thames Street.[93] Solid oak treads continued to be used in stair-turrets in London and elsewhere into the sixteenth century, as at Wash-house Court, Charterhouse (**48**). In a building contract for shops in Friday Street in 1410, each shop was to have two stairs, presumably to the first and second floors (**87**). Details of the timbers required for inserting a stair in a house in the parish of St Mary at Hill survive from 1477–9, and insertion of stairs into an existing building was by then no doubt a common practice.[94] In this case the risers and standards were made of elm board; '*brydgis for the stayere*' were apparently handrails. Ropes also sometimes served as rails.[95]

In the Treswell surveys a number of forms of stair can be distinguished, some of them traditionally medieval (i.e. known in medieval houses elsewhere) and others perhaps developments of the fourteenth and fifteenth centuries, products of the increased emphasis on first-floor living. The types were:

(i) exterior stair to a hall. An exterior stair of several steps, probably covered and in some cases with an oriel at the stairhead, is mentioned a number of times in the medieval period,

and was usually found at larger houses;[96] it is not evident in the houses surveyed by Treswell, with the possible exception of Foxe's Court (**142**). Here the main range had an entrance with two steps directly into the parlour, but an adjacent set of steps suggests a former small exterior stair to a doorway, now blocked, into the hall.

(ii) circular or semi-circular newel stair or vice, within substantial walls. This form, common in castles, could be made of stone or timber. There are no complete domestic examples yet recorded in the city, but the newel stair was standard in public buildings (e.g. the corner turrets of Guildhall and Leadenhall) and other masonry structures.[97] Ordinary houses often had a turning stair down to the cellar at the back of the ground-floor room which was probably partly hollowed out of the masonry of the thick cellar walls (**70/2**, **70/3**; an archaeological example at **129**).

(iii) straight flight of stairs, either between two walls or along one side of a room. This form in stone is found in undercrofts from the thirteenth century (**18, 138**) where a comparatively broad stair was required to move merchandise from the street into storage. By the late sixteenth century a straight timber stair was a common means of access from the ground to the first floor within a timber-framed building. Sometimes the stair used the chimney stack for support as it reached first-floor level (**189, 196**). In certain cases a flight of stairs gave access from the street or lane direct to the first floor (e.g. **179/2**).

(iv) enclosed timber newel stair. This is the most common form of stair within a room, and is shown many times in the Treswell surveys (e.g. **72, 76**). Sometimes the approach steps are lengthened, giving the impression of a dog-leg stair (**189**).

(v) newel stair on the exterior of a building, giving access also to the court. This form of stair, common in continental houses from the fifteenth century,[98] is found in the corners of substantial courtyards of buildings on the palatial scale from the second decade of the sixteenth century, and in later sixteenth-century houses around London.[99] There are also examples of a timber stair in the middle of a range, giving access from the court to two or three floors (Fig. 93; **56**). Similar square projections next to the main entrance to the building are found at the King's House, Tower of London, and in one case at King's Lynn.[100] The development of this form of stair is particularly noteworthy because its presence at the house entrance would suggest to the visitor that upstairs is an *alternative* to the ground floor, not a secluded section of the house to be reached *through* the ground-floor reception rooms; and such a stair would have encouraged the division of a multi-storeyed building into horizontal flats, as was the case in sixteenth-century Edinburgh houses.[101]

(vi) newel stair in an external projection, but without external access; the stair only served internal communication on several floors. It probably existed at Crosby Place (1466; **27**), where a stair within an appendage 12 ft square led, it has been proposed, from the parlour to the chamber above.[102] The form is known in Essex from the late sixteenth century[103] and in several London houses by the same general date. In a large house such as Foxe's Court (**142**) the former screens passage led to a square stair tower four storeys high crowned by a turret. A similar but more modest octagonal projection at St James's Hermitage, Monkwell Street (**140/1**), carried the

94.   (**48**) Charterhouse: the staircase (J. Crowther 1885)

95. Buildings in Little St Helen's, Bishopsgate (probably by J. T. Smith before 1799; published 1800)

stair up to the third storey, with a round turret above it. This form may have been used when a medieval hall was floored over, to give access to the new upper chambers. An external projection of this kind, containing an internal stair, was usually on the side of a range; a projecting turret containing a stair at the external corner of a brick range appears at Bridewell Palace in 1515–23[104] and in mansions influenced by the palace plan such as that within Charterhouse (48).

(vii) the wide stair rising by stages and half-landings round a solid core or an open stairwell was present from the mid sixteenth century in the main ranges of grand houses such as that at Charterhouse (Fig. 94). This was a regular form in Paris in the sixteenth century, and is said to be derived originally from Italian architecture. Two examples of this form of staircase are shown by Thorpe in a plan of a house outside London but reflecting London fashions: Copped Hall, Epping (Essex), built by Sir Thomas Heneage (who also owned Bevis Marks, 20) between 1564 and his death in 1595. Stairs of square plan with half landings at each corner around a central pillar are known in late fifteenth-century secular towers in Europe.[105]

(viii) a framed stair formed of two flights with half-landings within a rectangular stairwell, but without a masonry pillar or open space between is hinted at in the Treswell surveys (e.g. 150) and shown in the 1617 survey of Eton property at Bread Street (50); the type is known in Exeter houses of the late sixteenth century.[106] Both forms (vii) and (viii) of the framed staircase are shown many times in the Thorpe drawings of 1597–1603, showing that it was standard in fashionable London houses by 1600.

(ix) a final form of stair which is as yet recorded only in the mid seventeenth century at the Hoop and Grapes, Aldgate, but which might be expected in earlier houses, is that in which the stair communicates on each floor with a gallery between the main block and a rear building. This is another normal late medieval continental form.[107]

Stairs were not only a means of access to upper floors. Some fourteenth-century turrets or towers (the terms *turellus* and *garrita* are used) were the subject of litigation on the grounds that they overlooked a neighbour's property.[108] During the sixteenth century the stair-turret was taken higher than the range it served to form a look-out in the fashion of roof-top banqueting chambers found in Elizabethan country houses (Fig. 95).[109] This conceit is also found in sixteenth-century houses in French, German and Low Countries towns.[110] Other towers, of timber or of brick, were built as free-standing structures (72). It is perhaps these, rather than elongated stair-turrets, which John Stow condemned as vanities: the first such that he knew of, built in brick, was erected by Sir John Champneis, mayor, perhaps around the time of his mayoralty in 1534–5; the second, of timber, was built by Richard Wethell, merchant tailor, at his new house in Leadenhall Street probably in the middle of the century.[111] In 1594 Sir John Spencer added a tower, among other building works, to Crosby Place in Bishopsgate Street (22).

Thus by 1600, stairs took a variety of forms depending upon their destination and purpose. Stairs within the houses surveyed by Treswell were most often placed (at least at ground-floor level) within larger rooms, most commonly at the back of the room, whether it was a shop, kitchen or parlour. There were also, in lesser numbers, straight stairs leading up from entries or directly from the street to the first floor; stairs at the backs of houses down to the back yard tended to be winders. In other houses the grand staircase in its own space (48, 115) emphasised the stateliness of the first floor and the chambers on it. The grand stair is known from the mid sixteenth century (48) but the development of the Great Chamber above the parlour by 1466 at Crosby Place, and perhaps in similar but unrecorded houses, must have demanded a stately staircase two or three generations earlier.

Gallery, Long Gallery and Passage

The term *gallery* covers several different types of sixteenth-century construction; a passage or corridor, a lobby or vestibule, or a long room intended primarily for exercise and recreation.[112] A further specialised use of the term was for a covered walk around one or more sides of a garden, such as that built for the Marquess of Exeter's garden at his city house in 1530 by James Nedeham, one of the king's master-carpenters (114). In this section the term gallery is restricted to two types of room: a passage, either between buildings at first-floor level and above or, as in galleried inns, along a range of separate chambers; and a 'long gallery' or recreation room.

Constructions similar to galleries were present in London from the thirteenth century. About 1250 Adam de Basing built a structure which may have been a gallery across Aldermanbury, between two of his properties.[113] Such a gallery across a street was called an *hautpas*; there were several

between the two rows of houses on London Bridge, and one connected a house to Guildhall itself.[114] Other high-level passages across streets were constructed across Foster Lane (**84**) and in Seething Lane in 1381; what may be a third is shown across St Andrew's Hill on the Agas map. In addition there are references to galleries which, as they involved licensing by the City, appear to have been across the front of houses, or at least with access from the street or along public alleys. In 1533, for example, Sir John Alleyn, alderman, was allowed to set up posts for a gallery 4 ft wide outside his tenements near Tower Hill. It is possible that some houses, for instance those shown in Cheapside in the 1549 Coronation painting, had galleries forming parts of their façades at first-floor and higher levels.[115]

First-floor galleries between buildings, often between the main house and a rear block, are known in London from the early fifteenth century (**40**) and in post-medieval Exeter and Chester. Galleries of this type were made necessary by the restrictions on London sites: in comparison, galleries are generally absent in King's Lynn, where houses were mainly side-on to the street or with an alley down the property when end-on to the street.[116] In early fourteenth- and fifteenth-century examples in Southampton the gallery was used to communicate between two blocks of two-storeyed buildings by running through the open hall which lay between them.[117] In several central London properties in the early seventeenth century, galleries spanned a small open space between the two buildings (**13, 61**) and occasionally the house would have two

galleries on successive floors (**62**); but these are so far the earliest documented examples. An example of a gallery running along the side of a large open hall from the same period survives at Charterhouse (**48**). In larger houses a gallery was also found around one or more sides of a court, sometimes supported on posts (**69/2, 72/1**). Galleries are a feature of medieval inns in other towns; traces of what was probably a gallery along the back of the street range of an inn in London, perhaps of sixteenth-century date, were seen by Henry Hodge during the demolition of the Three Nuns, Aldgate, in 1881 (Fig. 96).

In the Three Nuns building, and in its analogies, the gallery was an integral part of the storey and did not project into the court. Galleries could also be outside the body of the building, sometimes supported down to the ground on posts; this would naturally happen when buildings had grown piecemeal into groups. The most elaborate arrangement of this second type was at Foxe's Court in Nicholas Lane (**142**), where the range incorporating the gate to the lane had, on the inner court side, galleries at first- and second-floor level. The first-floor gallery went on round part of the south side of the court, with a house of office at the corner. The 'long gallery' 44 ft × 3 ft on the second floor served three chambers which occupied the width of the range. A third gallery was placed on the third floor in the hall block on the north side of the court, giving access to five chambers. Here the term 'long gallery' may refer either to an access gallery or to the 'long gallery' of the more stately variety.

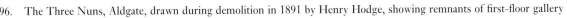

96.   The Three Nuns, Aldgate, drawn during demolition in 1891 by Henry Hodge, showing remnants of first-floor gallery

The 'long gallery' of the principal tenant at the Clothworkers' Throgmorton Street estate (**179/1**), was certainly of a larger kind, 11 ft wide and 30 ft long 'beside the window', which implies that the window was positioned at one end. Presumably this was the garden end, since the plan suggests the gallery lay over the buttery and parlour on the east side of the back yard of the house and terminated overlooking the large garden. An even larger 'long gallery' could be found at the great house in Fenchurch Street (**72/1**), which had served as Fullers' Hall in 1520–8. Here on the second floor of the range along one side of the garden was a gallery 68 ft × 15½ ft; it occupied the entire top floor of the range. At Clothworkers' Hall itself (**139**), a gallery on the second floor of the parlour block was 53 ft × 16½ ft, and had in it a chimney and a counting house. Presumably these true long galleries (having a width greater than 6 ft and so probably being intended for something more than communication between chambers) had the recreational functions attributed to them in royal palaces and noble houses. All three examples were alongside, or terminated with a view of, the private garden.

The term *passage* is used several times in the Treswell surveys. A ground-floor passage, whether outside or inside a building, was called an *entry*. A *passage* referred to similar corridors in upper chambers, though in one case they are called entries (**179/1**). Measurements are never given, since the form of reference is always to 'a passage into the kitchen' or some other room which is then described. In one case, at Darcy's large house in Fenchurch Street, reference is made to 'the passage up out of the hall' to the parlour; the layout of the first-floor rooms suggests that after climbing the stair from off the screens passage, one walked along a passage to reach the parlour which was over the high end of the hall.

Roof Leads

A roof-top walk on leads was provided for prisoners in the rebuilding of Ludgate prison in 1435. Sixteenth-century references to roof leads indicate that some domestic roofs were also covered in lead, and were flat, enabling them to be used as walks or airing spaces. Later engravings and reconstructions of seventeenth-century houses show that in addition small balconies could be formed on any floor, but often on the attic floor, by recessing the front of a storey several feet behind the front wall of the one below. Such a balcony would be entered from the recessed storey by a door and fronted with a balustrade.

A 'lead' or 'leads' are mentioned eight times in the Treswell surveys. In seven cases the term refers to a rooftop walk on the second or higher floors. At St James's Hermitage (**140**), for instance, the main tenant had a door out onto a lead at the top of a staircase turret; his neighbour Mr Gray (or his subtenant Mr Hunte) was allowed to walk on the roof of the chapel itself. At the Wildman, Cornhill (**62**), a lead is included in the description of the first floor without further detail; it could well have been a balcony overlooking the street, a feature of houses in principal streets which is known from engravings and other surveys (**50**).

Privy

Cesspits lined with wood, either boards or wattle, are found on London sites from the tenth century.[118] The thirteenth century seems a likely date for the introduction of stone cesspits to London; clearly they were accepted as a superior variant by the time of the surviving rolls of the *Assize of Nuisance* in 1301. The earliest reference so far located to a stone pit is for a house near Cheapside in the early thirteenth century,[119] and the earliest archaeological examples of stone pits date to the later thirteenth century (**138**). The first half of the fourteenth century saw the widespread adoption of stone cesspits, stimulated by the requirements of the *Assize*.[120] In 1422 the wardmote of Bassishaw could reasonably complain that the little rents of Richard Clerk at the Swan were defective because none of them had privies.[121] The great majority of the tenancies surveyed by Treswell in 1607–14 had individual privies.

The privy as a structure comprised three parts; the seat, usually built over joists; the garderobe chute, often lined with boards, which was called a *pipe*;[122] and the means of collection or disposal of the sewage below, usually a pit. The superstructure was usually of timber, which could both rot (with fatal consequences)[123] or be partially dismantled by a neighbour.[124] In the sixteenth century this was often called a *stool* (**69, 139**).[125] The pipe was between 1 and 2 ft wide, cut in the masonry of an adjacent wall. In the sixteenth century the words *towell*, *funnel* and *tunnel* are used.[126]

London houses, like those in towns elsewhere, also had privies on the first and upper floors. There are only hints that masonry walls had privies cut into them at first-floor level, as are found in other medieval towns.[127] There is however evidence in the Treswell surveys that privies with chutes or funnels were present on the upper floors of timber-framed houses (which were the great majority by 1600). At 21–22 Trinity Lane the tenancy (**181/4**) included a first-floor room 'with a funnel of a privy out of the room above', and the plan of the adjacent tenancy (**181/2**) shows two funnels going down the back of his ground-floor privy, presumably to a communal pit. In properties of the Clothworkers' Company next to the Fleet (**76**) there were three cases of privies at first-

97. (**31**) Watling Court, Bow Lane: base of stone cesspit, probably of fourteenth-century date, excavated 1978

floor level (shown by chutes) over a privy on the ground floor.

The privy shaft did not always communicate with a pit; along the waterfront it is likely that some medieval privies emptied directly into the river (as in the house, probably belonging to the abbey of St Peter of Ghent, which preceded the palace at Greenwich),[128] or as in one case in 1314 where a householder took advantage of the adjacent drain for the public privy at Queenhithe.[129] In the fourteenth century privies were built over the Walbrook and other streams, where they were occasionally removed,[130] though on other occasions allowed to remain;[131] privies over the Fleet are shown by Treswell in 1612 (76). Stone cesspits were however the norm. These were generally square or rectangular pits lined with chalk (Fig. 97; at site 31), often tapering in section, and could be of substantial dimensions, not only for the larger single households or properties (e.g. a privy 16 ft × 10 ft at Bucklersbury, 1405), but especially when they were designed from the start as double privies (e.g. 10 ft × 12 ft by 10 ft deep, the St Paul's shops contract of 1370, 90). A cesspit common to two houses in the parish of St Thomas Apostle is mentioned as early as c. 1160.[132] In other cases a privy became divisible between two properties which were formerly one,[133] or divided between three households.[134] In a dispute over rights to an alley a privy could be divided at the next cleansing with a brick wall.[135] In 1543 a property in St Dionys reportedly had three pipes to separate rooms: the owner's chamber, the maidens' chamber and the manservant's chamber.[136] In 1547 a privy in St Helens was found to be served by four stools of easement, three belonging to one owner and the fourth to another, thus suggesting a fair division of the cost of cleansing.[137] Privies are grouped in some of the suburban houses in the Treswell surveys (189, 196) or placed back-to-back on a boundary (110, 189), indicating a common pit. Presumably in these instances of common pits, the *Assize* (which required an individual cesspit to be a distance away from the property boundary) did not strictly apply.

There is little information on where the privy was in the London house for the thirteenth, fourteenth and fifteenth centuries. Analogy with rural manors[138] would suggest that the privy was off the solar, and in one case in 1314 it was in fact found there;[139] in a contract of 1310 for a small block of shops in the central parish of St Michael le Querne (141) the privies were attached to second-floor chambers which functioned as solars, above the first-floor halls. In the 1405 Bucklersbury contract (40), on the other hand, the 'common' privy was to be at the service end of the hall. In Treswell's surveys, the privy could be found on any floor of the house including the garrets, but there are some indications that it was often placed at a distance from the main living rooms: in cellars (189/8, 189/9), in the garret or on the fourth floor (34, 46, 61, 133/1) or at the far end of the yard or garden (110, 189, 196). Even in larger houses such as the 'great place' in Fenchurch Street (72/1), the main double privy was next to the brick tower in the garden. In many cases, when on the ground floor, the privy was either next to or sometimes entered from the kitchen, as has been noted above.

The ground-floor privies surveyed show a wide variety of sizes. The privy need not be small: dimensions include 6 ft × 3 ft (179, Fryth) or 9 ft × 4 ft (154, Cowndley) and a rather elongated ground-floor room 32½ ft long (55, Butler). The

majority of the ground-floor privies, however, were about 3 ft square (142, 150).

At intervals the cesspit was cleared out by labourers or special contractors called *gongfermers*. It was usual to break open the masonry of the vault to clean out the cesspit, and a bricklayer and carpenter would be required to rebuild the top and relay the joists,[140] though in certain cases the privy could be cleaned by going down a vent.[141] The practice of cleaning out the cesspits at intervals hampers archaeological deductions about the original dates of the pits themselves, since the pottery and other material in the pit will date only from after its last cleaning. From surviving accounts it is difficult to judge how long the intervals between cleaning were; clearly this would depend largely upon the size of the pit and the size of household using it. When a privy was moved or was no longer required, it was sealed off or 'covered' by a dauber.[142]

Close chairs and stools are mentioned in accounts and inventories from the late fifteenth century, though perhaps it is significant that these are all from royal or rich households. Close chairs are mentioned at the Coldharbour (170) in 1485. The king's servant John Porth had three close chairs in his house near Billingsgate in 1531, and at Crosby Place in 1549 there were two close chairs and one close stool. Two close chairs covered in black velvet were noted at York Place in 1530; there were also fifty-four pewter pots for chambers. By the later sixteenth century chamber pots were more common. A house at the Woolstaple, Westminster, in 1588 had chamber pots in two of its bedrooms, including the great chamber, and a close stool in the chamber next to the great chamber.[143]

Workhouses and Industrial Buildings

As in the case of shops, workrooms and industrial buildings figure in this study only when they formed or might have formed part of domestic complexes. Medieval industry rarely required heavy plant, and many types of work might therefore be carried out in any kind of room without modification. Rooms were easily adapted for work purposes: a kitchen could be modified into a forge, for instance. Forges in particular were easily erected, so that they occupied or encroached into the street in the thirteenth and fourteenth centuries.[144]

Industries tolerated within the city walls in the fourteenth century, though occasionally curbed, included tanning (later expelled), bell-founding, the dyeing of cloth and associated tenter-grounds, especially around Cannon Street, and brewing (see Chapters 2 and 3). In 1297 fullers' 'implements' were considered a hindrance in the streets, and were ordered to be removed; it is not clear what these were.[145] The equipment of a dyehouse and a brewhouse seem to have been interchangeable.[146] A brewhouse could be reasonably expected to be of solid construction, at least partly of brick and stone, because of the heat and smoke produced.[147] Other specialised structures mentioned in records before the Dissolution include a potter's *Werckhus*,[148] butchers' scalding-houses,[149] a workhouse for making gunpowder in a grocer's garden,[150] soap-making premises,[151] and a *crinosa* house, perhaps used for leather preparation.[152]

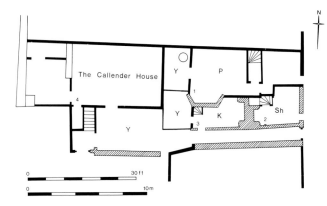

98. **(190)** 77 Wood Street (Treswell 1612)

During the later sixteenth century some of the dissolved monastic precincts were used for a variety of large-scale industrial purposes, including the making of glass at Crutched Friars and pottery at Holy Trinity Priory, Aldgate; description of these premises is however beyond the scope of this study.[153]

A number of the houses belonging to the Clothworkers' Company in 1612, when they were surveyed by Treswell, were occupied by members of the craft or their widows; and some of the houses show evidence of rooms or buildings being used in the trade. The term *wash house* is found twice (**55**, Fig. 59c; **70/4**, Fig. 58); this was a ground-floor structure at the back of the property, in one case with a chimney. Inventories of wash-houses in Norwich at this period indicate that they were used for the scouring of yarn.[154] In one of the Clothworkers' properties with a wash-house, in Fenchurch Street, a *work house* was to be found over the wash-house, but apparently reached only along the first floor of the range (also **70**). This was presumably a clothworker's workplace.

One of the few pieces of heavy machinery documented in medieval London was the horse-mill,[155] and Treswell's plan of more substantial industrial premises off Wood Street shows a *horse-plate* (*sic*, also *horse-place*; **190**, Fig. 98). Here a very compacted property, with a street range four-and-a-half storeys high on cellars, was divided into three tenements. Down the alley lay a Callendring House (where finished cloth was pressed by a great roller) and an adjacent space for a horse-gin to work it. The Callendring House, which had an arched cellar of brick, comprised only one ground-floor room; above it lay three storeys of domestic accommodation.

Stables, Barns, Outhouses and Sheds; Animals

Stables are mentioned occasionally throughout the period. In 1246 the abbot of St Alban's was judged to have encroached on Broad Street with his stable; references thereafter concern houses of both dignitaries and ordinary citizens.[156] On small central properties some ingeniously compact plans were devised to incorporate stables or haylofts. In 1372, for instance, the rector of St Augustine's by St Paul's was said to have had a stable over a vault, with a chamber above the stable;[157] a contemporary will mentions a garret which served as a hayloft.[158] Stables were a feature of larger properties and inns

throughout the fifteenth and sixteenth centuries, naturally in peripheral locations but also sometimes in central streets.[159] As pressure on space increased in the later sixteenth century, stables were converted into domestic accommodation.[160]

Five occurrences of stables are shown in the Treswell surveys (Figs. 48, 59a, 61, 191, 218). Two inns were surveyed: the White Horse, Barbican Street, and the Crowne, Aldgate. At the former (**12**) the absence of documentation including the text of reference makes analysis difficult, but it is clear that the eastern of the two halves into which the block had been divided contained two large stables among its buildings. To reach them the horse had to be led through the pedestrian entry from the street and through another building (which is not given a function on the plan, and may be a third stable). Both the larger stables had haylofts over. The stables at the Crowne (**10**) were on a more substantial scale; behind the public front yard of the inn, through a second gatehouse, lay a long yard surrounded by stables, all with haylofts over. Most had an entrance in the middle of a long side. At the far end of the yard was a small gate to the open spaces of the former extramural garden of Holy Trinity Priory. Stables were a feature of certain larger houses such as the Erber in Dowgate (**67**) and Lady Lucy's house off Old Bailey (**143**). One example of a small domestic stable was surveyed at West Smithfield (**189/1**). This was an open-sided shed behind the house, and the horse (or other animal) must have been brought through the house, which in this case did not even have a side entry.

The barn, a larger building than the stable, was no doubt rare within the city walls; only three references have been found, all for peripheral or suburban locations. St Bartholomew's Hospital had a barn in the parish of St Sepulchre in 1281; the Carpenters' estate in Lime Street included a barn which was shored up in 1495; and a barn was built in 1589 at Arundel House in the Strand, former residence of the Bishop of Bath (**157**; Fig. 45).[161] No doubt other religious houses besides St Bartholomew's had barns within their London precincts, akin to those known and occasionally surviving on religious estates in the London area.

Smaller sheds, chambers or ancillary spaces are mentioned rarely, implying that rooms or sheds were found for relatively unimportant functions as need arose, and without much alteration. Coalhouses, known from at least 1277,[163] are shown in the Treswell surveys (**154/3** and **154/4**, where the coalhouse is probably the unnamed chamber measuring 9 ft 2 in × 6 ft behind the house; **176**), and at Trinity Lane (**179**) a 'coleyard' was fenced off immediately behind the White Hart tavern. A boulting house was surveyed as part of the extensive tenancy of Mr Campion at Haywharf, Thames Street; it comprised a small chamber between the larder and the kitchen (**169**; cf. **175**).

Apart from stables, references to buildings or structures specifically for animals or domestic fowl are rare. Pigs roamed the streets in the thirteenth century, but were gradually banned; pigsties were sometimes moved away from property boundaries, but were otherwise tolerated.[164] References in city records to animals such as pigs and cows are rare after the fourteenth century; it is not clear whether this indicates a lack of official interest or the gradual disappearance of these animals from the properties of the citizens. If the latter, the

inference would be that during the fourteenth century it became more usual to buy ready-killed meat from butchers rather than to raise stock in backyards and gardens. This cannot however have been universal. A tenement in the suburban parish of St Andrew Holborn contained a cowhouse in 1351; in 1365 a baker in the large intramural parish of St Alphege was alleged to have oxen, cows and pigs which constantly broke down the walls of a neighbour's house.[165] Birds which were kept in yards or gardens included hens, ducks, and especially doves (e.g. at **200** in Southwark).[166]

Gardens

Until the middle of the sixteenth century, London would have seemed quite rural to modern eyes. Varieties of trees standing in the city, as mentioned in records, include ash, elm and pear;[167] presumably any oak had long ago been cut down for building works. Hedges were to be seen both inside and outside the walls; 'growings called Quykset' are mentioned in 1492.[168] In the fourteenth century a *herbarium* was located near the modern Bank road junction, and the city also contained orchards. By the time of Edward I, a nursery trade supplied trees, flowering plants and turf for laying, at least for royalty.[169]

Vineyards are known in suburban settings in the twelfth and thirteenth centuries;[170] the property which became the town-house of the prior of Lewes in Southwark contained, about 1255, gardens and *vinariis*,[171] but from the late thir-teenth century vineyards in London seem to have produced only verjuice, the acid juice of unripe grapes.[172] It is now thought that the weather generally cooled after 1300 until after 1530, thus greatly discouraging the large-scale cultivation of the vine;[173] a number of fifteenth- and sixteenth-century London gardens, particularly of livery companies, contained the plant, but normally only a single vine formed a feature of the garden.[174] Trellises, presumably for vines, are shown in several large gardens (e.g. at Grocers' Hall and south of Bucklersbury) on the copperplate map of *c.* 1559.

Several of the major livery companies had gardens attached to their halls, but the accounts, though often detailed, generally speak more of seeds or gardening tasks, and it is usually not possible to reconstruct the garden itself (see e.g. **128**, Carpenters' Hall; **178**, Drapers' Hall II). The amount of care given to the gardens, such as the provision of bowers and occasional vines, does however underline the impression that gardens in the city were precious, savoured enclaves, and that the gardens of the company halls were akin to the gardens of country houses and Oxbridge colleges today in their purposes and expert management.

By the time of the Treswell surveys, gardens were to be found only in some of the larger houses and in the peripheral or suburban areas. Most of the smaller properties on central streets had tiny yards, but the houses of one-room plan did not even have a yard. Three of the largest private houses, in Fenchurch Street (**72/1**), that of Lady Wood in Fleet Lane (**76/1**) and the nearby Christ Church property of Lady Lucy's house entered from Old Bailey (**143**), had gardens;

99. (**28**) Sir Paul Pindar's house, Bishopsgate: (a) elevation of banqueting house (N. Smith 1791)

(b) Details of plaster figures

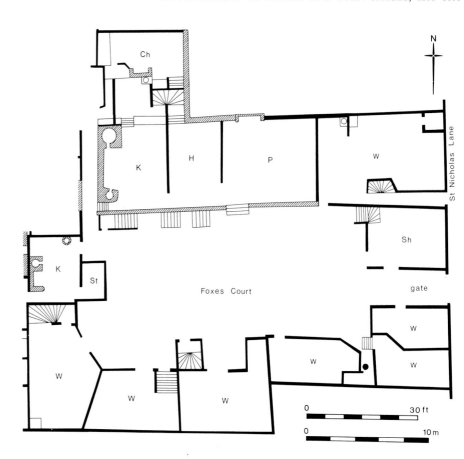

100. Access patterns at larger houses in 1612: (a) (*right*) (**142**) Foxe's Court, Nicholas Lane

(b) (*middle*) (**75**) Lady Wood's house, Fleet Lane

(c) (*far right*) (**145**) 3–4 Pancras Lane

Darcy had two (Figs. 48–9, 54). Darcy's larger garden, perhaps an orchard or at least with small trees, had a fountain in the middle; in two other cases the words *a grasse plotte* indicates a cultivated lawn (**76/1, 179/1**). In addition the garden at Clothworkers' Hall (**139**) was arranged in four ornamental 'knots' (Fig. 57). The Erber at Dowgate (**67**), surveyed slightly earlier in 1595, also had a formal garden, but it was walled off internally from an adjacent entry from Bush Lane (Fig. 218). This was privacy taken to an extreme.

Gardens of smaller houses are not detailed and are presented in outline only. The main tenant at the former St James's Hermitage, Monkwell Street (**140/1**), could step into an adjacent bastion (B13, excavated in 1965 and now preserved in the Barbican estate) as part of his garden, and the houses in Swan Alley must have been surrounded by large garden spaces. In the suburban settings of Bishopsgate or Southwark, gardens could reach considerable lengths and no doubt provided a source of income from market gardening. Within the city, the parlour, when on the ground floor (as in the majority of the examples in the surveys), was nearly always to be found overlooking the garden, and it is clear that the two went together; only occasionally is a parlour found without an adjacent garden.

Separate gardens, owned or leased by someone who lived elsewhere in the city, were also to be found: part of the Carpenters' estate in Lime Street, for instance, comprised a separate garden from at least 1485.[175] In the suburbs, and especially outside Bishopsgate, such gardens became pleasurable retreats in the later sixteenth century, and often contained summerhouses. These buildings were a feature of royal and monastic gardens from the early sixteenth century; Prior Bolton of St Bartholomew Smithfield (1505–32), for instance,

had two octagonal brick gardenhouses built at the priory estate which is now Canonbury House, Islington.[176] In the City the Marquess of Exeter, occupying the former Pulteney mansion in Pountney Lane, had an existing garden gallery replaced by a two-storeyed gallery round three sides of his walled garden with a summerhouse beneath on one side (**114**); a fireplace was to be included, presumably within the summerhouse. The copperplate map shows several summerhouses in the northern suburbs, especially outside Bishopsgate; Stow described them as a recent development.[177] Treswell surveyed one separate garden outside Bishopsgate, with a small timber-framed building possibly of this recreational character within it.[178] In its finest form, the summerhouse or gardenhouse could be called a banqueting house, which also owed much to royal models (**28, 115**; Fig. 99a–b).[179]

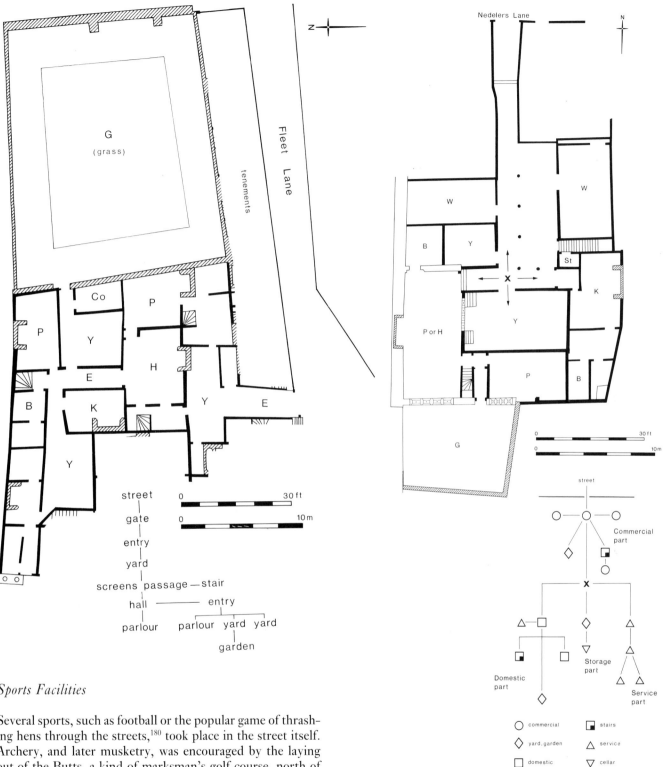

Sports Facilities

Several sports, such as football or the popular game of thrashing hens through the streets,[180] took place in the street itself. Archery, and later musketry, was encouraged by the laying out of the Butts, a kind of marksman's golf course, north of the city.[181] By the late fifteenth century courts for tennis and bowls could be found off central city streets, and plans of courts survive from the opening of the seventeenth century.

A tenement called the Tenyspley in the parish of All Hallows Staining is mentioned in 1481;[182] this may be the Clothworkers' tennis court in Fenchurch Street, in their possession by 1535 and surveyed by Treswell in 1612 (Fig. 54). Other tennis courts in the city are known in Thames Street next to the Steelyard in 1567 and nearby in Suffolk Lane in 1583.[183]

The Pewterers' Company had a bowling alley (probably adjacent to their hall in Lime Street) repaired in 1489–90,[184] and the Merchant Taylors' bowling alley within their hall complex is mentioned in 1571–2 (**177**). The Carpenters' Company constructed a bowling alley in 1547; like the one at Hampton Court, it had a floor of soap ashes, combined with house ashes and founders' earth (the latter easily obtained from the many founders who lived in the nearby parish of St Margaret Lothbury).[185] Hollar's bird's-eye view of Arundel

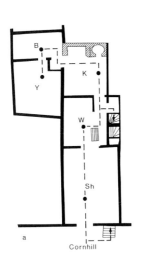
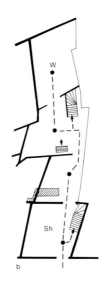
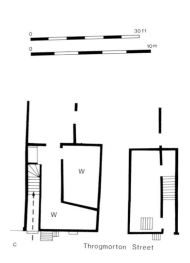

101.   Access patterns in smaller properties in 1612:

(a)   (**62**) The Wildman, Cornhill   (b)   (**133**) House at Mark Lane   (c)   (**179**) Tenancy at Throgmorton Street

House in the 1660s (Fig. 46) shows the bowling alley there as a long shed, the upper parts of its wide panels open to the elements. Bowling alleys were seen to be a centre of vice, like brothels and gambling houses, and were physically broken up by instruction of the mayor and sheriffs on several occasions during the later sixteenth century.[186] In 1612, nevertheless, the Clothworkers had two bowling alleys in close proximity off Coleman Street, at White's Alley (**55**) and Bell Alley (**56**). With its large gardens, summerhouses, banqueting houses and bowling alleys, the northern area of the city, both inside the wall and out, had a recreational tone during the second half of the sixteenth century.

Access Patterns through the Property

Although comparatively few complete house-plans have so far come to light for the medieval and Tudor period, the Treswell surveys of 1607–14 demonstrate a certain amount of variety in the way the internal spaces of houses were arranged. It is probable that some of this variety was influenced or even governed by the requirements of the users. Here are six examples, all from the better and more extensive residences or tenancies where such variety is more likely to have expressed itself.

The first two are traditional courtyard houses, that at Foxe's Court, Nicholas Lane (**142**) and Lady Wood's house in Fleet Lane (**76**). Though both had recently been rebuilt, they appear to represent large medieval houses in the post-medieval period (Fig. 100a–b). There is one significant difference between these two arrangements: Lady Wood's house is a town residence, with two parlours and a garden – the latter reached only through eight gates or doors from the outside street. The main house at Foxe's Court, tenanted by a clothworker in 1612 and probably having been rebuilt by one in the 1580s, has the yard as its node or nexus. Off the

yard are several warehouses; and in this case the shop opens not directly from the street, as is normal in London, but from the entry which is behind the street-gate. The complex is geared round the storage and protection of merchandise.

In a third example of a large house, that at Pancras Lane (**145**), the ground floor was evidently even further perceived as being divided into functional areas: commercial, domestic, storage and service (Fig. 100c). The buildings were so arranged that at a crucial single point (X on Fig. 100c) the visitor decided, or was directed, which way to go: left, into the hall (or parlour as it was then being called) and thereafter the garden or stairs to the upper chambers, including bedrooms; right, to the kitchen and service rooms, which also contained stairs to upper floors; or straight ahead to the main yard, from which access to the cellar beneath the hall range was alone gained. The functions of various areas of the ground floor, at least, were clearly defined.

Warehouses were off the main traffic routes within Foxe's Court; in smaller houses belonging to the Clothworkers' Company, and largely occupied by their members, trade considerations influenced the design to a greater extent, for instance the Wildman, Cornhill (**62**) – not a tavern, but a shop and warehouse complex – and a house in Mark Lane (**133/4**; Fig. 101a–b). Though a construction date for the Wildman is not available, the house at Mark Lane had been built by the Clothworkers' Company expressly for rent in 1562–3. These two houses show the primacy of trading or storage functions: at the Wildman four rooms – shop, warehouse and two cellars beneath them – formed both a circular route and a physical blockage between the street and the domestic accommodation, which could only be reached through the shop *and* warehouse; here, as noted previously, even the route from the kitchen to the hall on the first floor had to pass through the warehouse. In this restricted house, the private open space was not so much the small yard as the leads, or balconies, on the first and fifth floors. At Mark Lane (**133/4**) a similar but

less marked tendency was evident: again the route to the domestic accommodation was through the shop, even in a house comprising sixteen rooms or spaces.

A sixth example, a tenancy in Throgmorton Street (179/2; Fig. 101c), is of a phenomenon noted only once in the Treswell surveys of 1607–14 and once elsewhere in the present gazetteer, at the White Bear in Cheapside (50) in 1617. Here the whole tenancy was on the first floor or higher, with only stairs down to the street: the accommodation remained completely above the ground floor. Presumably this type was the residence of a person not desirous of wholesale storage like the clothworkers, or of large, open residences like Lady Wood. Perhaps there were examples in earlier houses, but they are not apparent from the evidence now available. The design of compact town-houses in Covent Garden, two decades later, would follow this model of a street-door leading directly to a stair, with no other ground-floor rooms.

Conclusions

Within Britain, London was probably in the forefront of architectural fashion as expressed in the houses of nobles who lodged in the city and in the houses of its more prominent citizens: in their different ways the stone tower, the parlour and the first-floor hall may be examples of this metropolitan progressiveness. Some rooms, such as the shop, the warehouse and especially the undercroft, changed their size, importance and perhaps function over time, presumably as a result of market forces which demanded different patterns of wholesale and retail trading; another influence which would have been felt first in the larger cities or those most likely to be exposed to new markets and new trading opportunities. The appearance of other rooms, such as the closet and study, the long gallery, the second parlour, the summerhouse and roof-top turrets, all during the sixteenth century, would appear to be a series of fashionable conceits which showed how the prosperous citizens of London could indulge in diluted forms of the architectural extravagance they saw around them in noble town-houses and royal palaces.

We can note the development of features which articulated a need or desire to live above the ground floor of the property; a need felt more in smaller houses than in those within extensive grounds. Here shops and warehouses took over the ground floor, and domestic functions were moved to the first and upper floors: the hall and kitchen from the early fourteenth century, the privy, and even in certain cases by 1600, the parlour. The small urban property, often forming a frontage to a street with a large house behind, grew upwards. The flat lead roof and balconies appeared to give a little more air. Stairs and staircases were developed to articulate this growth. And in so doing the stairs, by 1600, were often coming up directly from the street or from an alley, breaking the house into two separate worlds of trade and private lives.

The value of privacy in the home was developed by the thirteenth century; glass windows which were broken, and had therefore lost their smoky opacity, were to be reglazed. In 1293 the Earl of Lincoln, having acquired the first residence of the Blackfriars in Holborn, granted a plot of ground next to his gate into Holborn on condition that the building to be erected contiguous to his own residence would have a wall 10 ft high and with no window, arch or opening in it.[187] From these and references in the *Assize of Nuisance* for the fourteenth and fifteenth centuries, it is clear that the preservation of privacy was a continuing concern. This may have governed the design of medieval houses, but comparatively few complete house-plans have so far come to light for the period up to 1600. Besides privacy of the family from observation by other households, a concern with privacy of the individual within the household may be traced, though sketchily for the same general reason, in the multiplication of bedrooms and of chambers generally (compare the traditional use of the word *chambers* in legal circles to indicate a private reception room or domestic accommodation) in the London house from the fourteenth century. By 1600 a variety of arrangements of rooms can be observed. The way a substantial clothmerchant's house-and-warehouse complex was arranged reflected an emphasis on trade and the street outside. Where an extensive site allowed a number of ground-floor rooms, the parlour and garden were located as far as possible, in terms of access, from the street.

CHAPTER 5

The Fabric and Furnishings of the London House, 1200–1600

The built environment is partly a product of civic regulation in design and construction of buildings, including houses. London's growth in the eleventh and twelfth centuries may have been one reason why building regulations were drawn up at the end of the twelfth century against fire and to govern aspects of drainage and privacy; royal (and later civic) regulation attempted to restrain encroachment of structures into streets or other public spaces. One direct and notable result of the *Assize of Buildings* (in force by 1212) was that there were no widespread fires in the city between 1212 and 1666; a remarkable achievement which must be at least partly attributable to the requirement for 3-ft stone party-walls from the late twelfth century. A second consequence was a continuing concern by occupiers of buildings with standards of construction, hygiene and privacy, as exemplified by the rolls of the *Assize of Nuisance*. The concern of the civic authorities was however with boundaries and aspects of construction which might affect neighbours (such as roofs of flammable materials) rather than with standards of construction throughout the building.

The two carpenters and two masons who were the sworn Viewers of the city, and who gave specialist advice to the mayor and aldermen in these cases, were craftsmen of national and occasionally international note. Thomas Mapilton, for instance, who gave advice to the Grocers' Company about their new hall in 1430, has been credited with the rebuilding of St Stephen Walbrook in 1429 and the building of the Lollards' Tower at Lambeth Palace (Fig. 110) in 1434–5; he may also have gone to Florence to advise Brunelleschi on the building of the cathedral.[1] It seems fair to assume that from at least the opening of the fourteenth century, when the masons are known and their standing demonstrable, there was a certain perceived standard to London's buildings, whether public structures or private houses.

What did medieval London houses look like? No contemporary observer described them with the detail which the modern archaeologist or historian would wish. For many components, some quite large (such as the varieties of roof), there is very little information from the city itself and analogies, or substitutes, must be sought from similar buildings in other towns. The evidence is fragmentary, though archaeological excavation in particular is adding to knowledge at a growing rate. The underlying causes of variety can still be sought, as in the study of rooms and spaces in the previous chapter: the influence of fashion, the will and capacity to make statements of affluence, or the influences of high-density occupation at certain periods of London's history which might produce special features to be found only in crowded cities.

The fabric of the medieval house is considered, as it were, first from top to bottom: roofs and roof-coverings, windows and glazing, doors and floors, then hearths, fireplaces and chimneys, wells and water-supply, and finally gutters and drains. These were the skeleton of the medieval house. Fittings and decoration, including such potentially major items as boarded or plaster ceilings, are then reviewed, along with a brief account of mobile furnishings and furniture.

Roof Structures

Records or surviving examples of secular roofs in London are very scarce, and the range of roof-types present in the medieval and Tudor city can only be suggested by charting the developments demonstrated by houses in other towns and in the area around London.

The possibility that some early medieval buildings, probably of stone, in the city had low-pitched roofs in the Mediterranean manner, a hypothesis suggested by the style of some excavated fragments of rooftile, is described below. Such roofs, if they existed, were clearly a minority and would have been outdated by fashions of the twelfth and thirteenth centuries, such as aisled halls. No aisled halls have yet been identified in London, though it is likely that they were a common form, and their roofing styles can only be assumed from analogies in other towns and in the region.[2]

In the mid thirteenth century English carpenters 'picked up a French idea' in constructing roofs with the crown-post, an arrangement of braces on a tiebeam which gave support to a timber running longitudinally down the roof and thus stiffening its structure. The crown-post roof continued to be standard in better timber-framed buildings in the south-east of England until the middle of the sixteenth century, and many examples must have existed in London.[3]

During the fifteenth century, at least in the immediate area to the west and north-west of London, another form of roof was developed, in which longitudinal stability was transferred to purlins on the roofslopes. Its first recorded appearance is at the Harmondsworth Barn (Middlesex) in the early fifteenth century, where it may have been the work of Winchester carpenters.[4] In some buildings purlins were supported by a collar and a single short king-post, but far more common was the queen-strut roof in which two raking struts, sometimes curving, supported the purlins as they were clasped by principal rafters; queen-*post* roofs, in which two vertical posts support the collar, still survive at the Queen's House in the

102.   (47) Bishop of Chichester's Inn/Lincoln's Inn, Chancery Lane: interior of the Old Hall, looking south

Tower of London of 1528[5] and can be seen in large buildings near Dowgate in Hollar's panorama of 1647 (Fig. 24).

This clearing away of the crown-post during the fifteenth century also had the effect of making attic space more accessible, since the queen-posts in pairs in each truss, which could incidentally do service as door jambs for partitions, were the only obstructions. In a contract of 1492 for a brewhouse in the parish of St Martin in the Fields, for example, it was stated expressly that the roof was to have purlins.[6] Flat attic floors survive from *c.* 1500 at the town-house of Thomas Paycocke at Coggeshall, Essex, and in the Queen's House at the Tower of 1528. These developments suggest that the side-purlin roof and the exploitation of attic space must have gone together in London from at least the late fifteenth century; the ap-pearance of dormer windows in urban contexts by 1450 (see below) would suggest an even earlier date. Similar developments occurred in other towns at roughly the same time or shortly later. Side-purlin roofs without crown-posts became common in York in the late fifteenth century, and crown-posts disappeared from Lincoln at the same period.[7]

In the open halls which studded the city, and which were often expressions of private or corporate wealth, several suitably impressive styles of roof developed during the fourteenth century. One innovation was to carry the roof on lofty two-centred arches, which may be the meaning of the 'up-right roof' (a special term rendered in English, not the Latin of the rest of the contract) specified for the large house at Bucklersbury in 1405 (**40**); such arches or arch-couples, finely moulded, survive at the Bishop of Chichester's hall, now of Lincoln's Inn, erected in 1493 (**47**; Fig. 102). A more modest variant in which solid curved timbers support a raised tie-beam, in this case with a crown-post above, was employed at Barnard's Hall *c.* 1400 (**105**; Fig. 71). A second innovation was the hammerbeam roof, well known from its largest example at Westminster Hall (1394–1402), but found in a smaller scale at Winchester in 1325–6[8] and at Exeter by 1450.[9] The hammerbeam roof was employed at London in the sixteenth-century halls of the Inns of Court, at Gray's Inn (1556–60), Middle Temple (1570, possibly built by or under the advice of the carpenter from Longleat) and Staple Inn (*c.* 1581), which as a group chart the onset of Renaissance detail into formal woodwork.[10] Two other examples are recorded, one at Fishmongers' Hall, where two of the hammerbeams of the hall roof were renewed in 1639,[11] and in a house in the parish of St Katherine Cree, reported in 1588 as 'likely to fall into great ruin if not speedily repaired. The causes of decay are the weight of the roof which is hammer beam and of very large timbers; it is also overcharged with a lantern or lo[u]ver of great weight and is already spread 10 inches and more.'[12] From its location, this might be one of the convent buildings within the former Holy Trinity Priory. It seems likely that hammerbeam roofs were not usual in ordinary houses.

A further style of roof, at Crosby Place, is really a magnificent false ceiling of compartments in eight bays, conforming to a four-centred arch in profile (**22**; Figs. 40, 136); this is discussed with other ceilings (both of wood and plaster) below (pp. 118–22).

The fifty-odd company halls of which there is record must have displayed many roofs of notable craftsmanship. It is clear that for discerning clients with money, there was a range of styles to choose from. In 1496, for instance, when building their new hall, the Pewterers examined the halls of the Haberdashers, the Carpenters, the Papey Guild, and of 'the Dean' (of St Paul's?) at Hackney.[13]

Roof Coverings

At various times during the medieval and Tudor period in London, houses were covered with shingles, boards, thatch, ceramic tiles, blue slates, stone slates or lead.

In the thirteenth century the royal houses of Henry III, including many of the buildings at Westminster, were roofed with shingles; Westminster Hall was re-covered with shingles in 1307.[14] Shingles were allowed within the city under the building regulations of the early thirteenth century, but were probably a rare sight: the roof of St Paul's belfry was relaid in 1394–5[15] and only one domestic example has been noted, on a house of the abbot of St Alban's purchased in 1432 to extend the hospital of St Anthony, Threadneedle Street.[16] Modern experience of shingles suggests that they do not last as long as ceramic tiles, requiring restoration and perhaps renewal every hundred years and sometimes after shorter periods;[17] in the late fourteenth century they also cost about three times the price of tiles.[18] Boards were also allowed under the regulations, but their use seems to have been confined to smaller or ancillary structures, such as sheds or outside cesspits.[19]

Thatch, the most likely covering of Saxo-Norman secular buildings,[20] was banned in the building regulations of *c.* 1200, though isolated instances suggest the rules were occasionally broken, in both intramural and suburban streets;[21] outside the city, rural buildings continued to be thatched until the sixteenth century and occasionally later, into the early nineteenth century.[22]

Work on the earliest excavated examples of medieval ceramic roof tiles has shown that there were several varieties available by *c.* 1170,[23] the date of appearance of tiles in other towns such as Canterbury and Southampton.[24] Peg tiles, which had two holes for attachment by means of wooden pegs to the laths, were the standard form; other early and short-lived types were shouldered peg tiles (which only had one hole for attachment) and flanged and curved tiles. Use of the shouldered and of the flanged and curved tiles died out in the thirteenth century, perhaps because of the greater amount of hand-finishing required for each tile in both designs and, in the case of the shouldered peg tile, because the manner of laying and securing the tiles produced a roof twice as heavy as one of ordinary tiles.

The occurrence of the flanged and curved tile roofing system in the twelfth century, distinctly resembling the Roman manner of roofing but with tiles made in a medieval fabric, calls for further comment. The Roman roof was at a much lower pitch than its thirteenth-century successor (the latter illustrated, for instance, by aisled halls) in the regions of northern France and lowland Britain. The regional variations within present-day France, with steeper flat-tiled roofs generally to the north and less steep, flanged and curved tile roofs to the south, can be traced back to at least the fourteenth century.[25] The flanged and curved tile system is one employed exclusively on low-pitched roofs. It therefore seems

likely that certain stone buildings in twelfth-century London had roofs of low pitch; the source of this technology could be the Mediterranean areas of France or the region around Bordeaux, in which low-pitched tiled roofs predominate.[26] It is an attractive hypothesis, but at present without substantiation, that such roofs could also have been modelled on memories of ruined Roman buildings.

The use of tiles was enforced by the building regulations of the early thirteenth century; houses were occasionally particularised as 'covered with tiles' (*tegulis coopertam*) in documents up to the middle of the century, though some of these references referred to houses in suburban parishes, such as St Botolph Aldersgate and St Sepulchre, where tiled roofs may not yet have been the norm.[27] By this time broken rooftiles or wasters were regularly used for hearths, and tile roofs were the norm.[28] The *Assize* of 1276 ordered that tiles be well burnt and well leaded – taken to refer to the green lead glaze with which tiles were sometimes decorated – and of the ancient pattern (i.e. standard or dimensions).[29] The price of tiles was fixed at 5*s*. the thousand in 1350, after the Black Death had caused a rise in prices;[30] though occasionally the price rose to 5*s*. 6*d*. the thousand, the standard 5*s*. was still being charged in 1508.[31]

A move to standardise the quality and dimensions of tiles in the later fifteenth century provides some details of manufacture. In 1467–8 the tilers successfully petitioned the City for restoration of their franchise. They complained that tiles lasted no more than three to four years, instead of forty to fifty as formerly. Tiles should be made with better tempered clay, dug at Michaelmas (29 September) and left until Christmas, then cast up so that the marl and chalk in it would break out with the frost; and finally used in the March following. This scheme, with February substituted for Christmas, was enshrined in an Act of 1477; the standard size was to be $10\frac{1}{2}$in $\times$ $6\frac{1}{4}$in by at least $\frac{5}{8}$in thick.[32]

The places of manufacture of the earliest ceramic rooftiles in London have not yet been identified, though the clay is local. Tilers were to be found in St Sepulchre's parish, on the western fringe of the walled city by 1230;[33] in 1275–6 tilers bought the clay excavated from the Tower moat.[34] By the fourteenth century, tile-making centres for London had moved further to the east. Digging for clay is recorded in Stepney in 1366, though references to tile-houses or tile-garths are later.[35] Woolwich was another production centre on a large scale from at least 1375, selling products to sites in Essex and Westminster.[36]

Fragments of roofing slates have also been found in tenth-century contexts, though these may be residual from Roman buildings. Slate was in use in the south and west of England from the twelfth century (for example, at Southampton from *c*. 1170)[37] and pieces are found with sufficient regularity to indicate contemporary usage in medieval waterfront rubbish dumps in London from *c*. 1280.[38] There are also occasional documentary references to slate roofs in London from about 1340, when 5,000 slates for roofing at Westminster were carted from Milk Street.[39] The old hall of the Merchant Taylors, by then a subsidiary building, was covered with slates in 1406–7, as was the library at Guildhall in 1423–5.[40] A slate roof was however still thought worthy of remark by Stow, who noted that in 1593 the Merchant Taylors put one

103. (**193**) Bishop of Winchester's palace, Southwark: west end of the hall, *c*. 1330

on their almshouses in Hog Street by the Tower.[41] They had decided to roof their hall in slate in 1586 (see below).

There is also evidence of use of Horsham stone for roofing: in 1424–5, probably for the new hall then being built, the Drapers paid William Broker, 'Sclater de Horsham', in part payment for 'sclatte' which were presumably Horsham stone slates.[42]

Roofs of tile, slate or stone would need ridge tiles, which are found in London from the twelfth century. Ridge tiles were also known as 'creste' tiles,[43] and occasionally they were simply decorated to emphasise the ridge.[44] There was a distinction between ordinary tiles at 5*s*. the thousand and 'rooftiles', which cost up to one penny each;[45] these were presumably ridge tiles.

Other items of 'roof furniture' included finials, louvers and vanes. Finials were primarily decorative additions to the roof ridge; though certain hollow and perforated forms found outside London also served to ventilate smoke, the examples so far studied from the city appear to have been purely decorative. These employ crudely fashioned designs featuring animal or human heads and faces, resembling contemporary pottery aquamaniles which would have been made in the same kiln, and their use dates from the early thirteenth to the early fifteenth century.[46] Louvers are discussed below under chimneys. Vanes (i.e. weathercocks) were to be seen on many church towers[47] and occasionally on prominent buildings such as the Merchant Taylors' kitchen or the houses on the

Bridge, which in about 1542 were provided with eighteen vanes, painted with gold and sundry arms or fleurs-de-lys.[48] These are not shown by Wyngaerde (Fig. 9); perhaps this is additional evidence for a date earlier than previously suggested for the drawing, i.e. nearer 1540.

Lead as a roof covering is no heavier than thatch and lighter than tiles, but it was too expensive for widespread use at the domestic level.[49] References to lead roofs include parts of royal palaces (e.g. the chamber and the hall at Kennington Palace in the mid fourteenth century or a stair at Eltham Palace in 1397)[50] and the name *Leadenhall* in Cornhill, which perhaps signifies a roof of lead at a substantial thirteenth-century mansion. There may also have been times when lead was unfashionable. When the Merchant Taylors debated

whether to re-roof their hall in slate or lead in 1586, it was pointed out that lead was expensive and that none of the royal or noble houses, or the Inns of Court, were then covered in lead; it was therefore resolved that it would be more appropriate to cover the roof with slate.[51] The Taylors were slightly misinformed, as Somerset House (1547–52) had extensive lead roofs; but this reference incidentally shows that slates were considered more worthy than tiles or lead in the late sixteenth century. By the opening of the seventeenth century, however, balconies and small areas of roofs were being laid with lead to provide private open space and areas for drying washing, as noted in the previous chapter. The extent of these leads in a prominent tenement on a major street is shown in the 1617 plan of the White Bear in Cheapside (**50**; Fig. 209).

104.   Abbot's House, Westminster: west side showing late fourteenth-century windows (F. Nash 1805)

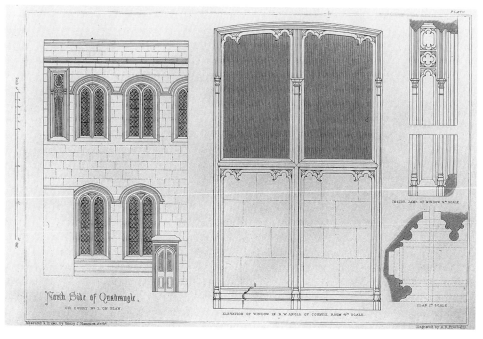

105.   (**22**) Crosby Place, Bishopsgate: details of windows (H. Hammon 1844)

106.   Guildhall: a window in the west crypt, probably late thirteenth century (restored)

Windows, Glazing and Privacy

Throughout the period there were differences in scale and decoration between basement windows and those for storeys above. Windows on the ground (basement) floor of twelfth-century stone buildings were narrow openings with semi-circular heads and deep internal splays (91, 198; Fig. 32b). On the first floor of stone buildings, two-light windows were probably to be found, though none has yet been recorded in London.[52] In the thirteenth century the usual form of stone window was of two cusped lights, with a quatrefoil piercing above; in royal buildings the transom made an appearance[53] and the taller windows required their own gablets in the roof.[54] Windows of this kind were to be seen at the hall of the Bishop of Ely in Holborn of 1286 (107; Fig. 69). During the fourteenth century stone windows in secular buildings followed styles in church windows;[55] an ambitious example in London was the translation of the circular rose window, fashionable in major churches in the late thirteenth and early fourteenth centuries, to the gable of the hall of the Bishop of Winchester in Southwark, perhaps of c. 1330 (193; Fig. 103). More commonly, but still in a rich establishment, the windows in the hall of the abbot's house, Westminster, of c. 1372–5 (Fig. 104) are of two lights beneath an elaborate traceried head.[56] Examples outside London indicate that by 1330 a common form was of two lights with cinquefoiled heads, split half-way down by a transom,[57] as shown in the

hall of Furnival's Inn, dating perhaps to the fifteenth century from its arch-couple roof (108; Fig. 72a).

Wooden window-frames are known in Saxon churches, in the middle of double-splayed openings in masonry;[58] archaeological excavation in London may one day produce similar evidence from secular buildings. The oldest surviving and unrestored examples from the city date from the late seventeenth century. In masonry buildings, timber would have provided simple lintels, sills and pads into which the iron fittings could be drilled, without mouldings or further decoration, as in thirteenth-century examples recorded in Bruges.[59] By the early fourteenth century, the general date of the earliest surviving timber-framed buildings in the London area, it is clear that windows were often a pre-planned feature of the framing, and could incorporate up-to-date traceried heads, mullions and transoms.[60] References to wooden-framed windows in London in the fourteenth and fifteenth centuries specify 'lintelled windows' (1342; 146) or 'handsomely lintelled' windows (1405; 40), indicating perhaps such traceried heads. Mullions (moynels) are mentioned in 1369 (89), indicating windows of at least two lights, again in a timber-framed building; in this case windows to shops are being described. A fifteenth-century two-light window of stone with some of its original fittings can still be found at Guildhall.

In the fifteenth century, too, the largest halls had great windows in their gables, as at Guildhall where large windows also ran along the sides.[61] The richer livery company halls and

107. (*above*) House in foreground of Wyngaerde's panorama of *c.* 1540

108. (**140**) St James's Hermitage, Monkwell Street (F. Nash *c.* 1800)

109. Alleyn's almshouses, Pepper Alley, Southwark (J. C. Buckler 1827)

the best merchants' houses such as Crosby Place had rows of windows along the walls of the hall, on a more modest but still palatial scale (Fig. 105). During the fifteenth century, also, smaller windows under a square hood or label became common; two-light examples survive, restored, in the west crypt of Guildhall after the rebuilding of *c*. 1430 (Fig. 106); at the Lollard's Tower, Lambeth Palace, of *c*. 1435 (Fig. 110); and at **140** (Fig. 108). Window-frames or surrounds in brick (the chamfered sill, the hood-mould, and the mullion) were introduced, sharing the style of frames in stone; examples in the region are found at the Bishop of Ely's palace at Hatfield (Hertfordshire) of *c*. 1485. By the late fifteenth century, in the London area, a window could reach six lights in a single row;[62] the 1547 painting of the Cheapside area shows cases of seven or eight lights. Eighteenth- and nineteenth-century illustrations of London buildings show further examples of timber windows, some with opening casements (Fig. 109), but it is not certain (and perhaps unlikely) that these windows were in their original form when delineated.

During the sixteenth century the window-frame of stone, brick or wood reflected changes in style and mouldings. Windows in the attic storey at Queen's House, Tower of London (1528),[63] have depressed four-centred heads; thereafter, by 1580 in the London area, preference grew for rectangular window-openings and ovolo-mouldings,[64] a change reflected in mouldings on roof-timbers, doors and panelling.

The Treswell surveys of 1607–14 are of limited value for the study of windows, since they show only the ground floors; and, apart from the outline of bay windows (discussed below), only exceptionally large examples of windows at the more substantial houses. These include a single case of a stone window in a hall gable (**145**) and several cases of windows in timber-framed walls; these could reach widths of eight lights in the end of a hall and seven lights in a parlour (**143, 145**).[65] Windows to other kinds of chamber are not shown.

Of particular interest for the development of taste in connection with town-houses is the history of the larger window of two lights, divided by mullion and transom into four parts. During the fifteenth century, in towns such as Bruges which might serve as a parallel for the buildings of London, rectangular windows were divided with mullions and transoms of stone or timber, the upper third glazed, sometimes with figures or heraldic devices, but not opening, and the lower two-thirds, beneath the transom, without glass but shuttered on the inside.[66] Such an arrangement might have formed the original aspect of windows high up in the walls of the hall at Furnival's Inn already referred to (Fig. 72), though access to the shutters would in that case have been difficult. Wyngaerde shows a further example in the side of a house in Southwark in the foreground of his panorama of *c*. 1540 (Fig. 107).

The first half of the sixteenth century, and perhaps the late

110.   Lollards' Tower, Lambeth Palace, 1435 (J. Wichelo *c*. 1800)

111.   (**118**) The Cock, Leadenhall Street (J. T. Smith 1798)

White Hart
INN
Bishopgate Street

113. **(99)** House at Crutched Friars: interior of courtyard (J. T. Smith 1792; cf. Fig. 130)

112. (*left*) **(29)** White Hart Inn, Bishopsgate (J. Wichelo *c.* 1800)

114. (*right*) **(105)** Barnard's Inn, Holborn: north elevation of hall

fifteenth, seems to have been the time for the development, in London, of an even more ambitious continuous row of double-height windows, usually on the first floor of a gabled property facing the street (Fig. 111; shown in Southwark near the bridge approach by Wyngaerde *c.* 1540, Fig. 42). Following the analysis of room functions in Chapter 4 above, such a row would have lit the room often called the hall. Where the property was wider than usual, the windows, sometimes on both first and second floors, could incorporate canted (projecting) elements to vary the elevation (Fig. 112);[67] a Treswell survey of 1586 of property in Tothill Street, Westminster, shows canted windows rising through the first and second storeys of a narrow gable.[68] Continuous runs of double-height casements could also be found in courtyards, lighting the hall or other principal chambers; and here two examples show the contrasting fashions of the mid sixteenth century. At a house south of Crutched Friars drawn by J. T. Smith, three sides of a splendidly decorated courtyard had continuous windows, lighting a first-floor suite of chambers, at least one of which had a marble fireplace, panelling and a plaster ceiling (Fig. 113; cf. Fig. 130 for interior view). The hall at Barnard's Inn, on the other hand, has ranges of double-height windows on both sides, originally interspersed with pilasters with Corinthian capitals in the Classical tradition, possibly dating from *c.* 1545 (**105**; Fig. 114).[69] Parallels in other towns would suggest that straight continuous runs of windows occupying the width of the property date from after 1500.[70] In 1599 Sir Paul Pindar's house in Bishopsgate incorporated extremely fashionable window-

forms in such a two-storeyed wooden façade, stretching as wide as the narrow elevation allowed (Fig. 115).

A further demonstration of wealth was the comparative profusion in London of oriel and bay windows. In the thirteenth century the term *oriel* meant a porch with a window at the top of an entrance stair to a first-floor hall or chamber;[71] an oriel of this type was to be added to a prosperous skinner's house in 1308 (**191**), and was probably what was meant by the term in the Bucklersbury contract of 1405 (**40**). During the fourteenth century the term was also used to describe a similar and probably more ambitious projecting window on the ground floor at the high end of the hall, jutting into the court; in later examples a comparable window jutted into the garden behind, to give lighting to the dais from both sides.[72] Stone oriel windows were to be found at certain livery company halls, such as the Merchant Taylors' (**177**, late fourteenth century), Grocers' (**149**, 1429; Fig. 53), Cutlers' (rebuilt 1458–9), and at Crosby Place (**22**) in 1466 (Fig. 116).[73] The form was still popular in halls of traditional plan in the late sixteenth century, when the hall of Charterhouse (**48**) was rebuilt by North or the Duke of Norfolk, and at the Inns of Court.

Oriel or bay windows were also constructed in timber, and analogies, some fragmentary, survive in the counties around London from the fourteenth century.[74] In 1405 a carpenter was to build an oriel for the St Paul's house in Bucklersbury (**40**) and in 1423 John Pekker, carpenter, was to build a bay window, like the one in a Charterhouse property on Cornhill, at Brewers' Hall (**1**); the same reference states that Warwick

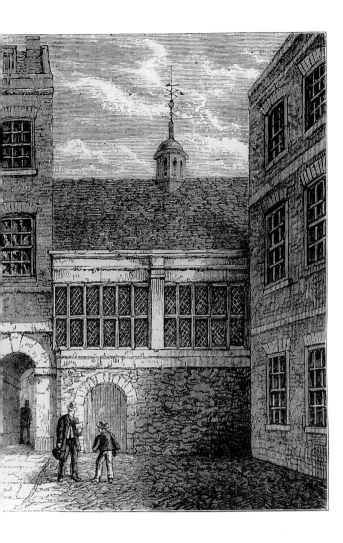

Inn (**185**) contained an oriel 'undersett' with stone.[75] The canted form, pushed out with further side walls at right angles to the main building, became semi-octagonal in plan, as at Crosby Place; and the semi-octagonal form is seen in brick in the Treswell plans, at the Clothworkers' Hall parlour of 1594 (**139**), and at the former Fullers' Hall in Fenchurch Street, in 1612 a private residence, in timber (**72**). In a more modest house off Coleman Street a bay window of timber protruded from the end of the house (**56**).[76] A bay window could also be built on the ground floor on the street side of a building, though permission or sanction was needed to extend it into the street.[77]

From the fourteenth century, bay windows, no doubt of timber, were to be found projecting from upper floors. At the Peter and Paul Tavern, Paternoster Row, in 1342 (**146**) both the hall and bed-chamber of the tavern, which lay on the second or third floors, were to have a bay window each. The 1405 contract for a house in Bucklersbury specifies two bay windows, for a chamber and a parlour, looking down into Bucklersbury and each 6 ft wide; the second floor would merely have lintelled windows (**40**). There are no surviving analogies in buildings around London to suggest what projecting windows on higher storeys would have looked like in the fourteenth or fifteenth century, but Smith's fine engraving of the house in Grub Street shows a bay window, perhaps co-eval with the framing of the house, of the mid sixteenth century (Fig. 93). From at least 1532 a bay window could incorporate clerestories (small flat lights), flanking it on either side.[78]

115. (**28**) Sir Paul Pindar's house, Bishopsgate: frontage after removal to Victoria and Albert Museum (R. Paul 1896)

116. (**22**) Crosby Place, Bishopsgate: oriel window (1908) [*Survey of London: Crosby Place*]

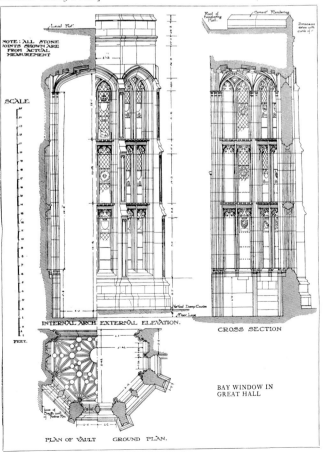

117.   81–84 Bishopsgate (J. Crowther 1886)

Several other types of projecting window built into timber-framing were developed during the sixteenth century. Two types were built to form bay windows of several superimposed storeys, most often two, but sometimes three, from the first floor upwards. Canted windows (i.e. with sides at an angle), fashionable in the late fifteenth century, continued so throughout the sixteenth. Windows of rectangular plan which might be called 'box windows' are seen in buildings of the reign of Henry VIII at Westminster, where they occurred only on the first floor.[79] By the time of Lord Rich's building speculation at Cloth Fair these windows could rise through three storeys, and other examples are known from Bishopsgate, where one house had a date of 1590 over the doorway (Fig. 117; cf. 50, windows dating possibly from the rebuilding of the tenement in 1595). A third design of projecting window was the 'round-compassed' or 'carrel' window, semi-circular in plan, found in royal contexts from the

1530s.[80] A probably more modest example was noted in 1568 in St Clement's Lane, when the Viewers reported that the 'jutty of a rownd compassed wyndowe' should be cut off and made even with the room next under it; but another was licenced by the Carpenters' Company in 1596.[81]

A final form of extravagance, in the late fifteenth and sixteenth centuries, was an exceptionally large flat window. By 1500 there must have been a number of examples of large glazed windows in public or semi-public buildings, and not only Guildhall and public places such as the Guildhall and Leadenhall chapels. The window of the hall of the Fraternity of the Holy Trinity in Aldersgate (7; Fig. 118b) serves as an indication of the size that could be attained, and which must also have been seen in livery company halls. In houses, large windows were a feature of the urban palaces built by courtiers on monastic sites after 1535. An example within the City was at Holy Trinity Priory, where Symonds' plans of about 1585

enable a suggested reconstruction to be made of the Ivy Chamber (Fig. 43b), perhaps dating from the building there by Thomas Audley before 1544, with windows occupying most of two opposite sides. In this case the height of the windows is not known. Such windows are a feature of other prodigy houses of this time (and especially of the 1540s to 1550s) elsewhere, e.g. Acton Court near Bristol. There may have been a window of this type, later reduced in size, at the house of Sir Thomas Pope at Bermondsey Abbey.[82] These two London examples would suggest that magnates who were courtiers in the 1540s were indulging in excessive amounts of glass in their London residences (and, in the case of Acton Court, occasionally in country seats) decades before the building of the well-known examples of Worksop Manor (Nottinghamshire, 1586) or Hardwick Hall (Derbyshire, 1590–7).

Several further types of window were more utilitarian. The garret or attic floor of houses could have windows built into the framing of the gable.[83] In addition, perhaps from the first half of the fifteenth century, dormer windows projected from the slope of the roof. The design of a louver described below, which might have been meant to resemble a little house with dormers, dates from shortly before 1430. A London account of 1458 mentions *gapyarys* windows, which may refer to dormers; the term *gapias* is used in a Canterbury contract of 1438.[84] Dormers are shown on houses in Southwark and the City by Wyngaerde in *c.* 1540 (Figs. 119–20) and Hollar in 1647 (Fig. 24); the warehouse range of the Steelyard shown in these panoramas may date from about 1475. Larger dormers which probably qualify as gables survive from 1586 in the street frontage to Holborn of Staple Inn (Fig. 170), but these must have been comparatively rare in the intramural city, as most houses did not present their eaves to the street.

Window-glass has been found on a small number of Saxon

118.   (**7**) Hall of the Fraternity of the Holy Trinity, Aldersgate: (a) figures from the windows (J. Carter 1783)

(b)   Interior looking east (J. Carter *c.* 1785)

119. Houses in Southwark in Wyngaerde's panorama of *c.* 1540, showing variety of window-forms including windows in a gable. Houses in the foreground are roughly on the site of **196** and may represent them.

120. Houses on west side of Borough High Street, Southwark Wyngaerde's panorama of *c.* 1540, showing a dormer window

sites both inside and outside London; fragments of eleventh-century window-glass have been found on the Watling Court site (**31**), suggesting that the large timber-cellared buildings there may have had glazed windows somewhere in their superstructure.[85] The glazing of church windows was general by the mid twelfth century, and the use of pictorial glass was common enough to be condemned by the statutes of the Cistercian Order.[86] In 1251 'white' glass was used at the house of the Bishop of Winchester in Southwark.[87] The earliest documentary reference to glazing in a normal London house is in a deed of 1263–4 cited in a case of 1321, and the earliest archaeological finding of lead cames for glass is from *c.* 1280 at Trig Lane.[88] In 1305 a defendant was instructed to block up or glaze (*vitro claudere*) windows through which his tenants had been throwing rubbish, overlooking church property in the parish of St Werbourga (St John Watling Street).[89] Windows in superior residences around London, such as Kennington Palace or the abbot's hall at Westminster (Fig. 104), were usually glazed after *c.* 1350.[90] London was a centre for glazing work for royal commissions from the late thirteenth century and the Glaziers were an organised mistery by 1328,[91] but the extent of their work for ordinary citizens has not yet been researched.

During the early fifteenth century references indicate that glass, sometimes painted or bearing benefactors' arms, was inserted in major secular buildings in the city such as Guild-hall and the adjacent Mayor's Court building, in livery company halls such as Merchant Taylors' Hall (repairs, 1416–17) and Carpenters' Hall (new building, 1441–2),[92] and on company properties.[93] By the end of the fifteenth century, as shown by the example of the Pewterers' Company, individual members were contributing to the glazing of plain window-panes, especially in the hall and parlour: the Pewterers by this method glazed the high window over the dais, the bay window (glazed by a total of nine contributors), five other windows in the hall, the bay window and at least two others in the parlour, and a window in the counting house.[94] Glass depicting coats of arms was set up in two rooms at Coldharbour II in 1485, significantly perhaps the great chamber by the water-side and the lady's chamber, where the arms of 'my lord and

my lady' were symbolically placed (**170**, and Table 1). Shortly after, the Fraternity of the Holy Trinity, Aldersgate, had glass with pictures of St Basil and two parishioners inserted in the window of the hall, possibly to celebrate its building (Fig. 118a). Heraldry in glass dating to before 1600 survives from 1520–32 at St Andrew Undershaft (the coats of arms of donors to the rebuilding of those years) and in two secular buildings: the windows of Barnard's Inn (from *c.* 1545) and Middle Temple Hall (*c.* 1570 onwards).[95] Just outside the period considered in detail here, in 1623–4, Lincoln's Inn chapel received a notable set of painted windows (badly damaged in an air-raid of 1915) which comprise saints against recognisable views, including the buildings of the Inn itself, Westminster and Baynard's Castle.[96]

Much of the plain window-glass and nearly all the coloured glass used in medieval London buildings seems to have come from abroad until the development of glassmaking in London itself in the late sixteenth century.[97] The degree to which London was supplied by the Wealden glassmakers, for instance those of Chiddingfold in Surrey who were established by the thirteenth century, is not known; at the very end of our period, Jean Carré of Arras introduced techniques of making vessel-glass in London and window-glass in the Weald,[98] but examples of window-glass definitely made in the Weald have not yet been identified.

The source of window-glass is usually only stated in accounts when it came from the Continent. Normandy crown glass came from near Rouen, the industry there developing about 1330; by the end of the century came thinner and flatter Lorraine glass, with a higher reputation.[99] Flemish glass was used in the windows of Merchant Taylors' Hall in 1420–1.[100] The native glass tended to be greenish in colour, from its constituents and the method of production.[101] This may have been why glass in London houses was often translucent rather than transparent; a case in 1305 has already been cited, and in 1341 the tenement of John Trappe, skinner, allegedly had four windows with broken glass through which the affairs of a neighbour could be seen, and which on inspection were ordered to be repaired (i.e. reglazed, so that they could not be seen through).[102]

TABLE 1

Coldharbour I (170), Glazing 1485

Rooms used by the noble occupants and guests

1. Hall
   4 ft of new glass besides the buttery: old glass repaired
   skowchyns to bear the coborde
2. Great Chamber (possibly on first floor); also called the [Great] Chamber over the hall on the waterside
   glass windows repaired, sizes not specified
   8 ft of ornamented glass 2 ft and a quarter
   52 quarrels of English glass in the windows
3. Great Chamber on the waterside (possibly different from 2)
   6 ft of new glass
   skochyn with my lady's arms set in the water side (in glass) – in this room?
   3 cases of iron for the great Chamber window by the water side, and hooks for same; one case of iron for a window in the same chamber
4. Chapel
   old glass repaired
   two pieces of glass set in chapel
   five windows scoured and set up
5. Wardrobe
   old glass repaired
6. My Lord's Wardrobe, also called the Great Chamber (possibly same as 2 or 3)
7. My lady's Wardrobe (possibly also Lady Elizabeth's wardrobe)
8. Lord Buckingham's Lodging
   piece of lattice in the high window, 15 ft
   2 panes of new glass, 8½ ft
   13 ft of Dutch glass in the windows
9. My Lady's Chamber
   2 panes of new glass, with arms of my lord and lady; 9 holes in same windows mended
   28 ft of Normandy glass in the windows
10. Closet next My Lady's Chamber
    6½ ft of old glass reset
    5½ ft of Dutch glass
11. Chamber over the hall (possibly different from 5)
    27 quarrels of English glass in 4 panes
12. Parlour by the garden
    glass repaired
13. My Lady Elizabeth's Chamber (possibly the same as 9, since no glass mentioned under this heading)
    6 Sawdelettes (saddle bars for windows) to the west window
14. Mr Fowler's Chamber
15. Chamber next the Chapel
    2 old windows repaired
16. Chamber over the Wardrobe
    12 ft of Normandy glass
17. Chamber of Sir Renold Bray
    14 ft of Normandy glass in 2 panes
    1 ft of Normandy glass in a lattice pane

18. The priest's chamber (possibly same as 17)
19. Chamber of John Denton
    14 ft of Normandy glass in 2 panes
    1 ft of Normandy glass in a little pane
20. Little Hall
    2 panes of Dutch glass containing 10 ft
    21 quarrels in the window; four panes of glass
21. The Great Chamber over the little hall
    14 ft of Dutch glass set in 2 windows
22. Parlour by the Thames

Service areas of the house

1. Gate, stable
2. Kitchen
   13 ft of Flemish glass
   a gapias window, 6 quarters of timber
   3 panes of Venice glass containing 26 ft; 26 quarrels of English glass, (each quarrel = 1 ft of glass); four other panes of glass
   3 empty pipes (then sawn)
   8 sawdelette bars for the windows
3. Ewery
4. Larder
   a new glass window made, 9½ ft of glass
   one pane of glass, probably English
5. Wet Larder
6. Dry Larder within the Kitchen
7. Pantry
8. Pastry
9. Buttery
   pane of glass containing 5 ft
   firment for the window
10. Buttery for little hall
    3 ft of Dutch glass
11. Countinghouse
    a piece of lattice
12. Chamber outside the gate
13. Chambers in Sege Alley
14. Stair to Great Chamber
    4 ft of Flemish glass at stair end next the Great Chamber
15. Stair over the Little Hall
    4½ ft of Dutch glass in a pane by the waterside next the stair
    8 quarrels set beneath this pane
16. Stair at the backside of Lord Buckingham's chamber (possibly same as 14)
17. Stair in the entry
18. Stair by the Cook's Chamber
19. Stair between the two gates
20. Stair without the gate
21. Wine cellar (and 'the cellar')
    2 ferments in the cellar repaired
22. Boiling House
23. Wood house
24. Watergate

Servants' quarters

1. Steward's Chamber
   3 pieces of lattice
   27 ft of English glass in a bay window
   10 sawdelettes (saddle bars) of iron for a window
2. Porter's Lodge
   wood for legges for windows and two fillets
3. Chamber of the Clerk of the Kitchen
4. Cook's Chamber
5. the Cater's (purveyor's) chamber
6. The Controller's chamber
7. Byrkhide's chamber
8. Abell's Chamber
9. The man's chamber over the new gate
10. The skinner's chamber

The details of glass supplied by Herman Glazyer for the refurbishment of Coldharbour II (**170**) in 1485 (Table 1) form a solitary landmark in the story of glazing in London, but also a reminder of the splendour to be seen in the some of the city's buildings. The account included four kinds of glass: English, Normandy, Venetian and Dutch (i.e. Rhineland), allocated without evident distinction between larger chambers, closets, stairs and the several halls. Even the kitchen was given 13 ft of Flemish glass (possibly same as Dutch), 26 ft of Venice glass and 26 ft of English glass; the Buttery received 3 ft of Dutch glass, and the Steward's chamber was embellished with 27 ft of English glass in a bay window. Some of the panes (i.e. panels) of imported glass were of considerable size: two chambers each had 14 ft of Normandy glass in two panes, and three panes of Venice glass contained 26 ft. The Coldharbour reference is thought to be the first in the British Isles to glass from Venice.[103] In 1541–2 a petition of the Glaziers offered to standardise the price of Normandy, Burgundy and Flemish glass to 4d. a foot for all three kinds;[104] presumably the visual differences were apparent only to the informed or the fastidious client.

Throughout the period, windows (that is, casements of iron or wood containing glass) were deemed precious and therefore movable, by both the owner and others. In 1470 William Smith, tailor in the parish of St Gregory, thought himself within his rights to remove the windows from his tenancy on vacating, in that they were not fastened to a principal post of the building;[105] in 1493 the churchwardens of St Mary at Hill paid a tenant 4s. for the lattice and windows that he left behind him, and allowed another tenant a quarter's rent for installing glass in her hall, parlour and chapel.[106] In 1537 a surgeon made a window with its glass one of his individual bequests.[107]

Unglazed windows, particularly of ground-floor or basement rooms, were commonly fitted with iron bars or a framework of bars let into holes on all four sides,[108] as shown in excavated examples: a wall probably part of the ground floor of Fisher's Folly in Bishopsgate (**25**; Fig. 121a) and an undercroft next to St Botolph Billingsgate (Fig. 121b). Alternatively, a lattice of wooden rods, round or square in section, was fixed outside the window to prevent birds flying in when the window was open or without glass, and to protect the glass when present; a lattice 12 ft long is mentioned in 1595.[109]

Unglazed medieval windows outside London commonly had shutters inside them, sometimes sliding from the side in grooves.[110] This may be the meaning of 'a long quarter [a beam-like timber] to make it slyders for a wendow' ordered for the house of the Carpenters' Company beadle in 1546–7.[111] By the seventeenth century there were several other kinds of shutters in general use inside glazed windows: a single leaf hinged on one side, pairs of shutters, and shutters making further economies of space by folding back on themselves and fitting into a recess in the window reveal.[112] This type is also shown in fifteenth-century paintings executed in other European countries, and thus may have been present in London at this earlier date.

Throughout the surviving rolls of the *Assize of Nuisance* of 1301–1437 complaints were made concerning the making of windows and their lack of glazing, apertures made in party walls and the consequent invasion of privacy, usually due to overlooking of the plaintiff's property by the defendant or his servants.[113] Three cases illustrate the concern, supported by custom, that windows on party walls should be 16 ft above the ground. In 1323 owners of a house in an unspecified parish were successfully prosecuted for having two windows 13 ft from the ground and unglazed; in 1338 a potter's hall, presumably on the ground floor, was found to have four windows only 4½ ft from the ground.[114] In 1427 a defendant claimed that the custom of the city exempted windows above the height of a man (a rather large 8 ft) and glazed with thick glass or barred with iron, as this would not disturb the privacy of neighbours, but this was not allowed.[115]

Further cases in the sixteenth century illustrate the neighbourly friction produced by close proximity. In 1537 a defendant was ordered to keep permanently closed a window through which he had been ejecting rubbish into a neighbour's gutter.[116] In a detailed judgement given in 1595, concerning a wash-house and the lights it impaired in the parish of St Leonard Eastcheap, 'the casements of the plaintiff's house shall open into the yard as they do now except for the furthest casement southward which is either to be nailed up or fitted with a pane of clear glass; all casements that are to be open shall have iron bars in the middle between the mullions' (*monyons*).[117] This suggests that by this date, clear glass was allowed, and there was more concern with rubbish; iron bars were to be placed on the inside of the window, so that objects could not be thrown through the casement when open.

Doors

Less is known about doors and doorframes than about windows in medieval London houses, partly because doors were the subject of less litigation (though *access to doors* was a recurring theme, as was complaint about rainwater falling near them). Doors which opened onto a neighbour's land could be prosecuted for invasion of privacy in the same way as overlooking windows.[118] A Saxon door has been excavated on a site in Pudding Lane but no medieval secular examples survive from the city.[119] At Lovat Lane the shape of a door, with low-arched head, was chiselled from the back wall of a cellar so that the door at the foot of the internal stair would lie flat against the back wall when opened (**129**). Superior door-

121.   Unglazed windows: (a) Bishopsgate Street, excavated 1988, probably part of the ground floor of Fisher's Folly (**25**)

(b)   Botolph Wharf, Lower Thames Street: windows of an undercroft, in one case with iron bars surviving, in excavations

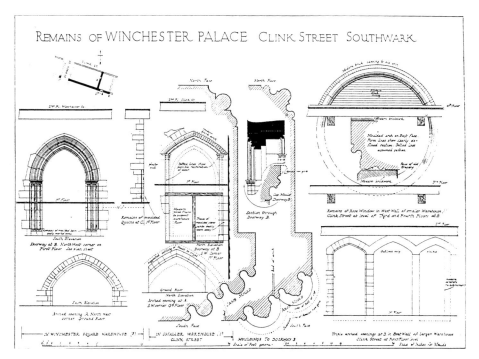

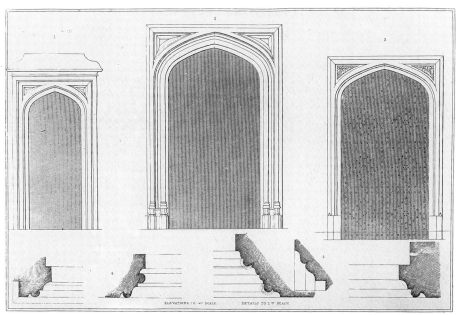

122. Medieval doorways: (a) (193) Bishop of Winchester's palace, Southwark: details of doorways and circular window [*Survey of London: Bankside*]

(b) Details of doors at Crosby Place, Bishopsgate (22) (H. J. Hammon 1844)

123. Thirteenth-century fragments reset at Lincoln's Inn (47), presumably from the Bishop of Chichester's Inn

124. (22) Crosby Place, Bishopsgate: view from St Helen's Churchyard (i.e. looking south-west), showing door with window above (F. Nash 1816)

125. (*below*) (28) Sir Paul Pindar's house, Bishopsgate: view of first-floor chamber (J. T. Smith 1817)

ways of stone survive at the Bishop of Winchester's palace (**193**; Fig. 122a) and Guildhall,[120] and several doorways were recorded in the nineteenth century at Crosby Place (Fig. 122b), including one with a window above it, lighting the passage behind (Fig. 124); fragments of stone jambs and door arches survive at the Bishop of Chichester's Inn (later Lincoln's Inn; **47**; Fig. 123) or have been excavated (**32**, **153**, **174**). A 'running door' (presumably sliding) is mentioned in records[121] and trap-doors to cellars were ubiquitous.

Engravings of the exteriors of better sixteenth-century houses (i.e. those whose robustness of construction ensured their existence for over 250 years) show examples of panelled street-doors of the middle of the century (e.g. Figs. 93, 112), either protected by a small pentice with grotesque corbels or bordered by grotesque and strapwork pilasters. A further feature of interest at the end of the period is the *portal*, or doorcase of wainscot on the inside of a door, which is mentioned at Thomas Cromwell's house in 1527 and in other, later high-quality residences (**115**, **145**) in larger chambers or grand entrances (shown at Sir Paul Pindar's house, **28**; Fig. 125). By the mid sixteenth century the portal was a feature of other principal chambers; two were recorded at The Kaye in Westcheap in 1562, in the great parlour and in the summer parlour.[122]

Floors

Only the most prestigious residences could afford floors of Purbeck marble, as at the hall of Crosby Place (**22**; Fig. 40), perhaps emulating the marble floor of Guildhall paid for by Whittington's executors, and the hall and screens passage of a similar residence probably refurbished by the mayor of 1603 at Leadenhall Street (**115**). Floors of simpler stone slabs are however occasionally mentioned in records and have been excavated in medieval houses.[123]

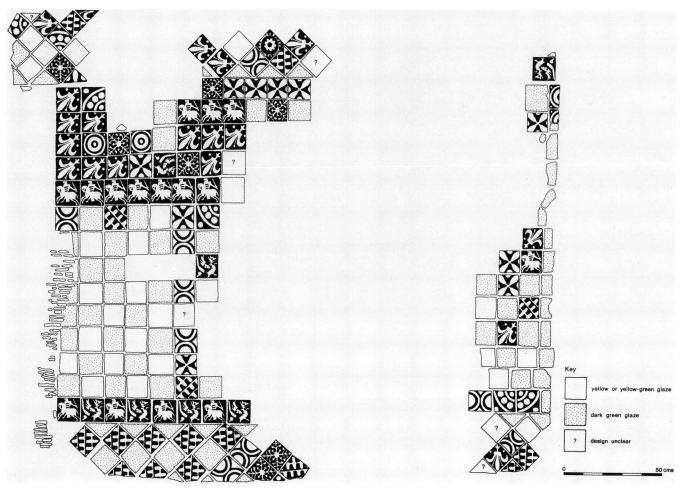

126. (172) Seal House, Upper Thames Street: fragmentary medieval tile floor, probably fourteenth-century, excavated 1974

Glazed floor tiles came into regular use during the second quarter of the thirteenth century in royal contexts.[124] Ward-Perkins, in 1940, concluded that tiles of the thirteenth century were uncommon in London, and that tiles came into general use in the city in the fourteenth century;[125] an assessment of recently excavated material in London is intended in the near future, and interim suggestions might modify Ward-Perkins's caution.[126] A tile kiln was recorded in 1870 in Farringdon Street, but none of its products have survived or been traced and it remains undated (maybe thirteenth or fourteenth century). Perhaps it is significant that this kiln was twice the size of examples elsewhere; London houses would have provided a large market for the products.[127]

Medieval floor tiles from city sites fall into two groups. The earlier, probably dating from the mid thirteenth century (perhaps as early as 1225–50) to the first half of the fourteenth century, are called 'Westminster' tiles since examples pave the muniment room at Westminster Abbey. They are found throughout the south-east of England; a pavement was recorded at Clifton House, a merchant's house in King's Lynn. In London a damaged pavement has been excavated in a late thirteenth-century building, probably the hall of a tenement, at Seal House, Thames Street (172; Fig. 126). The designs used by this tiler include mounted knights, lions, fleurs-de-lys, griffins and dragons, a common repertoire among tilers throughout southern England. 'Westminster' tiles are now being found, though not *in situ*, on a number of secular sites in the city.[128]

The second most important group of tiles in medieval London came from Penn in Buckinghamshire, where tiles were produced on a massive scale from 1332 to at least the 1380s.[129] Their distribution in Essex and Kent suggests the activity of London middlemen; they were widespread because they could be brought by river from Buckinghamshire to London, and the new technique they developed of making thinner tiles probably cut down production costs.[130] Penn tiles are found in a first-floor room in the Bloody Tower *c.* 1360; this example shows how floors were laid, when possible, in long panels.[131] Inferior copies of Penn tiles are found at the same period at Kennington Palace, where they were probably used initially in the hall and in the upper floor of a chamber.[132] Penn tiles have also been recovered as loose finds from many pre-Second World War excavation sites in the city, including several church and hospital sites.[133]

A small proportion of tiles may have come from Kent. At least one example of the tiles from the fourteenth-century kiln at Tyler Hill, near Canterbury, has also been identified in the Museum of London.[134] In 1443–5 the Fraternity of Holy Trinity, St Botolph Aldersgate, ordered 1,600 'donwyche' (Dunwich, Kent) tiles, for repair of their tenements, together

with a thousand from 'Newton~' (?); two sizes of tiles from Kent were available in 1532–44.[135]

From at least the outset of the fourteenth century floor tiles were also being imported from Flanders. The term *Flanders tile* referred both to tiles, or perhaps more properly in modern terms, small bricks, for use in fireplaces,[136] and to paving tiles. In 1302 four merchants of the Hanse were importing Flanders tiles, when they promised 10,000 'of the larger size' to an alderman.[137] Flanders tiles specifically for a chimney are mentioned in 1422, and for a kitchen, so probably also for a chimney, at Brewers' Hall in 1423.[138] Plain coloured Flemish tiles, more certainly for floors, were imported in large numbers into eastern England in the late fourteenth and fifteenth centuries.[139] These are generally yellow and green, but the green can verge on black, and this may explain the 'black and white' paving tiles bought by the London Bridge wardens in 1411.[140] Yellow and green Flemish tiles were imported for royal works in *c.* 1533 and 1536, and some are found in post-Fire buildings, indicating a long period of supply and currency.[141]

References to paving and paving tiles in London buildings suggest that tiles were a valued commodity. A tenement in the parish of St Bartholomew the Less was dignified by the name *le Pavedhalle* in 1348.[142] A tiled floor could be removed as a fitting, along with doors and windows;[143] this may be one reason why glazed tiles are (with the exception of the Seal House site) hardly ever found in their original pavements during archaeological excavations. They are normally found as single examples, or in small numbers, in dump layers associated with demolition of the buildings in which they presumably lay.

Floors were also of beaten earth, or sometimes beaten chalk.[144] By the opening of the seventeenth century cellar floors were also being laid in brick (**174**). Floorboards on joists were of course ubiquitous in chambers above the ground floor, but are also known in eleventh-century timber cellars[145] and occasionally in cellars or undercrofts (**132**, though undated – presumably pre-Fire; **174**, floorboards of pine laid over a brick floor in the sixteenth or early seventeenth century). Finally, rushes were also sometimes strewn about, even over tiles at Bakers' Hall.[146]

Hearths, Fireplaces and Chimneys

Open hearths, without any sign of chimney or restraining partitions, have been excavated within tenth-century buildings on Botolph Lane and Bow Lane.[147] During the later twelfth century roof tiles, often wasters or broken fragments, were used as a fire-proof base for hearths; waster tiles were sold in quantity for the purpose: for example, four baskets for the hearth of the Falcon brewery, Aldersgate Street, in 1438–9 (**7**). Elsewhere tilesherds were sold for foundation layers, though this has not yet been noticed in London.[148] A large fourteenth-century open hearth, bordered by decorated floor-tiles and therefore probably in the hall of the tenement, has been excavated on a property in Thames Street, as noted above (**172**).[149] The open hearth required an outlet for smoke in the roof, and fragments of ceramic louvers[150] have been found on several excavations. Two examples from Watling

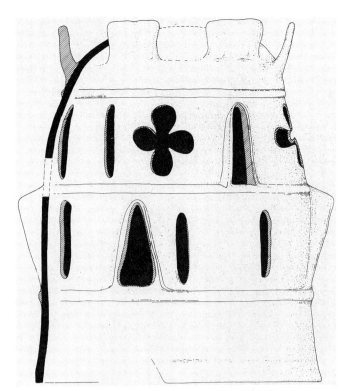

127. Beehive-shaped pottery louvre [Pearce *et al.* 1985]

Street have been dated to the late thirteenth to mid fourteenth century[151] and a notable example dated to *c.* 1360 was found in a waterfront dump at Trig Lane (Fig. 127); shaped like a beehive, covered with a white slip and splashed with clear glaze, it had no traces of soot inside and, as became the usual late medieval practice, may have been used for ventilation rather than to serve a central hearth. Another design, found in a deposit of *c.* 1430 at Trig Lane, may have been intended to resemble a little house, the smoke issuing from dormers in the roof-slopes.[152] Archaeological and documentary evidence suggests a period of currency for pottery louvers of *c.* 1220–1430.[153] In 1278 an earthen (i.e. ceramic) chimney was bought for Westminster from Ralph de Crockerlane, a lane probably on the site of the present Whitefriars Street,[154] and it is possible that this may have been one of the kiln-sites for 'London-type ware' which produced the excavated louvers – a pottery industry based in London, the production-sites of which have yet to be precisely located.[155]

By the opening of the fifteenth century the louver could also be a square or polygonal structure of timber, with slats or glass, as at Barnard's Hall (**105**) or Goldsmiths' Hall (**85**);[156] Guildhall had two.[157] At the other end of the domestic building scale, however, and as late as 1493–4, two tenants of the parish of St Mary at Hill appear to have shared a 'smoke hole' between their tenements.[158]

Early attempts to enclose the hearth generally included the construction of reredoses and smoke-bays. Early fourteenth-century regulations, later drawn up in *Liber Albus*, forbade placing any reredos where a fire was made for preparing bread, ale, or cooking meat (presumably a larger hearth than for mere heating), near partition walls of lath or boards, or elsewhere where there was danger of fire, and chimneys were no longer to be made of wood but only of stone, tiles or

128. Fireplaces: (a) detail
fireplace in brick in first-flo
range of Wash-house Cou
Charterhouse, early sixteen
century

(b)   Fireplace at Charterhouse

(c) (*right*)   (**22**) Crosby Place, Bishopsgate: details of fireplaces (H. J.
Hammon 1844)

ELEVATION ¼" SCALE.
DETAILS 1" SCALE.

Ancient Fire Place.

Measured & Drawn by H.J.Hammon, Arch¹.   Engraved by Geo.

plaster.[159] A wall called a reredos was put in the kitchen of the Brewers' almshouses in 1423,[160] and it is possible that by this time the term referred to a strengthening wall of tiles at the back of the fireplace, constructed of either roof tiles or special Flanders tiles. There is at present no evidence of the construction of smoke-bays in London houses, such as can be seen in houses in Middlesex,[161] but this could be the result of our almost total ignorance of the details of timber-framing in the city.

The development of the wall-fireplace and chimney was promoted in London by a pressure on land use which encouraged the division of open halls into several chambers and the development of the first-floor hall and kitchen during the fourteenth century. Four aspects may be examined: the position and gradual multiplication of fireplaces and chimneys within the London house, and the appearance and construction of these fireplaces and chimneys.

From the fourteenth century chimneys were placed on the outsides of buildings, both when added to an existing building and when ordered for a new building. Chimneys on property boundaries are often mentioned, either for being dangerous or for having been erected on the property of a neighbour[162] or of the commonalty, such as streets or lanes in common use.[163] As early as 1265, in the parish of St Sepulchre, a piece of ground 6 ft × 1 ft 6 in was given to a neighbour to build a chimney.[164] Chimneys in gable-ends of stone are specified in a contract for building the Peter and Paul Tavern, Paternoster Row (146), in 1342. Back-to-back fireplaces are specified in a St Paul's contract for a block of shops in 1370 (90) and it is likely that the axial stack shown in some of the Treswell plans (e.g. 26, 196) became common in London in the fifteenth century;[165] a building lease for a house belonging to Eton College in King Street, Westminster, specifies the building of a double chimney between parlour and kitchen in 1459.[166] During the fifteenth century, also, chimneys were inserted into existing houses.[167]

The disposition of fireplaces within the medieval house – in particular, which chambers they served – is rarely known. The contract of 1308 required the building of a chamber (i.e. a solar) with a chimney at one end of the hall (191); the 1317 contract, probably for Lovell's Inn (111), involved work on the flues of hall fireplaces. The Peter and Paul Tavern in Paternoster Row was to have two fireplaces in its basement in 1342; Crosby Place (22), built in 1466–75, had fireplaces in both hall and parlour (Figs. 40, 128c).

The Treswell plans show that by 1600 even the smallest houses in London possessed a chimney and several heated rooms. The kitchen invariably had the largest fireplace, often with an attached oven which might project into the yard or into an adjoining tenancy (168; see below on kitchens). A Type 1 house could have up to five hearths (called chimneys by Treswell) from its single stack, but generally two or three; Type 2 houses had a mean of between three and four hearths and Type 3 houses a mean of between four and five, with one case of thirteen hearths. The smallest houses were however better heated, room by room, than the two larger types, since more (often all) of the rooms could be served, relatively inexpensively, by a single chimney-stack. This cursory survey suggests that Type 1 houses had nearly two-thirds of their rooms heated, Type 2 had a little over a third of their rooms

heated and Type 3 about half. Thus the small and medium-sized houses of London in 1612 seem to have had fireplaces in about half their rooms, a luxury not found in other English towns.

The fireplaces in the 1370 St Paul's contract (90) were to be constructed of stone, tilesherds (as noted above) and Flanders tiles, 5½ ft wide between the jambs. The hall fireplace at Crosby Hall still survives, transposed with the hall to Chelsea. This fireplace and its companion which stood in the parlour (Fig. 128b) were of stone; such surrounds, common in prestigious houses during the later fifteenth century,[168] were called 'parells' (or apparels). The London mason Stephen Burton had a stock of them which he distributed among the beneficiaries of his will of 1488.[169] More modest sixteenth-century fireplaces of brick survive in the west range of Washhouse Court at Charterhouse: they have moulded jambs and four-centred arches in square heads (Fig. 128a–b).[170]

The fireplace, being the largest fixed feature of any room, increasingly took on monumental characteristics during the second half of the sixteenth century. Ornate fireplaces are known at the hall of the Fraternity of Holy Trinity in Aldersgate Street (7; Fig. 129) or survive at Charterhouse (48; Fig. 74b). Around 1600, in the most fashionable houses, the chimney breast could be adorned with figures and arches which matched the cornice of the room (Fig. 130); an upper chamber in Sir Paul Pindar's house had a marble fireplace with a sculptured panel, dating from the early part of the seventeenth century (Fig. 125).

Above the fireplace the flues were sometimes plastered, as in the 1317 contract for Lovell's Inn (111). Chimneys in smaller fourteenth-century houses were sometimes built of lath and rough plaster; despite the existing regulations, wooden chimneys were still being found and banned as late as 1469.[171] Medieval chimneys (usually of stone) are known from manor-houses in the countryside, but not so far from London. Sixteenth-century chimneys, some decorated with rubbed brick as in Tudor palaces and with prominent caps, are shown in the engraving from the 1547 Coronation painting of Cheapside and the streets on its north side (Fig. 131) and in the low-level panorama of c. 1550 (Fig. 41). Tall chimneys, some with apparently ornate caps (in one case, the cap appears to have sides formed by shields in brick), are shown in the foreground of the Hollar panorama of 1647 (Fig. 24).

The increasing number of chimneys in London houses from at least the fourteenth century is confirmed by references to various metal implements associated with the domestic hearth. Andirons or fire-dogs (pairs of horizontal bars on short feet placed on either side of the hearth to support burning wood) were an item of special bequest in 1328, being listed before the testator's rents.[172] At first the implements were simple and sparse. The inventory of Thomas Mockyng, fishmonger, in 1373 included, in his hall, a 'ferplace' of iron (?) and a pair of tongs.[173] When, during the later sixteenth century, andirons became more ornate, smaller fire-dogs called creepers were employed between them to support the logs, as in an inventory of a tenancy at Westminster in 1588. Here the fireplace in the great parlour had a pair of bellows and a creeper, while that in the great chamber had a pair of bronze andirons, a fire shovel, a pair of creepers and a pair of tongs tipped with brass.[174] Cast-iron firebacks survive

from 1487 and were being made in large numbers by the ironmasters of the Weald from at least 1548, a sideline of the contemporary expansion in the industry to meet Tudor demands for cannon;[175] but examples before 1600 have not so far been traced in London inventories or accounts.

Several types of simple oven were to be found within Saxo-Norman buildings: they were based on platforms of brickearth or rubble, sometimes surrounded by walls of brickearth reinforced with stakes. One example from a site near Botolph Lane comprised a gravel platform retained by planks.[176] Though there are occasional references to ovens on medieval properties,[177] their incidence or details of construction cannot be described fully until the time of the Treswell surveys.

Several kitchens shown in the ground-floor plans of 1612 had substantial ovens. In the case of Clothworkers' Hall (139), where there may have been two large fireplaces in line and a pastry room within the stack (i.e. intentionally hot), such facilities were clearly for communal feasting. In other cases the ovens were probably used for brewing, dyeing and the commercial production of food. One type of cooking facility was the 'range', a term current from the early fifteenth century,[178] which is shown in the Treswell plan of property at Giltspur Street (88/3) where it appears simply as two brick pillars at the back of a room. Two further types of oven are shown in the plans: a normal domestic oven at the side of a hearth, which could be quite large and therefore used for non-domestic purposes (West Smithfield, 189; Campion's brewery in Haywharf Lane, 169); and the larger oven, in which an oven or vat had its mouth in the back of the hearth

(12, 88). This larger type of oven was usually sited so that the body of the structure, of brick, tile and clay, lay outside the building.[179] The occurrence of four such ovens in adjacent premises (two worked by one tenant) at Pie Corner, Smithfield, suggests a row of cookshops, but the derivation of the name is said to be from an inn sign, that of the Magpie, rather than from the shops' function.[180] These houses were on the corner of Giltspur Street and Cock Lane, and a corner site for a cookshop may well have been prized; a single corner shop at the junction of Fenchurch Street and Philpot Lane (69/1) included two hearths and a substantial side-oven, perhaps for commercial production of food on a similar scale.

The fuel for the city's fireplaces and ovens was coal, turf, charcoal and (ordinary) wood. Coal had been worked in Britain in Roman times, but was rediscovered at the end of the twelfth century. The thirteenth century saw expansion in the mining industry and the wider use of coal in forging, burning of lime, evaporation of brine, brewing and baking.[181] Coal was being unloaded from ships in London in 1236.[182] Only wood and charcoal are mentioned in the Assize of 1276, but this was concerned with the overland haulage of these fuels by carters, and the coal came by sea.[183] In 1307 the king ordered that kilns in Southwark were to use charcoal or brushwood and not sea-coal because of the smoke produced, and goods chargeable for murage in 1315 included sea-coal and turf (both of which came by ship), and underwood, charged by the *shout* or *batella* (both smaller craft, usually working only along the river).[184] Sea-coal perhaps continued to be a special commodity; in 1425, for instance, the Brewers bought four quarters of coal for a single feast-day[185] and a wholesale change to sea-coal for

129.　(7) Hall of the Fraternity of the Holy Trinity, Aldersgate: interior elevation of south side (1742)

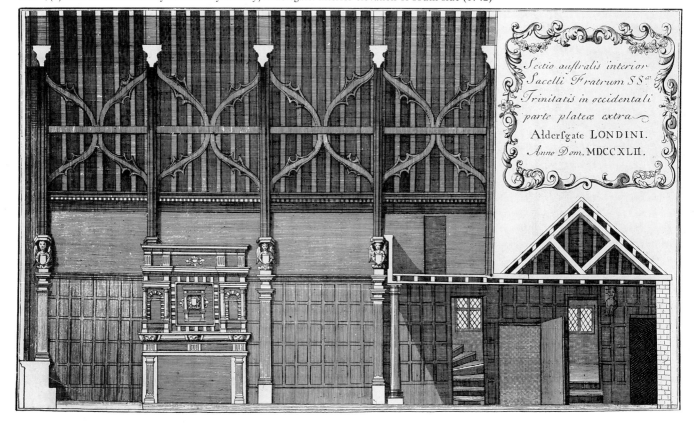

brewers, dyers and others has been ascribed to the later six-teenth century, though evidence is growing for its use by artisans in the thirteenth century.[186] Firewood, on the other hand, was constantly required, and was occasionally stacked in large heaps which affected party-walls by causing water seepage, or was stacked against adjacent windows or over common property such as the Walbrook.[187]

Coal smoke was thought to be particularly unhealthy, and the ordinances of the Blacksmiths in 1298 forbade their members to work at night to avoid damaging the health of neighbours.[188] A recent study has pointed out that complaints about air pollution in London contained in parliamentary rolls tended to peak in the summer months, when the building industry was burning much of its lime for construction work.[189]

Water Supply and Wells; Gutters and Drains

In London the civic provision of water followed closely on the lead set by standards of plumbing in both royal and monastic houses. In 1237, only four years after the probable date of the laying on of water at the palace of Westminster, piped water was brought from springs at Tyburn to Cheapside; in 1378 the conduit system was extended to Cornhill, and in stages thereafter throughout the city.[190] Tapping into the public water supply was a rare occurrence, and was usually stopped by the City authorities when they found out; only towards the end of the sixteenth century were certain prominent persons allowed a pipe, and this privilege was exceptional. In 1580

130. (99) House at Crutched Friars: interior view of first-floor chamber (J. T. Smith 1792; cf. Fig. 113)

131. Detail of engraving after the 1547 painting of Cheapside, showing a variety of chimneys

Peter Morice, a Dutchman, approached the City with a scheme to raise water from the Thames and supply parts of the city, but this does not seem to have catered for private houses. Morice was allowed to erect a piece of stonework next to the cloister of St Magnus (next to the bridge). From this, lead pipes would rise 30 ft to a frame on which was a barrel, from which pipes would descend via a cellar of the same structure to the street, then up Fish Street Hill with cisterns at St Margaret's church and in the Green Yard at Leadenhall.[191]

Waterbearers were the usual means of supplying Thames water to individual houses. In addition, many London houses had private wells. In the late thirteenth century some were made of casks, up to six deep, but the casks could rot and collapse with fatal consequences,[192] and stone-lined wells seem to have become standard in the fourteenth century.[193] The wells shown in the Treswell plans are all of brick, at least above ground; the new digging of wells to be fully lined with brick is, from present evidence, a feature of the post-Fire years. Mention is occasionally made of a windlass at the top or of the bucket and iron chain.[194]

A well could be located in the middle of a yard (76), in an alley (179)[195] or in the corner of a yard or court (88, 140). The Merchant Taylors had a well within their great kitchen (177), turned into a pump in 1577 and still surviving beneath the

132. (172) Seal House, Upper Thames Street: early thirteenth-century timber drain running from a quayside building into the river, excavated 1974

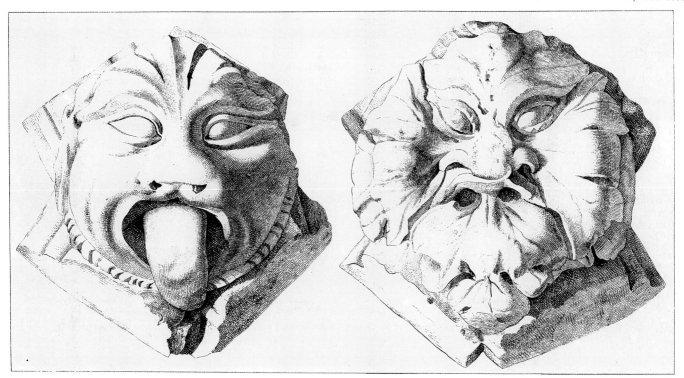

133. (119) Leadenhall Street/Fenchurch Street: two stone roof bosses from the undercroft, now in Museum of London (J. Emslie after J. Burt *c*. 1860).

floor.[196] Wells were often shared; one in 1378 was used by three households,[197] and Treswell shows several wells astride property boundaries. In several surveys it seems that subdivision, of apparently medieval date, divided an existing well (**3, 12, 147**).

Rainwater was also used as a water supply, either to cleanse privies or to run through the kitchen, sometimes with the aid of storage in cisterns.[198] Such storage facilities were clearly required in the company halls, where feasting and the associated tasks were regular occurrences; when the position of the cistern is known, as at Pewterers' Hall in 1547–9, it lay in the kitchen.[199]

Litigation about gutters and drains was fierce in a city in which a large proportion of the houses were built of timber, lath and daub and therefore highly susceptible to penetration by water. The arrangements for disposal of rainwater comprised gutters at roof level and drains, pits or channels at ground level. A gutter could be of timber, lead or shaped tiles but was rarely made of stone;[200] it was either attached with nails to the building or, along stone walls, carried on stone corbels.[201] A gutter most commonly ran along the boundary wall between two tenements, as a valley drain. This often caused complaint when one neighbour attempted to build to a higher level. Sometimes objects or filth were thrown out of upper windows into such valley drains.[202] These drains had to lead either back to the owner's land or to the street; such a practice was known 'from time out of mind' in 1302.[203] The gutter would end in a spout to throw water away from the building at both the street end and rear of the house, as shown in post-medieval illustrations.[204] Downpipes were rare, and apparently confined to pipes at roof level conveying water from one gutter to another;[205] downpipes in the modern sense seem to be an innovation of the Tudor palaces. Castellated lead downpipes are found today at Morton's gate to Lambeth

Palace (1490), but whether they represent an original feature is unknown.[206]

Along the ground, sometimes running in and out of buildings, drains of timber are mentioned throughout the period and are found on archaeological sites. On the waterfront, domestic or industrial drains (Fig. 132) could empty into the river, as did waste-pipes from privies. On inland sites, drains led to soakaway pits by the house or in the garden; a stone-lined soakaway has been recorded at Watling Court, south of Watling Street, in a position suggesting it lay in the garden of a prominent tenement (**31**).[207] Substantial arched drains of brick are found in the late sixteenth century, often beneath alleys, suggesting more comprehensive drainage schemes in the building revolution of the post-Dissolution years, though the era of drains connected to an overall system was still far off.[208]

Internal Decoration and Fittings

Carvings such as human and animal heads were found on corbels and presumably on the ends of door-hoods made of stone, though no examples of the latter are known. Figured corbels could support both roof-couples, as at Carpenters' Hall (two examples are shown in Fig. 144), and in undercroft vaulting either as ceiling bosses (Fig. 133) or where the ribs sprang from a wall (as in the undercroft at Merchant Taylors' Hall, Fig. 66). An angel-figure survives in the vaulting of the west crypt at Guildhall, of *c*. 1280 (Fig. 134). A head of a young man forming the support for a corbel, probably from a roof-truss, was exhibited at the British Fine Art Commission Summer Exhibition in 1939, allegedly from the site of Merchant Taylors' Hall (Fig. 135);[209] but it could just as well have come originally from a church as from a secular building.

134. Guildhall, west crypt: angel carving at junction of vault ribs, *c.* 1280

135. Carved corbel in stone, said to be from Merchant Taylors' Hall, Threadneedle Street (**235**), exhibited 1939

The general history of smaller domestic buildings outside London suggests that exposed beams and joists were both moulded and carved, especially from the late fifteenth century, and perhaps painted; but no examples have been recorded from the city. The ceiling of the Post Room in the Lollards' Tower at Lambeth Palace is a good example of a timber ceiling with elaborate mouldings of *c.* 1435, and similar ceilings may have been part of the scheme at Leadenhall in the 1440s.[210] The carved and painted ceilings at Crosby Place (**22**; 1466–75) are, like so much of the house, at present without detailed secular parallels. Besides the hall, which has survived, two other chambers originally also had elaborate ceilings. The hall roof is remarkable for being a false ceiling conforming to a four-centred arch, with four rows of panels divided by pendants (Fig. 136). The roof of the adjacent Great Chamber was similarly designed (Fig. 74a), with cusps and pendants, and also highly gilt; the flat ceiling of the chamber below apparently included arched principals adorned with cusps. This technique of dividing the ceiling into squares by applied mouldings of wood is found thereafter in Tudor houses, but its origins in secular construction before Crosby Place are not known.[211]

Plaster and papier-mâché work was introduced into England by Italian craftsmen, and plaster ceilings of native manufacture date from after 1550.[212] Dated examples within London include the Great Chamber at Charterhouse, erected, on the evidence of its armorial badges, in the time of Thomas Howard, Duke of Norfolk, before his execution in 1571 (**48**; Fig. 137);[213] two first-floor chambers in Paul Pindar's house, Bishopsgate, probably of *c.* 1599 (**28**; Figs. 138–9); and the ceiling of Prince Henry's Room, Fleet Street, of *c.* 1610 (**77**; Fig. 140). Several other examples have been recorded in suburban areas, spared by both the Great Fire

and subsequent fashions which would have removed them (Figs. 141–2). In two cases (Paul Pindar's house in Bishopsgate and Prince Henry's Room in Fleet Street, presumably originally a residence) the room containing the plastered ceiling is on the first floor by the street, in the position favoured by the hall or principal chamber in many London houses. It has been noted that wall paintings and plaster ceilings in Hertfordshire houses also survive in greatest number in this location, suggesting that such embellishments were especially to be found in the front first-floor room. It is likely that pattern-books were instrumental in providing the repertoire of designs: especially those of Cornelius Bos (1540s), Jan Vredeman de Vries (*c.* 1563), and Abraham de Bruyn (1584). A de Bruyn design may have been followed in a ceiling at Paul Pindar's house in Bishopsgate (Fig. 139; **28**).[214]

136. (**22**) Crosby Place, Bishopsgate: details of false ceiling in hall (H. J. Hammon 1844)

137. (a) (48) Plaster ceiling: Charterhouse, the Great Chamber, about 1570 (restored)

(b) Detail of 137a: the Howard arms

There are very few references to the colouring of walls in houses, either internally or externally. 'White casting' was generally employed elsewhere for many rooms, inside and out; plaster of Paris was also used for internal walls, as well as for fireplaces and chimneys (11). Walls were also simply plastered as background for the vivid textile hangings, as seems the case at Crosby Place. The Skinners whitewashed their hall for the coming Corpus Christi festival in 1492–3. The Drapers' parlour was painted green in 1495; this may mean painted walls or painted panelling.[215]

No evidence survives for wall paintings in medieval domestic buildings in the City of London, though fragmentary paintings survive in the Tower.[216] Elizabethan wall paintings were seen in the chambers at Lincoln's Inn (47) and three out of an original four scenes from a coloured frieze survive at Carpenters' Hall (128; Figs. 143–6); originally the frieze stood over the dais of the hall. The artist is not known: the painting was in place by 1596, and may date from the 1560s or 1570s. The paintings may have been the gift of William Ruddock, William Buttmor and Robard Quoyney, all wardens in 1561.[217] Shortly after came the fashion of classical

138. (28) Sir Paul Pindar's house, Bishopsgate: details of ceiling in first-floor room (R. Paul 1894)

139. (28) Sir Paul Pindar's house, Bishopsgate: plan of ceiling in second first-floor chamber (1906)

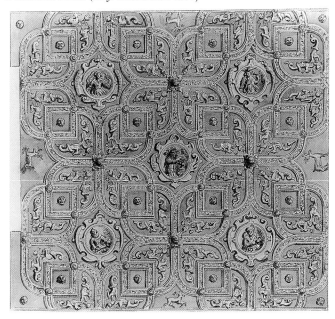

140.   (77) Prince Henry's Room, 17 Fleet Street: interior view showing ceiling of *c*. 1610, photographed *c*. 1890

141. (*left*)   Ceiling from house in Goodman's Yard, Minories

142.   Ceiling in a chamber at a house at the back of 84–85 Upper Whitecross Street (C. J. Richardson 1871)

143. (128) Carpenters' Hall, London Wall: west end of hall, showing truss and paintings [*ILN*, 3 January 1846]

144. (128) Carpenters' Hall, London Wall: two stone roof corbels from the roof of 1429 (F. W. Fairholt 1848). For their positions beneath the roof-trusses, see Fig. 234.

motifs, when in 1572–3 the company paid John Knight, painter, for a 'piece of Antyke work' over a window, probably in the hall.[218]

Internal woodwork was commonly painted, as shown in Holbein's portrait of the Hanse merchant Georg Gisze in his office at the Steelyard (Fig. 152). The Goldsmiths' parlour was given wainscot painted with oil in the fourteenth century; the roof and principal posts of Pewterers' Hall were painted in 1497–8. Wainscot was generally painted until the middle of the seventeenth century, and occasionally so were items of furniture, such as tables.[219]

Another subject worthy of more detailed study is the decorative use of ironwork in the medieval and Tudor house. Door-knockers were occasionally lively pieces, for example one representing a monkey's head, of fourteenth-century date, found in Thames Street (Fig. 151).

145. (128) Carpenters' Hall, London Wall: mid-sixteenth-century wall paintings: Noah (the fragment lost in the nineteenth century) (F. W. Fairholt 1848)

146. (128) Carpenters' Hall, London Wall: the surviving mid-sixteenth-century wall paintings: (a) King Josiah and the carpenters, alluding to the trustworthiness of carpenters in the Old Testament story

Christ with Joseph the carpenter

(c)   Christ in the Temple

147. (105) Barnard's Hall, Holborn: detail of early sixteenth-century panelling

148. (78) Middle Temple Hall, Fleet Street: hall screen of 1574, in 1968

Wainscot and Screens

Wainscot panelling was employed in royal palaces in the thirteenth century and included in the fitting-up of rooms at York Place in the Strand in 1307. It was most often painted, sometimes with figures. The Goldsmiths' parlour was wainscotted in the fourteenth century, as noted above. These examples may have been of tongue-and-groove clapboard (*seelyngbord*) overlapping at the front and flush at the back; this kind of panelling continued to be used in the region throughout the fifteenth century.[220]

Wainscot could take various other forms, particularly during the sixteenth century; though there are very few surviving fragments from the city itself. Simple ribbed oak panels could also be placed between structural studs; outside London this dates only to the late fifteenth century. From the mid fifteenth century panels with linenfold or similar vertical designs were mounted in framed rectangular panelling, as at Paycocke's house in Coggeshall (*c.* 1500); these moulded panels could accept Renaissance designs (such as the heads in profile in panels at Barnard's Inn hall, of *c.* 1525 (**105**; Fig. 147), or a series of four panels from a house in Leadenhall Street, now in the Museum of London) or mix them with traditional motifs.[221] From the first half of the sixteenth century also examples of almost square panels in simply moulded frames are recorded, and in the later sixteenth century classi-

149.   (6) 133–136 Aldersgate: interior of an upper chamber (J. P. Emslie 1879)

150.   (48) Charterhouse: screen of 1571

cal pilasters divided the panelling into groups of panels, with the fireplace as a centre-piece (as at a house in Aldersgate, 6; Fig. 149).[222] An inventory of 1598 of a house in Aldermanbury (Warner in the section on furnishings, below) describes the wainscot of a Long Parlour, including the 'Trymming of the chimney and the wainscot Portall', which may be this kind of room treatment.

Wainscotting, perhaps because of its expense, seems to have been employed at first only in smaller rooms such as parlours in the fourteenth century. The Mercers considered 'syllyng' their hall in 1477, and as late as 1527 the Goldsmiths were trying to decide whether to replace their stained hangings for the hall or have wainscot there, and three years later seem to have chosen tapestry. Grocers' Hall may not have been wainscotted until 1591, whereas the parlour had been since its erection in 1429; in addition only the dais end of the hall might be wainscotted, as at Carpenters' Hall in 1460 (**128**; Fig. 143 shows the remains of this dais in the nineteenth century).[223] The occurrence of wainscot in inventories of private houses increases throughout the sixteenth century, however, and it must have been relatively common among the well-to-do by 1600.

During the sixteenth century, and possibly before, major houses would have a decorated wooden screen demarcating the screens passage from the body of the open hall. The examples surviving in London reflect Renaissance decorative taste: the screens of 1571 at Charterhouse (**48**; Fig. 150), of 1574 at Middle Temple (**78**; Fig. 148), and of the early seventeenth century at Lincoln's Inn Hall (**47**; Fig. 102). Those at Gray's Inn and Staple Inn were destroyed in the Second World War.

Lighting

Methods of lighting are rarely mentioned in documentary sources. Houses must have been generally quite dark indoors except on special occasions. There were several types of lighting equipment: torches, candles and oil lamps. Torches are mentioned in livery company accounts, for instance the 24 fathom of cord acquired for torches at the Merchant Taylors in 1421–2.[224] When candles could be afforded they were usually of tallow, since wax candles were kept for church;[225] they could be placed in candelabra or candlesticks. The candelabrum was rare in domestic contexts but in 1368 the rector of St Martin Pomeroy, Thomas Kynebell, had two pendant chandeliers, and one standing chandelier – perhaps simple iron structures? – whereas a fishmonger had four candelabra weighing 71 lb in total in his hall in 1373. More modestly there were several kinds of candlestick: attached to the wall or often to the mantel of the fireplace, sometimes on a swinging bracket anticipating the seventeenth century sconce; in a pewter or wooden holder which stood by itself; or the pricket kind which was based on a spike to be driven into the floor or other surface.[226] Candlesticks seem to have replaced stone cresset lamps, which were a feature of the Norman period, though the latter continued to be used on ceremonial occasions, particularly outdoors.

Furnishings and Furniture

In this book only a brief and impressionistic review will be attempted of the movable furnishings and furniture in medieval and Tudor London houses. The subject is in need of more detailed study than can be offered here.

Besides references culled mainly from wills, the discussion draws on twenty detailed inventories and repair accounts at private houses:

1356	Stephen le Northerne, ironmonger
1368	Thomas Kynebell, rector of St Martin Pomeroy
1373	Emma Hatfield, chandler's widow
1373	Thomas Mockyng, fishmonger
1391	Richard Toky, grocer
1406	John Olyver, draper
1453	Thomas Gy, vintner
1454	goods of William Furnyvale
1485	repairs at Coldharbour II, Thames Street (**170**)
1485	inventory of Lumbard's Place, Botolph Lane, probably the goods of Maryn Conteryn (Conterino?), merchant of Venice (**30**)
1499	William Stede, haberdasher
temp Henry VII	Nicholas Withers, probably a draper
1509	Edmund Dudley, king's minister (**45**)
1531	John Porth, 'king's servant'
1543	Katheryne Brase, widow
1543	John Patryk, porter of the king's wardrobe
1549	Antonio Bonvisi, Italian merchant (**22**)
c. 1556	Austen Hinde, alderman
1588	list of furniture and household stuff sold to Sir John Trevor for his tenancy of a house at Westminster
1598	Nicholas Warner
1603?	John More, alderman[227]

In addition the furnishings of several company halls are known through inventories, the most useful of which are:

1490	Pewterers' Hall, Lime St (**121**)
1496	Blacksmiths' Hall, Lambeth Hill (**112**)
1550	Pewterers' Hall
1512	Merchant Taylors' Hall, Threadneedle Street (**177**)
1556	Ironmongers' Hall, Fenchurch Street (**73**)
1580	Skinners' Hall, Dowgate (**66**)
1585	Armourers' and Braziers' Hall, Coleman Street (**59**)
1586	Cutlers' Hall, Cloak Lane (**67**).[228]

Walls of the most important chambers, that is the hall and parlour, were decorated with painted cloths or occasionally tapestry. Painted or stained cloths were in use in the fourteenth century, hanging usually in the hall.[229] Stephen le Northerne, ironmonger, had among his possessions in 1365 two painted cloths; in 1391 Richard Toky had three painted cloths in his chamber, and in 1406 John Olyver had a 'steyned sale' (set of hall-hangings). Stained cloths (normally stencilled in patterns) with imagery were hung at Blacksmiths' Hall in 1496 and were found in the long gallery by the garden at Dudley's house in 1509. Painted cloths continued to be found in the inventories of the more substantial citizens, as represented by the sample list, until at least the end of the sixteenth century. Nicholas Warner at Aldermanbury in 1598 had painted cloths hanging in his Long Parlour (30 square

yards), Little Parlour (20 yards), Wife's Chamber, the Maid's Chamber, the Stone Chamber, and the Chamber over the Great Parlour.

By the fourteenth century, however, tapestry, in which the design is stitched and woven into the fabric, was available in London as throughout the country. The tapicers, weavers of wool tapestries, are known in the city from 1282.[230] Local mercers were selling what were probably London products to the court in 1317–18; the will of the sixth Earl of Arundel in 1392 mentions a halling (set of tapestries) of blue with red roses and coats of arms 'lately made in London'.[231] The size of a tapestry was fixed at 3 or 4 ells in length and 1½ or 2 ells in breadth; no tapice was to be decorated with arms unless it was made wholly of wool.[232] The Countess of Pembroke had a tapestry woven with the arms of the Earl in 1377, and designs incorporating leopards' heads or grey trefoils on a blue ground are mentioned in citizens' wills.[233] In 1406 John Olyver, a draper, had a second and apparently less valuable *sale* of red and black tapestry, with two bankers and twelve cushions of the same set.

Tapestries were also probably imported from the production centres at Arras, Artois, until its suppression in 1477, and later from Brussels and Flanders. 'Arras work' on cushions is mentioned in a London will in 1399, but the earliest reference to Arras hangings in London located so far dates from 1485, when Hugh Clopton was ordered to provide a hanging of Arras for Mercers' Hall, with bankers (seat covers) and twelve cushions, for trading misdemeanours; in 1510 the company's best hanging of Arras, given for the Guildhall but in the custody of the Mercers, was not to be further lent out to members, who had presumably been borrowing it for private functions.[234] At Dudley's house in 1509 the inventory writers found one Arras which belonged to the Great Parlour and another which hung over the chimney in the Great Chamber. An old hanging of Arras was located at the high dais in the hall, and in the Square Chamber they found two counterpoints of rich Arras, a little altar cloth of Arras, in a frame, with a little curtain in front of it, and even 'a pece of fyne counterfett Arys'. The Merchant Taylors had nine pieces of Arras 'rychely made of the lyf of Saint John' in their hall in 1512; the Arras was 'well lined with canvas, lyred [?], lowped and corded, and [to be] putte in 9 severall bagges of canvas'. The Goldsmiths, in 1530, went to the considerable expense of ordering a tapestry direct from Flanders, to their own design. A member of the company sent his servant there for eleven weeks to supervise the work; the life of St Dunstan was translated into Dutch and four artists took sixteen days to make a design in black and white. The Arras measured 195 Flemish ells, and cost over £250 – 'as much as a smaller company would have paid to build a hall'.[235] Clearly Arras or Flemish hangings were signs of exceptional private or corporate wealth.

Hangings made of less luxurious textiles occur regularly in inventories and wills; of say (a kind of serge) and buckram (linen), often brightly coloured.[236] In 1531, for instance, John Porth had a hanging of green say of 37 square yards in his parlour, and another in his main chamber of 50 yards, which would not have been of tapestry. The engraving from the painting of the Coronation of Edward VI in 1547 (Fig. 63) shows hangings displayed from goldsmiths' shops on the south side of Cheapside; some are plain or striped, and others contain figured scenes.

The subjects of pictures on the hangings, whether stained or woven, were heraldic, noble, legendary or biblical; fourteenth-century subjects included King Richard and Hector of Troy in 1361 and the history of the Prince of Wales in 1376.[237] The inventory of Dudley's house in 1509 included seven pieces of imagery, embroidered with the months of the year, to be set upon a cloth. In 1512 the Merchant Taylors had other hangings besides their Arras, and like the Arras they featured St John, their patron saint; in the hall was a hanging given by Margaret, wife of Stephen Jennings (who rebuilt St Andrew Undershaft in its present form), showing St John 'richely browdered, sette upon blewe velvet with a white Rose over the hed of Saint John, the sydes of grene velvet, browdered with floure de luces of venyce gold, and with these wordes browdered in gold *Entere tenere*'. Several hangings are shown draped from windows on Goldsmith's Row and the adjacent houses in the 1547 painting (see Fig. 63), and the subjects include George and the Dragon and the Annunciation. Specified subjects of hangings in late sixteenth-century wills from south-west Essex, where London taste may have been influential, include the story of Tobias, a forest scene and the Robin Hood story.[238]

The Reformation probably had a seriously damaging effect on the number of holy and religious subjects which survived the 1530s and 1540s; in 1538–9, for example, the Skinners paid for 'taking out of the Crown Triplex of the Bishop of Rome [i.e. the papal tiara] out of the cloths of the Hall and for mending other faults in the same cloths'.[239]

Three trades were principally involved in the making of furniture in London: carpenters, joiners and turners. Though furniture was traditionally made by carpenters, with pegged mortice and tenon joints or nailed together, the fifteenth century saw the introduction of joined chairs, stools, tables and beds in which more elaborate joints, especially the lap dovetail, were employed by joiners.[240] As described below, joined Flemish chests were heirlooms in London by 1350, and joined stools are mentioned in 1406. A joiner's account for providing furniture at Coldharbour II (**170**) in 1485 mentions two tables and trestles, stools, window lattices, forms (benches), wainscot, a close chair and repair of two chests. A second joiner supplied cupboards, two beds and a 'prece' (press?). By 1543 joined chairs could be found in the house of a haberdasher's widow (Brase), and Bonvisi had four at Crosby Place in 1549.

Continuing friction between the carpenters and the joiners finally required arbitration in 1632. The Court of Aldermen had to adjudicate the differences between the crafts of carpentry and joinery. The joiners were to make forms, beds, chests, cupboards, presses, wainscot, shop windows (i.e. shutters?), doors, signboards, all carved works, coffins of wainscot; the carpenters were to be concerned with all tables when nailed of deal, elm, oak and beech, stools so made, the laying of elm or oak floors (deal floors could be laid by either company), shelving and signboards when not of wainscot.[241]

The turners were much less of a threat to the carpenters. Although an organised body by the early fourteenth century, their making of furniture was confined to stools, chairs and occasionally, in the sixteenth century, parts of beds.[242] The

only turned pieces mentioned in this group of inventories are two chairs at the house of John Porth in 1531, but these must have been exceptional pieces; no doubt other beds or stools had turned components but were not described as such in inventories.

The main type of table was of boards laid on trestles (e.g. at Toky's house in 1391, Olyver's in 1406), of the type surviving, with trestles of late fifteenth-century style, at Penshurst Place. This simple type was long-lived; in 1550 the main table at Pewterers' Hall was still of this kind. A second type was called fixed or *dormaunt*, which was built as a unit, though the term fixed could also mean fixed to the floor.[243] *Una mensa dormiens* is a term used in the twelfth century (e.g. in the leases of St Paul's manors),[244] and in the later medieval period seems to be restricted to tables in more prestigious settings, such as Coldharbour (1485), which had six, or Merchant Taylors' Hall, which had a 'high table dormaunt with a particion slyding in the mydell' and four dormaunt side tables in 1512.[245] 'Framed' or 'wainscot' tables may also have been of this kind (e.g. at Bonvisi's house, Crosby Place, in 1549).

Folding tables are known from the late fourteenth century and little folding tables, some from Spain, in the sixteenth century.[246] Extendable tables, already noted at Merchant Taylors' Hall in 1512, were to be found in private houses by the late sixteenth century.[247] Round tables are mentioned regularly from 1531; a 'round table with a foot' in Porth's house may have been similar to pedestal tables common in France from the opening of the century. At his death, probably in 1603, the alderman John More had an 'oyster table'.[248]

Elaborate chairs[249] or thrones were symbols of authority in the royal or noble household, and this overtone lingered for some time within assemblies and perhaps the ordinary household. In 1568 the Carpenters resolved that the eldest master would sit in the chair at dinners and occasions; evidently there was still only one at high table.[250] There were no chairs at all in Blacksmiths' Hall in 1496, or at the Pewterers' Hall in 1490 or 1550 – forms sufficed. Within the private household, however, more variety was apparently to be found. In 1368 Thomas Kynebell, rector of St Martin Pomeroy, had twelve chairs in the hall (perhaps for vestry meetings?) and a long chair (settle?) in his chamber; inventories of the sixteenth century include chairs largely in the living rooms.[251] In 1527 the house of Thomas Cromwell had a small number of chairs, but stools and forms were clearly the normal mode of seating;[252] in 1549, on the other hand and probably exceptionally, Bonvisi had over thirty chairs at Crosby Place, including a suite of seventeen. 'Low chairs' for women and children are found by the middle of the sixteenth century (Hinde).

Chairs thought notable by the inventory writers included turned chairs,[253] joined chairs,[254] chairs with embroidered or leather backs and folding chairs.[255] Sir John Trevor's lodging at Westminster, using the furniture of a previous tenant, had ten chairs distributed through five chambers; these included examples with backings of needlework, black leather and Turkey work (see below). Trevor also had a wicker chair in his garret; these are known in London and elsewhere from the mid sixteenth century.[256] Further sorts of chairs came from abroad. Flanders or Flemish chairs are mentioned from the second decade of the fifteenth century, but the meaning of

this term is as uncertain for this period as it is when they were still popular in the seventeenth century.[257] French chairs, apparently a luxury item, were to be found in the gallery, parlour and little parlour of Dudley's house in 1509 (one in each setting), and Spanish chairs are mentioned a generation later.[258] Close chairs appear at the Coldharbour in 1485; thereafter their use became more common, though they probably remained a rarity in citizens' houses.[259]

The term 'settle' is not used in the London inventories before the mid sixteenth century; varieties then included 'long', and 'low joined long'.[260] Presumably the 'long chair' was the equivalent term in the fifteenth century. This seat for several people, often with carved ends, could be found in both the private house (Olyver, 1406) and the tavern (Gy, 1453).

Stools and forms were commoner forms of seating, especially in the domestic or company hall (e.g. Mockyng; Toky). Joined stools are mentioned in 1406 and joined forms in 1485.[261] As late as 1588, in Trevor's lodging at Westminster, the Great Parlour which formed the main reception room (a hall not being mentioned) contained five joined stools which went with the table.

From the main living rooms we can turn to the chambers with beds in them. Simple framed bedsteads are known from twelfth-century representations[262] and presumably formed the majority of those cited in London inventories and wills.[263] Joined beds are mentioned at Coldharbour in 1485 and in the will of Robert Herryson, clothworker, in 1540 and in the inventory of Jasper Hylltreman, Dutchman and shoemaker, in 1544; in the previous year Katheryne Brase, a haberdasher's widow, had two joined beds, one with painted hangings and the other 'with postes with gerthys' (straps, or elaborate examples of turning?).[264] A 'standing bed' is mentioned in 1454 (Furnyvale) and one of *estrichborde* in 1485 (Conteryn), but this term has not yet been satisfactorily explained; a common term after 1600, it may at the later period refer to any substantial bed, especially the 'four-poster' then in fashion.[265] This massive form reached its apogee shortly before 1600; examples are found in museums but cannot be identified specifically from London records.

Beds with canopies are known in twelfth-century France and were present at royal Westminster by 1242–7.[266] The bed hung with textiles became widespread as an heirloom in the fourteenth century. London wills mention 'a white bed embroidered with hounds, with a tester' (the hanging at the head of the bed) and demi-celour (the canopy over the bed) in 1375, and 'a bed embroidered with dogs with demi-celure' in 1382.[267] Nine years later Richard Toky, a grocer, had four beds in his chamber, the first with worsted tester, the second with a tester of say with roses, the third with a green tester and the fourth with a stained tester. In 1406 the draper John Olyver had eighteen 'beds', though perhaps these refer to sets of hangings he had for sale; two had tapestry testers of large assize (on sizes of tapestry, see hangings section above), four of embroidered worsted, and twelve of Winchester work with testers (William Furnyvale also had a coverlet of Winchester work in 1454). Bed-curtains and cushions were embroidered with lions, peacocks or other animals, most often crude heraldic figures. The hung bed with tester and celour continued to be found in London houses in the fifteenth and sixteenth centuries; Furnyvale, for instance, had a celour 'portrayed

151. Bronze door-knocker, ring missing, in the form of a monkey's head: from Thames Street; diameter 4.2 in, perhaps fifteenth century (Museum of London)

with an eagle'.[268] A conical celour called a sparver was found in richer European households from the late fourteenth century[269] and in English royal palaces by 1423; one was owned by Edmund Dudley, ex-minister to the king, in 1509.

Alternatively the tester and occasionally the celour could be made of boards, e.g. at an ironmonger's house in 1356 (le Northerne), and '2 grete celours of estericheborde for beddys' are mentioned in the inventory of the Saracen's Head brewhouse in Aldersgate in 1463.[270]

Trussing or trundle bedsteads were folding beds, used in nobler households for servants or for travel, kept under the main bed, though in the inventory of a house in St Nicholas Shambles in 1543 a 'tryndyll bedsted' was one of the main beds.[271]

An *aumbry, almarye* or *armoire*[272] could be built-in (sometimes simply shelves within an alcove) or free-standing, resembling the modern cupboard. The early thirteenth-century building regulations indicate that alcoves could be excavated in stone walls to a depth of 1 ft. When listed in wills the second, movable kind is presumably meant – as in the will of Thomas de Stanes, merchant, in *c.* 1293.[273] Two aumbries are mentioned in Toky's inventory in 1391 (both in the pantry or buttery, one hanging), and Olyver had one in 1406. The 1485 lease of a house in Botolph Lane mentions *almaryes* in the summer parlour and the kitchen. Special armoires are known in fourteenth-century France for plate, and in England for storing clothing or armour; in 1373 one with vats was found in the house of a London fishmonger.[274] An almarye constructed in the great kitchen of Brewers' Hall in 1423 needed seventeen quarters (stud-like timbers), 116 ft of oak boards, two elm boards for shelves, and a board of oak for a coalbin.[275]

Buffet, dresser or *cupbo[a]rd* were three overlapping terms for furniture used for displaying and storing plate in the hall, or storing plate and utensils in the kitchen. The hall form,

very often called simply *cupbord*, was a stepped structure with open shelves on which pewter or silver was shown, as on a modern Welsh dresser. A 'cuppeborde called vesseller' was bequeathed by John Croydon, fishmonger, in 1378[276] and cupboards are thereafter sometimes mentioned in wills and inventories (Olyver, 1406; 'a single cupboard' at the Pauleshede in 1453; Dudley had three cupboards in the hall, parlour and little parlour in 1509). The cupboard usually stood in the hall, as at Carpenters' Hall in 1499[277] or Merchant Taylors' Hall in 1512. Its position alongside the high table and its presentation of the owner's plate gave the cupboard an air of dignity; from at least 1503 to stand by the cupboard was part of the ceremonial of those ordained to be serjeants-at-law at Middle Temple.[278] In 1517 a cupboard was a priest's second concern in his list of bequests, after his bed and bolster.[279] By 1600 there were two main forms: the court cupboard, like two tables one on top of the other, and the livery cupboard, in which the upper part was enclosed. The latter derived in part from the *gardevyans* chest (see below). This may be the 'servytour bourd' at Carpenters' Hall which was given two garnettes (fastenings) in 1546–7.[280]

The kitchen form, the *dressoir*, was used in preparing and serving food; in 1485 for instance carpenters set up a dressing board 10 ft long in the larder, and three in the kitchen at Coldharbour; two 10 ft and one 12 ft long, all of elm. These sound like simple boards rather than more elaborate structures.

One type of cupboard which was called a chest (and which therefore might have existed with or without feet) was the gardevyans or meat-chest, later called the livery-cupboard. An early example is found at the Pauleshede in 1453 (inventory of Thomas Gy); there were six at Bonvisi's house, Crosby Place, in 1549. Edmund Dudley had two 'gardevyaunce' in his Little Wardrobe; he kept his 'dyvers obligacions concerning the kyng' and other evidences in them.

Chests, in the modern sense of the term, were both furniture and luggage. Generally they can be divided into chests with feet for fairly sedentary storage, and chests with no feet but domed lids, ideal for travelling. The latter were also known as trussing-coffers, taken on a *malesadell* (Toky, 1381). A variant of the travelling kind was the ship's chest.[281] Chests were used for storing coin, plate and jewels;[282] textiles, clothing, chapel ornaments, muniments and books;[283] armour, grain and bread.[284]

Chests were variously made of wainscot, joined, or sometimes bound with iron.[285] Chests made completely of iron were rare, but the Guildhall had one from *c.* 1427 (now in the Museum of London), and Bonvisi had another in 1549. It was also natural for the crafts to store their communal possessions, especially plate, napery and records in the company chest, which was often of substantial proportions and of exceptional strength. The Carpenters, for instance, had a chest from the earliest surviving accounts in 1438; in about 1452 one of the wardens was paid 4*s.* for binding it, presumably with iron. The 'grete chest', presumably the same, was repaired in 1466 and 1500; in 1503, now in the treasure house, it was given six bars of iron. A second chest was made for the parlour in 1501.[286] The company still possesses two iron chests which may be these two.

152. Interior of the office of Georg Gisze in the Steelyard by Hans Holbein junior, 1532 (Gemäldegalerie, Berlin)

Perhaps because of their association with foreign travel and valuables, examples from abroad are frequently noted. Flemish chests are mentioned from 1349, though it is far from clear what was meant by this term.[287] A great Gascony chest which belonged to the testator's father is mentioned in 1384.[288] From the mid sixteenth century the Dansk chest became a common possession of mariners,[289] and during the first half of the sixteenth century Flemish craftsmen refugees, settling on the outskirts of the city where craft jurisdiction could be avoided if at all possible, may have produced chests with inlaid marquetry panels.[290] John More, around 1603, had three 'Indian chests'. By 1600, however, it may have been unfashionable to have chests as furniture at all, at least in leading circles.[291]

During the sixteenth century the general storage function of the chest may have been at least partly taken over by the *press*, a term usually taken to mean a large cupboard with shelves.[292] These are mentioned in inventories from the 1530s (e.g. Porth's house in 1531, an old press of wainscot), usually in private or non-public rooms such as the garret or parlour.[293]

Hangings were sometimes en suite with bankers and cushions, for example in green say,[294] or the bankers and cushions were of the same set (e.g. at John Olyver's house in 1406 – perhaps here the *sale* of red and black tapestry mentioned immediately before in the inventory is also en suite).

Cushions are frequently mentioned in wills and inventories, and must therefore have been of some value and opu-

lence. In 1356 the ironmonger Stephen le Northerne had twelve cushions and five bankers. Toky in 1391 had thirteen cushions in his hall in three sets – red and blue worsted, red tapestry and another kind of tapestry; in Olyver's hall in 1406 the twelve cushions were en suite with two bankers. In 1454 William Furnyvale had twelve 'Flemish cushions', a term not yet explained. In the sixteenth century cushions could be of velvet damask (Dudley, 1509), of 'Nant makyng' (Porth, 1531), of Bruges satin (Brase, 1543) of leather and even of Arras (Bonvisi, 1549); many were embroidered with needlework.[295] In the Great Wardrobe at Dudley's house in 1509 were stored twenty-three cushions of carpet work, and cushions must have been often covered in this way.[296]

Carpets were originally expensive coverings for tables and chests (as shown, for instance, in Holbein's portrait of the Hanse merchant Georg Gisze in his office at the Steelyard, Fig. 152), and only later descended to floor level.[297] Le Northerne had five carpets in 1356, though this seems an exceptionally early reference. Nicholas Withers, probably a draper, had three carpets and six cupboard carpets when his inventory was drawn up in the reign of Henry VII; at Dudley's house in 1509 carpets were found in the Long Gallery, the Gallery next to the Great Chamber, and the Great Chamber itself (two short, one long), but not in any of the other rooms. Carpets are thereafter found regularly in inventories of the mid and late sixteenth century; some of them were 'Kentish' and one at Bonvisi's house in 1549 is described as 'a table carpet of Turkey work' – the imitation Turkish carpets made in this country during the sixteenth century. 'English carpets' are recorded at York Place in 1530. Wolsey's collection of carpets, which passed to the king in 1525 and 1529, included over 250 pieces; imports, Turkey work, and English work. Lower down the social scale, the will of Richard Myles in 1544 included a bequest of his 'lesser Turkey carpet' – presumably he had two.[298] A carpet could also be of 'Darneck' – from Doornik (Tournai) in the Low Countries, a centre of tapestry-weaving.[299]

Curtains mentioned in wills and inventories are likely in most cases to have been for beds rather than windows; this is underlined by the clear tendency for curtains not to be mentioned in rooms where there were no beds. Besides those which were en suite with the bed coverings, curtains could be of linen, blue buckram, green say, or canvas. Curtains were occasionally fitted to windows in prestigious houses or company halls from the late fifteenth century.[300] In 1497–8 the Skinners paid 'for the curtains and painting of them which hang afore the glas windows in this hall',[301] and at Dudley's house in 1509 two curtains of green say were noted in the great parlour, and two of similar material in the great chamber, in both cases specifically hanging in the windows. Significantly, perhaps, no window curtains are mentioned in the inventory of the other nineteen chambers examined. There are more regular references specifically to window curtains in London from the sixteenth century; twelve of 'sarcenet' (thin taffeta silk) are mentioned at Wolsey's York Place in 1530[302] and Katheryne Brase had window curtains of yellow and red in her house in 1543.

As far as this brief survey can show, furniture was generally specific to individual chambers in the medieval and Tudor London house. Where their positions in the house can be

determined beds were always in upper chambers and never on the ground floor; chairs and stools were usually in public chambers such as halls, parlours or galleries. There is no evidence for the suggestion, born of paintings from Bruges such as the *Arnolfini Marriage* (1444), that it was fashionable in London to have a chair by a bed. As the period progressed, chairs became generally more fashionable, and chests were relegated from the main living rooms to ancillary or storage rooms. But the overall impression gained is that while some richer persons might indulge in expensive furnishings, this was not a widespread phenomenon. Wainscotting of chambers, for instance, was rare until the end of the sixteenth century; painted hangings were common. Many of the citizens' inventories show instead a far greater expenditure on jewelry, plate, and especially napery and clothing.

To get the feel of the variety in quality of internal furnishings, however, it is instructive to compare two houses of about the same period; remembering that the two inventories, of Katheryne Brase in 1543 and of Edmund Dudley in 1509, are both unusual in their extent among surviving records.

The house of Katheryne Brase in the parish of St Nicholas Shambles was evidently a tavern, with the drinking house on the ground floor and eleven chambers on the two floors above. The drinking room was sparsely furnished with forms and a single table. In the hall above were painted cloths, chairs, two pairs of playing tables and a clock; this and one other chamber had chimney irons. The widow had seven surviving children, of whom at least two lived with her. There were six beds in the house, two in the same chamber, and all four main bedrooms had painted hangings. Chests, some containing bedding, were found in the bedrooms or ancillary chambers. Many of the textiles and pieces of furniture were old, and the only foreign items were two cushions of Bruges satin and six small pieces of Dornick carpet which distinguished the main bedroom. The interior of the house must have had a patently used, vernacular look.

In contrast, the mansion held at lease by Edmund Dudley at the corner of Cannon Street and Walbrook – the contents of which were described in 1509 when Dudley, a former minister of Henry VII, was arrested – was clearly exceptional; but a brief description of some of the main rooms brings out the wealth of textiles and the variety of colours seen by any visitor. This would have been on a scale to which the richer London merchants must have aspired. The hall contained an old Arras at the dais, but was otherwise lightly furnished. The great parlour had hangings of red and green buckram, and like the little parlour had window curtains of green say; each had one French chair. The long gallery was hung with blue and yellow buckram, two stained cloths with imagery and the third French chair. The great chamber contained a bed with embroidered hangings. Another bed-chamber had hangings of blue and red buckram, the bed in this case of white fustian. Other storage rooms contained many pieces of hanging or tapestry, pewter and silver, expensive clothing in satin, velvet and furs, and armour. At this level in society, wealth was expressed in the mobile furnishings of the home as much as in expensive clothing and jewellery.

At the level of the well-to-do citizen and his social superiors, it is evident that a thread of foreign fashion ran through the interior decoration of the London house. An important influence on furnishings and decoration, though sporadic, was from Flanders: Flemish chests in the late fourteenth century, and chairs in the fifteenth. One of the leaders of the Evil May Day apprentice riots in 1517 complained that Dutchmen brought over, among other things, wainscot ready-wrought, cupboards, stools, tables, chests and painted cloths.[303] After mixing with a taste for French and even Spanish furniture, the Flemish or Dutch influence affected houses most vividly in the grotesques and strapwork of the second half of the sixteenth century.

London houses were, as far as we can tell, of a higher standard in their embellishments than those in other English towns or in the countryside; they had new features earlier. They had glass in domestic windows from the fourteenth century (and in some cases from the mid thirteenth); by the late fifteenth century (and earlier in the fifteenth if Low Countries parallels are relevant) this glass contained armorial bearings in royal and other residences where coats of arms mattered. More commonly, houses had tiled floors and, even more frequently, chimneys of stone and brick. This would encourage the development of stairs, which were often attached to chimney-stacks, and therefore the further exploitation of upper storey space and the subdivision of open halls.

These basic expressions of affluence could be enhanced by further exposure to contemporary fashion, especially in stone carving and woodwork. The crown-post roof came perhaps from France in the late thirteenth century; though evidence is largely lacking, it is possible that London was a staging-post in its diffusion through England. During the fourteenth century, the hammerbeam and later the arch-coupled roof were found in prominent secular buildings in the city. Windows in stone or timber had carved, traceried heads by the early fourteenth century. Two forms of window became widespread in London during the early fifteenth century; a larger window of two lights divided by a transom (which would allow glass to be mounted in the upper lights) and a smaller window, often in stone or brick, beneath a square hood-mould. Later in the fifteenth century double-height windows could be seen stretching across the full width of narrow properties, as an embellishment of the principal chamber at the front of the house on the first floor, overlooking the street. At the end of the sixteenth century, Renaissance mouldings appeared on all kinds of moulded stone and timber-work.

As the period progressed, however, these statements of affluence were overlain and modified by other developments born of the density of urban living. The crown-post roof gave way to the side-purlin roof during the fifteenth century; the chronology of this development is not yet clear, since the purlin roof is documented in London and its immediate periphery only in the late fifteenth century, and the appearance of dormer windows a generation earlier would suggest that by 1450 the exploitation of roof space was becoming common.

153. (174) New Fresh Wharf, Lower Thames Street: Building H, corner of cellar with chequerwork walls, probably fourteenth century, excavated 1974

154. (138) 1–6 Milk Street: Building 6 (early twelfth century) viewed from the north, showing as foundations beneath modern stanchions, excavated 1977 (cf. Fig. 238). Milk Street is to the right; the main foundations to the left are the back of the house.

CHAPTER 6

Construction of Medieval and Tudor Houses in London

In the medieval and Tudor periods, London houses were built out of four basic materials: stone, timber, bricks and earth. In each case we may examine the types, sources and supply of material, and study the way it was used, how well the buildings stood up, and how far the character of the materials was conducive to architectural or decorative expression.

Stone

The main stones used on domestic building-sites were ragstone, chalk and flint. The earliest source of these stones must have been the considerable amount of Roman building rubble littering the early medieval city, or available for the comparatively small labour of digging out old Roman foundations, some of them very substantial. Apart from the city wall and gates, no Roman structure of stone is known to have survived into the late Saxon period, though there are some probable cases. On documentary grounds it can be suggested that a number of prominent stone structures did survive: the east gate of the Roman fort in Aldermanbury, for instance, or the early Roman bath complex at Huggin Hill, both of which may have been foci of local activity in the late Saxon period.[1] By the eleventh century, in general, there can have been few if any Roman masonry buildings to be seen within the city walls, and large-scale digging-out ('robbing') of both standing and buried walls and foundations was common practice. The third-century Roman riverside wall gradually disappeared until by 1100 stone buildings reused it as foundations for their front walls, facing north to help form the line of Thames Street. Saxon and early medieval (pre-1200) stone churches and secular stone buildings all contain some element of re-used Roman stone or tile in their fabric, suggesting that robbing of Roman structures continued until the thirteenth century.

Ragstone came in two varieties: Kentish (Maidstone) and from Surrey (Reigate or Merstham). Kentish rag had been quarried in Roman times and in the medieval period it was favoured for rough locations, such as river-walls in 1307 (163), in 1384 (175; 'maydenston') and in 1440 (164), and occasionally for exteriors of prominent buildings and as paving for kitchen floors.[2] Reigate or Merstham stone is a calcareous sandstone, which is softer than the Kentish but hardens on drying. It was used for London Bridge from 1176, and in great quantity by the masons at Westminster, on both abbey and palace, in the middle of the thirteenth century.[3] Although the variety is not specified, it seems likely that Reigate was intended when a mason's contract for the Peter and Paul Tavern in Paternoster Row in 1342 expressly required *bon pere de Rag* to be used for the walls of the cellar and ground floor, the steps leading to the cellar and to the hall and

the jambs of the cellar door.[4] Merstham stone was specified in the building of Grocers' Hall (149) in 1435–6.[5] Being initially soft, Reigate was much used for carving, and window- and door-frames, for example at Winchester Palace, Southwark (193), for the vaulting and battlements on the Bridge chapel in 1396 and in several medieval city churches.[6]

Flint, a silica nodule occurring in the chalk, was often used with chalk for rubble walling, roughly plastered on one or both sides.[7] The widespread use of flint dates from the second half of the thirteenth century. It may be significant that the building accounts of royal works at Westminster Abbey and Palace of 1249–70 never mention flint; the earliest occurrence of the English form of the word is in 1283, when a wall at the Tower used chalk and flint in quantity.[8] Knapped flints were laid in regular courses after 1250, and in the fourteenth and fifteenth centuries several church and secular interiors in London had chequerwork walls, in which flints were composed into black squares to alternate with a paler stone (usually chalk; Fig. 153). This effect is also roughly attempted in Guildhall east crypt (c. 1430) but more adroitly in the larger squares of chequerwork on exterior walls at Charterhouse (fifteenth century?) and at the Steelyard.[9] A house in the parish of St Olave Silver Street was called *le Flynt Hall* in 1399, presumably from the character of its walls.[10]

Examples of some other English stones have been noticed in churches or public buildings, but rarely on the sites of private houses. Wheatley stone, from around Oxford, is found in some London parish churches.[11] Stapleton (Yorkshire) stone, was used unwrought and ready hewn, for window jambs and sills at Grocers' Hall in 1428.[12] Beer stone (a fine chalk from Seaton, Devon) was bought for an unspecified municipal purpose in 1350.[13] Huddleston stone (Yorkshire) passed through London, since the clerk of works at Sion (Middlesex) sold some at London to the builders of Eton College in 1444–5.[14] Corfe stone from Dorset was used at the Tower in 1278; Portland stone, also from Dorset, was used at the Tower in 1349 and on the Bridge in 1350.[15] The hard grey-green limestone from Purbeck (Dorset), composed of small freshwater mussel and snail shells and which takes a high polish, was fashionable in southern England towards the end of the twelfth century and remained so for two centuries; but apart from the comparatively late occurrence in columns in the western crypt of Guildhall (1411–30), its use for buildings is not documented in the secular city.[16]

The most important foreign stone used in London was Caen stone, from Calvados in Normandy. This had a fine grain but weathered badly, and so was often soon replaced if exposed to the elements.[17] It was generally used in prestigious residences for the jambs of doors and windows (Fig. 32a–b) or loop-holes: for windows at Grocers' Hall in 1495–6, for five windows on the south side of St Stephen Walbrook in 1536–7, and by the Clothworkers' Company for repairs of property

155. **(177)** Merchant Taylors' Hall, Threadneedle Street: elevation of north wall, showing foundation arches, and plan, 1910–12 [Norman 1916]

ELEVATION.

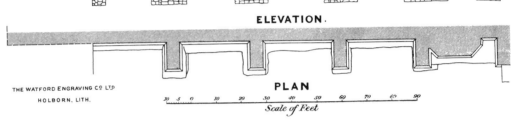

THE WATFORD ENGRAVING CO LTD
HOLBORN, LITH.

PLAN

10 5 0   10   20   30   40   50   60   70   80   90
Scale of Feet

156. **(177)** Merchant Taylors' Hall, Threadneedle Street: foundation arches recorded below the north wall, photographed in 1910–12 [Norman 1916]

in 1560–1.[18] Presumably the use of Caen in royal works made it more easily available for domestic use; in at least one case Caen stone was resold in London from royal works at Eton.[19]

The effect of royal and ecclesiastical building on the grand scale in the city and its environs must have stimulated certain fashions in stone usage. A useful analogy may be supplied by medieval Florence, where marble was used in private houses after the cathedral authorities organised the large supply they needed for the cathedral itself;[20] similar things may have happened in London.

Foundations and Walling

The secular stone buildings erected in the city from the late eleventh century were often greater in area than the largest timber cellars which preceded them on central properties, and in every case much heavier. New foundation techniques were therefore developed: the use of piles and, later, arches in stone. In a study of sites around Cheapside, three main techniques of construction of foundations beneath stone buildings have been identified: (i) chalk and gravel foundations without mortar, sometimes with piles; (ii) arched and mortared foundations; and (iii) mortared foundations without arches. Each of these techniques had a definable period of currency or widespread usage.[21]

The technique of foundations formed of unmortared layers of large stones interleaved with gravel, sometimes supplemented by piles, is found throughout the city and its environs in religious structures in the Saxon and early medieval period, and on secular sites from the twelfth century. On religious sites, it is used in the first, probably eleventh-century, church of St Nicholas Shambles; and at the first, possibly eleventh-century, church at St Bride's, Fleet Street.[22] Secular examples include buildings in the streets off Cheapside (**138**; Fig. 154) and on the waterfront, at Seal House, Upper Thames Street (**172**, Building A, early to mid twelfth century), and New Fresh Wharf, Lower Thames Street (**174**, Buildings A–D, mid twelfth to early thirteenth century). In the City of London there are at present no examples independently dated to later than the mid thirteenth century, and it seems likely that the technique, which is expensive in stone, was thereafter modified.

Several excavated stone buildings of the thirteenth century have arched foundations; pits had been dug in the bottom of the foundation trench at regular intervals and the foundation constructed as piers of stone linked by arches, brought to a level surface at or slightly below the level of a cellar floor, or a comparable distance below ground level where no cellar was intended (Figs. 155–6). An early example is Building 11 at Well Court, Bow Lane (**32**), possibly the vault mentioned on the site in 1269; it is suggested that a suitable date for construction would be the 1220s. A second example from a secular context, Building F at New Fresh Wharf in Thames Street (**174**), had walls on arches, supported by timber piles through reclaimed land, and may have comprised part of a rebuilding of the tenement known on documentary grounds to have taken place in 1293. The arched foundation was used at the same period in religious building: the crypt of the chapel of the Bishop of Ely at his mansion in Holborn (**106**), built in

1286–90; shortly afterwards arches were employed beneath the south wall of the choir of the Greyfriars' church, begun in 1306 and finished in 1337.[23] Thereafter the technique is widely employed for stone buildings in the fourteenth and fifteenth centuries, for church extensions, company halls and the better-built private houses.[24] The technique therefore broadly dates from the middle of the thirteenth century (and possibly from *c.* 1220) to the mid fifteenth century, when brick began to be widely used for foundation arches. In London the arched form was well adapted to the stabilising of large stone buildings erected upon the soft soil of previous occupation, and may have been developed for this purpose.

Foundations of chalk bonded with mortar, as opposed to pounded gravel, but without occasional arches, were the less ambitious complement to arched and mortared foundations. They were often not carefully layered, but the chalk was evidently poured with the mortar. They are first recorded below medieval secular buildings in London in the twelfth and thirteenth centuries[25] though in larger buildings arched foundations were often preferred. From the thirteenth century thinner mortared foundations or walls with no foundations at all are recorded in situations where very heavy loads did not have to be supported, e.g. cesspit walls or inner walls of cellars within the area covered by buildings.

Above the foundations in twelfth-century stone buildings, an almost standard technique of wall-building may be noted. Large rag blocks were laid to form the outer faces, the spaces between them being then filled with smaller chalk blocks, occasional flint and fragments of Roman tile, all mortared together (Fig. 157). The sides presented a random uncoursed appearance with wide joints occasionally filled with small stones. A twelfth-century town-house recorded in Southwark in 1839 (**198**) had a first-floor doorway edged in Caen stone, but nineteenth-century engravings suggest that the walls of

157. (**174**) New Fresh Wharf, Lower Thames Street: foundation and first course of west wall of twelfth-century Building D, excavated 1974

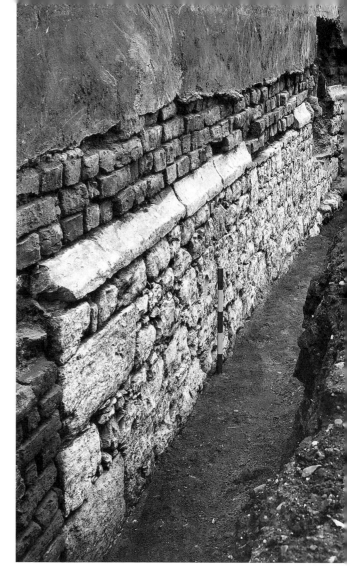

158. St Botolph Wharf, Billingsgate (Lower Thames Street): tooled ashlar (possibly reused from another structure) in a medieval undercroft, excavated 1982 (the same building as in Fig. 121b)

159. (**10**) The Crowne, Aldgate: part of the foundation of the west wall, exposed during building works in 1987

this building were of coursed stone rather than ashlar. Thus although prominent twelfth-century secular stone buildings in London probably had tooled ashlar quoins and details such as door and window surrounds, there is no evidence at present to suppose that they had ashlar exteriors, as at, for example, the Jew's House in The Strait, Lincoln (*c.* 1170–80).[26] The full dignity of squared ashlar was largely reserved, presumably on grounds of cost, for public buildings such as later at Guildhall or Leadenhall; though it was also employed on prestigious buildings such as Merchant Taylors' Hall and Fishmongers' Hall (as shown by Wyngaerde and the other panoramas), in certain undercrofts (Fig. 158) and, because of its durability, for river walls (Fig. 156).[27] Many other buildings, both religious and secular, had stone walls with roughly coursed and rough-hewn stone, embellished with larger but still rough-hewn quoins; both ashlar and roughly coursed walls sometimes had a hollow-chamfered offset of tooled stone between 2 and 4 ft above ground level (Fig. 159). This was presumably the 'water-table' of medieval and post-medieval building contracts.

A very few superior residences in the fourteenth century had crenellated walls. Among the first may have been the Savoy Palace, licensed in 1293 to be crenellated by Edmund of Lancaster.[28] The house of Richer de Refham in the parish of St Michael Paternoster had a stone *alure* (walkway behind a parapet) in 1306,[29] which may refer to crenellation, though the licence to crenellate is not in the usual source, the *Patent Rolls*. The *Rolls* give details of eleven licences between 1305 and 1385; two bishops, of Coventry in the Strand in 1305, and of Salisbury (**79**) in Fleet Street in 1337, and nine citizens, all but one in 1305–41.[30] A study of crenellation between 1200 and 1536 suggests that this aristocratic gesture was confined to nobles and religious lords, though the licence to crenellate did not necessarily result in building: since the licence sanctioned seignorial rights, 'very often bluster sufficed and no building was done'.[31] The only crenellated dom-estic building (i.e. apart from buildings such as Leadenhall, the Stocks, Mercers' and Fishmongers' Halls) visible in the sixteenth- and seventeenth-century panoramas is the main range of Pulteney's residence in Lawrence Pountney Lane, licensed in 1341 (**114**; Fig. 38).

The walls of later medieval buildings contained an increasing element of chalk on their interior faces (**138**, Building 10; **32**, Building 12). Further economies are found in fourteenth-century undercrofts, where the greater part of the wall below medieval ground level was often of chalk, though the interior face was often carefully composed of coursed, squared blocks (**129**; Fig. 160a–b) or could incorporate a colourful

S

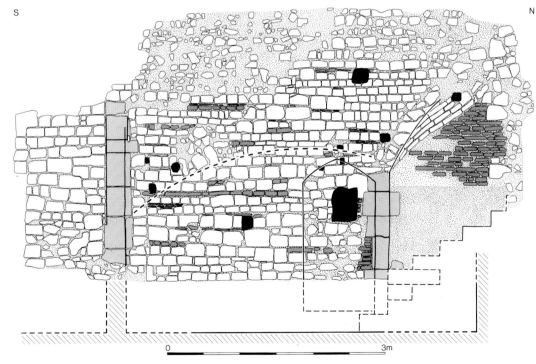

N 160. (129) 9 Lovat
Lane: (a) west (rear)
wall of undercroft in
1981

(b) Drawing
interpreting the
remains shown in (a)

0   3m

G15

161. (164) Trig Lane, Upper Thames Street: details of construction of stone river wall G15, *c.* 1440 [Milne & Milne 1982]

chequerwork of chalk and knapped flint (174; Fig. 153). A rough layering of ragstone and chalk, as well as a crude attempt at chequerwork in those types of stone, is seen in the walling of the east undercroft of Guildhall (*c.* 1430). By the late fifteenth century undercrofts were built in a mixture of chalk, rag and brick (as at 7–8 Philpot Lane, 148; Fig. 91). During the fourteenth and fifteenth centuries the most frequent use of stone in the ordinary house must have been for new cesspits (almost always chalk), as demanded by the *Assize of Nuisance*, civic regulations in force from about 1200.

A wall of stone was not always the permanent asset it may have seemed. There was a thin but constant stream of accidents when walls collapsed, and concern about walls which were alleged to be leaning dangerously.[32] As the period progressed, party-walls of stone also tended to be built thinner than the 3 ft demanded in the early thirteenth-century building regulations. In 1370 the back wall of a row of eighteen shops which rose to first-floor level was to be only 2 ft thick (108). A party-wall of stone only 2 ft wide was noted (and not criticised) in the parish of St Mary at Hill in 1348, though whether this was the wall of a building or of a yard is not known.[33] It is likely, moreover, that stone was largely confined to party-walls except in a minority of prestigious cases where

stone buildings were to be found; stone undercrofts often supported timber-framed buildings. By the time of the surveys of London houses by Ralph Treswell in 1607–14 there were very few houses with stone walls, and none with all four walls of stone; houses in stone must have been a rarity after the building of the great residences of the fourteenth century.[34]

Wood: Species and Sources

Oak was the most widespread timber used in buildings and other wooden constructions; it was used for structural timbers, laths and boards.[35] Oak for royal contracts, as in the case of the roof of Westminster Hall, came from royal woods in Hampshire, Berkshire, Surrey and Hertfordshire. The leaders of the church could also rely on royal or noble assistance for large structural timbers, as when the abbot of Westminster apparently asked the king for six large oaks for his hall.[36] The established religious establishments such as St Paul's could use wood sent as part of the *firmae* of their manors. The sources of oak for domestic building were also at least partly local; London Bridge bought oaks in Lewisham, Croydon and Coddington.[37]

Elm was supplied usually in the form of boards.[38] It was used for doors, window shutters, floors, benches, dressers and shelving;[39] and in privies, probably for the lining of their chutes (*pipes*).[40] The sources of elm were also local: the Bridge Account Rolls for the brief period 1381–97 mention eighteen specified places in Essex, Kent, Middlesex and Surrey as sources.[41] As with oak, London Bridge occasionally bought elms direct from magnates, such as from the Earl of Kent who held an estate at Stepney, or from the abbot of Chertsey who had sixty elms at Petersham. An elm tree in London was worth 10*s.* in 1358.[42]

Ash was used for handles of tools, the uprights in wattling and as planks in certain situations, especially pastry boards;[43] a table of ash was supplied to Coldharbour in 1485.[44] Beech was used for laths, occasionally for shelving,[45] and by 1607 beech puncheons (studs) were an allowed thinner alternative to oak.[46] Beech was sometimes used for scaffolding or other forms of poles, as was alder, fir and willow.[47] Wicker (horizontal and vertical rods woven together) was used chiefly for fences, weirs and in other external situations; two hurdles from an early fourteenth-century fence found in the medieval city ditch at Old Bailey (Fig. 163) were made of pliant rods of hazel, alder and a little oak.[48] During the tenth to twelfth centuries wicker was also used to line rubbish pits (167; Fig. 162).

The greater volume of wood must have come down river from such places as Kingston, however, since a distinct quarter of the waterfront at the west end of the city became associated with the timbermonger trade by the mid fourteenth century; the parish of St Benet Woodwharf is so called in 1374. Nearby in St Peter's Hill lay Woodmongers' Hall, though it is documented only when it had passed into other uses.[49] Woodmongers were among the will-making class in the 1370s – one with a fleet of small boats and a wharf; another was in partnership with a colleague in Kingston.[50] In the late fifteenth century it was usual to have timber brought

162. (**138**) 1–6 Milk Street: wicker-lined Pit 81, eleventh or twelfth century, excavated 1977

163. (*below left*) Wicker fence, probably fourteenth century, found in the backfilled city ditch north of Ludgate in 1982

from the waterside, and sometimes the client paid for carriage, wharfage and cranage of the timber.[51]

By the thirteenth century it was as cheap to import oak and fir (deal) from the Baltic as it was to bring it from anywhere in Britain outside the Home Counties; this was presumably a symptom of the extraordinary demand in London as well as of difficulties with overland transport. Eastland or Estrich boards (almost always of oak, but sometimes of deal in later accounts)[52] were employed in royal buildings in the mid thirteenth century and are mentioned in the stores of London Bridge in 1350.[53] The doors and shutters of the St Paul's shops of 1369 and the Friday Street shops of 1410 were to be of Eastland boards, presumably because they were better seasoned. In 1405 the chapter of St Paul's undertook to supply Eastland boards for the building of a courtyard house in Bucklersbury, whereas the framing was done by the carpenter. Estrich boards were also used to make lintels over the windows on the south side of Brewers' Hall in 1423, indicating perhaps that they were carved with tracery.[54]

The word *spruce* derives from *Prussia*, and must have referred to fir; spruce tables, coffers and chests are known from the late fourteenth century.[55] Furniture of other rare or possibly foreign woods are mentioned infrequently from the sixteenth century, for instance of cypress[56] and walnut. The Earl of Lincoln was selling walnuts from his garden in Holborn in 1295, and walnut was used as a timber tree at Abingdon in 1413.[57]

Study of the way timber was used may take account of several considerations: the character of timber-framing (sizes of timbers, bracing methods); the construction of floors and therefore upper storeys; the height of the various storeys; the first appearance, nature and decline of jetties; the decorative element in timberwork, including architectural embellishment; and what this evidence in total suggests about the styles of framing in London houses.

Building with Timber

In certain London building contracts the cross-sections of many of the principal timbers are specified, and these have been tabulated in Table 2. The methods of measuring timber by volume were codified by Richard More, a past master of the Carpenters' Company, in 1602. Volume of timber was calculated as a half times the sum of the breadth and thickness (in inches) times the length in feet. This gives an error of around 25 per cent. A 'foot' of stone or timber was one cubic foot, and a load of timber 50 cu ft. Timber was measured by a small piece of string (which went round the timber to ascertain its cross-section) and a foot-rule. Arithmetical methods were introduced towards 1600 under the influence of Leonard Digges's *Tectonicon*. Euclid's *Elements of Geometrie* was translated by Sir Henry Billingsley, mayor, and was also influential. The exact measurement of pi was not known to medieval and Tudor carpenters, but they calculated it as 'triple and almost one seventh part more'.

The regulations for timber sizes as laid down in 1607 are given in Table 3.[58] There were also accepted methods of calculating the amount of wood in waney timbers (planks without square edges), but by 1602 these were a comparative rarity in London; most timber seems to have been hewn into rectangular cross-section before arrival.[59]

TABLE 2

Sizes of Principal Timbers in Three Building Contracts

(sizes are in inches)

	1369	1383	1532
cellar joists	10 × 10		
sillbeam/groundsill	7 × 12	6 × 10	6 × 10
principal posts	14 × 12 (bottom) 12 × 10 (top)	12 × 9	12 × 10
groundfloor puncheon	12 × 9		
groundfloor summer	13 × 9	10 × 9	12 × 10 8 × 9, 9 × 9
mullions	6 × 9		
tie-beam/enterteys	10 × 9		12 × 14, 10 × 12
first floor joists	10 × 8	7 × 6	12 × 10, 5 × 3, 6 × 9
first floor sillbeam	6 × 8		
first floor puncheons	10 × 8		
first floor summer	12 × 8		
second floor joists	9 × 7	6 × 5	
second floor sillbeam	5 × 7		
second floor puncheons	9 × 7		
wallplates	10 × 8		
principal rafters		7 × 8	
rafters	6 × 5 (bottom) 5 × 4 (top)	6 × 5	
lyernes (tiebeams?)	6 × 8		

TABLE 3

Regulations for Timber Sizes, 1607

	Number in load	Cross-section	Length
solid timber	50 ft		
joists	30+	4 in thick throughout	8½ ft
puncheons	40 50	6 × 4 in (oak) 5 × 5 in (beech)	6½ ft 6½ ft
rafters	30+	4 × 4 in (bottom) 4 × 3 in (top)	12 ft+
double quarters	50	4 × 3 in	8½ ft
single quarters	100	3 × 2 in	8½ ft
boards			
stable planks	40	12 × 2 in	6½ ft
bedsides	60	10 × 2 in	6½ ft
quarter boards		1 in thick at thicker edge, ⅓ in at thinner edge	
seelinge boards		½ in thick at thicker edge ⅓ in at thinner edge	
planch boards		1 in thick (throughout?)	
laths	30 bundles	1 × ⅓ in	larger 5 ft (5 score to a bundle) smaller 4 ft (6 score to a bundle)

164. (*right*)   (**187**) Hosier Lane, showing construction of square panels (J. T. Smith 1795)

165. (*middle*)   The Old Fountain, Minories (J. T. Smith, before demolition in 1793; published 1798)

166. (*far right*)   Houses (probably belonging to the parish of St Bartholomew Smithfield) on the east side of Duke Street, now Little Britain (J. T. Smith 1807)

Two things may be observed immediately: firstly, that these examples suggest a general diminution in timber sizes between the middle of the fourteenth century and 1602; and secondly, that the variety of sizes of timbers available and used in 1369 was severely curtailed by 1602. Thirteen different cross-sections of timber were specified in the contract of 1369, but only five general thicknesses in 1602.

Standardisation of dimensions would aid prefabrication of buildings outside the city. Buildings were sometimes framed elsewhere, presumably near the source of the timber, and brought to London in a prefabricated state. For the large Bucklersbury house in 1405, St Paul's had the timber, including the arch-couple roof, framed at Hadleigh (Essex); in 1425 the new frame for Drapers' Hall came from Croydon, though other timber was bought at Hunton in Kent. A house 40 ft × 22 ft and 24 ft to the eaves built in 1510 was to be framed at Kingston on Thames and in 1515 the new London Bridge storehouse was framed at Charlwood (Surrey), carried to Kingston and brought by boat in 225 loads.[60]

Timber was not only used above ground. Beech piles were used to spread the load of stone foundations from the opening of the twelfth century.[61] From at least the thirteenth century larger timbers, sometimes from previous buildings, were also used within foundations, particularly when laid through reclaimed land.

Several separate traditions of building with timber were evident in the city by 1100. The main techniques of wall construction in the timber buildings of the late ninth to twelfth centuries were stave-building, walls of mud, planks or wattles supported by posts, and plank revetting of sunken areas, sometimes using a double cladding of planks, or earth walls.[62] The majority of the buildings would have had daubed or horizontally planked exteriors.[63] Some of these techniques may have continued well into the medieval period on smaller structures.

By the thirteenth century, on the basis of examples recorded in the environs of London, timber-framing using long, thin vertical panels might be envisaged in the city.[64] In the fourteenth century, regular but still rectangular panels are more likely; the framing of buildings began to reflect a structure based on trusses at intervals, with principal timbers emphasising the bays as major divisions in walls.[65] By the time of the first engravings of London houses in the late eighteenth century the majority of timber-framed houses were plastered over; occasionally solid framing in square panels, which might be of fifteenth- or sixteenth-century date, is seen (e.g. Figs. 164–5; in these two examples the antiquity of the structure (at least by c. 1800) is indicated by the build-up of street surfaces in front of the building).

The walls of medieval timber buildings were often braced across the corners of panels with diagonal or curving timbers, set either outside or inside the studs and connecting a principal timber, often a corner-post, with a horizontal beam either at ceiling or at floor level. Where two houses shared a timber wall and its principal posts, braces of each house might share a post.[66]

Surviving buildings in the region suggest that braces were of different forms at various times: braces were straight

DRAWN AND ETCHED BY J.T.SMITH.   DOMESTIC ARCHITECTURE.   DRAWN IN JULY 180
VIEW OF PART OF DUKE STREET, WEST SMITHFIELD.

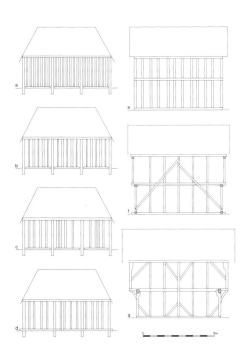

before the influence of Gothic forms in stone (*c.* 1230), but sometimes curved after this date. In the fourteenth century the 'Kentish' form of matching curved braces beneath a first-floor window was common, and an example can be seen in the room in the service accommodation at the Bishop of Bath's mansion, as drawn by Hollar in 1646 when it was Arundel House (Fig. 35). One engraving of houses in Duke Street (Little Britain) around 1800 shows a profusion of bracing, probably resulting from many periods of rebuilding and adaptation (Fig. 166). Ogee-curved braces were introduced in the early sixteenth century (the earliest dated ogee braces being found on immediately post-Dissolution houses such as that of Thomas Pope at Bermondsey)[67] and are shown by Wyngaerde on a house *c.* 1540; saltire or X-form braces are shown in the same panorama (Figs. 167–8). In the later six-

teenth century there was a return to straight braces, often confined to the first-floor corners[68] – a feature of the otherwise undated building, perhaps a lodging for retainers, shown on the north side of the court at Arundel House in another engraving by Hollar.

There were several periods when framing and bracing included timbers which were structurally superfluous, and when therefore it is highly likely that the external faces of timbers were exposed as a form of decoration or ostentation. By the early fourteenth century, in rural buildings of standing, selected gables such as parlour cross-wings had double curved braces which were more for show than for stability.[69] The widespread fashion of close-studding – in which buildings often had close-spaced timbers at the front, but more economical large framing on side and rear walls – is noted first

167. (*above*)   Bracing techniques employed in medieval buildings in London from evidence from waterfront excavations: (a–e) eleventh to thirteenth century; (f–g) thirteenth and fourteenth century [Milne 1992]

168. (*above right*)   Saltire bracing on a house on the west side of Borough High Street, Southwark, from Wyngaerde's panorama of *c.* 1540

169.   House in Sweedon's Passage, Grub Street: exterior view (C. J. Richardson 1871; cf. Fig. 93)

170.   (**103**) Staple Inn, Holborn: frontage of *c.* 1586 in 1983

171.   (**103**) Staple Inn, Holborn, photographed in the nineteenth century

172. House in Ship Yard, Temple Bar (R. B. Schnebbelie 1815)

173. (83) House at corner of Fleet Street and Chancery Lane (J. T. Sm[...] 1789)

in Kent at Wye College, c. 1445, and became common c. 1470;[70] it was remarked upon by a Venetian visitor to London in 1497. In the late sixteenth century there are examples of some studs (puncheons) not being jointed into the horizontal beams; they were there purely for effect.[71] The only authentic example of close-studding noted in London engravings (though representations of the building differ in their renditions of its magnificence) is a house in Moor Lane (Grub Street) (Figs. 93, 169). Although the frontage of Staple Inn to Holborn (Fig. 170) is today a fine example of this style, its previous appearance (Fig. 171) shows that it may originally have had panels without close-studding.

There is no evidence for the painting of these exposed timbers, whether studs or braces; they must have kept their natural colours, except when the whole house or storey was painted over.[72]

During the second half of the sixteenth century close-studding seems to have been replaced, in high-quality constructions in London, by a new fashion of square or rectangular panels with applied Renaissance mouldings (including classical blind arcading) and, at intervals along the front of the building, grotesque corbels growing out of elaborately carved vertical strips (6, 122; Figs. 172–3). This exuberant carving could be found in courtyards (Fig. 112) and was clearly en suite with contemporary styling of fireplaces and internal woodwork. It is usually attributed both to the influence of Renaissance-Mannerist pattern-books and to the influx of foreign joiners and carvers, particularly from the Netherlands.[73] The grotesque corbels were widespread on London buildings, including some of modest proportions

(Figs. 174–6), though it must be remembered that we only know of these examples because they were durable enough to survive two hundred years to be recorded.

Three-storey buildings are mentioned in London in 1314 and became increasingly common during the fourteenth century.[74] The height of storeys in a timber-framed house does not seem to be an indicator of date. The ground floor, at least where adjacent to the street, was to be 9 ft high in regulations of 1276. Thereafter examples can be given of contracts stipulating between 8 ft 9 in and 12 ft high for ground floors (Table 4). In 1602, a standard length for timbers called *quarters* was 8 ft 6 in (Table 2), suggesting a standard storey height.

TABLE 4

Documented Storey Heights in London, 1276–1466[75]

Floor	Date	Type of document	Height
ground	1276	civic regulation	9 ft
	1310	contract	10 ft
	1410	contract	10 ft 6 in
	1466	civic regulation	8 ft 9 in
first	1384	building lease	10 ft
	1405	contract	11 ft
	1410	contract	9 ft
second	1384	building lease	7 ft
	1405	contract	9 ft

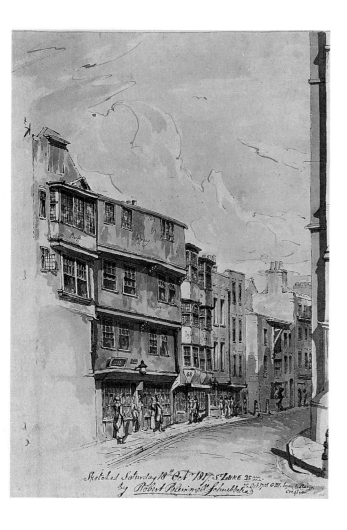

175. (54) Dick Whittington pub, Cloth Fair, in the nineteenth century

174. (*left*) Houses on west side of St Mary Axe opposite St Andrew Undershaft church (R. B. Schnebbelie 1817)

176. Buildings in Silver Street, Southwark (J. C. Buckler 1828)

Jetties first appear in London records in 1246, when a *getticium* bordering Ironmonger Lane was classed as a nuisance;[76] presumably the large number of solars also indicted were also criticised because they stuck out into the street.[77] In 1276 it was ordered that jetties, along with pentices and gutters, should be at least 9 ft above the ground so as not to impede horsemen. In a narrow lane or alley, where houses might face each other, there was a danger that a jetty of even normal dimensions might extend beyond the middle of the lane.[78]

Side jetties often of considerable length were prosecuted where they overhung neighbours' property or churchyards; in 1378 one was allegedly 14 yd 16 in (43 ft 4 in) long.[79] Overhangs of small dimensions might be a result of leaning, but the size of some indicates that jetties were occasionally contributory factors, as in one overhang of over 5 ft in 1323.[80] Jetties continued to be prosecuted under the *Assize* in the fifteenth century,[81] and in 1519 the Vintners were the unfortunate recipients of a judgement which ordered the cutting back of their new building in Fleet Street by 1 inch, the excess of the first-floor jetty into the street.[82] By the second quarter of the sixteenth century jetties were commonly of very slight projection (e.g. 18 Old Buildings, Lincoln's Inn, of 1524, Fig. 177)[83] and from the middle of the century jettying was falling out of fashion in the London area; many jettied buildings, for instance the once fashionable Wealden houses, were having their first-floor jetties underbuilt.[84] Cases in London from the 1560s indicate that jetties were being regarded as a nuisance to be removed, rather than tolerated.[85] By 1600 new buildings of four and a half storeys were being constructed without any

177. **(47)** 18 Old Buildings, Lincoln's Inn (1525), showing timber-framed building of mid-sixteenth-century date on left, photographed in 1923

178. **(6)** 133 Aldersgate (T. Shepherd *c*. 1850)

179. **(137)** Blue Boar, St Mary Axe (T. Dibdin 1854)

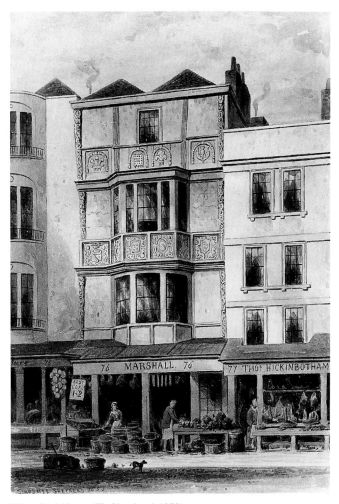

180. House on south side of Aldgate High Street, showing infill of laths, photographed in 1944

181. 76 Aldgate (T. Shepherd 1853)

jetties (**6**; Fig. 178). This suggests that recorded but undated buildings in the city with prominent jetties, such as the large house at the junction of St Mary Axe and Bevis Marks (**137**; Fig. 179), might date from the first half of the sixteenth century or before.

Dormer windows are probably a development of the first half of the fifteenth century in London; as shown in Wyngaerde's and Hollar's panoramas, dormers could light garrets occupying only the triangle formed by a sloping roof. The subsequent development of half-height walls to give the garret extra headroom is more difficult to date. A fixed point is provided by the street range of Staple Inn to Holborn of 1586, with its half-walls in the garret (Fig. 170). In this range the roof is supported on bent timbers which have the appearance of base-crucks, a feature present also in a similar building of the first half of the sixteenth century in Bruges;[86] a date of *c.* 1550 for the introduction of half-height garret walls into London is likely.

The filling of the timber frame was commonly lath and loam, finished with a skim of plaster; this was still the technique in the early seventeenth century (Fig. 180), and references to brick infilling of the frame are few. Internal walls were generally insubstantial; in 1390 a burglary at an inn could be undertaken by breaking through the wall of a guest's room.[87]

Exterior plaster panels with cartouches, strapwork designs or emblems (the Prince of Wales' feathers, the thistle) have been recorded on houses from the 1580s; they occur together with grotesque pilasters (e.g. Fig. 181) around the beginning of the seventeenth century. A group of four panels, presumably of plaster, recorded on the front of the lavish timber-framed banqueting house in the garden of Paul Pindar's house in Bishopsgate (Fig. 98) is intrinsically undated but perhaps contemporary with the rebuilding of the house *c.* 1600. Panels possibly of decorated plaster or of carved wood are shown on houses in Cheapside in 1547 (Fig. 183).

Larger timber buildings in Saxon London, such as those recently excavated on the Watling Court site at the junction of Bow Lane and Basing Lane, must have had timber floors above their deep and roomy cellars, but the carpentry of these buildings is almost totally unknown.[88] Surviving floors of the thirteenth century are usually lodged on stone walls, as in the case of the floor of the chapel of the Bishop of Ely in Holborn, now St Etheldreda's, Ely Place.[89] Joists were usually laid on their wider faces, though square-sectioned joists could be specified (e.g. in 1369, over the cellars of shops).[90] When substantial timbers were rarely straight, the former was necessary because only in this plane would they lie flat. The earliest recorded deep-sectioned (i.e. laid on a narrower face) joists recorded are at the Queen's House, Tower of London,

182.   Cheapside: the processional entry into London of Marie de Medicis, 1638

completed in 1528, and in the floor of Middle Temple Hall in 1561.[91]

Several kinds of boards are mentioned in London accounts: Estrich or Eastland boards, pipe boards, planchboard, elm board, quarterboard and evis board. With the exception of pipe boards, which were definitely larger and used for lining latrines, the types of boards were all about the same price[92] but had different functions in and around the house.

Planch board, mentioned at the Tower in 1324, averaged 10 ft × 1 ft 6 in and probably 1½ in thick; in 1568 a standard board 11 ft long is implied and in 1602 a planchboard had to be 1 in thick, probably throughout (see Table 3). It was used for gutters, garden fences and garden doors.[93] This type of board would seem to be the likeliest for flooring, but references are lacking. *Quarterboards* were boards made from trunks which had been quartered, i.e. split into four by cuts at right angles.[94] As Table 3 shows, these boards would tend to be triangular in section; the smaller boards could be called seeling boards – presumably these were the overlapping boards used in early wainscotting or seeling. Quarterboards were used for making a pentice over a window or in gutters.[95] *Evis boards* were eaves-boards, which were also triangular in section since their main purpose was to lie under tiles at the eaves to throw water away from the wall below.[96] They could also be used for making garden walls or fences.[97] *Clovenboards* or weatherboarding, in which boards overlapped, had been used for external constructions and in waterfront revetments since at least the twelfth century; the term *weatherboarding* occurs in 1554–5 and 1568,[98] and weatherboarded buildings are shown on the waterfront in both the Wyngaerde and especially the Hollar engravings (*c.* 1540 and 1647).

Apart from details of some grotesque corbels of the late sixteenth century, we are largely ignorant of any figured carving on the exteriors of domestic buildings. Documentation is similarly lacking for signs; places of public resort, such as major tenements, taverns and inns, were known by their signs in the thirteenth century, but great houses were often named rather from their appearance (Copped – i.e. with a pointed roof – Hall, *La Rouge Sale*, *Flynt Halle*) than from heraldic signs. In 1438–9 the Falcon on the Hope brewhouse in Aldersgate Street received a new sign requiring a bolt of iron weighing 12 lb, a 'shaftre' and the sign itself which was carved and painted; it took a carpenter three days to put it up.[99]

Taverns and alehouses had stakes protruding outside their doors; in 1387 the length of alestakes was restricted to 7 ft, both because they extended too far over the highway, and because their weight seriously affected the structure of the building to which they were attached.[100] Several tavern signs, on the ends of long beams, are shown in Cheapside in the 1638 engraving (Fig. 182).

The word *pentice* denoted two different structures: a long corridor or verandah-like structure connecting two buildings or a sloping rainwater roof over a window or door. In this sense it was also called a penthouse.[101] Pentices were the most common source of complaint in the 1244 Eyre and 1246 inquest. A pentice was usually built over a ground-floor door or over cellar-steps, and clearly impeded the highway. In 1276 it was ordered that pentices should be 9 ft high as mentioned above; thus the pentice might be fixed to the solar.[102] Even so pentices may well have afforded good protection in bad weather, since in 1345 the butchers were told to sell their meat beneath the penthouses of the houses adjoining the Stocks Market on fishdays, to allow the fishmongers to practise within the Stocks.[103] The copperplate and other panoramas of the late sixteenth century show houses with pentices on most of the major streets. Bargeboards, which were usually nailed on the outside of the frame beneath the two slopes of a roof in a gable, are shown on houses in Cheapside in the engraving of the 1547 painting of Edward VI's coronation procession (Fig. 63), and the 1638 engraving (Fig. 182).

Since the evidence for medieval and Tudor buildings is largely documentary (including lease-plans and panoramas), examples of carpentry joints in London are few, and they have been well studied. Recent archaeological excavations on medieval waterfront sites in the city are however adding to this corpus of joints, with new examples dated by dendrochronology.[104]

Brick

Imported Flemish bricks were used in great quantity for the curtain wall of the Tower of London in 1283, but although bricks were regularly imported in small numbers, it is now thought that south-east England produced its own bricks

from the beginning of the fifteenth century, after experience at Calais and works such as the city wall at Hull.[105] Yellow bricks of local manufacture have been noted in the curtain wall at Eltham Palace in the first quarter of the fourteenth century, at Northolt manor house (Middlesex) before 1350, at Kennington Palace in the middle of the century and at Charterhouse in 1372; they are found in excavated buildings in the city by about 1370.[106] The wardens of London Bridge engaged Dutch craftsmen to make bricks at Deptford from at least 1404; a small dock was constructed, and other buildings added soon after.[107] The rebuilding of the royal house at Sheen by Henry V in 1414, which included much brick from Calais, may have been the first royal venture in the new medium;[108] two million bricks were made locally for Eton College by 1451. There was also a watergate with a brick arch on stone jambs, of either Henry VI or Richard III's building, at Westminster Palace.[109] Richard Buckland, treasurer of the king's works at Calais between 1421 and 1436, was accused of stealing 20,000 of the king's bricks to repair his place in London; at the same time the new Drapers' Hall, in 1425, was using the relatively small number of 12,000 bricks in its construction.[110] Brick was increasingly used for chimneys and as a component of stone walls throughout the fifteenth century; at Crosby Place, Bishopsgate (1466), for instance, brick was used to vault the undercroft and fill in behind the impressive stone ashlar of the hall. Buildings largely or wholly of brick survive from the first half of the fifteenth century in the area around London, but near the city only from the 1480s: the Bishop of Ely's palace at Hatfield, 1485; the same builder, John Morton's, gateway at Lambeth Palace, c. 1490; and the Bishop of London's palace at Fulham, of 1506–22.[111] Within the City and Westminster, notable constructions in brick of the first four decades of the sixteenth century included Charterhouse's Wash-house Court (Fig. 208; early sixteenth century), Lincoln's Inn courts and gatehouse, the latter with an intended (but not completed) vault (1506–8, 1518 and 1534–5), Bridewell Palace (1515–22) and the Augmentations Office next to Westminster Hall (1536–7).[112]

Purchases of brick figure regularly in company accounts of the fifteenth and sixteenth centuries. Much was used for comparatively mundane purposes such as underpinning timber-framed buildings or for internal features such as a reredos in a kitchen and occasionally, though rarely, for partitions, i.e. as infilling of frames.[113] Perhaps significantly, on two occasions in the Carpenters' Company records, in 1484 and 1491, the bricklaying was carried out by masons.[114] Use of brick for extensions or even whole buildings, after the palaces and Lincoln's Inn of 1515–38, dates from the mid sixteenth century, as for the hall (1549) and parlour (1594) of Clothworkers' Hall and for unknown but substantial works at Weavers' Hall in 1542. In Treswell's surveys of 1610–12 there are a few brick buildings and a larger number of buildings with parts of their structure, besides the chimneys, built of brick; brick was also used rather than stone for garden walls and at least the upper parts of wells.[115]

On façades, brick could be used in a variety of decorative embellishments. The earliest known brickmakers in London, those engaged by London Bridge from 1404 and those working at Charterhouse around 1415, were foreigners from Flanders. Predictably similarities can be seen between many

183. Cheapside: detail of the 1547 painting, as later engraved by Grimm, showing decoration on house fronts on the south side of the street near St Mary le Bow

184. Detail of engraving derived from the 1547 Cheapside painting, showing brick roundels on the eaves of a house

185. A decorated brick found in Thames Street, late sixteenth century (MoL, A4626). The scene, from the story of Susannah and the Elders, shows the elders being led away under arrest.

fifteenth-century brick buildings in England and on the Continent; this includes a repertoire of decoration on brick surfaces which includes diaper patterns in darker bricks, banded arches, saw-tooth bands or strings. From the 1520s terracotta arms, roundels or door- and window-surrounds were apparently made in London.[116] There is a little evidence for these decorations on London buildings; in the foreground of the 1547 procession painting and the engraving from it (Fig. 184) is a house apparently with semi-circular roundels of brick along the eaves. Crow-stepped gables are shown in the same engraving, and still survive at Gray's Inn Hall of 1556–60.[117] From the late sixteenth century come a few examples of Dutch bricks embossed with biblical scenes, such as the story of Susannah and the Elders (Fig. 185), though none have been recovered from recent excavations. The choice of this story, the events of which are shown in several different designs, presumably reflects cocking a snook at civic authority, since it is the elders who get their just deserts; in the illustrated brick they are being led away under arrest.

Earth

Walls of unbaked earths, including mud mixed with lime and straw (known as cob in south-west England), were 'the stuff of rather humble buildings, mostly cottages, small farm-houses and their appendages', in pre-modern England.[118] Timber walls banked up with earth are known in tenth-century London buildings[119] and walls of earth forming tenement boundaries are mentioned from c. 1250.[120] They were frequently in need of rebuilding, as shown by cases in the *Assize of Nuisance* throughout the fourteenth and early fifteenth centuries; the majority of cases were located in suburban parishes or those within the walls but away from the city centres. Such walls could be as long as 200 ft, and were not necessarily only to be found on humbler properties: one ordered to be rebuilt in 1425 lay between the Domus Conversorum (House of the Converted Jews) in Chancery Lane and Clifford's Inn.[121] 'Mudwalls' were still to be seen near St James's Hermitage, Cripplegate, in 1516 and in Finsbury, immediately north of the City, in 1589. Other fourteenth- and fifteenth-century property boundaries were made of palings of wattle and daub and of daubed or plastered wood, which was probably the same thing.[122]

Conclusions

The secular buildings of the city, in 1600, were largely timber-framed. Stone buildings were a great rarity, though stone party or boundary walls could occasionally be seen. Brick was present but not prominently so. Records are particularly deficient as regards styles of timber-framing in the city, but it seems possible that the city shared in every conceivable style as it provided homes for a constant flux of immigrants both from the provinces and from abroad. The cosmopolitan air of buildings in late sixteenth-century London may have been a characteristic also of earlier centuries, when merchants from every European country stayed in the city for extended intervals.

Over the period, there was evidently a gradual standardisation of timber sizes; and stone, always expensive, was replaced by brick in almost every building context (foundations, boundary walls, window-frames and probably doorframes) by 1500. The chronology of these changes is still crude, so it cannot yet be known if London was a place where innovations were first implemented as far as building materials are concerned. It seems probable that jetties first occurred in towns, as an expression of a wish for more space on restricted sites; and jetties were clearly present in London by 1246, earlier than all known surviving examples in the countryside roundabout and, as far as can be told, examples in other British towns. In some decorative fashions, such as close-studding in the 1440s and the change to classical (ovolo) mouldings in timber-work in the 1570s, the capital adopted the new ideas at least as soon as they appeared elsewhere; unfortunately, the lack of physical evidence means that the timing of these and other innovations cannot at present be satisfactorily specified. It is possible that archaeological excavation, which is constantly unearthing timber-work on waterfront sites, may uncover parts of houses reused in the waterfront constructions. Such fragments, if datable by dendrochronology, may enable the development of building in London in timber, at least, to be charted more exactly.

Selective Gazetteer of Sites

Note

The sites are arranged by street-name in *c*. 1840; street-names pertaining then and later are given if available. Medieval street-names are used in the text when they are significantly different from those of 1840. The sites are shown on Maps 1–4 (pp. 236–41); where a site cannot be specified closely, the site-number is placed in the middle of the street. On a small number of sites, the address in 1840 is on a street built after the medieval period; in these cases it may be necessary to refer to Wild's map of 1840, or maps of a similar date, to locate the nineteenth-century street.

Abchurch Lane, see **142**

(1) Brewers' Hall, Addle Street (now Aldermanbury Square)

In 1403 William Betele, mercer, granted to John Hore, brewer, all his property in Adelane in the parish of St Mary Aldermanbury, which he had acquired from John Bosham and Thomas Welyngham. It stood between a tenement of St Paul's on the east, tenements of (a) Elsyng Spital, (b) once of John Makenhead, goldsmith, and (c) of St Paul's on the west, a tenement once of Stephen Bradele to the north and Adelane to the south. In 1404 Hore granted it to a group of clerks, including Sir Henry Jolipas (cf. **87**). The others quitclaimed to Jolipas by 1408, when he granted it to John Whitby, clerk, a chaplain, and eight citizens. Presumably the group represented the Brewers; they confirmed a life interest to Hore's wife Alice. In 1427/8 the sole remaining trustee, Whitby, granted the property to a further group, and in 1445 two of the survivors of this group granted it to another, this time all brewers.[1]

In 1423 building works included repairs to a cloister or tresaunce between the kitchen and hall, retiling of several buildings other than the hall, the making of an 'almarye' to stand in the kitchen and the construction of a hen-coop in the yard.[2] At the same time John Pekker, carpenter of Cambridge, was to amend the woodwork of the hall, and make a bay window on the south side like the bay windows in the new corner rent of the Charterhouse on Cornhill; the window was apparently to have six bays (i.e. segments) and a vault. Two other plain windows of two lights were also to be made on the south side of the hall. Another bay was to be underset (i.e. given a new sill-beam) after the manner of the bay window at the Inn of the Earl of Warwick (**185**). A building at the hall gate was also converted into an almshouse for poor brethren and sisters of the craft.[3]

In 1549 the four Viewers of the City arbitrated in a dispute between the company and Lewes Stokket, defendant, tenant of St Paul's property 'under the east end of the Brewers' Hall'.[4] The ground in dispute was a narrow strip containing posts which supported the first floor of part of Brewers' Hall (probably not the hall itself). Stow describes the hall as a 'fayre house'.[5] The post-Fire hall,[6] as shown on Ogilby and Morgan and in eighteenth-century engravings, lay at the back of a court, on the first floor.

The bombed hall site was partly excavated in 1958.[7] The east side of a north–south range on an alignment at an angle to the post-Fire hall was found, with fireplaces and one splayed window. In the post-Fire courtyard area were further foundations and a chalk well. It is possible that the north to south range was part of the domestic offices south-east of the medieval hall.

1. GL, MS 5503.
2. Accounts transcribed in *London English*, 152–61.

3. *Ibid.*, 147, 162–72. On Pekker, see Harvey, *English Medieval Architects*, 230.
4. *Viewers' Certificates*, 222.
5. Stow, i, 297.
6. Plan of site only, Mills & Oliver, *Survey*, v, 20.
7. Grimes 1968, 170–2.

(2) Addle Lane (later Street), 1383

In 1379 the executors of Rober Payn, joiner, sold a tenement in Addle Lane to Roger de Frenton, clerk, Thomas de Frenton and Thomas Carlton, broderer. In 1383 Carlton contracted with John Wolfey, carpenter,[1] to erect five shops and houses on the site. The five houses, forming a block 12 ft wide and 50 ft long, would each have a shop and two upper storeys, the first jettying 2½ ft and the second 2 ft into the street. The height of the ground floor would be 9 ft, that of the first floor 8 ft and the second floor 7 ft. Scantlings of principal posts, ground sills, somers and joists are given (see Chapter 6). The doors and *fenestres* (window-shutters) would be of Estrich board. The shops would have stairs and privies, partitions and possibly window-seats. The range would accommodate an alley, on one side of which (possibly behind the shops, though this is not clear) would stand a door with a porch and with a small chamber and window on either side. One chamber would contain the stairs to the hall. Behind three of the shops, which bordered a garden, Wolfey would erect a parlour on four posts (*pilers*), presumably principal posts, with two chambers in the manner of a *Tosalle* (unknown), 28 ft × 7½ ft (this presumably refers to the two chambers and not to the parlour).[2] It is not clear whether the parlour lay on the ground- or first-floor.

1. For Wolfey's career, see Harvey, *English Medieval Architects*, 344.
2. Tatchell 1962, 129–31.

(3) 7–9 Aldersgate Street

In his will of 1412 John Bradmore, surgeon, bequeathed the remainder of two tenements on the east side of Aldersgate, and two others in Barbican Street (**12**), to the Fraternity of the Trinity in St Botolph Aldersgate; he had lived in the southernmost of the Aldersgate tenements, which lay opposite the church.[1] By 1449–50 the property had three tenants.[2]

Edward VI granted the bulk of the fraternity property to William Harvey, Somerset Herald, in 1547;[3] this included properties **3**, **7** and **12**. In 1549 the Viewers decided that Harvey should have his lights into property **3** from the adjacent city ditch area, since there had at some time been a way there (i.e. probably on the outer lip of the ditch).[4] The three properties were all granted by Harvey to Robert Mellish in 1552 and by Mellish to the City for the use of the poor in Christ's Hospital in 1553.[5]

Property **3** was surveyed by Treswell in 1612, but (as also for **7** and **12**) without text of reference for the upper storeys (Fig. 76). This deficiency is puzzling, especially since one of the tenants was Ralph Treswell, presumably the surveyor himself, though he had a son of the same name. Treswell's tenancy (1) is described in a lease of 1623 as comprising a cellar and two storeys with garrets; a hall with a bay window and two clerestory windows lay on the first floor.[6]

The plan also shows part of the New Conduit, built in 1610 from

an endowment by Thomas Hayes; it was not replaced after the Great Fire.[7]

1. *Fraternity Register*, xviii.
2. *Ibid.*, 57.
3. GL, MS 10907.
4. *Viewers' Certificates*, 251.
5. GL, MS 13472.
6. *LSRT*, 34–5.
7. Strype 1720, i, 25.

(4)   19–20 Aldersgate Street

In the mid nineteenth century a house at this address featured two gables of three and a half storeys, each slightly jettied, and a ground floor divided into three shops (Fig. 186).[1] The building may be late sixteenth or early seventeenth century in date.

1. Photograph in GL.

(5)   Abbot of Walden's Inn, Aldersgate Street

Walden Abbey acquired land on the east side of Aldersgate from St Bartholomew's Priory in the reign of John, and on it built a town-house in about 1230. The abbey agreed with its neighbour, John de Coudres, to make a hedge between its land and his garden; that there should be no windows towards the garden except 12 ft high in the gable of the hall; and that there would be a barge-board on that gable, facing the garden; they also built a chapel at about the same time.[1] The agreement with Coudres was cited in 1323 when the neighbour, Thomas de Brackele, demolished half a common wall 40 ft long; the wall was to be rebuilt at Brackele's expense.[2] The Inn is mentioned as abutting the Jews' Garden in 1394 and 1447.[3]

1. *LTR*, xii, 49–51.
2. *Assize of Nuisance*, 272.
3. *Fraternity Register*, 87, 95.

(6)   133–136 Aldersgate Street

A single frame of four houses on the west side of Aldersgate was drawn and photographed in the nineteenth century (Fig. 178).[1] The block, of four and a half storeys, had canted bay windows running up three storeys from the first floor; at the corners and between two of the bays were carved grotesque pilasters. The northern two houses (nos. 133–4) may have originally been a single double-bayed house; the photographs suggest that the exterior was faced with both rectangular and square moulded panels. One of the upper chambers and the stair were sketched by J. P. Emslie (Figs. 149, 187). The interior and exterior decoration suggest a date in the late sixteenth century.

1. GL, MoL.

(7)   171–173 (later 190–194) Aldersgate Street (Trinity Hall)

In 1356 William Bever, merchant, granted to Thomas de Lynne, plasterer, and Maud his wife a tenement on the west side of Aldersgate in the parish of St Botolph which he had bought from the executors of Mary de Hungreye.[1] In 1392 Thomas de Lynne, plasterer, conveyed the property to Alan Brytte, carpenter; in 1417 Brytte, now described as a brewer, conveyed it, as a brewhouse

186.   (4) 19–20 Aldersgate Street, in the nineteenth century

187.   (6) 133–136 Aldersgate Street: staircase (J. P. Emslie 1879)

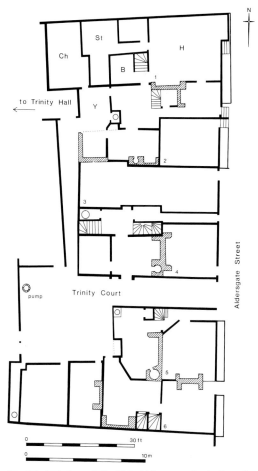

188.   (7) 171–173 (later 190–194) Aldersgate, including site of hall of the Fraternity of the Holy Trinity (Treswell 1611)

called the Falcon on the Hoop, to a group. The brotherhood of the Holy Trinity in St Botolph Aldersgate acquired the Falcon on the Hoop brewhouse from the executors of John Mason in 1431 and continued to lease it as a brewhouse; up to 1456, when their surviving records cease, there is no evidence that the hall was used by the fraternity. In 1463 their table, cups and linen were stored in the roof loft of the church. Eighteenth-century drawings and sketches of the hall show glass with an inscription referring to a church-warden of 1483–6 and 1503–4, and shields in stained glass including those of a churchwarden of 1495–6 and a warden of the fraternity in 1499–1500 (Figs. 13, 118a). By this time therefore the fraternity were presumably using the hall, as they certainly were at the time of the Reformation.[2]

The hall, six tenements to the south and eight tenements in Trinity Alley were granted to William Harvey in 1547, and passed to Christ's Hospital in 1553 (see 3). The parish leased the hall 'for assemblies and counsails' in 1548, and throughout the later sixteenth century from the hospital. In 1612 the Farriers' Company leased the hall for fifty-one years.[3] Treswell surveyed the property (not including the tenements in Trinity Alley) in 1610–11 (Fig. 188), but there is no text of reference and the upper storeys of the buildings can only be partly reconstructed.

A section through the first-floor Trinity Hall was engraved in 1742 (Fig. 129) and further drawings were made of the interior in the later eighteenth and early nineteenth centuries (e.g. Fig. 118b). The hall comprised at least four bays, with moulded arch-couples rising from corbels of angels holding shields. A fifth bay seems indicated by the interior view, but is not shown in the section. The roof had double tiers of cusped S-form wind-braces in each bay; a construction date of 1480–1500 seems likely. A fireplace was

inserted in the south wall c. 1600, perhaps also the date of panelling and fluted columns or pilasters placed beneath the angel corbels which are shown in the engraving.

South of the hall lay six tenements fronting onto Aldersgate, also part of the Bever property in 1356. Leases of 1572, 1577 and 1581 and views of 1630 and 1631 suggest that the buildings were of three storeys (the southernmost perhaps of four); tenancies (1) and (6) had cellars, that of the former described as 'arched with brick' in 1630.[4]

On the plan of 1610–11 four of the houses have individual fences about 3 ft in front of them, encroaching into the street, a feature not seen elsewhere in the Treswell surveys or found on any other contemporary site.

1.   *Fraternity Register*, 62.
2.   *Ibid.*, xvii–xviii.
3.   GL, MS 10907, 10907A.
4.   *LSRT*, 36.

(8)   Duke's Place and other buildings (including Woodmongers' Hall II) within the former precinct of Holy Trinity Priory, Aldgate (now covered by Mitre Street, Mitre Place and Creechurch Place)

In 1534 Henry VIII granted the site and all the possessions of the late priory of Holy Trinity to Thomas Audley.[1] At first Audley offered the priory church to the parishioners of St Katherine Cree in exchange for their own church; he may have intended to develop the Leadenhall Street frontage. When they refused, he pulled down the church and steeple, built in various parts of the priory and died there in 1544.[2] Building accounts of 1541–2 suggest overhauling of the kitchen, buttery and 'vaults', and the making of a new jakes in the court; refurbishment (especially of glazing) included the Comptroller's Chamber, the great chamber next to the hall, the great new chamber, the parlour, Lord Bayne's Chamber, the great gallery and the 'great chamber next the street side'.[3] The site passed via Audley's daughter to her husbands, the second of whom was Thomas Howard, Duke of Norfolk; the main house was thereafter known as Duke's Place. This name is attached to the former west range of the cloister from at least the time of Ogilby and Morgan's map of 1677, and it therefore seems likely that this was also the site of Audley's mansion, which would in turn have been based on the prior's lodging. Fragments of this range were observed in the early nineteenth century when it fell down.

The precinct of Holy Trinity Priory at the end of the sixteenth century can be reconstructed from plans of most of its buildings drawn by John Symonds probably about 1586.[4] There are separate plans at ground- and first-floor levels.

The main range between the Great Court and the cloister (i.e. the mansion of Audley and later Norfolk) was, on present evidence, doubled in width to the west in the monastic period. On the first floor, now on the cloister side, lay the hall; by 1586 the range fronting the court was divided into tenements, but its run of bay windows suggests a long room, perhaps a gallery, of some size. In view of the reduced circumstances of the priory's final years, this rebuilding on the first floor may have been part of Audley's scheme in the 1530s, the date of the nearest analogies for such window-arrangements (e.g. a series of four rectangular bay windows at first-floor level forming part of a range built on the east side of New Palace Yard, Westminster, in the reign of Henry VIII).[5] A further range called 'the gallery' bordered the south side of the garden occupying the southern half of the main court. The stone arches of the main gatehouse to Creechurch Lane survived until the early nineteenth century.

The body of the church was radically transformed. By 1586 the roofs of both chancel and nave had been removed, a way had been knocked into the chancel through the ladychapel, the north transept had fallen or had been knocked down, and two suites of rooms had been inserted at first-floor level: one suite over the ladychapel, and

190. (8) Duke's Place, Aldgate: one of the buildings in the great court (J. Crowther 1884); probably one of those on the plans by Symonds in about 1586

189. (8) Duke's Place, Aldgate: houses built above the arches of the choir of Holy Trinity Priory, Aldgate, drawn during demolition after the fire of 1800 by D. T. Powell

a second (called the Ivy Chamber) above the crossing overlooking the former chancel on one side and the ruins of the nave on the other (Fig. 43b). A gallery led from this apartment to the grand house. The gallery and the chamber within the crossing may be the rooms referred to in the accounts of 1541–2. Certainly by 1586 a mansion occupied the former prior's range and the western half of the precinct, and two suites of rooms had colonised the body of the church. The arcades of the twelfth-century choir were discovered when buildings above them were damaged in a local fire in 1800 (Fig. 189).

From the 1540s, also, parts of the precinct were let out to others. Counterparts of leases issued by Audley and the Duke of Norfolk were listed at the time of sale of most of the precinct (but not the mansion) to the City in 1592.[6] This was perhaps the occasion of the survey drawn by Symonds, then in Burghley's employ, though since Burghley was not directly involved the actual reason for drawing the plan remains unknown; it might have related to Howard's application to the Crown for a licence to alienate the property.[7] Six leases date from Audley's time (1540–4); other leases are listed, probably incompletely, and date from 1564–5, 1582–3, 1586–7 and 1591–2. Of the tenants shown in the survey, Edmond Auncell appears on the list of 1582–3 and two others, Richard Bedoe and Bryan Nayler, in 1591–2. Eleven main tenants or occupiers are named on the plans in 1592, and several areas of the ground-plan are marked 'Tenements' without further specification. Some of these buildings, rebuilt, were still visible in the 1880s (Fig. 190).

In the plans a William Kerwin occupied most of the western range of the cloister (i.e. the mansion), the west side of the cloister, and the garden occupying the southern half of the Great Court, in which he was erecting new buildings. Apart from the outline of their foundations shown by Symonds, the nature of these buildings is unknown; but by 1677, as shown on Ogilby and Morgan's map, the alley to the south of them was known as Sugar Baker's Yard. William Kerwin was Master of the Masons' Company in 1579 and the City Mason who rebuilt Ludgate in 1585–6.[8] Kerwin may have lived elsewhere, for he was a churchwarden of St Helen's Bishopsgate in 1570–1 and 1571–2[9] and was buried in St Helen's in 1594; his tomb survives.[10] It is therefore possible that he used part of the priory as his place of work, or as a builder's yard, or even as a quarry for building works such as Ludgate, for which he supplied at least some of the stone.[11]

There is also some evidence for the making of pottery, by foreign immigrants, in and around the precinct. A watching brief following excavations of 1979 on the west side of the cloister, that is in the range occupied by Kerwin and probably the centre of the Audley mansion, recorded a pit containing delftware wasters.[12] This lay in one of the ground-floor rooms of the western half of the range, fronting onto the Great Courtyard to the west. On Symonds' plan this room is shown with a large oven of domestic character in one corner. It seems unlikely that this was a kiln; the main objection, besides its comparatively small size, is that it lay in the middle of a building complex. The flue went up the side of what had been the Duke's Hall; the room was used as Woodmongers' Hall (II) in 1612 and by the parishioners of St James Duke's Place for worship, their church (on the Symonds plan, the former monastic chapter house) having fallen down in 1572.[13] The possibility that immigrant potters were at work in the precinct is explored in a forthcoming study.[14]

1. VCH, *London i*, 472.
2. Stow, i, 142.
3. PRO, E/101/674/24.
4. 1592 in Lethaby 1900; for refinement of the date of the plans to about 1586, see Schofield & Lea, in preparation.
5. Colvin 1966, 30–1 and Plate 11.
6. CLRO, Letter Book, AB, 106; Repertory, 22, f. 379.
7. Repertory, 22, ff. 414ᵛ–416.
8. GL, MS 4318; *Chamber Accounts*, xix, 23, 38–9, 179, 181.
9. GL, MS 6836.

10. RCHM, *City*, 23.
11. *Chamber Accounts*, 38.
12. MoL, sitecode HTP79.
13. Harben, *Dictionary*, 318.
14. Schofield & Lea, in preparation.

(9) 15–18 Aldgate, 1 Jewry Street

Vaults forming an L-shape beneath property at the corner of Aldgate and Jewry Streets, immediately inside the medieval gate, were seen during demolition of two houses of possibly Elizabethan date (Fig. 84).[1] Five bays were recorded, each bay almost square in construction but conforming to the site boundary corner of slightly less than 90 degrees. Pointed vaults of greensand ribs sprang from corbels, some carved but others only chamfered projections. At the vault centres were grotesque moulded stone lion faces, all made to take iron rings in their mouths, one of which has survived. The interior wall facing and the vault was of small squared chalk blocks. A semicircular arch in the centre of the south wall probably led to a further series of vaults, and a similar passage may have led off from the west end of the L shape. No windows were seen, and it was presumed the iron rings were for the suspension of lamps; but loading chutes had at a later date been cut into the north and east sides, and it is likely these were adapted windows. No entrance was found but was presumed to be on the site of the Victorian stairs, in the inner angle of the two arms. The vault would originally have been about 13 ft high. The stone bosses were retained by the Guildhall Museum.[2]

The corner property incorporating the L-shaped vault was leased by St Katherine's Hospital, with the assent of Holy Trinity Priory, Aldgate, to Robert de la Rocle in 1249 × 60; tenants are recorded until 1407/8.[3] The houses above the vaults, and other houses on the south side of Aldgate within the gate, are shown in a drawing of 1862.[4]

1. Loftus-Brock 1877.
2. MoL, Acc. Nos. 7253–5, 7257.
3. *HTA Cartulary*, 36–7.
4. GL.

(10) The Crowne, Aldgate (later 6–8 Aldgate High Street)

Between 1170 and 1197 Stephen, prior of Holy Trinity Priory, Aldgate, leased to Edric the Merchant land in the parish of St Botolph, Aldgate, which Richard the chaplain bought from Norman, son of Alfred Horeh, for 4*s. p.a.*[1] The priory cartulary records several tenants until 1268, when Albreda widow of Robert Lambard granted the property to William son of Stephen de Sharmbrok; in this grant the property is described as extending from the king's highway (Aldgate) on the south to the priory garden on the north, and between the cemetery of St Botolph to the west and the land of Mundekinus Trentmars (also priory property) to the east. In 1331 the priory leased the property to Thomas de Essex and his wife Isabella, the shop having burnt down; a new shop and solar were to be built by the tenant. In 1363, Thomas de Caxton, butcher, was in possession by right of his wife Alice, daughter of Nicholas Derman; he granted the property to William Cosyn, potter (*ollarius*). In 1398 Cosyn's heir Richard Knyght quitclaimed to Robert Burford, bellmaker. By 1458 the property had passed via Alexander Sprot to the church of St Botolph, to support a chantry.

In 1546 Thomas Bartlett and Richard Mody purchased it from the Court of Augmentations and sold it to John Margettson, brewer; two years later he sold it to David Gittins and John Lloyd, vintners. The tenement was then described as being 139 ft long on the east, 179 ft on the west, 73 ft wide on the north and 47 ft wide to the south, street side. In 1563 Gittins and John Lloyd sold the property to Johanne Turnbull, widow of Thomas Turnbull and formerly widow of Margettson, alebrewer; the property was thus probably a hostelry by this date. In 1569 she leased the Crowne to Richard Irme, woodmonger, and Johanna his wife for thirty years at £12 *p.a.* The attached schedule of fittings reads:

In the inner parlour: 7 panes of glass in the window there

Great Parlour: 7 panes of glass; wainscotted round; settles and all the roof ceiled with wainscott

The Hall: 14 panes of glass

The Great Chamber: 16 panes of glass and a screen

The chamber next the great chamber: 20 panes of glass

The corner chamber: 3 panes of glass

The Kitchen: a bar of iron in the chimney 'going throughout', a long ladder of 18 rungs, a short ladder of 12, a bucket of 4 hoops of iron for the well, a wheel and rope

12 doors with locks and keys and 2 bolts of iron, 'hangynge wyndowes' and 'shuttings wyndowes' to the parlour, hall and chambers; 5 stables 'with racks and moningiers.'

The Crowne must have been inherited by Thomas Margettson, merchant tailor, who sold it in 1581 to William Cooch, innholder, for £100.[2] By Cooch's will it passed to Christ's Hospital in 1584[3] and was surveyed by Treswell in 1610 (Fig. 61).

The documentary history does not enable suggestions to be made about the age of the various parts, although the front may have been quite ancient, as it had to be taken down in 1665. The text of reference describes ranges of three storeys on all three sides of the first courtyard, and two storeys round the second yard; a total of twenty chambers above the ground floor, fifteen of them heated.[4]

A watching brief of 1986 recorded part of the south-west side of the property, forming the boundary with the churchyard of St Botolph; the lower part of a stone wall with a chamfered plinth was observed (Fig. 159).[5] This is probably part of the south-west wall of the main range of the inn as shown by Treswell.

1. *HTA Cartulary*, 887.
2. All deeds in GL, MS 13133; for a fuller account see *HG*, ii.
3. GL, MS 13134.
4. CH View Book, ii, 132–4; *LSRT*, 39–40.
5. MoL, sitecode BOT86.

(11) Brittany Inn/Pembroke's Inn/Bergavenny House/ Stationers' Hall II, Ave Maria Lane

In 1317 Adam le Plasterer undertook to finish off the walls and flues of the hall of the Earl of Richmond with plaster of Paris. The 'inside and outside' of the walls are mentioned.[1] The site of the Earl's property in this case appears to be Brittany/Pembroke Inn, Ave Maria Lane.[2]

In 1331 John of Brittany, Earl of Richmond, granted his property in England, which included Britanny Inn, to Mary, widow of Aymer de Valence, Earl of Pembroke. In 1352 an inspection of encroachment near Ludgate by the City found that the countess had built a small tower (*turellum*) '*cum cameris et cellario*' on the common soil; in 1358 the great gate of the hostel of the Countess was mentioned.[3] In 1389 the earldom of Pembroke became extinct, and the property passed to William Beauchamp, created Baron Bergavenny in 1392. In the sixteenth century the house came to be called Bergavenny House, and was so known to Stow who described it as 'one great house builded of stone and timber' at the north end of Ave Maria Lane.[4] The house was sold to become Stationers' Hall II in 1611.

1. Salzman, *Building*, 425–6.
2. Though this has been doubted by Page 1923, 145, n. 64.
3. *Munimenta Gildhallae*, ii, 455; *Cal. LB, G*, 132.
4. Stow, i, 339.

(12) White Horse Inn, Barbican Street (later Barbican)

These two tenements were part of the property of the Fraternity of the Holy Trinity at St Botolph's (see **4**), passing to William Harvey in 1547 and to Christ's Hospital in 1553.[1] As with the other ex-fraternity property, there is no text with the survey by Treswell (Fig. 191). The front was rebuilt by 1624, when it was viewed, and repaired extensively in 1680, after being condemned as 'very defective'.[2] The inn appears on Ogilby and Morgan's map of 1677 (b59);

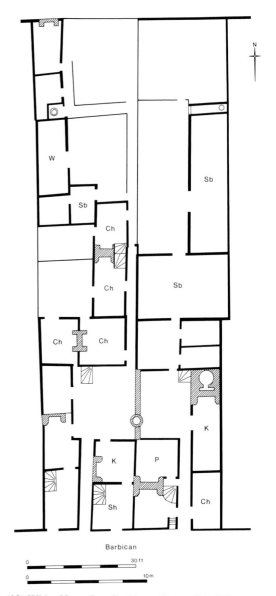

191.   **(12)** White Horse Inn, Barbican (Treswell, 1611)

the back buildings seem to have also been partially remodelled by this date.

1. *Fraternity Register*, viii, 43–4.
2. CH View Book, i, 27, 29; GL, MS 13475.

(13) Gisors or Gerard's Hall, Basing Lane

The Gisors family can be traced in London for at least three hundred years.[1] There were two generations before the first of whom anything is known, John (I) Gisors, alderman in 1243 and twice mayor; in 1242 he owned a house in the Vintry. The family owned much property in the city centre, and John (II) Gisors' 'new hall' in the parish of St Mildred Bread Street is mentioned in his will of 1296.[2] John (II) was a pepperer, but his father was a great wine merchant of Henry III's time, and the family continued being prominent vintners. The principal remains of this house, recorded in 1852, were the fine undercroft, which was probably used by John (III) as cellarage for wine bought from Gascons, for which in 1320–3 he was earning £10–12 a year. The place was known as Gerard's Hall by *c.* 1449.[3]

The undercroft formed the west side of a yard, its north side opening directly on the lane.[4] It had windows on three sides, the fourth side being the party-wall with the adjacent western property.

The undercroft (Fig. 82a–c) of 5 × 2 bays, measured 48 ft 2 in by 21 ft 2 in internally, the vaulting quadripartite and virtually square. Central columns 12 in in diameter stood on moulded bases, with moulded caps similar but not identical to each other. The walls were of roughly squared, coursed blocks, and the flooring may have been of Purbeck marble. At the north end of the west aisle a stone stair led to Basing Lane, divided from the undercroft by a wall which ran to the vaulting. In the middle of the flight was an arched inner doorway; an arched external doorway is presumed. In the south-west corner another smaller arched doorway led to an intramural passage and steps, probably up into the chamber above. Another arch in the west side of this passage may have led to a further undercroft, suggesting communication between properties. The undercroft was lit by six windows with internal arches on corbels, their sections similar to the groining. The bottom splay of each window was steeply angled so that the sill of the outside window was slightly higher than the crown of the vault. Externally the windows were small, but with moulded arches. Original external ground level was clearly below these windows, and engravings show that the topmost step was about 8 ft above the undercroft floor, which would raise the crown of the vaulting and the tops of the windows about 6 ft above the ground. Near the stair in the west wall several merchants' marks were carved, including two coats of arms. During demolition what was perhaps a ground-floor west door into the room above (perhaps the hall?) was seen, and a moulded stone recovered. This and the groining details, with the caps, date the building to around 1290. The undercroft was removed for the western extension of Cannon Street in 1852, the stones being numbered and taken to Crystal Palace for re-erection. Instead they were eventually ground up to make the prehistoric monsters in the gardens.[5]

Stow also noted arched gates of Caen stone to the lane. The kitchen lay in 1310 on the south side of the property, when it is mentioned in a boundary dispute between Thomas Gisors and a neighbour.[6]

1. Thrupp, *Merchant Class*, 345–6.
2. *Cal. Chart, R*, 1226–57, 269; *Cal. Wills*, i, 128.
3. Williams 1963, 118; *Paston Letters*, i, 54.
4. White 1853.
5. *Cal. Wills*, i, 644, n. 8.
6. Stow, i, 348; *Assize of Nuisance*, 156.

(14)   9–10 Basing Lane
Part of the bequest of John Watson to the Clothworkers' Company in 1555; two of these houses were ex-chantry property attached to St Andrew Baynard Castle.[1]

Two adjoining houses on the south side of the Lane (later nos. 9–10), surveyed by Treswell in 1612 (Fig. 192), were of similar design, though with differences. They were of two-room plan with separate kitchens, and in each case a gallery led from the house over the yard at first-floor level, to a room over the kitchen in the case of the east house. This house rose to four and a half storeys, the west house to three and a half; both had cellars under their shops.[2]

1. CD, Box 54.
2. *LSRT*, 44.

12–14 Basing Lane, see 31

(15)   20 Basing Lane (later 25 Cannon Street West)
Part of the bequest of John Watson to the Clothworkers' Company in 1555, it was rebuilt by the company in 1560–1. The accounts do not mention bricks, suggesting that lath and plastering may have been used.[1] Treswell's survey (Fig. 193) and text of reference of 1612 show a building of one room on the ground floor; hall, kitchen and study on the first floor; and chambers above to a height of four and a half storeys on a cellar.[2]

1. CD, Box 54; CRW, Accts., 1560–1.
2. *LSRT*, 45.

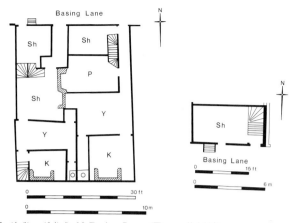

192. (*left*)   (**14**) 9–10 Basing Lane (Treswell 1612)

193. (*right*)   (**15**) 20 Basing Lane, later 25 Cannon Street (Treswell 1612)

(16)   Weavers' Hall, 22 Basinghall Street
The hall of the Weavers is mentioned in 1456, but Consitt[1] thought that this was probably a hired room, and that the company did not possess a hall until 1498. The hall is not mentioned in Harley MS 541 (*c.* 1475); and the earliest recorded association of the company with the site of their hall is 1498, when the 'bailiffs of the guild of weavers of London' acquired property in the parish of St Michael Bassishaw.[2] Private deeds from 1313 show that the property lay on the east side of Basinghall Street.[3] Repairs or extension are suggested by the purchase of 15,500 bricks and much carpentry in 1542; a parlour was built or rebuilt with contributions from the company in 1550–51.[4] In Stow's time the hall was the middle of three company halls on the east side of Basinghall Street, between Masons' Hall (not in gazetteer) and Girdlers' Hall (17).[5] Inventories of the hall survive from 1547 and 1575; in the latter year a buttery, a parlour next to the hall, and a parlour next to the kitchen are mentioned. In the last was 'a new lome to weave fether bed tykes'.[6]

1. Consitt 1933, 94, n. 5.
2. GL, MS 4677.
3. GL, MS 4662.
4. Consitt 1933, 252; *ibid.*, 272–6.
5. Stow, i, 285.
6. GL, MS 4646.

(17)   Girdlers' Hall, Basinghall Street
In 1420 a group of mercers sold two tenements and a garden on the east side of Basinghall Street to a group of five persons, including three girdlers. In 1431 Andrew Hunte left two tenements and a piece of land in the parish of St Michael Bassishaw to the vicar of St Lawrence Jewry and the wardens of the Girdlers; the hall was in use by 1439, when the main tenement was described as having a great gate and a solar over it. Girdlers' Hall in Basinghall Street is mentioned in Harley MS 541 (*c.* 1475). The company set up a bay window on the east side of the premises in 1496.[1]

1. Barker 1957, 35–6; GL, MS 5792.

(18)   Bakewell (Blackwell) Hall, Basinghall Street
In 1280 Sir Roger Clifford gave his great hall next to Guildhall to the City; apparently a John Fitzjohn had built it on the site of Jews' houses destroyed in 1263. In 1293 the City transferred it to John de Bauquell or Backwell, from whom it received its name. In 1395–6 the hall and a garden in St Lawrence Jewry were acquired by the City, to be used as a market-place for all kinds of woollen cloth; foreigners were instructed to bring their woollen cloth for sale here.[1]

In 1523 Thomas Cremour, draper and keeper of the seld of

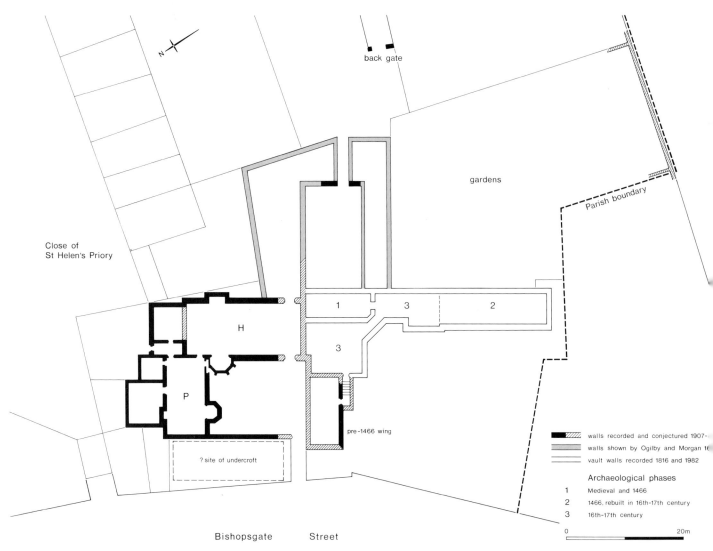

back gate

gardens

Parish boundary

Close of
St Helen's Priory

1   3   2

H

3

P

? site of undercroft

pre-1466 wing

N

walls recorded and conjectured 1907–
walls shown by Ogilby and Morgan 16
vault walls recorded 1816 and 1982

Archaeological phases
1   Medieval and 1466
2   1466, rebuilt in 16th–17th century
3   16th–17th century

0   20m

Bishopsgate   Street

194.   (22) Crosby Place, Bishopsgate: plan of the site after *Survey of London* and excavations of 1982

Blackwell Hall, rebuilt the place: on the 'nether floor' were two storeys with four gables, a clerestorey of windows and at least six bay windows, a chapel, closet and two new chimneys, with partitions, windows and doors.[2] In 1560 the house of Sir Thomas White was incorporated into the Hall as an alnager's office.[3] After more repairs in 1564–77 and 1584–7, the complex was pulled down in 1587 and rebuilt. Richard May, merchant tailor, bequeathed £300 towards the new building; the final cost was £2,500.[4]

Drawings by Schnebbelie of the hall and courts during final demolition in 1819 provide further details of its structural history. As Stow described it, the hall of the property lay north to south at the west side of a court entered from Basinghall Street. Stow remembered arms at several points around the house, especially in the walls of the hall, which he attributed, probably erroneously, to the Basing family. Kingsford suggests he was describing the Clifford arms from memory.[5] The hall was built on stone vaults including Caen stone, still visible in Stow's time.

1.   *Cal. LB, H*, 449.
2.   Repertory, 4, ff. 157[V]–158.
3.   CCPR, Blackwell Hall, 1560.
4.   Journal, 22, ff. 140–2; *LTR*, x, 49–51. For further works of 1612–15 see GL, MS 12848.
5.   Stow, i, 286–7; ii, 337.

(19)   **Derby House, [St] Benet's Hill (now College of Arms, Queen Victoria Street)**
Stow places this house on the east side of the Hill, next to Woodmongers' Hall (147).[1] It was acquired and rebuilt by Thomas Stanley, first Earl of Derby, who died there in 1497. The third Earl exchanged it with Edward VI for lands in Lancashire, and Queen Mary granted it to the College of Heralds in 1555.[2]

The house formed three sides of a quadrangle, entered by a gate from St Benet's Hill to the west; the hall lay in the south range and the east and west ranges enclosed a garden on the north side.[3] Kingsford records that some years prior to his writing, three tablets were found in the basement. Two, which showed the eagle's claw (a Stanley badge) and the Three Legs of the Isle of Man, were built into the east wall of the college; the third (presumably now lost) had the portcullis of Beaufort (Thomas Stanley married Margaret Beaufort, the mother of Henry VII).

The site of the house is covered by the present College in Queen Victoria Street (which lies across the southern part of the property).
1.   Stow, ii, 16–17.
2.   *LTR*, x, 105–6.
3.   Godfrey & Wagner 1963, 5–8.

(20) Abbot of Bury St Edmunds' Inn, Bevis (Buries) Marks

The modern street name (first mentioned in 1720) commemorates the house of the abbots of Bury St Edmunds, who appear to have held much of the site from the mid twelfth century, shortly after the foundation of Holy Trinity Priory, Aldgate, the precinct of which formed the property's east boundary. The Grocers' Company was founded at a dinner attended by twenty-two pepperers at 'the Abbot's place of Bury' in 1345. In 1422 the wardmote of Aldgate indicted a jetty in Bury's rent as being too low, to the nuisance of passers-by.[1] In 1528 the abbot and convent leased the house to two London merchants as keepers, one of the conditions being that they provided twelve beds with bedding when the abbot was in town. In 1540 Burys Markys was granted to Sir Thomas Heneage, in whose family it stayed for several generations.[2] In 1559 'Mr' Heneage agreed that in breaking ground to make a sluice before his gate he had broken into City ground, and succeeded in obtaining licence to continue.[3] Heneage House is shown on Ogilby and Morgan's map in 1677, but it is not clear where the hall of the house lay.

1. *Cal. Plea and Mem. R.*, 1414–23, 130.
2. *LTR*, x, 69–70; Stow, i, 146–7.
3. CCPR, Bevis Marks 1559.

Billiter Lane (later Street), see 72

Bishopsgate: the nineteenth-century division of Bishopsgate into Bishopsgate Street Within and Bishopsgate Street Without, each with its own series of street-numbers, is followed here.

(21) Bishopsgate Street Within/Leadenhall Street, see 120

(22) Crosby Place, Bishopsgate Street Within

Sometime before 1466 John Crosby leased from the nunnery of St Helen Bishopsgate a large house, once in the tenure of Caetano Pinelli, merchant of Genoa. In 1466, the year of his election as Member of Parliament for the City, Crosby renewed the lease. Crosby rebuilt the property between this date and his death in 1475 and was in the process of building in 1468;[1] his crest survives on a boss in the vault of the hall oriel.

The lease of 1466[2] suggests that additional properties were being added to Crosby's existing tenancy. Besides the Pinelli–Crosby house in Bishopsgate, the resulting property included a lane from the east gate of the house which ran south-east, six messuages on the Bishopsgate frontage between the existing house on the south and the Tower of St Helen's (presumably a gatehouse) to the north, one 'below the gate under the tower', with a vacant plot behind it stretching 58½ ft to the east, and two further messuages 'below the close' of the priory. The priory also allowed vehicular access through the close to St Mary Axe (street).

After Crosby's death the house was successively used as a lodging by Richard, Duke of Gloucester (1483), and Burgundian ambassadors (1495), and was leased by Bartholomew Reed (mayor, 1501), Sir John Rest (mayor, 1505), Sir Thomas More (1523), and Antonio Bonvisi (1524–47). Throughout the sixteenth and early seventeenth centuries Crosby Place was owned or tenanted by prominent citizens or ambassadors. The East India Company were tenants in 1627–33.[3]

The buildings of Crosby Place (site plan, Fig. 194; Ogilby and Morgan's map of the site, Fig. 195) are known through a combination of documentary study, antiquarian observations, archaeological excavation and recording during and after the removal of the hall to Chelsea in 1908. Various attempts to reconstruct the plan culminate in that of Godfrey in *Survey of London: Crosby Place* (adapted for Fig. 194), which shows the following elements:

(1) *Street range to Bishopsgate*. This presumably comprised the six tenements mentioned in 1466, and incorporated an entry. Six tenements, five to the north and one to the south of the foregate, are mentioned in 1589.[4] An undercroft with two 'fifteenth-century'

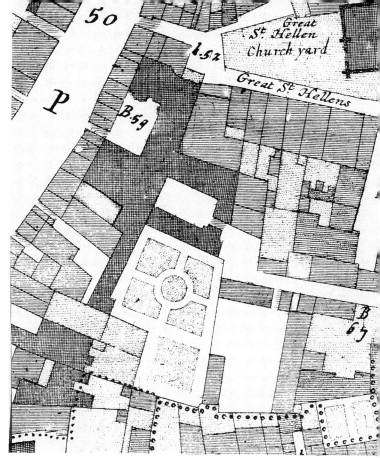

195.   (22) Crosby Place, Bishopsgate, from Ogilby and Morgan's map of 1677

arches was discovered in 1902 beneath 25 Bishopsgate Street Within, the building on the north side of the nineteenth-century (and presumably medieval) entry into the main court. This undercroft may be that shown as detached from the main vaults of the house by Nash in 1816 (Fig. 196), about 57 ft × 17 ft, with at least one arched stone rib and entrances in what must be the north and south ends. If so, it would have lain beneath the first three tenements north of the gate, its north end in line with the north wall of the hall to the east. The street range had a back wall of squared stones as high as the parapet of the hall behind, with no windows in it to the court.[5]

(2) The *hall* lay at the back of the rectangular courtyard, its screens passage in line with the entry from the street. It measured 69 ft × 27 ft, and 40 ft high. The ornate roof, windows and oriel window (Figs. 39, 40, 105, 116, 136) are described in detail above (pp. 102–3, 119). The hall had a side fireplace (Fig. 128c), probably original, and any central hearth it may also have had is likely to have been merely decorative;[6] the floor was of Purbeck marble. No dais was detected by nineteenth and early twentieth-century antiquaries who examined the building.

(3) The *parlour block* formed the north side of the court, entered from the high end of the hall (Fig. 74a). Goss[7] thought that the two-storeyed block was originally one undivided chamber, later divided by the intermediate floor, but this seems unlikely. The parlour on the ground floor and Council Chamber above, both of which had fireplaces (Fig. 128c) are described in Chapter 4 (p. 67, parlour section). The nature of the double-storeyed bay window on this side is uncertain; it seems to be largely conjectural.[8]

(4) *Rooms on north side of the hall and parlour*. From east to west four other rooms can be traced on the north side of the hall and the parlour. An engraving from the north of 1816 (Fig. 124) shows the ashlar northern façade of the two north-east apartments. The second room from the east was a corridor or vestibule to the parlour (see plan). Above its door was a run of three lights divided by chamfered mullions of brick or stone beneath a straight hood. A

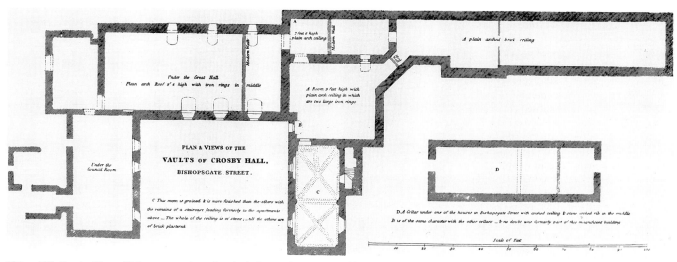

196.   (22) Crosby Place, Bishopsgate: plan of vaults below main ranges and inset plan of cellar below a house on Bishopsgate Street (F. Nash 1816)

drawing made at the time of demolition[9] shows that glazing bars still retained some diamond-shaped quarries. The third room was a staircase, in this position by 1566, but not datable by the antiquaries.[10] A staircase would have been required to reach the Council Chamber above the parlour, and it is likely that one lay in this position from 1466. The fourth chamber seemed to be a sixteenth-century addition.

(5) *Rooms on south side of the entrance court*. The south range, of smaller proportions to the parlour block, lay on an undercroft of two quadripartite bays, with freestone arches and chalk infill (plan, Fig. 196); presumably a fourteenth-century undercroft from the previous house. The undercroft had three windows, that to the south-

west larger than the others. The vaulting arrangement shows that the entrance at the north-east corner was original, and a stair led from within the south side up to the house above. The ground-level range was rebuilt by Crosby several feet shorter and was of two storeys. The ground floor had a window of two lights, with a centre corbel in the form of an angel, in its south wall. This has given rise to the suggestion that the room was a chapel, but the grounds are dubious (the undercroft does not by itself indicate a chapel above; and the corbel is a form found on secular buildings, cf. **118**).

(6) A *second court* lay to the east of the hall by the time of Ogilby and Morgan (Fig. 195); this was probably open space in the fifteenth century.

197.   (22) Crosby Place, Bishopsgate: view of the area from the William Goodman drawing (originally *c.* 1599?, but possibly a later copy) preserved at Merchant Taylors' Hall, showing what is probably meant to be Crosby Place; engraved 1825

(7) The *back gate and garden*. To the east of the buildings forming the second court lay a gate to the alley leading to St Mary Axe. This comprised a single depressed arch of several moulded orders, probably in brick, in a brick façade with ashlar stone jambs (Fig. 67). Hammond engraved three doors from unknown positions in the house, and recorded their mouldings (Fig. 122b).

(8) *Vaults and ranges subsequent to Crosby's time*. In 1594 Sir John Spencer added a warehouse (built on a garden?) to the south-east of the complex.[11] A long narrow building is shown in this position by Ogilby and Morgan. Spencer is also thought to have built a tower, which was said to be in need of repair in 1627.[12] The site of this tower is not certain, but a tower is shown behind houses which may represent Crosby Place in the engraving of Goodman's 1599 sketch-map (Fig. 197). Secondly, Ogilby and Morgan show a range running south from the south end of the hall. The brick vault for this range is shown by Nash (Fig. 196) and its sixteenth-century foundations were recorded during redevelopment in 1982.[13] The range above would have bordered the garden to the east in a manner very similar to a range also on a single cellar at **72** in Fenchurch Street. Between the new range and Bishopsgate Street Godfrey, following Papworth, shows in error several further vaults, and interpolates here the vault which properly lies beneath the street range further north.

The rebuilding of the hall of Crosby Place in Chelsea is described by Clapham & Godfrey.[14]

1. Stow, i, 172–3; Salzman, *Building*, 38.
2. Transcribed by Goss 1908, 20–2.
3. *LTR*, x, 102–4.
4. *Inq. PM*, III, 133.
5. *Survey of London: Crosby Place*, 42.
6. *Ibid.*, 47.
7. Goss 1908, 28.
8. Godfrey, in *Survey of London: Crosby Place*, 42–3.
9. Goss 1908, 27.
10. *Survey of London: Crosby Place*, 49.
11. *Ibid.*, 61.
12. Goss 1908, 84.
13. MoL, sitecode BOP82.
14. Clapham & Godfrey 1912, 121–38.

(23) Hall and Almshouses of the Fraternity of Parish Clerks, Bishopsgate Street Within

The Parish Clerks were granted a site, in what is now Clerk's Court and perhaps part of Wrestlers' Court (its continuation to Camomile Street) in 1448. A survey of 1543 describes a hall 30 ft × 25 ft, a pantry and buttery; a little house adjoining called a ewery, and a gallery over the nether end of the hall, with a little parlour at its west end; a parlour at the north end of the site, with an east side of 'faire glass' and a west side set with wainscott, 36 ft × 14 ft; a garden 70 ft × 21 ft on the east side of the property; and seven tenements or cottages, with the gate and yard of the hall, several without chimneys.[1] The hall was granted to Sir Robert Chester when the Parish Clerks were temporarily suppressed in the reign of Edward VI; in 1557 Sir Robert was involved in a boundary dispute over a brick wall forming part of the east side of the hall, which he subsequently took down.[2] By Stow's time (1598) the Parish Clerks were to be found in Brode Lane, in the Vintry, Thames Street.

1. Honeybourne, 'Value', 287–96.
2. Stow, i, 170–1; *Viewers' Certificates*, 375.

(24) 66 Bishopsgate Street Within (later 99 Bishopsgate)

An undercroft of at least four bays, divided by plain chamfered ribs forming four-centred pointed arches on corbels was observed here in the mid nineteenth century and engraved (Fig. 88).[1]

1. Hugo 1867.

(25) Fisher's Folly/Devonshire House, Bishopsgate Street Without (now Devonshire Street and Devonshire Square/Gardens)

Jasper Fisher, warden of the Goldsmiths' Company in 1567, bought six gardens off Bishopsgate from Sir Martin Bowes, and on them built a house before his death in 1579. By Stow's time it was called Fisher's Folly, an allusion to its sumptuousness.[1] By 1677, when it was Devonshire House, it comprised a large, rambling complex with one central courtyard, set back from Bishopsgate, and a large garden (later Devonshire Square) to the east, as shown by Ogilby and Morgan.

In 1989 a brick wall at least 35 m (115 ft) long was discovered during redevelopment, running east to west at the back of houses on the north side of Devonshire Street.[2] The bricks were laid in English bond and the wall incorporated three stone windows, unglazed but in one case with vertical iron bars (Fig. 121b). This seems to be a ground-floor or cellar range forming the north side of the Elizabethan house.

1. Stow, i, 166; ii, 298.
2. MoL, sitecode OPS88.

(26) 36–39 (later 37–40) Bishopsgate Street Without (now 182–184 Bishopsgate)

Three houses and a large garden, part of the bequest of Sir Martin Bowes to Christ's Hospital in 1565.[1] The properties originally belonged to the hospital of St Mary Spital, which in 1533 leased the

198. **(26)** 36–39 (later 37–40, now 182–184) Bishopsgate (Treswell 1611)

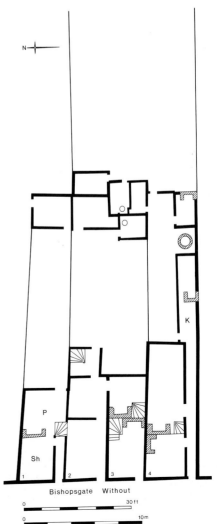

Bishopsgate Without

southernmost house (1) and garden to Richard Garnett, tailor, for eighty-one years years at 20s. p.a. In 1595 the property was leased by Christ's Hospital to John Clapham for sixty years at the same rent. Clapham is shown as tenant of the southern property on a plan by Treswell (Fig. 198). He died intestate, but his widow Anne, as Lady Anne Darrell, secured the residue of the lease in 1642, when the property was known as the Three Tuns Tavern. In 1652 the property passed to Gilbert East, who laid out £100 on repairs; the property had been greatly rebuilt from that shown in the plan by 1693, when a plan shows that East added a further brick building at the rear.[2]

Treswell's plan is one of the earliest datable in the Christ's Hospital collection, of 1607. In that year the hospital leased (2) to Richard Plowman for twenty-one years at £4 p.a., paying a fine of £25. The lease mentions a 'plott hereunto annexed'. A plan which is clearly by Treswell, and which had presumably been attached to this deed initially, now accompanies the next surviving lease of 1661.[3]

All the houses were two rooms deep, though of different lengths; the middle property was of double width. They were of two storeys with garrets, except for the small tenancy (3) which, the text on the lease-plan of 1607 adds, was only of two storeys.[4]

1. GL, MS 12949.
2. GL, MS 12949B, M and N.
3. GL, MS 12949E.
4. LSRT, 66–7.

(27) Soaphouse Alley, Bishopsgate Street Without

This property, on the west side of Bishopsgate Without and north of St Mary Bethlem, was bequeathed by John Walsshe, goldsmith, as 'le belle on the hop' to his wife Agnes in 1384,[1] with remainder to the son of Thomas Poyntel, a fellow goldsmith. Subsequent owners, recorded in deeds of the Tallow-Chandlers' Company, included a stockfishmonger who bequeathed the property to the parish of St Magnus, which in turn sold it in 1424/5 to a tailor, partnered by a brewer who released his claim a month later. In 1444 it passed to a haberdasher, and to groups including drapers in subsequent years. In 1460 it is described as lying between Bishopsgate and 'le Morediche'; perhaps here the ditch which formed the City boundary nearly 700 ft east of the street. In 1462 John Spencer, draper, now the sole owner, leased it to Robert Leveson, weaver; a previous tenant had been Thomas Salman, 'hakeneyman'. In 1477 the will of William Blackman, chandler, included a partial inventory of the shop: a counter in the shop and a selour (?) for candles, 6 pairs of mustardstones, a salt bin with six shelves and a chest; 2 pairs of scales with pewter measuring pots, 900 lead weights 'grete and small', balances and beams; 17 tuns for vinegar and 29 butts, pipes and hogsheads for vinegar work; 2 melting pans, 2 small melting pans, 2 moulds for white candles and 2 moulds for midsummer candles. By 1480 the property was in the hands of the Tallow-Chandlers' Company. In 1541 (as rehearsed in a deed of 1556) the property contained 'fathowses boylyng howses yardes coopers howses wells and garden'. The property was known as Sopehouse Alley in 1619, and is shown on Ogilby and Morgan's map of 1677 (d32).

1. Cal. Wills, ii, 24.
2. Monier-Williams 1897, 105, 177, 285–95.

(28) Sir Paul Pindar's House, Bishopsgate Street Without

In 1530 John Haselwood de Maydewell, of Northampton, conveyed to Sir William Hollys four messuages in the parish of St Botolph Bishopsgate. This property, now described as three messuages and a garden, passed from Thomas Hollys to Robert Wood in 1542. By the time of the death of John Wood in 1583 the estate had increased with the acquisition of the Half Moon to the north and other properties. John's mother Joan, his heir, sold the Half Moon to Ralph Pindar in 1597; it seems that Pindar also acquired the three tenements to the south for his brother Paul, who returned to England

from Italy in 1599 and rebuilt them.[1] The street façade was of three and a half storeys, the north bay (or property) occupied by a large gateway. The middle bay was occupied by a first- and second-floor frame of ornate woodwork, forming a double-height continuous window on each floor, which is now preserved in the Victoria and Albert Museum (Fig. 115). The exterior form of the south bay is not known, but at ground level included a street door to the upper chambers. On the first floor at the front of the house, a single room had an ornate plaster ceiling (Figs. 125, 138) and a fireplace with a plaster panel, dated 1600, showing Hercules and Atlas supporting a globe (Fig. 124). A second room had a similar ceiling with a central figure of St Christopher (Fig. 139) and other rooms in the house also had ornate ceilings.

About 340 ft to the rear of the Bishopsgate frontage stood a three and a half storey building, 20 ft × 40 ft, called the garden lodge or banqueting house (Fig. 99a–b). Its south face was enriched with four stucco panels representing Spring and Summer (above) and Peace and Plenty (below). Within were further plaster ceilings and a sixteenth-century fireplace.[2]

1. Goss 1930, 3–9.
2. Ibid., 10–11; Hugo 1867, Plate ix and Fig. viii.

(29) White Hart Inn, 199–200 Bishopsgate Street Without

In 1582 the White Hart, immediately south of the gate of St Mary Bethlem Hospital, was bequeathed by Roger Robynson to his wife Alice; he had bought it of James Batte of Burton (Yorkshire).[1] Stow noted 'a fair inn for receipt of travellers' next to the church of St Botolph.[2] Engravings and drawings show a three-and-a-half-storey façade with windows on two floors running the width of the property; the entry beneath was vaulted (Fig. 112). A date-plaque reading 1480 shown on the façade in several illustrations of the building cannot refer to the fenestration, which has a mid-sixteenth-century appearance.

1. Inq. PM, iii, 316.
2. Stow, i, 164.

(30) Lumbardes' Place, Botolph Lane

In 1472 John Bedham, fishmonger, bequeathed his house on the east side of Botolph Lane to the parish of St Mary at Hill.[1] In 1477–9 the parish was receiving £13 6s. 8d. annual rent from Lewis Lumbridge and the house was thereafter sometimes known as Lumbardes' Place.[2] In 1477–9 repairs included substantial tiling of floors (two tilers and two labourers for eighteen days), both paving tile and small paving tile being used.[3] In an inventory of 1485, when the 'great place' was leased to Maryn Conteryn (Conterino?), merchant of Venice, the following rooms are mentioned: a parlour, buttery, summer parlour, kitchen, larder house, house next the gate, garden and well; a chief chamber and ten other chambers, all with beds in – one called Antonyes Chamber, others specified as being over the parlour, kitchen, next to St Botolph's churchyard or over the gate. The tenement also had a postern gate, and mention is made of a great new standing almerye (cupboard) with three leaves (doors) and four plate locks in the chamber by the summer parlour.[4]

1. Recs. SMH, 16.
2. Ibid., 76, 114.
3. Ibid., 88–9.
4. Ibid., 28–9.

(31) 11–14 Bow Lane, 12–14 Basing Lane
(later 39–53 Cannon Street) (Watling Court site)

The Watling Court site, excavated in 1978–9, comprised an area on the west side of Bow Lane at its junction with Basing Lane (removed for the extension to the west of Cannon Street in 1852) corresponding to all of or parts of eleven medieval properties. Virtually no medieval ground-surfaces were recorded due to the truncation of strata by later basements; only the deeper foundations, cellars and pits (including wells and cesspits) survived to be recorded.[1]

199. **(31)** Watling Court, Bow Lane: plan of site *c.* 1450, with building foundations excavated in 1978 placed within the property boundaries established by documentary research. The buildings are numbered and shaded; the tenements are also numbered [Schofield *et al.* 1990].

Buildings along Bow Lane in the period 850–1020 are inferred from the regular placing of rubbish pits and cesspits parallel to the street but some distance from it; ground-level buildings, it is suggested, would have lain along the street. A sunken building at right angles to Bow Lane may have been constructed before 1000. In the short period 1000–1050 four further buildings with large timber-built cellars, two of them successively in the same place, were constructed behind the street frontages and at right angles to them (Fig. 26); these were also backfilled during the same short period. In the second half of the twelfth century a stone building (Building 6) was constructed against Basing Lane. Fragments of similar stone foundations of buildings south of and at right angles to Watling Street were also recorded. Behind them, to the south, lay a stone building (Building 7) in the middle of the site.

The documentary context of these buildings can be outlined for the years around 1350 (Fig. 199). Before *c.* 1270 a large property comprised tenements in Bread Street to the west and a garden, which became a separate tenement (1) known as *La Rouge Sale* after *c.* 1272. All the tenements in Cordwainer Street (Bow Lane) (nos. 4–8) were probably in single ownership in *c.* 1270, but three units (nos. 5–7) had been established before 1290. Similarly tenements 2–3 in Basing Lane, formerly associated with each other, had separate histories from 1298. For the present purpose the histories of only three tenements will be noted: Tenements 1, 4 and 5.

Tenement 1 (*La Rouge Sale*) had entrances to Watling Street to the north and Basing Lane to the south. A detailed description of the premises of the mid fifteenth century mentions a great parlour, a great chamber with chapel and a hall arranged around inner and outer courtyards. The archaeologically recorded Building 7, probably of twelfth-century date, formed part of this complex; it was extended to the east on a small undercroft (Fig. 199, Building 12) sometime in the thirteenth or fourteenth century, and one possibility is that this was for the chapel which is first mentioned (as an adjunct of the great chamber, both being built on cellars) in 1453. From the beginning of surviving documentation in the late thirteenth century, the property was owned by a succession of distinctive residents, including civic office-holders.

Tenement 4 formed the corner of Bow Lane and Basing Lane; its structural centre was probably the stone Building 6 of the twelfth century, which had been built across the site of the demolished timber cellar of the early eleventh century, perhaps indicating continuity of location for an important building within the tenement (Fig. 26). During the period 1200–1400 Building 6 was probably extended to the north (Building 11) and a stone well dug; another stone foundation (Building 10) was laid parallel to the east within the property, indicating subdivision. By 1280 the property comprised two houses in Basing Lane and four shops in Cordwainer Street. In 1413 a strip of the property forming the west end was granted away

(tenement 4a); and in 1438 a further strip was granted from the new west end (tenement 4b), up to the boundary formed by the (presumably still standing) Buildings 6/11. In 1441 the remainder of the property was described as a brewhouse called *le Keye on the Hope* in Basing Lane; in 1453 tenement 4a was described as two shops, but the premises were ruinous. In 1455 tenement 4 was bequeathed to the Skinners' Company, who also owned 4a and 4b by 1519.

Tenement 5, adjacent to the north, was part of a larger holding along the west side of Bow Lane in *c.* 1270; by 1305 three separate properties (tenements 5–7) can be distinguished. As tenements 6 and 7 owed quit-rents to the owner of 5, it is possible that the separation was made by the owner Hugh Moton before his death (before 1290), and that he may have lived in the south part, tenement 5. Several stone cesspits (e.g. Fig. 97) of thirteenth- or fourteenth-century date were found within tenement 5 but not in the others, suggesting some special distinction. Tenement 5 was subdivided into two equal parts in 1352; the north part passed to the Drapers' Company in 1535. The south part, tenement 5b, was described as two dwelling-houses and shops in 1535.

1. MoL, sitecode WAT78. This account is derived from Schofield, Allen & Taylor 1990.

(32) 44–48 Bow Lane (Well Court)

The Well Court site, excavated in 1979, comprised two medieval properties on the east side of Bow Lane.[1]

A street-surface probably of the first Bow Lane, and dated to the period 850–1020, was excavated within the present cellars; a timber building (Building 1) had preceded the street at this point, but subsequent structures (Buildings 2–6) formed parts of the east street frontage in the period to up to *c.* 1100. Behind the frontage, within the property, was traces of a sunken timber cellar (Building 7), of unknown orientation, of the same short period (1050–1100) as similar buildings on the Watling Court site across Bow Lane to the south-west (31). Rents identifiable as deriving from part of the site were included among those given to Canterbury Cathedral Priory at the end of the eleventh century when Living the priest gave St Mary le Bow church to the priory.

In the twelfth century a large stone building (Building 8) was built at right angles to Bow Lane and with gable against the street, encroaching slightly into the street. It was 9 m (29 ft 6 in) wide and 18 m (59 ft) long, and comprised two cellars (the front one slightly larger), possibly with an entrance at the rear (Fig. 200). Documentary evidence suggests that by *c.* 1200 the site comprised three properties, the northern two being a subdivision of the Canterbury property; Building 8 lay on the third, south part, which was owned by William, son of Isabel, a former sheriff of London and Middlesex and a substantial landowner in the city (d. 1197/8). In the mid thirteenth century all three holdings came into the possession of William, son of Richard (d. 1269), one of the most powerful citizens of London in the 1250s–60s: sheriff in 1250–1 and alderman of Tower Ward; mayor in 1258 and 1259. The Well Court property included his residence, and the boundaries and some of the buildings can be conjecturally reconstructed for the early fourteenth century, i.e. reflecting the layout of William's residence or works of two generations after him (Fig. 201). The site now comprised two major properties, the larger (the residence of William) to the south. By this time the stone Building 8 seems to have been modified, since a row of buildings along the street passed across it but reused the division between the front and back cellars; presumably this subdivision within Building 8 had also been evident in storeys above the basement. Behind lay a second stone building (9) of thirteenth- or fourteenth-century date, of which only fragments of the west and south walls were recorded. The north property, about one third the size of its companion to the south, included two further recorded stone buildings: an impressive, vaulted undercroft (Building 11) along the side of the property at the front (probably a vault mentioned in 1269), and a building (12) also of thirteenth- or fourteenth-century date lying across the property, at the rear of a small yard. This building was also vaulted, at least in its northern half, which was recorded. Thus by *c.* 1300 the site comprised two large houses, their main buildings at right angles to the street at the ends of alleys; the frontages were composed of shops, and the north tenement included a large undercroft running back from the street beneath the north end of the shops.

From the subsequent documentation of the properties two particular details of the buildings along Bow Lane are noteworthy. In 1387 the prior of Elsyng Spital, which owned most if not all of the site, complained that a tenant – John Bradlee – had removed a counter for drapery in the shop, a pavement of Flanders tile in a large chamber, a screen or partition (*parclos*) of Eastland board 13 ft long in another chamber, three locks and four bolts, another partition in an entry (*huys*) 24 ft long in the said large chamber, a cupboard of Eastland board in the parlour, a crest of Eastland board over the screen in the same parlour, and a *rierdos* (possibly from a fireplace, or panelling) of Eastland board, together with a quantity of Maidstone stone.[2] This tenement, which from this description contained at least three rooms in addition to the shop, was probably one of the smaller units along the Bow Lane frontage. Secondly, the range along the street in front of the southern property can be reconstructed in three-dimensional outline in the first half of the seventeenth century: part comprised three storeys with garrets (the fourth storey having a leaded balcony over the street) on cellars, with the hall on the first floor overlooking the street, and a smaller house of two storeys with garret to the south.

1. MoL, sitecode WEL79. This account is derived from Schofield, Allen & Taylor 1990; there a documentary study by D. Keene summarises his fuller account of the property as **104/23** in *HG: i, Cheapside*.
2. *Cal. Plea and Mem. R., 1381–1412*, 129–30.

(33) 34 Bow Lane, 1–3 [St] Thomas Apostle

A corner property, known in 1612 as the Black Lion, fronting west onto Cordwayner Street (the south part of Bow Lane) and north on Turnbase alias Backe Lane. John Watson bequeathed it, with property in Basing Lane (**22, 23**), to the Clothworkers' Company in 1555.[1]

The property, as surveyed by Treswell in 1612 (Fig. 202), comprised three and a half storeys on cellars on the north side of an entry to Bow Lane.[2] The substantial wall forming the north side of the Black Lion at ground level was of stone, with three internal stubs or buttresses. The hall was at the front at first-floor level, overlooking Bow Lane and sailing over the entry; the principal stair to the first-floor chambers rose from the entry directly behind the shop, and a backstairs communicated between the first floor and the ground-floor kitchen.

1. CD, Box 54.
2. *LSRT*, 50–1.

(34) Salters' Hall, Bread Street

In March 1454/5 Thomas Beaumond, salter, bequeathed to the wardens of the Fraternity and Guild of Corpus Christi in All Hallows, Bread Street, all his land on the east side of the street 'where there is now built a hall called *Saltershalle*, and six houses newly built on the same land' between the George on the Hoop to the south and All Hallows church to the north.[1] The land may originally have been bequeathed by two previous wardens of the fraternity.[2] The hall, mentioned in *c.* 1475, was burned down in 1539 and rebuilt, only to burn down again wholly or in part in 1598.[3] In 1641 the company moved their hall to the former mansion of the priors of Tortington, Oxford Place (not in gazetteer), in St Swithin's Lane.[4]

1. *Cal. Wills*, ii, 534.
2. Herbert, *Livery Companies*, ii, 560–1.
3. BL, Harley MS 541; Watson 1963, 28.
4. Watson 1963, 77.

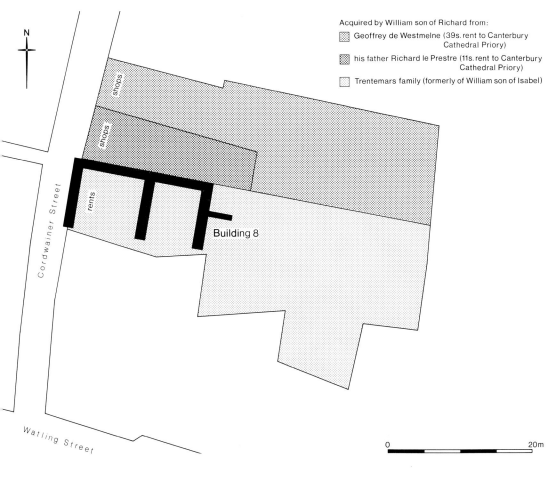

Acquired by William son of Richard from:

▨ Geoffrey de Westmelne (39s. rent to Canterbury Cathedral Priory)

▨ his father Richard le Prestre (11s. rent to Canterbury Cathedral Priory)

▨ Trentemars family (formerly of William son of Isabel)

shops

shops

rents

Building 8

Cordwainer Street

Watling Street

0   20m

200. (**32**) Well Court, Bow Lane (Cordwainer Street): main buildings on the site in the early thirteenth century, from excavations of 1979 and documentary research [Keene in Schofield *et al.* 1990]

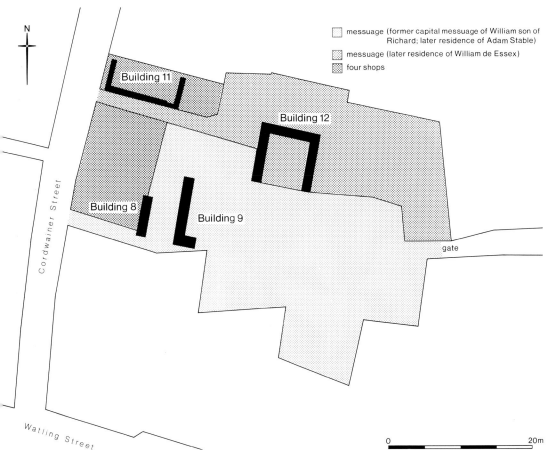

☐ messuage (former capital messuage of William son of Richard; later residence of Adam Stable)

▨ messuage (later residence of William de Essex)

▨ four shops

Building 11

Building 12

Building 8

Building 9

gate

Cordwainer Street

Watling Street

0   20m

201. (**32**) Well Court, Bow Lane (Cordwainer Street): main buildings on the site in the early fourteenth century, from excavations of 1979 and documentary research

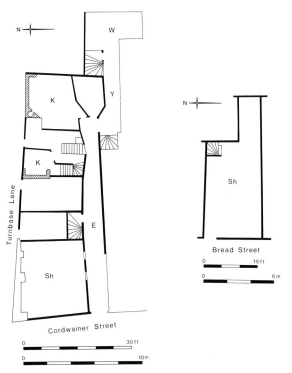

202. (*left*)   (33) 34 Bow Lane, 1–3 St Thomas Apostle (Treswell 1612)

203. (*right*)   (34) 36 Bread Street (Treswell 1612)

(35)   36 Bread Street

On 24 July 1582 the treasurer of Christ's Hospital took possession of a tenement called The Ship, under the will of Thomas Hall, salter, late treasurer of the hospital.[1] Treswell's plan of 1611 (Fig. 203) and text of reference show it to be of three and a half storeys on a cellar, with the hall and kitchen on the first floor. The privy was in the garret on the third floor.[2]
1.   *Charity Comm.*, 97.
2.   *LSRT*, 52–3.

(36)   Abbot of Tewkesbury's Inn, Bride Lane

Tewkesbury Abbey (Gloucestershire) acquired this site in 1314–15, under the will of Peter de Leycester, canon of Lichfield. The use of the Inn by the abbey must have been brief, since in 1360–1 it was leased. It was claimed by the king in 1374; by then it had degenerated into a stable on Bride Lane between St Bride's church and the gate of the Inn of the abbot of Faversham (not in gazetteer). Part of the Tewkesbury site had become St Bride's parsonage by 1380.[1]
1.   Honeybourne, *Fleet*, 44, 73–8; Dyson 1981, 16–17.

(37)   Bishop of St David's Inn, Bride Lane

The Bishop was apparently renting property from the Templars in 1301, and probably bought the site, comprised of at least three tenements, from the Order of St John, who acquired the property on the suppression of the Templars in 1307. In 1415 the Inn had ten shops belonging to it, probably known as the Bishop's Rent. Miss Honeybourne specified the site as forming a square block north of Bride Lane and bordering on the Fleet, south of the Abbot of Winchcombe's Inn.[1]

In 1847 an undercroft was discovered on the site of 15 Bride Lane, which falls within the area of the Inn.[2] An illustration shows the west wall, with a window (said to have its iron bars intact) and a stair to the left, presumably to Bride Lane. Quadripartite vaulting is suggested by the arrangement of ribs, and walling of chalk.
1.   Honeybourne, 'Value', 330–3.
2.   *JBAA*, ii (1847), 341–2.

(38)   Prior of Okebourne's Inn, Bristow Street (formerly Castle Lane)

In 1352 the Blackfriars obtained permission to enclose a lane running east and west from the gate of the prior of Okebourne to the new city wall by the Fleet, in order to enlarge their precinct;[1] the Inn lay west of the East Water Gate (St Andrew's Hill, Puddledock) and south of the later Duke Humphrys (Castle Lane). The priory, as an alien house, was suppressed in 1415; the Inn seems to have been granted in 1441 to King's College, Cambridge, who were in possession of it in 1473.[2]
1.   *Cal. Close R.*, *1349–54*, 502.
2.   *LTR*, xi, 62; *Survey of Sources*, 19.

(39)   Abbot of St Alban's Inn, Broad Street

This Inn was purchased for the abbey by Abbot William in 1214–35, and is described as having a chapel, kitchen, garden, orchard, well, stable and apartments besides a court.[1] In 1246 the abbot was accused of building a porch and stable which encroached on the highway of Broad Street by 4 ft.[2] Part of the property, comprising a house, a garden and a further piece of land, were sold to the adjacent Hospital of St Anthony in 1429;[3] in 1432, when the hospital built a new hospice, arrangements were made for access to the rebuilt wall of the Inn.[4]
1.   *Gesta Abbatum*, i, 259.
2.   *Eyre 1244*, 418.
3.   *Cal. Pat. R.*, *1422–9*, 517–18
4.   Graham 1932, 1–8, with a reconstruction of the site in outline.

(40)   House of St Paul's, Bucklersbury, 1405

In 1405 the Dean and Chapter of St Paul's contracted with John Dobson, carpenter, to erect a group of buildings on their property on the south side of Bucklersbury in the parish of St Sithe.[1] The previous buildings on the site having been demolished, the plot would measure 38 ft along the street, 45 ft along the west side, 57½ ft along the south side and 58 ft 'linearly' (*mensurando linialiter*) along the east side. The likely arrangement of the buildings in the contract (reconstructed in Fig. 204) suggest that this means 'measured directly' between the two corners of the tenement, not allowing for necessary intermediate irregularities to accommodate all the buildings described. The Dean and Chapter would have two large cellars dug, one along the west side and one at the back of the property, with a cesspit at the east end of the latter. Dobson would erect a street range with a shop, 'sotelhouse' (meaning not clear) and entry, a first floor comprising a parlour and chamber each with a bay window 6 ft wide, jettied front and rear, and a further full storey over. The first-floor storey would be 11 ft high and the second 9 ft high. At the rear of the internal courtyard, on the larger cellar, he would erect first a warehouse 9 ft high and then on that a hall, 33 ft × 20 ft and 16 ft to the wallplate, with an 'upright' roof incorporating an archcouple in the middle. It would have a bay window at the dais end, two other two-light windows to the court and an oriel at the door.

On the west (dais end) side of the court would be a gallery full of windows connecting the hall and the first floor of the street range; on the second floor, a parlour 20 ft × 11 ft with a flat, battlemented roof, a small chamber leading to the second floor of the street range. At the east side of the court, over subsidiary buildings (stable, coalhouse, woodhouse and privy) would be a kitchen in line with the hall, 16 ft × 15 ft, buttery and pantry, with rooms over the latter. A further room would sit half over the hall and half over the kitchen, above the screens passage.

The buildings can be reconstructed if the east boundary is expanded slightly to accommodate the service buildings.[2]
1.   Salzman, *Building*, 478–82.
2.   Cf. Pantin 1963, 455–60.

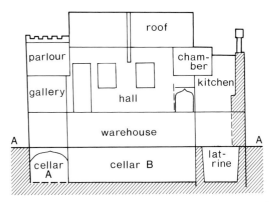

section A-A

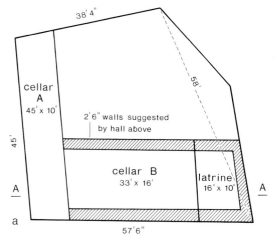

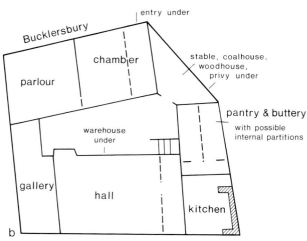

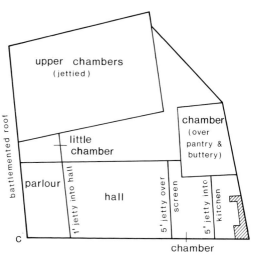

(41) Le Barge, Bucklersbury

The history of this large house on the south side of Bucklersbury has been outlined by Kingsford.[1] The Bokerels or Bucherells were settled in London by the early twelfth century. The house (as opposed to the street) called Bucklersbury is first mentioned in 1270. In 1343 the house had three entrances, from Bucklersbury, from Budge Row, and a postern to Walbrook. The name *Le Barge* first appears in 1414; in 1440 the property passed to the Hospital of St Thomas of Acon. The Barge was divided into tenancies, in one of which Sir Thomas More lived in 1505. Part of the site was acquired by the Mercers' Company at the Dissolution. Stow saw 'a great stone building, yet part remaining' on the south side of the street.[2]

1. *LTR*, x, 78–80.
2. Stow, i, 259.

(42) Servat's Tower, Bucklersbury

This stood on the north side of Bucklersbury, with the Walbrook as part of its east boundary. First mentioned in 1305, when William Servat, alderman of Walbrook 1309–19, Member of Parliament 1309 and 1313, and Collector of Customs, had licence to build and crenellate a tower above the gate of his dwelling house. By 1317 it had passed via a Genoese merchant to Edward II, who granted it for life to his queen, Isabella; in 1338, in the time of Edward III's queen, Philippa, it was known as the 'Queen's Tower of Sernat'. In 1344 and 1367 the King's Exchange for gold and silver lay here. Lessees during the second half of the fourteenth century included two Lucchesi merchants and prominent drapers (e.g. William Holbech, alderman 1358–67, sheriff 1361–2). In 1383 the Grocers met there temporarily. The building, 'an ancient and strong tower of stone', was pulled down shortly before Stow wrote.[1]

1. Stow, i, 260; Honeybourne, 'Richard II', 67–8; *HG*, i, **156/12**; Keene 1987, 8–16.

(43) Undercroft, south side of Cannon Street

In 1851 T. Dibdin drew an undercroft 'under the old houses [in] Cannon Street, opposite London Stone' (Fig. 89). At least six bays of the undercroft are shown, with transverse stone ribs of low-arched profile dying into the walls. The site of this impressive building has not been further identified.

(44) Corner of Candlewick (now Cannon) Street and St Swithin's Lane, 1523–4

On 12 April 1523/4 Richard Parker, parson of St Swithin's, together with Richard Marbery and Robert Alford, churchwardens, contracted with Robert Isotson, carpenter, for a new house-frame of oak without sap or windshake on a void plot belonging to the parish 'against the east end of the church', 64 ft 3 in × 19 ft 1½ in. In this frame were to be three messuages or tenements, four storeys high; the principal messuage at the south end, by Candlewick Street, with a shop and warehouse together 28 ft × 19 ft 1 in. The scantlings of timbers and the proportions of the principal messuage were to be made after the form of a new house built in the parish of St Thomas Apostle wherein Edwards Grene, mercer, dwelt. The other two messuages were each to be 26 ft in length with a shop on the street side, their scantlings and proportions as in the house built in Abchurch Lane in which James Halley then dwelt. The principal messuage was to be set up and ready for tiling by St John's Day 1525, and the other two by the same date in the following year. The wardens would find all manner of nails, boards and ironwork.[1]

The site must be opposite the church (the normal meaning of 'against'), on the east side of the street, since the medieval church occupied the same area as its Wren successor, and the latter's east end fronted on the narrow lane.[2]

1. GL, Add. MS 419, No. 44.
2. Grimes 1968, 200.

204. **(40)** House in Bucklersbury, 1405 contract: section at A-A, (a) cellar plan, (b) first floor, (c) second floor

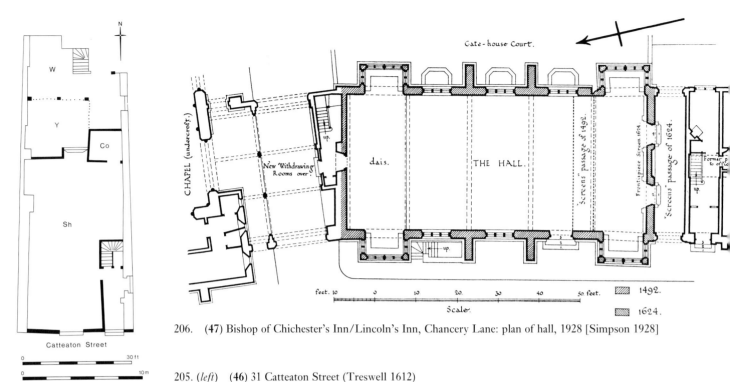

206. (47) Bishop of Chichester's Inn/Lincoln's Inn, Chancery Lane: plan of hall, 1928 [Simpson 1928]

205. (*left*) (46) 31 Catteaton Street (Treswell 1612)

(45) Dudley's house, Candlewick (now Cannon) Street and Walbrook

Edmund Dudley, minister of Henry VII, had a large house at the east corner of Candlewick Street and Walbrook. In 1509 Dudley was convicted of treason and his goods taken into safe keeping. An inventory of the house has been transcribed and discussed by Kingsford.[1] It is valuable as a picture of the contents of rooms in a courtier household in the early sixteenth century. The rooms listed are: Hall, Great Parlour, Little Parlour with a counting house within it, Long Gallery against the garden, Square Chamber, Little House for the Bows, Armour Chamber, Gallery next to the Great Chamber, Closet within the same chamber, Great Wardrobe, Little

207. (47) Bishop of Chichester's Inn/Lincoln's Inn, Chancery Lane: plan of site, 1677 (Ogilby and Morgan)

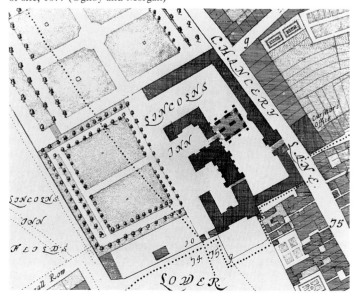

Wardrobe, Closet without the Little Wardrobe door, Low Gallery by the garden, The Great Gallery at the end of the Low Gallery, My Lady Lytton Chambre, Buttery and Kitchen. The chambers were furnished with Arras, stained cloths, and furniture; stored in various places were a large stock of bows and arrows, a quantity of furs, coffers with writings and other evidences, a large amount of armour, books, and plate.

1. Kingsford 1921, 17–21, 39–42.

(46) The Leadenporch, 31 Catteaton Street (now part of Gresham College, Gresham Street)

This house, on the north side of Catteaton (later Gresham) Street, passed to the Clothworkers' Company by the will of John Lute in 1585;[1] it was known as The Leadenporch. It was the only house surveyed by Treswell in 1612 to have stone walls on both sides of the ground floor (Fig. 205). The length of the cellar (31 ft) and the survival of a return on the west side of the ground floor in 1612 strongly suggest that the original building was a stone house with an internal area of 30–31 ft square, similar to the twelfth-century house at Corbet Court, Gracechurch Street (91). It is therefore possible that this was one of the stone houses of the Jewry, its focus Old Jewry in the south-east.

Treswell's text of reference describes the property as being three and a half storeys high on a cellar; the kitchen lay behind the hall on the first floor. The adjective 'fair' is applied to the upper rooms more than in any other Treswell survey.[2]

1. CD, Box 58.
2. *LSRT*, 54.

(47) Bishop of Chichester's Inn/Lincoln's Inn, Chancery Lane

In 1227 Henry III granted to Ralph Neville, Bishop of Chichester and Chancellor, a place with a garden on the east side of the New Street (subsequently Converts' Lane, and Chaunceler's Lane in 1340).[1] The grant of confirmation of 1233 refers to property which the Bishop already possessed on the west side of the lane. The Inn was on the west side of the street by 1357; a bakehouse and brewery, evidently old and on the edge of the property, are mentioned in

1374.[2] Fragments of a thirteenth-century doorway (Fig. 123) are preserved in the fabric of the later hall.

In 1422 the Bishop leased the Inn to apprentices of the Common Law, and it became known as Lincoln's Inn (Fig. 206); the Society of Lincoln's Inn acquired the freehold in 1580.[3] A Long Garden, now the site of Stone Buildings, is mentioned in 1445.[4] Eleven new chambers were built in 1450–1; a porch is mentioned in 1456–7 and a chapel from the early fifteenth century.[5] The hall, rebuilt by the Society in 1489–92, was originally of four bays, of brick with stone dressings on an undercroft of brick; it was enlarged to the south in 1623 with two rectangular oriels which match those at the other, high end (Figs. 102, 206). The roof has three transverse frames, with S-shaped cusped wind braces between them.[6] The cornice is topped by a row of quatrefoil pierced squares as at Crosby Place (22), of perhaps twenty years before (and there in stone, not timber).

The accounts describe a new building of 1506–8: John Frankham, brickmaker, produced 200,000 bricks by digging in the Coneygarth, part of the Inn, and John Tull, mason, provided all necessary stonework. This new block included a Council Chamber.[7]

Old Buildings, the brick court between Chancery Lane and the hall, and including the gatehouse, dates from the same period of rebuilding and was finished 'about 1520'.[8] The gatehouse of 1518–19 had blue diapering on both sides, and inside the toothing for a brick vault, never completed. The original door of two leaves and a wicket still remains. The ranges to the north and south, of which the latter remains, though rebuilt, were of four storeys with occasional protruding octagonal stairs in the court. In a first-floor room at no. 3 Old Square a series of fresco paintings were discovered during demolition in 1885. They consisted of arabesque ornaments in black outline, with touches of red, yellow and blue, and representations of a gardener, a woman with fruit, a cupid, dolphins and floriate ribands: a watercolour by J. P. Emslie was included in the Gardner collection (present location not known).

The smaller continuation of Old Square or Old Buildings west of the hall – 16–20 Old Buildings – includes a greater proportion of original brickwork and the stairs have both some original windows and oak newels. The south range incorporates a timber-framed front (Fig. 177). The *Black Books* show that this range was being built in 1525–34 by Richard Mower and Richard Bocher, who dug more bricks from the Coneygarth; oak and iron bars for the construction were 'borrowed' from the king's store.[9]

The passage of 1583 which communicates between the two courts, south of the hall, is a unique example of late sixteenth-century decoration of a passage in the city.

1. *LTR*, x, 88–90.
2. Williams, *Early Holborn*, ii, 1547.
3. *LTR*, xi, 33.
4. *Black Books of Lincoln's Inn*, i, 16–17.
5. *Ibid.*, i, 20, 25, 30; xvii.
6. Hewett 1980, 212, 313.
7. *Ibid.*, 146, 148, 151, 154.
8. RCHM, *West London*, 45; the *Black Books* accounts do not identify them directly.
9. *Black Books of Lincoln's Inn*, i, 211, 242, 244, 249–50.

(48) Charterhouse, Charterhouse Square

The Charterhouse was forcibly suppressed in 1537 and the buildings stayed in royal hands until 1545, when the priory was granted to Sir Edward, later Lord, North, a privy councillor. He began rebuilding and transforming the priory into a town-house. Thomas Howard, Duke of Norfolk, continued building between 1565 and

208. (**48**) Charterhouse: Wash-house Court from south, in 1924

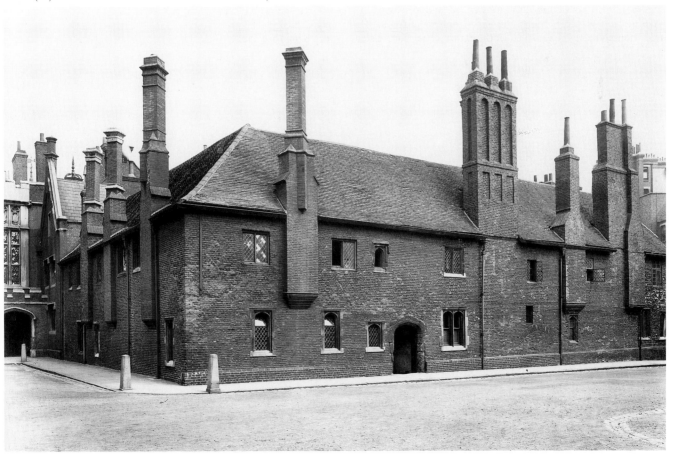

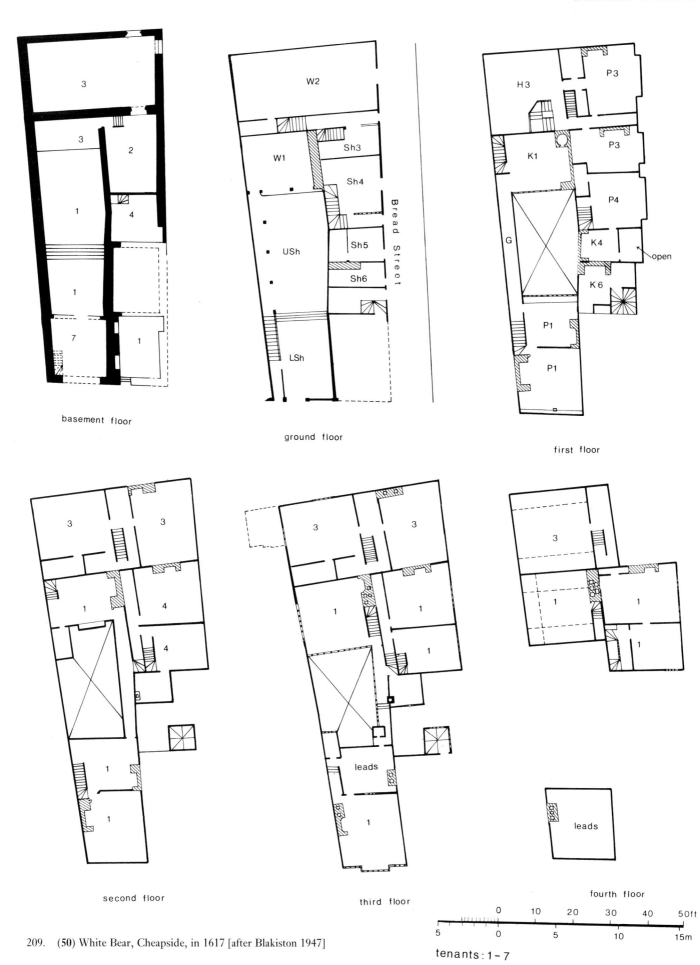

basement floor

ground floor

first floor

second floor

third floor

fourth floor

209. (50) White Bear, Cheapside, in 1617 [after Blakiston 1947]

tenants: 1–7

his execution in 1571, and from the existing remains[1] it is difficult to differentiate the work of the two owners.

The medieval priory consisted of a square cloister surrounded by twenty-six cells, on the south side of which were grouped communal buildings and areas in a west to east axis: the lay-brothers' quarters, recently rebuilt by the last prior, the Little Cloister and the church with the founder's tomb. The lay-brothers' quarters (Fig. 208; for a fireplace in an upper chamber, Fig. 128a) were retained and a kitchen range extended to the north (demolished probably in the late eighteenth century). The Little Cloister was pulled down and widened to form an impressive court of stone buildings entered from the south. The church, apart from its tower, was demolished, since the eastern range of the new court crossed it at right angles. From the outer south-east corner of the court a further new range (also probably demolished in the eighteenth century) extended east facing Charterhouse Square. Dressed stone from the priory buildings, especially the cell doorways, was reused throughout the new work; the majority of the new ranges were built of coursed ragstone.

At the back of the inner court lay the new hall (Fig. 44), entered by a porch (shortened and refaced in the late seventeenth century). Inside, some of the original woodwork as left by Howard survives after war damage: the carved oak screen bearing his initials and the date 1571 (Fig. 148). A door at the dais end leads to a stair within a square stairwell, said to be new in 1571 (Fig. 94; destroyed in the Second World War). Its replacement leads to the Great Parlour, also damaged but now restored with the arms and crest of Howard in the ceiling (Fig. 137a). A long external walk, also of 1571, was constructed on the site of the west walk of the cloister, at first-floor level.[2]

In 1611 the mansion was sold to Thomas Sutton, who founded a hospital and free school there.
1. Plan in RCHM, *West London*, 23.
2. RCHM, *West London*, 21–9; Knowles & Grimes 1954.

(49) Goldsmiths' Row, Cheapside

A goldsmiths' quarter, based on Cheapside, seems to have existed since at least the opening of the thirteenth century; two shops with solars in the Goldsmithery (*aurifabrica*) in Cheap (*in foro*) are mentioned in 1235, and Goldsmiths' Row is placed east of Friday Street in 1238–9.[1] In 1277–8 the Goldsmithery is said to be in the parish of St Vedast; in 1329 it employed four wardens. A will of 1373 mentions St Augustine 'in the Goldsmithery of London', suggesting the area then extended to St Paul's Gate.[2]

The Goldsmiths' Row of the later Middle Ages, a single building, lay on the south side of Cheapside between Bread Street and Friday Street, nearly all in the parish of St Peter Westcheap. According to Stow the Row was built by Thomas Wood, goldsmith, in 1491, as a single frame four storeys high, garnished on the street side with the Goldsmiths' Company arms and the likenesses of woodmen riding on monstrous beasts, cast in lead and painted or gilt. Stow says[3] this building contained ten dwelling houses and fourteen shops, but the records of the Goldsmiths indicate otherwise. Robert Botiller bequeathed three houses and three shops in Cheapside to Thomas Wood, his former apprentice, in 1470,[4] with the intent they should eventually pass to the company. By his will, proved in 1504, Wood left money to his tenants, all goldsmiths, six in houses with shops and a further four with shops only.[5] In 1533, when the Goldsmiths' Company acquired the property, it comprised seven tenements with shops, four separate shops and a tavern called the Egyll.[6] In 1558, 1566 and 1569 the clerk of the company compiled lists of the goldsmiths in Cheapside, which Reddaway[7] analysed as accounting for thirty-three tenancies in four parishes; but it is not possible to correlate any part of his findings with this block of property. The eleven tenements (the seven tenements and four separate shops of 1533) and the Egyll tavern are shown on a post-Fire plan in the company's archives.

The frontage to Cheapside is shown in the painting 'The Coronation Procession of Edward VI' (1546–7), now lost but known through a watercolour copy at the Society of Antiquaries, and later engraved by Grimm. Two buildings are shown on the south side of Cheapside. The main frame to the west (Fig. 63) is apparently of four goldsmiths' shops, on three floors with attics. The east frame (Fig. 183) comprises at least four storeys with attics indicated by eight gables. In this building ornamental work is shown from window to bressumer on each of the two upper floors; scrolls on the second and roses on the third, with more scrolls above the third floor. The first-floor decoration has been omitted, and the windows rise from a moulded beam directly above the ground floor. Fourteen continuous lights may be counted on the second floor, reaching from side to side of the property. Since these two frames are intended to represent nearly all the south side of Cheapside between St Mary le Bow and St Paul's Gate, the painting can only be regarded as impressionistic.
1. *Cal. Inq. PM.*, i, 917; *Cal. Chart R., 1226–57*, 202; *SMC Cartulary*, 350.
2. *Cal. Wills*, i, 29, 372, ii, 80.
3. Stow, i, 345.
4. Goldsmiths' Company, Reg. of Deeds, ff. 319–320[V], 322[V].
5. PCC, 2, Holgrave.
6. Goldsmiths' Company, Wardens Accts. and Court Minutes V, E, 25.
7. Reddaway 1963, 181–206.

(50) White Bear, 47–48 Cheapside

A rectangular block with one main frontage to Cheapside and several smaller tenancies along Bread Street, but not including the corner site. This was the property of Eton College by 1453.[1] When surveyed in 1617 (Fig. 209, redrawn from original) the block comprised seven tenancies:[2]

(1) The White Bear: a street range of four storeys on cellars, the ground floor extending behind the range as an 'upper shop'. At the rear was a block comprising a warehouse on the ground floor, kitchen on the first (reached from the street range by a gallery carried on pillars over the upper shop), two further chambers and a garret above. The property had been rebuilt in 1545 by Fulke Skydmore, mercer;[3] further chambers, probably those on the third and fourth floors, were added by Baptist Hicks in 1595. This may have been the date of construction of other galleries for the second and third floors which ran on the other side of the property to chambers over the kitchen.

(2) (Sydway: these names are of the Eton tenants in 1617) A ground floor warehouse and cellar in Bread Street.

(3) (Milton) A small shop in Bread Street, two cellars, and three floors above (2), with a garret over the rear.

(4) (Gould) A shop in Bread Street and two floors over.

(5) (Milliner) and (6) (pointmaker) Ground-floor shops in Bread Street, the former with no other accommodation, the latter with a kitchen above.

(7) (West) The occupier of the corner property, not an Eton tenement, was apparently exchanging front cellars with the White Bear.
1. PRO, Eton Records, vol. 16 (London), no. 2.
2. Blakiston 1947.
3. PRO, Eton records, vol. 16 (London), no. 5.

(51) House of the Prior of Christ Church, Canterbury, Cheapside

In 1965 the west end of an undercroft was recorded immediately west of the present tower of St Mary le Bow (Fig. 81).[1] The walls survived to a height of 12 ft, and were over 4 ft thick. Moulded corbels supported ribs forming a quadripartite vault of one rectangular bay, evidently the west end of an east to west undercroft along

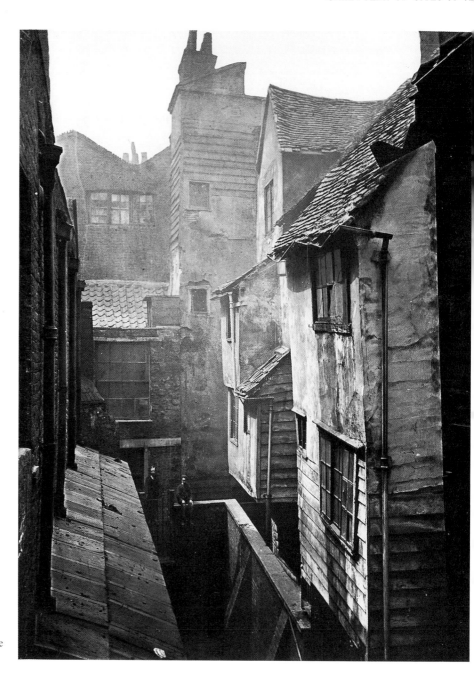

210. (**54**) Rich's houses, Cloth Fair: (a) the back of 54b, photographed *c.* 1875

the street. The south jamb of a recess or entrance was found in the west wall, and the splay of one window in the north wall.

Documentary study by Keene & Harding[2] suggests that this was part of a property belonging to Christ Church, Canterbury, from the twelfth century. The property was damaged when the steeple of St Mary le Bow fell in 1271, and the discovered portion appears to be part of a new undercroft of 1272–9. 'Michael the mason' who was associated with it may be Michael of Canterbury, responsible for the Cross in Cheap (1291) and the first part of St Stephen Westminster (by 1292). The ground floor over the vault was divided by 1315–16 into at least four selds with solars, some separately let, above. The cellar was used as a tavern by 1341; by 1370, the selds are no longer mentioned. By the early sixteenth century the tavern was still on the site, though it had moved out of the undercroft.

1. Grimes 1968, 168–70; Fig. 81 is the original survey now in HBMC archives.
2. *HG, i, Cheapside*, site **104/20**.

(52)   Mercers' Hall, Cheapside

The trade of the mercers had been associated with the eastern end of Cheapside since the thirteenth century; by 1391 they met in *la sale* of the Hospital of St Thomas Acre or Acon. A *petite chambre* and a chapel formed part of their rooms by 1417; the latter was within the church of St Thomas. The hall had a lead roof, a fireplace, a chest for evidences, and glazed windows which in 1448 were decorated with the Maiden's Head, the company's emblem. In 1510–18 the company took advantage of financial difficulties at the hospital to enlarge and rebuild their hall. At first the rebuilding was to include an enlargement of the church of St Thomas, but in 1513 the company negotiated for the enlarged chapel and hall to be built by themselves. The hall site, probably extending over the entry to the church of St Thomas, had a frontage of 76 ft 4 in to Cheapside; in 1517 a further acquisition of property from the hospital increased this to 98 ft 8 in. The new building was finished by 1522, and in 1524, 'the altar [of the chapel] now standing naked', the Mercers

(b) The front of 54a, photographed in the nineteenth century [Webb 1921]

looked at a *platt* for a *table* (altar-piece) by Walter Vandale of Antwerp, carver, who wanted £90 Flemish for it, which was agreed.[1] An early sixteenth-century statue of Christ now at Mercers' Hall may be part of this work. The hall parlour and kitchen lay on the first floor, partly over the Mercers' Chapel on the ground floor. The copperplate map of *c.* 1559 shows a battlemented façade, presumably of stone, with a central entrance. On the rest of the ground floor was a separately let shop and probably a lower parlour.

After the dissolution of the hospital in 1538 the company acquired the site of the church, the master's lodging and other adjacent hospital property by 1542; but in 1550 the north part of the hospital and church site was sold off. The fragmentary sixteenth- and seventeenth-century remains reported in 1929[2] do not contribute significantly to the hall's history.[3]

1. *Mercers' Acts*, 673–4.
2. RCHM, *City*, 69–70.
3. This entry is derived from work by Keene & Harding (*HG, i, Cheapside*, site **105/16**).

(53) Cutlers' Hall (now College Hill Chambers), Cloak Lane

Stow traces the history of this house from 1295, when the property of Richard de Wilhale lay on the south side of Cloak Lane (then Horshoe Bridge Street), between College Hill ('the way called pater noster Church') on the west and the Walbrook on the east (which formed a boundary with Tallow-Chandlers' Hall II further east).[1]

The Bladers, Haftmakers and Sheathmakers united in 1428–9 to form the Cutlers' Company.[2] They built a hall with adjoining almshouses in Cloak Lane by 1440. Accounts suggest a hall with an oriel (rebuilt 1458–9), a ladies' chamber, a new parlour in 1465, a little parlour, counting house and kitchen; later a yeomanry hall; a garden with a well and vinery.[3] The hall is mentioned in the Harley MS 541 list of *c.* 1475, 'in the parish of St Michael fast by the Ryall'. An inventory of hall fittings survives from 1586; rooms then mentioned were the hall, parlour, buttery, cellar, pantry, little parlour or dining house, kitchen and yeomanry hall.[4] The Fire-damaged site was surveyed by Oliver in 1688.[5] Ogilby and Morgan show the post-

211. (**54**) Cloth Fair (J. Crowther 1884)

Fire hall as a small courtyard house on the south side of Cloak Lane, with a main L-shaped range forming one side of the court and the street frontage.

1. Stow, i, 244–5.
2. *Ibid.*
3. GL, MS 7164; Welch 1916, 159–63, 316, 319–20.
4. GL, MS 7164, ff. 5A–8.
5. Mills & Oliver, *Survey*, iv, 104v.

(54) (a) 6–9, (b) 12–22, (c) 24 Cloth Fair
At the Dissolution of the monasteries, the priory of St Bartholomew Smithfield passed to the first Lord Rich. When Robert, third Baron Rich, later created Earl of Warwick, came into possession in 1581, he began to develop the former fairground on the north side of the priory church, and laid out several streets on its east part. Several parts of this late sixteenth-century private housing venture re-

mained until the early twentieth century. The most imposing group (**54a**) was built in 1590–7 along the south side of Cloth Fair, backing on to the site of the demolished nave of the priory church, which was itself turned into a churchyard.[1] Photographs (e.g. Fig. 210b)[2] show them to be three and a half storeys high (no. 6 four and a half storeys) with two-storeyed rectangular wooden bay windows (three-storeyed in the case of no. 6); all were two rooms deep.

The second group (**54b**) was built in a similar position eastwards, backing onto the choir and ladychapel (Fig. 211). Warwick House, no. 22, bore the arms of the Rich family, and leases for the house date from 1582; the others have leases dating from 1598.[3] They were also of three and a half storeys; at the back were small projecting chambers (Fig. 210a).

Of a third row on the north side of Cloth Fair facing these buildings, photographs show only the Dick Whittington public

house (**54c**; no. 24) at the east end (Fig. 175; further photographs in the Guildhall Library show two other jettied houses to the west). These houses were smaller; the Dick Whittington (despite its claim to be fifteenth-century in origin, not used as a pub until the late nineteenth century) was of three storeys, forming the end of the row and jettied slightly on the second floor, the corners supported by grotesque corbels (now preserved in the Museum of London). This row was probably built by 1598; in 1616 it was known as Longtyled-house Rowe.[4]

1. Webb 1921, ii, 232–42.
2. In GL, and MoL; the series of photographs by the Society of Photographing Old Relics of London, issued 1875–86.
3. Webb 1921, ii, 239.
4. *Ibid.*, 237.

Sites 55–7 Bell Alley and White's Alley, Coleman Street

This group of properties belonged to Rewley Abbey, a Cistercian house in Oxford. In 1528 the abbot leased three gardens in Whites Alley to Thomas Abraham the elder, leatherseller. By March 1543 the lands were in the possession of William Lambe (d. 1580) who left them, with other property (e.g. **140**) to the Clothworkers' Company. The company accounts show that houses were built on the gardens in 1598; the absence of building accounts in company records implies that the tenants were responsible. They were surveyed by Treswell in 1612 (Figs. 212–14).

These lands comprised three blocks: (**55**) is now represented by 4–5 Copthall Buildings (and probably some of the property next to the west); (**56**) by 1–2 Copthall Buildings; and (**57**) by 8–10 Telegraph Street.

(55) Swan Alley (now 4–5 Copthall Buildings)

Two gardens with houses built on their north sides, let to two principal tenants (Fig. 59b and c). That to the west (Fig. 59b) was of two and a half storeys; its parlour had a semi-octagonal bay window taking up much of the end of the building. The unrestricted setting enabled the house to be entered in its long side, an example of a lobby-entrance house in London. A bowling alley occupied a strip along the south edge of the garden, entered from White's Alley. The house in the east (Fig. 59c) was also a lobby-entrance house, of two and a half storeys, with two studies on first and second floors, each 10 ft 6 in × 10 ft, looking into the garden. A cellar lay under the parlour.[1]

1. Weinstein 1980, 61–80; *LSRT*, 59–64, where the original Treswell plans show the extent of the gardens attached to the houses.

(56) Bell Alley (now 1–2 Copthall Buildings)

A pair of gardens also included buildings on the north side of the west garden, and on the south side of the east garden.

The west house was on a terrace raised above the garden by a low wall and steps. It comprised ground-floor rooms in an L-shape, with two rooms on the first floor and a garret over one of them (Fig. 212). The east house was a lobby-entrance house on two floors without garrets, an unusual feature being that the stair to the first floor was included within the porch, and not attached to the chimney stack (Fig. 213).[1]

1. *LSRT*, 62–3, showing the extent of the gardens.

(57) Bell Alley (now 8–10 Telegraph Street)

This complex of rooms (Fig. 214) was divided in 1612 among three tenants. The largest (2) rose to three and a half storeys at the back of a small yard entered from Bell Alley on the north. The two smaller tenancies (1 and 3) occupied the buildings fronting the alley to the north, rising to two and a half storeys in both cases and probably joining over the entry. Only the tenant with the largest number of rooms and the highest house (2) had a small cellar and presumably sole rights to the large garden to the east.[1]

1. *LSRT*, 64.

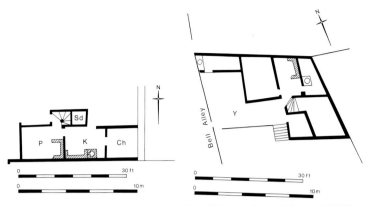

212. (*left*) (**55**) Bell Alley/White's Alley, Coleman Street (Treswell 1612)

213. (*right*) (**56**) Bell or Gough's Alley, Coleman Street, now 1–2 Copthall Buildings (Treswell 1612)

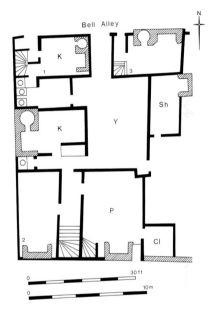

214. (**57**) Bell or Gough's Alley, Coleman Street, now 8–10 Telegraph Street (Treswell 1612)

(58) 79 Coleman Street

A photograph of 1871[1] shows the street front of a house, plastered over but evidently timber-framed, of four storeys with a jetty below the third storey (Fig. 215). The second and third storeys have projecting windows which, though rebuilt, may have derived from later sixteenth- or early seventeenth-century originals. A date in the second half of the sixteenth century is possible for this building, about which nothing else has so far been traced.

1. GL.

(59) Armourers' and Braziers' Hall, Coleman Street

The site, comprising the Dragon and two shops, was acquired by the company in 1428;[1] the hall is mentioned in Harley MS 541 (*c.* 1475), and was used by the Founders, who at that time had no hall of their own, in 1497.[2] An inventory of 1585 of furniture in the hall mentions three tables, a cupboard, and a 'George of complete Armor over the screen'.[3]

1. Barron 1913.
2. Parsloe 1964, 4.
3. Barron 1913.

215.   (58) Tudor house, Coleman Street, photographed *c.* 1875

(60)   Drapers' Almshouses, Woodruff Lane
(later 9 Cooper's Row)

In 1518 Sir John Milbourne built thirteen almshouses for poor
members of the Drapers' Company on land on the west side of
Woodruff Lane, backing onto the east end of the Crutched Friars'
church.[1] Stow says they were constructed of brick and timber.[2] A
drawing by Nash shows a range, probably of two storeys, of brick
with stone window dressings (Fig. 64). A four-centred arched gateway in a square label, also of stone, gave entrance through the range
(Fig. 68). Above, also under a square label, is a relief of the Virgin
surrounded by angels, with two shields on either side let into the
façade (arms of the Drapers, bottom left). Below the relief is an
inscription dated 1535; this probably commemorates both the building in 1518 and Milbourne's death in 1534.[3] The almshouses escaped the Great Fire, and thus the representation of them on Ogilby
and Morgan's map of 1677 as two ranges on either side of an alley
perpendicular to Woodruff Lane seems to show their original
arrangement.
1.   *Drapers' Recs.*, ii, 83; Strype 1720, ii, 78–9.
2.   Stow, i, 148.
3.   *Drapers' Recs.*, ii, 83 n.

(61)   16 Cornhill

On the south side of Cornhill near the Royal Exchange, backing
onto part of 'the stone house in Lumbard Street' (124?) in
Treswell's survey in 1612 (Fig. 216). It is first mentioned in 1445,
when William Chadworth and Laurence Sprynges, executors of
Alice Boydnell, granted it to John Stokker.[1] The property appears to
have stayed with the Stokker family until 1565, when Henry
Stokker sold it to John Lute, who bequeathed it with other property

(69) to the Clothworkers' Company. When surveyed in 1612 it
comprised a street range of four and a half storeys on cellars, with a
first-floor gallery leading to a 'new building' at the rear which incorporated a ground-floor kitchen. The gallery had an 'entry' over it,
which also communicated between the front and rear blocks. The
privy lay on the third floor.[2]
1.   CD, Box 58.
2.   *LSRT*, 65.

(62)   The Wildman, Cornhill

First appears in the records of the Clothworkers' Company in 1549,
as a tenancy of Mrs Thorowgood, who paid a quarter's rent.[1] This
suggests that the property was acquired during that year, and possibly that Mrs Thorowgood, presumably a widow, was the sitting
tenant. The company does not possess any documentation which
explains how it acquired the property.

The property (split into two tenancies by 1612) was in the parish
of St Christopher, and the north to south length of 63 ft between
Cornhill and Threadneedle Street in Treswell's survey (Fig. 217)
would place it in the narrow triangle of housing between the first
Royal Exchange and the end of Poultry. The property surveyed in
1612 was evidently a union of two smaller properties, one on
Cornhill to the south and the other on Threadneedle Street to the
north. The text of reference describes the Cornhill part as having a
street range of five and a half storeys on a cellar, and the
Threadneedle part as four and a half storeys on a cellar 38 ft long
(i.e. under building and yard). The first-floor hall contained a
study.[2] For an access diagram, see Fig. 101a.
1.   CRW, Accts., 1549–50.
2.   *LSRT*, 66–7.

(63)   Leadenporch, Crooked Lane

First mentioned in 1398.[1] Stow describes this house as one of the
most ancient in the lane, belonging to Sir John Merston in 1461–2.
By his own time it had been turned into a tavern called the Swan,
selling Rhenish wine.[2] In 1831, during construction of the northern

216. (*left*)   (61) 16 Cornhill (Treswell 1612)

217. (*right*)   (62) The Wildman, Cornhill (Treswell 1612)

approach to London Bridge, part of the north wall of a vaulted undercroft with two lancet windows was found immediately south of St Michael Crooked Lane church. Mouldings on a central pier and capitals of smaller columns at the sides suggest a late twelfth-century date. These remains have been attributed to the Leadenporch, but there is no direct evidence of its position in the lane.[3]

1. *LTR*, xi, 28.
2. Stow, i, 219.
3. *Gentleman's Magazine*, 1831, Part i, 295–6, 196; *Archaeologia*, **29** (1831), 191; Harben, *Dictionary*, 345.

(64) Cordwainers' Hall, Distaff Lane (later 7 Cannon Street)

In 1393 a dwelling-house was granted to a group of cordwainers. Further adjacent premises were conveyed to the company in 1479 and the hall was rebuilt after a substantial bequest in 1559; it was finished in 1577.[1] The post-Fire hall is shown on Ogilby and Morgan as a small building at the back of a small court on the north side of the lane.[2]

1. HR, 209(2); Mander 1931, 108–10.
2. GL, MS 7528 is a plan of 1667 at a scale of 5 ft to the inch.

(65) Tallow Chandlers' Hall II (now 4 Dowgate)

In 1335 Henry Fraunkeleyn, having purchased from the executors of Andrew de Staunford, skinner, the property north of Copped Hall (**66**) stretching north to the junction of Dowgate with *Horsshobregglane* (Cloak Lane), sold it to Reginald de Conduit, mayor, in 1334.[1] As with Skinners' Hall (Copped Hall) to the south, the Walbrook formed the western boundary. The Tallow Chandlers' Company (incorporated in 1471) bought the property in 1475–6 with a bequest of John Steward, chandler.[2] The position of the Dowgate hall when rebuilt after the Great Fire (on Ogilby and Morgan's map, 1677, Fig. 54) suggests that, like its neighbour to the south, it was formerly a courtyard house with the hall arranged north to south on the west side of a court entered from Dowgate.

1. Monier-Williams 1897, 80.
2. *Ibid.*, 85. The previous hall (unlocated) is mentioned in 1465: *Cal. Pat. R., 1461–7*, 367.

(66) Skinners' Hall (now 8 Dowgate)

This house was known at an early date as Copped Hall (a name known elsewhere in the City and Southwark, probably signifying a prominent gable). First mentioned in 1267, it was rented by Julia Hardel from John Renger. Several subsequent owners are known, including Edmund, Earl of Cornwall, in 1295.[1] In 1326 Copped Hall included five shops.[2] Harben[3] asserts that the Skinners were temporarily in possession in the reign of Henry III, and had the property restored to them by Edward III about the time of their incorporation (1327); but Lambert could not find the evidence for this. Company deeds seem to show private ownership throughout the fourteenth century, though it passed to a group of trustees about 1380. Eight skinners are mentioned as trustees in a deed of 1408; from this date the association with the craft is certain.[4] The hall is mentioned in the list of prominent halls in the city of *c.* 1475.[5]

An inventory of the hall in 1580, after repairs, mentions a parlour, counting house, ladies' parlour, kitchen, pastry, buttery and store-house.[6] The hall probably lay at the back of a court entered from Dowgate; in the medieval period the Walbrook stream formed the property's western boundary (cf. Fig. 54).

Wadmore[7] suggested that some of the walls may have resisted the Great Fire, to be incorporated into the present fabric. Norman & Reader[8] observed the medieval Walbrook stream in the garden of the hall during building works in Cloak Lane in 1905. Two walls to the west of the stream seem to mark different lines of embankment during the medieval period. The outer was 2 ft wide and of chalk, the inner to the east 2 ft 8 in wide, of chalk and greensand blocks with occasional bricks.

1. *LTR*, x, 100–1; *Skinners Recs.*, 60–8.
2. *Cal. Inq. PM.*, vi, ed. II, 703.
3. Harben, *Dictionary*, 170.
4. *Skinners Recs.*, 61, 63.
5. BL, Harley MS 541.
6. *Skinners Recs.*, 204.
7. Wadmore 1881, 121.
8. Norman & Reader 1906, 230.

(67) The Erber, Dowgate Hill

First mentioned in 1340 when Edward III granted the property to Geoffrey Scrope. This large property, about 50 yards by 70 yards in extent, had three frontages, to Dowgate Hill in the west, Carter or Chequer Lane to the south and Bush Lane to the east. Later owners included the Earl of Wiltshire in 1399, the Earl of Salisbury in 1429, the Earl of Warwick ('the Kingmaker') in 1460 and Edward IV's brother George, Duke of Clarence, in 1472–8.[1] Besides being a royal or noble residence, the Erber had other uses: in 1392 Richard II made a grant of the office of keeper of the common beam and balance hanging in the Erber.[2] A rental and a series of accounts rendered to the Countess of Salisbury between 1521 and 1524 and an account for the period when the property was again in the king's hands in 1539 provide some details, including the names of several chambers and outbuildings. The property was purchased by the Drapers' Company in 1539.[3] Stow[4] describes it as a great old house, lately rebuilt by Sir Thomas Pullison (mayor 1584–5).

An anonymous plan, dated 1596, survives in the archives of the Drapers' Company (Fig. 218).[5] It presumably represents the house shortly after the rebuilding by Pullison. The property divided into two parts, the larger part to the south containing the main house and Scott's Yard to the north. The hall of the house, of stone and evidently (from the use of steps) on an undercroft, lay north to south at the back of a court entered from Dowgate Hill on the west. To the south were the kitchen, new stables and a store yard with its own gate to Dowgate. Behind the main range was a paved yard with galleries on the east and west sides and subsidiary chambers on the south side; beyond lay a garden, and a back gate to Bush Lane. It is not possible to identify the extent of the new building except in the case of the stables in Scott's Yard.

1. *LTR*, x, 114–16; Honeybourne, *Richard II*, 50–1.
2. *Cal. Pat. R., 1391–6*, 144.
3. Kingsford 1921, 28–31, 50–2.
4. Stow, i, 231.
5. Thompson 1939–40, i, 121.

(68) Innholders' Hall, Elbow Lane

Not mentioned by Stow, and little is known of the pre-Fire site. The hall is first mentioned in 1522.[1] The rebuilt hall is shown on Ogilby and Morgan in the south-east corner of Elbow Lane and Little Elbow Lane, the major building arranged north to south on the east side of a small court.

1. Harben, *Dictionary*, 315.

Farringdon Street, see 76

(69) 11–12 Fenchurch Street

This block of property on the west corner of Fenchurch Street and Philpot Lane was acquired by John Lute in 1541 and bequeathed with other property (see **57**) by his will of 1585 to the Clothworkers' Company.[1]

Three tenancies are shown in Treswell's survey of 1612 (Fig. 62b).[2] Each of the tenants (1–3) had a shop on the Fenchurch Street frontage; the largest (1) lay on the corner with Philpot Lane, and as it had two doors to Fenchurch Street and two fireplaces, this was probably originally two shops. (3)'s shop was a lock-up, for the entry next door led to his chambers on the upper floors; his kitchen was on the third storey. (1)'s kitchen was on the ground floor and included a large oven. Tenancies (1) and (2) were four and a half storeys high,

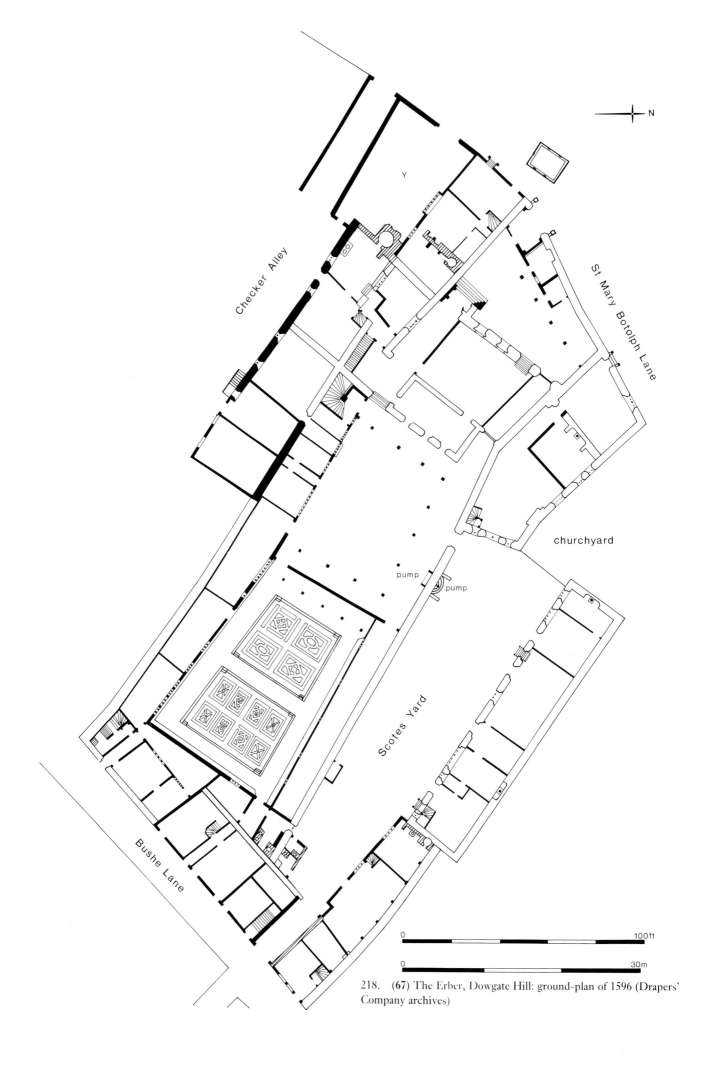

N

Checker Alley

St Mary Botolph Lane

churchyard

pump
pump

Scotes Yard

Bushe Lane

0   100ft

0   30m

218.   (67) The Erber, Dowgate Hill: ground-plan of 1596 (Drapers'
Company archives)

but (3) was apparently only two and a half. Behind was a yard with a gallery on the west side and further buildings of (2).

The cellar stairs in Fenchurch Street led to a large cellar on the corner under (1). No privy is mentioned in the description of (3).

1. CD, Box 1.
2. *LSRT*, 70–1.

(70)   47–48 Fenchurch Street

This block of four houses was bequeathed by Roger Gardiner to the Shearmen's Company in 1520, when it was described as six tenements.[1] It was surveyed by Treswell in 1612 (Fig. 58).[2] The three houses to the west (1–3) were of two-room plan; the two outer ones rose to three and a half storeys, the middle one to two and a half. All had kitchens on the ground floor behind the shop, though one (3) had a shed in the yard which had a prominent chimney, possibly a former separate kitchen. All three had a room called a hall on the first floor over the shop, though in each case unheated; the stack from the kitchen passed up through the rear rooms.

The east half of the block was occupied by a larger house, incorporating two further small tenancies in the street range (4–6). The layout of the major tenancy in this half (4) suggests the adaptation of a medieval hall along the east side of the property, with its kitchen to the south.

1. CD, Box 5; CDW, 47–50.
2. *LSRT*, 72–3.

(71)   Earl of March/Northumberland Inn, Fenchurch Street/Aldgate

In 1360 Roger Mortimer, Earl of March, died in the possession of a tenement, shop and garden in the parish of St Katherine Coleman, with quit-rent to Holy Trinity Priory; the garden comprised part of a former garden called *Colemanhawe*.[1] In 1426, after the death of Edmund Mortimer, the Inn was granted to Henry Percy, second Earl of Northumberland, and was probably the one in his possession at his death in 1455, when it was described as ruinous and waste. The Inn and garden lay on the south side of what is now Fenchurch Street, somewhere east of St Katherine Coleman church and within its parish. The fourth Earl of Northumberland recovered it in 1472 and sold it two years later; in the sixteenth century the gardens were converted to bowling alleys, which were among those broken up by the mayor and sheriffs in 1533. Northumberland Alley, which led from Fenchurch Street to Crutched Friars, is first mentioned in 1600 and shown by Ogilby and Morgan.[2]

In 1982 excavations took place on a site north of Rangoon Street (a nineteenth-century creation, largely removed in 1982) about 30 m (100 ft) south of Fenchurch Street and 60 m (200 ft) east of the site of St Katherine Coleman church.[3] A large timber-framed hall was inferred from two east to west rows of rammed chalk and gravel post-pads, occupying an area 7 m × 9 m, though whether the main axis lay east to west or north to south was unclear. At the south-east corner of the structure a substantial chalk cesspit contained a rich mixture of organic and food debris, window-glass, glass lamps and pottery of 1350–1500. The cesspit was rebuilt in brick in the later sixteenth century. This building may have stood on the site of the Inn as a subsidiary building (perhaps later part of the bowling alley) but further documentary work is required to determine the boundaries of the Inn.

1. *HTA Cartulary*, 80–1.
2. *LTR*, xi, 44–5, 59; Stow, i, 149.
3. MoL, sitecode RAG81; Bowler 1983.

(72)   115 and 118 Fenchurch Street, 12–14 Billiter Street

This large block of property on the west corner of Billiter Lane (later Street) and Fenchurch Street was surveyed by Treswell as part of the Clothworkers' Company estate in 1612 (Fig. 54).[1]

In 1314 Sir John Perry granted to the Hospital of St Mary Spital,

Bishopsgate, the tenement he had by gift of John, son of John Rogemounde in the parishes of All Hallows Staining and St Katherine Cree, between the tenement of Gilbert and two others on the west and the tenement already belonging to the hospital on the east, on the way from Aldgate to *Garscherche* (i.e. Fenchurch Street) in the south and the tenement once of Matthew le Chaundler to the north. In 1520 the block, now including the Billiter Lane frontage, was sold by the hospital to the Wardens of the Fullers' Company; it was possibly used as their hall until the amalgamation with the Shearmen to form the Clothworkers' Company in 1528.[2]

The property can be described in three parts: (a) the great house behind both frontages, (b) the range astride the main gatehouse of the great house to Fenchurch Street, and (c) the small houses forming the façade to Billiter Lane, including a subsidiary gate to the large house.

(a) *The great house* (1). An entry from Fenchurch Street passed into a courtyard, at the back of which lay the hall with a semi-octagonal bay window. A first-floor gallery around three sides of the yard led to chambers on two of the sides; there was a second storey over the buttery and kitchen, but only partly over the hall, which appears to have had no rooms over it. From the hall a three-storey range, including a gallery, lay at right angles along one side of the larger of two gardens. In the second garden, by the kitchen, was a brick tower, first mentioned, as 'insufficient', in 1593.[3]

(b) *The range to Fenchurch Street* (2–3). In 1556–7 the company, noting that the houses at Billiter Lane were about to fall down, assigned moneys to their rebuilding, and appointed one Revell to be carpenter.[4] It is possible that this was either Nicholas Revell (*fl. c.* 1520)[5] or a relative. Three tenements were rebuilt in 1557–8;[6] the rent rose from 58s. *p.a.* to £8 (the great house behind rented at £4 *p.a.* at this time). It seems likely that this is the prominent block shown in this position in the copperplate map of *c.* 1559–60 and the woodcut map based upon it; in 1612 the corner block rose to four and a half storeys on cellars.

(c) *The houses along Billiter Lane* (4–11). This row of one-room plan houses, comprising eight houses and the subsidiary gatehouse of Darcy's tenancy, was composed in 1612 of houses of differing dates; they rose to between two and a half and three and a half storeys. Two sub-groups can be distinguished. In 1536–7 the company bargained with Thomas Delyke, carpenter, for two new houses, paying £12; and with Walter Coper, probably a mason, for making foundations and chimneys and for tiling, paying £19.[7] The frame was viewed at Croydon by men of the company, and the rents fixed at 26s. 9d. The building accounts for the new houses[8] indicate three houses (three cellar windows, three privy seats, mention of the 'middle house'), but subsequent accounts indicate four houses at the new rent. Three of the new houses seem to be the three forming the north end of the row in 1612, backing on to the gallery range of the large house; despite the same rents, the three houses were of differing sizes.

In 1571–2 the tenant of the great house took tenancy of one of the houses in Billiter Lane and may then have made it into a subsidiary gate; in 1603–4 this and two adjacent houses were converted into a gatehouse by rebuilding into two storeys and garret. The other houses in the row have no individual histories in the period 1528–1612 covered by the Clothworkers' accounts, and each may have been built before 1528.

1. *LSRT*, 74–7.
2. CD, Box 15; Girtin 1958, 13; CCO, 1605–23, 224 (1619–20).
3. CCO, 1581–1605, 142.
4. CCO, 1536–58, 27[v], 278.
5. Harvey, *English Medieval Architects*, 250.
6. RW, Accts.
7. CCO, 1536–58, 69.
8. RW, Accts., 1537–8.

(73)   Ironmongers' Hall, Fenchurch Street

The area occupied by the hall is shown in the survey of adjacent properties on three sides by Treswell in 1612 (Fig. 56). The earliest deed in company possession is of 1344, when Robert de Kent and his wife Felicia granted to Richard atte Merk a vacant plot of ground surrounded by their tenements, with a certain part of a great gate and a solar built thereon.[1] The mistery of Ironmongers is known from at least 1328, and in 1457 a group of ironmongers bought the house from the executors of Alice Stiuard, in anticipation of their incorporation in 1463–4.[2] An inventory of 1556 mentions a counting house, court chamber, little spence (a term used as synonymous with both larder and pantry) beyond the court chamber, inner garret and great garret, parlour 'joined round about' (wainscotted) and buttery. The hall was rebuilt in 1578 by Elias Jarman, who also framed a new adjoining tenement towards the street. An inventory of 1643 mentions in addition a linen chamber, gallery, armoury and a parlour over the court room. Furniture and fittings mentioned in 1592 include two cupboards with a desk to set plate on, an iron chimney-back, tables and wooden scutcheons.[3]

1.   Nicholl 1866, 421.
2.   *Cal. LB, E*, 232; Nicholl, *op. cit.*, 421–30.
3.   Nicholl, *op. cit.*, 432, 434–7.

(74)   Tennis Place (later 118) Fenchurch Street

A property in the parish of All Hallows Staining called the Tennyspley was owned by John Yonge, tailor, in 1481.[1] The present property is first called the Tennisplace in the Clothworkers' Company records in 1535.[2] In 1533 John Dale had sold the property to Margaret, Countess of Kent, who entrusted it with other property (see **183**) to the company in 1538.[3]

In Treswell's survey of 1612 (Fig. 54) a main tenant, Richard Holman, and three sub-tenants (1–3) are named. The frontage, two and a half storeys high, was divided between (1), who had only a ground-floor tenancy, and (2), who had large rooms above. (3) held chambers along the rear of the property, also two and a half storeys high. The tennis court, held by (3), is also shown.[4]

1.   *Comm. Court, 1374–1488*, 207.
2.   CDW, 223–4.
3.   Confirmed in her will of 1540, CD, Box 21.
4.   *LSRT*, 78.

(75)   45 Fish Street Hill

A pen-and-ink drawing signed 'KL' and dated 1825, formerly in the collection of Gerald Cobb and now, with his papers, in the National Monuments Record, shows one side of an undercroft beneath 45 Fish Street Hill (Fig. 87). One complete wall 36 ft long and the start of two others at right angles are shown in plan and elevation. Two bays of vaulting are comprised of low pointed arches along the wall rising from semi-octagonal embedded columns with moulded caps and bases; though the caps and the upper part of the vault are conjectural. In the right-hand bay is a stone doorway with low-arched head and chamfered jambs. No compass points are given but it may be presumed that this was either a north or a south wall, along the longer axis of the property.

Fish Street Hill, see also **Old Fish Street Hill (144)**

(76)   1–6 Fleet Lane, 16–21 Farringdon Street, Modern Court

By his will of 1538/9 Walter Wilcockke bequeathed property in Seecollane or Fletelane to Thomas Bonyfaunte; the same property was bequeathed in 1539 to the Clothworkers' Company by Robert Peele, vicar of Chilham in Kent.[1] There is no indication how large this bequest was, but by the time of Treswell's survey in 1612[2] property which represented at least a part, and probably all, of the bequest is shown on both sides of Fleet Lane as it met the Fleet.

Nos. 16 Farringdon Street and 1 Fleet Lane were created after the Great Fire by straightening up the south corner of the lane; the Fleet ditch became Farringdon Street.

The property shown in Treswell's survey of 1612 (Fig. 49) falls into three parts: (a) the great house (Lady Wood), (b) the other buildings north of the lane (left on the plan) and (c) buildings south of the lane, backing on to the Fleet Prison.

(a) *Lady Wood's house* (1): there is no text of reference in Treswell's survey, and information about all floors except the ground floor shown on the plan is therefore lacking. Extensive repairs to the great house in Fleet Lane in 1560 included the use of Caen stone and 'hard stone ready wrought';[3] though none of the walls shown by Treswell is of his usual thicker 'stone' type. The house shown in 1612 comprised hall, parlour and kitchen with other chambers at the back of a small yard entered from Fleet Lane; on the east side was a large garden with a 'grasse plotte'. For an access diagram for this site, see Fig. 100b.

(b) The *buildings on the north side of Fleet Lane* (2–17) comprise a row of one-room plan houses to the east of the great house, and others to the west, including Blacksmith's Court or Flowerdeluse Alley. Treswell specifies in the text of reference that the majority of the occupants in both groups were tenants of Lady Wood. The seven tenancies forming a row along the Lane, backing on to the garden or the house itself, were of two and a half to three and a half storeys, and showed some differences in their internal arrangements on the ground floor. Only one (6) had a cellar. The buildings west of the gate into the great house comprised two sections: two tenancies fronting the lane (9 and 10) of three and a half and two and a half storeys respectively; and Blacksmith's Court, which bordered the Fleet Ditch. At the street end, the tenant of (10) held a two-and-a-half storey house (11), but sublet it. Behind, the alley comprised a number of small tenancies within two or two-and-a-half storey buildings. Although two tenants (16–17) on the east side of the court had two-and-a-half storey houses to themselves, those on the west side were split into smaller tenancies: (12) and (15) had widows with single ground-floor chambers, with other tenants above; between, (13) was a tenancy of three rooms and (14) two separate tenancies (ground floor to one, upper chambers the other). The upstairs tenants of (12), (14) and (15) all had privies overhanging the Fleet, as did three of the ground-floor tenants.

(c) The irregular shape of the available space *south of Fleet Lane* probably contributed to the mixed shapes and sizes of the seven tenancies (18–24) surveyed in 1612. The street frontage was uniformly four and a half storeys high except for (22), which was only two and a half storeys. Features of interest include the position of the well in the yard to the east; the cellar of (18), entered from the inner yard and not from the street; and two instances of ovens separate from kitchen fireplaces, in tenancies (23) and (24), but close to fireplaces from which the coals would have been brought.

1.   CD, Box 66.
2.   *LSRT*, 79–82.
3.   RW Accts., 1560–1.

(77)   Inner Temple Gate (Prince Henry's Room), 17, Fleet Street

In June 1610 John Bennett, newly appointed Serjeant-at-Arms, applied to the authorities of Inner Temple to rebuild the Inner Temple Gate to Fleet Street, together with his house called the Prince's Arms, adjoining to and over the said gate and lane. The new building would be 19 ft north to south, with a jetty of 2 ft 4 in besides the window. The building, which survived the Great Fire, was bought by the London County Council in 1900 and restored; it was also moved back 5 ft for the widening of Fleet Street.[1] All the timberwork is modern, with the exception of eight carved panels which are preserved from the previous (early modern) building; they may be original or themselves reproductions. The present form

of the building reproduces general features of early seventeenth-century London houses; it is of three and a half storeys, jettied on the first and second, and with a baluster rail at the attic floor. Inside on the first floor is an ornate plaster ceiling (Fig. 140) incorporating the feathers of the Prince of Wales, and contemporary panelling on the west side. There is no known connection with Prince Henry (son of James I) or the Duchy of Cornwall; the feathers may be an allusion to the name of the house in 1610.

1. Norman 1905, 370–1, 376–8.

(78)   New, Inner and Middle Temple, Fleet Street

In 1158–62 the Knights Templar acquired land south of Fleet Street, to which they moved from Holborn, and land below Baynard's Castle I, probably on the east side of the Fleet outside the city wall, for a mill. Accounts from their dissolution in 1307–8 show that the Fleet Street estate comprised chambers, kitchen, stable with horse-mills, brewery, dormitory and the surviving church; the mill on the Fleet was broken up and sold for the timber.[1] In 1336 the Temple was divided into two parts: the old consecrated portion (later Inner Temple) was granted to the Knights of St John, and the west part (the New Temple, later Middle Temple) kept in the king's possession. The freeholds were finally purchased by the two Societies in the seventeenth century.[2]

Three buildings survive to provide parallels for more domestic structures in the City. These are the Inner Temple gatehouse (77) and two described here: medieval fragments at Inner Temple Hall, and the Elizabethan Middle Temple Hall.

The hall of Inner Temple, lying south of the Temple church, was rebuilt in 1816, totally rebuilt in 1868–70 and again in 1955 after war damage. An engraving of the hall between 1816 and 1868 is given by Thornbury (Fig. 72b).[3] A roof of at least five bays, separated by arch couples rising from sculptured corbels, is shown, the detail very similar to the roof of Lincoln's Inn hall (47) of 1493. At the west end of the hall two superimposed medieval vaulted rooms survive; these appear to be the remnants of a fourteenth-century tower. Plans of 1867 and two surviving doorways on the north side indicate further medieval chambers. One round-headed doorway in twelfth-century style recorded in 1756 may be the original entrance from the cloister (which ran around the court between hall and church) to the hall.[4]

The present hall of Middle Temple was being built in 1562, when the treasurer of the works requested assistance or advice of the chief carpenter at Longleat (Wiltshire), where a similar roof survives; the hall was largely finished by 1570. It is of brick with stone dressings, and rectangular oriels at the west end. The roof is of double hammerbeam construction, with classical mouldings of Renaissance form: a sunken channel on the side of the beams, with quarter-round mouldings. The screen at the east end of the hall is generally dated 1571, the doors being added in 1671. The site of the previous hall, which lay under what are now Pump and Elm Courts, was then rebuilt as chambers.[5]

Other buildings and structures mentioned in records include a gatehouse of the Middle Temple to Fleet Street, built c. 1520 by Sir Amyas Paulet, treasurer, in brick on stone foundations (demolished 1694);[6] a river-wall, built 1523–33; and a courtyard called Brick Buildings, in building 1568.[7] The gatehouse is shown on the wood-cut map of c. 1558.[8]

1. Williams, *Early Holborn*, ii, 1315–58.
2. *Ibid.*, 1335–6, 1346.
3. Thornbury 1872–8, i, 162.
4. RCHM, *City*, 143–7; Godfrey 1951, 136.
5. RCHM, *City*, 148–51; Hewett 1980, 314, Fig. 375; Williamson 1924, 227–33.
6. Williamson, *op. cit.*, 139–40.
7. *Ibid.*, 142–3, 227.
8. Prockter & Taylor 1979, site ×61.

(79)   Bishop of Salisbury's Inn, Fleet Street

Miss Honeybourne suggests the outline of the site, south of Fleet Street. The Inn, south of Fleet Street, was acquired from St Giles' Hospital, through Herbert, Archdeacon of Canterbury, who was elected to Salisbury in 1194. Additional property was acquired from the Templars by c. 1206. The earliest reference to the Bishop's house here is 1290; the lane of the Bishop is mentioned in 1324,[1] and called Salisbury Lane in 1417. Excavations on the site in 1986–7 revealed a mid-fourteenth-century Thames riverside wall and large-scale dumping to reclaim land behind it.[2] The porch of the hall is mentioned in 1401. In 1564 the Inn was sold to Sir Richard Sackville, who enlarged it. Ogilby and Morgan show the lane opening into a court (Salisbury Court) in 1677.[3]

1. *Cal. Wills*, i, 307.
2. MoL, sitecode BOY86.
3. Honeybourne, 'Value', 334–8; Honeybourne, 'Fleet', 68–73.

(80)   Abbot of Winchcombe's Inn, Fleet Street

The Inn of Winchcombe Abbey (Gloucestershire) lay on the south side of Fleet Street on the corner with Fleet Bridge (now Ludgate Circus).[1] It was acquired during the abbacy of Walter de Wykewane, 1282–1314; there is a reference to the abbot's house in 1345.[2] It then consisted of houses, buildings, gardens and a quay (to the Fleet on the east); of these, the lower hall, some chambers and the stables could be reserved by the abbot as his quarters when in London. The Inn abutted south on the Inn of the Bishop of St David's (44). In February 1477 a report was made on the house by two London masons, Thomas Hylle and Stephen Burton.[3] Hylle may have been the mason Thomas atte Hill who built the wall of the Lollard's Tower (Fig. 107) in 1434,[4] though this sounds unlikely; Burton dealt, among other things, in ready-made fireplaces.[5]

1. Honeybourne, 'Value', 428–31.
2. *Possessory Assizes*, 31.
3. Royce 1892, ii, 563.
4. Harvey, *Early Medieval Architects*, 155–6.
5. *Ibid.*, 40–1.

(81)   Abbot of Cirencester's Inn, Fleet Street

The abbot of Cirencester may have owned property between Holborn and Fleet Street from before 1253; a hall of the abbot in the parish of St Bride's is mentioned in 1358, but the Inn is not mentioned until 1416. It was called the *Popyngaye* by 1430.[1] In 1538 the City Viewers judged that the abbot's property should measure 6¾ ells (27 ft) along the street; but a further 20¼ in to the east belonged to a neighbour, Thomas White.[2] Perhaps the frontage had been rebuilt too wide shortly before. In 1544, granted by Henry VIII to Alexander Hudson, the Inn was described as 'dyvers messuages small cottages and one garden plott'.[3]

1. *Assize of Nuisance*, 496.
2. *Viewers' Certificates*, 130.
3. Honeybourne, 'Value', 349–54; Honeybourne, 'Fleet', 83–7.

(82)   Clifford's Inn, Fleet Street

This property belonged in the reign of Edward I to Malculum de Harley, who held various posts in the administration of estates in royal hands.[1] In 1310 it was granted to Robert Clifford, Guardian of the Marches of Scotland, who died at Bannockburn in 1314. In 1344 the widow of his second son Robert demised the property to apprentices of the Bench, and it thus became an Inn of Chancery, although the Cliffords remained in residence. The Clifford family continued to maintain an interest, with interruptions, until the transfer of the property to a trust in 1902.[2]

Ogilby and Morgan show the Inn as a courtyard house north of St Dunstan's church, entered from Fleet Street. A protuberance at the south-west corner of the hall, into the court, presumably represents an oriel window. The south aspect of the hall is shown by Crowther in 1884 (Fig. 219). A two-centred, moulded, fourteenth-century

219.   **(82)** Clifford's Inn, Fleet Street (J. Crowther 1884)

doorway survived at the south-east corner of the hall until the Second World War;[3] it may originally have led to a buttery.[4] This would place the service rooms at the east end of the hall.

1.   Williams, *Early Holborn*, ii, 976.
2.   *LTR*, x, 91–2; Williams, *op. cit.*, ii, 1006–13.
3.   *LTR*, x, Plate opposite p. 92; RCHM, *City*, 157.
4.   Norman 1903, 253.

(83)   Fleet Lane/Chancery Lane

A house at the west corner of Fleet Street and Chancery Lane is shown in an engraving by J. T. Smith of 1789 (Fig. 173); a water-colour of the same view dated 1794 is in the British Library.[1] It is of four storeys and garret, richly embellished with grotesque carvings and with exterior panelling forming classical arches (on the Fleet Street front only), the elevation divided by prominent moulded string-courses beneath each storey except the garret. The house is not dated but a date of *c.* 1590 may be proposed. Other houses down Chancery Lane in the same engraving also have grotesque corbels, and probably date from the second half of the sixteenth century.

1.   Add. MS 42506, f. 81 (reproduced in Payne 1987, title page).

(84)   Barentyn's House, Foster Lane

Drew Barentyn, goldsmith and mayor in 1398, had at his death in 1415 a hospice in which he dwelt, with fifty-four shops and solars in the parishes of St John Zachary, St Anne and St Mary Staining. Stow says 'he dwelled right against Goldsmiths' Hall. Between the

which Hall and his dwelling house he builded a gallery, thwarting the street, by which he might pass from the one to the other'.[1] This gallery or *hautpas* is shown at the north end of Foster Lane on the woodcut panorama (based on the copperplate map of *c.* 1559). Barentyn's considerable house must have therefore lain near the north end of Foster Lane on its west side, backing onto the precinct of St Martin-le-Grand.[2] Since part of his estate was in St Ann's parish (as delineated on Ogilby and Morgan's map in 1677), Barentyn presumably owned property on the south side of St Anne's Lane, which ran from St Martin-le-Grand (street) east to Foster Lane (i.e. now the west end of Gresham Street).

1.   Stow, i, 305.
2.   *LTR*, x, 53.

(85)   Goldsmiths' Hall, Foster Lane

The executors of Sir Nicholas Segrave sold property in Foster Lane to William de Clyf, clerk, in 1323; he sold it to nineteen goldsmiths acting for their craft in 1339. Reddaway suggests that a new hall was built in 1362–3, together with a kitchen, pantry, buttery and at least two chambers. A parlour was added in 1382, its frame costing £25; it had chimneys and a privy, was roofed in tiles and connected with the hall. At first the parlour was a retiring and private room for the wardens, but later the livery were dining there.[1] Stow described it as 'a proper house, but not large'.[2]

1.   Reddaway & Walker 1975, 29–30, 39.
2.   Stow, i, 305.

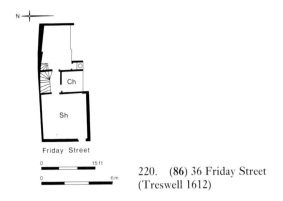

220.   (86) 36 Friday Street
(Treswell 1612)

(86)   36 Friday Street
In 1599 Peter Blundell gave £150 to the Clothworkers' Company; out of this they purchased this house on the east side of Friday Street.[1] The house was of four and a half storeys on cellars (Fig. 220).[2]
1. CD, Box 74.
2. *LSRT*, 83.

(87)   Friday Street (west side), 1410
In 1410 Master Walter Cook and Sir Henry Jolipas (cf. 1), clerks, contracted with John More, timbermonger, and John Gerard, carpenter, to build three houses on the west side of Friday Street between the tenement of John Frensshe, goldsmith, on the north and the tenement of Cook, Jolipas and others on the south. A new cellar occupying the entire plot was to be dug, over which More and Gerard would lay joists and floors. On the ground floor would be three shops, each with a counter and partitions, with two floors over. On the first floor would be a hall, larder and kitchen for each house, each hall with benches, screens and suitable windows, jettying over the ground floor. On the second floor would be a principal chamber, a withdrawing chamber and a privy; presumably, though not certainly, as individual sets rather than in common, since each house would have two flights of stairs (between the three floors). The ground floor would be 10½ft high, the first floor 9ft to the wallplates and the second floor 8ft to the tie-beam. The houses were to be roofed with gables to the street, as shown on a plan (*un patron*), which also specified details of the lintelled window required on the street frontage. The sizes of timbers used were to resemble those in the Rent of Robert Chichele in Soper Lane.[1]
1. Salzman, *Building*, 483–5. A model by C. Hewett is in the medieval gallery of the MoL.

(88)   Giltspur Street and Cock Lane
Henry Suckley or Suckliffe, merchant tailor, granted four messuages at Pie Corner, Smithfield, to a trust in 1558; they passed by his will to Christ's Hospital in 1586, presumably on the death of his wife Agnes.[1] A survey and plan by Treswell (Fig. 62a) dates from before 1611, when the tenancy allocated to John Welles on the plan was granted to Thomas Hartley.[2] Comparison with a view of the main block in 1624 adds further details of rooms, such as cellars, which probably existed in 1611, and tells of recent internal changes attributable to the period *c.* 1611–24.[3]

The rectangular block of property divided into two parts: (a) a row of four tenancies facing Giltspur Street to the east (bottom of the plan) with small yards behind, and (b) a court entered from Cock Lane, in which were smaller dwellings.

(a) The four tenancies (1–4) on the west side of Giltspur Street were part of the row or street called Pye Corner. Stow[4] derived the name from an inn sign; in 1677 Ogilby and Morgan gave the name to Giltspur Street between Cock Lane and Hosier Lane. The large ovens shown by Treswell suggest that these houses were involved in the cooked food trade. The houses were of two and a half or three and a half storeys. In the front room of (3), against the back wall, were two square brick pillars supporting a 'range'.

(b) The court on the south side of Cock Lane. Five of the six small tenancies (5–10) shown on the plan have some added text. (8) and (9) both had '3 rooms one over the other', which probably indicates three storeys, i.e. two upper chambers; but the stair to (9)'s upper chambers was not shown within his ground-floor room, perhaps it was outside. The ground floor of the range to Cock Lane comprised small tenancies of (5–7). (7) had chambers behind in the court, one over the other; (6) had a chamber over (7)'s ground floor, and (5) seems to have encroached onto (6) at first floor or higher. The access to all these upper chambers must have been from the court behind.
1. *Inq. PM*, ii, 17–19; *Charity Comm.*, 98.
2. CHMB, 3, 121ᵛ; *LSRT*, 85–7.
3. GL, MS 12834/1, 16–20.
4. Stow, ii, 22.

(89)   St Paul's Bakery (later Godliman Street), 1369
In 1369 the Dean and Chapter of St Paul's contracted with Roger Fraunkeleyn and John Page, carpenters, to build a range of shops at St Paul's Bakery The length of 86 yards and references to a corner indicate that the range was to be L-shaped, along the entire west side of Godliman Street and along the north side of Knightrider Street. Fraunkeleyn and Page were to erect twenty shops, with gables to the east and west, and a gate with a wicket between the first two at the north end. The shops would have lintelled windows to the street, with two bay windows at the corner. The shops were to be as large as the underlying cellar, and each one would have an internal partition, stairs, a wooden privy pipe, and benches in the hall. The doors and *fenestres* (window-shutters?) would be of Eastland boards, and all the other timber components, including gutters, of heart of oak. Measurements of many timbers are specified (see Chapter 6).[1]

This range of buildings was still standing in 1649, though rebuilt and extended higher.[2]
1. Salzman, *Building*, 441–3.
2. St Paul's Parliamentary Survey, GL, MS 8164.

(90)   St Paul's Brewery (later Godliman Street), 1370
In 1370 the Dean and Chapter of St Paul's contracted with Piers de Webenham, mason, for the masonry groundworks of a range of shops on a vacant plot 'at St Paul's Brewery'. Webenham would demolish a standing wall to a height of 1ft, suitable for receiving the sill beams of eighteen new shops, each 25ft long and 11ft wide (presumably aligned at right angles to the street). The old rubble of the wall would be used elsewhere in the foundations. Webenham would make another wall of the length of the shops (i.e. the rear wall) which would be 2ft thick and rise to the first-floor joists. At the south end of the building the underpinning foundation would cross between the other two, and also be 1ft high. This suggests that the range was to lie north to south. In the east part of the building he would make enclosing walls to divide the cellars below the shops, which 'will rise in height as far as the aforementioned joists'. This can only refer to the first-floor joists, and perhaps indicates that the shops had cellars under part of the ground floor – the east part – and the dividing or party-walls of the cellared portion were in masonry to the first floor. Certain other foundations would carry principal posts as parts of the shops. Further, there would be ten chimneys in the shops, eight of which were to be double and under mantels of Flemish tile, hearths of stone and tilesherds, the chimneys rising 1ft above the roof of the shops, each chimney 5½ft between the jambs. There were also to be ten privies of stone, eight of them double, 11ft × 10ft deep. The Dean and Chapter would provide all materials except Flemish tile and plaster, which the mason would provide; saving that he would receive ten marks to pay for a shipload of Flanders tile.[1]

Because the relevant carpentry contract has not survived, this

building can only be half envisaged. It presumably lay north to
south, though on which side of the street is not specified. In its east
half were to be cellars, which could be below either the front shop or
the rear room (two rooms are assumed from the length of 25 ft).
Presumably each had a solar over (cf. the 1369 contract (**89**) above).
They were all provided with a privy and a chimney.

St Paul's Brewery is usually placed on the east side of Godliman
Street, opposite the Bakery.[2] The frontage to the street is only 125 ft
long; perhaps the 198 ft of frontage for these shops was achieved by
making it a corner site, as with the 1369 contract for shops opposite,
although the contract seems to imply a building lying in one direction only.

1. Salzman, *Building*, 443–4.
2. Harben, *Dictionary*, 460, 468.

(91)   Corbet Court, Gracechurch Street

A 'Norman' stone building, discovered about 1870, lay to the north
of All Hallows Gracechurch (or Lombard) Street, on the south side
of Corbet Court (extending between Corbet Court and Bell Yard),
on the west side of Gracechurch Street, but not aligned to it. The
east wall was built on an underlying larger wall, believed to be
Roman but probably post-Roman, of chalk rubble with a few Roman
bricks in gravelly mortar, about 9 ft thick and surviving up to 10 ft
high. The Norman building measured 39 ft × 39 ft 3 in, and was
of two by three rectangular bays (Figs. 29–30). Transverse and
longitudinal arches were of broad flat ribs of rectangular blocks.
Responds were formed by corbels of two chamfered projections
lying on top of each other. The two central piers had been replaced
at a later date with neatly squared stone.

Two windows were found in both the east and west walls, set
about 5 ft above the conjectured original floor level. At the south-
east corner there may have been a half-bay continuation of the east
aisle. A door at the north end of the west aisle led to a porch, on the
west side of which was a door to a newel staircase to the upper floor.
The porch itself had an arcade internally on each side, of circular
columns with cushion capitals, supporting a semi-circular vault
springing from a moulded string course. Loftus-Brock, who recorded the structure during demolition of the post-Fire houses
above, thought that the original floor level was about 18 ft below
Corbet Court.[1] The walls were of Kentish rag and plentiful Roman

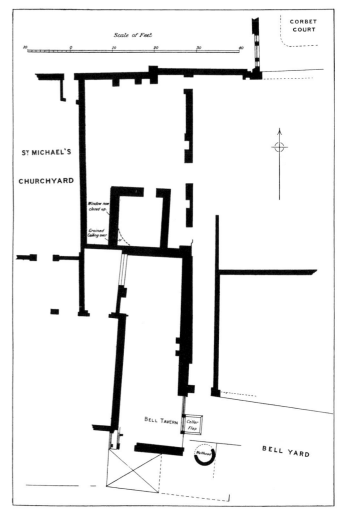

221.   (**92**) 7–12 Gracechurch Street: position of vault recorded 1912
[Norman 1916]

222.   (**93**) 28–30 Gracechurch Street: vaulted undercroft recorded
1928, section and plan

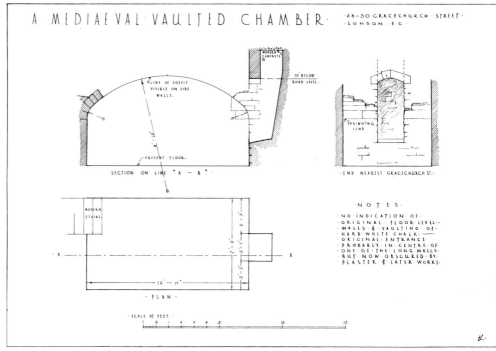

bricks (from the underlying forum), used specially in the barrel vault over the entrance passage. Caen stone was used for the arcade and elsewhere as freestone.

1. Loftus-Brock 1872, 176–9.

(92)   Bell Yard, 7–12 Gracechurch Street

A small vaulted chamber was recorded at the rear of Bell Yard, adjacent to St Michael's churchyard, in 1912 (Fig. 221). It measured 11 ft 6 in north to south by 10 ft 5 in east to west and 12 ft 6 in high; the vault was of rubble construction, and apparently ran east to west. A recess interpreted as a blocked window was recorded in the west wall.[1]

1. Norman 1916, 12–13.

(93)   28–30 Gracechurch Street

A rectangular undercroft measuring 12 ft 11 in east to west by 7 ft north to south was recorded here in 1927 (Fig. 222). The surviving floor level was about 19 ft below the level of Gracechurch Street and 6 ft 9 in below the vaulting, but the original floor level was not determined. The walls and vault were constructed of 'hard white chalk' (clunch?), and the vault was of depressed four-centred form without ribs. At the east end, nearest Gracechurch Street, a rectangular cavity with a low-arched head formed a light well up to the modern surface. The position of this chamber within the modern property is not known.[1]

1. P8 GM files, MoL.

(94)   Gray's (Grey's) Inn, Gray's Inn Lane

Property forming the site of Gray's Inn is first mentioned in 1280, and in 1294 was granted by St Paul's to Reginald de Grey, justice, of Cheshire. At his death in 1307 the land comprised at least thirty acres, a dovecote and a windmill. Apprentices of the Common Law became associated with the Inn about 1370, and by the late fifteenth century a trust figures on the title deeds, in the manner of the livery companies.[1] Stow thought the buildings dated from the time of Edward III.[2] The earliest surviving features are blocked early sixteeth-century windows in the chapel (sixteenth-century walls, rebuilt 1698). The present hall was built in 1556–60; it is of brick with stone dressings on an undercroft.[3] It incorporates two earlier stone doorways, dating to the first half of the sixteenth century.

1. *LTR*, x, 130–1; Williams, *Early Holborn*, i, 629–75.
2. Stow, ii, 87.
3. RCHM, *West London*, 52–5; Pevsner, *London II*, 211–12.

(95)   63–65 Gray's Inn Lane

A frame of three houses on the east side of Gray's Inn Lane, opposite the entrance to Gray's Inn, was photographed in 1875 (Fig. 223). A late nineteenth-century plan shows them then to have been of two-room plan on the ground floor with axial chimneys-stacks; the larger house to the south, no. 63, was of four rooms, two either side of a longitudinal passage. A date of 1591 or 1595 was carved upon a bracket on the front of no. 65 (note on the plan).[1]

1. Bristol City Archives.

223.   **(95)** Houses in Gray's Inn Lane, photographed in 1875

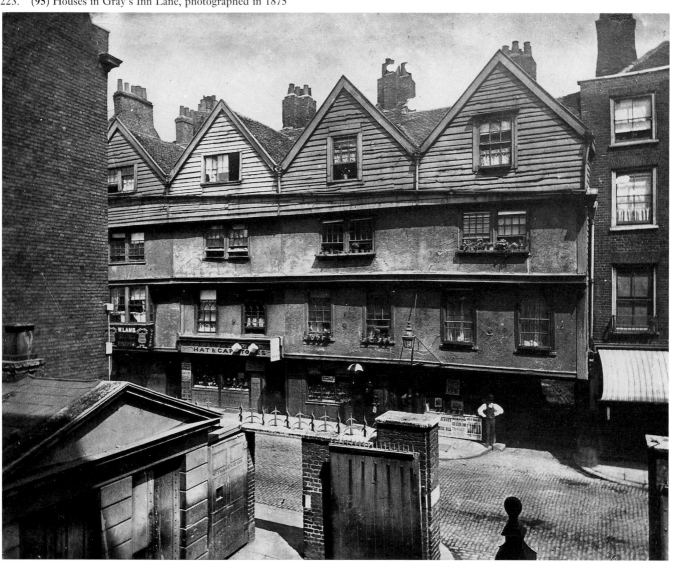

(96)   Leathersellers' Hall II, Great St Helen's, Bishopsgate
In 1542 Henry VIII granted part of the convent of St Helen's,
Bishopsgate, to Sir Richard Williams, who sold it to Thomas
Kendall, leatherseller, in 1544; he immediately demised it to his
company.[1] The company occupied the first-floor dorter on the east
side of the cloister, north of the priory church. Company records
mention repairs and adaptations, especially in 1566–7 when the
parlour was built.[2]

Illustrations of hall and parlour before their destruction in 1799
(Figs. 55–6) show that the hall was of four bays, with rich panelling
of 1608 to the ceiling; the thirteenth-century door from the nuns'
dorter to their frater was retained, as were the vaults below. The
ceiling probably dates from 1610, when the hall was re-roofed.[3] The
parlour of 1566–7, built on the former chapter house (Fig. 55) was
of one and a half storeys above the ground floor, with dormers
apparently added in the seventeenth century. Its east end was
largely glazed, in lights of three tiers. The fireplace was evidently
half way along the long, blind south side, in a position similar to that
in the Clothworkers' parlour of 1594 (**139**).
1.   Stow, ii, 299 (notes by Kingsford).
2.   Black 1871, 73.
3.   For the dates of the two ceilings, *ibid.*, 74.

(97)   Embroiderers' Hall, 36 Gutter Lane
John Throwstone, embroiderer (afterwards goldsmith and sheriff),
gave £40 towards the purchase of the hall site; he died in 1519. Stow
places the hall in Guthrun's (Gutter) Lane.[1]

The site, on the east side of Gutter Lane, was surveyed by Mills
& Oliver[2] in 1668.
1.   Stow, i, 314.
2.   Mills & Oliver, *Survey*, iv, 70.

(98)   Bakers' Hall II, Harp Lane
The company bought the property from a member, Richard Roper,
in 1506; previously the house had been the property of Richard
Chicheley, chamberlain of London 1434–49, and before him of
Richard Lyons, a prominent vintner murdered during the Peasants'
Revolt. The Elizabethan hall lay north to south on the east side of
the lane, at the back of a court with deep buildings along the street
frontage. The hall was partly of brick and partly timber-framed, and
roofed in tile. Large gates on yellow posts with a hanging lantern led
to a covered way. Besides the hall there was a summer or Clement
(after St Clement) parlour, a winter parlour with a room for the
yeomanry over, an 'upper hall', chamber for the clerk, beadle's
quarters, kitchen with a bow window, buttery, armoury and other
chambers. The garden had a well and a bowling alley.[1]
1.   Thrupp 1936, 163–5; GL, MS 5174/1–2.

(99)   'Whittington's Palace', Hart Street
A notable late sixteenth-century house was recorded by several
antiquaries at the very end of the eighteenth century. Its location is
given as 'four doors from Mark Lane' and on the south side of Hart
Street; this would place it close to St Olave's church. The recorded
exterior (Fig. 113) formed three sides of a courtyard (the north side

224.   (**100**) 48–50 Hart Street (Crutched Friars) (T. Shepherd *c.* 1850)

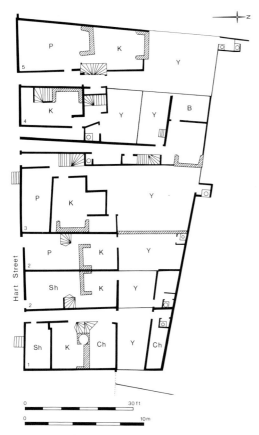

225. (101) Houses on north side of Hart Street (later Crutched Friars) (Treswell 1612)

having been rebuilt), but no courtyard is shown in this part of the street by Ogilby and Morgan.

The engravings show that the court's east, south and west sides were probably built at one time, and stood at least three storeys high. Grotesque carvings formed pilasters on the ground floor and as corbels supported jetties of the first floor and rows of windows on the first and second floors. Under the first-floor windows were carved the arms of the twelve major livery companies. One original first-floor chamber remained (Fig. 130); about 25 ft × 15 ft, it had wainscot with carved arches above, and a plaster ceiling. A second 'anteroom' had a ceiling dated 1609 and the initials P.M.M., with heads of several Caesars and two coats of arms; to one observer this room seemed to have been fitted out later than the exterior.[1] There is no known connection with Richard Whittington.

1. *Gentleman's Magazine*, 1796, Part ii, 545.

**(100) Houses on north side of Hart Street
        (later 48–50 Crutched Friars)**
A pencil drawing by T. Shepherd of three houses on the north side of Crutched Friars, immediately east of the railway viaduct, is in the Guildhall Library (Fig. 224). No. 50, of three storeys and garret, has a mansard roof. Nos. 48–49 are of four storeys, with slight jetties. A note on the sketch, probably referring to no. 48, calls it the Cheshire Cheese.

**(101) Houses on north side of Hart Street
        (later Crutched Friars)**
By her will of 1596 Thomasine Evans bequeathed six properties in Crutched Friars to the Clothworkers' Company.[1] These lay on a wedge-shaped piece of land on the north side of Hart Street, immediately west of the south end of Northumberland Alley. In 1612 the buildings (then five tenancies) were generally of two rooms on each floor with yards behind (Fig. 225).[2] Tenancy (2), formerly

two buildings, still retained its two street doors, and the juxtaposition of the entry with that of the adjacent (3) brought all three doors together. (3) had a parlour alongside the street, an unusual position. This tenancy rose to four and a half storeys, whereas its neighbours were three and a half or two and a half storeys; all were on cellars. The text of reference for (5) is lacking.

1. CD, Box 51.
2. *LSRT*, 68–9.

(102) Bishop of Lincoln's Inn, Holborn
Robert de Chesney or de Querceto, Bishop of Lincoln 1148–68, purchased from the Templars their first site in Holborn, comprising houses, a chapel and gardens; this purchase was confirmed by Henry II in 1162. References to the house continue until 1545, by which time it had been acquired by Thomas Wriothesley, Earl of Southampton, and was called Southampton House until 1636.[1]

Stow recalled that 'Master Roper hath of late builded much here, by means whereof the ruines of the old Temple were seene to remaine builded of Cane stone, round in form as the new Temple by Temple barre and other Temples in England'.[2] Southampton Buildings were built on the site in 1652.

1. MLH, xi, 63–4.
2. Stow, ii, 87.

(103) Staple Inn, Holborn
The documentary history of this site is given by Williams,[1] though his elaborate argument connecting the site with the Staple of Wools is without foundation. The present site originally comprised two adjacent properties on the south side of Holborn, the east of which is first mentioned *c.* 1183, when it was 29 ft wide and 597 ft long. The west property is first mentioned in 1271 as an abuttal on the east property, and in 1307 William de Brimmesgrave quitclaimed his interest in it; a William atte Stapeldehalle is known in 1292.[2] The name may derive from OE *stapel* = post, and refer to an aisled hall. The name is attached to the east property from 1333, when Richard Starcolf, mercer, bequeathed *le Stapledehalle* to be sold for pious uses; Stapled Hall in Holborn is mentioned in 1407 and 1436.[3] It was known as Staple Inn by 1415, and by the early fifteenth century was associated with the students of law as an Inn of Chancery; it was attached to Gray's Inn in 1520. The west property continued in separate ownership, passing to St Sepulchre's parish through the will of Richard Harsham, 'ferror', in 1391. In 1415 it was known as the Star on the Hoop. The Inn was put on the market in the mid sixteenth century as chantry property, and by 1580 the Company of Staple Inn had acquired it. The existing buildings of the enlarged Inn date from 1581–6, the period of unification of the two properties.

The layout of Staple Inn in 1676 is shown on Ogilby and Morgan's map of 1677 (Fig. 73); the hall formed the rear range of a courtyard entered from Holborn, with a large garden to the south. The hall of 1580–1 is of four bays, of brick with stone dressings, with kitchen and pantry (rebuilt) to the west; the hall has been rebuilt after severe war damage. A canted oriel window (with a main face of sixteen lights, 4 × 4, in 1830) protruded into the court at the north-east corner. A drawing of 1830 by Shepherd[4] shows that the main entrance to the screens had a moulded ogee door frame of stone, and a glazed main louvre and a subsidiary louvre over the screens. The roof has been damaged but Hewett[5] suggests its main components may be intact; it is of hammerbeam style with king-posts. A mid- or late sixteenth-century classical screen within the hall survived until the Second World War.[6]

The street range to Holborn (Figs. 170–1, 226) is in two parts. In 1586 the Company of Staple Inn leased two houses, now nos. 337–8 High Holborn (i.e. the westernmost buildings), to Vincent Engham, principal in 1586, who had built them.[7] There is no information on the building date of the major part of the street range to the east, and it has been much altered, particularly in restorations of

226. (103) Staple Inn, Holborn: the main block to the street of 1586 (J. T. Smith 1800)

1894 and 1936. There is no evidence that it was originally close-studded as it now appears; engravings and nineteenth-century photographs (Figs. 171, 226) show an exterior of bland rough plastering, and that the majority of the windows were by then sash-windows. Hewett[8] erroneously considers the present windows to be original, and notes that pegging of the studs is frequently only at every fifth stud – a possible sign of insertions into what were originally rectangular panels. The simple scroll corbels now on the main range also appear to be modern (i.e. *post*-1894). Devoid of accurately datable features, the main range can only be dated to the 1580s because it was probably part of the rebuilding scheme implied in the documents.

Engham's two houses on the west are of four and a half storeys, and the furthest west of the two has a small projecting room on the second floor (a study?). Both are of one-room plan on the ground floor with no access to the court behind. The five bays of the main range, three and a half storeys high, are also separate shops of one-room plan.[9] The eighteenth-century stairs at their rear allow access to upper floors from the court only (i.e. not to the shops), perhaps reflecting an original division between the ground-floor shops and chambers above, which would be lodgings for the Inn. The central bay incorporates the stone gateway to the Inn, which presumably also dates from the late 1580s; it has diminishing pilasters, moulded imposts and a round arch with reeded ornament and panelled soffit (recently restored). The gate or door leaves are also of this date.

A break in the building line of the east range of the courtyard perhaps indicates the site of the Stapled Hall of 1333, at right angles to the street.

1. Williams, *Early Holborn*, ii, 1160–74, 1192–1226.
2. *Cal. LB*, *A*, 144.
3. HR, 62(25); HR, 135(47); *Cal. Close R., 1435–41*, 47.
4. Williams, *op. cit.*, 1178.
5. Hewett 1980, 231.
6. RCHM, *West London*, 57–9.
7. Williams, *op. cit.*, 1184.
8. Hewett, *op. cit.*, 233.
9. Plan in RCHM, *West London*, 58.

(104)   Abbot of Malmesbury's Inn, Holborn

The earlier histories of the component properties of this Inn can be traced from the mid thirteenth century.[1] Three messuages on the south side of Holborn were given to the abbey by Thomas Coubrigge and William Camme in 1369; the pope's licence was confirmed by the Archbishop of Canterbury in 1383, when mention is made of the 'inn newly built, next the great garden, and the kitchen on the west side of the inn'. The property was quickly enlarged by the acquisition of tenements to the east and west (the latter in 1387). The Inn, which lay immediately east of Staple Inn, was usually leased. It was known as Lincoln's Inn until 1417 because between 1331 and 1364 it was occupied by Thomas de Lincoln, King's Sergeant; in 1399 the property included at least four shops. In 1544 the Inn, now called *le Castell*, included rooms which the abbot and monks could enjoy at fifteen days' notice: the hall, chapel and four chambers in front of it, the kitchen, stabling and pasture in the little garden next to the Inn, and the great garden.[2]

1. Williams, *Early Holborn*, ii, 1080, 1099, 1155.
2. Honeybourne, 'Value', 375–86.

(105)   Barnard's Inn, Holborn

In the early fourteenth century this site comprised two adjacent properties, known as the Flourdelyse and the Aungel on the Hope in 1381, with a garden which stretched to Fetter Lane on the east, where it was fronted by seven shops. Shortly after 1422 the property was known as Macworth Inn, after John Macworth, Dean of Lincoln and Chancellor to Henry V. By 1435 the Inn was called Barnard's Inn, after Lionel Barnard, its principal, and was a house of legal learning (possibly since 1415).[1] The Inn is mentioned as 'new built' in 1439.[2] Its hall, mentioned in 1450, was rebuilt in 1510.[3] For the site, see Fig. 73.

The hall has survived, much restored, at the south end of a court entered from Holborn. Measuring 36 ft × 22½ ft, it has walls of coursed ragstone, now fronted with brick. In the present basement a small portion of the south wall is displayed, showing roof tiles laid between several courses, a decorative feature which suggests the existence of a medieval cellar beneath the hall. Old prints (e.g. Fig. 114) show a round-headed arch or doorway in the north wall at ground-level immediately west of the passage which communicated between the front courtyard and the former garden to the south; this doorway presumably was from a former screens passage. The hall is of three bays, divided by trusses comprised of a hollow chamfered tiebeam supported by arched braces springing from modern wooden corbels (Fig. 71). Crown-posts support a longitudinal collar. Two of the bays on the north side and all three on the south side have their upper parts filled with double-height windows, six lights wide, separated by restored wooden mullions and transoms. A fireplace at the west (dais) end may be original, but a matching fireplace at the east end is a later insertion. Oak linenfold panelling around the walls and ten carved panels with heads in profile over the fireplaces have been dated to *c*. 1525 (Fig. 147);[4] but they are perhaps part of the rebuilding of 1510. The lantern to the roof is thought to be medieval, but is generally inaccessible. The Royal Commission described it as octagonal, with a small opening with trefoiled head in each face, finished with a Gothic moulded cornice and an ogee-shaped roof of lead carrying a ball and vane.

Other buildings of the Inn are shown in early photographs (National Monuments Record). The gabled front to Fetter Lane, rebuilt in the late sixteenth century, was pulled down in 1909–10.[5]

The dating of Barnard's Inn hall, important as the only surviving medieval secular timber structure of domestic scale in the City, is not precise. The carpentry would support a date in the later fourteenth or first half of the fifteenth century.[6] Barron[7] suggests that the hall was built between 1405, when the properties were described as dilapidated, and 1439, when the Inn was described as 'new built'; but the new buildings could have been of other structures than the

hall. Nevertheless an early fifteenth-century date for the hall is retained here.

1. Williams, *Early Holborn*, ii, 1060–79.
2. Barron 1979, 19.
3. *LTR*, x, 54.
4. RCHM, *City*, 159.
5. *LTR*, x, 54.
6. Hewett 1980, 182, 305.
7. Barron 1979, 19.

(106) Ely Place, Holborn

An inquisition of 1290 found that John de Kirkeby, Bishop of Ely from 1286, held a hall, chambers and part of a new chapel in Holborn of Alice More, and the rest of the chapel and stable of Hugh le Carpenter. Kirkeby left the property to the bishopric of Ely.[1] In 1302–3 the Inn was described as a messuage with a great gate and nine cottages (shops in 1376).[2] When surveyed in 1357, the Inn comprised a hall, roofed in lead, three principal chambers, other chambers *pro secretis episcopi*, chambers for the household, domestic offices and a grange for hay; a cloister was partly in ruins. Thomas Arundel, Bishop 1374–88, rebuilt the Inn and gatehouse; Stow saw his arms in the stonework.[3] In 1376 there was also a middle gatehouse with rooms over it, part of the lodgings of royal personages,

such as the Black Prince who lodged in 1357, and their retainers; here John of Gaunt died in 1399.[4] An oratory is mentioned in 1383.[5] Accounts of the Keeper of the Palace for 1399 mention an armoury next to the hall and 'the oratory of the house next the chapel'; repair of the kitchen in that year included temporarily raising the roof.[6] In 1531 the chapel, cloister and gallery were used for extra seating at a feast.[7]

The topography of the medieval Inn can be reconstructed from late eighteenth-century drawings and the survival of the chapel as St Etheldreda, Ely Place; a plan of 1776 and a view from the north shows the major buildings of the by then much-reduced property (Figs. 36–7). The gatehouse to Holborn shown in the plan is not shown by engravers; presumably no ancient work survived above ground. The hall (see also Fig. 69) lay east to west at the back of a large court, and was of four bays and a screens passage, with windows (stylistically of *c.* 1300) comprising two trefoil-headed lights and a quatrefoil pierced head. A side fireplace had been inserted on the north side by the eighteenth century. A porch on the south side was built of diapered brick with an elaborate entrance incorporating a design, presumably armorial, under an ogee-shaped moulded arch. The kitchen lay on the north side of the hall, at right angles to it.

West of the hall were three rooms (presumably the three principal chambers of 1357) and, north of them, a rectangular cloister with

227. **(107)** Bishop of Ely's Inn, Holborn, shown in background of Wyngaerde's panorama of *c.* 1540. Baynard's Castle II is shown bottom right.

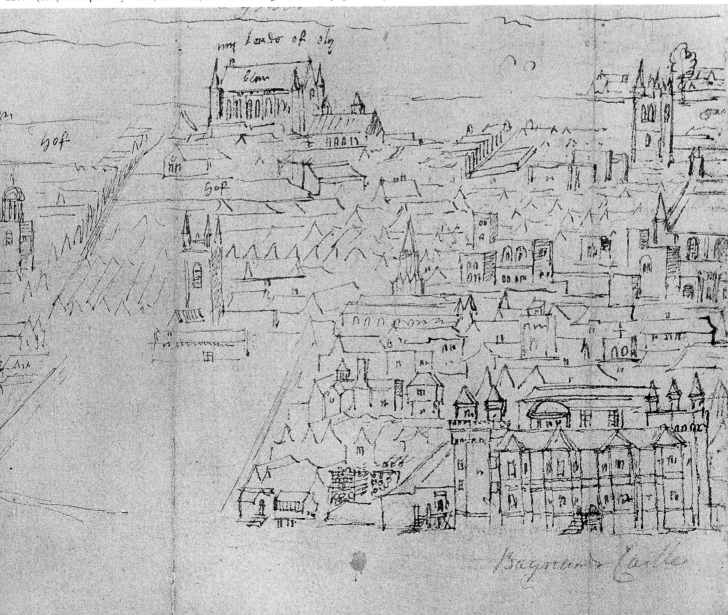

chambers over at least the west and north sides (Fig. 37). At the north-west corner was an octagonal turret, presumably a stair, and a small gabled two-storeyed structure added to the north side. It is possible that this was the oratory. Building work in 1985 exposed part of the west alley of the cloister, exposing 9 m (29 ft 6 in) of tile pavement, its full width 3 m (10 ft). The tiles were of fourteenth- to fifteenth-century Flemish type, glazed green and yellow and laid chequerboard fashion. A fragment of the cloister wall on the west side was also recorded, with white plaster on the cloister side.[8]

The chapel, now St Etheldreda's, was entered as today from a conventional south door which was reached by a stair from the cloister. Despite much restoration it remains important as the only extant private chapel of a prominent personage in the medieval city; its tracery shows 'the evenness of the Geometrical just on the point of disintegrating into the illogicalities of the coming Dec style'.[9] Engravings show that the chapel formerly had high octagonal pinnacles (the sides formed by narrow traceried panels) on the corners, and traceried niches between the windows on both inside and outside walls. Beneath lies the crypt, also originally lit by traceried windows; it formerly had a well.[10] The floor of the chapel and the posts supporting it (the latter with later stone bases) date from the late thirteenth century.[11]

The hall and chapel were prominent features of the city's skyline when viewed from the south (Fig. 227). It is possible that both were begun by Kirkeby but finished by his successor, William de Luda (d. 1298). The gatehouse (Fig. 69) and cloister (Fig. 37) presumably dated from the rebuilding by Thomas Arundel in 1374–88. The building date of the brick porch cannot be ascertained from the present documentary evidence, but might be around 1500.

1. *Cal. Wills*, i, 90–1; Williams, *Early Holborn*, i, 386–9.
2. Honeybourne, 'Value'; Williams, *op. cit.*, 349.
3. Aston 1967; Stow, ii, 35.
4. Williams, *op. cit.*, 352–3.
5. Aston 1967, 196.
6. MS in Cambridge University Library; from notes by D. Sherlock.
7. Stow, ii, 36.
8. MoL, sitecode ELY85. The tiles were left *in situ*.
9. RCHM, *West London*, 44–5; Pevsner, *London 2*, 205–6.
10. Williams, *op. cit.*, 352.
11. Hewett 1980, 123–4.

(107) Furnival's Inn, Holborn

In 1376 Thomas atte Bower, spicer, granted his inherited lands in Holborn to Sir William Furnival. At his death in 1388 Furnival held two messuages and thirteen shops in Holborn.[1] The Inn was an Inn of Chancery by 1408, and so continued until about 1818.[2] Its situation and component ranges are shown by Ogilby and Morgan in 1677 (Fig. 73). Williams[3] says the hall was rebuilt in 1587–8, but drawings of 1819 (e.g. Fig. 72a) suggest that this may have been superficial (e.g. fitting of the late sixteenth-century panelling, or recasing the walls in brick) or concerned other buildings. In the drawings the hall has a fifteenth-century arch-coupled roof and fourteenth- or fifteenth-century windows, including an oriel to the courtyard.

1. Williams, *Early Holborn*, i, 505, 508.
2. *LTR*, x, 123–4.
3. Williams, *op. cit.*, 489.

(108) Bath Place (later Brooke House) Holborn

In 1416 Sir William Hankford, Chief Justice of the King's Bench, added four acres to the north of his garden in Holborn next to Furnival's Inn. By 1418 this was a newly-built messuage with a garden and four shops. The property passed by descent to Fulk Bourchier, whose son John was created Earl of Bath. Kingsford suggests[1] that the house became the later Bath Place, which was west of Furnival's Inn, and which Stow noted as 'of late for the most part

new builded'.[2] Bath Place later belonged to Fulk Greville, created Lord Brooke in 1620, and so became Brooke House. This is shown on Ogilby and Morgan's map in 1677 as a large house arranged on three sides of a deep court, entered centrally through a range from Holborn (Fig. 73). Slight protuberances on the south face of the range at the rear of the court may indicate an oriel and a porch to the hall. The east range has three regularly spaced rectangular protuberances on its outer east side, suggesting stairs and/or garderobes, like the ranges at Bridewell Palace (1515–22) but on a smaller scale. Presumably the house shown is that resulting from the mid to late sixteenth-century rebuilding.[3]

1. *LTR*, x, 133–4.
2. Stow, ii, 37.
3. The later history of the house is given by Barron (1979, 57–8). The front to Holborn was drawn in 1619 by John Smythson (RIBA, Smythson III/6; Girouard 1983, Plate xv).

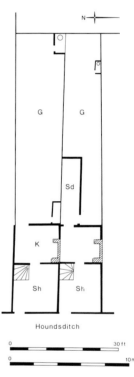

228. (110) 140–141 Houndsditch (Treswell, 1611)

(109) 140–141 Houndsditch

These two houses on the east side of Houndsditch were confirmed by Thomas Browne and Robert Wilson to John Arnold in 1562/3. Arnold granted them to John Warreyn in 1564; Warreyn granted them to his son George Warren, leatherseller, in 1576. Lawrence Ponder was one of Warren's tenants in 1583, and his widow Anne is seen to have occupied the south of the two properties in Treswell's survey of 1611 (Fig. 228).[1] Warren meanwhile sold the two properties to John Wriothesley, haberdasher, in 1586, and he sold them to Thomas Lawrence, goldsmith, in 1588.[2] Lawrence is recorded as the donor of the properties to Christ's Hospital in 1593, but no deed or will is preserved.[3] Both houses were of two and a half storeys, and of identical plan on the ground floor. They differed however on the first and garret floors, jettying to different extents into the street. Neither had a cellar.

1. *LSRT*, 88–9; probably based on a lease-plan of 1607.
2. GL, MS 13442.
3. *Charity Comm.*, 101.

(110)   Lovell's Inn, Ivy Lane

At his death in 1328 Robert de Holand held a messuage and ten shops in the parish of St Faith, and a brewhouse in the parish of St Nicholas Shambles. At her death in 1423 Maud de Holland, who had married John de Lovell, owned a hospice and fourteen shops in the former parish. The Inn stayed in the Lovell family until 1488, and seems to have been gradually broken up in the sixteenth century.[1] It probably occupied most of the east side of Ivy Lane, where Ogilby and Morgan show Lovell's court astride the parish boundary. In 1529 the City Viewers examined a variance between St Bartholomew's Priory, plaintiff, and Christopher Barker, alias Richmond, defendant, who owned Lovell's Place. The result was that a building of the plaintiff had to be withdrawn (i.e. demolished); mention is made of a former privy of Lovell's Place, probably at the north-west corner of the house, and a buttress of stone at the back of a chimney.[2] In the reign of Elizabeth there is mention of a footway to Paternoster Row, presumably that shown on Ogilby and Morgan's map. The house must have largely disappeared by the time of Stow, who records that it was 'of old time . . . one great house' in Ivy Lane.[4]

1. *LTR*, xi, 39–40.
2. *Viewers' Certificates*, 84.
3. CCPR, Lovell's Inn, 1596.
4. Stow, i, 343.

(111)   Bishop of Hereford's Inn, Lambeth Hill

Ralph de Maidstone, Bishop of Hereford, purchased Monthalt or Mounthalt, the residence of the Mounthauntes of Norfolk, in about 1234 and gave it to his successors in the see.[1] Its chapel was converted into the church of St Mary Mounthaw in 1346.[2] In 1400 the Inn was on the east side of Lambeth Hill, with the chapel of St Mary in its south-east corner, against Fish Street Hill.[3] Stow saw 'an ancient house and large rooms builded of stone and timber . . . greatly ruinated, and . . . now divided into many small tenements: the Hall and principal rooms are an house to make sugar loaves in, etc.'[4]

1. Stow, ii, 4.
2. Parry 1912, 90.
3. Honeybourne, 'Value', 324–8.
4. Stow, *ibid*.

(112)   Blacksmiths' Hall, Lambeth Hill

Though the Blacksmiths are known to have drawn up ordinances in 1298, they did not have a hall until the late fifteenth century. In 1434 they met at the Hospital of St Thomas Acon.[1] In 1494–5 the wardens obtained a lease from the City of the hall site, apparently with two adjacent shops, on the west side of Lambeth Hill, in the parish of St Mary Magdalen (Fish Street), on the south side of the church.[2] An inventory of the hall in 1496 mentions the pantry, parlour, hall, gallery, chamber over the parlour, pastry house and kitchen, with their furnishings.[3] From the dimensions and positions of the hangings, the hall lay north to south. The post-Fire hall complex is shown by Ogilby and Morgan (C29), but it is not clear which part is the hall.

1. Adams 1951, 16–17.
2. *Ibid.*, 13; Stow, ii, 17.
3. Adams, *op. cit.*, 19–21; see also Chapter 6.

(113)   Blossoms Inn, [St] Lawrence Lane

First mentioned in 1374; in 1463 order was made to transfer the sale of worsted cloth, lead and nails, previously sold there privately, to Leadenhall. Part of it was a hostelry by 1480; here lodged some of the retinue of Charles V during his visit of 1522. It was in the possession of the College of Ottery St Mary by the time of its granting to Edward Seymour, Earl of Hertford, in 1546. Stow describes it as a large inn for the receipt of travellers.[1] The post-Fire inn is shown by Ogilby and Morgan as a courtyard of buildings (B48) at the north-west corner of Lawrence Lane and what is now Trump Street, with long entries from both. Excavations on the site

in 1956 found a chalk-lined well with many objects dating to *c.* 1500; among them debris suggesting the making of buckles.

1. Stow, i, 270; *LTR*, x, 71–2.
2. PRG, 386. For the objects, see Goodall 1981, 63–4, Fig. 61.

(114)   Pulteney's (Pountney's) Inn (later Manor of the Rose) Lawrence Pountney Lane (centred on 3–31/2 Lawrence Pountney Hill)

Sir John de Pulteney had property in the parish of St Lawrence Pountney by 1336, and this house is perhaps the one which he had licence to crenellate, along with Penshurst Place in Kent which he was building, in 1343;[1] it was called his principal messuage in his will in 1348. Later owners or occupiers included the Black Prince (1349–59), the Earl of Arundel (1385–97), the Duke of Suffolk and his heirs (by 1439 to 1521) and the Duke of Buckingham (1506–21). In the early sixteenth century the house was also known as the Manor of the (Red) Rose. In 1525 it was granted to Henry Courtenay, Earl of Devon and afterwards Marquess of Exeter, and granted again by the Crown to the Earl of Sussex in 1540. In 1561 the house was sold and then split into two halves. One was transferred by Richard Botyl to his company of Merchant Taylors to be converted into Merchant Taylors' School; the other half was described as four messuages and a garden in 1567.[2] The part bought by Botyl comprised the west gatehouse, a long court or yard, the winding stairs at the south end of the court, on the east side, which led to the leads over the chapel, two galleries over the south end of the court and part of the chapel (not located, presumably in the east range).[3] Ogilby and Morgan show both the school and the other mansion (C38) in rebuilt form, occupying an irregularly shaped block between Suffolk and Duxfield Lanes.

Details of four parts of the Pulteney mansion have been recorded: a tower, a crenellated block, a late thirteenth- or fourteenth-century undercroft, and an early sixteenth-century garden gallery.

In all three pre-Fire panoramas used in this study a tower is shown immediately west of St Lawrence Pountney church (Figs. 23–4, 41), of perhaps four storeys, with either clasping buttresses (Hollar) or a diagonal buttress at the south-east corner (low-level panorama), a low-pitched roof and three chimneys. In the views by Wyngaerde and Hollar a crenellated range is shown running west from the tower, though it appears to be north to south in orientation on Wyngaerde and, if anything, east to west on Hollar; on the latter five ornate windows are indicated in the south wall. This range must have been a principal building, presumably the hall, with the tower at its south-east corner.

Norman[4] described a late thirteenth- or early fourteenth-century undercroft of two quadripartite bays which survived until 1894 beneath 3 Lawrence Pountney Hill, i.e. not part of the Merchant Taylors' moiety (Fig. 85a–b). An entrance, probably medieval, was formed from the lane to the east; at the far end of the two vaulted bays, a small door led to a narrow vaulted passage running north to south (across the building) with traces of decorated floor tiles still remaining *in situ*. Beyond this to the west were two square chambers, one vaulted. Norman suggested that this might have supported the crenellated or hall range, and that the below-ground passage would equate with the screens passage above. If the undercroft, 40 ft × 20 ft, represents the size of the hall and its alignment, then Hollar must be right in making it east to west.

A parish map of 1805 (Fig. 229) supports the suggestion that the part not granted to the Merchant Taylors included the site of the crypt at no. 3, probably the tower site which was probably later no. 4, and all of Lawrence Pountney Place to the south-east. This must have been the site of the garden (east of the court demised to the Merchant Taylors) where in 1530 the Marquess of Exeter contracted with James Nedeham, one of the king's carpenters, to replace the existing gallery with a first-floor gallery with twelve bay windows, fireplaces and a summerhouse.[5]

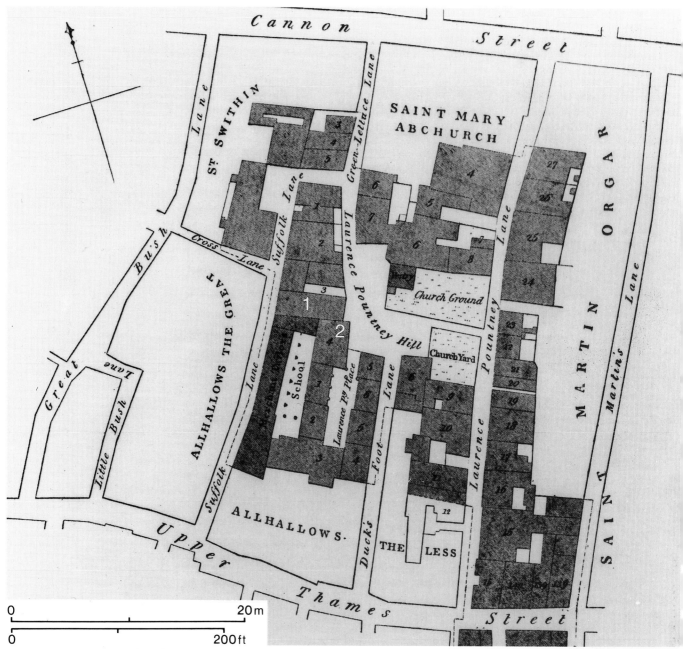

229.   (**114**) Pulteney's Inn, Lawrence Pountney Hill: map of parish of St Lawrence Pountney (1805), showing sites of (1) the recorded undercroft, which probably lay beneath the hall, and (2) suggested site of the tower seen in panoramas [Norman 1901]

These elements therefore suggest a hall 40 ft × 20 ft (crenellated 1341) on an arched undercroft of the late thirteenth or early fourteenth century running between Suffolk Lane and Lawrence Pountney Hill, a tower at its south-east corner, a court with building (probably including the kitchen, since there is no room for it over the small chambers shown in Fig. 85a) to the south-west along Suffolk Lane, and the garden to the south-east along the Hill (later Duxfield or Duck's Foot Lane).

1.   *Cal. Pat. R*, 1340–3, 331.
2.   *LTR*, xi, 74–8.
3.   Norman 1901, 269.
4.   *Ibid*.
5.   Salzman, *Building*, 575–6.

(**115**)   **Zouche's Inn/Robert Lee's house/East India House, Leadenhall Street**

William, second Lord Zouche of Haryngworth, held two messuages and seven shops in Lime Street Ward at his death in 1382. In 1431 the hospice of Lord Zouche was granted to John Carpenter, and described as being to the west of the garden of Lord Zouche; evidently a large property was being subdivided. Stow described Lord Zouche's tenement as being in Cornhill (the part later called Leadenhall Street), west of Pembridge's Inn.[1]

The Zouche property passed to the Crown as chantry property in 1548, and was sold to Thomas White and Stephen Kirton, aldermen. Kirton probably occupied the house until his death in 1553; his widow Margaret lived there until 1573. In the years immediately before 1600 the property was acquired and rebuilt by Robert Lee, mayor 1602–3. After his death in 1605, his son Robert leased the property in 1607 to William Craven, merchant tailor and mayor in 1610–11.[2] An attached schedule (Appendix below) gives details of

sixty-two rooms and external yards with their furnishings, probably as rebuilt by Robert Lee in *c.* 1600.

From Cornhill (Leadenhall Street), the visitor passed through two gates: the outer strengthened with a flat bar of iron 8 ft long, the inner with a portcullis of wood over it, raised or lowered by a winch. Each gate had a pedestrian wicket. Inside the inner gate, to one side, was a urinal of lead with a tin laver set on four pillars fed by Thames water (presumably from Morice's scheme of the 1580s?). A gutter of stone, garnished with arms, and a drainpipe from the eaves above flushed the urinal. Nearby was a frame for towels, and a long rack of buckets. Entered from the yard, probably near the gate, were a lodge, a porch, counting house, and an old parlour. Next was the kitchen, 18 ft × 15 ft, with a still house and a pastry, above which was the scouring house and armoury; and next in the schedule, and therefore probably adjacent to the kitchen, was a dry larder and a buttery, with passage down to the cellars. A great door (presumably from the main yard) led to the screens passage of the hall, the internal screen carved and supporting the arms of Elizabeth I. In the hall, which like the screens passage was paved with squares of blue and white marble, was a 'gilt beame' (perhaps an ornate back to the dais) with five candlesticks and 'an Angell over' and a court cupboard incorporating a frame for the Lord Mayor's sword. The great parlour adjacent was wainscotted and carved; the chimney-piece had pillars of jet garnished with alabaster imagery, the arms of Elizabeth I and carvings of St George on horseback, Justice and Charity. A door led via a porch to the garden, in which was a raised flower-bed or knot, a pump and a banqueting house, paved with green and yellow tiles.

A great staircase, probably between the hall and parlour, led to the first floor where the dining chamber and main bedchambers were to be found. The former was on the garden side, wainscotted, with a chimney-piece carved and gilt with the story of the Creation. Other chambers on the first and upper floors included two galleries, a room over the screens, the men's chamber (with an adjacent flat lead to walk on, with a balustrade), and two chambers for the maids. On the south side of the main range, presumably reached through the screens, a *lobby* (the earliest known use of this term in a London context) probably led to work rooms: an upper and lower warehouse, the former containing a workplace for a tailor, a wash-house, stable, separate hayloft, back yard and gate to Lime Street. The East India Company leased the property in 1648, thus beginning their association with the site. A second schedule of 1660–1 adds a small number of further details.[3]

An engraving of 1851 by W. B. Rye from a drawing by Vertue (Fig. 230) shows the street elevation of 'Old East India House'; but this building, the third floor or garret of which was fronted by a hoarding bearing an eighteenth-century naval painting, is probably The Ship, a tenement between Craven's house and Leadenhall Street. The freehold of The Ship was sold to the Company in 1710 and its site was subsumed beneath the subsequent Company building.[4]

1. Stow, i, 151–2; *LTR*, xii, 65–6.
2. GL, MS 1123.
3. GL, MS 1125.
4. Harding & Metcalf 1986, 59.

(116)   Leadenhall Street, probably nos. 27–33

When in 1590 a frame of three houses was being set up in place of a garden which stretched back from Leadenhall Street, between Billiter Lane and Lime Street, excavations for cellars disclosed a brick wall fronting the street, and founded on a stone wall which was evidently the front of an early medieval undercroft. Stow describes a 'gate of stone' with iron hinges, clearly a central entrance, flanked by two square windows barred with iron. The wall was 'two fathoms deep', and Stow concluded that it belonged to a house burnt in the fire of 1132.[1]

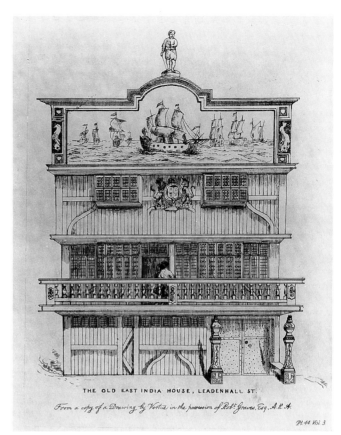

THE OLD EAST INDIA HOUSE, LEADENHALL ST.
From a copy of a Drawing by Vertue in the possession of Robt. Graves, Esq. A.R.A.
Pl. 44 Vol. 3

230.   (115) East India House (Robert Lee's house), Leadenhall Street: frontage of 'Old East India House' redrawn by W. B. Pye in 1851 after a drawing by G. Vertue

1. Stow, i, 138–9.

(117)   Abbot of Evesham's Inn (later Principal Place), 42–49 Leadenhall Street

In 1314 the prior and convent of Holy Trinity Priory leased to John de la Marche land in the parish of St Katherine Cree bordered on the north by the chapel of St Michael and its cemetery to the southwest of the chapel. The rent was 53*s.* 4*d.* for this and one other tenement in the same parish. Some subsequent occupiers paying rent (presumably quit-rent) are noted in the cartulary; the latest is the 'Abbot of Evesham' in 1426.[1] In 1366 Margery, widow of Thomas Broun, gave five messuages and thirty-six shops to Evesham Abbey;[2] the cartulary shows that this included the property in question. In 1541 the Crown granted the property to Edward and Alice Cornwallis;[3] in 1556, now called 'Principal Place', it was described as a large messuage with a large garden adjoining, when it formed the estate of Alice Cornwallis, along with sixteen tenements or houses and three stables in Billiter Lane which were presumably attached and which may have formed the Billiter Lane frontage indicated in the priory lease.[4] Alice's son Thomas sold the houses in 1562 to Sir Nicholas Throckmorton, who died in 1571.[5] Stow mentions the 'fair house with diverse tenements adjoining' and places it between Billiter Lane and Sugar Loaf Alley.[6] The house is shown on Ogilby and Morgan, in the area outside that of the Great Fire, as Whitchurch House, which in 1678 was leased by the African Company. Excavation on the site in 1975 uncovered foundations of early medieval character.[7]

It is proposed elsewhere[8] that this property comprised the site of the chapel of St Michael, mentioned in the description of the boundaries of the soke given to the priory by Queen Matilda in 1108.[9] It is not mentioned in the cartulary after 1314, and was presumably part of the Broun property by 1366 when the site passed to Evesham.

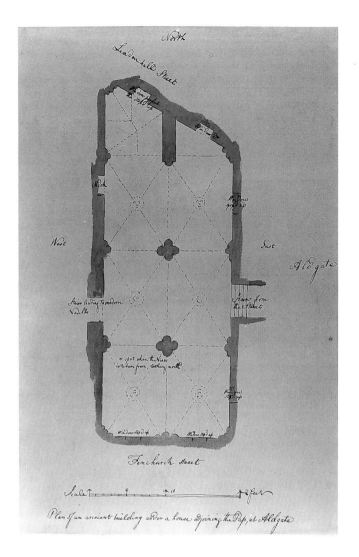

Plan of an ancient building under a house adjoining the Pup, at Aldgate

North view in the inside of an ancient building under a house adjoining the pump at Aldgate. Mem. The ground is raised nearly to the top of the columns.

231. **(119)** Undercroft at junction of Leadenhall Street and Fenchurch Street: (a) (*left*) plan,

(b) (*above*)   Interior looking north (both J. Carter 1784)

1. *HTA Cartulary*, 55–7; the reading *cimiterium* rather than *civitatis*, apparently read by the editor of the cartulary, is confirmed by Husting Roll 46(67).
2. Honeybourne, 'Value', 355–60.
3. *Letters & Papers*, xvi, 55.
4. *Inq. PM*, i, 143.
5. *Inq. PM*, ii, 143–4.
6. Stow, i, 138.
7. Woods, Rhodes & Dyson 1975.
8. Schofield & Lea, in preparation.
9. *HTA Cartulary*, 11.

(118)   Bricklayers' Hall and other houses at 53 Leadenhall Street

The Tilers' and Bricklayers' Company obtained their first joint charter in 1568;[1] previously the Tilers had a hall in Broad Street.[2] Thomas Audley had sold tenements in Leadenhall Street including the Cock and Hoope to Thomas Alderton, carpenter, in 1537; four years later a group purchased the property from Elizabeth Dyall. It was then described as the Cock on the Hoope and two tenements, and measured 35 ft wide along the north, street side, 33 ft along the south, 146 ft on the east and 108 ft on the west. Not damaged by the Great Fire, the hall is shown by Ogilby and Morgan as a square building at the end of an alley, reached through the Cock Tavern, and the street frontage (not part of the hall) was engraved by Smith (Fig. 111). On the frontage were angel corbels, presumably indicating a construction date of *c.* 1450–1550 for part of the structure.
1. Bell 1938, 18.

2. BL, MS 451 (*c.* 1475); the hall is located in the parish of All Hallows London Wall in 1555 (HR, 247 (149)).

(119)   Undercroft, junction of Leadenhall Street and Fenchurch Street

An undercroft at the junction of Fenchurch Street and Leadenhall Street, often mistaken by antiquaries for a crypt beneath the lost St Michael's church near Aldgate (for a proposed site of which, see **117**), was recorded from the late eighteenth century (Fig. 231a–b). Further measured drawings were made by F. A. Burt in 1870 (Figs. 83a–b, 133). Three north to south bays together were 36 ft 6 in long; the two aisles were together 16 ft 6 in wide. Central columns were made of a cluster of four shafts, their height 12 ft from the original floor to the junction of the vaulting-ribs. Two stone bosses were recovered, and are now in the Museum of London. Two windows originally lit the north end, and a third window the east bay at the south end. The undercroft was entered by a flight of steps on the west side at the north end. The undercroft is usually dated to *c.* 1300.[1]
1. *Trans. LAMAS, Proceedings 1870–4*, 1–8.

(120)   153 Leadenhall Street

This entry covers records of what may have been two different structures.

A fire of 1766 at the corner of Leadenhall and Bishopsgate Streets exposed a stone structure aligned east to west, 40 ft × 26 ft, of four arches long by two aisles wide (Fig. 232a). This is shown on the map as site **21**.

232. **(120)** 153 Leadenhall Street: (a) the building drawn in 1766 (*Gentleman's Magazine*)

(b)   Medieval arches in the cellar of the eighteenth-century house in 1815

When 153 Leadenhall Street was rebuilt in the mid eighteenth century, a medieval structure was incorporated; a new flight of steps led down from the street and the lower portions of columns in the cellar were cased with brick. It was noted by Wilkinson in 1825 (Fig. 232b) and on demolition in 1896.[1] Illustrations show two walls, at opposite ends of a structure which appears to lie north to south, each pierced by two pointed arches rising from octagonal corbels; the illustration in the *Daily Graphic* shows the south end with the stair to the street. Since both walls were pierced with arches, they must originally have comprised inner cross-walls for an even larger building; a further illustration during demolition shows that there was space beyond the south wall towards the street.

1. *Londina Illustrata*, i, 43; *Daily Graphic*, 3 July 1896.
2. *Gentleman's Magazine*, 1766, 55–6; 1795, ii, 810.

(121)   Pewterers' Hall, 15 Lime Street

During the second half of the fifteenth century the Pewterers' Company hired the refectory of the Austin Friars for their gatherings; after incorporation in 1474, they set about looking for a hall. In 1475 the company obtained possession of a site in Lime Street, and from trustees it came via William Smallwood, a past master and notable benefactor, to the company in 1486. By this time the building was sufficiently fitted out to allow a dinner for the wives to be held in it. An inventory of 1490 mentions the hall, parlour, counting house, garden and well. Several windows, including a bay window 'the high window over the high dais' were glazed by seventeen individual members of the company. The parlour also had a bay window, and both it and the counting house were wainscotted; the parlour may have been on the first floor.[1]

The company decided to rebuild the hall in 1496, and viewed the halls of the Haberdashers, Carpenters and 'at pappey', which presumably means the hall of the Brotherhood of Papey. They also spent 10*d*. 'at Hackney with the carpenter to have a view of the Dean's [of St Paul's?] roof there'.[2] The hall was built by Simon Birlyngham, carpenter,[3] and was of brick and timber. Several of the craft went a second time with the carpenter to view the 'hall at hackney' as their roof was being given a painted louvre and being painted inside, two years later;[4] this suggests that the Pewterers' roof was modelled in some respects on the Dean's.

An inventory of the hall in 1550 mentions the hall, buttery with two cellars, pantry, kitchen, larder house, parlour over the hall, garret over the parlour, and an inner yard which is probably meant to be the hall is shown on the copperplate map of *c*. 1559. All the glass on the east side of the hall was reset in 1558;[5] this implies that the hall lay north to south. The hall is probably that marked C62 on Ogilby and Morgan's map of 1677.

1. Welch 1902, i, 19, 45, 59, 68–76.
2. *Ibid.*, 82–3.
3. Harvey, *Early Medieval Architects*, 26.
4. Welch, *op. cit.*, 85.
5. *Ibid.*, 167–9, 206.

(122)   Tiptoft's Inn, Lime Street

Robert Tiptoft had an Inn in Lime Street in 1369–72; his grandfather had been Giles de Badlesmere, and the Inn may have been part of Badlesmere Inn. On his death in 1372 the property, on the east side of Lime Street, was partitioned between his three daughters.[1] The central third, probably including the nucleus of the medieval house, went to Margaret Tiptoft who married into the Scrope family, and they appear to have held the property until 1501 when Richard Knyght, fishmonger, bequeathed a messuage, tenteryard and six tenements on the east side of Lime Street, formerly belonging to Lord Scrope, to the Fishmongers' Company.[2] The remaining third to the south became the house of Thomas Warham in 1454 (**123**).

1. Harding 1986, 38–41.
2. *LTR*, xii, 43–4; Metcalf 1977, 39.

(123)   Thomas Warham's house(s), Lime Street

In 1454 Edmund Wydwell and Reginald Harneys confirmed to Thomas and William Warham, both members of the Carpenters' Company, and three others, two tofts in Lime Street in the parishes of St Dionys and St Andrew Undershaft.[1] It is possible that Thomas Warham, who bequeathed the property to the company in 1477 (proved 1481),[2] was party to a case of testamentary devise, in which the company (which was not incorporated until 1477) ensured receipt of property intended for it;[3] certainly the company paid for repairs in 1480 and 1481.[4] The property included several gardens let separately, and a timber yard and a timber house; the tenants were all members of the company, in at least one case also receiving alms. The cellar was let separately. In 1488 a rebuilding took place involving 3,000 tiles, 250 rooftiles and 5,500 bricks, with 27 ft of border stone for the chimneys, which were probably being inserted for the first time.[5] The floors were renewed and five stairs made. Further renovations followed in 1491, with the making of internal partitions, window lattices, a pale, and a brick wall of 13,000 bricks. A stable is mentioned in 1492, a well repaired in the same year, and a barn underpinned with brick in 1495. In 1501 one of the tenancies had a new parlour built by the fellowship, using 17,000 bricks, and probably including a bay window; the walls were wainscotted with evis (Estriche) board. Minor repairs are recorded into the sixteenth century.[6]

1. *RCC*, ii, 257.
2. PCC, 4, Logge.
3. Alford & Barker 1968, 49–52.
4. *RCC*, ii, 59, 60.
5. *Ibid.*, 64, 69, 71, 75, 77–8.
6. *Ibid.*, 92–4, 97–8, 108–12, 138–9.

(124)   Pope's Head, Lombard Street

In 1291 Gregory de Rokesley, mayor in 1274–80 and 1284–5, left his house in Lombard Street to his nephew Walter. In 1318 the house was acquired by the Florentine Society of the Bardi; the property extended from Cornhill to Lombard Street. In 1338 the estate was forfeit and granted to Sir William de la Pole, the Hull and London merchant. His son Michael was created Earl of Suffolk, and before 1415 Michael, second Earl of Suffolk, conveyed 'le Popeshed' in Lombard Street to the Bishop of Exeter and others. At this time the property comprised the Pope's Head, known in the fifteenth century as a tavern, and other houses. At the Reformation the name was briefly changed to the Bishop's Head; part of the complex, separate from the tavern, was the Sarazen's Head before 1538. In 1583 this lay on the west of the alley which ran from Cornhill to Lombard Street. In Stow's time the Pope's Head (*sic*) tavern lay at the south end of the alley, and in 1615 the Pope's Head was conveyed by Sir William Craven (mayor in 1610) to the Merchant Taylors' Company.[1] A plan of about 1660[2] shows the tavern as a loose-knit collection of rooms around a small yard east of the alley, with at least two ground-floor parlours overlooking Lombard Street. The Merchant Taylors' estate comprised the east part, by Horwood's time (1792–9) forming nos. 1, 7–9 Pope's Head Alley and 73 Lombard Street.[3]

Stow saw the arms of England, dating from before the time of Edward III, 'faire and largely graven in stone' on the Cornhill side of the complex, over the door of the Sarazen's Head side. He also reported a surmise that the Pope's Head was originally a house of King John, a tradition presumably rising from its ancient stone character.[4] Another room, not necessarily of stone, was alluded to as 'King John's chapel' in a lease of 1668; this was west of the kitchen of the Pope's Head, and so may have been on the Cornhill frontage, near the royal arms.[5]

1. Stow, i, 199; *LTR*, xi, 70–3.
2. *LTR, ibid.*
3. Herbert, *Livery Companies*, ii, 508–9; Clode, *MT Memorials*, 304.

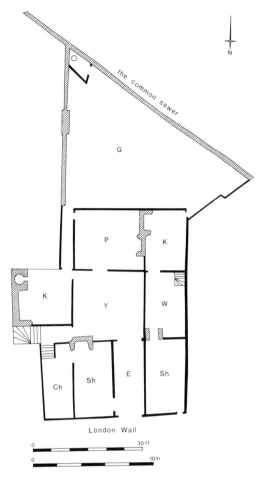

the common sewer

G

P K

K Y W

Ch Sh E Sh

London Wall

0 ___ 30 ft
0 ___ 10 m

233. **(274)** Leathersellers' Hall I, London Wall (probably Treswell 1614)

4. Stow, i, 199.
5. *LTR, ibid.*

(125) Cardinal's Hat, Lombard Street

In 1227 Willam de Blemonte granted to Holy Trinity Priory, with other quit-rents, 2s. p.a. from a stone house of Robert Burrell which was of de Blemonte's fee.[1] The cartulary records two further owners after Burrell before the property was granted to Missenden Abbey (Buckinghamshire), which sold it in 1252–3 to Geoffrey Godard, merchant, when it was described as two messuages extending from Lombard Street to Cornhill. In 1362 the tenement was described as a tavern called the Cardinalishatt, with three shops adjacent, two on the east side and one on the west; one end of the tavern (*sic*) abutted south onto Cornhill.[2]

1. *HTA Cartulary*, 1014.
2. *Ibid.*, 488–91.

(126) Curriers' Hall, 6 London Wall

In the list in the British Library, Harley MS 541 (*c.* 1475), the Curriers had a hall in the parish of St Mary Axe. The Curriers' garden, bordered by a brick wall on the south, was in the parish of St Alphege in 1548.[1] A fragment of an inventory of 1558 mentions the hall and parlour. The site of the hall, south of London Wall about half a mile to the west, was entrusted to the company in the will of Thomas Sterne, 1516.[2] The hall is not mentioned by Stow, though in 1598 Curriers' Row was to be found on the south side of London Wall near Carpenters' Hall (128).[3] The site of the hall was surveyed in October 1669,[4] and the post-Fire building is shown by Ogilby and Morgan as L-shaped, at the back of a court (A60).

1. *Viewers' Certificates*, 220.
2. GL, MS 14357.
3. Mayer 1968, 65; Stow, i, 176.
4. Mills & Oliver, *Survey*, iv, 193[v].

(127) Leathersellers' Hall I, 50–55 (now 49) London Wall

By 1477 the Leathersellers' Company possessed a hall in London Wall.[1] In 1543 the company acquired part of the conventual buildings of St Helen's nunnery in Bishopsgate, and moved their hall there (96). The hall site was then let out. In 1613 the Court resolved that the Old Hall should be divided into 'reasonable dwelling-houses'. Black, in his history of the company, declared that the west part of the estate was separated off and divided into three shops, with kitchens, a parlour and a garden behind; and that this was surveyed by Robert (*sic*) Treswell the elder in 1614.[2]

A plan of the former hall site (Fig. 233) on vellum survives at the present Leathersellers' Hall.[3] In general style it closely resembles Treswell's other surveys of 1610–12, but is not signed or dated. An MS Schedule of Ancient Deeds, drawn up by Black *c.* 1834, does however speak of a larger plan, signed by Treswell and dated 1614, which Black copied in sketch form. This shows that the Leathersellers' estate in this area comprised two separate blocks south of London Wall. The surviving plan is probably a copy, presumably contemporary and by Treswell, of part of this larger plan, which has not survived. The plan shows a street range of two and a half storeys, with an entry leading to a small yard surrounded by two kitchens and a parlour; behind lay a garden, its south boundary formed by the covered course of the Walbrook.

1. Black 1871, 72.
2. *Ibid.*, 73.
3. *LSRT*, 90–1.

(128) Carpenters' Hall, London Wall

In January 1428/9 Roger Jordan, prior of the Hospital of St Mary Spital, leased five cottages and a waste piece of land in the parish of All Hallows London Wall to two carpenters, Richard or Peter Sextein and Richard Punchon. They immediately regranted the lease to a group of the craft; the cottages were replaced by the hall and four houses, the hall apparently behind a street range formed by the houses fronting on to London Wall. In 1519–20 the hospital sold the freehold to Thomas Smart, carpenter, and by his will of 1519 (not proved until 1575) the land passed to the company; a property called The Beare to the east was added by purchase in 1514/15.

A paved outer gateway, the gate strengthened with iron spikes and painted with red lead, led to a courtyard containing box-trees and an integral garden or plot. The four houses fronting on to London Wall had ten tenants. The door of the hall was a prominent entrance with its own roof. Inside, on the walls, were escutcheons and a gilded table (*tablat*) with names of brothers and sisters of the craft. At the west end lay the dais, with the door to the parlour. The hall had a hearth; a chimney, probably of stone, may have been in the hall. The roof was built by William Serle in 1429–31. An arch-couple roof was recorded in 1846;[1] it sprung from figured stone corbels, two of which have been recorded, though now lost (Figs. 143–4, 234). A bay window was added in 1442. Glazing is mentioned in 1482, and boards for the bay window in the same year may be shutters.

Eighteenth- and nineteenth-century maps show a range stretching south from the west end of the hall, and especially since the site was not damaged in the Great Fire of 1666, it seems likely that this was the site of the (main) medieval parlour. This had an earth floor in 1441, a cupboard and its own hearth. The parlour was rebuilt in brick in 1500–1.

The service rooms included kitchen, buttery, pantry and larder. In 1442 the new oven in the kitchen used 1,000 roof tiles, presumably in a stacked-tile base as well as the superstructure; the (main) hearth lay under a reredos in 1492. In 1507 the kitchen was rebuilt. Two mantle-trees were bought for large fireplaces; there were two ovens, one larger than the other. A 'house over the ovens' was constructed. The use of 13,000 bricks suggests a building wholly or

234.   (128) Carpenters' Hall, London Wall: interior looking west (mid nineteenth century)

largely of brick. A pump is first mentioned in 1500, when it was repaired; it was replaced in 1507, when its position was said to be in the well, first mentioned when cleaned out in 1442.[2]

Wall paintings of the mid sixteenth century were discovered in 1845 and largely survive, preserved at the present hall. On the west side of the hall, surmounted by an embattled oak beam, was a series of four fresco paintings. The subjects were divided by columns painted in distemper; the ground-work was laths, with a thick layer of brown earth and clay held well together with straw, and a layer of lime. The subjects were (1) Noah receiving the commands from the Almighty for the construction of the ark and Noah's three sons at work (this one is lost); (2) King Josiah ordering the repair of the Temple (2 Kings xxii), mentioning carpenters and builders and masons as having no reckoning of money made with them, 'because they dealt faithfully'; (3) Joseph at work as a carpenter; (4) Christ teaching in the synagogue: 'Is this not the carpenter's son' (Figs. 144–6). Each painting had a black-letter inscription. Above the picture, in the spandrel of the arch, were painted the company's arms, and the names 'Shreeves' and 'Robard' then survived from an inscription. The artist is not known; the paintings were in place by 1596, and may have been the gift of William Ruddock, William Buttmor and Robard Quoyney, wardens in 1561.[3]

Substantial outlays in 1572–3 suggest that a gallery was set up in the hall for the first time; it was glazed on the hall side. The hall itself was also wainscotted to match the gallery. Repairs or new work were undertaken in the kitchen in 1585, the larder and parlour in 1586, and a gallery in 1588; by this time there was also a little parlour. In 1593 the hall was enlarged to the east, and included a new counting house.[4]

1. *Illustrated London News*, 3 January 1846.
2. All contemporary details from *RCC*, ii.
3. Jupp 1848, 222–3; Alford & Barker 1968, 225–8 and colour plates, including one of the lost panel.
4. *RCC*, v, 28–9, 183–5, 196–8, 228–32; GL, MS 4326/5.

(129)   9–10 Lovat Lane

In 1981–2 fragments of an undercroft measuring 10 m (33 ft) × 4.5 m (15 ft) and aligned end-on to the street to the east were recorded. The chamfered north jamb of an off-centre street entrance was found in the east wall, and later blocking probably concealed a medieval splayed window. The west end of the undercroft survived largely intact (Fig. 160a–b) as a wall of squared chalk blocks, with a spiral stair in the north-west corner. The door at the foot of the stair would have fitted into a slight hollowing out of the adjacent wall. A vault with diagonal ribs was indicated by a scar of chalk blocks. The west wall passed to the south of the undercroft indicating another structure on that side; the west stone jamb of a communicating door had been reset in the post-medieval period, but perhaps succeeded a medieval doorway. The ribs and walls were built of finely cut blocks of chalk, which, along with the diagonal direction of the ribs, may suggest a construction date in the fourteenth century; bricks were employed in the stair wall and steps, suggesting fifteenth-century work, perhaps repair.[1]

1. Gadd 1982; MoL, sitecode LOV81.

(130)   Waxchandlers' Hall, Maiden Lane

Originally the property of the Knights Hospitallers, the hall site was a brewhouse from at least 1331, named in 1421 as the Cock on the Hope, at the corner of Ing Lane (later Maiden Lane) and Guthrun

(Gutter) Lane. The property contained shops, including a *shopa corneria* in 1488.[1] In 1367 the architect Henry Yevele bought the brewhouse and five adjacent shops and sold them in 1396. In 1501 a group of wax chandlers acquired the property, and by 1525 refurbishment of the buildings behind the Cock (which continued to be let separately) had been undertaken. The hall itself was on a cellar with a stone stair, and the buildings were arranged around a small courtyard entered from Maiden Lane. In 1530–2 the 'Assumpcion of our lady in the parlour' was mended by a glazier, and further repairs followed in 1536–8. An inventory of 1550 mentions a chamber, parlour, hall, an upper chamber, buttery, larder house and cellar. In 1566 the City Viewers reported an encroachment by the Waxchandlers onto land of the parish of St John Zachary by the construction of ovens.[2] Ogilby and Morgan show the post-Fire hall on the east corner of Gutter Lane and Maiden Lane.

1. GL, MS 9506.
2. Dummelow 1973, 26–8, 162–4.

(131) Haberdashers' Hall, Maiden Lane

In 1458 a group of haberdashers acquired this property from Sir Richard Walgrave. In the same year the company contracted with Walter Tylney, carpenter, that he would set up the frame of their hall and other tenements; in 1461 another contract with Robert Wheatley, carpenter, concerned the porch, screen, hall doors, armourie, entry from the kitchen to the parlour, the *seeling* over the head of the parlour, stairs to the Raven Chamber, and dresser boards and other things in the kitchen.[1] Haberdashers' Hall is mentioned in a boundary dispute with Beaumont's Inn in 1460,[2] and a little later in the list in Harley MS 541 (*c.* 1475). Its site at the northeast corner of Maiden Lane and Staining Lane is noted by Stow.[3] A block of ten almshouses, endowed in 1539, stood on the east side of Staining Lane, adjoining the hall.[4] Ogilby and Morgan show the post-Fire hall on the same site, a courtyard building with the hall east to west at the rear. In 1677 Oliver surveyed the site of the Haberdashers' 'ancient parlor', evidently on the north side of the site and measuring 56 ft 3 in east to west and 26 ft 9 in north to south at the east end, 27 ft 12½ in north to south at the west end.[5]

1. GL, MS 15874, 25–7.
2. *Cal. Plea & Mem. R, 1458–82*, 14.
3. Stow, i, 291, 298.
4. *Ibid.*, 304.
5. Mills & Oliver, *Survey*, v, 181[V].

(132) 50 Mark Lane

An undercroft of two bays was recorded during post-Second World War redevelopment (Fig. 235a). The walls were 2–2½ ft thick, of chalk and flint with interiors of chalk ashlar; they had no foundations, since the ballast lay directly beneath. In the middle of the longer east and west sides were semi-circular engaged columns of limestone with simple base mouldings, resting on sub-structures of stones (Merstham rag), and attached shafts of limestone were found in all four corners, suggesting quadripartite vaulting. Fragments of ragstone ribs and possibly of a capital in limestone were found in later contexts.[1] The floor of the undercroft produced fifteenth-century sherds, but the simplicity of the shafts and their apparent likeness to those at Gerard's Hall led the excavator to suggest a building date before the fourteenth century.[2]

1. GM 21158–60.
2. Harris 1958.

(133) 62–63 Mark Lane

Four houses forming the south-east corner of the junction of Hart Street and Mark Lane; they were part of the bequest of Oliver Claymond (see also **142**), an early master, to the Clothworkers' Company in 1541.[1] The houses were totally rebuilt by the company in 1562–3, apparently with a single frame; the accounts described them as a 'great place' and three others.[2] The larger house

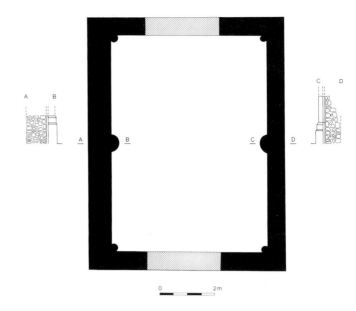

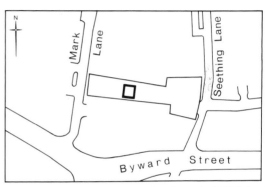

235. **(132)** 50 Mark Lane: (a) plan of undercroft, 1958 [after Harris 1958]

(b)   Plan of site

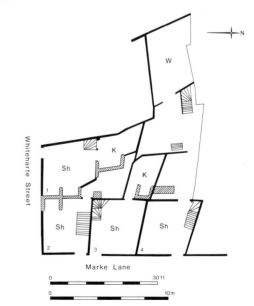

236. **(133)** 62–63 Mark Lane (Treswell 1612)

(Ivatt) included a yard, warehouse and larger cellar, which the others did not; but otherwise they were all similar three-and-a half storey buildings on cellars (Fig. 236).[3] The dimensions for the first floor of the corner tenancy (Rymell) suggest that at the corner its jetty sailed 2 ft into Mark Lane (the major street) and 1½ ft into Hart (Whiteharte) Street.

1. CD.
2. QW, Accts., 1562–3.
3. *LSRT*, 92–3.

(134) Northumberland Inn/Queen Joan's Wardrobe, [St] Martin's Lane

The history of this site can be traced from 1298, when it adjoined an intramural way, later built over, between Aldersgate and Newgate.[1] In 1352 Henry, second Lord Percy, owned a tenement and eight shops within Aldersgate. The fourth Lord Percy, first Earl of Northumberland, granted them to his son Henry (Hotspur), after whose death in 1403 the Inn was granted first to Richard, Lord Grey of Codnor, in 1404 and, enlarged by a grant of a further ruinous Inn and twelve shops and solars, to Henry IV's queen, Joanna of Navarre, in 1405. Throughout the fifteenth century the house was granted for short periods to nobility, but was in the possession of the fourth Earl of Northumberland at his death in 1489.[2] In 1552 the City ordered a view of the little old tower (i.e. one of the interval towers on the city wall) on the backside of Northumberland Place, which Edward Arundel, now farmer of Northumberland Place, desired to hire from the City and build upon.[3] In Stow's 1603 edition

the property is described as a printing-house, on the west side of St Martin's Lane.[4]

1. *Recs. of Two City Parishes*, 145.
2. *LTR*, xi, 57–8.
3. CCPR, Northumberland Inn, 1552.
4. Stow, i, 309.

(135) Abbot of Waltham's Inn, [St] Mary at Hill

The abbot of Waltham (Essex) established a town-house in the late twelfth century, enlarged by a further plot in 1201. A chapel is mentioned in 1218–21, 'in the court adjoining the church of St Mary at Hill'. From accounts of 1540–1 Miss Honeybourne reconstructed the place as a courtyard house on cellars entered through a gatehouse range set back from St Mary at Hill (Lane), the hall backing on to Lovat Lane to the west, with domestic offices on the north side of the court, and a dormitory and a chapel on the south side.[1] A modified reconstruction from the accounts (Fig. 237) has been proposed by Gadd, partly from observation of walls and foundations on the site in 1981.[2] The observed walls may have derived originally from the ecclesiastical house, but some details at least seemed more likely to derive from a post-Dissolution building, such as that documented in 1550–62 by Thomas Blanke, haberdasher. His son Thomas became Lord Mayor in 1582, and may have kept his mayoralty there.[3]

1. Honeybourne 1952, 34–46.
2. Gadd 1983.
3. *Inq. PM*, iii, 135–7; ii, 23; Honeybourne, *op. cit.*, 44–5.

237.   **(135)** Abbot of Waltham's Inn, [St] Mary at Hill: reconstruction based on excavation and documentary records by D. Gadd, 1981

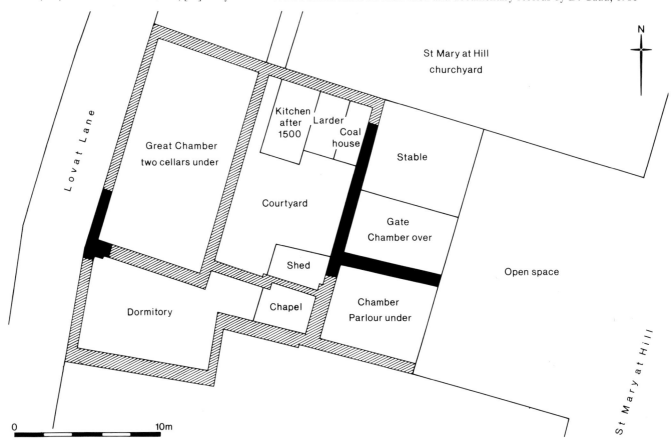

(136) Fletchers' Hall, [St] Mary Axe

Not in the list of halls of *c.* 1475 in Harley MS 541; the Fletchers hired the Carpenters' Hall in 1488.[1] In 1532 the company paid rent to the Crown after the dissolution of Holy Trinity Priory, suggesting that the hall site was originally priory land; they bought the freehold soon after.[2] Stow placed the hall near the north end of St Mary Axe (Street) on the west side.[3] It does not appear by name on Ogilby and Morgan's map, though it would be in the area undamaged by the Great Fire; its site is shown by Hollar on his map of company halls (1666) and by Rocque in 1744–9.

1. *RCC*, ii, 76.
2. Oxley 1968, 61.
3. Stow, i, 146.

(137) Blue Boar, [St] Mary Axe/Bevis Marks

Nineteenth-century watercolours (e.g. Fig. 179) and photographs show a large timber-framed house at the east corner of St Mary Axe and Bevis Marks. It was of three storeys with garrets; the first and second floors were jettied to both streets, and the three garret gables further jettied to St Mary Axe, its frontage. The two south bays had bay windows on first and second floors. This was evidently a house of distinction, probably dating (from its overall appearance) from the middle or second half of the sixteenth century (there are no grotesque corbels to be seen, perhaps suggesting a date before *c.* 1560). No pertinent documentary records have so far been traced.

(138) 1–6 Milk Street

This site was excavated in 1976–8;[1] archaeological evidence for the period after *c.* 1100 was confined to the deeper stone foundations of substantial buildings, cesspits and wells.

The establishment of Milk Street (the name is extant from *c.* 1140),[2] inferred by the recording of buildings along its east side, can be placed probably in the tenth century and with more certainty by the opening of the eleventh. During the second half of the eleventh century there was a great increase in the digging of rubbish pits and cesspits, as on the Watling Court and Well Court sites south of Cheapside (31–2), but in contrast there were no sunken timber-built cellars aligned at right angles to the street on the Milk Street site. The fragmentary rebuildings can be placed in a documentary framework of property boundaries which is evident by 1350 (Fig. 238). Six tenements can be discerned.

Tenement 1 to the south, adjacent to St Mary Magdalen church,

was granted in 1202–4 to St Paul's Cathedral; it then included stone houses. The property, with probably adjacent property in the parish of All Hallows Honey Lane, had passed into the possession of Henry de Frowyk I by *c.* 1284, and they remained with the family for about 250 years. When the suggested alignments of property boundaries for this period are superimposed on the archaeological remains (Fig. 238) it can be seen that an early stone-lined cesspit (Pit 116, with fills dating to 1230–70) lay within this property; its contents included several wooden items, including bowls. A part of the property to the south, adjacent to the church, was apparently sold to the parish for a graveyard shortly before 1527, and much of the rest was absorbed by an expansion of Tenement 2 at the same time.

Tenement 2, on documentary evidence, formed a small rectangle along the Milk Street frontage next to 1. Prior to 1212/13 this property belonged to Pentecost the robe-trimmer (*parmentarius*). In 1276 it belonged to the Crown, and was in the hands of Cresseus son of Elias, Jew of London; in the same year the king granted it to Sir Stephen de Chendut, who granted it back to Cresseus for a large sum in silver. Sir John de Enefeld was in possession by 1315, and John Coterel, mercer, in 1342. In his testament of 1463 Sir William

238. (138) 1–6 Milk Street: plan of site *c.* 1350, with building foundations (of 1100–1400) excavated in 1976 placed within property boundaries established by documentary research [Schofield *et al.* 1990]

0   20m

Cantelowe (alderman of Cripplegate ward 1446–61; sheriff 1448–9; Member of Parliament for the City 1453, 1455; master of the Mercers' Company in 1450, 1456 and 1462) bequeathed the property as his dwelling house, with a tenement annexed: evidently the front part of Tenement 3 to the north (3a). His son Henry, in his own will of 1490, left money 'towards the fynysshing and garnysshing of my new place in Mylkestrete' – presumably the enlarged mansion. This house however still only occupied a strip along the street, with no depth behind. In 1525 the property passed to Thomas Kytson, mercer (the builder of Hengrave Hall in Suffolk), who extended it by buying much of Tenement 1 from the parish of St Mary Magdalen (Fig. 239). Kytson probably also rebuilt the property; at his death in 1541 an inventory mentions his dwelling house in Milk Street, in which there was a chapel. In 1584 the property was sold to Christ's Hospital and one of the tenants, from 1605 to 1612, was the Stationers' Company. No archaeological traces attributable to the buildings on this property were recorded, except for the cesspit noted under Tenement 1 and the stone building beneath Tenement 3.

Tenement 3 was the site of Building 6 (Figs. 27, 154), a stone building at right angles to the street; though the west end was outside (or coincided with) the boundary of the site, it probably fronted onto Milk Street. Two parallel foundations protruding from its east end may indicate a stair to the upper floor; between them was evidence for a doorway into the lower chamber, which may have been vaulted. This building's north side observed a boundary which may have been marked by a concentration of pits from the early eleventh century (Fig. 27). A construction date of around 1100 is proposed from material in underlying pits, making it one of the earliest medieval secular buildings from recent excavations. The tenement belonged in 1276 to Bonamicus the Jew of York. In 1315 it was in the possession of Sir John de Enefeld, who held Tenement 2, and who undertook not to disturb the light of the windows on the tenement's east side. In 1317 the property was described as newly built, but the archaeological evidence relates only to the twelfth-century building. Between 1334 and 1336 the property was divided into two; the back (east) half was absorbed into the contiguous Tenement 1 between 1349 and 1361, and the front half was annexed to Tenement 2 by the time of William Cantelowe in 1460 (Fig. 239). The lack of archaeological information for this period means that it is impossible to say whether the basement storey of the twelfth-

century Building 6 survived the partition of 1334–6; but the building above it, as rebuilt by 1317, must have had an influence on the property boundary around it which did not disappear until the two halves were absorbed away finally, perhaps in the sixteenth century. In Cantelowe's time the front half was still regarded as a separate tenement, though annexed to his own.

Tenement 4, adjacent to the north of 3, belonged in the early thirteenth century to Martin de Virly, citizen of Rouen, and in 1249 to Leo le Bland, Jew. In 1401 Thomas Dyster, mercer, dwelt there on lease; he was evidently a man of great wealth, and when he died in 1411 an inventory of his goods amounted to £4,336 9s. 3d.[3] The only archaeological features of note on this property were a stone-lined cesspit towards the rear (Pit 117) which contained material of the late fourteenth century and the remains of a papal bull of 1378–89, and the foundation of a rebuilt west wall against the street, of unknown but medieval date.

Tenement 5, again to the north, is notable for the survival of parts of the walls of a cellar at the front of the property, with the base of a stair which would have communicated with the street. Though undated archaeologically, this cellar is equated with a vault mentioned in 1293 as being annexed to the adjacent tenement to the north.

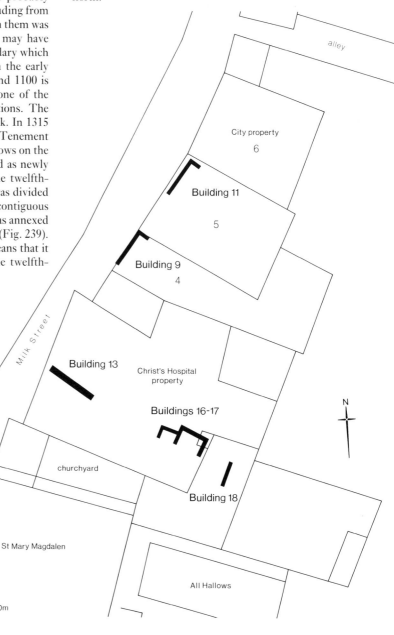

239. (**138**) 1–6 Milk Street: plan of site *c.* 1660, with building foundations (of 1400–1700) excavated in 1976 placed within property boundaries established by documentary research

1. MoL, sitecode MLK76; Schofield, Allen & Taylor 1990, where the documentary work is by C. Taylor.
2. Ekwall, *Street-names*, 76.
3. *Cal. Plea & Mem. R., 1413–37*, 21–4.

(139) Clothworkers' Hall, Mincing Lane

In 1170–97 Stephen, prior of Holy Trinity Priory, Aldgate, granted property in the parish of St Dunstan in the East to Alfred the roofer (*Cooperator*) which Pain the fishmonger, his brother, had held, for a rent of 1s. 8d. p.a.; this tenement was increased by the grant of another, presumably adjoining and presumably much larger, to Edeua daughter of Walter, in 1197–1221.[1] The joint quit-rent of 5s. 8d. p.a. continued to be paid, and this with the coincidence of owners' names for the two parts confirms that this property eventually became Clothworkers' Hall. Deeds in the company's possession survive from 1349; the property passed via William de Stanes, apothecary, to Sir Reginald de Grey and others, who released their claims to de Grey and his wife in 1376. The house extended from Mincing Lane to the churchyard of All Hallows Staining. In 1397, when de Grey's son Reginald sold the property, it was known as Grey's Inn. In 1399 William Marker, stockfishmonger, and Nicholas Glover were the owners; and the property continued to be passed between groups containing fishmongers in the early fifteenth century. One such group contained twenty-four names, including two aldermen.[2]

In 1456 they sold it to a group of Shearmen, and the association with clothworkers began;[3] Shearmen's Hall is mentioned in the list of c. 1475 in Harley MS 541. The Shearmen united with the Fullers in 1528 to form the Clothworkers' Company, and the hall in Mincing Lane became Clothworkers' Hall. Repairs in 1539–40 suggest that the parlour was in a two-storey range.[4]

In 1548 the company decided to rebuild the hall. A 'new frame' was expected;[5] but shortly afterwards a bricklayer, Henry Davyron, bargained to bring up and make the sides of the walls of the hall with brick, 18 ft high. James Maylam of East Mallinge in Kent, shipwright, brought timber for the hall by water.[6] The hall, with its parlour of 1594[7] and garden, was surveyed by Treswell in 1612 (Fig. 57).[8] The hall lay between a courtyard entered through a gatehouse – which contained the beadle's house (2) – from Mincing Lane and the garden, in which were two knots. The buttery, pantry and kitchen were probably parts of the pre-1548 house. The south block had two floors over, including the Ladies' Chamber, dry larder, plate chamber, little comptinghouse, armoury and pastry (above the kitchen ovens, approached by the little stair shown in the kitchen). Both parlour and hall were on undercrofts; subtenant (1) had a long vault under his tenancy and the north side of the court, and leased the vault beneath the hall itself.

1. *HTA Cartulary*, 202, 204.
2. CD, Box 6.
3. Girtin 1958, 13; CD, Box 6.
4. RW, Accts., 1539–40.
5. CCO, 1536–58, 202.
6. QW, Accts., 1548–9.
7. QW, Accts., 1594–5.
8. *LSRT*, 94–6.

(140) St James's Hermitage/Lambe's chapel, Monkwell Street

The Hermitage of St James's, situated on the city wall between Cripplegate and the north-west corner of the defences, was said, in 1255, to have been given by Richard I to his chaplain Warin in 1189; but another record speaks of it as founded in the reign of John.[1] By 1289, when it was extended by the incorporation of an adjacent lane, the hermitage was a cell of the Cistercian house of Garendon (Leicestershire); at this time a hermit, Friar Robert, was mentioned. In 1338 William de Lyouns, 'heremite', of the Cripplegate hermitage, was restrained from repairing the wall of the hermitage by his neighbour, Thomas Sporon, goldsmith, but allowed to continue by the City. The Countess of Pembroke founded a chantry in the hermitage for the soul of her husband, Sir Aylmer de Valence (d. 1323); and in 1364–5 it was used for ordinations. In 1382 the abbey leased a further garden – 165 ft long – from the City.[2]

By 1539, the hermitage site was owned by Robert Draper of Camberwell (Surrey), and he leased it to William Lambe, clothworker. The site was granted to Lambe in 1543. A contemporary biography of Lambe asserts that he lived 'in the house next to St James chapel'. The site passed to the Clothworkers' Company in 1580.[3]

The undercroft of the chapel,[4] datable on architectural grounds to c. 1140, was removed during rebuilding in 1872 and partially re-erected (the individual stones not in correct order) by the Clothworkers' Company on the site of the nave of All Hallows Staining, Mark Lane.

When surveyed by Treswell in 1612 (Fig. 66) the estate was in two parts, north and south of a long brick wall which divided the two entrances to Monkwell Street. The larger, north part comprised a medium-sized house (1) (presumably that occupied by Lambe) of two and a half storeys, with a garden and access into the redundant corner-tower on the city wall (Bastion 12, which still survives). Tenant (2) ran a school in the highest buildings, of three and a half storeys, next to Monkwell Street on the east. He was also the tenant of the undercroft below the chapel, and used it as a cellar. Tenant (3) had rooms adjacent to the chapel and access to the leads over it; the chapel itself was not let out. The south side of this range was drawn by Nash c. 1800 (Fig. 108).

The southern property comprised an alley going past a two-room building (5) of two and a half storeys to a small court in which were five one-room plan houses (6–9) of two and a half storeys each. The first-floor and garret dimensions agree to the extent that all five may have been built in a single construction. Apart from those mentioned, none of the properties on either part had cellars.[5]

1. *Cal. Pat. R., 1247–58*, 402; Harben, *Dictionary*, 319.
2. *Cal. Pat. R., 1281–92*, 401; *Assize of Nuisance*, 333; *Memorials*, 553; CD, Box 19.
3. *Letters & Papers xviii(i)*, 201; CD, Box 19.
4. Cf. Schofield, *Building of London*, Fig. 41.
5. *LSRT*, 97–9.

(141) Newgate or Paternoster Row, 1310

In 1310 Sir John Mundene, clerk, bargained on behalf of St Paul's with Richard de Rothing, carpenter, to build a frame of three shops on the north side of the highway in the parish of St Michael le Querne, west of the entrance to Mundene's house and between the road and Mundene's kitchen to the north. The carpenter was to have as much of the timber of the previous building as he cared to salvage. The ground storey was to be 10 ft high to the joists of the first floor, on which were to be two halls with chimneys, a buttery, pantry and kitchen, 'according to the size of the place' (perhaps service rooms with each of the halls). On the second floor would be two chambers with privies. The building would take four months to construct.[1]

The site of the building in this contract is not yet identified. The parish of St Michael included both the east end of Newgate and Paternoster Row, either of which could be the street in question.
1. Salzman, *Building*, 418–19.

(142) Foxe's Court, [St] Nicholas Lane/23–24 Abchurch Lane

In 1363 Elias Chaunceler granted back to Sir Edward Kendale the property he owned between St Nicholas Lane and Abchurch Lane. In 1377 the property had passed, perhaps by way of an Elizabeth Kendale in dowry, to William de Bughbrigge, clerk, who granted it to Sir John Cobham, three citizens and two other clerks. In 1382 this group quitclaimed to John de Bosham, one of their number; and in

1390 Bosham, a mercer, demised the property to three more clerics: John Turk, John Poydras and Robert Turk. This group then leased all '*illud magnum hospitium*' which a Daniel Damar had held to John Basse *pannarius* (draper), together with nine shops and solars which Basse had recently built, for sixty years at a rent of 12 marks. At the same time they leased two further shops in Abchurch Lane, between this block of property to the east and 'the entrance of the large gate' of John Turk *et al.*, to Simon Engram, 'lyndraper'. In 1397 John, son of John Basse, sublet his property to John Attilburgh, prior of Bermondsey Abbey, and Richard Forster of London; Attilburgh sublet it again to John Burford, 'belyeter', who also held the Crown, Aldgate (**10**) at this time.[1]

Between 1397 and 1424 the freehold passed from Turk, Poydras and Turk to Richard Jepe, rector of All Hallows Honey Lane. Robert Turk must have willed it to Thomas Trumpington to support a chantry in All Hallows for the Turk family, since Trumpington willed it in 1425 (proved 1428) to Jepe for this purpose. Jepe granted it to a large group of citizens, including John Carpenter; the three survivors, Clemens Lyly, draper, John Chisehill and Thomas Mullying, quitclaimed to Simon Eyre in 1448. Eyre granted the property to his son Thomas and Elizabeth his wife, and Thomas granted it to Richard Heton, Richard Quatremayne and Richard Peverell in 1459. This group sublet to a physician, Matteo Dominico de Serege (?) in 1468, and to John Saunder, draper, in 1470. Saunder or Saunders, called a 'sherman' in 1488, owned the property by the time of his death in 1504. One notable set of subtenants were Fernando de Castro and Diego de Castro, merchants of Burgos in Spain, who leased the property for £10 *p.a.* in 1488. In this lease Saunder undertook to 'make defensible [the property] and the sieges of the same do to be purged and the pavement of the same do to be repaired as ofte as nede shal be'. In 1491 Alphonse de Burgos was tenant at the same rent; and it was noted 'that there remayneth in the chamber over the parlor a standing close bedde of Estriche borde' belonging to Saunder. By his will of 1504 Saunder left the property to his wife, and on her death to his daughters Agnes, wife of Oliver Claymond, and Mary, wife of Richard Nicholl. Claymond was one of Saunder's executors; he had sole control of the property by 1520. In 1533 Claymond, an early master of the new Clothworkers' Company, granted the property to a group of clothworkers; it was fully granted to the company by reversion after Claymond's widow's death, under the terms of his will in 1540. The company then leased it to a succession of tenants. Notable among these was John Foxe, clothworker, who leased the property in 1585–6 for £80 *p.a.*, whereas the rent in 1582–3 had been £24; thereafter the main house on Nicholas Lane was called Foxe's Court.[2]

The estate surveyed by Treswell in 1612 comprised two parts (Fig. 48). A great house (1) lay on the north side of a court entered from Nicholas Lane through a three-storey street range. The house comprised a hall, perhaps originally 28½ ft × 20 ft, entered by steps and on a cellar. The hall had evidently been divided by 1612 into a smaller hall and parlour, the original door being blocked up and a new entrance made directly into the parlour which formed the upper two-thirds of the original hall. Beyond the screens was a kitchen with a large stack which occupied nearly all the end of the range. The range to Nicholas Lane contained first- and second-floor galleries on the court side, with access down to the court; each floor had several rooms running the width of the range, as in galleried inns. The hall range was four storeys high, and a subtenancy (2) on Nicholas Lane rose to four storeys with garrets. Around the south and west sides of the courtyard were warehouses, three of two storeys and one of only one storey.

The second part of the estate (though probably inseparable from it from earliest times) comprised a frontage of eleven houses (3–13) to Abchurch Lane. The nine northern houses were on the site of nine built shortly before 1390 by John Basse (see above); it is possi-

ble that the arrangement of rooms and kitchen on the ground floor, and possibly some of the fabric, dated from his building.

The five houses to the north (9–13) were of two-room plan with separate kitchens across a small yard (Fig. 80); in one case the two ground-floor rooms had been thrown together, and in the same house the kitchen was replaced by a shed. The coincidence of alignment of partitions, stairs, and some correspondence in dimensions of upper chambers, together with a uniform height of three and a half storeys, suggests that all five were part of one frame and built as a unit. The houses also shared the feature of a heated chamber on the first floor next to the street which probably functioned as a hall.

South of this group of five houses were more individual buildings (3–8); their construction may have been dictated by the presence of the adjacent great house. A gateway to Abchurch Lane is mentioned for instance in 1390, and was probably somewhere on this part of the site. The shops, two of one-room plan and four of mixed one- and two-room plan, were of three and a half storeys with one exception.[3]

1. CD, Box 59, 1–12.
2. *Cal. Wills*, ii, 447; CD, Box 59, 14–33, 39; *Cal. Wills*, ii, 646.
3. *LSRT*, 100–3.

(143) Lady Lucy's House (later Dean's Court) Old Bailey (later 38–40 Fleet Lane, 1–5 Dean's Court, 28–31 Seacoal Lane)

In 1528 William Tymbigh, prior of Charterhouse, leased this property to Sir John Mordaunt for ninety years. The property was purchased by Sir Edward North and sold to Henry VIII, who granted it to Christ Church in 1546.[1] The tenant in 1600 was Sir Edward Lucy; Lady Lucy appears as the tenant in 1610, when Treswell surveyed the property, presumably for the college (Fig. 52).[2] The plan is not dated, but is endorsed '1610'. A draft for the same is also extant.[3]

The plan, which is drawn on paper, shows a substantial house at the end of a long alley on the west side of Old Bailey (unnamed, but called Dean's Court by the time of Ogilby and Morgan's map in 1677). The ground floor of the house comprised a hall, kitchen and pantry, and two parlours; the high end of the hall and both parlours had large windows which are shown in section (an unusual feature for the Treswell plans, see also **145**). There is no text of reference, but four stairs are shown on the ground-floor plan, of which two may have led to cellars and two probably led upwards (from the hall and the parlours). Around the garden were single-storeyed chambers and privies; a further set of steps, which because of the fall of the land must have led downwards, went into a stable yard which contained a building marked 'the stable and Coche howse'.

1. Christ Church Oxford, MS Estates 45, 2; Book of Evidences, 1, 464–6.
2. *LSRT*, 104–5; Christ Church Deeds, London, St Sepulchre's, 1–9.
3. Christ Church Deeds, London, St Sepulchre's, 4.

(144) (Old) Fishmongers' Hall, 9 Old Fish Street Hill

A Fishmongers' Hall in this street is mentioned in BL Harley MS 541 (*c*. 1475). A tenement called Old Fishmongers' Hall was leased to William Blewe in 1602, when it was described as comprising a tenement and four cellars under the same.[1] An inventory of 1601 mentions hall, parlour, kitchen, chamber over the parlour and courtyard. The hall was boarded with boards painted like wainscot, with settles on the south side; the parlour was wainscotted, with a built-in court cupboard; the courtyard had a well.[2] In 1612 the Glaziers leased the hall from the Fishmongers, and a plan of 1618 shows the ground floor (Fig. 240): a court entered from (Old) Fish Street Hill, with both kitchen and parlour on the left, the hall with extensive windows forming the back, west side of the court. Parts of the buildings had walls 3 ft thick, indicating stone walls.

1. GL, MS 5758/6.
2. Ashdown 1919, 38–9.

(145)   3–4 Pancras Lane (formerly Needlers Lane)

The property, perhaps originally two separate tenements, was united by the late thirteenth century. It was probably inhabited by Simon Corp, pepperer, in the early fourteenth century, and by William de Causton, mercer, in the mid fourteenth century.[1] In 1587 Arnold James, brewer, leased part of the property to Thomas Thorowgood, draper, and attached to the lease is a small schedule of fittings which included wainscot around the parlour, a wainscot portal and door; in the chamber above the parlour chamber, one portal and door of wainscot; two counting houses next the chamber over the parlour, ceiled with wainscot; the chamber over the parlour chamber, with a portal and door of wainscot; and the kitchen with a cistern of lead weighing $4^{1}/_{2}$ cwt and a pump. The house was bought from James by Christ's Hospital in 1602 out of £500 bequeathed to them by Peter Blundell.[2]

When surveyed for the hospital by Treswell (Fig. 70),[3] the property was divided between two main tenants. This is one of only two Treswell plans which include details of windows (cf. 143): two prominent four-light stone windows to the hall and parlour, and a third on the slighter east wall of the hall, probably of timber. There is no accompanying text of reference, but the upper floors of most of the buildings may be reconstructed from a lease of 1611 to one of the tenants, Edward Baber.[4] The buildings appear to be only two storeys high, with garrets. Especially noteworthy is the room with pillars, which was not, as may appear, an open yard but – as the schedule attached to the lease makes clear – an enclosed space. For analysis of the access patterns through this property see Fig. 100c.

The brick wall which divided the garden was inserted just before the lease was drawn up, to divide Baber's tenancy from that of Jackson; evidently Baber was taking over some of Jackson's rooms. It therefore seems likely that the plan was drawn in or shortly after 1611.

1. For those eminent merchants, Thrupp, *Merchant Class*, 333, 329.
2. GL, MS 12935. The detailed history of this site has been traced in *HG, i: Cheapside*, site **145/14–15**.
3. *LSRT*, 106–7.
4. GL, MS 12935.

240.   **(144)** Old Fishmongers' Hall, Old Fish Street Hill, surveyed in 1618

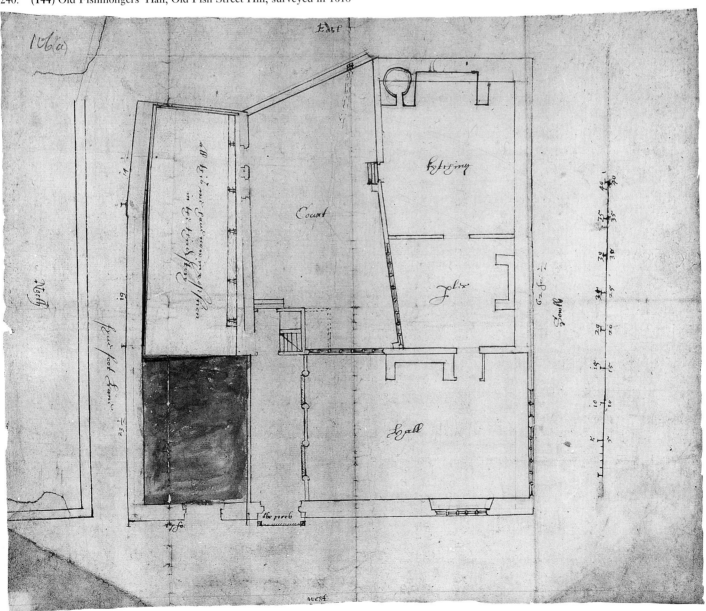

(146) Peter and Paul Tavern, Paternoster Row

In 1338 Robert le Foundour and other executors of John de Pykenham, paternosterer, granted to Hugh le Marbrer five shops and solars on the north side of Paternoster Row in the parish of St Michael le Querne.[1] This property may formerly have been the street range of a larger estate, since the property on all three sides apart from the street was owned by the same person in 1338. In 1342 William Marbrer, vintner, made separate contracts with a mason and a carpenter to rebuild the property as a tavern.[2] Phelip de Cherche, mason, was to excavate to a depth of 17 ft, and in the north-west corner dig for a privy, 7 ft square, as deep as the water-table would allow. The vault of the garderobe was to be of chalk, with a pipe in the wall up to the first floor. The walls of the cellar were to be of rag, 3 ft thick, standing up to 2 ft above the pavement level. The arches (of the vault) were to be of freestone (*Franche pere*) and the filling of the vault of chalk. There were to be four windows in the cellar facing the street; on the other side the wall was to be carried up to the first floor. Stairs down to the cellar and to the first floor were also to be of ragstone. At each end of the cellar would be a fireplace, carried up in stone to the level of the first floor.

The contract with the carpenter, Richard de Felstede,[3] gives the position and dimensions of the plot, apparently on the *south* side (i.e. not as stated in 1338) of the street, 12¼ ells (*aunes*) long and 7¼ ells wide. Richard was to make a house with two gables to the street (i.e. in the longer street façade), of three storeys with both upper storeys jettied. In one gable would be a garret, in the other, on the second floor, a hall with kitchen and larder on its north side (on the street side, see below). Part of the ground floor was to be partitioned and provided with seats to make a tavern, as also throughout the first floor. The remainder of the ground floor would be a chamber. The bedchamber (not located, but probably in the other garret) would have a bay window with two other lintelled windows; the same arrangement would apply to the street side of the hall.

In 1347 William Marbrer, taverner, granted a yearly 38s. 6d. in dower from the tenement to Lettice, widow of Hugh le Marbrer.[4] In 1375, William Marbrer being dead, his apprentice and executor Leo granted the property to John Mokyngge, vintner; and in 1429 Robert Mockyngge granted the property, named *le Petre et Paule* to his heir or to charitable uses. The latter evidently became the case since the tavern passed through a number of groups of trustees from 1430 to 1450.[5] A Peter Bylton, bookbinder, had been a witness to the transfers in 1430 and 1431, and he became one of the trustees in the transfers in 1450. Peter Bylton was the principal bookbinder for London Bridge during the first decades of the fifteenth century; in 1404 he held four shops in Paternoster Row.[6] It seems likely that he was in occupation by this time, and possibly from 1430, since his will of 1454 refers to his tenement called the Peter and Paul, and with the agreement of the other trustees he granted the property to London Bridge.[7]

1. CLRO, Bridge House deeds, G22.
2. Salzman, *Building*, 432–4.
3. Felstede had worked on several royal castles in 1322–6, and in 1347 agreed to make the roofs for the hall, pantry, buttery and kitchen of Kenilworth Castle (Harvey, *English Medieval Architects*, 107).
4. CLRO, Bridge House deeds, G59.
5. *Ibid.*, G69, H62, H64, H52, H81, H85.
6. Christiansen 1987, 17, 27, 48–51.
7. CLRO, Bridge House deeds, H81, I22, I26, I29, I35.

(147) Woodmongers' Hall and Smith's Almshouses, [St] Peter's Hill

From at least the fifteenth century the woodmongers were congregating in the parish of St Andrew Castle Baynard. No hall is mentioned in Harley MS 541 of *c.* 1475; the earliest reference is in 1581 when it was already defunct. David Smith, embroiderer to Elizabeth

I, purchased it from Edmund Helles, woodmonger, shortly before his (Smith's) death in 1587, when he left it with other property to the mayor and commonalty on trust for Christ's Hospital. The hospital took possession in 1607.[1]

The site was surveyed by Treswell in 1611 (Fig. 65a).[2] The six almshouses each comprised a ground-floor chamber of brick with a chimney, and a first floor and garret, probably timber-framed, which jettied one foot into the court. The upper chambers were not heated, but each had a house of office.

The stone building next to the almshouses included an upper room called Woodmongers' Hall. The plan and text of Treswell's survey indicate that Thomas Swayne held a cellar and two rooms on the ground floor; the south wall on the ground floor was a stout stone wall with two buttresses. There is no further information from the 1611 survey about the upper floors of this building, or about the part of it called Woodmongers' Hall. A view of 1628 describes the hall as a second-floor room.

The Woodmongers were still active in 1609–10, when they sued the Blacksmiths to have a William Stephens made free of the latter company; and in 1612 there is a reference to Woodmongers' Hall in Duke's Place (8).[3]

The site of the almshouses is now beneath Queen Victoria Street.

1. *Inq. PM.*, iii, 106–9; CHMB, 1, 105ᵛ.
2. *LSRT*, 108–9.
3. Adams 1951, 50; Harben, *Dictionary*, 318.

(148) 7–8 Philpot Lane

In 1979 a medieval undercroft was recognised beneath the standing buildings, of immediately post-Fire date, forming 7–8 Philpot Lane. It lies north to south on the west side of the lane, running south from the present post-Fire entry into Brabant Court. Four bays of a brick tunnel vault are divided by chamfered transverse ribs of greensand stone (Fig. 91). The original south end is probably within the present south wall of no. 8, and thus the full length has been preserved. A post-Fire entrance to the street, probably on the site of the medieval entrance, lay in the north-east corner; two other entrances are post-Fire intrusions. Traces of two medieval window-openings have been seen in the east wall, with an enlarged modern opening at the site of a third, and one in the west wall. Excavation in 1984 found that the medieval floor level had been reduced in the post-medieval period, probably in the seventeenth century.[1]

1. MoL, sitecode HIL84; Lea 1985.

(149) Grocers' Hall, Poultry

Robert Fitzwalter, Baron (d. 1234), had a house in Old Jewry. His grandson Robert enlarged the site by acquiring the chapel of the Friars of the Sack on the corner of Old Jewry and Lothbury in 1305; the chapel had formerly been a Jewish Synagogue. In 1411 the chapel was sold to the Grocers' Company, who acquired the rest of the Fitzwalter Inn by 1433.[1] The main part of the site was granted by a group of Grocers to the wardens in 1429.[2] The company had begun building in 1427, when during a brief building season of 8 May to 5 June the foundations of the west gable of the hall were dug. In the following year the foundations of the hall were complete, the gable walls raised 10 ft and 9½ ft above the water-table (offset), and the north wall raised in part to its full height of 23 ft. Foundations for the parlour and 'chambre with the vawte' (an undercroft), for the buttery and pantry were dug, with privies and chimneys; the parlour and tresaunce were latticed, glazed and 'selyd' (panelled). The chamber had a bay window; the parlour apparently contained a 'celour' with battlements, and vines were planted in front of its windows. Stapylton stone was used for window jambs and sills, and the 'crestable' of the south wall of the hall was of Merstham stone. The company had a chapel, presumably the previous chapel of the friars, with two windows into it from the hall.[3] A large garden had a stone and brick tower at its north-east corner.[4]

The rebuilt hall is shown on Ogilby and Morgan's map as a large

building lying east to west at the back of a court entered through a long alley (Grocers' Alley – formerly Coneyhope Lane?) from Poultry. Post-Fire engravings show the hall with a semi-octagonal (stone) bay window on the court side; the window has three tiers of fifteenth-century lights (Fig. 53).

1. *LTR*, x, 120–1.
2. *Cal. Pat., R., 1429–36*, 78.
3. Heath 1869, 4–6.
4. Stow, i, 263, 278; ii, 334–5.

241.   **(150)** 28 Pudding Lane (Treswell 1610)

(150)   28 Pudding Lane

The tenement, formerly chantry property, was granted in 1549 by Edward Welsshe and Simon Aynesworth to Nicholas Howe, butcher. His widow Helen married John Gylmyn; they made an arrangement whereby they conveyed the property to Sir Roland Hill, who conveyed it back to them with reversion to the Christ's Hospital on Helen's death.[1] In 1573 Helen, now married to her third husband Cornelius de Vos, but acting on her own behalf, leased the property to Richard Holgate, carpenter, on the condition that within two years he take down the stone wall on the street side and set up a substantial timber frame of two storeys; the property was then known as the Boar's Head. Cornelius de Vos and his wife granted the reversion of the property to the City and Christ's Hospital in 1577.[2]

The front of the building in the plan of 1611 by Treswell (Fig. 241) was probably as Holgate built it in 1573–5. From Treswell's measurements, it seems that there was no jetty to the street. The tenancies comprised (1) one-room plan, three and a half storeys on a cellar; (2) two rooms, two and a half storeys; (3) rooms with one chamber and a gallery over; (4) six chambers in three and a half storeys.[3] If the agreement of 1573 referred only to the future building of (2), then it seems likely that the stone wall mentioned comprised the former frontage of (2). This would imply that (1), the larger portion with a ground-floor room called a hall in 1611, was the former main range of the whole property.

1. GL, MS 13184.
2. GL, MS 13186–7.
3. *LSRT*, 110–11.

(151)   Bishop of Bangor's Inn, Shoe Lane

On the west side of Shoe Lane, immediately south of St Andrew Holborn. Most of the land and some of the buildings on it were the gift of Thomas de Brancestre and Isabella his wife to the see in 1280–1; it was immediately extended by the Bishop. The Inn may have been leased as early as 1349.[1]

The Great Fire stopped just south of the house. Several engravings of one gable made just before demolition in 1820 show a two-storeyed, semi-octagonal bay window, the fenestration continuing on both floors to the corners of the building. In one engraving of 1818 a coat of arms is shown in the central light of the ground-floor bay window. The window is crowned by an ornate cornice of late sixteenth-century type. Shadows on the engravings suggest this may be the west end of an east to west block, perhaps a parlour, since it appears to border a garden.

1. Honeybourne, 'Value', 306–11.

(152)   Holborn Old Hall, Shoe Lane

By 1224 the first Dominican friars in London were settled on a site in Shoe Lane, where they held a general chapter of the Order in 1250. After their removal to the area subsequently known as Blackfriars, they sold the house in 1286 to Henry de Lacy, Earl of Lincoln; a little later there is mention of the great hall and chapel. Kingsford suggests that since the conveyance to Lacy and his will were enrolled in the Court of Husting they must have related to property within the City, and that this site is the later Oldbourne Hall; and he traces the descendants of Lacy as owners of the Hall to 1602. In 1382 the property was probably that described as a great tenement with a garden and sixteen shops. By Stow's time Oldbourne Hall, which lay on the east side of the lane, had been divided into tenements.[1]

In 1616 Margaret Husbandes of Edmonton (Middlesex), widow of Edward Husbandes, sold the capital messuage of the manor of Holborn, sometimes called Derby Hall and then called the Windmill, to Richard Husbandes, citizen and draper. The buildings were all in one block, but then divided into at least six tenements or parts: (1) (Giles Longe) a hall, kitchen, buttery, five chambers, two garrets, stable and hayloft, a yard with three further stables, a coachhouse with haylofts, the yard 22½ yards east to west and 17 yards north to south; (2) (Giles Longe) a hall, passage, three chambers, garret, two closets and a little yard; (3) (Margaret Gilbert) a chamber; (4) (William Underwood) a chamber formerly a kitchen, a garden adjoining with a fair workhouse therein, 11 yards east to west and 10 yards north to south; (5) (Margaret Husbandes) a hall, kitchen, coal house, three chambers and a garret; (6) (Mary Jones) a passage, hall, kitchen, pantry, a little dark room, six chambers, two closets and a garret, a little yard and a garden, 40 yards north to south and 18½ yards east to west, a privy on the south.[2]

1. *LTR*, x, 136–8; *Cal. Wills*, i, 218; Stow, ii, 38.
2. Williams, *Early Holborn*, i, 749; for a summary of the property's post-medieval history see also Barron 1979, 52–4.

(153)   Neville's Inn, Silver Street

At his death in 1357 Ralph Neville of Raby had an Inn, which he apparently rarely used, at the junction of Silver Street and Mugwell Street, on the east corner. In 1368 his son John acquired an adjoining tenement, and in 1374 leased from the City a garden 96 ells (288 ft) long alongside the city wall. At the time of John's death in 1388 this was described as a great tenement, implying consolidation or rebuilding. Stow recites the grant of the garden, which he places on the west side of Noble Street, adding that the house, 'one great house of stone and timber', lay at the north end (thus presumably) adjacent to the church of St Olave, which may account for the narrowest width of the garden (8 ells and 2 ft 6 in) being at the north end – this is approximately the distance between the church and the city wall on Ogilby and Morgan's map.[1]

Excavations on the site in 1947 found several chalk wall foun-

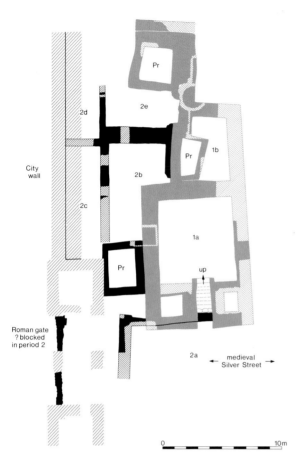

242. **(153)** Neville's Inn, Silver Street: simplified plan of excavated buildings, 1947 [after Grimes 1968]. The earlier of two phases is shown in grey. The letters a to e refer to rooms or spaces.

dations suggesting a north to south range of stone buildings or chambers, with two chalk-lined cesspits to the west in the narrow space between the building(s) and the city wall (Fig. 242). At the south end of the excavated area lay a deeper medieval cellar, with stairs up into the rest of the building in its north wall; here were steps and traces of Reigate stone jambs, probably of an arched doorway. One of the cesspits produced a coin of Edward III (1327–77), suggesting (though not strongly) that the buildings and cesspits may be the rebuilding presumed between 1368 and 1388. From their construction technique, a fourteenth-century date for these buildings is acceptable, indicating that they were probably part of Neville's Inn at some time.[2]

1. *LTR*, xi, 49–51; Stow, i, 315.
2. Grimes 1968, 164–7.

(154) Dudley Court, Silver Street

In 1547 Thomas Colley purchased much property which had belonged to Holy Trinity Priory, Aldgate, in Silver Street. His estate passed to John Dudley of Hackney, Sergeant of the Pastry to Elizabeth I, and his son Thomas, grandson of Thomas Colley. The estate of Thomas Dudley was thereafter partitioned among his five sisters. Three of the tenements of one portion passed to Arthur Jackson, clothworker, from whom they were purchased in 1599 by Christ's Hospital with part of a covenant made by Dame Dorothy Edmonds in 1596. The properties are shown in the plan by Treswell in 1611 (Fig. 75b).[1]

The two small tenements (1) and (2) are of a form common in the Treswell plans: one room on each floor with newel stair in one corner, often attached to the chimney stack, facing the entrance. Both houses were three and a half storeys high. As they backed onto

neighbouring property which provided a fixed vertical plane, their upper floor measurements may reliably be taken to indicate the amount of jettying of the upper storeys. (1) would therefore jetty 1½ft on the first floor, and another 6in on the second, which was flush with the garret; while (2) would jetty 2ft on the first, and 3in on both second and garret floors. The text of reference for (3) is not precise, but a building of two and a half storeys is indicated.

1. GL, MS 13242; *Charity Comm.*, 101; *LSRT*, 112–13.

(155) Butchers' Hall, Stinking Lane (now King Edward Street)

The Butchers hired Carpenters' Hall in 1474;[1] by 1544 they leased the hall of the Fraternity of St Giles, possibly in Beech Lane, in the largely extramural parish of St Giles. After the fraternity lost the hall to the Crown as chantry property soon after 1545, the Butchers leased the parsonage of the redundant St Nicholas Shambles in Stinking Lane. Much rebuilding followed; the hall was wainscotted and a great window, probably looking north over gardens, glazed with coats of arms. On the first floor a parlour was created from two former rooms, and elsewhere the kitchen refurnished.[2] Parts of the foundations of the hall were located in excavations of 1975–6.[3]

1. *RCC*, ii, 48.
2. Jones 1976, 46–50.
3. MoL, sitecode GPO75.

(156) Bishop of Exeter's Inn (later Paget's Place, Leicester House and Essex House), Strand

Walter de Stapledon, who became Bishop of Exeter in 1308, was probably the first builder of this house, on land acquired from the Knights of St John after 1310; his murdered body was thrown on a heap of sand in the house, 'where he had made great building', in 1326. In 1384 a range between the house and the street is mentioned; this included a tavern and shops to the east of the gate. The hall was rebuilt by Edmond Lacy, Bishop 1420–55. It was granted in 1549 to William Paget, who enlarged it, as did the next owner, the Earl of Leicester (from 1563). By the time of the 'Agas' woodcut (*c.* 1559) a tower can be recognised as part of the south façade, but it is not known whether this is Paget's building or from the previous house. A detailed probate inventory of the house and contents was made at the time of Leicester's death in 1588, and the plan of the house *c.* 1640 has been reconstructed from maps and map-views.[1] In 1656, as Essex House, after Robert Devereux, Earl of Essex (Fig. 46, extreme right), it comprised two courts separated by a range, the south range of up to three storeys incorporating the tower, and extensive gardens.

1. Kingsford 1923, 8–41.

(157) Bishop of Bath's Inn (later Arundel House), Strand

First mentioned in a deed of 1231–8, and described as outside Temple Bar in 1376. In 1509 the Inn comprised orchards, gardens, and tenements including two called 'le Cardinallis Hatt' and 'the Tabard'. The Keeper's mansion at this time was on the east of a tenement between the place and the hall on the south and the Strand on the north; the Cardinal's Hat lay in a similar position. In 1545 Bath Place passed to Sir Thomas Seymour, who greatly rebuilt it; and in 1549 the property was bought by the Earl of Arundel. By 1580 it was called Arundel House, and a survey in 1589[1] together with drawings of the main buildings by Hollar in 1646 and 1656 (Figs. 35, 46–7, 243) enables some reconstruction to be made.

The Great Court, set some distance back from the south side of the Strand (plan, Fig. 243), comprised a five-bayed hall with a porch (Fig. 35); the form of windows suggests a construction date of 1300–50, and it is clear that the courtyard surfaces had been built up at least 4 ft against the north wall of the hall during its lifetime (human figures are seen at a lower level within the porch, indicating steps down). East of the screens stood a timber-framed building at right angles to the hall on its own undercroft, which had a central door to

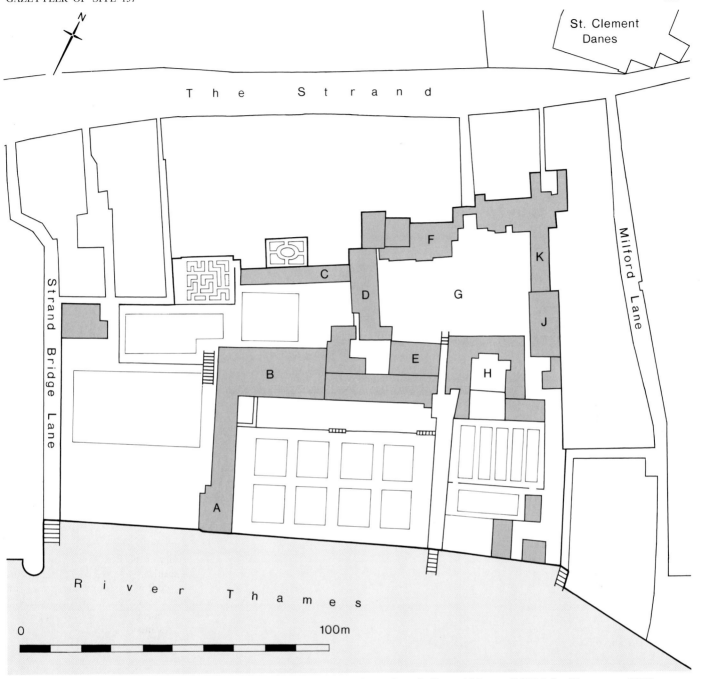

The Strand

St. Clement Danes

Strand Bridge Lane

Milford Lane

River Thames

0   100m

243. (157) Bishop of Bath's Inn/Arundel House, Fleet Street: site plan redrawn from Ogilby and Morgan (1677) [after Hammerson 1975]

the court. Further east, and to the south, were kitchens, laid out round a kitchen court. On the north side of the main court lay a building about 75 ft long which was probably a lodging (not the storehouse suggested by Kingsford, which probably lay behind it to the north) with framing suggesting a date of 1550–1600. It was a long two-storeyed building with entrances at ground- and first-floor level on the court side. On the west side of the court was a barn, 'new' in 1589, and on the east a storehouse apparently being used as a stable in 1646 (both shown in Fig. 47).

Hollar's map-view of 1656 and Ogilby and Morgan show a parlour block, three storeys high in Hollar's drawing, running west from the hall (Figs. 46, 243). This was built by c. 1559 when it is shown in the 'Agas' woodcut panorama, and appears to be of sixteenth-century date. A 'great brickhouse and galleries' are mentioned in the survey of 1589 and this perhaps refers in part to this block and to a two-storeyed gallery built after c. 1559 in a southerly

direction ending in a two-bayed block at the riverside, which is shown by Hollar in 1656. The gallery was probably added or completed by Thomas Howard between 1604 and about 1620. It was lit by five semi-octagonal projections on each side which are probably two-storeyed bay windows. Other buildings mentioned in the survey of 1589 include a bowling alley, which is also shown by Hollar (Fig. 46).

Excavations on the site during redevelopment in 1972 uncovered fragments of the Tudor building. A cesspit with material of the third quarter of the sixteenth century, including Venetian goblets, was found in a position which was probably below the barn on the west side of the Great Court. The walls, of squared chalk blocks, were at least 1.9 m (6 ft) high; the lowest excavated level within the structure, which was not the earliest floor-level, produced material of the fourteenth to sixteenth centuries. The vault was roofed with chalk blocks, supported on four-centred greensand arches at inter-

vals of 1.5 m (5 ft). On architectural grounds the vault is probably of fourteenth-century date, contemporary with the building of the great hall. A ground-level wall of chalk was found running immediately west of and parallel to the vault, which was probably the east wall of the barn, dated from pottery to the medieval or post-medieval period.[2]

Fragments of the north and south walls of the west parlour wing were also observed. The north wall was of chalk, and may be part of an earlier parlour block; the south wall was of brick decorated with a pattern of greensand blocks, on a brick plinth. The base of one buttress, a V-shaped projection of brick with greensand quoins, was also seen.

1. Kingsford 1922, 267–76.
2. Hammerson 1975, 209–51.

(158) Bishop of Carlisle's Inn (later Russell or Bedford House), Strand

First mentioned in 1238; shared with the prior of Carlisle in 1402, when the Bishop's Inn included a new stable, and a gatehouse was to be built. A further grant from the Bishop to the prior in 1402 mentions a stone wall on the riverside, and the prior was to make a stew for fish in the Bishop's garden. In 1539 the Bishop moved to the Bishop of Rochester's former place in Lambeth, and the Strand Inn was assured to Lord Russell, afterwards Earl of Bedford. In Stow's time it was called Russell or Bedford House.[1] Francis, the fourth Earl, built a new Bedford House on the other side of the Strand (not in gazetteer: see Fig. 47).

The house is shown on Hollar's bird's-eye view of the Strand in 1656 (Fig. 47); a gate (presumably that of 1402) and a broad alley lay on the west side of a court of buildings, its range towards the river of three storeys with garrets. Smaller properties lay between the main house and the Strand to the north.

1. *LTR*, x, 83–5; Stow, ii, 95.

(159) Salisbury House, Strand

In 1599 Sir Robert Cecil, afterwards Earl of Salisbury, erected a house on land which he had acquired between Carlisle Place (the Bishop of Carlisle's Inn) and Durham Place. The construction was supervised by Simon Basil, Surveyor of the Works. Stone came from Berwick, Oxford and Canterbury. The house is shown by Hollar in 1656 (Fig. 47); the main part was of three or four storeys, with two courts each bordered on the Strand only by a wall of a railing and an ornamental gate.[1]

1. *LTR*, x, 85; *Survey of London: Strand II,* 18, 120–3.

(160) Bishop of Norwich's Inn/York Place, Strand

In 1237 the quay of the house of the Bishop of Norwich was repaired; in 1382 the house is placed at Charing Cross. In 1536 Norwich Place was assured to the Duke of Suffolk, in exchange for Suffolk Place (195) in Southwark; it then comprised seven tenements. It was bought by the Archbishop of York in 1557 and was known as York Place; the Duke of Buckingham acquired it in 1622, and the watergate of 1626 by Nicholas Stone survives from his building.[1] A painting attributed to Cornelius Bol (1589–1666? or later) in the Dulwich Gallery shows the house and the watergate.

1. *LTR*, xi, 59–61; RCHM, *West London,* 136–7.

(161) Bishop of Durham's Inn, Strand

The house of the Bishop of Durham in London is mentioned in 1237, when Alexander the Carpenter, who also worked at Westminster Palace in 1234–40, was allowed £3 9s. 10d. for its repair and in 1238 its site can be suggested as lying south of the Strand.[1] Major building works by Anthony Bek (Bishop 1285–1310) and Thomas de Hatfield (Bishop 1345–81) were attributed by Leland and Stow.[2]

A reference of 1380 mentions the chapel with a vaulted chamber beneath; a partial inventory of beds, coverlets and cushions of 1528 mentions a nether parlour and a great chamber.[3] The house is shown in a plan of 1626 drawn to illustrate a report on a disturbance; it

comprised an inner and outer court apparently separated not by a range of rooms but by a wall. A large gatehouse formed the entry from the Strand on the north to the first court; the main range and hall lay at the back of the inner court, with the chapel at the east end, parallel to the hall but connected by a north to south range from the high end.[4] A parlour block of four storeys (Hatfield's building?) is shown in views from the south. The screens passage came through the hall to a watergate which formed part of a two-storeyed galleried range flanking the hall on the river side. In 1592 Norden wrote 'the Hall is stately and high, supported with lofty marble pillars. It standeth upon the Thames very pleasantly'.[5] Presumably this indicated that the hall, which stands out by its height on the panoramas, had pillars rather like Winchester Castle hall (1222–35); this would suggest that it was built by Bek in the late thirteenth century.

Durham House passed to the Crown in 1536 and was thereafter used for diplomatic entertainment and lodging.[6] Cecil built an exchange, 'Britain's Burse', along the Strand frontage in 1608–9. Most of the ancient buildings were pulled down in 1660, and in 1769–70 the Adelphi was built on the site. The great gatehouse was drawn *c.* 1790 by Smith for his *Antiquities of Westminster* (1807).

1. *Cal. Close R., 1231–4,* 413; *1237–42,* 208.
2. Stow, ii, 90.
3. GL, MS 231.
4. Wheatley 1916.
5. Introduction to *Speculi Britanniae Pars.*
6. *Survey of London: Strand II,* 18, 84–94; *LTR,* x, 107–11.

(162) Drapers' Hall I, [St] Swithin's Lane

The site of the first Drapers' Hall seems to have been a tenterground in the reign of Edward I, originally part of the estate of Henry Fitzailwin centred on the house which became Tortington Inn (not in gazetteer) to the north. In 1348 the land had shops upon it; in 1408 Richard Forster and Thomas Carleton granted the property to a group of drapers. Work on a new hall started after Easter 1425, under the direction of John Salisbury, carpenter, with Simon Eyre, draper, handling much of the payments for workmanship and materials.[1] Some of the company visited the place of the Celestines at Sheen and the hall of the Bishop of Bath in the Strand (157) as potential models, and discussed the building with the aldermen and others. The frame was viewed at Croydon.

First a well was dug, and a vault excavated; both structures required 197 tons of ragstone from Aylesford in Kent, and nine boatloads of 'pendant chalk' may have been for the vaulting of the cellar. Some timber came from Huntone in Kent; thirteen carpenters worked under Salisbury, paid weekly by Eyre. There were still seven carpenters on site in November. Masons were employed on a lesser scale, and the buying of a stone for axesharpening suggests they dressed some stones, perhaps the quoins and tablement, on site; there is little indication of use of ready-dressed stone (for doors or windows) in the accounts. Twelve thousand bricks were used, at 5s. 5d. the thousand, but these are comparatively small numbers and stone was probably also used for walls above the ground; the walls may have been of brick faced with stone, as at Crosby Place (1466) (22).

Details in the accounts imply that the hall lay north to south, since a plumber was paid for 'le ledying de les bataylement & le hautpas en le suthpart de la sale' – at £23 6s. 8d. the largest individual purchase in the building programme. This was evidently a flat lead roof. The 'hautpas' might be the high table (the dais) or the screens passage – in the same year expenditure on 'le nove gistyng de le hautpas de le suth part de la sale' might be for joists for the dais or for a gallery over the screens. The hall also had a bay window.[2]

Other buildings erected at this time included a pantry, buttery, larder, and 'squelerie' (presumably pastry), and a parlour, known as the Chambre, with a privy attached. The kitchen is mentioned in

1429–30. In this year, as the hall neared completion, Thomas Wynchcombe, carpenter, was paid for a table in the hall, trestles, a winding stair, a door, and a lattice in the parlour, four stools and four 'Popeyz' (presumably poppy-heads, i.e. carved bench-ends); two of the 'popeyz' were carved with four angels, and these were gilded. The parlour was decorated with scutcheons of the company arms.[3]

At the same time an adjacent property, originally also in the ownership of Fitzailwin and in the company's possession by 1428, was incorporated into the hall complex. This property extended in 1336 from the garden of the prior of Tortington on the north to Candlewick Street in the south.[4] It was known as the *Bakhouse*, and was presumably used by the company, though it was subsequently let as a rent.

The Drapers moved to their second hall in Throgmorton Street (**178**) in 1544.

1. *Drapers' Recs.*, i, 303–17, 348.
2. *Ibid.*, 317.
3. *Ibid.*, 337.
4. *HTA Cartulary*, 426–7.

(163)   Abbot of Chertsey's Inn, [Upper] Thames Street

In 1289–90 John de Lelhan left his messuage and wharf in the parish of St Peter the Less to be sold to pay his debts; Lelhan is called 'haymonger' in 1296–7 when Robert Chykewell, fishmonger, granted the property, 9¼ ells wide along Thames Street and 8½ ells 2 in wide along the Thames, to Chertsey Abbey, with a rent of 5*s.* *p.a.* to Merton Abbey.[1] Chykewell's own tenement abutted the granted property to the west, and the property of William Bernard, dyer, lay to the east; the granted property did not therefore border on Bosse Lane to the east. In 1307 the abbot constructed a new quay of stone in his hospice, an event important enough to be recorded in the annals of the abbey. In 1317–18 the wall of stone on the east part of the hospice was built and in 1322–3 the stone wall on the west part.[2]

Archaeological excavations on the adjacent block to the east in 1974–6 (see **164**), largely between Bosse Lane and Trig Lane, also located the south-east corner of a river wall on the west side of Bosse Lane, dating to sometime during the first half of the fourteenth century (Fig. 244).[3] This suggests that the quay wall of 1307 was extended along the neighbouring property or properties east to Bosse Lane, either at the same time or shortly after.

1. *Cal. Wills*, i, 89; *Chertsey Cartulary*, 293.
2. *Ibid.*, 281, 291, 554. For later history of the property, *LTR*, x, 86–7.
3. Milne & Milne 1982, 25 (Group 8), Fig. 16 and Plate 21.

(164)   Trig Lane, Upper Thames Street

Excavations on this site in 1974–6 uncovered a succession of revetments and river walls dated by dendrochronology to the period *c.* 1290 – *c.* 1480 (Figs. 161, 244–7). The excavation lay across the southern ends of three medieval properties between Trig Lane to the east and Bosse Alley to the west. It demonstrated that reclamation had reached a point 45 m (148 ft) south of Thames Street by the mid thirteenth century, suggesting that earlier, possibly twelfth-century reclamation may have lain in the large intervening space up to the street in the north. A lane on the west is first mentioned in 1256, and in 1291 is 'the lane by which the Fishwharf is approached'. In 1256 the south portion of the adjacent tenement comprised houses, buildings, a quay and a little chamber above the Thames. Traces of two buildings (A and B), one a small structure interpreted as a storage compartment but possibly a privy, were found dating to the mid to late thirteenth century and late thirteenth century respectively. Shortly after 1345, on dendrochronological grounds, the east part of the waterfront was extended and a building (C) with stone foundations laid north to south about 2 m (6 ft 6 in) west of the lane (Fig. 245). An internal drain along its west side went

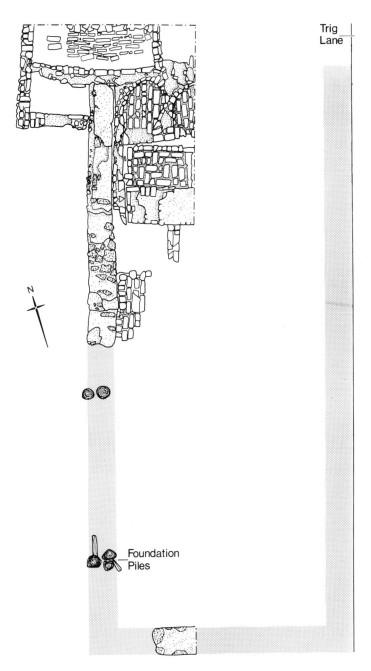

Trig
Lane

Foundation
Piles

⊞ **Bricks**

🪨 **Ragstone**

0   2m

244.   (**164**) Trig Lane, Upper Thames Street: Building E, fifteenth century. The bases for vats or ovens at its north end may indicate use as a dyehouse.

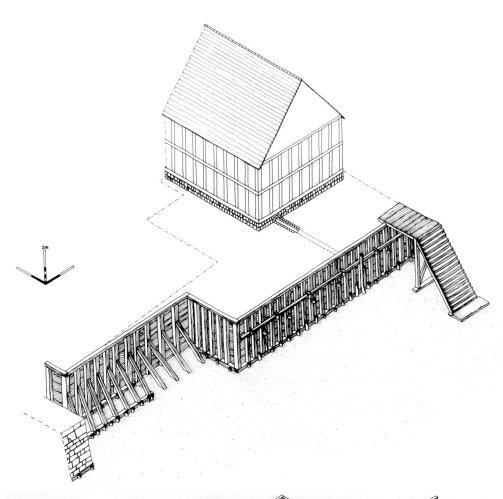

245. (164) Trig Lane, Upper Thames Street: Building C and contemporary waterfront revetments, *c.* 1350. The river wall bottom left, constructed probably 1307–22, was on a property west of Bosse Lane (cf. 163). Trig Lane is to the right [Milne & Milne 1981].

246. (164) Trig Lane, Upper Thames Street: partial reconstruction of the riverside end of the site in the late fourteenth century, showing individual river stairs to properties

247. (164) Trig Lane, Upper Thames Street: river wall of *c.* 1440, uniting the previously separate properties. In the middle is the base of a river stair.

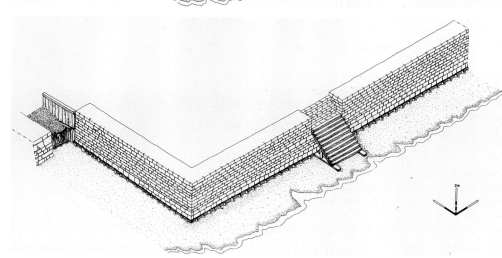

out over the new extension to empty into the river; an adjacent private landing stair is implied by posts in the foreshore. The waterfront was again extended *c.* 1380 (Fig. 246), and the building levelled for a yard surface by *c.* 1430. A replacement, Building D, was only fragmentarily recorded; contemporary with the latest quay wall of *c.* 1440 (Fig. 247), a further large building containing at least two sub-circular ovens or vat-bases (Building E) was traced alongside Trig Lane (Fig. 244). Apart from the north part of the westernmost tenement, all the property between Bosse and Trig Lanes was owned by the fishmonger Trig family between 1389 and 1420.[1]

1.   MoL, sitecode TL74; Milne & Milne 1981; 1982.

(165)   Brokenwharf, [Upper] Thames Street

An inquisition of 1259 found there used to be a wharf at Brokenwharf, and that no one claimed right in it except Hugh Bigod, who might erect a wharf there. In 1319 the Earl of Norfolk (whose family name was Bigod) had there a ruinous messuage and a void plot, nine shops and eight solars; these were still standing in 1381–2.[1] Desebourne Lane bordered the property on the west, and in 1370 the Earl of Suffolk, then in possession of Broken Wharf, complained that John Tornegold, fishmonger, who held the tenement to the west and the lane itself (measuring 213 ft long, 7 ft wide at the street, and 1 ell wide at the river) had raised the level of the lane on his side with stones and timber, and blocked the river end with a gutter, so that water thrown out of his tenement by his tenants entered the Earl's messuage.[2] In 1973 a section across what is probably this alley, under its later name of George Yard, was observed; ragstone walls and alley surfaces were seen; from the latter, but not the earliest, came pottery of 1350–1450.[3]

The house may have contained a chapel in 1415; described in 1477 as a mansion, Broken Wharf was in and out of the possession of the Dukes of Norfolk until 1542, when it was bequeathed to the Corporation of London, and purchased in 1583 by Thomas Sutton, founder of Charterhouse school. An inventory of 1582 mentions the hall, parlour, chamber over the kitchen, little chamber over the buttery, kitchen, coalyard, beer house, stable, mill loft, yard, 'Tonnemen's chamber', brewers' chamber, hayloft, cooper's shop, 'myllpace' (presumably a horse-mill), oven-pit and a new house at the gate.[4] In 1594–5 Bevis Bulmar erected a water engine or pump on the site, possibly in the courtyard. Stow saw 'one large old building of stone with arched gates'; the hall had by then become a brewhouse.[5]

Excavations on the site in 1986 recorded stone foundations probably comprising a thirteenth- or fourteenth-century south wall of the property and both timber and masonry walling along the west side of an extension to the south, perhaps of fifteenth-century date.[6]

1.   *LTR*, x, 77–8.
2.   *Assize of Nuisance*, 577.
3.   Notes by J. Haslam in MoL Archive.
4.   GLRO, Charterhouse estates muniments, Acc. 1876, F4/11.
5.   Stow, ii, 10–11.
6.   MoL, sitecode SUN86; Hunting 1988, 18, 30–1.

(166)   Vintners' Hall, [Upper] Thames Street

The modern hall lies astride the parish boundary between St James Garlickhithe and St Martin Vintry, indicating its origin in two adjacent tenements which possibly formed part of a bequest of Ralph Hardel in *c.* 1259. In 1306–7 the property seems to have comprised a hall alongside a lane (later Stodeye Lane) to the east, with a solar called *Chapmanchambre*, with a cellar beneath, on the south (westwards from the hall?). The 'stone gable' of the hall is mentioned as a northern limit in 1396, indicating it lay north to south along the lane.[1] The house was bequeathed to the Vintners by Guy Shuldham, vintner, in 1446, when it consisted of a hall and kitchen with coalhouse, a pantry and buttery, a yard with a well, a

parlour with a counting house and two chambers above the counting house; the property was apparently not in the possession of the company until 1496, when John Porter's will reaffirmed the provisions of Shuldham's. In 1364 and 1406 a wharf belonging to others bordered the hall's ground on the south.[2]

It is likely that the post-Fire hall shown on Ogilby and Morgan's map (1677) occupied exactly the same site; a hall lay across the plot (possibly a rebuilding of the solar of 1306–7, sometime before 1446) with a courtyard in front, containing the well, by then turned into a pump.[3]

Excavations immediately to the south of the present (post-Fire) hall in 1989 established that the west wall of the present hall lay on an earlier chalk foundation which continued south beyond the south-west corner of the building. A series of medieval tile hearths lay south of the southern end of the present building, presumably also part of this former structure, which may have been the medieval kitchen.[4]

1.   *Cal. Wills*, i, 3; HR, 34 (121); *ibid.*, 124 (91).
2.   Crawford 1977, 35; Nichols 1870, 442–3.
3.   RCHM, *City*, 193; Crawford 1977, Plates 2 and 3; plan of site in Mills & Oliver, *Survey*, v, 41[V].
4.   MoL, sitecode VHY89.

(167)   Northampton Inn, [Upper] Thames Street

In the mid thirteenth century Arnold son of Thedmar, alderman of the City and one of the German merchants, had a house east of the original nucleus of the Cologne Merchants' Guildhall in Thames Street. By the fourteenth century it had a gate and five shops, with a group of cellars behind which functioned as a tavern (Fig. 22). By 1384 the property belonged to John de Northampton, mayor 1381–3. Part of it, comprising a mansion with the dyehouse, two mansions on steps and a cellar in the lane, was granted after Northampton's imprisonment in 1384 to Richard Medeford, afterwards Bishop of Chichester, but was restored to Northampton in 1391. By 1437 part of the property was absorbed into the mansion of John Reynewell, which was in the same general location on the east side of the lane. Stow saw Reynewell's mansion, which he described as a great house. Reynewell bequeathed it to the City, and they in turn granted it to augment the Steelyard in 1475.[1]

1.   Stow, i, 234; *LTR*, xi, 55–6; Keene 1989.

(168)   All Hallows Lane, [Upper] Thames Street

This lane, leading from Thames Street to the Thames at the west end of the church of All Hallows the Great, was known as Haywharf Lane in the fourteenth and possibly fifteenth centuries, but as Church Lane or All Hallows Lane during the sixteenth century.[1] In 1480 William Gardyner bequeathed his property in the lane to the Shearmen's Company. The property appears in the Clothworkers' accounts for 1529 with seven tenants.[2]

When surveyed by Treswell in 1612 (Fig. 248) the property comprised buildings of single-room plan (1–6) on the west side of the lane. A further building, also single-roomed in plan, is shown on an inset on the original plan (not in Fig. 248) somewhat to the north; the adjacent Steelyard lay along the lane in between. The buildings, of utilitarian aspect, were two to three and a half storeys high. From one chamber in (5) a large oven protruded to the south possibly into a small yard. This tenancy also included two chambers and a garret for a widow, upstairs.[3]

At the south end was a half unit 'open to the steares', i.e. the Clothworkers' Stairs which are shown adjacent to the common stairs at the end of the lane. The Clothworkers' Stairs were frequently repaired during the period 1528–1612 covered by the company accounts. In 1553 the need for repairs was blamed on the clothworkers' washing of their 'bukkes' (baskets), which was banned. In 1562–3, 372 loads of rag and 20 loads of flint were brought from Limehouse for repair work, which went on during night tides. A second load of 36 1/2 loads of rag came by lighter, the

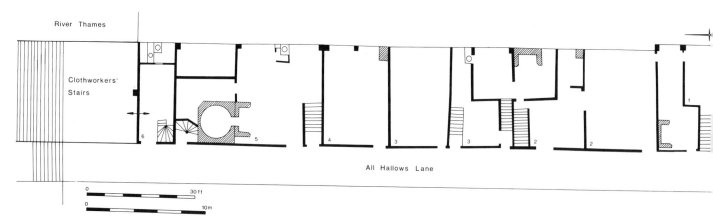

248.   (168) All Hallows Lane, Thames Street (Treswell 1612)

total cost being £118 10s. 10d. In 1565–6 the wooden steps were replaced, and further major repairs to the stairs and end house carried out in 1597–8; this may be the 'newe house' noted by Treswell on the plan.[4]

The south end of the lane and the stairs are shown by Hollar in his engraving of 1647 (Fig. 24). The company stairs are shown, but not the separate common stairs; this is an error common to all the panoramas except the unique woodcut of London of c. 1560 in the Pepysian collection.[5] Immediately to the north Hollar shows a single-storey building of two gables, which must be the unit shown 'open to the steares' by Treswell, and then six buildings of two or perhaps three storeys with garrets. This suggests that the buildings shown by Treswell were roofed individually on their long axis, as would be expected, at right angles to the lane.

1.   Harding 1980, 15.
2.   CDW; RW, Accts.
3.   *LSRT*, 116–17.
4.   CCO, 1536–58, 235[V]; RW, Accts., 1562–3, 1565–6; QW, Accts., 1597–8.
5.   *Building of London*, Fig. 107.

(169)   Coldharbour I, [Upper] Thames Street

In the medieval period the name Coldharbour was applied successively to two separate and adjacent houses on either side of Wolsey Lane, leading south from Thames Street. The earlier references are to the house on the west of and including the lane. In the thirteenth century the house belonged to John de Gisors; Sir John de Pulteney (d. 1349) acquired it in 1334. By 1355 the property was bisected by a second, unnamed lane which ran from the east end of All Hallows the Great church to the wharf, with tenements on either side of it; in 1366 the property comprised five mansions, nine cellars (called shops in 1408) with solars and a wharf. Since the property did not enjoy any frontage to Thames Street, the shops must have been along the lane. After 1408 the house passed out of use as a residence of note and became commercial premises; in 1431 it was let to a draper and a shearman, but appears to have been used in part for brewing. In 1436 John Aynes, carpenter, took a lease on condition that he rebuild a ruinous tenement into two new ones, in the manner and materials of existing buildings to the south.[1] James Finch, shearman, was in possession when he granted the property to his company of Shearmen in 1509.[2] In this year the property included

249.   (169) Coldharbour I/Haywharf, Thames Street (Treswell 1612)

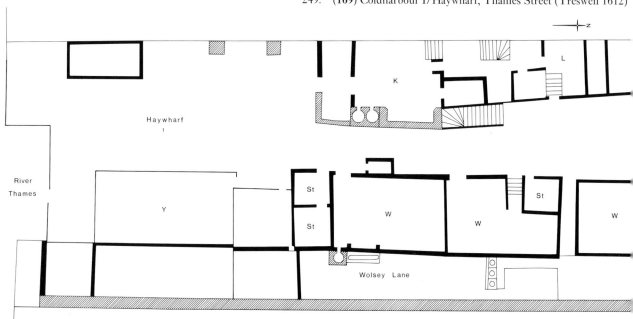

thirty-six tenants; in 1528 there were thirty, some holding only a cellar or a garret. By 1553, however, the rent was paid by three major tenants who sublet, and by 1560–1 only one major tenant, the Campion family, is named.

In 1537 the Clothworkers' Company accounts mention 'bricking up the whole of the Crane'. In the years 1553–7 the company several times required the major tenant, Elizabeth Gates, to take down a rotten stable and hayloft.[3] At about this time the river front of the property appears on the low-level panorama (Fig. 41).

Treswell surveyed 'the Brewhouse and two tenements sometime in twelve tenements' in 1612 (Fig. 249).[4] The lane and its buildings were then divided into seven tenancies. William Campion, clothworker, leased (1) and the adjoining property with its dyehouse in 1597, and Treswell notes 'Mr Campion's Brewhouse' on the next property to the west. Campion's buildings on the Clothworkers' property included a kitchen and boulting house, but they may be incomplete on the plan, for the boundary to the west slices them off rather sharply. The text of reference describes this major building complex as of three and a half storeys, including a large parlour on the first floor; the ground-floor plan and measurements suggest that a large timber-framed house comprised both east and west sides of the lane, and that all the major rooms lay on the first floor. To the north along the lane were six further tenancies (2–7), of two and a half or three and a half storeys. Mr Campion held a separate large warehouse in the alley, between (2) and (3); it seems likely that an eighth tenant had rooms over the warehouse.

Forming the east boundary of the whole long property lay the Common Sewer or Wolsey's Lane. This appears to have been, in 1612, a strip of ground rather than a channel, though it was crossed by walls and fences several times, and by privy buildings which blocked it twice. In 1569 Henry Campion was accused of having enclosed and stopped up a lane at Thames-side near Coldharbour with a brick wall, and the Chamberlain of the City was instructed to open it up and repair the stairs so that it could be a common lane as before – evidently to no effect.[5]

Below the text of reference, alongside the plan (but omitted from Fig. 249), is Treswell's record of a view of the property in July 1613 (i.e. exactly one year after the surveys had been conducted) by the Master and Wardens, Treswell, Thomas Haydon, carpenter, John Morgan, bricklayer, and others. The Viewers noted that two plates engraved with the Clothworkers' name (*sic*, but perhaps a badge is meant) were set on the southern waterside corners of the property; and they decided that four further plates should be set up to delineate the northern bounds.

The riverside aspect of both Coldharbours is shown in all three major panoramas – Figs. 23 and 38 (Wyngaerde, *c.* 1540), Fig. 41 (low-level anonymous panorama, *c.* 1550?) and Fig. 24 (Hollar,

1647). For site **169**, both Wyngaerde (Fig. 23, extreme right) and the low-level panorama show a substantial building at the water's edge, incorporating a crenellated tower with two large windows (best seen in Fig. 41). This building is presumably Coldharbour I, though the tower may in fact be 'la Tour' of the adjacent tenement Coldharbour II (**170**).

1. Harding 1980, 11–29.
2. CD, Box 61.
3. RW, Accts.; CCO, 1536–58, 252, 268, 275[V].
4. *LSRT*, 118–19.
5. Repertory, 16, 498; 17, 365.

(170) Coldharbour II, [Upper] Thames Street

The name Coldharbour was acquired by a prestigious residence immediately east of the earlier Coldharbour; as the latter descended the social scale, so the former rose in the late fourteenth century. Between 1370 and 1377 it was bought by Edward III's mistress, Alice Perrers, who extensively rebuilt it. In 1401, known as 'la Tour', it was granted by Henry IV to his brother the Earl of Somerset, and it continued in noble or royal occupation throughout the fifteenth century.[1] The name Coldharbour probably refers to this house in 1410, and certainly in 1447. An account of repairs ordered by Henry VII's mother, Countess of Richmond, after a brief occupancy by the College of Heralds in 1484–5 mentions many rooms, their glazing (see pp. 107–8) and furnishings.[2] The rooms included the great hall (probably on the riverside), buttery, every, little hall with buttery, great chamber above the great hall, another great chamber over the little hall, my Lady's chamber, Lady Elizabeth's chamber, Duke of Buckingham's chamber, chapel, several other chambers, kitchen, wet and dry larders, pantry, pastry, boiling-house, porter's lodge, wood-house and wine cellar.

After the death of the Countess in 1509, Henry VIII granted Coldharbour for life to George Talbot, Earl of Shrewsbury (d. 1538); Edward VI gave it to Francis Talbot, Earl of Shrewsbury (d. 1560), and his heirs in 1553.[3] In 1598 Stow recorded that Coldharbour (presumably the second of that name) was entered by an arched gate under All Hallows the Less, and that the 'last deceased earl took it down, and in place thereof built a great number of small tenements, now letten out for great rents to people of all sorts'. Kingsford thought this referred to the death of the recent Earl in 1590.[4]

The house is shown in the low-level panorama (Fig. 41), and by Wyngaerde at about the same time (Fig. 38), but in both cases little specific can be suggested. In the Wyngaerde view, a courtyard surrounded by ranges on all sides is suggested; the east wall of the east range may have had diapering in brick, suggested by cross-hatched diagonal lines in the drawing. Hollar (Fig. 24) shows the property as

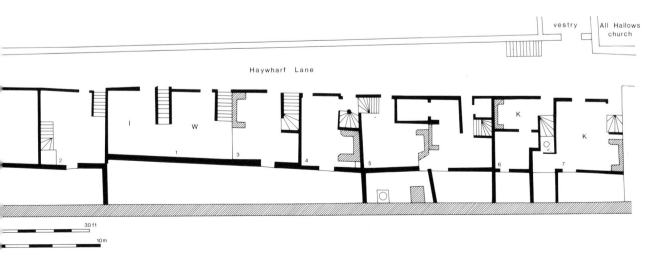

rebuilt after 1553. Two separate buildings can be seen. To the east was a large arched watergate (which must have reflected the main thoroughfare) within a building of three storeys and garrets, the latter with half-height walls (a feature seen at Staple Inn in 1586), presumably the Earl's building shortly before 1590; the size of windows on the first and second floors suggests that this was the Earl's residence rather than the tenements seen by Stow, which could have occupied the northern parts of the site. A smaller building lay to the west, its distinctive window pediments suggesting an early seventeenth-century date. After the Great Fire this building was the Watermen's Hall (marked C58 on Ogilby and Morgan's map), and it might be suggested, though at present evidence is lacking, that this building was the pre-Fire Watermen's Hall.

1. Harding 1980, 20–3.
2. Kingsford 1921, 43–50.
3. Harding, *op. cit.*, 22.
4. Stow, i, 237; Kingsford, *op. cit.*, 27.

(171)   Swan Lane, [Upper] Thames Street

Excavations on the east side of Swan Lane, the modern successor of the medieval Ebbgate, took place in 1981–3. By the twelfth century there had been several periods of land reclamation south of the presumed line of the Roman riverside wall, and fragments of buildings appeared behind the waterfront, which by the end of the twelfth century had an irregular indented line indicating several separate properties.[1] These divisions were clearer in the thirteenth-century remains, which included a large building (11) or yard inside which, along its east side, were a number of hearths (Fig. 250).[2] Across an alley to the east lay a further building (13) with similar hearths. These buildings were probably dye-works, the alley between them leading to a protruding jetty which gave access to the river. The building west of the alley (11) is thought to have lain within a tenement recorded as 52 ft wide in 1402;[3] the excavated building was 13 m (42 ft 7 in) wide, so presumably there was a widening of the tenancy nearer Thames Street. The alley was prob-

250.   (**171**) Swan Lane, Upper Thames Street: plan of thirteenth-century dyehouse, excavated 1978–9 [Shepherd, in prep.]

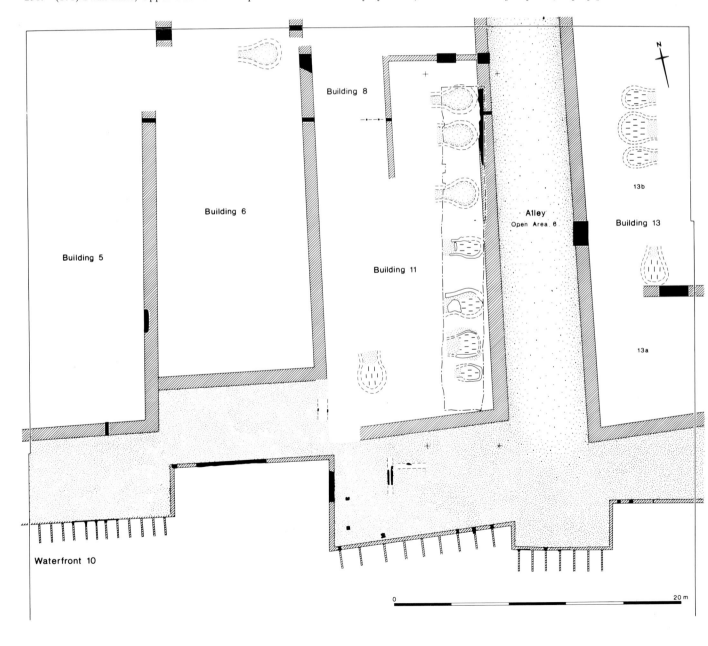

ably that which led to the Swan Lane stairs, later Old Swan Lane.
1. MoL, sitecode SWA81. The archaeology and documentary history of the excavation up to about 1200 is reported in Steedman, Dyson & Schofield 1992.
2. For strata after about 1200, see Shepherd, in preparation, the source of Fig. 250.
3. HR 131/37; T. Dyson in Steedman, Dyson & Schofield 1992, 93–4.

(172) Seal House (Fishmongers' Hall extension), 106/108 [Upper] Thames Street

Excavations on this site in 1974–6 uncovered details of three adjoining properties; the main excavation of 1974 comprised a north to south trench down the axis of the largest, central property, from a short distance south of the medieval frontage to Thames Street on the north to the position of an early thirteenth-century revetment at the south end.[1]

Two stages of land reclamation, marked by revetments, were dated to *c.* 1140 (Waterfront I) and *c.* 1170 (Waterfront II) by dendrochronology. Also in the twelfth century a building (A) with stone foundations was erected on the reclaimed land near the street. In the early thirteenth century a second building with stone foundations (B) was added on the south side of Building A. Hearths within it suggest a possible industrial function, and from it a wooden drain led to a new revetment further into the river (Waterfront III), dated by dendrochronology to *c.* 1210 (Figs. 132, 251). The earliest documentary reference to the property is in 1269–71 when it was occupied by Nicholas Horn; he owned another house, two tenements to the east, and the same family owned the intervening tenement in 1315. William de Eure, ironmonger, bequeathed the property in 1298.

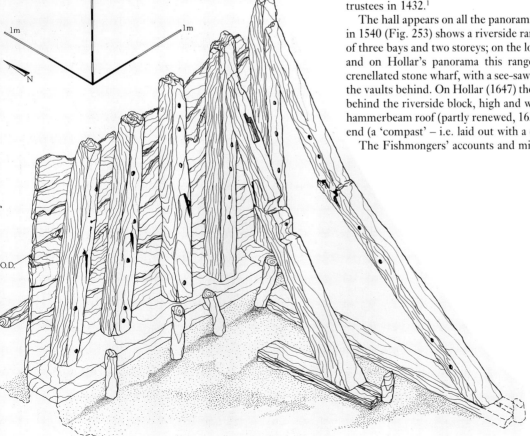

After changes (possibly only internal) to Building B (pending analysis, termed Building C) in the early fourteenth century, the south end of the property was redeveloped also in the early fourteenth century with a new stone building (D) and an extended revetment; Buildings A and B were replaced by a set of rooms on lighter foundations (Building E) comprising a hall, suggested by the partial survival of a decorated tile floor (Fig. 126), service rooms and kitchen. The property was transferred to a stockfishmonger, Lucas, in 1343, and remained with stockfishmongers until 1392, when it was sold to support a chantry in St Michael Crooked Lane; it was thereafter known as Our Lady. The property was still occupied by stockfishmongers in 1509, and was sold to the Fishmongers' Company in 1590. Further rebuildings on the site (Buildings F and G) date from the fifteenth and sixteenth centuries.[2]
1. MoL, sitecodes SH74, SH76.
2. Morgan & Schofield 1978; T. Dyson, Seal House Documentary Archive Report, MoL; Schofield & Dyson, in preparation.

(173) Fishmongers' Hall, [Upper] Thames Street

The ground which shortly after the company's new charter of 1433 became the hall site had been the site of a large private house from *c.* 1350. It passed through a succession of fishmongers and their apprentices, three of them mayors: John Lovekyn (d. 1368), Sir William Walworth (d. 1385), and William Askham (d. 1415). A lease of 1395 gives some measurements, though not enough to give dimensions to the buildings. The western boundary can be recreated to give a total length to the Thames of 233 ft. The north part of the plot measured 68 ft to a 'certain wall in the kitchen'; then 78 ft to a vacant plot; then 73 ft of the vacant plot, on the south-west corner of which was a water-house or tower, newly built by Walworth, with a privy in its north wall and a *hautpas* (gallery or raised buildings?) stretching north from it along the west wall (of stone) for 33 ft 10 in. From the north-west corner of the tower to the wharf was a further 14 ft; the tower may have been 11 ft 2 in north to south, coming almost to the north edge of the quay. The property passed to trustees in 1432.[1]

The hall appears on all the panoramas of 1544–1647. Wyngaerde in 1540 (Fig. 253) shows a riverside range, presumably the parlour, of three bays and two storeys; on the low-level panorama (Fig. 252) and on Hollar's panorama this range is crenellated. Below is a crenellated stone wharf, with a see-saw crane and a large doorway to the vaults behind. On Hollar (1647) the hall is shown at right angles behind the riverside block, high and with a lantern. The hall had a hammerbeam roof (partly renewed, 1639), and an oriel at high table end (a 'compast' – i.e. laid out with a compass – window).[2]

The Fishmongers' accounts and minutebooks begin in 1592; by

251. **(172)** Seal House, Upper Thames Street: isometric view of Waterfront III, *c.* 1220 [Schofield 1975]

252. (173) Fishmongers' Hall, Thames Street: view of the parlour block from the south in the low-level panorama of *c.* 1550

253. (173) Fishmongers' Hall, Thames Street: from Wyngaerde's panorama of *c.* 1540

this date both hall and parlour block were in the positions shown by Hollar. It is likely, from what is known of other halls, that the hall of the early seventeenth century was on the site of Askham's original hall, along the side of the plot behind a street range. If this were so, it must have lain north of the 'vacant plot' described in the 1395 lease, which then became the site of the company's parlour on the riverside (between *c.* 1400 and *c.* 1550).

1. GL, MS 6697; Metcalf 1977, 13.
2. Metcalf, *op. cit.*, 8–32.

(174) New Fresh Wharf, 2–9 [Lower] Thames Street

Excavations here in 1974–8 uncovered sequences of buildings on the northern halves of six properties on the south side of Thames Street, dating from the tenth century to the Great Fire.[1] Seven properties or tenements could be identified from documentary evidence between the churches of St Magnus and St Botolph Billingsgate; excavation uncovered details of Tenements 2–7, numbered from the west.[2]

Embankments of clay, stones and timber were built out from the decaying late Roman riverside city wall in the early eleventh century, apparently all of one phase and stretching to what may have been a common line about 22 m (72 ft) south of the wall. They had individually constructed parts, divided by fences, which are interpreted as properties. To the west the properties stopped at an inlet formed by earlier rubble banks; the west bank of this inlet may have been part of the site of St Magnus church.

Tenement 2: river silts filled up the inlet in the twelfth century, obscuring it by the early to mid thirteenth century. Building F comprised two piled and arched wall-foundations, the first forming the boundary with Tenement 3 and the second parallel and 1 m (3¼ ft) to the west, forming an alley down the east side of the property. A newly built house on the property is mentioned in 1293, but this could be to the south.

Tenement 3 was also part of the inlet until the thirteenth century and in 1278 a wharf on the property is mentioned, but must have been off the excavated area to the south (as for all thirteenth-century and later wharves on the site). The first recognised building, Building G, was constructed in the fourteenth century. After a heightening of the ground, which included a layer of oyster shells 0.9 m (3 ft) thick, walls of ragstone and flint with chalk were laid out to form a range filling the property, with gable to the street; it would have used the public alley of Rothersgate to the east as communication. The front part was subdivided into two rooms with floors slightly below street level; behind were two further rooms, at a still lower level. The property was subdivided between 1308 and 1326; possibly the substantial wall between the third and fourth rooms formed the subdivision. The southern half was granted at this time to Adam Pikeman, fishmonger. Vintners were in possession of the northern half between 1350 and 1405; in the latter year the property's wharf was said to be on the point of collapsing into the Thames and was ordered to be rebuilt.[3] At cellar level the property stayed in this form until the Great Fire.

Tenement 4: two wharves with adjoining land in Roderesgate were granted by Holy Trinity Priory, Aldgate, to Brounlocus in 1147–67;[4] fragmentary masonry foundations of the early twelfth century (Buildings A and B) stretched to within about 4 m (13 ft) of the wharf (Fig. 28). Only part of the wall of the former survived, but the latter comprised two rooms 6 m (20 ft) and 8.5 m (28 ft) long, the larger room to the south (and wharf). Both buildings stood at ground level with alley surfaces (i.e. Rothersgate) to the west. The implied unification of the two properties was corroborated in the fourteenth century when a new Building K filled the double property. At least eight rooms were observed, and Rothersgate probably served as access down the west side.

Tenement 5: scattered twelfth- to thirteenth-century foundations (Building E; Fig. 28) were succeeded in the fourteenth century by

Building L, a two-room street range with an alley running down the east side and other rooms behind, one of which had a hearth and may have been a kitchen. In 1349 the property, owned by the fishmonger family Pikeman in 1293–1351, was known as *le Brodegate* – and anciently as Burgateskey in 1454. It was owned by fishmongers until 1402 when it was divided between two dyers.

Tenement 6: Building D, of the twelfth century, filled part of the plot with a yard or wide alley to its west (Fig. 28). End-on to the street, from which it may have been set back, it comprised a large rectangular room with a smaller room to the north; the floors of both were about 1 m (3¼ ft) below medieval street level. In 1269–71 the property was described as being once owned by Laurence the clerk. In the early fourteenth century Building D was demolished and the property rebuilt as Building H (Figs. 153, 254). A street range two rooms deep had an alley down the eastern side of the property, with further buildings behind. The rear cellar of the street range had all four walls faced in chequerwork (Fig. 153), and an intramural chute from presumably the first floor emptied into a cesspit beneath the alley. During the fourteenth century the property was owned by fishmongers, a woolmonger and a chandler by 1421. It was divided into north and south portions by 1589–1615.

Tenement 7: Building C, of the twelfth century, was a rectangular building possibly with a ground floor vaulted in two to three bays, with a door to the quay at its south-east corner (Fig. 28). The quay seems to have jutted out into the river from the line of the adjacent properties to the west in the form of a stone quay wall, of which the south-west corner was recorded. In 1269–71 the property was granted by Wybert of Arras to Peter of Kingston, and in 1286 it belonged to Henry, son of Robert de Burgh, pepperer. In 1407 it was owned by John Wakele, vintner, and was described as including a hall, alley and chambers. It is possible that an unrecorded rebuilding included a new alley, presumably down the east side. The survival on the eastern property boundary of a window to a fifteenth-century undercroft on the next property (recorded on the adjacent Billingsgate Lorry Park site, 1984), would suggest an alley on that side. The property was bequeathed to the Vintners' Company in 1438 by Thomas Crofton, executor of Geoffrey Dalling. There are occasional references to repairs in the Vintners' accounts thereafter.[5] Tenement 7 was rebuilt as Building J in the sixteenth century; a street-range equivalent to two rooms deep, of exactly the same depth as its neighbour to the west (Building H), with an alley on the east leading to cellared buildings behind (Figs. 69, 244, 247). Debris from the property's destruction in the Great Fire included stone window-mullions.

1. MoL, sitecodes NFW74, SM75, FRE78.
2. The archaeological and documentary evidence to about 1200 for the site is in Steedman, Dyson & Schofield 1992; from 1200 to about 1600, in Schofield & Dyson, in preparation.
3. *Assize of Nuisance*, 645.
4. *HTA Cartulary*, 257.
5. GL, Vintners' Calendar, ii, 218; MS 15443; MS 15333/1, 2.

(175) Pakemann's Wharf/Browne's Place, [Lower] Thames Street

This property was acquired by John Chertsey, his brother Simon Sudbury, Bishop of London, and others before 1375.[1] In 1384 Chertsey leased the property, now called Pakemann's Wharf, to Richard Wyllysdon, tallow-chandler, and his wife Anne on condition that they rebuild it. The existing wharf (whether of timber or stone is not stated) was to be extended into the river by 4 ft, and made only of Maidstone stone (i.e. Kentish rag). A street range 40 ft deep was to be erected, three storeys high, the individual storeys measuring 12 ft, 10 ft and 7 ft high respectively. All timber was to be heart of oak and no reused timber was to be employed. Behind the range there was to be a hall 40 ft × 24 ft, a parlour, kitchen and buttery 'as to such a hall should belong', and chambers and houses

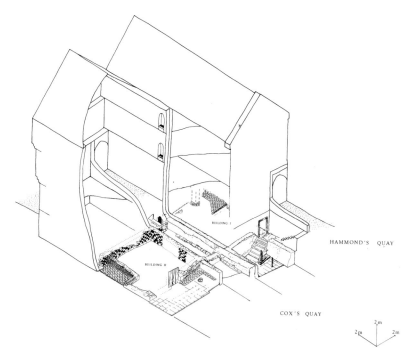

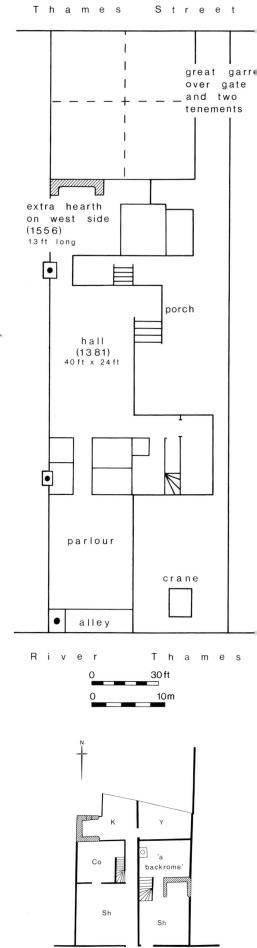

254. **(174)** New Fresh Wharf, Lower Thames Street: reconstruction of Buildings H and J, fourteenth and sixteenth century respectively, from excavations of 1974 [Schofield 1977]

255. (*right*) **(175)** Pakemann's Wharf, Thames Street: reconstruction of the site in 1463

256. (*bottom right*) **(176)** 174 Upper Thames Street (Treswell 1612)

for merchandise to fill out a further 80 ft to the wharf, which with the cartway was to be left open. In addition the hall, parlour, kitchen, buttery and other chambers would all be cellared 7 ft high.[2] Chertsey left the reversion of the tenement to Holy Trinity Priory, to whom it passed in 1432. Stephen Browne, grocer, was in occupation and renewed the lease in 1444, on such favourable terms that Kingsford suggests he had made improvements. It passed to Agnes, the wife of Browne's son John, in 1463, and her portion is described; evidently the main buildings had been constructed as specified in 1384, and further buildings are described. This part of the waterfront is also shown by Wyngaerde in *c.* 1540 (Fig. 257).

Kingsford and Godfrey[3] reconstructed the ground-plan of 1463, but on a plot about 140 ft wide. A more likely size[4] is 50 ft wide, so a fresh reconstruction is required (Fig. 255). Buildings mentioned in 1463, but possibly dating from 1384, are the boulting house (apparently in or at the back of the street range), larder-house, porch with nine steps to the hall, chapel, counter, second parlour with chambers over, a cloth-house with entry, an alley with privy at the end of the parlour, the great garret or coalhouse over the gate and the two tenements to the street. The chapel was roofed in lead, and probably did not have any chambers over it. The kitchen was on the west side of the plot in 1566, when Christopher Draper, then the owner, was allowed to set out an arch of brick to build an extra chimney and oven, encroaching for an area of 13 ft × 9 ft along the alley next door;[5] it is therefore likely that the service rooms, hall and parlour were also laid out along the west side of the tenement, and that the gateway and cartway were therefore on the east side.

1. Kingsford 1925, 137–58.
2. Salzman, *Building*, 464.
3. Kingsford 1925.
4. Identification of the plot within St Dunstan's parish by Harding, 'Port of London'.
5. Repertory, 16, f. 15.

(176)   174 [Upper] Thames Street
This property on the north side of Thames Street was bequeathed to the Clothworkers' Company by William Frankland in 1574. By the time of Treswell's survey in 1612 (Fig. 256)[1] there were two

257. **(175)** Pakemann's Wharf, Thames Street: the area in Wyngaerde's panorama of *c.* 1540 showing a range with large windows on a vault on the approximate site of Pakemann's Wharf: the parlour?

tenants; it is possible that the house had earlier been occupied by one. The building was of two and a half storeys, with a separate kitchen on the ground floor now used by one tenant only. No cellars are mentioned.

1. *LSRT*, 122.

(177) Merchant Taylors' Hall, Threadneedle Street

The site of Merchant Taylors' Hall belonged in the mid thirteenth century to Roger fitz Roger, whose son John sold it with other property to Ralph de Alegate or Crepin in 1281.[1] In 1297–8 Ralph de Alegate, clerk, sold to Walter de Glovernia his stone gateway, with the stone chamber erected over it, and the new stone work (stock-piled materials?) for constructing a hall adjoining the same gateway to Cornhill, with the adjoining garden as far as the gable of the stone chamber of the great mansion to the south. In 1298–9 Crepin conveyed to Walter his mansion upon Cornhill, with the exceptions outlined in the previous deed, in the parishes of St Peter and St Michael Cornhill, St Benet Fink and St Martin Outwich. In 1332 Edmund Crepin, son of Walter Crepin (= Glovernia), sold the mansion to John de Yakeslee, tentmaker to the king; the house now included a second great gate to Bradestrete (Threadneedle Street).

In 1345 Yakeslee conveyed it to John Aystwich, who in 1347 granted it to William Galeis and twenty-five other trustees, many of them of the Fraternity of Taylors and Linen Armourers.[2]

In 1392 the premises were described as two messuages and eleven shops, of which one messuage called 'Taillourshalle' and the eleven shops were in the parishes of St Benet and St Martin, and fronted Bradestrete to the north, and the second messuage was in the parish of St Peter Cornhill, fronting Cornhill to the south. Hopkinson suggested that this second messuage could only be on the site of 2 White Lion Court, Cornhill (since the fraternity did not acquire any other property in the parish for a further three hundred years). In 1399–1400 the messuage was known as 'le vielle hostielle', and this may have been the hall under construction in 1297–8.[3]

The medieval company hall complex (Fig. 53) comprised the following parts: (a) the hall, (b) the kitchen, (c) the chapel and the crypt beneath, (d) other chambers and the garden, (e) the street range to Threadneedle Street and a separate courtyard of almshouses. Of these, the hall, kitchen and crypt survive, though rebuilt many times.

(a) The hall (93½ft × 43½ft internally) is of five bays, separated by buttresses, with the screens passage forming a sixth eastern bay.

258.   (177) Merchant Taylors' Hall, Threadneedle Street: view of south side of hall from garden, photographed in 1930 [Hopkinson 1931]

Arched foundations of chalk and ragstone springing from rectangular foundation piers (which also support the buttresses) were recorded along the north wall in 1910 during building works (Figs. 154–5). Similar arches were recorded along the east wall in 1919.[4] Above ground level the walling of the north side was of squared and coursed ragstone, with a chamfered plinth about 2 ft above medieval ground level. In the second bay of the hall a blocked stone doorway with a four-centred head was recorded; the head of a second doorway in the third bay was in brick, and appears post-medieval. Much of the facing stone has been replaced by brick, perhaps after the Great Fire. The main windows of the hall were products of 1793, when the ancient windows 'were enlarged and incorporated in the windows'.[5] At the west, dais, end, a semi-octagonal 'buffet', of mid-fifteenth-century date with a diminutive fan-vault with cusped cells, projected to the north. On the south side the arch of a bay window of *c.* 1400, larger than the buffet, was uncovered in 1913 and is now visible on the exterior of the south wall (Fig. 258). The window would have looked onto the garden.

An inventory of 1512 refers to a *cupborde* with four feet in the south window – presumably a reference to the oriel – and to a Cupborde Room on the north side of the hall – presumably the north buffet. In 1547–8 expenses are recorded for the 'new making of the great stone window in the upper end of the hall'. The floor of the medieval hall, apparently of earth until paved with tiles in 1646, is preserved beneath the present floor.[6]

(b) In 1388 John Churchman, who owned adjoining property fronting onto Bishopsgate Street, settled a dispute with the company (of which he was a member) over a strip of garden adjacent to his own tenement and that of the fraternity by donating

the strip and building a wall on the new boundary, which ran up to the company's kitchen. The wall has been identified by its length as one reaching the present kitchen, which was thus in this position by 1388. The wall in question was examined in 1951 and found to be of ragstone patched with yellow bricks; a small section can be seen at the hall. Large expenses of £149 in 1425–6 and £17 in 1432–3 relate to the enlarging of the kitchen. In 1425 John Goldyng, carpenter, was paid 7s. 4d. for drawing the design of the kitchen and for his work on the hall; presumably this relates to the kitchen roof.[7] In 1433–4 members of the company went to see the kitchen roof at Kennington Palace, and the Viewers of the City viewed the hall kitchen roof. It had a gilded vane. The kitchen (37½ ft sq.) is now entered by three four-centred arches, moulded in two orders, in the north wall (Fig. 77). In the east wall is a blocked doorway with a two-centred head; a doorway in the west wall, in 1931 thought to be of Tudor date, is not now visible. High up on the west wall is a blocked two-light window. Two large fireplaces, one against each of the east and west walls, are of late seventeenth-century date but may be in the same positions as their medieval predecessors. In the south-west corner, in a recess, is a stone-lined well. The foundations of the kitchen, tested at the south side, were found to be at least 16 ft deep.[8]

(c) Accounts for 1400–1 may refer to a chapel at the hall; accounts of 1403–4 refer to 'le chapel del sale', and repairs to it are recorded in 1407. In 1430 the chapel adjoined the hall; and in 1455–6 the *capellam infra aulam* is placed alongside an adjoining tenement which can be located on Bishopsgate Street. A bull of Callixtus II of 1455 allowed masses to be celebrated in the chapel of 'Taillours Halle'. Hopkinson[9] suggests that the chapel became the Bachelors'

Chamber by 1555 (i.e. after the Dissolution of chantries), and that the latter can be placed over the existing crypt on the east side of the hall beyond the screens (plan, Fig. 53). The crypt (Fig. 86) is now of two bays, with walls and vault of chalk with Reigate stone dressing. The vault is quadripartite with deep hollow-chamfered ribs springing from moulded and sculptured corbels; on the west wall, a winged beast and grotesque face, on the east wall the head and shoulders of a man and a bat. The southern springers for a third northern bay (destroyed 1853) still remain; this third bay projected beyond the north wall of the hall. The beginning of a fourth bay could be seen in 1828. The crypt is entered by a doorway with two-centred head, restored in 1930. The crypt is dated to *c.* 1375 by the Royal Commission on Historical Monuments (England).[10]

(d) In 1389 the fraternity settled a dispute with the Austin Friars about their encroachment into land west of the hall as a result of building a chimney in a chamber newly built by them. This chamber was known as the King's Chamber by 1492. A parlour was rebuilt in 1547, including a cleansing of the privy 'going into the pastry'. The garden is mentioned in 1415, and in 1490 it had an Erber which could accommodate a cupboard. A bowling alley is mentioned in 1572/3.[11]

(e) In 1405 the company acquired property from John Churchman, including a messuage and five shops in Broad Street (later Threadneedle Street) at the west end of St Martin Outwich (i.e. immediately east of the hall). On this site the company built seven almshouses around a courtyard in 1414. These were not part of the hall site but were separated from its Broad Street entrance by two other tenements. A quit-rent of 7s. to Holy Trinity Priory payable on the Churchman tenement enables it to be identified with that from which Martin Baker granted 3s. of quit-rent to the priory *c.* 1230; Ralph Crepin paid this in 1307. The almshouses are shown on William Goodman's map-view of the parish of St Peter Cornhill dated 1599 (later engraved, Fig. 197). They appear as a two-storeyed range along the street, the first floor having windows with arched heads. The street range in front of the hall is also shown as three storeys with garrets, of three bays with a central entrance on the ground floor. There was presumably a small courtyard behind this range and on the north side of the hall.

A stone corbel, carved with a king's head, was said to have come from the site of the hall when exhibited in 1939 (Fig. 135); its present whereabouts are unknown.

1. Hopkinson 1931, 5.
2. HR, 28(49); 28(48); 60(44); Hopkinson 1913, 7–8, 11.
3. Hopkinson 1913, 14–17.
4. Norman 1916, 1–7; Hopkinson 1931, Plate opposite p. 24.
5. Hopkinson 1931, 33.
6. Clode, *MT Memorials*, 84, 572; Hopkinson 1931, 37.
7. Hopkinson 1913, 69–70; W. F. Grimes, note in *Trans. LAMAS*, xi, 1952, 85–6; Clode, *MT Memorials*, 569–70. Goldyng was appointed King's Carpenter in 1426, and may have designed the roof of Eton College (Harvey, *English Medieval Architects*, 121).
8. Hopkinson 1931, 55–7.
9. *Ibid.*, 42–52.
10. Allen 1828, iii, 251; RCHM, *City*, 36.
11. Hopkinson 1931, 58–9, 72; Clode, *MT Memorials*, 572.
12. Hopkinson 1913, 29, 38; 1931, 30; *HTA Cartulary*, 771–3.

(178) Thomas Cromwell's house/Drapers' Hall II, Throgmorton Street

'In place of old and small tenements' Thomas Cromwell, minister of Henry VIII, built a house in London in 1532.[1] He had purchased the ground in two plots, giving a frontage of 155 ft 9 in along Throgmorton Street. James Nedeham, Surveyor of the King's Works and designer of the roof of the hall at Hampton Court, may have been involved in its building.[2] This involved arbitrarily moving the northern boundary of the garden 22 ft further north at the expense of the neighbours, who included Stow's father.

After Cromwell's execution in 1540, the Drapers bought the house in 1542–3 for £1,200. A survey of the hall and two adjoining tenancies in 1544 mentions: a great gate, paved yard, low gallery on north side of the yard, 'wyndyng' staircase with bay windows leading into the hall with leads above, a hall with two bay windows and clerestories, buttery, pantry and cellar, 'a dark chamber with lattes window' over the buttery and parlour 'to look down into the hall, a parlour with bay window and chimney, a second buttery with clerestory containing a jewel house, a kitchen with two chimneys and stairs to the hall, pastry house with ovens, scullery, two larder houses (the last five with clerestories), a coal house; on the east side of the gate, three and a half storeys including the Ladies' Chamber, and a privy on the first floor.[3]

The representation of the house on the copperplate map (*c.* 1559) and the 'Agas' woodcut show a street façade or gatehouse of three crenellated turrets or windows at the first floor, over one large and one small gateway in an otherwise blank wall. There is a suggestion of a fourth turret at the north-west corner of the building.

The Drapers also re-arranged and replanted Cromwell's large garden, about 1½ acres in extent. In 1546 two bowling alleys and a sun-dial were added, and the beds laid out in knots. Besides roses, lillies, marigolds and columbines, the plants were mostly herbal or medicinal, or fruit; the hedges were of whitethorn and privet.[4]

1. Stow, i, 179.
2. *Drapers' Recs.*, ii, 280; Harvey, *English Medieval Architects*, 210–11.
3. *Drapers' Recs.*, ii, 279–80.
4. *Ibid.*, 67–8.

(179) 31–32 Throgmorton Street, 9–13 Copthall Court

In 1556 Thomas Ormston, clothworker, bequeathed his property in Lothbury (the east part later named Throgmorton Street) to the Clothworkers' Company, with a life interest to his wife. The property does not appear in company accounts until 1592/3, when it was let as a great house and four tenements.[1]

When surveyed by Treswell in 1612 (Fig. 75a) the site was divided in two parts, east and west, demonstrated by the boundary between the gardens.[2] On the east side lay a large house (1) at the back of a small court entered from Throgmorton Street; the street range – incorporating (3) – was three and a half storeys high. The large house of three storeys and garrets had a semi-octagonal bay window facing the garden, and this continued up to the first floor (the 'round window'). A long gallery led from the chamber over the kitchen towards the garden on the first floor, on the east side of the inner yard, with another bay window at its north end near the garden. A feature of the street range (also of three and a half storeys) was unusual: at the west end stairs led to the first-floor and higher chambers of (2), who had no ground-floor room (although he held the cellar beneath (1)'s warehouse).

Along the east side of the great house, in Copthall Alley, was a row of three smaller units (4–6) containing five tenancies: two of the three ground-floor tenants (5 and 6) had one room each, and the third (4) a first-floor room above his own, but without internal access to it. The first floor over the other tenants was occupied by (7) and (8), each with a room and garret over, reached by a single stair from the alley.

1. *Charity Comm.*, 218–19; RW, Accts.
2. *LSRT*, 123–5.

(180) Angell Dune's house, Tower Street

Stow mentions a 'fair house' built by Angell Dune, grocer and alderman, on the north side of Tower Street at the west end, near or next to St Margaret Pattens church. The house was later owned by Sir John Champneis, alderman and mayor (1534), skinner (d. 1536). He 'builded . . . an high tower of brick, the first that ever I heard of

in any private man's house to overlook his neighbours in this City; but this delight of his eye was punished with blindness some years before his death'.[1] Tower Street lies on the crest of the slope above the Custom House waterfront area, and a tower would have given a good view downstream. A tower is shown in this general area by Wyngaerde in c. 1540 (Fig. 257, top right).

1. Stow, i. 133.

(181)   21–22 Trinity Lane (formerly Knightrider Street)

In 1553 Nicholas Brisstowe and Lucy his wife granted one large messuage called the White Hart in Knightrider Street to Henry Roberts, brewer; Roberts leased it for twenty-one years to John Jackson, founder. In 1563 Roberts demised the property to Jackson and Andrew Palmer, goldsmith, for their lives, with reversion to his own heirs; at this time the White Hart was described as three messuages (i.e. it had been subdivided). Under Roberts' will of 1566 his widow took possession of the property. In 1589 the owner of the White Hart, then a brewhouse, was Thomas Haselwoode, brewer; two tenants, Robert Cawsey and James Alcocke, were named.[1]

William Mascall, mercer, by his will of 11 September 1608 gave £160 to Christ's Hospital, out of which the hospital appears to have bought the property shown in Treswell's survey of 1611 (Fig. 60a), though no deeds showing the actual investment of the money survive. These houses were however in the possession of the hospital in 1605, before the gift, and it is possible that the governors 'decided to appropriate them as an investment of Mascall's gift, or rather as a security for the performance of his intention'.[2]

Except for (7), the houses were three and a half storeys high, and comprised a tavern (1) and six other tenancies. On the first floor of (1) part of the floor was open to give light to the drinking rooms on the ground floor below; perhaps this was some form of gallery. The stone walls, two of which are (uniquely in the surveys) back-to-back, seem to comprise the relics of a stone house. In (2), the tenancy of Thomas Alcocke (presumably a relation of James Alcocke recorded in 1589), are shown pipes for two privies on upper floors, passing behind the ground-floor privy to the pit below. Tenancy (7), occupying part of the tavern frontage, comprised four and a half storeys.

1. *Inq. PM*, ii, 68–70; *ibid.*, iii, 131.
2. *LSRT*, 126–7; *Charity Comm.*, 109.

(182)   Ormond Place, Knightrider Street

At the west end of the street, on the south side, Stow noted a newly-built tavern and other houses in a plot of ground where Ormond Place stood.[1] In 1467 Edward IV granted the Inn to his queen, Elizabeth Woodward; it was then ruinous.[2]

1. Stow, i, 239, 247–8.
2. *LTR*, xi, 64–5.

(183)   Countess of Kent's Almshouses
(later 28–30 Tudor Street)

Margaret, Countess of Kent, built a row of five almshouses on the site of a garden within the Whitefriars' precinct shortly before 1538, when she entrusted them to the Clothworkers' Company as part of an endowment of property (see also the Tennis Place, Fenchurch Street; **74**). This was confirmed in her will of 1540.[1]

The timber-framed almshouses, when surveyed by Treswell in 1612, comprised ten single rooms, five on the ground floor and five on the first floor, the latter reached by a stair at one end of an external gallery (Fig. 65b). The ground-floor chambers varied slightly in size around an average of 13 ft square; the chambers above were of similar dimensions. All had individual chimneys and houses of office.[2]

1. CDW.
2. *LSRT*, 129–30.

(184)   Walbrook and Bucklersbury (4–5 Woolchurch Haw)

The detailed history of this site from the early fourteenth century is given in *HG*, iii, site **118/14**. The property was granted to the Clothworkers' Company by the will of John Rogers, clothworker, in 1558, when it comprised four old houses. By 1571 it comprised three tenements; and in the text of reference of the Treswell plan of 1612 (Fig. 259), they are called 'those two tenements sometimes three and now one'. The structure reflected the three-part division, with three street-doors; but Treswell notes only one tenant. A structural division is present between the shop on the south and the other two units to the north, presumably reflecting the time when the three parts were only two. In 1612 the property was of three and a half storeys on cellars; hall, buttery, parlour and kitchen were all on the first floor.[1]

1. CDW, 77–86; *LSRT*, 131.

(185)   Warwick Inn, Warwick Lane

First mentioned in 1351, when it already belonged to the Warwick family. The house is indirectly mentioned in 1423, when the Brewers asked their carpenter to model details on the bay window at the Earl's Inn (**1**). Among fifteenth-century owners was Richard Neville, the Kingmaker, who in 1458 lodged there having come from Calais with six hundred attendants. Stow gives details of his extravagant household, implying a large establishment, which is confirmed by reports of John Paston in the 1470s. In the reign of Henry VII the property fell to the Crown and was held by a series of keepers. In 1541 this post was held by the Yeoman of the Revels, and in 1543–4 theatrical equipment was stored there; this function was transferred to Blackfriars in 1547–8. By Stow's time it was still recognisable as an ancient house, but was probably divided into tenements.[1]

Excavations in 1880 and 1966 revealed buildings of several medieval phases. The excavation of 1966 (Fig. 260) uncovered (1) traces of two rooms, one aligned parallel with Warwick Lane, of a thirteenth-century masonry building, with foundations of alternate chalk and gravel; (2) a rebuild on the same alignment of two rooms in line, one a cellar, probably also dating to the thirteenth century; and (3) a much larger group of rooms with a common east wall overlaying the second building, but expanding to the west. This comprised an east to west room 57 ft × 19 ft 7 in, a possible garderobe at the west end, and at least three chambers on the south

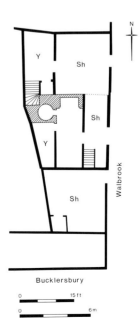

259.   (184) House at corner of Walbrook and Bucklersbury, later 4–5 Woolchurch Haw (Treswell 1612)

side. The garderobe and west end of this structure were also recorded in 1880. This complex was built over destruction debris of the previous building which contained fourteenth-century material.[2] If the post-Fire Warwick Court shown on Ogilby and Morgan's map represents the whole area of the pre-Fire Warwick Inn, then the excavated buildings were found under the north side and at the north-east corner of the Inn. It is not clear whether they represent principal or subsidiary buildings in what may have been a very large complex.

1. Stow, i, 87–8; *LTR*, xii, 53–5.
2. Marsden 1969; *Archaeologia*, **48** (1884), 222–4.

(186)   34 Watling Street

An undercroft one bay wide and five bays long, at right angles to and on the south side of Watling Street, immediately east of St Mary Aldermary (though probably separated from it by an alley, as shown by Ogilby and Morgan in 1677), was almost totally destroyed in 1825. The springers for the north-west corner survive in a small space in the present basement of 34 Watling Street. A plan and section drawings of *c.* 1825 by C. Busby, now in the library of the Society of Antiquaries (Fig. 90a–b), shows the undercroft to be 74 ft 4½in × 15 ft 5½in, with slightly rectangular bays, plain chamfered ribs forming quadripartite vaulting and plain circular bosses. The plan was not oriented but it seems likely that a doorway in one end was at the north, street end; at that end also was a recess which may have originally been a window. Along the east side, in each bay except the northernmost, was a splayed window opening; a further opening in the northernmost bay may have been a window altered by later building.[1] The surviving fragments were re-examined in 1987 and the primary floor-level ascertained. The undercroft wall was of ragstone rubble, with traces of original plaster around the surviving north-west springer (Fig. 90c). The doorway, vault ribs and bosses together indicate a building date in the range 1400–1500.[2]

1. Society of Antiquaries Library, Red Portfolio I, 4–5; RCHM, *City*, 83, Plate 144.
2. Samuel 1987.

(187)   Abbot of Glastonbury's Inn, West Smithfield

This Inn lay between Hosier Lane and Cock Lane but behind the houses on each, with an entrance from Smithfield to the east. The Inn was acquired by the abbot and convent in 1426–7. By 1677 the Inn was called The Dolphin. A separate property on the south corner of Hosier Lane, for which the abbot paid the hospital a quit-rent, is shown in an engraving by Smith (Fig. 164).[1]

1. Honeybourne, 'Value', 366–9; Moore 1918, ii, 51–2; *SBH Cartulary* 185; *Cal. Pat. R.*, 1422–9, 331, 477–8; *SBH Cartulary*, App. I, 64.

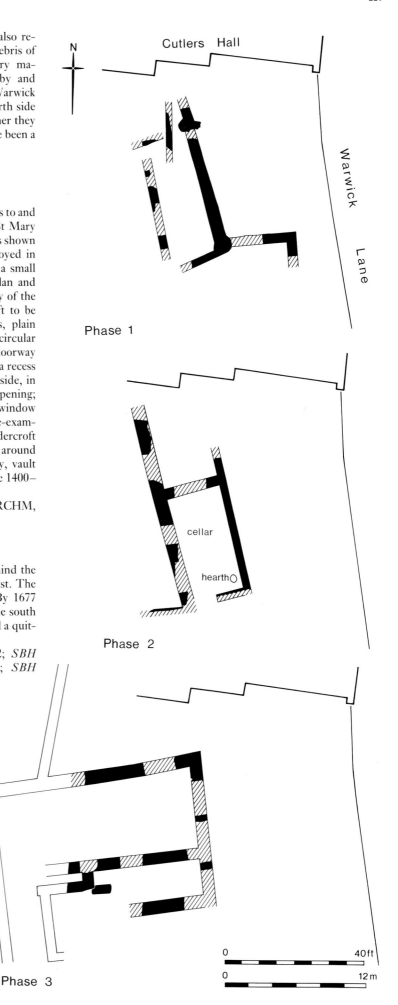

260.   (185) Warwick Inn, Warwick Lane: plan of main buildings revealed by excavation [after Marsden 1967]

**(188)   Gateway of St Bartholomew's Church,
              West Smithfield**
The gateway now appears as two and a half storeys of timber-
framing over the thirteenth-century entrance to the churchyard;
originally this was one of the western doors to the priory church, the
west end of which lay on the street. The house above was rebuilt by
Philip (later Sir Philip) Scudamore, parishioner, in 1595.[1] Restoration after damage in a Zeppelin raid in 1916 showed that much of
the timber was reused, including one piece from an ecclesiastical
screen, possibly from St Bartholomew's itself. The present windows
date from the restoration. As the front was hung with tiles before the
restoration, the present arrangement of the framing cannot be assumed to follow the original one.
1.   Webb 1921, ii, 68.

(189)   90–94 West Smithfield, 28–30 Cow Lane
In 1536 Thomas Cutbert, barber, brother and heir of Robert
Cutbert, granted the Maidenhead in Cow Lane to Edward Barbour,
Katherine his wife and others. By his will of 1580 William Heron
bequeathed the lands to the Clothworkers' Company. In 1603 the
company leased them to John Walker on condition that he rebuild
four small tenements on the south side, between Smithfield and the
entry to the Maidenhead. His will of 1609 records that he duly did
so at a cost of £200.[1]
    When surveyed by Treswell in 1612 (Fig. 59a), the Heron estate
comprised five large, two-room plan houses of two and a half or
three and a half storeys on cellars facing Smithfield (1–5), all with
prominent chimneys and ovens, the four tenements (6–9) rebuilt by
Walker on the Cow Lane frontage, of similar size, and the Maidenhead, then called Pheasant Court, to the west. Presumably the
Maidenhead had been a hostelry; by 1612 it was divided into ten
tenancies (10–20), some of them single chambers. Ten tenants had
ground-floor rooms; seven of these had upper chambers also.
Further subtenants were of two kinds: one apparently lived
('dwelleth') in a cellar with a chimney beneath (18) and (19), and
two widows each had a first-floor chamber over (16). Two cellars
under (16) and (17) were held by a further tenant who was not
otherwise a tenant on the site.
    The building forming (16) and (17) was apparently of lobby-
entrance plan, a form otherwise found only in the more open, out-
lying parts of the city (see **55**).[2] In 1612 this origin must have been
obscured, as it was divided into a total of five separate tenancies.
Pheasant Court seems to be amongst the lowliest class of housing
surveyed by Treswell for the Clothworkers.
1.   CD, Box 52.
2.   *LSRT*, 132–4.

(190)   77 Wood Street
Two houses on this property are first mentioned in 1364, when
John, son of John Casewell, fishmonger, granted them to Robert de
Esse; in 1520 the property was bought by the Shearmen's Company
from two members, William Estwyk and John Olyver, and a mer-
chant tailor. The houses became part of the Clothworkers' estate

when the Shearmen and the Fullers united to form the
Clothworkers' Company in 1528. During the sixteenth century the
property was divided between two tenants; by 1612 (Fig. 98) there
were four tenancies. On the north side was (1), a house of two and
a half storeys without a cellar; on the south, a house originally of
two-room plan had been split into two houses of one-room plan (2)
and (3), both four and a half storeys tall, on cellars.[1]
    At the rear of the property was (4), the Talbot, a building of three
and a half storeys on an arched brick cellar which contained, on its
ground floor, a 'Callendring House'. The Calender was a large
wooden box filled with stones cemented together, weighing 10 tons
or more. It pressed finished cloths by its movement over two rollers
on a table, by means of ropes winding on a shaft turned by a horse-
gin (as in this case) or tread-mill.
1.   CD, Box 56; *LSRT*, 135.

**Sites 191–2: sites within the City north of the river, but
unlocated or only generally located**

(191)   House of William Hanigtone, 1308 (unlocated)
In 1308 William Hanigtone, skinner, contracted with Simon of
Canterbury, carpenter, that Simon would build a hall and a chamber
(*camera*) with a chimney, a larder between the hall and the chamber,
a solar above the chamber and larder, an oriel at the head of the hall
ultra summum scamnum (beyond high table), a step with its oriel at
the hall door, two *claustures* (partitions) in the cellar *ex transverso*
beneath the hall, one *claustura* to a privy, and two pipes to the privy;
a stable stretching between the hall and the old kitchen, 12 ft wide,
with a solar above and a garret above the solar; and at the head of the
solar, a kitchen with a chimney and an oriel between the hall and the
old chamber, 8 ft broad.[1]
    The house is unlocated, but at his death in 1312–13 William
Hanigtone held property in the parishes of St John and St Stephen
Walbrook, near Skinners' Hall.[2]
1.   Salzman, *Building*, 417–18; for Simon of Canterbury, who rose
     to be 'the most important carpenter in the City' in the 1330s, see
     Harvey, *English Medieval Architects*, 46.
2.   *Cal. Wills*, i, 237–8.

(192)   Parish of St Benet Paul's Wharf, 1510
On 8 July 1510 the prior of Charterhouse contracted with William
Dewilde, carpenter, that Dewilde would set up a house in the parish
of St Benet Paul's Wharf, with two lofts, one 'oversett' (jettied),
with two stairs to the said lofts, two doors on the street side and with
as many 'plain' windows as the prior should think fit. The house
would be 40 ft long and 22 ft wide, and 24 ft high to the eaves. It
would be framed in Kingston upon Thames and then brought to
the site.[1]
    A height to the eaves of 24 ft suggests that the house was to have
two and a half storeys. The mention of two doors to the street
presumably indicates that one led directly into the front chamber
(for a shop?), and the other to a passage to the rear chamber, as in
surveyed examples by Treswell (e.g. **142**).
1.   Salzman, *Building*, 569.

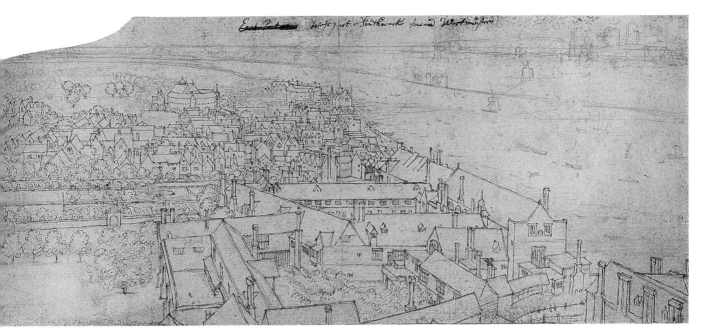

. **(193)** Bishop of Winchester's Inn, Southwark: original drawing by Hollar in 1647. The rose window (Figs. 103, 122a) was at the far, west end of hall.

Southwark

Sites in Southwark are arranged in three groups: those west of the main street, those along the main street (Borough, Borough High Street), and those along both sides of Tooley Street to the east.

(193)   Inn of the Bishop of Winchester, Southwark

The town-house of the Bishop of Winchester has been the subject of several studies (and another is in preparation)[1] and therefore only an outline is presented here.

A fifteenth-century copy of a recognisance of *c.* 1147–50 by Henry of Blois, Bishop of Winchester and brother of King Stephen, tells of 'many inconveniences and losses that I and my predecessors have substained through the lack of a house to use for royal business and other affairs in the neighbourhood of London . . . and therefore . . . I have procured the house and land that were of Orgar the Rich and many other lands lying around them of the soke of the church and monks of Bermondsey'. According to Fitzstephen, Becket was received at the Bishop's house on his way to Canterbury in 1170. A quay between the house and the adjacent priory of St Mary Overey is mentioned in 1174. Later building history indicates that twelfth-century buildings were on different alignments to those of the thirteenth and fourteenth centuries; an old hall is mentioned in 1220–1, when the stone hall known from surviving fragments and later engravings was in construction.

From the thirteenth century the main range of hall, parlour and kitchen lay east to west virtually on the bank of the Thames, all on the first floor on undercrofts (Figs. 34, 261–2). The hall was at least 82 ft long, and was either extended to the east in the fourteenth century or was originally 117 ft long, with the east one or possibly two bays partitioned off to form a chamber. Both hall and bishop's chamber were provided with white glass windows in 1251–2. There are no documentary records for the making of the surviving rose window in the west gable of the hall (Figs. 103, 122a). It is of Reigate stone, comprising a central hexagonal design, surrounded by cusped triangles, and held together with an original iron band. It is 11 ft 10 in in diameter, and was glazed. Wood suggests a date of *c.* 1320–

30,[3] citing a parallel for the window at the east end of the hall of the Bishop of St David's (at Llandaff) of *c.* 1327–46, though the design is different.

At first-floor level in the wall below the rose window, three flat-pointed ashlar arches originally penetrated through the wall, presumably marking entrances to the kitchen and service rooms. In the south-west corner of the hall a doorway with equilateral pointed moulded head and worked jambs, caps and bases marks the screens entrance (Figs. 103, 122a).

On the south side of the hall and also on the first floor lay the bishop's chapel, first mentioned in 1213–14, and two courtyards of buildings, including stables, brewhouse, servants' quarters, a men's prison and a women's prison, and a new bishop's chamber built in 1356–7. Some rebuilding took place under Bishop Stephen Gardiner (1531–55) and a gallery along the south side of the hall, details of which survived into the nineteenth century, may have been built by the Marquess of Northampton in 1552–3. Many of the buildings of the complex, as shown by Hollar in 1647 (Fig. 261), have sixteenth-century chimneys.

1. *Survey of London: Bankside*, 46–56; Carlin, 'Southwark', 79–119; Carlin 1985; Yule in preparation.
2. Carlin, 'Southwark', 80.
3. Wood 1965, 29, 357.
4. Carlin, 'Southwark', 93–119.

(194)   The Mealmarket, Fowl Lane, Southwark

Four tenements here were probably rebuildings or fragmentations of the two tenements originally owned by St Mary Overey Priory, Southwark, as detailed under **196** below; in a survey by Treswell of 1611 (Fig. 60b) two main tenants and two houses could still be discerned, but now there were four occupants: the southern half (1–2) comprised one of the former properties, and the northern half comprised the Red Bull tavern (4) and a separate small tenancy (3). The houses were three and a half storeys high on cellars.[1]

1. *LSRT*, 140–1.

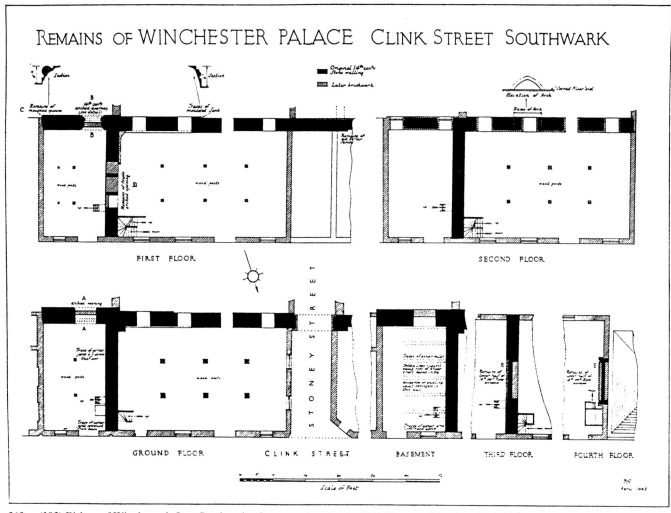

REMAINS OF WINCHESTER PALACE CLINK STREET SOUTHWARK

262.   (193) Bishop of Winchester's Inn, Southwark: plans at various levels, 1943 [*Survey of London, Bankside*]

(195)   Suffolk Place, Southwark

In 1516 Charles Brandon, son of Henry Tudor's standard-bearer at Bosworth, bought eleven messuages and eight gardens in Southwark probably to enlarge the property there which can be associated with the family from the 1460s. In 1518–20 he built a house there, the works being under the supervision of Robert Hutton. In 1536 the house and adjoining park were acquired by Henry VIII in exchange with Brandon for Norwich Place, Charing Cross; but although maintained and with its park stocked with game, it was rarely used. In 1545 a Mint was established there until 1551. After a small amount of use by Edward VI and Mary, the house was granted to the Archbishop of York in 1556 and sold by him in 1557. In the same year building materials from the house were sold to the Crown and by 1562 the property was subdivided into gardens and tenements.[1] In 1649 a parliamentary survey of the adjacent Mint in Southwark found that Sir Edmund Broomefield, late alderman of the City, occupied the mansion house of Suffolk Place, which comprised a hall, parlour, kitchen, buttery, larder, cellar and other low rooms, six chambers above stairs with garrets, two other upper chambers, a stable, coach-house, outhouses, orchards, gardens, and a courtyard which contained a long fish-pond, containing in all $3\frac{1}{2}$ acres.[2]

The house appears in the foreground of Wyngaerde's panorama (*c.* 1540; Fig. 42).

1.   *LTR*, xii, 35; Carlin, 'Southwark', 176–80.
2.   Giuseppi 1899, 64–5.

(196)   44–48 (later 34–38) Blackman Street (now 291–299 Borough High Street), Southwark

In 1537 the prior of St Mary Overey, Southwark leased to William Cawsey, saddler, for sixty years two tenements in the parish of St Mary Magdalene, Southwark on the west side of an unspecified highway; these are probably wholly or partly the properties described above (194) as in the Mealmarket, Southwark. Also leased were six tenements and a garden in Blackmanstreet in the parish of Newington. By 1544 all these properties were in the hands of John Pope and Anthony Foster, who confirmed them to George Hoord; in 1559 a Richard Bortsek of Newington also quitclaimed his interest in the six tenements in Blackmanstreet to Hoord. By his will of 22 December 1562 (proved in the Prerogative Court of Canterbury) Hoord left all his lands in Southwark to Christ's Hospital.[1]

On the Treswell plan of 1611 (Fig. 263), however, seven tenements are shown; it is not clear which, if any, is an addition, or whether one of the properties had been subdivided by the time of the plan. Nor are the upper storeys of the houses described, since no text survives with Treswell's plan.[2] The houses are apparently shown in the foreground of Wyngaerde's panorama of London, drawn *c.* 1540 (Fig. 119), and the form of one of them is known from a lease of 1585 by the hospital to Gilbert Appertington, in which the tenant was required to rebuild the house by 1588 'of good, stronge substanciall and well seasoned tymber of Oke, which shall contain two stories high and a half, the first of them to be tenne fote highe,

263. (196) 44–48 (later 34–38) Blackman Street, now 291–299 Borough High Street, Southwark (Treswell 1612)

the second storie eight foote and the halfe storie fower foote or more besides the rofe'; this is probably the later no. 46, tenancy (4).[3]
1. GL, MS 13387.
2. *LSRT*, 138–9.
3. GL, MSS 13389, 13390.

(197) Abbot of Battle's Inn, Tooley Street, Southwark
Before *c.* 1150–67 Merton Priory (fd. 1114–17) held a town-house on part of this site. Battle Abbey acquired it with other properties piecemeal in the late twelfth and early thirteenth centuries. In 1528 the house comprised a gate, hall, buttery, kitchen, the abbot's chamber, a chapel with a chamber below it, and a dorter; the site lay in the southern half of the present Hay's Wharf, Tooley Street.[1]
1. Carlin, 'Southwark', 349–52.

(198) Earl of Warenne's Inn, Tooley Street, Southwark
From the time of William Maitland's *History of London*[1] and especially after recording of a twelfth-century stone building on the site in 1829, some antiquaries thought that this property was part of the town-house of the prior of Lewes, which lay to the east (**199**).[2] This is now thought unlikely; it is possible, as suggested by Corner that it was the London residence of the Earl of Warenne in the thirteenth century. By 1274 however the property and others around it were owned by John de Boklaunde.[3]

The mid- or late-twelfth-century building uncovered during demolition in 1829 stood at right angles to Tooley Street and about 100 ft south of the street; a yard lay to the east in 1829 (Fig. 31). The main range was 40 ft 6 in long by 16 ft 6 in internally, the basement groin-vaulted in four bays. The west side (i.e. away from the yard) had a round-headed splayed window in each of the two middle bays, and the south end had two smaller similar windows (Fig. 32a–b).

The bays were marked by semi-circular columns in the walls and capitals of several designs. Leading from the north-east bay was a smaller range at right angles to the first, of two bays at basement level (Fig. 264).[4] A section through the long axis of the building shows part of the east wall of the room above the vault, with a round-headed doorway above the second bay from the north (i.e. the bay next to the smaller range at lower level). The door was edged in cut stone, as were the windows below and the vault ribs; this was said to be Caen stone.

It is possible that the smaller range at right angles to the main range was part of a fore-building supporting a stair to the door on the first floor; but an equally possible theory, considering the position of windows in the basement of the main range and that the upper doorway was in the *next* bay to that above the extension, is that the main range comprised a solar block to a former ground-floor hall extending to the east. The upper doorway would then be at the head of stairs from the hall, and the absence of windows in the east side of the basement would be explained by the presence there of the hall. The smaller extension at the north-east corner of the block might be a chapel.
1. Maitland, *History of London*, 1756 ed., 1389.
2. Wilkinson, *Londina Illustrata*, i, 139, Plates 83–5; Gage 1831.
3. Corner 1860; Carlin, 'Southwark', 270–1.
4. Drawings by J. C. Buckler, Society of Antiquaries Library, Surrey Red Portfolio, S-Z, 8; the drawings reproduced in Brooke & Keir 1975, Plates 32–3, and engraved in Gage 1831, Plates 20–5.

(199) Prior of Lewes' Inn, Tooley Street, Southwark
Building operations of 1832 revealed a rectangular twelfth-century undercroft on the east side of Carter Lane (off Tooley Street) at its

264. (198) Earl of Warenne's Inn, Tooley Street, Southwark: view of the north-eastern, smaller wing (J. C. Buckler 1831), cf. Figs. 31–32a–b

south end (Figs. 31, 33). It was of four quadripartite bays, with elliptically arched ribs rising from plain pilasters on the walls. In the centre was a single round column with scalloped capital; a doorway led east from the north-east bay, and windows were recorded in the north, east and south walls.[1] This might imply that the undercroft lay under the east end of the range.

In 1371 the priory of Lewes (Sussex) leased to William de Wyngtryngham, carpenter,[2] a plot outside the gate of the Inn, on the west side, 23 ft wide from the gate to Wyntryngham's own house and 30 ft deep, on condition that he build on it a house with a solar 23 ft long and 12 ft wide (i.e. across the width of the plot, presumably at the front) with its doors 'over against the ditch which leads from our said hostel to the other road by our gate', presumably a reference to the road or lane leading from Tooley Street south to the hostel gate. In 1373 Wyntryngham obtained a similar but more substantial building lease for land inside the gate. Here were to be two rows of shops running north to south, the east containing five shops and the west six shops; each shop was to be 12 ft deep, with a first-floor jetty, modelled on the rent or range of shops of Adam Franceys at the east end of the Austin Friars' church (except for the details of chimneys and the stone wall behind the latter). The east range would be 84 ft long, the west range 106 ft long, 'which six shops shall be 22 feet beyond the said gate and 84 feet within' – i.e. the sixth shop, 22 ft wide, would be outside the gate on the west side and presumably matched the building 23 ft wide which Wyntryngham had put up two years previously. At the south end of the two rows, and connecting them, were to be two stables, 14 ft deep and with solars above but without jetties, 'for storing therein whatever the said Prior and convent shall wish'. Between the two stables was to be a gate with a room above. Other terms of the agreement mention gardens to go with the shops.[3]

At the Dissolution the Inn was granted to Thomas Cromwell; by 1582 part had become the Walnut Tavern. Stow saw 'one great house builded of stone, with arched gates, which pertained to the Prior of Lewes . . . it is now a common hosterie for travellers, and hath to sign the Walnut Tree'.[4]

1. Gwilt 1834, 604–6; Corner 1860; Carlin, 'Southwark', 275–7.
2. Wyntryngham supervised the erection of the hall roof of Windsor Castle in 1361–5, and was rewarded for service by John of Gaunt in 1372–3 (Harvey, *English Medieval Architects*, 337).
3. Salzman, *Building*, 446–8.
4. Stow, ii, 64; *LTR*, xi, 32.

(200) Inn of the Prior of Christ Church, Canterbury, Tooley Street, Southwark

The priory acquired the site in the late twelfth to early thirteenth century, and had established a town-house there by the 1240s. In 1274–5 the Inn comprised a gate, hall, kitchen, garden, and vineyard; the roof of the hall was shingled in 1276–7, and the prior's chamber and stable re-roofed in tile in 1315–16. Other buildings included a chapel (1320–1) and dovecote (built 1323–4). Shops are mentioned in 1254, and a shop or shops by the gate in 1276–7. During the fifteenth century parts of the site were leased to dyers, fullers and masons; in 1512–13 the main house may also have been leased. By 1555 the house had been converted into an tavern called the Flower de Luce.[1] The site now lies beneath London Bridge Station.

1. Carlin, 'Southwark', 288–94.

(201) Inn of the Abbot of St Augustine, Canterbury

The site adjoining the east side of St Olave, Southwark, was bought by the abbey in 1215. Stow described it as 'a great house of stone and timber . . . which was an ancient piece of work, and seemeth to be one of the first builded houses on that side [of] the river'.[1] It had a wharf by 1330; this was located in excavations in 1971.[2] In 1538 the abbot and convent leased the house to Sir Anthony Sentleger, who obtained a grant of the property from the Crown in 1540.[3] In Hollar's panorama of 1647 the roof of a long building running north to south is shown immediately east of St Olave's church; this may be part of the Inn.

1. Stow, ii, 64–5.
2. *Cal. LB, E*, 243; Sheldon 1972, 5.
3. Carlin, 'Southwark', 362.

Appendix

Robert Lee's house, Leadenhall Street (115) – Schedule of 1607 (GL, MS 1123)

IN PRIMIS a Long flatt barr of Iron to the outward gates of viiji foote long with Two keepers with lock & key and a stock to the wickett with lock and key And a flatt bolte and a round bolt with theire keepers to the said wickett and a Rounde Barr of Iron to the said gates fastened to the Lodge.

ITEM an Inner paire of Gates with a Portcullis of wood over them and a Wickett with a springe lock in the same Gates with a winche of Iron to shutt the samd wickett and a Barr of five foote long fastened to the wall over the Pissing Leade and fower bolts of Iron and an Iron chayne and a Ring to the same Gates & wickett.

In the yard next leaden hall streete
Item a Leade to make water in with a Pipe of Leade into the Syncke, the same Leade is an ell in length and half an ell in depth And a pipe of Leade to bring the Rayne water into the saide Pissing place.

Item a Laver of Tyne having fower Pillers And Three Cocks of Brasse And in length a yard and more with the Cocke of Brasse to bring the Thames water into it And a washer of Brasse to clense the said Laver and a faire Gutter of freestone to carye the water into the pissing place garnished with Armes.

Item a frame to hang a Towell

Item a long Rack to hang Bucketts on and a frame of Two stepps and a wickett with a Bolte for the waterbearer to putt water into the kitchin.

Item a Doore to the Celler with lock and key and Twelve Iron pykes to the same and a Doore with a Bolte within the said Celler doore to make Cleane the Syncke.

Item all the Entrye and yard paved with Purbeck stone And Three Rings in the stones to make Cleane the Syncke.

Item in the Lodge a doore with bolte & lock & key and Two falling wyndowes with theire Frames.

Item the Porche paved with Purbeck stone with Two seates of waynscotte with pillers and backs of waynscote to the same, about a yard in height from the said seates.

In the Compting Howse
Item the same wainscotted round about and a doore with doble plate lock, and three keys to the same.

Item a square Table covered with Buckrome and ij benches to the same And a foote pace at the utter end of the same Table And Five Boxes under the same Table and Six shelves about the said Compting howse A nest of iij boxes at the wyndowe And iiij falling wyndowes.

In the Old Parlor
Item the Wainscote rounde aboute the same Parlor, paynted and a doore to the Compting howse with a doble plate lock & iij keys and a handle to it, A doore to the lodge with a smale lock; a doore to the Litle Buttery within the said Parlor with a lock key and a handle and Fower shelves within the said Buttrye and a dore to the yard with an Architect over it, And a Latch and a Ketche of Iron to the same Doore.

Item and Iron back in the Chymney and Two falling skreene shelves with iij to them and ij Curtayne Rodds to ye wyndowe.

In the yard and Entrye next the old parlor & kitchin
Item a greate Doore with ij great bolts with theire Keepers And a Ring of Iron and a dresser dore to the kitchin with a lock.

Item all the said yard and the walke at the East end thereof paved with Purbeck stone and a Bench of Waynscotte with pillers in the said [?] with a backe of Wainscote to the same ij foote and a halfe in height and ij Corner pillers wainscotted upp to the Ceeling And a Bench with a back of waynscote and a falling skreene shelf betwene the said Two Pillers.

Item Three wodden racks for to lay pykes on it the said Entrye and the said Entrye paved with white and blew marble stones iiij square and an Architect over the porche leading out in the yard into the said old parlor.

In the Entrye turning to the Pastrye & kitchin
Item a Great Door with an Iron handle and latche and the Entrye paved with Purbeck stone and ij grates of Iron into the Cellers.

Item Six Narrowe shelves and a broad shelf.

In the Pastrye
Item a doore with a lock & key to it.

Item a faire Moulding boord about xiij ten foote long almost iij foote broad and Fower ynches Thick with a returne from the same boord to the doore and one broad plancke all along under the said Mouldinge boord.

Item a long shelf with a Retorne to the doore over the said mouldinge boord and the wall lyned with boords behinde the same Mouldinge boord half a foote heigh & more.

Item Fower lydds of Iron to the Ovens there.

Item a dresser boord behinde the doore with a Broad shelf under it, and a narrowe shelf over it.

In the Kitchin
Item a doore with a Locke and a key to it And a dresser doore with a Bolte.

Item a Long Dresser boord on the South side of the said Kitchin of xviij foote longe and ij foote broad and iij ynches thicke with a Broad shlf all alonge under the said dresser boord with frames to the said dresser & shelfe and a long shelfe over the same dresser.

Item a faire Cesterne of Leade with a Cocke of brasse and pipes of Leade to bring the Thames water into the same.

Item a dresser boord at the Eastend of the said kitchin of xv foote longe, ji foote broad & more and Three Ynches thick with a boord shelfe under it ix foote long and frames to the said dresser & shelfe.

Item one long boord shelfe under the said dresser one narrowe long shelfe under the same Boord shelfe and over the said dresser and Fower smale shelves.

Item Two Barres of Iron crosse the great Chymney and one Barre of Iron all alonge between the said Crosse Barres and iiij Iron Creepers fastened in the Range and iij wodden racks for spitts over the said Chymney

Item Tow Crosse barrs of Iron in the Boylinn Chymney and a longe Barre betwene the said Crose Barres And a long Boord with a paire of Hinges to keepe the [ ] in the same Chymney

Item a Frame for a Towell at the Kitchin doore and the same Kitchin paved all with fair Purbeck stones.

Item a doore to the still house with locke & key and Three shelves in the same.

In the Skullerye yard
Item the same yard paved all with Purbeck stones and Fyve grates of Iron to convey light into the Celler.

Item an old dresser and a wyndow behind the same

Item a Furnace with a Copper & Tabred [?] with Leade & a dore out of the Kitchin into the said yard

Item a faire Cesterne of Lead with a Cock of Brasse & pyn of Leade to Convey the Thames water into the same.

In the scorowinge howse over the pastrie

Item a Troughe to scowre in and a foote pace to the same

Item a presse for pewter with iij bottoms & ij locks & keys to the doores of the same and ij shelves over the said scorwinge Trough.

Item iiij shelves in the Entrye betwenw the scowringe house and Armorye.

Item a Doore at the stayrsfoote to the scowwringe house with a stock lock to it and a doore from the skowring house to the entrey to the Armorye with a litle lock to it And a dore from the said Entrye to the Armorye with a lock and key to it And a Rack in the said Armorye to hang Armour on.

In the Drye Larder

Item Two half doores of waynscote and a double spring locke and key to the Lower of them And a round bolte upon a plate to the upper doore and a handle to the Lower doore

Item the said Drye Larder paved all over with purbeck stones

Item Thirtene shelves about the said Larder

In the Butterie

Item Two half doores of wainscote and a doble spring lock and key and handle to the Lower of them And a bolte uppo a plate to the upper of the same dores

Item the said Butterie paved with Purbeck stones

Item Two shelves in the same butterye

Item a passage into the Cellers grated with a dore to the same with a Lock to it and a Rack to hang potts on.

In the hall and Entrye behinde the skreene

Item one great Dore with a doble plate springe, lock & key, a Rack to hang hatts on and a Case for a Clock with a dore and a handle.

Item a faire Carved skreene garnished with Imagery with the late Queenes Armes upon it and ij skreene boordes with Irons to them.

Item a faire gilt Beame, with Five brass candlestickes and an Angell over

Item Two long Benches at the sides of the said hall covered with greene Cloth and a long bench with ij retornes at the upper end of the hall covered with Greene Cloth.

Item a faire standing Courte Cupborde with ij particons and Two Drawers under it and one lock & key to it being all Carved & garnished with Imagerie and a frame for the Lond Maiores sword at the end of the said Courte Cupbord

Item the said Entrie behinde the skreene and the said hall paved with square Marble stones white and blew.

In the Great Parlor

Item the said parlor waynscotted rounde about verye faire with gilt knobbs and Carvynge & garnishinge of Imagerie all about the same waynscote.

Item one fayre Portall garnishes with Armes and Imagerie with ij doores and one lock & key and iiij bolts sett upon Carved plates and Two Iron Rings to the same dores.

Item one faire back of one Elle in length and a yard in height for the Chymney and one bench with pillers Two returnes covered with greene Cloth and fringed with silke frynge at the west end of the said parlor And one faire wainscote dore with Two bolts sett upon plates leadinge from the parlor to the Garden porche.

Item one faire Carved Chymney peice with pillers of Jett garnished with Imagerye wrought in Allabaster and having the late Queenes Armes and a George on Horsebacke Carved in the same with many knobbs gilt in it and the pictures of Justice and Charitye carved in the same.

In the Garden

Item the Portche benched and backed with wainscote on both sides

Item the walke paved all with purbeckstone

Item Nyne Carved postes with Railes & Turned pillers

Item a faire pumpe of Leade with an Iron sweepe with a great weight of Leade at the end of it and a cock to the said pumpe

Item an Iron grate into the Cellers under the warehouse sett in stone and a fall dore over the same grate.

Item two stone stepps of Fowerfoote a peice into the knott.

Item a stronge Doore with a Doble locke & key and bolts leadinge out of the banquettinge howse into Sir Robert Wrothes Garden and Three stone stepps to the said banquettinge howse and the same howse paved with greene and yellow Tyles

Item Two great wainscote Dores with doble plate locks to the Entrye to the great stayres and the saide Entrye paved with Purbeck stones

In the Great Dyning Chamber

Item a great wainscote dore wrought with a doble plate lock and key to it

Item all the side of the said chamber towards the garden wainscotted & Carved

Item a very faire Chymney piece carved and gilt knobbs

Item a faire mantle Treee with the Jambes of freestone very Curiouslie carved & gilt with the storye of the Creation

Item a waynscote dore with a Bolte leading into the withdrawing Chamber and a dore out of the with drawing Chamber into the Entrye leadinge to the Mens Chamber.

In the Great Beddchamber & withdrawing chamber

Item the same Chamber very faire wainscotted rounde about with a Portall with a springe locke & key & one smale bolte

Item the Mantle Tree of Freestone carved and a foot pace to the Chymney of blew Marble

Item a Portall dore out of the said Great chamber into the with drawing Chamber with lock and key & latch to it.

Item the said with drawinge chamber wainscoted rounde about with a dore to the south of Fyve and Two samle wrought bolts to the said doore

Item a waynscote dore in the said house of offyce with a Latch and a Bolte to it

In the chamber next the said great bedchamber

Item the said Chamber waynscotted rounde about with a Portall dore of wainscote and a springe lock & key and wrought bolte to the said dore and a back to the Chymney and a foote pace of paynted Tyles.

In the paynted Chamber

Item a Wainscote Portall Doore with a spring locke & key and a foote pace to the Chymney with paynted Tiles.

In the Gallerye

Item Two settles & Backe of Wainscote at the ends of the said Gallerye and a backe for the Chymney And paynted Tiles for a foote pace to the same Chymney.

Item Two doores of wainscote & glasse to go into the platt formes of the Gallerye and ij other smale portalles at the Est end of the said gallerye with Latches to them and wyndowes of Boordes to goe into the gutters

In the skreene Roome

Item a Settle at the end thereof & iiij racks of wood to lay pikes and halberds on, And a waynscote portall dore to the same.

In the Chamber & compting house over the butterye

a Back for a chymney a Table in the Compting house covered with Buckerom and viij shelves in the same.

Item a wainscote dore with a springe lock & key to the said chamber and a doore with locke & key to the Comptinge howse.

In the Mens chamber

Item a dore to the said Chamber with a locke & key and ij doores to the howses of office with out latche & a foote pace with paynted Tyles to the Chymney and a Case of boors for the Jack weight

Item a dore to the Chamber over the Mens chamber with a locke & key.

Item a dore to the Leades with a bolte and a frame of Rayles fower square with posts and turned pillers of the Inner courte

Item another halfe square of rails over the outward Courte with

postes & Turned pillers and a Benche with Two Irons at the end of the Leades.

Item fower walkes about the said Railes platformed with Leade with stepps of leade

Item a Comptinge house at the end of the Lower gallerye shelved rounde about with iij shelves & a stronge doble doore to it with a spring locke & a key & a wainscote particon before the saide Comptinge howse with a dore & a latche to the same.

In the Chamber over the old parlor

Item a wainscote dore with a spring lock & key to it and ij flatt bolts uppon plates and an Iron barr behinde the saide doore

Item all the said Chamber wainscotted rounde about with a portall dore and latche towards the Compting howse and a doore with a latche & ij flatt bolts towards the streete chamber and a skreene shelf with ij Irons

Item a back of Iron to the Chymney & a foote pace with painted tiles

In the Compting house

Item a strong double doore with a double plate locke & key to it

Item a Table Covered with greene and shelves round about the said compting house

Item a doore into the house of offyce there with a lock & key a latche & a bolte to the same.

In the streete chamber

Item iij Cupbords of wainscote in the Entrye with iij locks & j key to the same iij Cupbords.

Item the said Chamber wainscotted round with a dore cominge in at with lock & key

Item one faire presse of wainscote to laye plate in having v bottoms & iiij Inner doores with 3 [sic] strong locks screwed on, with ij keys & 4 [sic] flatt bots upon plates to the said Inner Dores

Item ij outward doores of wainscote with ij locks & a key to them.

Item one other fair presse of waynscote for Lynnen having v bottoms & ij drawers in it & vj dores with v locks & keys And ij bolts uppon plates & ij Catches to the said presse.

Item an other presse of waynscote for apparell with ij bottoms & ij Racks with pyns to hang apparell on.

Item a dore to a litle compting house with a lock & key to it and vj shelves in the said Compting howse.

Item a wainscote dore goeing into the Maides chamber

In the ij Chambers for the maydes

Item 4 [sic] doores with out spring lock one stock locke & iij bolts and a staye to goe downe the stayres

Item stayes to goe downe ye stayres out of the lower gallery to the old parlor.

In the Lobby

Item one dore going out of ye hall with a handle & ij great flat bolts uppon plates

Item a dore into the back yard with ij great flatt bolts uppon plates & a Ringe of Iron to the same.

Item a dore into the garde with ij great round bolts uppon plates

Item the same Lobbye paved all with purbeckstones

In the Upper warehouse

Item a particon of deale boords at the East end of the Inner warehouse with a dore & lock & key to it and within the particon ij broad shelves to laye goods on; & without the same particon one broad shelve with returne And a narrower shelf to laye Comodyties on.

Item a Trapp dore with ij leaves into the lower warehouse & a wheele a wynche & a rope to drawe upp goods with all

Item a doore with locke & key goeing into the outward warehouse

Item betweene the said doore & the wyndowes towards the garden one broad grounde shelf of deale backed with deales on either side of the said warehouse

Item a nest of vi smale boxes and ij falling wyndowes of wood

Item in the outward warehouse a working roome for a Tailor with a broad table to worke on & a smale frame under it & ij shelves therein & a dore with a lock & key to it

Item an other litle roome with ij shelves & a dore with lock & key to it

Item iij falling wodden wyndoes & a dore with one bolte at the stayer hedd goind out of the said warehouse

Item in the Entrye going into ye yard ij frames to hang bucketts on

In the Lower Warehouses

Item iij dores with locke & keys & a dore with ij leaves & a hinge iij shelves in the outward warehouse & ij hookes of Iron to hang beams on.

In the Washouse.

Item a Furnace with a copper & tabred with leade & ij shelves in the same & a Cock of brasse & pipe of Leade to bring ye Thames water in.

Item a dore with lock and key to it & the said washouse paved with purbeck stones.

Item a long Cesterne of Leade with a particon and a washer in it.

In the Stable.

Item a dore with a woodden latche and a locke & key & a Racke & a Maynger & iij postes & iij barres & a Racke to hang Sadles on & ij falling wyndoes

In the heylofte.

Item a doore with locke & key to it and a doore to the streete with ij bolts to take in haye & a Pulley over the said doore

Item iij doores locks & keys to the iij roomes over the heylofte

Item Frames & particons to keepe pygeons in ye garrett over ye said iij chambers

In the Backe yard.

Item a Crosse barre to the backe gate with locke & key with a wickett in it & a locke & key & ij great flatt boltes to the said wickett

Item a Bell with a Frame & a doore with a latche & a Lattice over it into the pryvie house & a particon of deale boords & a Lattice over it to the said pryvie house

Item a Cocke of brasse & a pipe of Leade to convey water from the pumpe in the garden to the said backe yarde

Item xvj doores to the Cellers with locks & j key & a particon grated in ye Celler under ye Buttrye

Item pipes of Leade to convey the Thames water into the kitchin & skullery yard & pipes of Leade to bring the Rayne water from the Topp of the house into the Yards And all the wyndowes of the said house soiled with Leade

Item the Clothes all about the said house . . .

Manor of Portpole

94 ● 95 ●

Putepolestrate

Lyverelane

Holborn Bars

108 ● 107 ●

102 ● Holeburnstrete 106 ●

103 ● 104 ●

105 ●

Garden

Bishop of Chichester's Garden

Conyerslane

St Andrew Holborn

Holborn Bridge

151 ●

152 ● Garden

Newstrate

Shollond

Field of the Blackfriars

Fleet River

Fickett's Field

47 ●

76 ●

81 ●

Fletestrete

82 ●

St Dunstan in the West

Ch. Yd.

Gate

83 ●

Temple Bar

St Clement Danes

La Straunde

77 ●

To Savoy Palace

78 ●

Quarters of Prior & Chaplains

New Temple (Knights Templars)

Cokarelane

Carmelite Friary

(Whitefriars)

79 ●

183 ●

Fleet Bridge

Fletestrete

80 ●

St Bride

37 ●

36 ●

Venella S. Bride

Bridewell Palace

Lay Brothers' Hall

Orchard

c 1270

c 1520

Line of Waterfront

Fleet River (Tidal)

Templars' Mill

Barbican

Black Friars

Baynard's Castle (Disused)

Gate

R   I   V   E   R

T   H   A   M

St John's Gate

Cow Bridge

Fagswell Brook

City

West Smithfield Bars

Goldnelane

Chikenelane

Chikenelane

189 ●

Cowelane

Cockeslane

187 ●

Wendegoselane

88 ●

St Sepulchre

Lymebrennerslane

Snore Hylle

Sacolelane

Smalebriggelane

Sacolelane

Sacolelane

76 ●

143 ●

Smalelane

Fleet Prison

La Baillie

Newgate

Gaol

185 ●

11 ●

Ludgate

St Martin

Lutgatestra

38 ●

St A Castle

Tamisestrete

Wharf

Watergate

KEY

● site known

○ site uncertain

——— extent of Great Fire 1666

- - - precinct boundary

0 ————————— 220 yds

0 ————————— 250 m

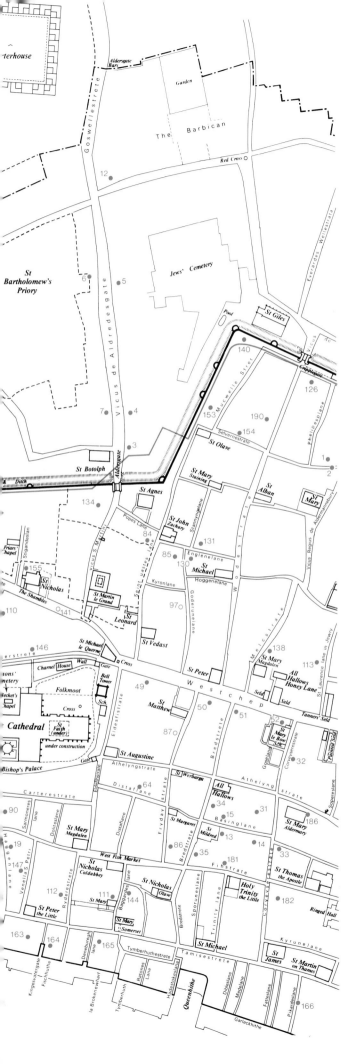

Map 1   The western half of the City of London, showing the gazetteer sites

Maps 1 and 2 use the base-maps of the Historic Towns Atlas for the City of London (Lobel 1989), which is gratefully acknowledged. The base-map shows the City around 1270. To this have been added certain significant buildings constructed in later years up to about 1600 (e.g. Leadenhall, Bridewell Palace, the Royal Exchange); and the line of the later waterfront. The sites in the gazetteer are shown in red. The streets in Maps 3 (the Strand) and 4 (Southwark) are based on John Rocque's 'Plan of the Cities of London and Westminster', surveyed 1739–46 and published in 1747. All the maps are at the scale of 1:5000.

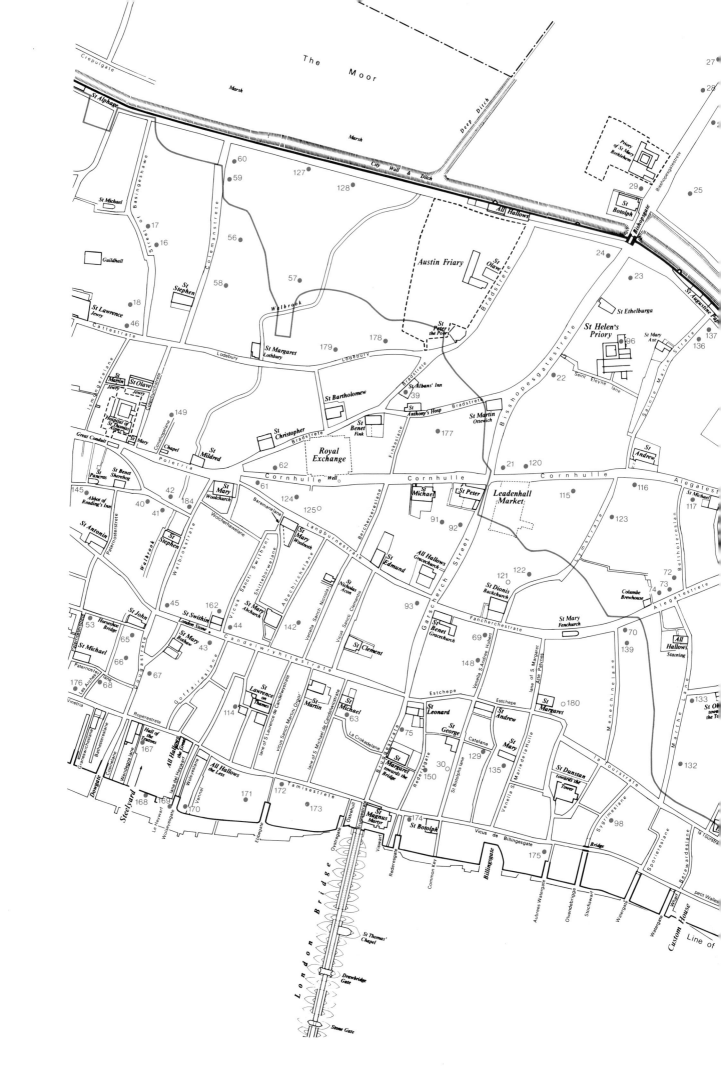

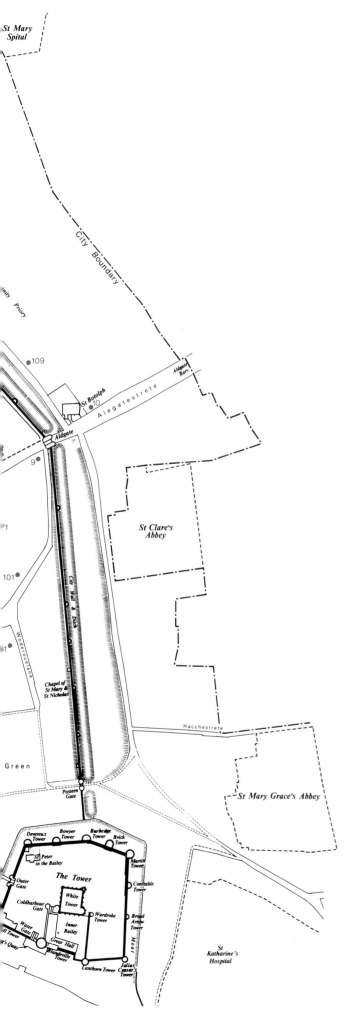

Map 2 The eastern half of the City of London, showing the gazetteer sites. For details of its composition, see note under Map 1.

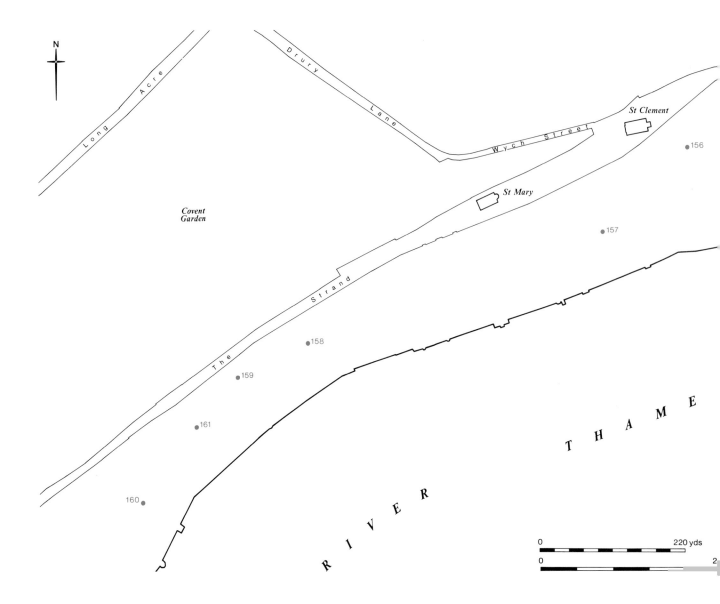

Map 3   The Strand area west of the City, showing the gazetteer sites. For details of its composition, see note under Map 1.

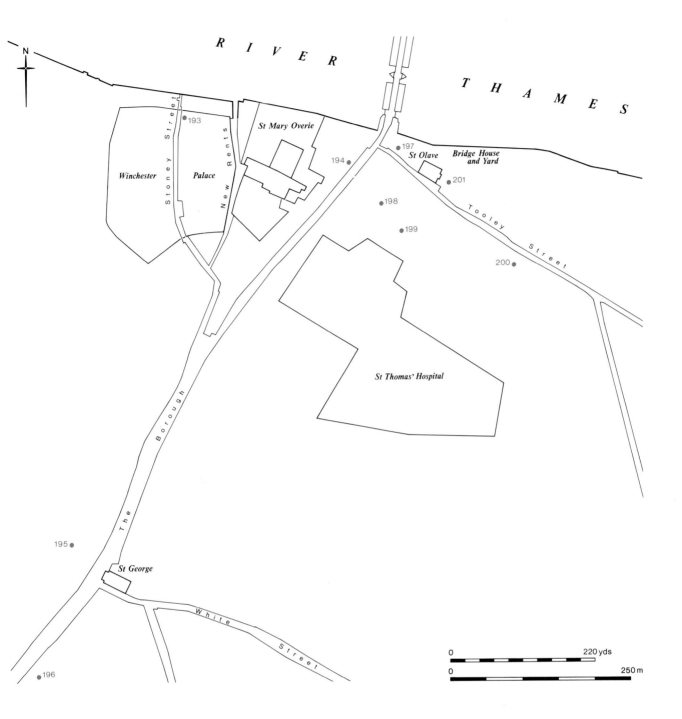

R I V E R

T H A M E S

Winchester

Stoney Street

●193

New Rents

Palace

St Mary Overie

194 ●

●197

St Olave

Bridge House
and Yard

● 201

●198

●199

Tooley

Street

200 ●

St Thomas' Hospital

The

Borough

195 ●

St George

White

Street

●196

0   220 yds

0   250 m

Map 4   Southwark, showing the gazetteer sites. For details of its composition, see note under Map 1.

Notes to Chapters 1 to 6

CHAPTER 1

1. For detailed descriptions of surviving medieval and Tudor buildings, see RCHM, *West London* (1925); *City* (1929); *East London* (1930); Godfrey 1964; Pevsner, *London 1* (1957, rev. Cherry 1973), *London 2* (1952, repr. 1969); cf. *Building of London* (1984), 6–7. Buildings in the Tower are not included in the present gazetteer: see RCHM, *East London*, 93–5; Hewett 1980, 186–8, 217; Salzman, *Building*, 579–80.
2. Barron, *Guildhall*; Marsden 1981.
3. The 500 buildings dating from the sixteenth and seventeenth centuries in present-day Norwich are thought to represent the residences of only the most affluent 5–10 per cent of the city's population (Priestley & Corfield 1982, 94 and n. 5).
4. Wilson 1976.
5. RCHM, *West London*, 53–7; *City*, 147–56; Hewett 1980.
6. RCHM, *West London*, 79–81, 85–6.
7. For summaries of recent archaeological work in the city, see Grimes 1968; Hobley & Schofield 1977; Schofield & Dyson 1980; Dyson & Schofield 1981, 1984; Schofield 1993; DUA *Archive Catalogue*. A detailed bibliography of reports on excavations, particularly since 1973, can be found in Schofield 1987.
8. Schofield 1981, 24–31.
9. E.g. Tatton-Brown 1974, 1975; Milne & Milne 1982.
10. For house fittings, see Egan, in preparation. The moulded stones from secular undercrofts encountered on archaeological excavations are the subject of archive reports (see DUA, *Archive Catalogue*, *passim*).
11. For examples and descriptions of the approach, see T. Dyson, 'Documentary Survey' in Milne & Milne 1982, 4–9; Harding 1980, 1985; Carlin 1985; *HG, i* (1986); Keene 1987.
12. *Sources for Property Holding*, 12–36.
13. *Sources for Property Holding*, 12. Apart from the Clothworkers', the records of the Carpenters' Company (*RCC*, i–vi), the Drapers (*Drapers' Recs.*, i–ii) and the Mercers (*Mercers' Acts*) have been found useful.
14. Reddaway & Walker 1975, 182–4.
15. The first recorded perambulation of their estate by the Carpenters' Company to view the need for repairs, which were notified to the tenants, was June 1558, though the next recorded view was not until 1567 (*RCC*, iii, 64, 94). Thereafter views were regular, almost annual occurrences (*ibid.*, 107, 119, 144, 161). The records of other companies show a similar pattern.
16. Schofield, *London Surveys of Ralph Treswell* (*LSRT*).
17. *LSRT* describes the majority of the City estate of Christ's Hospital in 1607–12, though there were probably some further properties not surveyed by Treswell and therefore not in *LSRT* (records in GL).
18. *Sources for Property Holding*, 37–112; Honeybourne, 'Value'.
19. For monastic cartularies, see Davis 1958; for an impression of the extent of religious property-holding by 1392, see *Church in London*; for the picture in 1548, *London and Middlesex Chantry Certificate*. For St Paul's, the main printed sources have been HMC, *Ninth Report* and *Early Charters of St Paul's*; other cartularies used include *Chertsey Abbey Cartularies*; *SMC Cartulary*; *HTA Cartulary*; *SBH Cartulary*; *Westminster Abbey Charters*.
20. *Sources for Property Holding*, 113–43.
21. Basing, *Fraternity Register*.
22. These are mainly printed in Salzman, *Building*; see also Tatchell 1962.
23. The main printed indexes used have been those of the Court of Husting (*Cal. Wills*; 1258 onwards), the Prerogative Court of Canterbury (*PCC*; 1558–1603), the Consistory Court of London (*Cons. Court Wills*; 1492–1547) and the Commissary Court of London (*Comm. Court*; 1374–1570). Cf. *Sources for Property Holding*, 219.
24. For the inventories used here, see Chapter 5, n. 227.
25. *Sources for Property Holding*, 168–92.
26. For one published wardrobe account of the household of Bogo de Clare in 1275–6, see p. 35 and notes there cited.
27. *Sources for Property Holding*, 8–11; Christianson, 1987, 3–5. For a description of the estate in the early fourteenth century, *Cal. LB, C*, 237–9.
28. Jones & Smith 1950; *Sources for Property Holding*, 1–11.
29. *Assize of Nuisance*, ix–xi.
30. Dated about 1480–3 (Payne 1987, 12).
31. Reproduced in 1881–2 as Publication 1 of the London Topographical Society. For the dating of the panorama and Wyngaerde's career, see Howgego 1978, 5–10, and *King's Works iv (Part II)*, 9.
32. Reproduced in Prockter & Taylor 1979; the relations of the copperplate, woodcut and Braun and Hogenberg maps are discussed in the introduction by J. Fisher, v–vii.
33. London Topographical Society, Publication 77, 1944; *Building of London*, Fig. 107; for Norden, Hurstfield & Skelton 1965; for Visscher, Howgego 1978, 8–9; London Topographical Society, Publication 4, 1909.
34. Howgego 1978, 8; reproduced as London Topographical Society, Publication 19 (1906–7) and again as Publication 112 (1970). The sketches and Hollar's techniques are discussed in Orrell 1983; for Hollar's career, see Hind 1922; Adams 1983, 8, 13–17.
35. Howgego 1978, 4–5; this was engraved for G. Vertue's *Vetusta Monumenta* (1787) (Adams 1983, 88).
36. E.g. four fifteenth-century plans discussed by Harvey (1952, 1–8); four sixteenth-century plans of Southwark (Carlin 1990).
37. *LSRT*. The Treswell plans have been redrawn to uniform scales for the present study, and individual tenancies numbered within the sites. *LSRT* contains photographs of the original plans and details of the named tenants.
38. Stow, i, 38; 138–9.
39. Sneyd, *Relation*, 45; for other examples, Malfatti 1953; Groos 1981; Barron, Coleman & Gobbi 1983.
40. Strype's edition of Stow in 1720 includes plates engraved by J. Kup (e.g. of Charterhouse and Grocers' Hall). All the surviving pre-Fire parish churches of London were engraved by West and Thoms in 1736.
41. Adams 1983, 153–4.
42. *Ibid.*, 78–9, 153, 158–9, 162–8.

CHAPTER 2

1. Marsden 1980; Perring 1991.
2. Kingsford, *LTR*, x, 122; *Cal. Plea & Mem. R.*, 1413–37, 125–6.
3. *Eyre 1276*, 56–7.
4. *Memorials*, 43–4; 25.
5. *HTA Cartulary*, 729 (1170–97); *SBH Cartulary*, 867, 876 (1213–14 and 1338); *Cal. Wills*, i, 218 (1310–11); ii, 269 (1388).
6. *Memorials*, 23 (1288); *Assize of Nuisance*, 15–16, 198–200, 382–3.
7. *Cal. LB, I*, 137–8; and see **66**. For an earlier injunction of 1337 see Stow, i, 27.
8. Stow, i, 14, 27.
9. *Cal. EMCR*, 113; for archaeological observations, Lambert 1921, 94–109.
10. E.g. *Cal. Plea & Mem. R.*, 1414–37, 117 (1421). For a medieval arch carrying a Walbrook tributary under the wall, see Maloney 1990, 80–1.
11. Stow, ii, 76–7.
12. Stow, i, 12.
13. E.g. a detailed inquisition on the Fleet in 1356: *Memorials* 280, *Cal. LB, G*, 50.
14. Williams, *Early Holborn*, i, 231.
15. *Chronicles*, 258.
16. CCPR, Fleet Ditch, 1566, 1574, 1585, 1587; *Repertory*, 21, ff. 201–2, 319ᵛ–320ᵛ.
17. Stow, i, 13.
18. Strype 1720, i, 228–9.
19. Williams, *Early Holborn*, i, 388, 610.
20. *Ibid.*, 674 (1470).
21. E.g. Thompson *et al.* 1984, 18.
22. Keene 1975. Domestic properties are recorded outside most of London's gates by the early twelfth century; excavation (MoL, sitecode ALG84) has indicated eleventh-century occupation outside Aldersgate.

23. E.g. *Eyre 1244*, inquest into purprestures, 1246, nos. 350–1, 470; *Cal. Wills*, ii, 164–5 (Holborn, 1374); cf. *Winchester Studies*, i, 434.

24. *Ekwall, Street-names*, 114.

25. Potters are found in eastern parishes of the City, both inside and outside the walls, in the period 1270–1330. In 1270–87 seven can be traced, owning property in the parishes of St Katherine Cree (*HTA Cartulary*, 36, 40, 48; *Cal. Wills*, i, 50) and St Andrew Undershaft (*HTA Cartulary*, 810, 813, 1290, 1300), and by 1300 others are found outside the walls in the parish of St Botolph Aldgate (*ibid.*, 905, 909, 915, 917, 955). The term *ollarius* is also used of a bell-founder, and it is clear that some of these 'potters' were (also?) bell-founders, e.g. Peter de Weston (*ibid.*, 36, 40) who made a bell still hanging in the church at Kingsbury, Middlesex.

26. Tanners in Seacoal Lane and near the Fleet *c*. 1180, *SBH Cartulary*, 163–5. The will of William de Hadham, tanner, in 1308 mentions his tenement in *Sekollane* and his brasier, with all his utensils of wood, silver and iron, and bundles of skins (*Cal. Wills*, i, 199). Tanners also operated in Southwark (Johnson 1969, 37).

27. Honeybourne, 'Fleet', 54–5; Williams, *Early Holborn*, i, 57; *Cal. Plea & Mem. R. 1413–37*, 125–6.

28. *Cal. LB, L*, 149; *SBH Cartulary*, 599; Appendix I, 111.

29. VCH, *Surrey ii*, 249–50.

30. Honeybourne, 'Fleet', 55–6. *Cal. Wills*, ii, 192, 374–5; *Memorials*, xvi, n. 7.

31. *Cal. Close R. 1369–74*, 31–2, 177–8; *ibid.*, *1377–81*, 363–4; *ibid.*, *1389–92*, 409–10, 521, 567.

32. McDonnell 1978, 15, 40–1.

33. *HTA Cartulary*, 871, 975–6.

34. *Survey of London: Bankside*, 94–5.

35. Honeybourne, 'Fleet', 45–7, 52 and n. 5.

36. *Early Charters of St Paul's*, 323–4; Salzman, *Building*, 270.

37. *Cal. EMCR*, 152, 155; *Cal. LB, A*, 2.

38. *Cal. Close R. 1346–9*, 236; Thrupp, *Merchant Class*, 121; Salzman, *Building*, 467–8; Carlin, 'Southwark', 378–80.

39. Unwin 1980, 239; shown in the Pepysian collection woodcut panorama (*Building of London*, Fig. 107) and in later views of the bridge.

40. Williams, *Early Holborn*, i, 647.

41. Cipolla 1981, 171; *Memorials*, 401; *Liber Cust.*, i, 128–9; *Cal. LB, C*, 52–3; *Cal. LB, D*, 239–40.

42. Rosser 1989, 45.

43. Stow, i, 10.

44. *Cal. Plea & Mem. R. 1381–1412*, 56. For studies of the city's defences in the medieval period, see Bell, Cottrill & Spon 1936, 39–70; Grimes 1968, 71–9.

45. *Coggeshall, Chronicon*, 171.

46. *Cal. Pat. R. 1232–47*, 22.

47. Grimes 1968, 81 and Fig. 19; Westman 1987.

48. *Cal. Pat. R. 1272–81*, 252; *Cal. Chart. R. 1257–1300*, 211.

49. GL Print Room, Photographs 373/8; *Archaeologia*, 63 (1912), 304; *MoL Archive Catalogue*, 154 (sitecode NBS84). The bricks are in MoL, Acc. Nos. 11456–7.

50. Stow, i, 10; Lambert 1921, 94–109 and Fig. 14.

51. In 1492–4 the company paid Guy Herendon, freemason, £10 for their part in the work (*Skinners' Recs.*, 151).

52. Grimes 1968, 82–3; and at Duke's Place, near Aldgate, in an excavation of 1977 (Maloney & Harding 1979; MoL, sitecode DUK77).

53. *Cal. Plea & Mem. R. 1413–37*, 130 (1422).

54. Stow, i, 19–20.

55. For excavations of the ditch, see Grimes 1968, 78–90; Marsden 1970, 6–9; Maloney & Harding 1979.

56. *Assize of Nuisance*, xxviii–xxix; *Cal. LB, K*, 188. This was stated as a law in 1435; *Cal. Plea & Mem. R. 1381–1412*, 163, n. 2.

57. *MoL Archive Catalogue*, 138 (sitecode LUD82); cf. *Liber Cust.*, ii, 454–5.

58. CCPR, Aldersgate, 1553.

59. For efforts to keep the ditch clear, see CCPR, Bishopsgate Without, 1568; Cripplegate Without, 1576, 1578; CCPR, Leases, 1588. An overall survey of the defences was made in 1578 (CCPR, Aldgate, 1569; CCPR, Bevis Marks, 1569; Repertory, 19, f. 320ᵛ (1578)) and again in 1666 by William Leybourn, whose drawn Survey (CLRO) includes outlines of all the gates as they then stood (several after rebuildings of the early seventeeth century; this is the source of Fig. 4).

60. These three gates all first appear in Ethelred's fourth law-code, attributed by Liebermann to *c*. 1000, but perhaps closer in date to the time of Edward the Confessor. I am grateful to Tony Dyson for this note.

61. *HTA Cartulary*, xiv, 4; RCHM, *Roman London*, 97; Marsden 1969, 20–6.

62. Stow, i, 29; Lethaby 1900; *Cal. LB, K*, 98; Marsden 1969; CLRO, Comptroller's City Lands Plan, 160.

63. *Memorials*, 57, 127; Stow, i, 32. CCPR, Bishopsgate, 1559, 1577.

64. Strype 1720, i, 17; Pennant 1813, 362. A drawing of 1688 in the Pepysian collection at Magdalene College, Cambridge, shows the north side of the gate, with a single statue of a bishop over a fifteenth-century arch (Pepys Drawings, 86a).

65. Stow, i, 33–4, and ii, 275; *Cal. LB, E*, 304; City Lands Plan Book (CLRO), i, 55.

66. *Cal. LB, F*, 15; Harben, *Dictionary*, 7; RCHM, *Roman London*, 98.

67. Norman 1904, 132–6; RCHM, *Roman London*, 98–9; *Cal. LB, I*, 49–50; *Cal. LB, K*, 19, 39, 49, 119; Imray 1968, 8–9. Repairs are recorded in 1448, 1455, and 1462: Journal 5, 3ᵛ, 47ᵛ, 260ᵛ; Journal 6, 62ᵛ, 87ᵛ.

68. Stow, i, 38; *Chamber Accts.*, xv, xix, 201.

69. Stow, i, 36–40; Marsden 1970, 8–9.

70. Leases for Aldersgate, Aldgate, Bishopsgate, Cripplegate, Ludgate (before its conversion into a prison), the Tower postern and the gate to Guildhall in the period 1374–1591: *Memorials*, CCPR, *Letter-Books*, *passim*.

71. The gate (or tower) partly fell down into the Tower ditch in 1440 (Stow, i, 28). For excavation on the site preceding its present display, Whipp (in preparation). A plan of the north tower of the Tower Postern in the eighteenth century is in CLRO, City Lands Plan Book, i, 32.

72. *Cal. LB, I*, 137; *Memorials*, 614–16; Stow, i, 32–3; ii, 274; RCHM, *Roman London*, 97.

73. Maloney & Harding 1979; *HTA Cartulary*, 12.

74. CCPR, Christ Church within Newgate, 1552; dimensions given, CCPR, Christ's Hospital, 1591. The north side is shown in one of the 1617 St Bartholomew Hospital plans (London Topographical Society, Publication 87, 1953–4).

75. RCHM, *Roman London*, 99–104; Merrifield 1965, 111–13; Marsden 1980, 171–4; Egan & Maloney 1985.

76. RCHM, *Roman London*, 104–6; Merrifield 1965, 323–5 and references therein. Norman and Early English carved stones were used in the building of B16, on the east side of King Edward Street (*ibid.*, 324); twelfth- or thirteenth-century pottery was found below B11A, discovered in 1965 (Grimes 1968, 71–8).

77. Stow, i, 9.

78. CLRO, Liber Horn, f. 183; Strype 1720, i, 62.

79. *Cal. Pat. R. 1232–47*, 106–7.

80. *Memorials*, 56, 115.

81. CCPR, All Hallows London Wall, 1499; and cf. *Cal. LB, E*, 49.

82. E.g. CCPR, Northumberland Inn, 1552; Aldgate, 1578; Duke's Place, 1579, 1580; Aldgate, 1583.

83. Williams, *Early Holborn*, i, 9; Page 1923, 178–9. For the Bars at Canterbury (the earliest mentioned in 1149), Urry 1967, 196–7.

84. CCPR, Temple Bar, 1554, 1584; Hilton-Price 1896. As this suggestion is made in the present study, the site is not included as a domestic structure in the gazetteer.

85. Dyson 1978; Robertson, *Laws*, 71.

86. *Early Charters of St Paul's*, 189; Honeybourne, 'Fleet', 41–4.

87. The dimensions are derived from the general conclusion arising from several recent archaeological excavations that the line of the quay shown on Ogilby and Morgan's map in 1677 shows approximately the pre-Fire line.

88. RCHM, *East London*, 74–95. For suggestions as to the sites of Baynard's Castle I and Montfichet's Tower, see *Building of London*, 39–40; Lobel 1989, 59–62.

89. *King's Works*, iv, 50–2; Gadd & Dyson 1981.

90. (St Paul's) Dugdale 1658, Longman 1873, Penrose 1879, 381–92, Cook 1955; (St Mary Overie) RCHM, *East London*, 58–66; (Holy Trinity Aldgate) Lethaby 1900, and work in progress by the author and R. Lea (MoL, sitecodes HTP79, LEA84); (St Bartholomew's Priory) RCHM, *City*, 123–7, Webb 1922; (Inner and Middle Temple) *Gentleman's Magazine*, Part i, 1783, 284–5, Godfrey 1953; (St John Clerkenwell) Clapham & Godfrey 1913, 165–78; (St Helen Bishopsgate) Wilkinson, *Londina Illustrata*, i, engs. 24–30, RCHM, *City*, 19–24; (hospitals) Clapham 1911–15, Honeybourne 1963–7.

91. For building at the friaries see [Blackfriars – first site] *Cal. Close R. 1231–4*, 214, *1234–7*, 457; (second site) Clapham 1912 and Norman 1916, both modified by recent excavations (MoL, sitecodes APO81, LBY86), RCHM, *City*, 114–15; (Greyfriars) *Archaeologia*, 63 (1912), 274–6, the plan of 1617 in the archives of St Bartholomew's Hospital (reproduced by London Topographical Society, Publication 88, 1955), Johnson 1974, Herbert 1980; (Whitefriars) Clapham 1910, Martin 1927; (Austin Friars) Cater 1912 and 1915, RCHM, *City*, 32–4, Grimes 1968, 124–5; (Crutched Friars) Povah 1894, 291, *HTA Cartulary*, 165, CCPR, Crutched Friars, 1516, 1536; (Charterhouse) **48** in present gazetteer.

92. *Sources for Property Holding*, xvii–xix.

93. For parish churches surviving in 1929, RCHM, *City*. For excavations of

church sites, Grimes 1968, 182–209; Marsden 1968, 14–16; Thompson 1979.

94. The best summary of the water system is Stow, i, 12–19. For Fleet Prison, see a forthcoming monograph based on excavations of 1988–90, McCann in preparation. For market buildings, see note 109 below.

95. Dyson 1975.

96. For the architecture of the bridge, see Knight 1831, 1834; Home 1931; *Medieval Archaeology*, 12 (1968), 184; Christianson 1987, 1–13. The earliest reference to the Bridge House is in 1280 (Jones 1953, 60). For an inventory of the stores of building materials at Bridge House in 1350, see *Memorials*, 261–2.

97. This account of Guildhall is based upon Barron, *Guildhall*; Wilson 1976 and Marsden 1981.

98. Barron, *Guildhall*, Plate 28.

99. *Cal. LB, L*, 45–8; Stow, i, 160.

100. Samuel 1989.

101. For arcaded squares in bastide towns, see Beresford 1988, 33–4; Lauret *et al.* 1988. For famines, Dyer 1989, 267–8.

102. *Cal. LB, L*, 45–8.

103. *Eyre 1244*, 108; *Liber Cust.*, i, 46, 47; *Cal. LB, C*, 15; *Cal. LB, E*, 103; Stow, ii, 6–11. A new quay is mentioned in 1357 (*Cal. LB, G*, 97). For the *Romeland*, see *Cal. Wills*, i, 122 (1311), *Cal. LB, G*, 221 (1367–8), Journal 15, 256ᵛ (1545). For the rebuilding of 1525, see Stow, ii, 10. Rebuilding of the quay wall took place in 1560–1 (Repertory, 14, 331, 332b, 511); Lyon's 'new house' or Garner was rebuilt by 1566, when the City decided that meal, wheat and other grain coming from the west by water were to be sold there (Repertory, 16, 133, 184; Repertory, 21, 472ᵛ). A building called the Market House is mentioned in 1573 (Repertory, 19, 331, 498; cf. Repertory, 22, 198ᵛ) and its post-Fire position at the north-east corner of Queenhithe shown in a plan of 1686 of property belonging to the Fishmongers' Company (Fishmongers' Company, Plan Book). This seems to be a different building from the Garner.

104. CCPR, Billingsgate *Romeland*, 1523, 1525, 1544, 1549, 1583; Journal 15, 256b (1545); Mills & Oliver, *Survey*, iv, 190ᵛ. For Haseley, see Barron, 'Government of London', 226, n. 2.

105. Stow, i, 135; Tatton-Brown 1974; 1975. *Cal. LB, E*, 211.

106. *Liber Albus*, 241; *Cal. Pat. R. 1258–1266*, 77; Norman 1909; Harben, *Dictionary*, 549–50.

107. Parker 1971, 114.

108. Burgon 1839, ii, 118–19; Girouard 1985, 140–1, Figs. 115–16. Gresham also used van Paesschen to design a large house for himself in Broad Street, later Gresham College; this was of brick, with a colonnade of white marble columns inserted in 1601.

109. For medieval and Tudor markets, see also Masters 1974; Archer *et al.* 1988.

110. Pope's house at Bermondsey is the best recorded of these houses, through the drawings and watercolours of J. C. Buckler: in several repositories, notably the Guildhall Library Print Room.

111. Keene 1985, 6.

112. Hoskins 1953.

113. Bowden 1967, 628–9.

114. Keene 1985, 20.

115. Keene 1989; the figures for 1560 from Finlay & Shearer 1986, 42, Table 2.

116. Finlay & Shearer 1986, 42.

117. Keene 1985, 20.

118. Holt 1985 (repr. 1990), 142–3.

CHAPTER 3

1. The most recent summaries of work on Saxon London are Brooke & Keir 1975, 83–184; Dyson & Schofield 1984; Vince 1990; 1991.

2. The following paragraphs are based on two archaeological reports: Horsman *et al.* 1988 on the Bridgehead-Eastcheap area, and Schofield *et al.* 1990 on the streets around Cheapside.

3. Dyson 1978.

4. Miller 1977; Horsman *et al.* 1988.

5. Horsman *et al.* 1988, 13–20.

6. L. Miller, Miles Lane Archive Report, Group 124 (MoL, sitecode ILA79).

7. Horsman *et al.* 1988, Fig. 5.

8. Northampton: Williams 1979, 140–1; Lincoln: Perring 1981, Fig. 34.

9. Williams 1979, 143; Perring 1981, Fig. 34; Durham: Carver 1979, 71.

10. Long, narrow plots are recorded in the mid tenth century at Coppergate, York; but at Exeter, where blocks were perhaps laid out in the tenth century, the plots were of uniform length, but not necessarily uniform width (Allan *et al.* 1984, 402). For Lübeck, see Hammel 1986.

11. Sawyer 1968, No. 208; Birch 1893, No. 1288. Dyson & Schofield (1984, 306–8) suggest that *Staeningahaga* may be the site of the properties of the forty burgesses of Staines recorded in London in Domesday.

12. Brooke & Keir 1975, 155–7; *Eyre 1321*, lvi–lvii.

13. Schofield *et al.* 1990.

14. Platt & Coleman-Smith 1975, 83–5, 233, Fig. 68; RCHM, *Stamford*, 129, Plate 58.

15. The Warenne building could also be a first-floor stone hall; stone manor houses and first-floor halls of the twelfth century (e.g. Boothby Pagnell) are reviewed by Barley (1986, 108–13).

16. Corner 1860; Carlin, 'Southwark', 275–7; Vogts 1930, 489–90; Buttner & Meissner 1983, 28, Fig. 2; Wood 1965, 8–9.

17. Crummy 1981, 53–70; Winchester Studies i, 346.

18. *SMC Cartulary*, 6, 200, 229–30, 254; *HTA Cartulary*, 122, 485; Harvey, *Early Medieval Architects*, 161.

19. Macleod 1990.

20. Richardson 1960, 2.

21. Lipman 1967, 65.

22. Several Jews were occupying houses in Milk Street in 1236–7: *Cal. Close R., 1234–7*, 213, 263, 298, 418, 462. A synagogue lay in Coleman Street (Stow, ii, 334).

23. Harben, *Dictionary*, 321.

24. Crummy 1981, Fig. 53; Stephenson 1984–5.

25. Urry 1965, Maps 2/5 and 2/6.

26. Ayers 1987, 172–4. For the locations of stone houses in King's Lynn and their relations to the expanding waterfront, see most recently Clarke 1981, 132–3 and Figs. 120–1.

27. Cologne: Vogts 1930, 509; Regensburg: Strobel 1976; Prague: Buttner & Meissner 1983, 26–8.

28. *Liber Albus*, 284.

29. Discussed in *Assize of Nuisance*, ix.

30. *Liber Cust.*, i, 86–8. Although the custumal of John's reign headed *Lex de Assissa* cannot be later than 1216 and may be of the late twelfth century, the *Assisa de Edificiis* (also known as the *Assize*) in its earliest surviving form has no such indications of early date, and can only be dated to before the last quarter of the thirteenth century, when it probably gave its name to the collection in which it appears, *Liber de Antiquis Legibus* (*Assize of Nuisance*, ix–xi). Since the *Lex de Assissa* describes nearly all the regu-lations in the *Assize*, they are taken here to represent a body of regulation probably in existence by 1200 (I am grateful for advice from W. Kellaway on this point). The rules of 1212 about roofing are to be found only in *Liber Cust.*, i, 86–8.

31. *HG*, i, St Mary le Bow, sites **19/21**, Fig. 10; sites **31, 138**.

32. Faulkner 1975, 125–7.

33. Armitage *et al.* 1981.

34. Schofield, *LSRT*.

35. On the Archbishop's holding, Johnson 1969, 22–4. Other early houses in the City were the Inns of the abbot of Peterborough, Carter Lane (before 1210: Honeybourne, 'Value', 388), and of the abbot of Colchester, Mincing Lane (about 1230: Kingsford, *LTR*, x, 93–4).

36. *Eyre 1244*, 353. A further Inn, not in the gazetteer, was that of the Bishop of Chester (the diocese of Lichfield and Coventry; Kingsford, *LTR*, x, 87–8). It became part of the site of Somerset House.

37. For the Inn of the abbot of Faversham, see *Eyre 1244*, 353; Dyson 1981, 13–17; Honeybourne, 'Fleet', 44, 73–4.

38. Harvey, *Early Medieval Architects*, 45–6; but this is only a possibility, based on the similarity between St Etheldreda's and St Stephen's.

39. The London steward of the Bishop of Chichester, however, had to sell some horses because *grave et onerosum est sustentare equos Londoniae* (Shirley 1862, 497).

40. Giuseppi 1920; the site of the wardrobe has been suggested by Keene (1987, 10).

41. Stow, ii, 15; *Viewers Certificates*, 185.

42. Curnow 1978, 59. This suite includes an elaborate tiled floor, fireplace, large window with seats and garderobe.

43. Wood 1965, 22, 96–9.

44. For these inns, see Honeybourne, *Richard II*, 40–1; Kingsford, *LTR*, xii, 21–2; x, 68–9.

45. Alexander & Binksi 1987, 335; for episcopal palaces elsewhere, Wood 1965, *passim*; Barley 1986, 58–64.

46. RCHM, *West London*, 79–86.

47. Colvin 1983, 129–30.

48. Bony 1979, 20–1; Colvin 1983, 136.

49. D. Keene has drawn attention to the similarity between the first market hall in London, built about 1274 at the Stocks, and called the *Halles*, after its counterpart in Paris (lecture, 1987; and *HG*, iii, site **118/17**). In the late

50. For the house of the English merchants at Bruges, Devliegher 1975, 376.
51. Bond 1840, 207–326.
52. *Ibid.*, 261.
53. *Ibid.*, 240. *Literae Cantuarienses*, i, 285, 311, 379, 403; Salzman, *English Trade*, 107.
54. For the Tabard, Kingsford, *LTR*, xii, 38; for Colchester Inn, *ibid.*, x, 93–4.
55. *King's Works*, i, 122.
56. *Ibid.*; for comment see Harvey, *Early Medieval Architects*, 74, 210.
57. Blunt 1969; Whinney 1984, 4–11.
58. Harvey, *Early Medieval Architects*, 64–5; for the Bridewell range, see Gadd & Dyson 1981; *Building of London*, Fig. 111.
59. Another possibility is a house designed and built for James Yarford, alderman, about 1520 by Humphrey Coke and Nicholas Revell (Harvey, *Early Medieval Architects*, 64); the site of this house is not known.
60. Webb 1921, ii, 76–9.
61. The Apothecaries acquired the former Guest House of the Blackfriars in 1632 (Wall *et al.* 1963, 61–3). Other cases in Stow, i, 246–7; ii, 15.
62. Stow, i, 163.
63. Stow, i, 133; Dekker's *Jests to make you merry*, quoted in Brett-James 1935, 36.
64. BM, Lansdowne MS 78, f. 67; quoted by Brett-James 1935, 37.
65. Stow, ii, 193.
66. *Sources for Property Holding*, 533.
67. BL Harley MS 541.
68. Stow, ii, 190–2.
69. *Memorials*, 346 (1370).
70. Fletchers, Fruiterers, Glaziers and Plumbers (**136**; Stow, i, 242; 248).
71. Stow, i, 297.
72. Williams, *Early Holborn*, i, 10.
73. For excavated examples of town-houses of the religious in York, see Hall *et al.* 1988, 52–4; in medieval Edinburgh, Schofield 1975–6.
74. HR 62(52); 165(25).
75. Tony Dyson, in Steedman *et al.* 1992.
76. *Cal. Wills*, i, 109; *Assize of Nuisance*, 396, 577.
77. Houses forming frontages in Wood Street are mentioned in 1202, but their plan is not known (*HTA Cartulary*, 663).
78. For houses of 'Wealden' form in the immediate periphery of London cf. Old Cottage, Cowley Road, Cowley, Middlesex (late fifteenth to sixteenth century: RCHM, *Middlesex*, 11, Plate 29); 1–4 Tudor Cottages, Foots Cray, Kent (Airs 1983, 107); Old Rectory House, Northfleet, Kent (Newman, *Kent*, 439); a house in Church Street, Chiswick, appears to be of Wealden form (RCHM, *Middlesex*, 9, Plate 27). There are several surviving examples in Hertfordshire, and they may have been present in Hertford itself (Pevsner, *Herts*, 364–5, 373; Munby 1977, 177). For Wealdens in other towns, cf. houses in Hertford and Hitchin (Smith 1992, 148–9); 13–23 Upper Lake, Battle, a row of nine forming a rent of Battle Abbey, *c.* 1468 (Martin & Martin 1987, 16–17); 3 Church Street, Canterbury, fifteenth to early sixteenth century (Pantin 1963, 212–13); and 55 Spon Street, Coventry, fifteenth century (*ibid.*, 216). The example at 49–51 Goodramgate, York, is a hall range at right angles behind a street frontage, a configuration possible in London streets (RCHM, *York*, v, 138–40).
79. Rigold 1963, 353.
80. Mercer 1975, 60–1; Hewett 1980, 225–6; Quiney 1984.
81. Biddle 1967, 264–5.
82. *LSRT*, 155.
83. Clark 1983, 5: as a rough analogy, in a sample of Canterbury drinking houses of 1560–1640, alehouses had a mean number of 4.8 principal rooms, taverns 10.0, and inns 14.0 (*ibid.*, 64). For these building-types at Westminster, see Rosser 1989, 122–33.
84. Thrupp, *Merchant Class*, 42.
85. *Memorials*, 386–7.
86. *Fraternity Register*, 53–4, 101, 121. For contents of other brewhouses, see *Cal. LB, L*, 232 (in parish of St Mary Somerset, 1486); Weinstein 1985, 20; for a brewhouse within the former mansion of the Bigods at Brokenwharf, Thames Street (**165**), in 1582, GLRO, Charterhouse Estate Muniments, Acc. 1876, F4/11. St Paul's brewhouse is mentioned in 1182–98 (*SBH Cartulary*, 584).
87. *Cal. Plea & Mem. 1413–37*, 252; *1437–57*, 83; *Mercers Acts*, 396, 423.
88. Thrupp, *Merchant Class*, 42; Clark 1983, 11; *Cal. LB, H*, 12. In at least one case, beer (*cervisia*) could also be bought at a tavern: *Select Cases of Trespass*, 171 (1386).

89. Cf. *Memorials*, 409 (1377). Subterranean taverns are noted at the Mermaid, Carfax, Oxford, by 1333 (Salter 1926, 155–6).
90. **194**; and the Sun at Westminster (*LSRT*, 142–3).
91. *London Topography*, 239 (originally in *Gentleman's Magazine*, 1788, Part ii, 581–3). This inventory also gives much detail of the well-stocked cellar and of the variety of pewter in the kitchen.
92. Consitt 1933, 280–1; Welch 1902, i, 48, 53.
93. E.g. the churchwardens of St Michael Cornhill: *St M C Accts.*, 16, 19, 93; the churchwardens of St Mary at Hill: *Recs. SMH*, 70, 179, 203, 230, 274.
94. Power 1978, 177.
95. CCPR, Hosier Lane, 1596, Fenchurch St, 1596.
96. *Cal. LB, C*, 84.
97. *Cal. Plea & Mem. R. 1381–1412*, 79.
98. *Comm. Court 1374–1488*, 57, 107–8, 116, 122, 127.
99. *Cal. Plea & Mem. R. 1323–64*, 220–1.
100. *Ibid.*, *1364–81*, 260.
101. *Ibid.*, *1381–1412*, 172–4.
102. *Assize of Nuisance*, 521 (1364); *Cal. Plea & Mem. R. 1413–37*, 123; *1364–81*, 203.
103. Cf. the George Inn, Rochester (undercroft of *c.* 1320: Newman, *Kent*, 494); Golden Lion, Romford (fifteenth century); Golden Fleece, South Weald (fifteenth century: Pevsner, *Essex*, 361); White Hart, Brentwood (late fifteenth century; Pevsner, *Essex*, 102); Woolpack Inn, Coggeshall (second half of sixteenth century: Hewett 1969, 145–8).
104. *Description of London*, 504.
105. Salzman, *Building*, 418–19.
106. Keene 1985, 12–13.
107. Imray 1968, 16–20.
108. E.g. *Cal. Wills*, i, 618; *Assize of Nuisance*, 632.
109. *Possessory Assizes*, 13–14, 18, 60.
110. *Cal. Wills*, i, xl–xli; *ibid.*, ii, 176, 203–4; *Possessory Assizes*, 41, 60; cf. *Liber Albus*, 339.
111. *SBH Cartulary*, 157–8 (1432–56).
112. For examples over a short period, 1578–89, see *Inq. PM*, iii, 8, 66, 83, 149–50.
113. E.g. Stow, i, 166.
114. Brett-James 1935, 67–8.
115. *Ibid.*, 69.
116. *Ibid.*, 70–8.
117. Known in Venice, for instance, in the fifteenth century and in Edinburgh in the sixteenth century (Schofield 1975–6).
118. *Recs. SMH*, 113.
119. Schofield *et al.* 1990.
120. Pantin 1963.
121. *Ibid.*, 203–28.
122. *Ibid.*, 228–39; Parker 1971, on King's Lynn.
123. Pantin 1947, 136–8.
124. For two-room houses in other towns, see Portman 1966, 5, 25–6 (Exeter); Carter 1977 (Norwich). A less compact form has a hall forming the back ground-floor room, rising through two storeys: e.g. 20 Jordan Well, Coventry (Pantin 1963, 220–1).
125. Parker 1971, 100–1; O'Neil 1953; Atkin 1985, 253.

CHAPTER 4

1. Winchester Studies i, 347; *HTA Cartulary*, 663, 761.
2. *Eyre 1244*, 451, 472.
3. E.g. Cologne: Vogts 1930, 575–6. For early mentions of gates on London houses, *Assize of Nuisance*, 36 (1302), 175 (1311).
4. *Cal. Wills*, i, 86; *Cal. Close R. 1419–22*, 182–3.
5. See **174**; *Cal. Wills*, ii, 252; Kingsford, *LTR*, x, 75 (1543).
6. Wood 1965, 155–65.
7. RCHM, *West London*, 22, 47; on the carpentry of the Charterhouse gate leaves, see Hewett 1980, 183.
8. Horsman *et al.* 1988, 89.
9. E.g. the Music House, Norwich (Wood 1965, 153).
10. E.g. *Eyre 1244*, 352, 407, 415, 427–8.
11. *HTA Cartulary*, 517.
12. *Cal. Plea & Mem. R. 1413–37*, 126–7.
13. Barron, *Guildhall*, 26–7.
14. HR, 121(30); *Cal. Plea & Mem. R. 1458–82*, 52; site **46**.
15. *Cal. EMCR*, xv; *SBH Cartulary*, Appendix I, 200; *Select Pleas of Trespass*, 82.
16. *PN Mddx*, 116; *Cal. Wills*, i, 394.
17. Suggested by Harben, *Dictionary*, 546.
18. Mercer 1975, 9; for fourteenth-century examples of aisled halls, see

Nurstead Court, Nurstead, Kent (Newman, *Kent*, 439–40); Baythorne Hall, Birdbrook, Essex (Hewett 1980, 140–1).

19. Barley 1986, 49.
20. *Ibid.*, 47. The earliest dated crown-post roof in the London area is at Headstone Manor House, Headstone, Middlesex, in 1344 (Airs 1983, 105).
21. For examples of early unaisled, timber-framed halls, see the guest house at Priory Place, Little Dunmow, Essex (late thirteenth century: Hewett 1980, 129–30); Wynter's Armourie, Magdalen Laver, Essex (*c.* 1290, *ibid.*, 110–11); Southchurch Hall, Southchurch, Essex (*c.* 1300: *ibid.*, 134); for discussion of the type, see Mercer 1975, 11–14.
22. RCHM, *York*, v, lxi.
23. Harvey, *Early Medieval Architects*, 208; Portman 1966, 73–4; Castle 1977, 7–9, 14, 17–18.
24. RCHM, *Stamford*, liv.
25. *SBH Cartulary*, 77; *HTA Cartulary*, 493. The term is found in twelfth-century Winchester: Winchester Studies i, 339. For general discussion see Wood 1965, 67–80.
26. *Eyre 1244*, 430, 469.
27. *Eyre 1276*, 54; *Assize of Nuisance*, 586.
28. *Cal. Wills*, i, 363; *Coroner's Rolls*, 60; *HTA Cartulary*, 441.
29. *Coroner's Rolls*, 60, and cf. 66, 102.
30. *Coroner's Rolls*, 4.
31. *Cal. Plea & Mem. R.*, *1374–81*, 155; *Cal. Wills*, ii, 30; cf. i, 363.
32. The term *soller* was used in sixteenth-century Essex to mean an upper room of any kind, including a loft (Emmison 1976, 3–4).
33. *Cal. Wills*, i, 332, 407; *Cal. Plea & Mem. R.*, *1364–81*, 154–6; *Assize of Nuisance*, 311.
34. *Piers the Plowman*, i, 292.
35. E.g. The Kaye, Cheapside, 1562 (Mercers' Company, First Register of Leases, 307); Sir John Trevor's house, Westminster, 1588 (*LSRT*, 148).
36. *LSRT*, 142–3.
37. *RCC*, ii, 139 (Carpenters); Parslow 1964, 97 (Founders).
38. And at the Inn of the abbot of Hyde, Southwark, where the abbot obtained a licence to hold a chapel in his house in 1307 (Corner 1864, 52).
39. RCHM, *West London*, 79–83.
40. Wood 1965, 227–46.
41. E.g. **175**; *HTA Cartulary*, 818; *Cal. EMCR*, 82; *Cal. Wills*, ii, 339, 621; Harvey 1987, 188; *Cal. LB, K*, 108. A comparable chapel has been recorded in Cologne (Vogts 1930, 569–71) and another of 1372 survives as part of the town museum in Ulm.
42. Hopkinson 1931, 42, 52.
43. *Cal. EMCR*, 82; Bridge Acct. Rolls 17/3/xxv; *Recs SMH*, 202. For Lady Colet, *Mercers' Acts*, 572; for Kytson, Gage 1822, 116–17. The Kytson house was on site **138**, but few details were recorded during the recent excavations there.
44. For examples see *Cal. Wills*, ii, 99, 103, 206; for portable altars which were consecrated by the bishop, Pendrill 1937, 226.
45. Wood 1965, 166–8.
46. Cf. the tower in Inner Temple, **78**.
47. Hewett 1980, 209; Wood 1965, 247–56; RCHM, *York: SW*, lxviii.
48. Newman, *Kent*, 456–7.
49. Faulkner 1975, 98.
50. *OED* definition, relating it to *lard*.
51. The word *dispensa* is used in an inventory of 1390; the contents imply it was a buttery (*Cal. Plea & Mem. R.*, *1381–1412*, 209–13). Pantry: Adams 1951, 19–20. Buttery: **141**, **40**; *RCC*, ii, 91; Dudley's house (**45**), with fittings.
52. *Cal. Plea & Mem. R.*, *1381–1412*, 209–13; *Recs. SMH*, 26; *Journal*, 7, 131.
53. *LSRT*, 148.
54. Beier & Finlay 1986, 20.
55. *Historical Gazetteer*, i, St Mary Colechurch parish, Figs. J–L; St Mary le Bow parish, Figs. J–K.
56. *Cal. Wills*, i, 51 (1280); i, 349, 406; Dyson 1974, 36–7, 63; *HTA Cartulary*, 111–12, which mentions three shops beneath a single solar on the south side of Fenchurch Street in 1305.
57. *Cal. Inq. PM*, i, 'Henry III', 897; *Cal. Wills*, i, 374–5.
58. RCHM, *York* v, 143–5; *Memorials*, 261.
59. Jones 1976, 73. Stalls, as opposed to shops, were generating rent for Holy Trinity by about 1215 (*HTA Cartulary*, 1011). The construction of stalls in the street, and of Middle Rows, has regrettably not been dealt with here.
60. *HG*, i, St Mary Colechurch parish, Figs. M–N; St Mary le Bow parish, Fig. M.
61. CCPR, St Peter Cornhill, 1570, where this depth is evidently a product of building in line with the porch of the church; CCPR, St Benet Gracechurch Street, 1581, 1582, where the buildings were to be 4 ft 2 in wide; CCPR, St

62. Jones 1976, 76–7. The stalls are shown in the drawing of Eastcheap in Hugh Alley's *Caveatt* (1598), f. 11 (Archer *et al.* 1988, 57).
63. Mercers' Company, First Register of Leases, 307.
64. Ramsay 1982, 42–3. The earliest recorded warehouse at Bruges is of 1574, a stand-alone structure end-on to the street, as big as a house: Devliegher 1975, 300–1, Fig. 445.
65. For instance at 58 French Street, Southampton (Platt & Coleman-Smith 1975, 107) and as recently restored.
66. *RCC*, iii, 146.
67. Holst 1986.
68. Platt & Coleman-Smith 1975, 79–112; Winchester Studies i, 339–40; Vogts 1930, 489–90, 509.
69. Kissan 1940, 57–69.
70. *Description of London*, 504; Stenton 1934, 28.
71. *Eyre 1244*, 413, 445, 447, 455, 474, 476. There were far more cases of illegal pentices, especially in Cheap (381–95).
72. E.g. **32**. This may however be for lack of examples, e.g. of vaulted cellars below medieval company halls.
73. *Westminster Abbey Charters*, 370; *Cal. EMCR*, 194; cf. *Cal. Plea & Mem. R. 1458–82*, 34–5.
74. Williams 1963, 50–1, 329–30; *HTA Cartulary*, 430.
75. Stow, i, 238.
76. E.g. *Cal. Wills*, ii, 63; *Memorials*, 342.
77. *Cal. Wills*, i, 478 (1340); the *Seler* underneath St Thomas Acon (*London English*, 190; cf. 184, 191). These are possibly references to taverns where ale was also sold.
78. CLRO, Bridge House Rental f. 671; *Cal. Fine R. 1405–13*, 236.
79. *Cal. Plea & Mem. R. 1413–37*, 126–9, 132, 136.
80. Devliegher 1975, 328; Parker 1971, 89; RCHM, *Middlesex*, 86.
81. GL, MS 7783.
82. E.g. CCPR, Laurence Lane, 1575.
83. Faulkner 1966; Platt & Coleman-Smith 1975; Heighway 1985; RCHM, *Stamford*; Urry 1967; Holst 1986.
84. Turner 1988.
85. Thornton 1978, 296. The term is frequently used and illustrated in Thorpe's *Book of Drawings* (drawings largely of 1596–1603).
86. *LSRT*, 149 (a house at Westminster, 1611).
87. Thornton 1978, 297.
88. Babelon 1977, 110–11.
89. *King's Works*, iv, 310, n. 3.
90. Thornton 1978, 306; cf. Thorpe, *Book of Drawings*, 65, a plan of a house probably built in 1607.
91. On books in medieval London houses, see e.g. Thrupp, *Merchant Class*, 161–2.
92. *LSRT*, 72, 70, 102, 96.
93. *Eyre 1244*, 78; MoL, sitecode SUN86; RCHM, *West London*, 30.
94. *Recs. SMH*, 85.
95. *MT Memorials*, 568 (1421–2); *Fraternity Register*, 121 (1443).
96. *Coroner's Rolls*, 2, 113; *Assize of Nuisance*, 632. In a contract of 1308 (**191**) *gradus* must mean a flight of steps rather than one step, as it is sometimes translated; cf. *Eyre 1244*, 78.
97. An example in timber of *c.* 1435 survives at the Lollard's Tower, Lambeth Palace (RCHM, *West London*, 81, 83).
98. E.g. Achtersikkel, Ghent (personal observation) and houses in Tours (Guillaume & Toulier 1983, 16–17).
99. E.g. Bridewell Palace, Dyson & Gadd 1981, Fig. 9; Lincoln's Inn, RCHM, *West London*, Plate 71; Charterhouse, *ibid.*, 23; Eastbury Manor, Barking (1571), *Survey of London: Eastbury*.
100. RCHM, *East London*, plan in rear pocket; Parker 1971, Fig. 20.
101. Schofield 1975–6, 187–90.
102. A two-storeyed example is found at Tickenham Court, Somerset, also in the fifteenth century (Wood 1965, 334).
103. Barley 1961, 141, quoting examples in Essex in 1615–42; Hewett 1973, 70–3, an example of the late sixteenth century similar to the house shown here in Figs. 93 and 169.
104. Dyson & Gadd 1981, Figs. 1, 12; Master's Court at Charterhouse (**48**), late sixteenth century, originally standing free at the outer corner of the court, and later incorporated into further building (RCHM, *West London*, 26).
105. Babelon 1977, 97–9; Thorpe, *Book of Drawings*, 51, Plate 13; Sint-Jorisstraat 71, Bruges of *c.* 1493 (Devliegher 1975, 355–6).
106. Portman 1966, 80 (a house of 1567).
107. E.g. in Paris (Babelon 1977, 104–5).
108. *Assize of Nuisance*, 31, 362–6.

109. E.g. Longleat (Wiltshire) rebuilt in the 1570s (Girouard 1983, 46–54).
110. E.g. Toulouse (Tollon 1983, 54, Plate 75); Cologne (Vogts 1930, 505–6) or Bruges (Devliegher 1975, 448, 452–3).
111. Stow, i, 133, 151–2.
112. *King's Works*, iv, 17–21.
113. Williams 1963, 119.
114. Home 1931, 85–6. In 1429 William Estfield obtained permission to build a gallery from his house to the east end of Guildhall (Barron, *Guildhall*, 48, n. 76).
115. CCPR, Tower Hill, 1533; a gallery across a façade is recorded at 227 High Street, Exeter, in the seventeenth century (Portman 1966, 34).
116. Pantin 1963, 460–5, 469; Portman 1966, 34; Parker 1971, 88.
117. Platt & Coleman-Smith 1975, 94–96 (Red Lion, High Street).
118. Schofield *et al.* 1990.
119. *HG*, i, St Mary Colechurch parish, sites **19–21**, Fig. 10.
120. *Assize of Nuisance*, 2, 69. A similar late thirteenth- or early fourteenth-century date is suggested for the introduction of stone cesspits in Southampton (Platt & Coleman-Smith 1975, 34, 206, 209–10, 238–9).
121. *Cal. Plea & Mem. R. 1414–37*, 118.
122. CLRO, Bridge House Acct. Rolls, 11/12/xlviii; *Cal. Plea & Mem. R. 1413–37*, 254–5. In the sixteenth century a pipe could be built outside a wall if it was in brick: *Viewers' Certificates*, 16 (1511).
123. *Coroner's Rolls*, 167–8 (1326).
124. *Assize of Nuisance*, 325 (1333).
125. E.g. also *Viewers' Certificates*, 16 (1511). The term 'stool room' is used for the privy in royal houses of the 1530s, e.g. *Kings Works*, iv, 14–15.
126. *Cal. Plea & Mem. R. 1413–37*, 254–5 (the parsonage of St Michael le Querne parish, 1413); *Viewers' Certificates*, 270 (1550).
127. E.g. at Bergerac (Dordogne); Grandchamp 1992, 118.
128. Dixon 1972, 9.
129. *Assize of Nuisance*, 214.
130. *Assize of Nuisance*, 383; *Cal. Plea & Mem. R. 1413–37*, 154 (1422); *Memorials*, 614–15. A privy over the Cowbridge stream near Smithfield is mentioned in 1250 (*SBH Cartulary*, 143).
131. *Memorials*, 478.
132. Godfrey 1942, 8. In the central parish of St Mary Wolchurch a privy was divided between two households in 1253–4 (*SBH Cartulary*, 467).
133. *Assize of Nuisance*, 165; cf. *Cal. Plea & Mem. R. 1458–82*, 36–7.
134. *Assize of Nuisance*, 325 (1333). This might have been a common privy in a yard.
135. *Cal. Plea & Mem. R. 1458–82*, 122; cf. 32, 36–7.
136. *Viewers' Certificates*, 170.
137. *Ibid.*, 209.
138. Outside London on a rural site, e.g. Old Soar, Plaxtol, Kent: Wood 1965, 380. The privy is found in this position in medieval houses in other towns, e.g. Church House, Crane Street, Salisbury (fifteenth-century): RCHM, *Salisbury*, 73–5.
139. *Assize of Nuisance*, 214.
140. Salzman, *Building*, 284–5; *Recs. SMH*, 210; *RCC*, ii, 25.
141. *RCC*, iii, 3; cf. also Salzman, *Building*, 284, vents over privies in 1450.
142. As in 1508–9 at the Gote in Cheap: *Drapers' Recs.*, i, 384.
143. *Letters & Papers*, IV, Part 3, 2766; *LSRT*, 148.
144. *Assize of Nuisance*, 617; *Eyre 1244*, 350–1, 470; *Assize of Nuisance*, 483, 547.
145. *Assize of Nuisance*, 251 (tanning); 298 and 488 ('le Tythyngwowes', a tenter-yard); for tenter-yards, see also *Assize of Nuisance*, 589 (apparently near a dye-house); *Possessory Assizes*, 72; *Cal. Wills*, ii, 554–5; *Memorials*, 35.
146. In 1431 a dyer's equipment at Haywharf, Thames Street, was left in the charge of a brewer (*Cal. Plea & Mem. R. 1413–37*, 252); in 1510 the Mercers leased the Katherine Wheel in Thames Street to a dyer, but in 1514 to a brewer (*Mercers' Acts*, 396, 423).
147. *Viewers' Certificates*, 85. For a plan, possibly incomplete, of a brewhouse, see **169**.
148. *Cal. Wills*, i, 196.
149. *Assize of Nuisance*, 569.
150. Thrupp, *Merchant Class*, 461.
151. First mentioned 1506 (Thrupp, *Merchant Class*, 10; cf. **33**).
152. *crinosa* = hairy; *Inq. PM*, 94.
153. For glass-making at Crutched Friars, see Sutton & Sewell 1980; for delftware production at Holy Trinity Priory Aldgate, MoL, sitecode HTP79.
154. Priestley & Corfield 1982, 112–13.
155. *Cal. Plea & Mem. R. 1413–37*, 252; *1437–57*, 83; *SBH Cartulary*, Appendix I, 92.
156. *Eyre 1244*, 418, **46**; *Assize of Nuisance*, 510; **123, 204, 266, 268**.

157. *Assize of Nuisance*, 585.
158. *Cal. Wills*, ii, 91. In Westminster in 1613 eight cows were tied up in a kitchen, with hay to feed them stored in upper rooms (Clark 1983, 113).
159. *Fraternity Register*, 54–5; *RCC*, ii, 92, 196; CCPR, Wood Street, 1553; *Inq. PM*, iii, 94; GL, MS 7783/47; *Possessory Assizes*, 273.
160. CCPR, Old Bailey, 1574.
161. *SBH Cartulary*, 69; *RCC*, ii, 108; **157**.
162. For St Paul's barns, see *Domesday of St Paul's*, 21–7, 33–8, 129–32, 136–9. A barn probably of the twelfth century survives at Grange Farm, Coggeshall (Hewett 1980, 47–9); barns of the thirteenth century at Cressing Temple, Essex (Hewett 1969, 63; 1980, 104–5); fourteenth century, at Manor Farm, Ruislip (RCHM, *Middlesex*, 107; Airs 1983, 104), Harmondsworth, Middlesex (RCHM, *Middlesex*, 61–2); fifteenth century, at Upminster Hall, Essex (Airs 1983, 105); and sixteenth century, on several farms in Middlesex (Pevsner, *Middlesex*, 45; RCHM, *Middlesex*, 56; Airs 1983, 105–6).
163. *Memorials*, 12; *Cal. Plea & Mem. R. 1381–1412*, 213; *London English*, 155–6.
164. On pigs and pigsties, see *Cal. LB, A*, 217; *Liber Albus*, i, 270; *Coroner's Rolls*, 57; *Assize of Nuisance*, 263, 332; *Cal. Plea & Mem. R. 1364–81*, 39.
165. *Possessory Assizes*, 96; *Assize of Nuisance*, 524.
166. *Assize of Nuisance*, 607; *London English*, 160–1. Keeping ducks inside a house was illegal: *Cal. Plea & Mem. R. 1413–37*, 119. Dovecotes are mentioned in 1259 (*Cal. Wills*, i, 5, without location), at Tower Hill in 1379 (*ibid.*, ii, 210), in the parish of St Giles Cripplegate in 1422 (*ibid.*, ii, 440), and in the parish of St Botolph Bishopsgate in 1448 (*Cal. Close R. 1447–54*, 75).
167. *Viewers' Certificates*, 55 (1523); *Assize of Nuisance*, 64 (1304); *Memorials*, 7 (1276) respectively.
168. *Assize of Nuisance*, 188 (1313); Williams, *Early Holborn*, i, 423, quoting the cost of hedging the garden at Ely Place in 1372–3; the quickset hedges are mentioned in a lease of 1492 for a property north of Holborn (*ibid.*, 613). Thorns were used to hedge a garden at Tower Hill in 1493–4 (*Recs. SMH*, 202).
169. *Assize of Nuisance*, 66, 70, 519.
170. *HTA Cartulary*, 961 (1140–6).
171. Carlin, 'Southwark', 276.
172. E.g. the Bishop of Ely's garden and the Earl of Lincoln's garden, both in Holborn (Cecil 1910, 25–6, 34–5).
173. Platt 1976, 94–5; Brimblecombe 1987.
174. E.g. the garden of St Anthony's Hospital, Threadneedle Street (1432) (Graham 1932, 4); Grocers' Hall, **149**; Carpenters' Hall, **128**; Pewterers' Hall, **121**.
175. *RCC*, ii, 69.
176. *King's Works*, iv, 138; RCHM, *London II: West London*, 67.
177. Stow, ii, 78, 370.
178. *LSRT*, 48–9.
179. *King's Works*, iv, 315.
180. *Cal. Plea & Mem. R. 1381–1412*, 291–2.
181. Stow, i, 104; *ibid.*, ii, 77; musketeers are shown at practice in this area on the copperplate map of *c.* 1558.
182. *Comm. Court*, 207. In his history of medieval gardens, Harvey prints a manuscript illustration of *c.* 1465 showing a sports garden with archery and an open-fronted summerhouse, adding 'such places of entertainment were widely spread over the Continent by the fifteenth century and there were doubtless some in England' (1981, 49, Fig. 25).
183. *Inq. PM*, ii, 60–1. Sir Thomas Wyatt had a tennis court within the walls of the dissolved church of the Crutched Friars, according to Stow (i, 140).
184. Welch 1902, i, 71.
185. *RCC*, ii, 22–3.
186. Stow, ii, 294, 368.
187. Williams, *Early Holborn*, i, 683.

CHAPTER 5

1. On Mapilton, see Harvey *Early Medieval Architects*, 194–6.
2. For examples, see Smith 1958; Wood 1965, 35–49; Barley 1986, 46–7; Fletcher & Spokes 1964. Examples in the immediate region date from 1344 (Airs 1983, 107). In towns, fifteenth-century examples survive at Kingston upon Thames and Romford (Essex).
3. The roof at Penshurst Place, Kent, the country seat of John Pultney, incorporates crown-posts, in this case perhaps designed by the king's carpenter, William Hurley (Wood 1965, 308; Harvey, *Early Medieval Architects*, 155, though documentary evidence is lacking).
4. Airs 1983, 105.

5. Hewett 1980, 217.
6. Salzman, *Building*, 553.
7. RCHM, *York v: The Central Area*, lxix.
8. At Pilgrim's Hall (Wood 1965, 324).
9. The Law Library, originally a courtyard house (Portman 1966, 9–11).
10. RCHM, *West London*, 53–4, 58–9; Hewett 1980, 220, 314.
11. Metcalf 1977, 31.
12. CCPR, St Katherine Creechurch, 1588.
13. Welch 1902, i, 82.
14. *King's Works, i*, 124, 506; *Building Accts. Henry III*, 325; Salzman, *Building*, 228–9.
15. Harvey 1975, 153.
16. Graham 1932, 2.
17. Taylor 1972, 331.
18. The St Paul's shingles (above, note 15) cost 18*s.* the thousand with carriage; in the late fifteenth century tiles were generally 5*s.* 5*d.* the thousand without carriage.
19. E.g. *Assize of Nuisance*, 325 (1333).
20. Horsman *et al.* 1988, 107.
21. *Memorials*, 46–7 (1302); *Cal. Plea & Mem. R. 1364–81*, 237; *1413–37*, 125 (1422).
22. Jones 1953, 63–4; CLRO, Bridge House Rental, 1460–84, transcr., 692 (willow used for binding reeds in thatching houses at Lewisham, 1474).
23. Armitage *et al.* 1981. Work by I. Betts (e.g. in Schofield *et al.* 1990) suggests rather that peg-tiles may have been introduced just before 1200, ousting the other forms.
24. Urry 1967, 192–4; Platt & Coleman-Smith 1975, 24.
25. Chapelot & Fossier 1985, 318–19.
26. The Italian stone houses of the eleventh and twelfth centuries cited as parallels for Romanesque houses in London in Chapter 3 also have low-pitched roofs.
27. E.g. *SMC Cartulary*, 226 (1216/23); *SBH Cartulary*, 143 (*c.* 1250).
28. Hearths made of stacked rooftiles are found on several sites, e.g. **171–2, 174**; site reports in MoL archives.
29. *Cal. LB, A*, 218.
30. Salzman, *Building*, 229–30; *Memorials*, 308–9.
31. E.g. *Recs. SMH*, 82, 85, 102, 137; *RCC*, ii, 17, 128, 186.
32. *Cal. LB, L*, 77; Salzman, *Building*, 230; Celoria & West 1967.
33. Whitechapel, in the reign of Henry VII; Stepney (Brick Lane), 1549–50 (McDonnell 1978, 113–14).
34. See Chapter 2 above, n. 30.
35. Salzman, *Building*, 230.
36. *Ibid*.
37. Platt & Coleman-Smith 1975, 25. Slate from the west was in use in Sussex from the thirteenth century (Holden 1965).
38. Rhodes in Milne & Milne 1982, 90.
49. Harvey 1975, 131.
40. *MT Memorials*, 566; Barron, *Guildhall*, 33.
41. Stow, i, 125.
42. *Drapers' Recs.*, i, 304.
43. Salzman, *Building*, 231; *Building Accts. Henry III*, 375 ('curved tiles').
44. Pearce *et al.* 1985, 47; information on recent work on ridge tiles from I. Betts.
45. E.g. *RCC*, ii, 34, 171, 236.
46. Pearce *et al.* 1985, 48–50, Figs. 78–9. The latter date is when examples were discarded, and does not necessarily (as with all archaeological artefacts) indicate the date-range of production.
47. See for example the churches on the copperplate map of *c.* 1559.
48. Home 1930, 202.
49. Taylor 1972, 378.
50. Dawson 1976, 101; Salzman, *Building*, 265.
51. Hopkinson 1931, 26–7. The Merchant Taylors were slightly misinformed, as Somerset House (1547–52) had extensive lead roofs. This reference also shows that slates were considered more worthy than tiles in the late sixteenth century.
52. For the type, see House 1 in Cuckoo Lane, Southampton, Platt & Coleman-Smith 1975, 86–90. Comparable stone houses of this period in Italy frequently had chambers lit by the doorway only (Andrews 1982, 8).
53. In the hall of Winchester Castle, 1222–35 (Wood 1965, Plate IVc).
54. As originally at Winchester; and at Stokesay Castle, Shropshire, *c.* 1240 (Lloyd 1931, 329).
55. Wood 1965, 352–8.
56. Harvey 1978, 105.
57. Lloyd 1931, 332.
58. Hewett 1980, 21–3.
59. Devliegher 1975, 132–3.

60. E.g. the Prior's Chamber, Prittlewell, Essex (Hewett 1969, 80, Fig. 29); lower down the social scale, the Old Sun Inn, Saffron Walden (Hewett 1980, Fig. 160).
61. Barron, *Guildhall*, Figs. 1–5.
62. Synards, Otham, Kent (Mercer 1975, 177); St John's Institute, Hackney, early sixteenth century (RCHM, *East London*, 45).
63. Hewett 1980, 217.
64. E.g. a window of 1580 at the Bedford Almshouses, Watford (Castle 1977, Fig. 18). Hewett (1980, 217) also gives a date of the 1580s for ovolo mouldings, but he is perhaps basing this on the Staple Inn frontage of 1586, which, as shown here (**122**), is restored and not demonstrably ancient. The overall statement is however probably true for London.
65. Cf. also a further Treswell survey of a house in Westminster in 1611, *LSRT*, 145–6.
66. The Arnolfini marriage painting of 1434 (National Gallery), painted in Bruges, shows a small guard-rail let into the sill. In this case the sides of the window-frame are in brick.
67. Here the date panel shown must be inaccurate as applied to the windows; which are themselves undated, but analogies elsewhere would suggest a date in the later sixteenth century.
68. *LSRT*, Plate 2.
69. The earliest arms in the glass at Barnard's Hall date from 1545, thus perhaps giving some indication of date. Pilasters between windows first appeared in London at Somerset House (Thorpe, *Book of Drawings*, Plate 41).
70. E.g. 46–47 High Street, Exeter: Portman 1966, 78–9.
71. As at Westminster in 1237–9 (Wood 1965, 117, no. 2; cf. Salzman, *Building*, 94–5).
72. At Penshurst Place, Kent (1341), the oriel at the dais incorporates the stair up to the main chamber, thus combining both functions (Lloyd 1931, 187, Fig. 80).
73. For a detailed description of this oriel, see Norman 1908, 59.
74. E.g. Stanton's Farm, Black Notley (Essex), *c.* 1340; Ockwells Manor, Bray (Berkshire), *c.* 1465 (Wood 1965, 117–18).
75. *London English*, 162–5.
76. For the semi-octagonal form and the bay window in the gable, in both cases rising through ground and first floor, Thorpe, *Book of Drawings*, Plate 44. A design for Sir Baptist Hicks, who also rebuilt site **50** in Cheapside itself in 1595.
77. Salzman, *Building*, 581; CCPR, Old Bailey, 1553.
78. Clerestories are noted at site **4** in 1623 (*LSRT*, 34); they are a feature of houses of around 1600 in other towns (e.g. King's Lynn).
79. Colvin 1966, 30–1, Plate 11.
80. 'A great carrall window' was made for the queen's dining chamber at the Tower in 1533 (Salzman, *Building*, 94).
81. CCPR, Clement's Lane, 1568; GL, MS 7783, No. 42. The location of the latter site is not known.
82. *Building of London*, 143, Fig. 117.
83. As at Paycocke's House, Coggeshall (Essex), of *c.* 1500.
84. Salzman, *Building*, 511, n. 5.
85. Horsman *et al.*, 91–3; window glass has also been found at eighth-century Hamwih (Southampton) and at the tenth-century Saxon palace of Old Windsor (Berkshire) (Harben 1961, 53–4).
86. Salzman, *Building*, 175.
87. Site **201**.
88. *Assize of Nuisance*, 255; Rhodes in Milne & Milne 1982, 90. Other pieces of cames and glass have been recovered from excavations at Swan Lane, the earliest dating from the late thirteenth century (MoL, sitecode SWA81).
89. *Assize of Nuisance*, 81.
90. Dawson 1976, 89–91; for Westminster: Lethaby 1925, 144–5.
91. Salzman, *Building*, 37, 181. For a history of the Glaziers, see Ashdown 1919.
92. Barron, *Guildhall*, 30–1; Merchant Taylors' Hall, where the *haut fenestre de vitre* was repaired in 1416–17 (Hopkinson 1931, 36); Carpenters' Hall in 1441–2 (*RCC*, ii, 11–12).
93. E.g. *Drapers' Recs.*, i, 344.
94. Welch 1902, i, 73–4, 87.
95. RCHM, *City*, 6–7, 159, 150 respectively. The King's Arms were placed in the great west window of Merchant Taylors' Hall in 1547–8, and the windows of the hall given benefactors' scutcheons in 1588/9 (Fry & Thomas 1934, 11, 13).
96. RCHM, *West London*, 49 and Plates 234–5.
97. Godfrey 1975, 10–13. A works was set up at Newgate by Anthony Becker and John Carré in 1567, but discontinued in 1580 (CCPR, Newgate, 1579, where Jacopo Verzelini, apparently using a separate glass-house, is mentioned): cf. Ashdown 1919, 12, 23.

98. In 1567 Carré obtained a licence to make glass in the Burgundy and Lorraine manner, and for this purpose introduced some Lorraine glass-makers into the Weald. There was a thriving glassmaking industry in the Weald by 1600 (Kenyon 1967, 120–42).
99. *Ibid.*
100. Fry & Thomas 1934, 111.
101. Godfrey 1975, 6–7.
102. *Assize of Nuisance*, 362.
103. Kingsford 1921, 46–7; Marks 1991, 165–6.
104. Ashdown 1919, 21–2.
105. Salzman, *Building*, 185.
106. *Recs. SMH*, 200; Pendrill 1937, 219–20.
107. *Cons. Court Wills*, 108; cf. *ibid.*, 88.
108. Barron, *Guildhall*, Plate 25d; *Assize of Nuisance*, 312.
109. *RCC*, ii, 187 (1508); GL, MS 7783, No. 18 (1595); cf. Salzman, *Building*, 186.
110. Lloyd 1931, 335.
111. *RCC*, iv, 12.
112. Thornton 1978, 81.
113. *Assize of Nuisance, passim.*
114. *Ibid.*, 261, 341.
115. *Ibid.*, 652.
116. *Viewers' Certificates*, 119.
117. CCPR, St Leonard, 1595.
118. *Assize of Nuisance*, 77, 234, 613; for invasion of privacy cases involving doors, *ibid.*, 163, 379, 492, 626.
119. Horsman *et al.* 1988, 89–91.
120. In the fifteenth-century porch, but also, presumably dating from *c.* 1280, smaller doorways in the western crypt (Barron, *Guildhall*, Plates 22 and 24).
121. *Recs. SMH*, 139 (1487–8).
122. *Letters & Papers*, iv, Part 2, 1454–7; Mercers' Company, First Register of Leases, 307.
123. Barron, *Guildhall*, 25. For domestic examples, *Cal. Plea & Mem. R*, 1364–81, 172; site **174**.
124. Salzman, *Building*, 146–7; Eames 1968, 1.
125. *London Museum Catalogue*, 233.
126. The Museum of London is preparing a corpus of medieval house fittings for publication in its *Medieval Finds from Excavations in London* series.
127. Price 1870, 31–6; Eames 1980, i, 27.
128. Eames 1980, i, 207. Westminster tiles are found at Lambeth Palace chapel, perhaps contemporary with the chapel of 1225–50 (Degnan & Seeley 1988).
129. *Ibid.*, 222–3.
130. Drury 1981, 133; Platt 1978, 121.
131. Curnow 1978, 60–1. Penn tiles were often specified in accounts of royal building works between 1344 and 1388 (Eames 1980, i, 222).
132. Dawson 1976, 104–5.
133. *London Museum Catalogue*, 237–8.
134. Drury 1981, 134; the tile is in the *London Museum Catalogue*, Fig. 82, no. 69.
135. *Fraternity Register*, 22. In 1532/44 John Bude, tilemaker, of Wyllwyege in Kent brought 700 of great paving tiles 18 in square and 700 small, 7 in square (Godfrey 1947, 113).
136. Salzman, *Building*, 99, where 'white tiles of Flanders' are mentioned; are these the same as small white-yellow bricks found on London sites? Henry Yevele supplied 7,000 Flanders tiles to pave the courtyards of Westminster Palace in 1365 (Harvey, *Early Medieval Architects*, 359).
137. *Cal. LB, B*, 115.
138. Clode, *MT Memorials*, 508; *London English*, 154.
139. Drury 1981, 130.
140. Salzman, *Building*, 146.
141. *King's Works*, iv, 104–5. For post-Fire use of Flemish tiles, see archive report on Seal House, Thames Street (**172**) excavations in MoL archives.
142. *Cal. Wills*, i, 511.
143. Keene in Schofield *et al.* 1990, 99 (a floor taken from a first-floor chamber in Bow Lane, 1387); *Assize of Nuisance*, 646 (1405).
144. E.g. at Seal House (**172**); and at Kennington Palace (Dawson 1976, 28), both fourteenth-century examples.
145. Horsman *et al.* 1988, 85.
146. Rushes: used at Brewers' Hall, 1425 (Unwin 1908, 195); Carpenters' Hall on Feast Days, e.g. in 1477 and 1491 (*RCC*, ii, 52, 91; cf. ii, 131); rushes on tiles, at Bakers' Hall (Thrupp 1933, 164). Rushes were still being used in the great parlour of Grocers' Hall in 1631 (Heath 1869, 13).
147. Horsman *et al.* 1988, 97.
148. The waster tiles were sold in quantity for the purpose: for example, four

149. baskets for the hearth of the Falcon brewery, Aldersgate Street, in 1438–9 (**9**; *Fraternity Register*, 72).
149. Seal House (**172**) excavation archive report, MoL archives.
150. Following *OED*, a *louver* or *femerell* (cf. *fumariolum*) was originally for the passage of smoke, but by the sixteenth century was a timber construction principally to aid ventilation.
151. Dunning 1961, 83–4.
152. Pearce *et al.* 1985, 50–1, Figs. 80–1.
153. A similar period of 1250–1425 is suggested at Leicester (Allin in Mellor & Pearce 1981, 63).
154. Salzman, *Building*, 100. For the lane, see *Cal. LB, B*, 267 (1283); *Cal. Wills*, i, 66 (1291); *ibid.*, i, 101 (1349).
155. Pearce *et al.* 1985, 5–6.
156. The Louver or femerell for the hall roof was made in 1448 (Reddaway & Walker 1975, 134).
157. Barron, *Guildhall*, 32.
158. *Recs. SMH*, 201.
159. The regulations were copied into the fifteenth-century *Liber Albus*, 288. For the use of plaster of Paris in flues in 1317, see site **11** (Lovell's Inn).
160. *London English*, 154.
161. Airs 1983, 107–9. A smoke-bay was formed when an open hall was partly floored over, leaving the ground-floor hearth a space which rose through both storeys.
162. E.g. *Assize of Nuisance*, 77 (1305), 447 (1355), 629 (1383), 655 (1423); *Viewers' Certificates*, 10 (1509), 81 (1529).
163. *Cal. Plea & Mem. R. 1413–37*, 139 (Trig Lane, 1421); *ibid.*, 157 (Chancery Lane, 1421).
164. Williams, *Early Holborn*, i, 31.
165. Such chimneys were also widespread in Norwich by the end of the fifteenth century: Atkin 1985, 253.
166. Blakiston 1960, 51–5.
167. For examples, the houses in the street range in front of Carpenters' Hall (**128**), 1477 (*RCC*, ii, 52); a house next to Blacksmiths' Hall (**112**), 1496–8 (Adams 1951, 24).
168. Wood 1965, Plate xlii.
169. Harvey 1986, 40–1.
170. Some of the Charterhouse examples may also be early instances of corner fireplaces.
171. *Cal. Plea & Mem. R. 1364–81*, 165; *Cal. LB, L*, 85.
172. *Cal. Wills*, i, 346.
173. *Cal. Plea & Mem. R. 1364–81*, 155.
174. *LSRT*, 148. In the seventeenth century bronze andirons came principally from Flanders (Thornton 1978, 261); whether Flemish examples might have been imported into London at an earlier date is not yet known.
175. For the fire back of 1487, Geddes 1991, 181. A fine group survive in Hastings Museum (Baines 1958). Common by the seventeenth century, fire backs were decorated in relief with coats of arms, cyphers or mythological figures (Thornton 1978, 260).
176. Horsman *et al.* 1988, 98–9.
177. *HTP Cartulary*, 195; CLRO, Bridge House Acct. Rolls, 11/8/xx; Drapers' *Recs.*, i, 331.
178. At Eltham in 1403 (Salzman, *Building*, 98).
179. Cf. ovens at Westminster Abbey (Black 1976, 150 and Fig. 10).
180. Stow, ii, 22.
181. Donkin 1976, 109.
182. Page 1923, 272.
183. *Cal. LB, A*, 218. In 1307 the king ordered that kilns in Southwark were to use charcoal or brushwood and not sea-coal because of the smoke produced (*Cal. Close R. 1307–13*, 537).
184. *Cal. LB, E*, 65–6.
185. *London English*, 188.
186. Trevelyan 1952, 48. Brimblecombe (1982, 18–19) argues, on the contrary, that coal was more available than wood for artisans in the thirteenth century.
187. *Assize of Nuisance*, 16, 55, 60, 183, 199, 312, 524.
188. *Cal. EMCR*, 34. The atmosphere at night tends to be more stable than during the day.
189. Brimblecombe 1982, 19.
190. Salzman, *Building*, 273–5; for the conduits, Harben, *Dictionary*, 166–8. Part of a new conduit at Aldersgate is shown in one of Treswell's plans in 1610 (**4**). It is not clear what is meant by Fitzstephen's (probably hyperbolic) statement that London had 'sewers and acqueducts in its streets' in the 1170s (*Description of London*, 506).
191. Repertory, 17, 307, 375; *Remembrancia*, 500–1. For a summary of the city's water-supply in 1600, see Brett-James 1935, 53–6.
192. *Cal. LB, B*, 276–7.

193. For examples of recently excavated wells see Schofield *et al.* 1990, 171–3.
194. *Cal. LB, B*, 270; *Recs. SMH*, 28–9.
195. Cf. *Assize of Nuisance*, 219.
196. *Memorials*, 575.
197. *Assize of Nuisance*, 633.
198. *Drapers' Recs.*, i, 337; a cistern in a house is mentioned in 1333, apparently in a courtyard (*Assize of Nuisance*, 318).
199. Welch 1902, i, 159, 167; Parsloe 1964, 155.
200. Gutters of timber or lead are frequently described or recommended in the rolls of the *Assize of Nuisance*. Shaped ceramic tiles which probably functioned as valley gutters have been found on excavations (Armitage *et al.* 1981). A stone gutter on a property belonging to the Fraternity of the Holy Trinity, Aldersgate, is mentioned in 1432–3 (*Fraternity Register*, 126), and stone gutters were probably common on buildings of distinction.
201. *Assize of Nuisance*, 351 (39, citing deed of 1269–70).
202. *Ibid.*, 370.
203. *Ibid.*, 20; see also note 207.
204. For the type, see the buildings of Henry VIII's reign at Westminster, in Colvin 1966, Plate 11; for small (possibly sixteenth-century) houses in Southwark, *Building of London*, vi. For spouts at rear of houses, *Assize of Nuisance*, 424 (1350).
205. *Assize of Nuisance*, 283; *Cal. Plea & Mem. R. 1437–57*, 151.
206. Downpipes are shown at Oatlands, Surrey, by Wyngaerde in 1559 (*Kings Works*, iv, Plate 17).
207. *Assize of Nuisance*, 222, 277, 572, 584.
208. Cf. CCPR, Wood St, 1590.
209. British Fine Art Commission Summer Exhibition 1939; photograph from Courtauld Institute, B39/1640.
210. For buildings in the area around London, including Colchester, Coggeshall and Lambeth (Hewett 1980, 280–1 and Figs. 293–303). Moulded joists and beams are found in fifteenth-century houses in Exeter, usually in the principal ground-floor room if there was no hall (Portman 1966, 12).
211. *Survey of London: Crosby Place*, 52–3. A similar, perhaps even more ornate, roof (as opposed to a false ceiling) of the later fifteenth century survives at Weare Gifford, Devon (Wood 1965, Plate xlviiib).
212. E.g. 4 Watchbell Street, Rye (1556–60), where chambers on both ground and first floors were designed to have plaster ceilings from the start (Martin & Martin 1987, 29–30).
213. RCHM, *West London*, 25 and Plate 46.
214. Puloy 1982, 144.
215. *Skinners Recs.*, 135; Herbert, *Livery Companies*, ii, 465.
216. Pevsner, *London*, I, 209.
217. Jupp 1848, 222–3; Alford & Barker 1968, 225–8.
218. *RCC*, v, 30.
219. Jourdain 1950, 17; Herbert, *Livery Companies*, ii, 465.
220. Wood 1965, 393; Lloyd 1931, 394, Figs. 673–5. For York Place, Kingsford, *LTR*, xii, 63–5.
221. Lloyd 1931, Fig. 396; Cescinsky & Gribble 1923, 243. Jourdain (1950, 14) suggests the original design for linenfold panelling may have come from France.
222. E.g. the room in the kitchen wing, Eastbury Manor (Barking), first half of sixteenth century; *Survey of London: Eastbury*, 24–5, Plates 14 and 26. Eastbury may have been owned at his death by John More, whose inventory of *c.* 1603, in a badly damaged portion, mentions the house.
223. For wainscotting of livery company parlours, see Welch 1902, i, 75 (Pewterers, 1499); Parsole 1964, 87 (Founders, 1539–40); hall of Mercers, *Mercers Acts*, 99–100; of Goldsmiths, Prideaux, i, 44–5; of Grocers, Heath 1869, 13; of Carpenters, *RCC*, ii, 32. See also illustrations of the panelling, perhaps dating from rebuilding in 1587, at Furnival's Inn hall, **107**.
224. Clode, *MT Memorials*, 568.
225. Pendrill 1937, 222.
226. The various types of medieval candlesticks recovered from excavations in Britain are reviewed by Goodall (1981).
227. The sources are: Le Northerne, *Memorials*, 282–4; Kynebell, *Cal. Plea & Mem. R. 1361–84*, 91–3; Mockyng, *ibid.*, 154–6; Hatfield, *ibid.*, 158–9; Toky, *Cal. Plea & Mem. R. 1381–1412*, 208–13; Olyver, *Cal. Plea & Mem. R. 1413–37*, 2–5; Gy, *Cal. Plea & Mem. R. 1437–57*, 138–9; Furnyvale, *ibid.*, 78–81; Coldharbour, Kingsford 1921, 43–50; Lumbardes' Place, *Recs. SMH*, 28–9; Stede, PRO E154/2/7; Withers, PRO E154/7/5; Dudley, Kingsford 1921, 39–42; Porth, *Recs. SMH*, 36–45; Brace, *Cons. Court Wills*, 178; Patryk, *ibid.*, 192; Bonvisi, *Inq. PM*, i, 113–16; Hinde, PRO PROB 2/257; Trevor, *LSRT*, 148; Warner, Washington, Folger Library, Z.c.22 (33); More, PRO E154/7/5. I am grateful to Dr C. Barron for some of these references.
228. Welch 1902, i, 68–76; Adams 1951, 19–21; Welch 1902, i, 164–9; Clode, *MT Memorials*, 84–92; Nicholl 1866, 421–60; *Skinners' Recs.*, 204; (E. J.) Barron 1913, 300–13; GL MS 7164, ff. 5A–8.
229. Wood 1965, 402.
230. *Cal. LB, A*, 71–2. Several small fragments of tapestry have been recovered from recent waterfront excavations: Crowfoot *et al.* 1992.
231. Wood 1965, 403.
232. Consitt 1933, 69.
233. *Cal. Wills*, ii, 195; *ibid.*, ii, 190, 262.
234. *Cal. Wills*, ii, 341; *Mercers Acts*, 176, 378; Barron, *Guildhall*, 32. Nicholas Withers, probably a draper, had a bed-covering of Arras in his house, the White Herte in Cheapside, in 1499.
235. Unwin 1908, 179.
236. E.g. Trevor. On the definitions of say and buckram in the seventeenth century, see Thornton 1978, 114, 117. F. Pritchard warns (personal comment) that these terms may not have meant the same things in the fourteenth century.
237. *Cal. Wills*, ii, 190; *ibid.*, ii, 41.
238. Emmison 1976, 22. In the latter two cases, one wonders if the nearby Epping Forest was equally influential.
239. *Skinners' Recs.*, 173.
240. Gloag 1972, 7.
241. Alford & Barker 1968, 78–80.
242. Stanley-Stone 1925, 16. Chairs and stools were proof-pieces for journeymen turners in 1609 (*ibid.*, 114), and a recognised part of their repertoire in the early seventeenth century (*ibid.*, 265).
243. Eames 1977, 223–6.
244. *Ibid.*
245. Clode, *MT Memorials*, 84.
246. Mockyng; Furnvale, Dudley, Porth, Bonvisi. The Spanish table, a portable table with trestle-like legs, was common in England in the sixteenth century; Thornton 1978, 282 and Fig. 212.
247. CCPR, Queenhithe, 1573.
248. Eames 1977, 226. By the end of the sixteenth century round tables were to be found in several towns and villages of south-west Essex (Emmison 1982, 45, 100, 133).
249. Following Eames (1977) I use the following definitions: chair, a single seat with a back; stool, a single seat without a back; form, a seat for two or more without a back; bench, a seat for two or more with a back.
250. *RCC*, ii, 110.
251. Trevor, 1588.
252. *Letters & Papers, IV*, Part ii, 1454–7.
253. Porth, Brace. For the type, see Gloag 1972, 32.
254. For the type, see Gloag 1972, 33 (in the Victoria and Albert Museum).
255. Bonvisi in both cases. The latter were also called coffer-maker's chairs.
256. *Cons. Court Wills*, 156 (five chairs of straw, 1543); Emmison 1982, 150 (Waltham, 1598). Thornton (1978, 207–8) suggests that wicker chairs could be acceptable in 'quite smart' surroundings in seventeenth-century England.
257. 1423, *Cal. Plea & Mem. R. 1413–37*, 165; Thomas Gy, 1453 (see note 227); 1454, *Cal. Plea & Mem. R. 1437–57*, 142; two Flanders chairs covered in leather were recorded at Thomas Cromwell's house in 1527 (*Letters & Papers, IV*, Part ii, 1456).
258. Porth, Bonvisi. For discussion of Spanish chairs, see Thornton 1978, 374, n. 71.
259. Dudley (1509); Porth (1531); Brace (1543); Bonvisi (1549). At York Place in 1530 there were two close chairs covered in black velvet, and fifty-four pewter pots for chambers (*Letters & Papers, IV*, Part iii, 2766).
260. *Cons. Court Wills*, 161, 178, 209 (from 1542); Trevor 1588.
261. Olyver: Coldharbour. Some forms were 'stakyd', i.e. had their legs (stakes) drilled through the seat. Though this is mentioned infrequently (e.g. Porth's inventory) it must have been common.
262. Eames 1977, 73–4.
263. E.g. *Cal. Wills*, ii, 228 (1380).
264. *Cons. Court Wills*, 130, 204; Brace. Joined beds or bedsteads are found in Essex inventories from 1565 (Emmison 1982, 20, 33, 43, 71, 75).
265. Thornton 1978, 154–7.
266. Eames 1977, 75.
267. *Cal. Wills*, ii, 201–2, 235.
268. For another example of 1515, *Cons. Court Wills*, 37.
269. Eames 1977, 84–5.
270. *Fraternity Register*, 54.
271. Dudley; Trevor; Brace. Cf. Emmison 1976, 136.
272. Here the terms *aumbry* and *armoire* are taken as synonyms, following Eames 1977, 1–54.
273. *Cal. Wills*, i, 113.
274. Eames 1977, 6; *Cal. Plea & Mem. R. 1364–81*, 155.
275. *London English*, 159–60; for an aumbry at Carpenters' Hall, *RCC*, ii, 52, 126.
276. *Cal. Wills*, ii, 207.

277. *RCC*, ii, 126.

278. Hopwood 1904, 8.

279. *Cons. Court Wills*, 44.

280. *RCC*, 12 (1546–7).

281. *Cal. Wills*, ii, 250; for ship's chests, *Cal. Wills*, ii, 576 (1477); Porth and Brace inventories. Several medieval chests are preserved in London; a thirteenth-century boarded chest at the Victoria and Albert Museum (illustrated in Gloag 1972, 8); a chest of hutch type, with lap dovetail joints, dated *c.* 1480 by dendrochronology, in the Pyx Chapel of West-minster Abbey (Eames 1977, 149–50); and a chest of standard type in the Abbey Library, *c.* 1480–1500 (*ibid.*, 177).

282. *Cal. Wills*, ii, 62 (1361); Eames 1977, 122 (St Thomas Acon, 1450).

283. *Cal. Wills*, i, 665 (1351); *Cal. LB, E*, 74 (1320); Bonvisi, inventory 1549.

284. *Cal. Wills*, i, 274 (*c.* 1317); ii, 199 (1377).

285. Wainscot: *Cons. Court Wills*, 117, Brace, joined: *Cons. Court Wills*, 118. Brace, bound with iron: Patryk.

286. *RCC*, ii, 2, 15, 40, 131, 139, 152. The Pewterers had an iron-bound chest called a standard in 1494 (Welch 1902, i, 72).

287. For early examples, *Cal. Wills*, i, 582–3 (1349); ii, 11 (1358). Gloag (1972, 22) suggests that some may have been made by English joiners and ornamented by Flemish carvers. It is possible that Flemish chests are a generic term for chests with elaborately carved fronts; for general discussion, see Eames 1977, 146–8, and Tracy 1988, 176–7. Thornton (1971, 68) suggests that in the sixteenth century the inlaid chests originating around Cologne may have been known as Flemish, from their likely route to Britain.

288. *Cal. Wills*, ii, 250.

289. Emmison 1976, 20; Thornton 1971, 66–9.

290. One London example is known; the chest preserved at Southwark Cathedral, said to be the gift of Hugh Offley, mayor in 1556 (RCHM, *East London*, 63–4); an inlaid chest in the Museum of London has no known London connection, since it was bought in the early twentieth century. On the late sixteenth-century fashion for inlaid woods, see Lloyd 1931, Fig. 690; Jourdain 1950, 20–1.

291. Thornton (1978, 294–5) suggests that chests went out of fashion in the early seventeenth century in royal and polite houses.

292. The term is not used by Eames (1977) in her study of medieval furniture. A 'closse presse and a pressure for books' are mentioned in the inventory of William Stede, haberdasher, in 1499.

293. Porth; Bonvisi (who had four joined presses); Trevor (a press in garret); and the presses at **115**, see Appendix. Cf. presses in Essex wills of 1567–95: Emmison 1982, 32, 33, 75, 91, 133.

294. E.g. *Mercers Acts*, 572 (1523).

295. E.g. *Cons. Court Wills*, 115; Brace. Stede, in 1499, had twelve cushions to go with the twelve joined stools in his hall. On a grander scale, the parlour at Merchant Taylors' Hall in 1512 contained eighteen new cushions of the gift of John Skevyngton during his mastership, with 'Angells holdyng tharmes of the said Mr Skevyngton and with the markes of the said 4 wardens and tholy lambe'; and six other cushions embroidered with the holy lamb (inventory of 1512; see note 228).

296. An early seventeenth-century cushion cover in Turkey work is preserved in the Victoria and Albert Museum.

297. In the fifteenth century carpets could be found on the floor in royal settings in Provence, as shown in contemporary paintings.

298. Kentish carpets in the inventories of Porth, Brace; for carpets of unspecified manufacture, *Cons. Court Wills*, 156, 158, 190, 192. For York Place, *Letters & Papers*, IV, Part iii, 2766–7; King 1985. For Myles, *Cons. Court Wills*, 215.

299. Trevor; Thornton (1978, 109) suggests that the name may have covered several kinds of continental tapestry.

300. Dudley; *Cons. Court Wills*, 155, 130; Brace, Trevor. Thornton (1978, 137) cites further references.

301. *Skinners' Recs.*, 153.

302. *Letters & Papers, IV*, Part iii, 2767.

303. Unwin 1908, 248.

CHAPTER 6

1. Dyson & Schofield 1984, 296–7, 307.

2. E.g. at the Tower in 1389 (Salzman, *Building*, 469). The White Tower of London is also of Kentish rag with Caen dressings (Taylor 1972, 65–6). It is however probable that much of this stone came from demolished Roman structures within the city. Guildhall and Leadenhall, of 1420–50, employ large amounts of Kentish ragstone. Grocers' Hall (**149**) used some Kentish rag in its walling in 1429–30, and to pave the kitchen in 1469–70 (*HG, iii*, site **132/1**).

3. Taylor 1972, 116–17.

4. *Building Accts. Henry III*, 236, 242, 268, 418; VCH, *Surrey*, ii, 277–8.

5. Heath 1869, 418.

6. E.g. at Winchester Palace (**193**; *Survey of London: Bankside*, 54); for the vaulting and battlements on the Bridge chapel, 1396 (Bridge Acct. Rolls, 14/11/lxii); and in several medieval city churches.

7. Taylor 1972, 193–202, and medieval walls from excavations in the city.

8. It may be significant that the building accounts of royal works at Westminster Abbey and Palace of 1249–70 (*Buildings Accts. Henry III*) never mention flint; the earliest occurrence of the English form of the word noted by Salzman was in 1283, when a wall at the Tower used chalk and flint in quantity (Salzman, *Building*, 139).

9. The effect is also roughly attempted in Guildhall east crypt, and cf. the panels of chequerwork on the exterior of the wall of Charterhouse (possibly fifteenth century) and at the Steelyard (Norman 1909). It is also found in churches: carefully laid in small squares, as at site **174**, in the south aisle of the adjacent church of St Botolph Billingsgate (MoL, sitecode BIG82); or a general chequerwork appearance, as at the fourteenth-century north chapel at St Bride's (Grimes 1968, 190–1).

10. Kingsford, *LTR*, x, 122.

11. Jope 1961, 109–11.

12. Heath 1869, 6.

13. *Memorials*, 262; Baker 1970, 185.

14. Knoop & Jones 1933, 55.

15. Salzman, *Building*, 133.

16. Purbeck was used for carved heads over doors or in wall-arcades in English churches from the mid twelfth century (Gardner 1935, 115). The base of a wall shaft of Purbeck has been recovered from the site of a mansion built before the end of the twelfth century in Southampton (Platt & Coleman-Smith 1975, 25 and n. 19). Henry III's new buildings at the Tower in 1239–40 may have been decorated with Purbeck (*King's Works, i*, 714); and a Purbeck capital has been recovered from excavations at Kennington Palace (Dawson 1976, 77). Purbeck was extensively used at Westminster Abbey in the thirteenth century, and to provide the pillars to finish the nave in 1387–1404 (Salzman, *Building*, 134–5; *Building Accts. Henry III*, 439).

17. Elsden & Howe 1923, 76–7.

18. **198**; Salzman, *Building*, 135–7; Caen was used for windows at Grocers' Hall in 1495–6 (*HG, iii*, **132/1**), in 1536–7 for five windows on the south side of St Stephen Walbrook (Milbourn 1881, 363–4), and by the Clothworkers' Company for repairs of 1560–1 at **76**.

19. Knoop & Jones 1933, 54.

20. Goldthwaite 1980, 229.

21. Schofield *et al.* 1990, 164–7.

22. On religious sites, it is used in the first, probably eleventh-century church of St Nicholas Shambles (Thompson 1979); and at the first, possibly eleventh-century, church at St Bride's, Fleet Street (Grimes 1968, 185). For secular sites, see e.g. **138**.

23. Johnson 1974; Herbert 1979.

24. Church extensions: St Margaret Lothbury, MoL DUA archive; St Alban Wood Street, St Swithun and St Bride's, Grimes 1968, 205; Merchant Taylors' Hall (**177**). For houses, New Fresh Wharf (**174**) and elsewhere in Thames Street: e.g. sites south of the street, west of St Peter's Hill, Williams, 1982. For parallels in King's Lynn, Clarke & Carter 1977, 10; the example included horizontal planking, which is also known in London examples (Schofield 1977).

25. Schofield *et al.* 1990, 167.

26. Wood 1965, Plate IA. Availability of materials was probably an important consideration. The recently-excavated stone building of *c.* 1175 in Norwich had a flint rubble exterior (with ashlar dressings) and probably a rendered interior (Ayers 1987, 157).

27. For examples of the early fourteenth century and *c.* 1440, see Milne & Milne 1982, 25, 38–42; good examples of ashlar work in a utilitarian context were recorded in 1915 when the reservoir of the Greyfriars' conduit in Queen Square was demolished (Norman 1916, Figs. 1–2).

28. Coulson 1982, 98, n. 20.

29. *Assize of Nuisance*, 95.

30. The licences are: Bishop William Langton of Coventry/Lichfield, house by Temple Bar, 1305 (*Cal. Pat. R. 1301–7*, 367); William Servat, tower by gate (Bucklersbury), 1305 (*ibid., 1301–7*, 379); John de Pelham, house in Silver Street and a second house in Distaff Lane, 1311 (*ibid., 1307–13*, 398); John de Wengrave, house in Bread Street, 1314 (*ibid., 1313–33*, 118); Robert de Kelsey, house in West Cheap, 1315 (*ibid.*, 292); John de Cologne, house in Cornhill, 1337 (*ibid., 1334–8*, 505); Bishop Robert of Salisbury, house in Fleet Street, 1337 (*ibid.*, 498); John de Molyns, house in Castle Baynard Ward, 1338 (*ibid., 1338–40*, 62); Sir John de Pulteney, house in London, 1341 (*ibid., 1340–3*, 331); Matilda de Wel, a house in the Carmelites, Fleet

Street, 1385 (*ibid.*, *1385–9*, 42). I am grateful to Charles Coulson for information on these licences.

31. Coulson 1982, 81.
32. *Eyre 1244*, 80 (1232), 90 (1234–5); *Assize of Nuisance*, 69 (1328); *ibid.*, 388 (1344); *HTA Cartulary*, 82–3 (1421).
33. *Assize of Nuisance*, 408.
34. Salzman, *Building*, 240–5.
35. Salzman, *Building*, 237; *King's Works, i*, 529; Robinson 1911, 20–1. In 1299 Henry le Waleys, mayor, and Roger de Colebroc bought £16 of timber from the Earl of Cornwall's park at Isleworth, perhaps for the Greyfriars' church then in construction (*Cal. LB, B*, 90).
36. E.g. *Domesday of St Paul's*, xlvi.
37. CLRO, Bridge House Acct. Rolls, 4/9/xxviii, xxxiv; *ibid.*, 4/11/xlvi.
38. Salzman, *Building*, 250.
39. *RCC*, ii, 92, 117, 151; for floors, *ibid.*, 152–3; CLRO, Bridgemasters' Acct. Rolls, 11/9/xxviii.
40. At Coldharbour II (**170**) in 1485.
41. CLRO, Bridgemasters' Acct. Rolls, 1384–96, *passim*.
42. *Cal. LB, G*, 102.
43. Salzman, *Building*, 251; *RCC*, ii, 274 (1507).
44. Kingsford 1921, 44.
45. E.g. at Coldharbour II (**170**). Doors and shutters of beech are mentioned at the Tower in 1324 (Salzman, *Building*, 249).
46. Jupp 1848, 149–50.
47. *Building Accts. Henry III*, 42, 158, 236; 'a long pole of alder for the boket in Taymes', Coldharbour II, 1485 (Kingsford 1921, 46); the halling in Drapers' Hall was hung on poles of fir in 1433–4 (*Drapers' Recs.*, i, 325).
48. This information is derived from an archive report on the hurdles by Vanessa Straker, MoL, sitecode LUD82.
49. *Cal. Plea & Mem. R. 1364–81*, 172.
50. John de Potenhale, *Cal. Wills*, ii, 133; John de Tamworth, *ibid.*, ii, 167; Elias Garlond, *Cal. Plea & Mem. R. 1364–81*, 252.
51. *RCC*, ii, 84, 59.
52. Salzman, *Building*, 245–8.
53. *Memorials*, 261.
54. *London English*, 166.
55. A spruce table in 1391 (*Cal. Plea & Mem. R. 1381–1412*, 209), and spruce coffers or chests were widespread e.g. *Fraternity Register*, 55; Coldharbour II (**170**) 1485 (Kingsford 1921, 49); and at Dudley's house (**45**) in 1509 (Kingsford 1921, 40).
56. Tables, e.g. inventory of John Porth, 1531, *Recs. SMH*, 36–45; cypress furniture is said to be very rare (Eames 1977, 216).
57. In Essex walnut was used for stools (Emmison 1976, 18 (1578)); chairs 18 (1586); 146 (1591); in London for a small bedstead, 1583 (CLRO, Mayor's Court Roll, 4B, f. 21).
58. More 1602, 2–23, 50.
59. *Ibid.*, 8.
60. Jones 1953, 63.
61. Described in detail in Schofield *et al.* 1990, 165.
62. Horsman *et al.* 1988, 75–82.
63. *Ibid.*, 77; Schofield *et al.* 1990, 167.
64. Hewett 1980, 293–4. For a good example of thirteenth-century framing in a building in West Street, Ware (Hertfordshire), Gibson *et al.* 1982, 126–38.
65. Examples of fourteenth- and fifteenth-century framing from surviving houses in Essex may furnish the range of possibilities: Hewett 1980, 127, 129–30, 140–1, 145, 179, 209.
66. *Assize of Nuisance*, 204.
67. RCHM, *East London*, 94. *Building of London*, Fig. 117. Ogee braces are found in small towns such as Battle, in East Sussex, by 1569 (Martin & Martin 1987, 30–1).
68. An early example dates to 1575 (Hewett 1973, 77–8).
69. Hewett, 1980, 140 (Baythorne Hall, Birdbrook (Essex); about 1300).
70. This is noted first in Kent at Wye College *c.* 1445 and became common *c.* 1470 (Gravett 1971, 8; Newman, *Kent*, 80).
71. E.g. *RCC*, ii, 151 (1571).
72. Mercer 1975, 117.
73. On the grotesque style in woodwork in England, see Mercer 1962, 75–80.
74. *Assize of Nuisance*, 206, 493, 544. A grant of a 'shop with two solars' on the west side of Bridge Street in 1309–10 may refer to either superimposed solars or separate first-floor chambers (*HTA Cartulary*, 286).
75. References are as follows: ground floor, *Cal. LB, A*, 217; **141**; **175**; **87**; *Cal. Plea & Mem. R. 1458–82*, 34–5; first floor, **175**; **40**; **87**; second floor, **175**; **40**.
76. *Eyre 1244*, 396, 481.
77. E.g. *Eyre 1244*, 405–63, *passim*. The earliest surviving jetties of manorial or

similar residences in Essex, of the late thirteenth century, tend to be only on the cross-wings (e.g. Priory Place, Little Dunmow; Hewett 1969, 68; cf. Hewett 1980, 286, 293), perhaps suggesting that if they were following a London fashion, it was of first-floor solars. It might therefore be suggested that solars (a general term for an upper chamber) were commonly jettied by the second quarter of the thirteenth century in London.
78. *Assize of Nuisance*, 545 (1368).
79. Jetties 38 ft long and 2 ft 6 in wide (1346; *Assize of Nuisance*, 399), 32 ft 2 in long and 2 ft wide (1357; *ibid.*, 492), 14 yards 16 in long and 21¹/₂ in wide, overhanging the churchyard of St Martin Vintry (1378; *ibid.*, 619). For other cases involving churchyards, see *Assize of Nuisance*, 546 and *Cal. Plea & Mem. R.*, *1458–82*, 55 (St Clement Eastcheap, 1368 and 1469); cf. *Assize of Nuisance*, 574 (St Leonard Eastcheap, 1370).
80. *Assize of Nuisance*, 261.
81. E.g. *Cal. Plea & Mem. R. 1458–82*, 55.
82. *Viewers' Certificates*, 35.
83. RCHM, *West London*, 47.
84. Mercer 1975, 28; Mason 1964, 40.
85. CCPR, Wood St, 1562, St Martins Lane, 1591.
86. Hewett 1980, 232, and Fig. 232; Devliegher 1975, 172.
87. *RCC*, ii, 57; *Cal. Plea & Mem. R. 1381–1437*, 172–3.
88. Horsman *et al.* 1988, 85.
89. Hewett 1980, 123–4, 279.
90. Harris 1978, 18–19.
91. Hewett 1980, 217, 282, Fig. 305.
92. I.e. 3–4 ft for 1*d.*, or 2*s*. 2*d*–2*s*. 4*d*. the hundred foot (references from *Recs. SMH* and *RCC*, ii give a detailed picture for the years 1477–*c.* 1514).
93. Salzman, *Building*, 242; *RCC*, iii, 106 (1568), where the phrase used is 'eight foot [i.e. 8 cu. ft.] of season plaunche borde of the length of xj fote of assysse'. For uses of planch board, *RCC*, ii, 101, 106, 122.
94. Salzman, *Building*, 242; Cescinsky & Gribble 1922, i, 19, Fig. 7.
95. *RCC*, ii, 99, 101.
96. Salzman, *Building*, 244; *RCC*, ii, 104, 139.
97. *RCC*, ii, 104.
98. Parsloe 1964, 131; *RCC*, ii, 107. Overlapping boards were recorded in the revetment of *c.* 1170 at Seal House, Upper Thames Street, **172**.
99. *Fraternity Register*, 128.
100. *Liber Albus*, 389.
101. E.g. *RCC*, ii, 131 (1500).
102. *Assize of Nuisance*, 234.
103. *Memorials*, 203.
104. Milne 1992.
105. Salzman, *Building*, 140; *King's Works, i*, 427, n. 4; Platt 1976, 51.
106. Hurst 1961, 244; Dawson 1976, 23, 78.
107. Harvey 1972, 36–7.
108. *King's Works, i*, 999.
109. *Ibid.*, 282. There was also a watergate with a brick arch on stone jambs, of either Henry VI's or Richard III's building, at Westminster Palace: Colvin 1966, Plates 9 and 10.
110. *King's Works, i*, 431; *Drapers' Recs.*, i, 313.
111. Bishop of Ely's palace at Hatfield, 1485; the same builder, John Morton's, gateway at Lambeth Palace, *c.* 1490; Bishop of London's palace at Fulham, 1506–22.
112. **48**; Gadd & Dyson 1981; Colvin 1966, 33, 35; *ibid.*, Plate 31, 49–50.
113. *RCC*, ii, 92, 95. Perhaps significantly, on two occasions in the Carpenters' Company records, in 1484 and 1491, the bricklaying was carried out by masons: *RCC*, ii, 65–7, 92.
114. *Ibid.*, 92.
115. *Cal. Pat. R. 1416–22*, 22; discussed by Smith 1985, 7–8.
116. Smith 1985, 12–18. A motif in darker, probably vitrified bricks in the form of a simple cross is found on a house in Zilverstraat, Bruges, dated on its façade to 1468 (Devliegher 1975, 461–2; for other emblems, *ibid.*, 26–7). For terracotta, see Moore 1991, 218.
117. RCHM, *West London*, Plate 84.
118. Taylor 1972, 287–93.
119. Horsman *et al.* 1988, 81–2.
120. *SBH Cartulary*, 143.
121. *Assize of Nuisance, passim*. An earth wall 16 ft high was required in one case in 1342 (*ibid.*, 380), to confirm with rules about privacy; this seems a dangerously unwieldy height to specify out of doors, and it may have been part of a house.
122. CCPR, St James in the Wall, 1516 (i.e. **140**); CCPR, Finsbury, 1589. Other fourteenth- and fifteenth-century property boundaries, besides those of stone (and later brick), were made of palings of wattle and daub and of daubed or plastered wood, which was probably the same thing (*Assize of Nuisance*, 278–9, 595).

List of Abbreviations

These are works concerned mainly with primary sources (archaeological, documentary, cartographic) of London material, relevant theses and standard secondary studies of material in London and elsewhere.

Accts. AH London Wall	C. Welch, *Churchwardens' Accounts of the Parish of Allhallows, London Wall, 1455–1536* (1912)
Accts. St Christopher le Stocks	E. Freshfield (ed.), *Accomptes of the Church-wardens of the Paryshe of St Christofer's in London 1575–1685* (1885–95)
Accts. SMC	W. H. Overall (ed.), *The Accounts of the Churchwardens of the Parish of St Michael, Cornhill . . . from 1456 to 1608* (*c.* 1869–71)
Anglo-Saxon Chronicle	G. N. Garmonsway (ed.), *The Anglo-Saxon Chronicle* (1953, rev. 1954)
Assize of Nuisance	H. M. Chew & W. Kellaway (eds), *London Assize of Nuisance 1301–1431*, LRS, **10** (1973)
Barron, 'Government of London'	C. M. Barron, 'The Government of London and its Relationship with the Crown 1400–1500', unpub. PhD thesis, University of London (1970)
Barron, *Guildhall*	C. M. Barron, *The Medieval Guildhall of London* (1974)
Birch, *Historical Charters*	W. de G. Birch (ed.), *Historical Charters and Constitutional Documents of the City of London* (rev. ed., 1887)
BL	British Library
Black Books of Lincoln's Inn	J. D. Walker (ed.), *Records of the Society of Lincoln's Inn: the Black Books, i* (1422–1585) (1897)
Building Accts. Henry III	H. M. Colvin (ed.), *Building Accounts of King Henry III* (1971)
Building of London	J. Schofield, *The Building of London from the Conquest to the Great Fire* (1984)
CAD	*Descriptive Catalogue of Ancient Deeds in the Public Record Office* (6 vols., 1890–1915)
Cal. Chart. R.	*Calendar of Charter Rolls preserved in the Public Record Office* (6 vols., 1903–27)
Cal. Close R.	*Calendar of Close Rolls preserved in the Public Record Office* (62 vols., 1892–1963)
Cal. Fine R.	*Calendar of Fine Rolls preserved in the Public Record Office, 1272–1368* (22 vols., 1911–62)
Cal. Inq. PM	*Calendar of Inquisitions Post-mortem and other analogous documents preserved in the Public Record Office, 1216–1406* (18 vols., 1904–88)
Cal. LB, A, etc.	*Calendar of Letter-Books preserved among the archives of the Corporation of the City of London: A to L* (11 vols., 1899–1912)
Cal. Lib. R.	*Calendar of Liberate Rolls preserved in the Public Record Office, 1226–60* (4 vols., 1916–37)
Cal. Pat. R.	*Calendar of Patent Rolls preserved at the Public Record Office, 1232–1582* (72 vols., 1893–1986)
Cal. Plea & Mem. R.	*Calendar of Plea and Memoranda Rolls preserved among the archives of the Corporation of the City of London, 1323–1437* (ed. A. H. Thomas, 4 vols., 1926–43) and *1437–82* (ed. P. E. Jones, 2 vols, 1953–61)
Cal. Wills	*Calendar of Wills enrolled in the Husting* (ed. R. R. Sharpe, 2 vols., 1889–90)
Carlin, 'Southwark'	M. Carlin, 'The Urban Development of Southwark *c.* 1200–1550', unpub. PhD thesis, University of Toronto (1983)
CCO	Clothworkers' Company Court Orders
CCPR	Card Calendar to Property References in the Journals and Repertories (CLRO)
CD	Clothworkers' Company Deeds
CDW	Clothworkers' Company Book of Deeds and Wills
Chamber Accounts	B. R. Masters (ed.), *Chamber Accounts of the Sixteenth Century*, LRS, **20** (1984)
Charity Comm.	*Report of the [Charity] Commissioners*, vol. 32, Part VI (1840)
Chertsey Abbey Cartularies	M. S. Giuseppi, C. A. F. Meekings & P. M. Barnes (eds), *Chertsey Abbey Cartularies* (Surrey Record Society, 12, 2 vols. in 5 parts, 1915–63)
CH Evidence Book	Christ's Hospital Evidence Book, GL MS 12805
CHMB, 1–4	Christ's Hospital Court Minute Books, GL MS 12806: 1, 1556–63; 2, 1562–92; 3, 1592–1632; 4, 1632–49
Chronicles	C. L. Kingsford (ed.), *Chronicles of London* (1905)
CH Treas. Accts. 1–3	Christ's Hospital Treasurer's Accounts, GL MS 12819: 1, 1552–8; 2, 1561–1608; 3, 1608–16
Church in London	A. K. McHardy (ed.), *The Church in London, 1375–1392*, LRS, **13** (1977)
CH View Book	Christ's Hospital View Books, GL MS 12834/1–2
Clode, *MT Memorials*	C. M. Clode (ed.), *Memorials of the Guild of Merchant Taylors* (1875)
CLRO	City of London Record Office
Coggeshall, Chronicon	J. Stevenson (ed.), *Radulphi*

	de Coggeshall, *Chronicon Anglicanum*, Rolls Series, **66** (1875)
Comm. Court	M. Fitch (ed.), *Index to the Testamentary Records in the Commissary Court of London, 1374–1570* (2 vols., 1969–74)
Cons. Court Wills	I. Darlington (ed.), *London Consistory Court Wills, 1492–1547*, LRS, **3** (1967)
Coroner's Rolls	R. R. Sharpe (ed.), *Calendar of the Coroner's Rolls of the City of London* (1913)
CRW	Clothworkers' Company Renter Warden
d.	died
Description of London	William Fitzstephen, *Description of London*, trans. H. B. Wheatley in his edition of Stow's *Survey*, Everyman (1912, rev. 1956), 501–9
Domesday of St Paul's	W. H. Hale (ed.), *The Domesday of St Paul's of the Year 1222*, Camden Society, **69** (1858)
Drapers' Recs.	A. H. Johnson, *The History of the Worshipful Company of the Drapers of London* (4 vols., 1914–22)
DUA	Museum of London, Department of Urban Archaeology (from 1991, part of the Museum of London Archaeological Service)
DUA *Archive Catalogue*	Museum of London, Department of Urban Archaeology, *Archive Catalogue* (3rd ed. 1987)
Early Charters of St Paul's	M. Gibbs (ed.), *Early Charters of the Cathedral Church of St Paul, London*, Camden Society, 3rd series, **58** (1939)
Ekwall, *Street-names*	E. Ekwall, *Street-names of the City of London* (1954, corr. repr. 1965)
Eyre 1244	H. M. Chew & M. Weinbaum (eds), *The London Eyre of 1244*, LRS, **6** (1970)
Eyre 1276	M. Weinbaum (ed.), *The London Eyre of 1276*, LRS, **12** (1976)
Eyre 1321	H. M. Cam (ed.), *Year Books of Edward II, xxvi (Part I): The Eyre of London 1321*, Selden Society, **85** (1968)
Fraternity Register	P. Basing (ed.), *Parish Fraternity Register: Fraternity of the Holy Trinity and SS Fabian and Sebastian in the Parish of St Botolph without Aldersgate*, LRS, **18** (1982)
GL	Guildhall Library
GM	Guildhall Museum
Harben, *Dictionary*	H. A. Harben, *A Dictionary of London* (1918)
Harding, 'Port of London'	V. Harding, 'The Port of London in the Fourteenth Century: Its Topography, Administration and Trade', unpub. PhD thesis, University of St Andrews (1983)
Harvey, *Early Medieval Architects*	J. Harvey, *Early Medieval Architects*, 2nd ed. (1978)
Herbert, *Livery Companies*	W. Herbert, *History of the Twelve Great Livery Companies of London* (2 vols., 1836–7)
HG	*Historical Gazetteer of London before*
	the Great Fire: D. Keene & V. Harding, i, *Cheapside* (1986); D. Keene & M. Carlin, ii, *St Botolph without Aldgate* (in prep.); D. Keene & D. Crouch, iii, *Walbrook* (in prep.)
HMC, *Ninth Report*	Royal Commission on Historical Manuscripts, *Ninth Report, Part 1* (1834)
Honeybourne, 'Fleet'	M. B. Honeybourne, 'The Fleet and Its Neighbourhood in Early and Medieval Times', *London Topographical Record*, **19** (1947), 1–8
Honeybourne, 'Richard II'	M. B. Honeybourne, 'The Reconstructed Map of London under Richard II', *London Topographical Record*, **22** (1965), 29–76
Honeybourne, 'Value'	M. B. Honeybourne, 'The Extent and Value of the Property in London and Southwark Occupied by the Religious Houses (including the prebends of St Paul's and St Martin le Grand), the Inns of the Bishops and Abbots and the Churches and Churchyards, Before the Dissolution of the Monasteries', unpub. MA thesis, University of London (1929)
HR	Husting Roll(s), CLRO
HTA Cartulary	G. A. J. Hodgett (ed.), *The Cartulary of Holy Trinity Aldgate*, LRS, **7** (1971)
Inq. PM	G. S. Fry (ed.), *Abstracts of Inquisitiones Post Mortem relating to the City of London Returned into the Court of Chancery, Part I, 1485–1561*, LAMAS (1896); S. J. Madge (ed.), *Part II, 1561–1577*, LAMAS (1901); G. S. Fry (ed.), *Part III, 1577–1603*, LAMAS (1906)
JBAA	*Journal of the British Archaeological Association*
Journal	Journal of the Court of Common Council (CLRO)
King's Works, i–iv	H. M. Colvin (gen. ed.), *History of the King's Works, i* and *ii, The Middle Ages* (ed. R. Allen Brown, H. M. Colvin & A. J. Taylor, 1963, repr. 1971); *iii, 1485–1660 (Part I)* (ed. H. M. Colvin, D. R. Ransome & J. Summerson, 1975); *iv, (Part II)* (H. M. Colvin, J. Summerson, M. Biddle, J. R. Hale & M. Merriman, 1982)
LAMAS	London and Middlesex Archaeological Society
Langland, *Piers the Plowman*	W. Langland, *Piers the Plowman* (ed. W. W. Skeat, 1886)
Letters & Papers	*Letters and Papers Foreign and Domestic of the Reign of Henry VIII*
Leybourn, Survey	W. Leybourn, 'Survey of the Defences and Encroachments within 16 ft Upon Them, 1676', (CLRO)
Liber Albus	H. T. Riley (ed.), *Liber Albus* (1861)
Liber Cust.	*Liber Custumarum*, in H. T. Riley (ed.), *Munimenta Gildhallae Londoniensis*, ii (1859–62)

Literae Cantuarienses	*Literae Cantuarienses: The Letter-book of the Monastery of Christ Church, Canterbury*, Rolls Series (3 vols., 1887)
London and Middlesex Chantry Certificate	C. J. Kitching (ed.), *London and Middlesex Chantry Certificate, 1548*, LRS, **16** (1980)
London English	R. W. Chambers & M. Daunt (eds), *A Book of London English, 1384–1425* (1931)
London Museum Catalogue	London Museum, *Medieval Catalogue* (1940, repr. 1954; 1967 edition used)
London Topography	G. L. Gomme (ed.), *The Topography of London*, Gentleman's Magazine Library, 2 vols. (1904–5)
LRS	London Record Society
LSRT	J. Schofield (ed.), *The London Surveys of Ralph Treswell*, London Topographical Society, **135** (1987)
LTR, x–xiii	C. L. Kingsford, 'Historical Notes on Medieval London Houses', *London Topographical Record*, x (1916), 44–144; xi (1917), 28–81; xii (1920), 1–66; xiii (1923), 33–54 ('London Topographical Gleanings')
ME	Middle English
Memorials	H. T. Riley (ed.), *Memorials of London and London Life in the XIIIth, XIVth and XVth Centuries* (1868)
Mercers' Acts	L. Lyell & F. D. Watney (eds), *Acts of Court of the Mercers' Company* (1936)
Middle Temple Recs.	C. H. Hopwood (ed.), *Middle Temple Records: Minutes of Parliament I, 1501–1603* (1904)
Mills & Oliver, *Survey*	P. Mills & J. Oliver, *Survey of Building Sites in the City of London after the Great Fire of 1666*, ed. P. E. Jones and T. F. Reddaway, London Topographical Society, **97–9, 101, 103** (1962–7)
MoL	Museum of London
Munimenta Gildhallae	H. T. Riley (ed.), *Munimenta Gildhallae Londoniensis*, 3 vols. in 4, Rolls Series (1859–62)
Newman, *Kent*	J. Newman, *West Kent and the Weald*, Buildings of England Series (2nd ed., 1976)
OE	Old English
OED	*Oxford English Dictionary* (1888–1928)
Paston Letters	N. Davis (ed.), *Paston Letters and Papers of the Fifteenth Century*, 2 vols. (1971)
PCC	Prerogative Court of Canterbury
PCC	S. A. Smith & L. L. Duncan (eds), *Index of Wills Proved in the Prerogative Court of Canterbury, iii, 1558–83* (1898, repr. 1968); S. A. Smith & E. A. Fry (eds), *iv, 1584–1604* (1910)
Pevsner, *Essex*	N. Pevsner, *Essex*, Buildings of England Series (2nd ed. rev. E. Radcliffe, 1965)
Pevsner, *Herts.*	N. Pevsner, *Hertfordshire*, Buildings of England Series (2nd ed. rev. B. Cherry 1977)
Pevsner, *London, I–II*	N. Pevsner, *London I: The Cities of London and Westminster* (3rd ed. rev. B. Cherry, 1973); *London II: Except the Cities of London and Westminster*, Buildings of England Series (1952, repr. 1969)
Pevsner, *Middlesex*	N. Pevsner, *Middlesex*, Buildings of England Series (1957)
Plan Book	Clothworkers' Company, Plan Book ('Book of Treswell Surveys')
PN Mddx	J. E. B. Gover, A. Mawer & F. M. Stenton, *The Place-names of Middlesex* (1942)
Possessory Assizes	H. M. Chew (ed.), *London Possessory Assizes: A Calendar*, LRS, **1** (1965)
PRG	C. Harding, 'Post-Roman Gazetteer', MS in MoL
PRO	Public Record Office
QW	(Clothworkers' Company) Quarter Warden
RCC	B. Marsh (ed.), *Records of the Carpenters' Company, i, Apprentice Entry Books 1654–1694* (1913); ii, *Wardens' Accounts 1438–1516* (1914); iii, *Court Book 1533–73* (1915); iv, *Wardens' Accounts 1546–71* (1916); B. Marsh & J. Ainsworth (eds), v, *Wardens' Account Book 1571–91* (1937); vi, *Court Book 1573–94* (1939); A. M. Millard (ed.), vii, *Wardens' Account Book 1592–1614* (1968)
RCHM, *City* etc.	Royal Commission on Historical Monuments (England), *London I: Westminster Abbey* (1924); *London II: West London* (1925); *London III: Roman London* (1928); *London IV: London (The City)* (1929); *London V: East London* (1930)
RCHM, *Essex*	Royal Commission on Historical Monuments (England), *Essex i: North-west Essex* (1916); *ii: Central and South-west Essex* (1921); *iii: North-east Essex* (1922); *iv: South-east Essex* (1923)
RCHM, *Middlesex*	Royal Commission on Historical Monuments (England), *Middlesex* (1937)
RCHM, *Salisbury*	Royal Commission on Historical Monuments (England), *City of Salisbury, i* (1980)
RCHM, *Stamford*	Royal Commission on Historical Monuments (England), *The Town of Stamford* (1977)
RCHM, *York v*	Royal Commission on Historical Monuments (England), *City of York: v, the central area* (1981)
Recs. of Two City Parishes	W. McMurray, *The Records of Two City Parishes . . . SS Anne and Agnes, Aldersgate, and St John Zachary, London* (1925)
Recs. SMH	H. Littlehales (ed.), *The Medieval Records of a London City Church (St*

	Mary at Hill) 1420–1559, Early English Text Society, **125** (1904), **128** (1905)
Remembrancia	*Analytical Index to the Series of Records Known as the Remembrancia . . . AD 1579–1664* (1878)
Repertory	Repertory of the Court of Aldermen (CLRO)
RIBA	Royal Institute of British Architects
Robertson, *Laws*	A. J. Robertson (ed.), *The Laws of the Kings of England from Edmund to Henry I* (1925)
RW	(Clothworkers' Company) Renter Warden
Salzman, *Building*	L. F. Salzman, *Building in England Down to 1540* (1957, 2nd ed. 1965)
SBH Cartulary	N. J. Kerling (ed.), *The Cartulary of St Barthomew's Hospital* (1973)
Select Cases of Trespass	M. S. Arnold (ed.), *Select Cases of Trespass from the King's Courts 1307–99*, Selden Society, **100** (2 vols., 1985–7)
SESML	Social and Economic Study of Medieval London
Skinners' Recs.	J. J. Lambert (ed.), *Records of the Skinners of London, Edward I to James I* (1933)
SMC Cartulary	W. O. Hassall (ed.), *The Cartulary of St Mary Clerkenwell*, Camden Society, 3rd Series, **71** (1949)
Smith, *Ancient Topography*	J. Smith, *Ancient Topography of London* (1810)
Smith, *Antiquities*	J. Smith, *Antiquities of London and Environs* (1791)
Sneyd, *Relation*	C. Sneyd (trans.), *A Relation, or Rather a True Account, of the Island of England . . . about 1500*, Camden Society, **37** (1847)
Survey of London: Bankside	Sir H. Roberts & W. H. Godfrey (eds), *Bankside (the Parishes of St Saviour and Christchurch Southwark)*, Survey of London, **22** (1950)
Survey of London: Crosby Place	P. Norman (ed.), *Crosby Place*, Survey of London, **9** (1908)
Survey of London: Eastbury	P. Norman, *Eastbury Manor House, Barking*, Survey of London, **11** [n.d., 1914?]
Survey of London: Strand II	Sir G. Gater and W. H. Godfrey (eds), *The Strand (the Parish of St Martin-in-the-Fields), part ii*, Survey of London, **18** (1937)
Survey of Sources	D. Keene & V. Harding, *A Survey of Documentary Sources for Property Holding in London before the Great Fire*, LRS, **22** (1985)
Stow	J. Stow, *Survey of London* (1598) ed. C. L. Kingsford, 3rd ed. (2 vols., 1971)
Thorpe, *Ancient Laws*	B. Thorpe (ed.), *Ancient Laws and Institutes of England*, Record Commission, **66** (1840)
Thorpe, *Book of Drawings*	J. Summerson (ed.), *The Book of Architecture of John Thorpe in Sir John Soane's Museum*, Walpole Society, **40** (1966)
Thrupp, *Merchant Class*	S. Thrupp, *The Merchant Class of Medieval London 1300–1500* (1948)
VCH, *London* etc.	Victoria History of the Counties of England, *London i* (ed. W. Page, 1908); *Middlesex i* (ed. R. B. Pugh, 1969); *Surrey ii* (ed. H. E. Malden, 1905)
Vestry Mins. St Bartholomew Exchange	E. Freshfield (ed.), *The Vestry Minute Books of St Bartholomew Exchange 1567–1676* (1890)
Vestry Mins. St Christopher le Stocks	E. Freshfield (ed.), *Minutes of the Vestry Meetings and Other Records of the Parish of St Christopher le Stocks* (1886)
Vestry Mins. St Margaret Lothbury	E. Freshfield (ed.), *The Vestry Minutes Book of St Margaret Lothbury* (1887)
Viewers' Certificates	J. S. Loengard (ed.), *London Viewers and Their Certificates*, LRS, **26** (1989)
Westminster Abbey Charters	E. Mason (ed.), *Westminster Abbey Charters 1066–c. 1214*, LRS, **25** (1988)
Wilkinson, *Londina Illustrata*	R. Wilkinson, *Londina Illustrata . . . Graphic and Historical Memorials of Churches and Theatres . . . in the Cities and Suburbs of London and Westminster* (2 vols., 1818–25)
Williams, *Early Holborn*	E. Williams, *Early Holborn and the Legal Quarter in London* (2 vols., 1927)
Winchester Studies i	M. Biddle (ed.), *Winchester in the Early Middle Ages*, Winchester Studies i (1976)
Winchester Studies ii	D. Keene, *Survey of Medieval Winchester*, Winchester Studies ii (2 vols., 1985)

Sources and Bibliography

PRIMARY SOURCES

I. ARCHAEOLOGICAL AND OTHER ARCHIVES DEALING WITH PHYSICAL REMAINS

Museum of London, Archive of former Department of Urban Archaeology
Archive excavation reports and other records from the following medieval domestic sites (the year of excavation shown by the last two digits of the MoL sitecode):

ALG84   7–12 Aldersgate Street, EC3 (G. Egan, 1986)
APO81   Apothecaries' Hall and 22–6 Blackfriars Lane, EC4 (D. Bluer & P. Allen, 1985)
BIG82   Billingsgate Lorry Park, Lower Thames Street, EC3 (S. Roskams, 1989)
BOP82   28–32 Bishopsgate, EC2 (C. Evans, 1988)
BOT86   St Botolph Aldgate churchyard, E1 (C. Maloney, 1987)
BOY86   City of London Boys' School site, Whitefriars, EC4 (C. Spence, 1988)
DUK77   2–7 Duke's Place, EC3 (J. Maloney, 1989)
ELY85   Ely Place, EC1 (G. Malcolm, 1986)
FRE78   Fresh Wharf, Lower Thames Street, EC4 (L. Miller, 1981)
GPO75   81 Newgate Street, EC1 (S. Roskams *et al.*, 1990)
HIL84   7 Philpot Lane, EC3 (R. Lea & A. Westman, 1986)
HTP79   Mitre Square, 10–11 Mitre Street, EC3 (J. Schofield, 1985)
ILA79   Miles Lane, 132–7 Upper Thames Street, EC4 (L. Miller, 1989)
LBY85   7 Ludgate Broadway, EC4 (J. Hill, 1986)
LEA84   71–7 Leadenhall Street, 32–40 Mitre Street, EC3 (S. Rivière, 1985)
LOV81   9 and 22–5 Lovat Lane, EC3 (D. Gadd, 1982)
LUD82   42–6 Ludgate Hill, 1–6 Old Bailey (P. Rowsome, 1985)
MLK76   1–6 Milk Street, EC2 (S. Roskams, P. Allen & J. Schofield, 1988)
NBS84   35–8 New Bridge Street, EC4 (P. Chitwood, 1986)
NFW74   New Fresh Wharf, Lower Thames Street, EC3 (L. Miller & J. Schofield, 1989)
OPS88   156–84 Bishopsgate, EC3 (S. Poole, 1989)
RAG81   61–5 Crutched Friars, 1–12 Rangoon Street, EC3 (D. Bowler, 1983)
SH74   Seal House, 106–8 Upper Thames Street, EC4 (J. Schofield, 1977)
SM75   New Fresh Wharf, Lower Thames Street, EC4, Area III (L. Miller & J. Schofield, 1987)
SUN86   Sunlight Wharf, Upper Thames Street, EC4 (D. Bluer, 1988)
SWA81   Swan Lane, Upper Thames Street, EC4 (G. Egan & R. Harris, 1990)
TL74   Trig Lane, Upper Thames Street, EC4 (G. Milne & C. Milne, 1977)
VHY89   Vintners' Place, Upper Thames Street, EC4 (R. Brown, 1992)
WAT78   Watling Court, 41–53 Cannon Street, 11–14 Bow Lane (D. Perring, 1983)
WEL79   Well Court, 44–8 Bow Lane, EC4 (P. Allen & D. Perring, 1989)
WTS86   34 Watling Street, EC3 (M. Samuel, 1988)

Other archives and museums
British Museum
National Monuments Record, Royal Commission on Historical Monuments (England)
Victoria and Albert Museum

II. MANUSCRIPT SOURCES

Published records, including many parts of the manuscript series noted here, are listed in the bibliography.

Corporation of London Record Office
Court of Husting, Husting Rolls (1300–1600)
Viewers' Reports, 1509–53
Letter-Books M–P, AB
Journals (1416–1600) and Repertories (1485–1600) of the Court of Common Council and Court of Aldermen
Court of Orphans, inventories

Comptroller's (City Lands) Deeds, Grant Books (1589–1672), and 'Plans of City Lands and Bridge House properties' (2 vols., *c.* 1680–1720)
Bridge House Estates, Small Register, 1358; Rentals (1404–1600); Grant Book (1570–1622); Deeds
Bridgemasters' Account Rolls, 1382–94, 1395–8
City Cash Accounts (1633–70)
Survey of City Wall by William Leybourn, 1676

Guildhall Library
Deeds, wills, rentals, accounts, plans and surveys of property belonging to the following City companies:

Armourers and Brasiers
Bakers
Blacksmiths
Brewers
Butchers
Carpenters
Cordwainers
Fishmongers
Girdlers
Grocers
Haberdashers
Ironmongers
Mercers
Merchant Taylors
Painter-Stainers
Parish Clerks
Pewterers
Saddlers
Salters
Skinners
Tallow Chandlers
Turners
Vintners
Wax Chandlers
Weavers

Records of City parishes and St Paul's:
Churchwardens' accounts, vestry minutes, memoranda of rents from:
All Hallows London Wall
All Hallows Staining
St Alban Wood Street
St Botolph Aldersgate
St Botolph Aldgate
St Margaret Bridge
St Margaret Pattens
St Martin Orgar
St Paul's Parliamentary Surveys, 1649–57

Records of Christ's Hospital:
Deeds, Leases, Papers and Loose Plans
Treasurer's Account Books, 1552–1616
Court Minute Books, 1556–1649
View Books 1–2
Evidence Book with Surveys by Treswell, 1607–11

Records held by individual Livery Companies
Clothworkers' Hall:
     Deeds, Leases and Wills
     Court Orders, 1528–1616
     Quarter Wardens' Accounts, 1528–1616
     Renter Wardens' Accounts, 1528–1616
     Plan Book of Treswell Surveys, 1612
Drapers' Hall:
     Plan of Erber, 1596
Fishmongers' Hall:
     Plan Book by W. Leybourn, 1686
Goldsmiths' Hall:
     Leases and Plans, Register of Deeds, Accounts
     Plan Book
Leathersellers' Hall:
     Court Minute Books, 1608–14; Plan of Old Hall Site, 1614
Mercers' Hall:
     First Register of Leases

Public Record Office
Inventories, post-Dissolution accounts on monastic sites (classes PROB, E)
Eton College Records and Register

Greater London Record Office
Deeds and Inventory, Brokenwharf (Charterhouse School Muniments)

British Library
Harley MS 741

Christ Church, Oxford
Christ Church Estates, Leases and Plan, 1610

Folger Shakespeare Library, Washington, USA
Inventory of Nicholas Warner, Z.c.22. (30)

III. DRAWINGS, ENGRAVINGS AND PAINTINGS

In the collections of:
Ashmolean Museum, Oxford
British Library
British Museum, Department of Prints and Drawings
Courtauld Institute of Art
Dulwich Art Gallery
Gemäldegalerie, Berlin
Greater London Record Office
Guildhall Library, Print Room
Kenwood House
Magdalen College, Cambridge
Museum of London, Department of Prints and Drawings
National Gallery
Society of Antiquaries of London

BIBLIOGRAPHY

Adams, A., 1951, *History of the Worshipful Company of Blacksmiths*
Adams, B., 1983, *London Illustrated 1604–1851*
Airs, M., 1982, *Tudor and Jacobean: 1500–1640*, The Buildings of Britain Series
Airs, M., 1983, 'Timber-framed Buildings' in *London 2: South* (ed. B. Cherry & N. Pevsner), 104–12
Alexander, J., & Binski, P., 1987, *Age of Chivalry: Art in Plantagenet England 1200–1400*
Alford, B. W. E., & Barker, T. C., 1968, *A History of the Carpenters' Company*
Allan, J., Henderson, C., & Higham, R., 1984, 'Saxon Exeter' in *Anglo-Saxon Towns in Southern England* (ed. J. Haslam), 385–414
Allen, T., 1828, *The History and Antiquities of London*
Andrews, D., 1982, 'Medieval Domestic Architecture in Northern Lazio' in *Medieval Lazio: Studies in architecture, painting and ceramics* (ed. D. Andrews, J. Osborne & D. Whitehouse), British Archaeological Reports, S125, 1–122
Archer, I., Barron, C. M., & Harding, V., 1988, *Hugh Alley's Caveat: The Markets of London in 1598*, London Topographical Society, Publication **137**
Archer, J. W., 1851, *Vestiges of Old London*
Armitage, K., Pearce, J., & Vince, A., 1981, 'Early Medieval Roof-tiles from London', *Antiquaries Journal*, **61**, 359–62
Ashdown, C. H., 1919, *History of the Worshipful Company of Glaziers*
Aston, M., 1967, *Thomas Arundel: A Study of Church Life in the Reign of Richard II*
Atkin, M., 1985, 'Excavations on Alms Lane [Norwich]' in *Excavations in Norwich 1971–1977 Part II*, East Anglian Archaeology, **26**, 144–260
Ayers, B., 1987, *Excavations at St Martin-at-Palace Plain, Norwich, 1981*, East Anglian Archaeology, **37**
Babelon, J.-P., 1977, *Demeures Parisiennes sous Henri IV et Louis XIII* (Paris)
Babelon, J.-P., 1983, 'Paris: un quartier residentiel, la couture Sainte-Catherine, durant la seconde moitié du XVIᵉ siècle' in *La maison de ville à la Renaissance* (ed. A. Chastel & J. Guilaume) (Paris), 31–6
Baines, J. M., 1958, *Wealden Firebacks*, Hastings Museum
Baker, T., 1970, *Medieval London*
Balestracci, D., & Piccinni, G., 1977, *Siena nel trecento: assetto urbano e strutture edilizie* (Florence)
Barker, T. C., 1957, *The Girdlers' Company*
Barley, M. W., 1961, *The English Farmhouse and Cottage*
Barley, M. W., 1986, *Houses & History*
Barron, C. M., Coleman, C., & Gobbi, C., 1983, 'The London Journal of Alessandro Magno 1562', *London Journal*, **9** (2), 136–52
Barron, C. M., with Hunting, P. & Roscoe, J., 1979, *The Parish of St Andrew Holborn*
Barron, E. J., 1913, 'Notes on the History of the Armourers and Braziers' Company', *Trans. LAMAS*, New Series **2**, 300–13
Bell, W. G., 1938, *A Short History of the Worshipful Company of Tylers and Bricklayers of the City of London*
Bell, W. G., Cottrill, F., & Spon, G., 1936, *London Wall through Eighteen Centuries*
Beresford, M., 1967, *New Towns of the Middle Ages: Town Plantation in England, Wales and Gascony* (repr. 1988)
Biddle, M., & Keene, D., 1976, 'Winchester in the Eleventh and Twelfth Centuries' in *Winchester in the Early Middle Ages* (ed. M. Biddle), Winchester Studies i, 241–448
Birch, W., ed., 1893, *Cartularium Saxonicum* (3 vols.)
Black, G., 1976, 'Excavations in the Sub-vault of the Misericorde of Westminster Abbey, *Trans. LAMAS*, **27**, 135–78
Black, W. H., 1871, *History and Antiquities of the Worshipful Company of Leathersellers*
Blair, J., & Ramsey, N., (eds.), 1991, *English Medieval Industries*
Blakiston, N., 1947, 'Milton's Birthplace', *London Topographical Record*, **19**, 1–12
Blunt, A., 1969, 'L'influence Francaise sur l'architecture et la sculpture decorative en Angleterre pendant la première moitié du xvie siècle', *Revue de l'art*, **4**, 17–29
Bond, E. A., 1840, 'Extracts from the Liberate Rolls, Relative to Loans Supplied by Italian Merchants to the Kings of England, in the Thirteenth and Fourteenth Centuries; with an Introductory Memoir', *Archaeologia*, **28**, 207–326
Bowden, P., 1967, 'Agricultural Prices, Farm Profits and Rents' in *The Agrarian History of England and Wales: iv, 1500–1640* (ed. J. Thirsk), 593–695
Bowler, D., 1983, 'Rangoon Street', *Popular Archaeology*, **5**, no. 6, 13–18
Brett-James, N., 1935, *The Growth of Stuart London*
Brimblecombe, P., 1982, 'Early Urban Climate and Atmosphere', in *Environmental Archaeology in the Urban Context* (ed. A. R. Hall & H. K. Kenward), Council for British Archaeology, Research Report 43, 10–25
Britton, F., 1986, *London Delftware*
Brooke, C. N. L., & Keir, G., 1975, *London 800–1216: The Shaping of a City*
Burgon, J. W., 1839, *The Life and Times of Sir Thomas Gresham, Knt* (2 vols.)
Buttner, H., & Meissner, G., 1983, *Town Houses of Europe* (Antique Collectors' Club)
Carlin, M., 1985, 'The Reconstruction of Winchester House, Southwark', *London Topographical Record*, **25**, 33–58
Carter, A., 1977, 'The Building Survey' in 'Excavations in Norwich 1976–7', *Norfolk Archaeology*, **36**, 298–304
Carver, M. O. H., 1979, 'Three Saxo-Norman Tenements in Durham City', *Medieval Archaeology*, **23**, 1–80
Castle, S. A., 1977, *Timber-framed Buildings in Watford*
Cater, W. A., 1912, 'The Priory of Austin Friars, London', *JBAA*, **18**, 25–82
Cater, W. A., 1915, 'The Austin Friars, London', *JBAA*, **21**, 213–21
Cecil, Hon. Mrs E., 1910, *A History of Gardening in England* (3rd ed.)
Celoria, F., & West, H., 1967, 'A Standard Specification for Tiles in 1477', *Journal British Ceramic Society*, **4.ii**, 217–20
Cescinsky, H., & Gribble, E. R., 1922, *Early English Furniture and Woodwork* (2 vols.)
Champness, R., 1966, *The Worshipful Company of Turners of London*
Chapelot, J., & Fossier, R., 1980 (trans. 1985), *The Village and House in the Middle Ages*
Cipolla, C. M., 1981, *Before the Industrial Revolution: European Society and Economy, 1000–1700* (2nd ed.)
Clapham, A. W., 1910, 'The Topography of the Carmelite Priory of London', *JBAA*, **16**, 15–32
Clapham, A. W., 1911–15, 'Three Medieval Hospitals of London', *Transactions of St Paul's Ecclesiological Society*, **7**, 153–60
Clapham, A. W., 1912, 'On the Topography of the Dominican Friary of London', *Archaeologia*, **63**, 57–84
Clapham, A. W., & Godfrey, W. H., 1913, *Some Famous Buildings and Their Story*
Clark, P., 1983, *The English Alehouse: A Social History 1200–1830*
Clarke, H., 1981, 'King's Lynn' in *Waterfront Archaeology in Britain and Northern Europe* (ed. G. Milne & B. Hobley), Council for British Archaeology, Research Report **41**, 132–6
Clarke, H., & Carter, A., 1977, *Excavations at King's Lynn 1963–1970*, Society of Medieval Archaeology, Monograph **7**
Clifton-Taylor, A., 1972, *The Pattern of English Building*
Colvin, H. M., 1958, 'Architecture and Town Planning' in *Medieval England* (ed. A. L. Poole), 37–97
Colvin, H. M., 1966, 'Views of the Old Palace of Westminster', *Architectural History*, **9**, 23–184
Conder, E., 1894, *Records of the Hole Crafte and Fellowship of Masons*
Consitt, F., 1933, *The London Weavers' Company: i, From the Twelfth to the Close of the Sixteenth Century*
Cook, G. H., 1955, *Old St Paul's Cathedral*
[Corinti, C.], 1976, *Firenze antica nei disegni di Corinto Corinti* (Istituto geografico militare, Florence)
Corner, G. R., 1860, 'Observations on the Remains of an Anglo-Norman Build-

ing . . . now believed to have been the Manor House of the Earls of Warren and Surrey in Southwark', *Archaeologia*, **38**, 37–53

Coulson, C., 1982, 'Hierarchism in Conventual Crenellation: an Essay in the Sociology and Metaphysics of Medieval Fortification', *Medieval Archaeology*, **26**, 69–100

Crawford, A., 1977, *A History of the Vintners' Company*

Crummy, P., 1981, *Aspects of Anglo-Saxon and Norman Colchester*, Council for British Archaeology, Research Report **39**

Curnow, P. E., 1978, 'The Bloody Tower' in *The Tower of London: Its Buildings and Institutions* (ed. J. Charlton), 55–61

Currie, C. R. J., 1988, 'Time and Change: Modelling the Attrition of Old Houses', *Vernacular Architecture*, **18**, 1–9

Davies, R. T., ed., 1963, *Medieval English Lyrics*

Davis, G. R. C., 1958, *Medieval Cartularies of Great Britain: A Short Catalogue*

Dawson, G., 1976, *The Black Prince's Palace at Kennington, Surrey*, British Archaeological Reports, **26**

Degnan, S., & Seeley, D., 1988, 'Medieval and Later Floor Tiles in Lambeth Palace Chapel', *London Archaeologist*, **6**

Devliegher, L., 1975, *Les maisons à Bruges*, translated into French from the original, *De Huizen te Brugge* (Tielt & Amsterdam)

Dietz, B., 1986, 'The North-East Coal Trade, 1550–1750: Measures, Markets and the Metropolis', *Northern History*, **22**, 280–94

Dixon, P., 1972, *Excavations at Greenwich Palace 1970–1*, Greenwich and Lewisham Antiquarian Society

Donkin, R. A., 1973, 'Changes in the Early Middle Ages' in *A New Historical Geography of England* (ed. H. C. Darby), 75–135

Drury, P., 1981, 'The Production of Brick and Tile in Medieval England' in *Medieval Industry* (ed. D. W. Crossley), Council for British Archaeology, Research Report **40**, 126–42

Drury, P., & Pratt, G. D., 1975, 'A Late Thirteenth and Early Fourteenth-Century Tile Factory at Danbury, Essex', *Medieval Archaeology*, **19**, 92–164

Dugdale, W., 1658, *The History of St Paul's Cathedral in London*

Dummelow, J., 1973, *The Waxchandlers of London*

Dunning, G. C., 1961, 'Medieval Chimney Pots' in *Studies in Building History* (ed. E. M. Jope) 78–93

Dyson, A., 1974, 'A Calendar of the Cartulary of the Parish Church of St Margaret, Bridge Street', *Guildhall Studies in London History*, **1** (3), 163–91

Dyson, T., 1975, 'The Pre-Norman bridge: A Re-appraisal, *London Archaeologist*, **2**, 326–7

Dyson, T., 1978, 'Two Saxon Land Grants for Queenhithe' in *Collectanea Londiniensia . . .* (ed. J. Bird, H. Chapman & J. Clark), LAMAS, Special Paper **2**, 200–15

Dyson, T., 1981, 'The Terms "Quay" and "Wharf" and the Early Medieval London Waterfront' in *Waterfront Archaeology in Britain and Northern Europe* (ed. G. Milne & B. Hobley), Council for British Archaeology, Research Report **41**, 37–8

Dyson, T., & Schofield, J., 1981, 'Excavations in the City of London: Second Interim Report, 1974–1978', *Trans. LAMAS*, **32**, 24–81

Dyson, T., & Schofield, J., 1984, 'Saxon London' in *Anglo-Saxon Towns in Southern England* (ed. J. Haslam), 285–314

Eames, E., 1968, *Medieval Tiles: A Handbook*

Eames, E., 1980, *Catalogue of Medieval Lead-glazed Earthenware Tiles in the Department of Medieval and Later Antiquities, British Museum* (2 vols.)

Eames, P., 1977, *Medieval Furniture* (Furniture History Society Journal, **13**)

Elkington, E., 1933, *The Coopers' Company and Craft*

Elsden, J. V., & Howe, J. A., 1923, *The Stones of London*

Emmison, F. G., 1976, *Elizabethan Life: Home, Work and Land* (Chelmsford)

Emmison, F. G., 1982, *Essex Wills (England), i, 1558–65* (National Genealogical Society, Washington DC)

Englefield, W. A. D., 1923, *The History of the Painter-Stainers' Company of London*

Faulkner, P. A., 1958, 'Domestic Planning from the Twelfth to the Fourteenth Centuries', *Archaeological Journal*, **115**, 150–83 (repr. in Swanton, 1975, 84–117)

Faulkner, P. A., 1966, 'Medieval Undercrofts and Town Houses', *Archaeological Journal*, **123**, 120–35 (repr. in Swanton, 1975, 118–33)

Fehring, G., 1984, 'Stadtarchäologie in Deutschland' in *Archeologia urbana e centro antico di Napoli: atti del convegno 1983* (ed. S. A. Muscettola & P. Gastaldi) (Naples), 49–58

Finlay, R., & Shearer, B., 1986, 'Population Growth and Suburban Expansion' in *London 1500–1700: The Making of a Metropolis* (ed. A. L. Beier & R. Finlay), 37–59

Fleming, A., *c.* 1580, *Some Account of William Lambe* (repr. 1875, copy at Clothworkers' Hall)

Fletcher, J. M., & Spokes, P. S., 1964, 'The Origin and Development of Crown-post Roofs', *Medieval Archaeology*, **8**, 152–83

Fry, Sir F. M., & Thomas, W. L., 1934, *The Windows of Merchant Taylors' Hall*

Gadd, D., 1983, 'The London Inn of the Abbots of Waltham: A Revised Reconstruction of a Medieval Town House in Lovat Lane', *Trans. LAMAS*, **34**, 171–8

Gadd, D., & Dyson, T., 1981, 'Bridewell Palace: Excavations at 9–11 Bridewell Place and 1–3 Tudor Street, City of London, 1978', *Post-Medieval Archaeology*, **15**, 1–79

Gage, J., 1822, *The History and Antiquities of Hengrave in Suffolk*

Gage, J., 1831, 'Letter Addressed by John Gage . . . Accompanying Drawings of Remains of the Prior of Lewes' Hostelry, in their Parish of St Olave, Southwark', *Archaeologia*, **23**, 299–308

Gardner, A., 1935, *English Medieval Sculpture*

Geddes, J., 1991, 'Iron', in Blair & Ramsey (eds.), 167–88

Gibson A., Partridge, C., & Day, I., 1982, 'Investigation of a Thirteenth-century Building at No 2 West Street, Ware', *Hertfordshire Archaeology*, **8**, 126–43

Girouard, M., 1983, *Robert Smythson and the Elizabethan Country House*

Girouard, M., 1985, *Cities and People: A Social and Architectural History*

Girtin, T., 1958, *The Golden Ram: A Narrative History of the Clothworkers' Company 1528–1958*

Giuseppi, M. S., 1899, 'The Parliamentary Surveys Relating to Southwark', *Surrey Archaeological Collections*, **14**, 64–71

Giuseppi, M. S., 1920, 'The Wardrobe and Household Accounts of Bogo de Clare', *Archaeologia*, **70**, 1–56

Gloag, J., 1972, *Guide to Furniture Styles: English and French 1450–1850*

Godfrey, E. S., 1975, *The Development of English Glassmaking 1560–1640*

Godfrey, W. H., 1942, 'London Properties of the Cluniac Priory of St Pancras, Lewes, Sussex', *London Topographical Record*, **18**, 1–26

Godfrey, W. H., 1953, 'Recent Discoveries at the Temple, London', *Archaeologia*, **95**, 123–40

Godfrey, W. H., 1964, *A History of Architecture in and around London*

Godfrey, W. H., & Wagner, Sir A., 1963, *The College of Heralds*, Survey of London, **16**

Goldthwaite, R., 1980, *The Building of Renaissance Florence*

Goodall, I., 1991, 'The Medieval Blacksmith and his Products' in *Medieval Industry* (ed. D. W. Crossley), Council for British Archaeology, Research Report **40**, 51–62

Goss, C. W. F., 1908, *Crosby Hall: A Chapter in the History of London* (W. Heffer, Cambridge)

Goss, C. W. F., 1930, *Sir Paul Pindar and his Bishopsgate Mansion* (W. Heffer, Cambridge)

Gotch, J. A., 1901, *Early Renaissance Architecture in England*

Gould, A. W., 1912, *History of the Worshipful Company of Fruiterers of the City of London*

Graham, R., 1932, 'A Plan of the Site and Buildings of St Anthony's Hospital, Threadneedle Street, *c.* 1530', *London Topographical Record*, **16**, 1–8

Gravett, K., 1971, *Timber and Brick Building in Kent*

Griep, H.-G., 1959 (repr. 1984), *Das Bürgerhaus in Goslar* (Tübingen)

Grimes, W. F., 1968, *The Excavation of Roman and Medieval London*

Gros, G. W., 1981, *The Diary of Baron Waldstein*

Guillaume, J., & Toulier, B., 1983, 'Tissu urbain et types de demeures; la cas de Tours' in *La maison de ville à la Renaissance* (ed. A. Chastel & J. Guillaume) (Paris), 9–24

Gwilt, C. E., 1834, 'Exhibitions of drawings of a crypt . . . on the site of the hostelry of the Prior of Lewes, in St Olave's Southwark', *Archaeologia*, **25**, 604–6

Hall, R. A., MacGregor, H., & Stockwell, M., 1988, *Medieval Tenements in Aldwark and Other Sites*, Archaeology of York, **10/2**

Hammel, R, 1986, 'Hereditas, area und domus: Bodenrent, Grundstücksgefüge und Socialstruktur in Lübeck vom 12. bis zum 16. Jahrhundert', in *Hausbau in Lübeck*, Jahrbuch für Hansforschung, **35**, 175–200.

Hammerson, M. J., 1975, 'Excavations on the Site of Arundel House in the Strand, WC2, in 1972', *Trans. LAMAS*, **26**, 209–51

Hammon, H. J., 1844, *The Architectural Antiquities and Present State of Crosby Place, London, as restored by John Davies, architect, delineated in a series of plans, elevations . . . from original drawings by H. J. Hammon: with an historical and descriptive account*

Harding, V., 1980, 'The Two Coldharbours of London', *London Topographical Record*, **24**, 11–30

Harding, V., 1985, 'Reconstructing London before the Great Fire', *London Topographical Record*, **25**, 1–12

Harding, V., & Metcalf, P., 1986, *Lloyds at Home: The Background and the Building*

Harris, E., 1958, 'A Medieval Undercroft at 50 Mark Lane, London EC3', *Medieval Archaeology*, **2**, 178–81

Harris, R., 1978, *Discovering Timber-framed Buildings*

Harvey, J., 1972, 'Four Fifteenth-century London Plans Relating to Bridge House Property in Deptford, without the Bar of Southwark, without St George's Bar towards Newington, and in Carter Lane in the City', *London*

Topographical Record, **23**, 35–59

Harvey, J., 1975, *Medieval Craftsmen*

Harvey, J., 1978, *The Perpendicular Style 1330–1485*

Harvey, J., 1981, *Medieval Gardens*

Haslam, J., 1972, 'Medieval Streets in London', *London Archaeologist*, **2**, 3–8

Haslam, J., 1973, 'The Excavation of a Section across Aldersgate Street, City of London, 1972', *Trans. LAMAS*, **24**, 74–84

Heath, Baron, 1869, *Some Account of the Worshipful Company of Grocers* (3rd ed.)

Hembry, P., 1978, 'Episcopal Palaces, 1535 to 1660' in *Wealth and Power in Tudor England: Essays Presented to S. T. Bindoff* (ed. E. W. Ives, R. J. Knecht & J. J. Scarisbrick), 146–66

Herbert, P., 1979, 'Excavations at Christchurch, Greyfriars, 1976', *London Archaeologist*, **3**, 327–32

Hewett, C. A., 1969, *The Development of English Carpentry 1200–1700: An Essex Study*

Hewett, C. A., 1973, 'The Development of the Post-medieval House', *Post-Medieval Archaeology*, **7**, 60–78

Hewett, C. A., 1980, *English Historic Carpentry*

Hind, A. M., 1922, *Wenceslaus Hollar and his Views of London*

Hobley, B., & Schofield, J., 1977, 'Excavations in the City of London, 1974–5: First Interim Report', *Antiquaries Journal*, **57**, 31–66

Holmes, M., 1966, 'An Unrecorded Map of London', *Archaeologia*, **100**, 105–28

Holst, J. C., 1986, 'Beobachtungen zu Handelsnutzung und Geschossbildung an Lübecker Steinhäusern des Mittelalters', *Hausbau in Lübeck*, Jahrbuch für Hausforschung, **35**, 93–144

Holt, R., 1985, 'Gloucester in the Century after the Black Death', *Trans. Bristol and Gloucestershire Archaeology Society*, 103, (1985); repr. in *The Medieval Town: A Reader in English Urban History 1200–1540*, ed. R. Holt and G. Rosser (1990), 141–59

Honeybourne, M. B., 1952, 'The Abbot of Waltham's Inn', *London Topographical Record*, **20**, 34–46

Honeybourne, M. B., 1963–7, 'The Leper Houses of the London Area', *Trans. LAMAS*, **21**, 3–61

Hope, Sir W. St J., 1925, *The History of the London Charterhouse from its Foundation until the Suppression of the Monastery*

Hopkinson, H. L., 1913, *A History of the Site of Merchant Taylors' Hall in the City of London*

Hopkinson, H. L., 1931, *The History of Merchant Taylors' Hall*

Horsman, V., Milne., G., & Milne, C., 1988, *Aspects of Saxo-Norman London 1: Building and Street Development near Billingsgate and Cheapside*, LAMAS, Special Paper, **11**

Hoskins, W. G., 1976, *The Age of Plunder: King Henry's England 1500–1547*

Howgego, J., 1978, *Printed Maps of London circa 1553–1850* (2nd ed.)

Hugo, T., 1866, *An Illustrated Itinerary of the Ward of Bishopsgate in the City of London*

Hunting, P., 1988, *St Paul's Vista: A History Commissioned by Lep Group to Mark the Redevelopment of the Sunlight Wharf Site* (Lep Group, London)

Hurst, J. G., 1961, 'The Kitchen Area of Northolt Manor, Middlesex', *Medieval Archaeology*, **5**, 211–99

Hurstfield, J., & Skelton, R. A., 'John Norden's View of London, 1600', *London Topographical Record*, **22**, 5–26

Imray, J., 1968, *The Charity of Richard Whittington*

Johnson, D. J., 1969, *Southwark and the City*

Johnson, T., 1974, 'Excavations at Christ Church, Newgate Street, 1973', *Trans. LAMAS*, **25**, 220–34

Jones, P. E., 1953, 'Some Bridge House Properties', *JBAA*, **16**, 59–73

Jones, P. E., 1976, *The Butchers of London*

Jones, P. E., & Smith, R., 1950, *A Guide to the Records in the Corporation of London Records Office and the Guildhall Library Muniment Room*

Jope, E. M., ed., 1961, *Studies in Building History*

Jourdain, M., 1950, *English Interior Decoration 1500 to 1830*

Jupp, E. B., 1848, *An Historical Account of the Worshipful Company of Carpenters*

Keene, D., 1975, 'Suburban Growth' in *The Plans and Topography of Medieval Towns in England and Wales* (ed. M. W. Barley), Council for British Archaeology, Research Report, **14**, 71–82

Keene, D., 1984, 'A New Study of London before the Great Fire', *Urban History Yearbook 1984*, 11–21

Keene, D., 1985, *Cheapside before the Great Fire*

Keene, D., 1987, 'The Walbrook Study: a Summary Report', MS in library of Institute of Historical Research, University of London

Keene, D., 1989, 'New Discoveries at the Hanseatic Steelyard in London', *Hansische Geschichtsblätter* (Cologne), **107**, 15–25

Keene, D., 1990, 'Documentary Report on Well Court Site', in Schofield *et al.*, 89–113

Kenyon, G. H., 1967, *The Glass Industry of the Weald*

Kingsford, C. L., 1920, 'Two Forfeitures in the Year of Agincourt', *Archaeologia*, **70**, 71–100

Kingsford, C. L., 1921, 'On Some London Houses of the Early Tudor Period', *Archaeologia*, **71**, 17–54

Kingsford, C. L., 1922, 'Bath Inn or Arundel House', *Archaeologia*, **72**, 243–77

Kingsford, C. L., 1923, 'Essex House, formerly Leicester House and Exeter Inn', *Archaeologia*, **73**, 1–5

Kingsford, C. L., 1925, 'A London Merchant's House and its Owners, 1360–1614', *Archaeologia*, **74**, 137–58

King, D., 1985, 'The Carpet Collection of Cardinal Wolsey', in *Oriental Carpet and Textile Studies*, **I** (ed. R. Pinner & W. B. Denny), 41–54

Kissan, B. W., 1940, 'An Early List of London Properties', *Trans. LAMAS*, **8**, 57–69

Knight, W., 1831, 'Observations on the Mode of Construction of the Present Old London Bridge, As Discovered in the Years 1826 and 1827', *Archaeologia*, **23**, 117–19

Knight, W., 1834, 'Account of Some Antiquities Discovered in Excavating for the Foundations of London Bridge, and of the Ancient Northern Embankment of the Thames in its Neighbourhood', *Archaeologia*, **25**, 600–2

Knoop, D., & Jones, G. P., 1953, *The Medieval Mason*

Knowles, D., & Grimes, W. F., 1954, *Charterhouse*

Lambert, F., 1921, 'Some Recent Excavations in London', *Archaeologia*, **71**, 55–112

Lappenberg, J. M., 1851, *Urkundliche Geschichte der Hansischen Stahlofes zu London* (Hamburg)

Lauret, A., Malebranche, R., & Séraphin, G., 1988, *Bastides: villes nouvelles du Moyen Age* (Toulouse)

Lavigne, M., 1983, 'Lyon: le quartier Saint-Jean' in *La maison de ville à la Renaissance* (ed. A. Chastel & J. Gauilaume) (Paris), 37–42

Lea, R., 1985, 'Archaeology of Standing Structures', *Popular Archaeology*, **6**, No. 14, 22–30

Lethaby, W. R., 1900, 'The Priory of Holy Trinity, Aldgate', *Home Counties Magazine*, **2**, 45–53

Lethaby, W. R., 1925, *Westminster Abbey Re-examined*

Lewis, E., Roberts, E., & Roberts, K., 1988, *Medieval Hall Houses of the Winchester Area* (Winchester City Museum)

Lipman, V. D., 1967, *The Jews of Medieval Norwich*

Lipson, E., 1915, *The Economic History of England i: The Middle Ages*

Lloyd, N., 1931, *History of the English House* (repr. 1975)

Lobel, M. D., 1989, *The City of London from Prehistoric Times to c. 1520*, The British Atlas of Historic Towns, III

Loftus-Brock, E. P., 1872, 'Notes on the Norman Crypt', *JBAA*, **28**, 176–9

Loftus-Brock, E. P., 1880, 'Description of an Ancient Crypt at Aldgate, Recently Demolished', *JBAA*, **36**, 159–64

London Museum, 1940, *Medieval Catalogue* (repr. 1954; 1967 ed. used)

Longman, W., 1873, *A History of Three Cathedrals Dedicated to St Paul in London*

Maitland, W., 1756, *History of London*

Malfatti, C. V., 1953, *Two Italian Accounts of Tudor England*

Maloney, J., & Harding, C., 1979, 'Duke's Place and Houndsditch: The Medieval Defences', *London Archaeologist*, **3**, 347–54

Mander, C. H. W., 1931, *A Descriptive and Historical Account of the Guild of Cordwainers*

Marks, R., 1991, 'Window Glass' in Blair & Ramsey (eds), 265–94

Marsden, P., 1967, 'Archaeological Finds in the City of London, 1963–4', *Trans. Lamas*, **21**, 189–221

Marsden, P., 1968, 'Archaeological Finds in the City of London, 1965–6', *Trans. LAMAS*, **22**, Part 1, 1–17

Marsden, P., 1969, 'Archaeological Finds in the City of London, 1966–8', *Trans. LAMAS*, **22**, Part 2, 1–26

Marsden, P., 1970, 'Archaeological Finds in the City of London, 1966–9', *Trans. LAMAS*, **22**, Part 3, 1–9

Marsden, P., 1980, *Roman London*

Marsden, P., 1981, 'The Pre-1411 Guildhall of London', *London Archaeologist*, **4**, 115–20

Martin, A. W., 1927, 'Excavations at Whitefriars, Fleet Street, 1927–8', *JBAA*, 33, 293–320

Martin, D., & Martin, B., 1987, *A Selection of Dated Houses in Eastern Sussex 1400–1750*, Rape of Hastings Architectural Survey: Historic Buildings in Eastern Sussex, **4**

Mason, R. T., 1964, *Framed Buildings of the Weald* (2nd ed., 1969)

Masters, B. R., 1969, 'The Mayor's Household before 1600', in *Studies in London History Presented to P. E. Jones* (ed. A. Hollaender & W. Kellaway), 95–114

Mayer, E., 1968, *The Curriers and the City of London*

McCann, W., in prep., 'Fleet Valley Excavations'

McDonnell, K., 1978, *Medieval London Suburbs*

Mellor, J. E., 1981, *The Austin Friars, Leicester*, Council for British Archaeology, Research Report, **35**

Mercer, E., 1962, *English Art 1553–1625*

Mercer, E., 1975, *English Vernacular Houses*

Merrifield, R., 1965, *The Roman City of London*

Metcalf, P., 1977, *The Halls of the Fishmongers' Company*

Milbourn, T., 1881, 'Church of St Stephen Walbrook', *Trans. LAMAS*, **5**, 327–402

Miller, L., 1977, 'New Fresh Wharf, 2: The Saxon and Early Medieval Waterfronts', *London Archaeologist*, **3**, 45–53

Milne, G., 1992, *Timber Building Techniques in London, c. 900–1400*, LAMAS, Special Paper, **15**

Milne, G., & Milne, C., 1978, 'Excavations on the Thames Waterfront at Trig Lane, London 1974–6', *Medieval Archaeology*, **22**, 84–104

Milne, G., & Milne, C., 1981, 'Medieval Buildings at Trig Lane', *London Archaeologist*, **4**, 31–7

Milne, G., & Milne, C., 1982, *Medieval Waterfront Development at Trig Lane, London*, LAMAS, Special Paper, **5**

Monier-Williams, M. F., 1897, *Records of the Worshipful Company of Tallow Chandlers*

Moore, N., 1918, *The History of St Bartholomew's Hospital* (2 vols.)

Moore, N. J., 'Brick' in Blair & Ramsey (eds), 211–36

Moorhouse, S., 1981, 'The Medieval Pottery Industry, in *Medieval Industry* (ed. D. W. Crossley), Council for British Archaeology, Research Report, **40**, 96–125

More, R., 1602, *The Carpenter's Rule* (repr. Amsterdam, 1970)

Morgan, R., & Schofield, J., 1978, 'Tree Rings and the Archaeology of the Thames Waterfront in the City of London' in *Dendrochronology in Europe* (ed. J. Fletcher), British Archaeological Reports, **S51**, 223–39

Munby, L. M., 1977, *The Hertfordshire Landscape*

Museum of London, Department of Urban Archaeology, 1987, *Archive Catalogue*

Nicholl, J., 1866, *Some Account of the Worshipful Company of Ironmongers* (2nd ed.)

Nichols, J. G., 1870, 'The Muniments of the Vintners' Company', *Trans. LAMAS*, **3**, 432–47

Norman, P., 1901, 'Sir John de Pulteney and his Two Residences in London, Cold Harbour and the Manor of the Rose, Together with a Few Remarks on the Parish of St Lawrence Pountney', *Archaeologia*, **57**, 257–84

Norman, P., 1904, 'Roman and Later Remains found during Excavations on the Site of Newgate Prison, 1903–4', *Archaeologia*, **59**, 125–42

Norman, P., 1905, *London Vanished and Vanishing*

Norman, P., 1909, 'Notes on the Later History of the Steelyard in London', *Archaeologia*, **61**, 389–426

Norman, P., 1916, 'Recent Discoveries of Medieval Remains in London', *Archaeologia*, **67**, 1–26

Norman, P., & Mann, E. A., 1909, 'On the White Conduit, Chapel Street, Bloomsbury, and its Connexion with the Greyfriars' Water System', *Archaeologia*, **61**, 347–56

Norman, P., & Reader, F. W., 1906, 'Further Disoveries Relating to Roman London', *Archaeologia*, **60**, 169–250

O'Neil, B. H. St J., 1953, 'Some Seventeenth-century Houses in Great Yarmouth', *Archaeologia*, **95**, 141–80

Orrell, J., 1983, *The Quest for Shakespeare's Globe*

Oxley, J. E., 1968, *The Fletchers and Longbowstringmakers of London*

Page, W., 1923, *London: Its Origin and Early Development*

Pantin, W. A., 1947, 'The Development of Domestic Architecture in Oxford', *Antiquaries Journal*, **27**, 120–50

Pantin, W. A., 1961, 'Medieval Inns', in *Studies in Building History* (ed. E. M. Jope), 166–91

Pantin, W. A., 1963, 'Some Medieval English Town Houses: A Study in Adaptation', in *Culture and Environment: Essays in Honour of Sir Cyril Fox* (ed. I. Foster & L. Alcock), 445–78

Parker, V., 1971, *The Making of King's Lynn*

Parry, J. H., ed., 1912, *Registrum Johannis de Trillek*, Canterbury & York Society (2 vols.)

Parsloe, G., 1964, *Wardens' Accounts of the Worshipful Company of Founders of the City of London 1497–1681*

Paul, R., 1894, *Vanishing London*

Payne, A., 1987, *Views of the Past: Topographical Drawings in the British Library*

Pearce, J. E., Vince, A., & Jenner, M. A., 1985, *Medieval Pottery: London-type Ware* (A dated type-series of London medieval pottery: 2), LAMAS, Special Paper, **6**

Pendrill, C., 1937, *Old Parish Life in London*

Pennant, T., 1813, *Some Account of London* (5th ed.)

Penrose, F. C., 1879, 'On the Recent Discoveries of Portions of Old St Paul's Cathedral', *Archaeologia*, **47**, 381–92

Perring, D., 1981, *Early Medieval Occupation at Flaxengate, Lincoln*, Archaeology of Lincoln, **IX-1**

Phillips, H. L., 1915, *Annals of the Worshipful Company of Joiners of the City of London*

Platt, C., 1976, *The English Medieval Town*

Platt, C., & Coleman-Smith, R., 1975, *Excavations in Medieval Southampton 1953–1969* (2 vols.)

Portman, D., 1966, *Exeter Houses 1400–1700*

Povah, A., 1894, *The Annals of the Parishes of St Olave Hart Street and All Hallows Staining, in the City of London*

Power, M. J., 1978, 'East and West in Early-modern London' in *Wealth and Power in Tudor England: Essays Presented to S. T. Bindoff* (ed. E. W. Ives, R. K. Knecht & J. J. Scarisbrook), 167–85

Power, M. J., 1985, 'John Stow and his London', *Journal of Historical Geography*, **11**, 1–20

Price, J. E., 1870, 'Medieval Kiln . . . discovered near Farringdon Road', *Trans. LAMAS*, **3** (1866–70), 31–6

Priestley, U., & Corfield, P., 1982, 'Room and Room Use in Norwich Housing, 1580–1730', *Post-Medieval Archaeology*, **16**, 93–123

Prockter, A., & Taylor, R., eds, 1979, *The A to Z of Elizabethan London*

Puloy, M., 1982, 'Decorative Plasterwork in Hertfordshire', *Hertfordshire Archaeology*, **8**, 144–99

Ramsay, G. D., 1982, *The English Woollen Industry 1500–1750*

Reddaway, T., 1963, 'Elizabethan London: Goldsmith's Row in Cheapside, 1558–1645', Guildhall Miscellany, **2**, 181–206

Reddaway, T., & Walker, L. E. M., 1975, *The Early History of the Goldsmiths' Company 1327–1509*

Richardson, H. G., 1960, *The English Jewry under Angevin Kings*

Robinson, J. A., 1911, *The Abbot's House at Westminster*

Rogers, K., 1928, *The Mermaid and Mitre Taverns in Old London*

Rosser, G., 1989, *Medieval Westminster 1200–1540*

Royce, D., ed., 1892, *Landboc sive registrum Winchelcumba* (2 vols.)

Salter, H. E., 1926, *Oxford City Properties*, Oxford Historical Society, **83**

Salzman, L. F., 1923, *Medieval English Industries*

Salzman, L. F., 1964, *English Trade in the Middle Ages*

Samuel, M. W., 1987, 'The Undercroft at 34 Watling Street', *London Archaeologist*, **5**, 286–90

Samuel, M., 1989, 'The Fifteenth-century Garner at Leadenhall', *Antiquaries Journal*, **69**, 119–53

Sawyer, P. H., 1968, *Anglo-Saxon Charters: An Annotated List and Bibliography*

Schofield, J., 1975, 'Seal House', *Current Archaeology*, **49**, 53–7

Schofield, J., 1975–6, 'Excavations South of Edinburgh High Street, 1973–4', *Proceedings of Society of Antiquaries of Scotland*, **107**, 155–241

Schofield, J., 1977, 'New Fresh Wharf: 3, The Medieval Buildings', *London Archaeologist*, **4**, 66–73

Schofield, J., 1978, 'Bastion 10A: A Newly Identified Bastion in the City of London', *Trans. LAMAS*, **29**, 91–8

Schofield, J., 1981, 'Waterfront Buildings in the City of London', in G. Milne & B. Hobley (eds), *Waterfront Archaeology in Britain and Northern Europe*, Council for British Archaeology, Research Report, **41**, 24–31

Schofield, J., 1987, 'Archaeology in the City of London: Archive and Publication', *Archaeological Journal*, **144**, 424–33

Schofield, J., 1993, 'The Capital Rediscovered: Archaeology in the City of London, *Urban History*, **20**, 211–24

Schofield, J., in prep., 'Medieval Parish Churches in London'

Schofield, J., Allen, P., & Taylor, C., 1990, *Medieval Buildings and Property Development in the Area of Cheapside*, Trans. LAMAS, **41**, 39–238

Schofield, J., & Dyson, T., 1980, *Archaeology of the City of London* (MOL)

Schofield, J., & Dyson, T., in prep., *Medieval Waterfront Tenements*

Schofield, J., & Lea, R., in prep., *Holy Trinity Priory, Aldgate*

Sefton-Jones, M., 1923, *Old Devonshire House by Bishopsgate*

Sheldon, H., 1972, 'Excavations at Toppings and Sun Wharves, Southwark, 1970–72', *Trans. LAMAS*, **25**, 1–116

Shepherd, L., in prep., 'Swan Lane'

Sherwell, J. W., 1889, *History of the Guild of Saddlers*

Shirley, W. W., 1862, 'Royal and Other Historical Letters Illustrative of the Reign of Henry III', Rolls Series, **27** (2 vols.)

Simpson, Sir J. W., 1928, *Some Account of the Old Hall of Lincoln's Inn*

Simpson, W. S., 1868, 'On the Parish of St Peter Cheap, in the City of London, from 1392 to 1633', *JBAA*, **24**, 248–70

Simpson, W. S., 1905, 'The Palaces or the Houses of the Bishops of London', *Trans. LAMAS*, New Series, **1**, 13–73

Singer, C., Holmyard, E. T., Hall, A. R., & Williams, T. T., 1957, *A History of Technology: iii, c. 1500–c. 1750*

Smith, J., 1807, *Antiquities of Westminster*

Smith, J. T., 1955, 'Medieval Aisled Halls and their Derivatives', *Archaeological Journal*, **112**, 76–94 (repr. in Swanton, 1975, 27–44)

Smith, J. T., 1958, 'Medieval Roofs: A Classification', *Archaeological Journal*, **155**, 111–49 (repr. in Swanton, 1975, 45–83)

Smith, J. T., 1965, 'Timber-framed Building in England', *Archaeological Journal*, **122**, 133–58 (repr. in Swanton, 1975, 1–26)

Smith, T., 1985, *The Medieval Brickmaking Industry in England 1400–1450*, British Archaeological, Reports, **138**

Somerville, R., 1960, *The Savoy: Manor, Hospital, Chapel*

Stanley-Stone, A. C., 1925, *The Worshipful Company of Turners of London: Its Origin and History*

Steedman, K., Dyson, T., & Schofield, J., 1992, *Aspects of Saxo-Norman London, 3: The Bridgehead and Billingsgate to 1200*, LAMAS, Special Paper, **14**

Stenton, Sir F. M., 1934, *Norman London*, repr. in D. M. Stenton (ed.), *Preparatory to Anglo-Saxon England* (1970), 23–47

Stephenson, D., 1984–5, 'Colchester: A Smaller Medieval English Jewry', *Essex Archaeology and History*, **16**, 48–52

Strype, J., 1720, *A Survey of the Cities of London and Westminster Present* (3 vols.)

Sutton, A., & Sewell, J. R., 1980, 'Jacob Verzelini and the City of London', *Glass Technology*, **21**, No. 4, 190–2

Swanton, M. J., ed., 1975, *Studies in Medieval Domestic Architecture*, Royal Archaeological Institute

Tatchell, M., 1962, 'A Fourteenth-century London Building Contract', *Guildhall Miscellany*, **2**, 129–31

Tatton-Brown, T., 1974, 'Excavations at the Custom House Site, City of London', *Trans. LAMAS*, **25**, 117–219

Tatton-Brown, T., 1975, 'Excavations at the Custom House, Part II', *Trans. LAMAS*, **26**, 103–70

Thompson, A., 1979, 'St Nicholas in the Shambles', *Current Archaeology*, **65**, 176–9

Thompson, A., Grew, F., & Schofield, J., 1984, 'Excavations at Aldgate, City of London, 1974', *Post-Medieval Archaeology*, **18**, 1–149

Thompson, W. A., 1939–40, *History of the [Drapers'] Company's Properties and Trusts*

Thornbury, W., 1872–8, *Old and New London* (3 vols.)

Thornton, P., 1971, (commentary in) Lindsay Boynton, 'The Hardwick Inventory of 1601', *Furniture History*, **7**

Thornton, P., 1978, *Seventeenth-century Interior Decoration in England, France and Holland*

Thrupp, S., 1933, *A Short History of the Worshipful Company of Bakers of London*

Tollon, B., 1983, 'Toulouse' in *La maison de ville à la Renaissance* (ed. A. Chastel & J. Guillaume) (Paris), 51–8

Toy, S., 1932, 'The Crypt at Whitefriars, London', *JBAA*, **38**, 334–7

Tracy, C., 1988, *English Medieval Furniture and Woodwork* (Victoria and Albert Museum)

Trevelyan, G. M., 1952, *Illustrated English Social History*, vol. 2

Turner, R. C., 1988, 'Early Carpentry in the Rows of Chester', *Vernacular Architecture*, **19**, 34–41

Unwin, G., 1908, *The Gilds and Companies of London* (4th ed., 1963)

Urry, W., 1967, *Canterbury under the Angevin Kings*

Vince, A., 1985, 'Saxon and Medieval Pottery in London: A Review', *Medieval Archaeology*, **29**, 25–93

Vogts, H., 1930, *Die Kunstdenkmaler der Stadt Koln* (Düsseldorf)

Wadmore, J. F., 1881, *The History and Antiquities of the Skinners*

Wall, C., Cameron, H. C., & Underwood, E. A., 1963, *A History of the Worshipful Society of Apothecaries of London: i, 1617–1815*

Watson, J. S., 1963, *A History of the Salters' Company*

Webb, E. A., 1913, 'The Plan of St Bartholomew, West Smithfield, and the Recent Excavations', *Archaeologia*, **64**, 165–76

Webb, E. A., 1921, *The Records of St Bartholomew's Priory and of the Church and Parish of St Bartholomew the Great, West Smithfield* (2 vols.)

Weinstein, R., 1980, 'Clothworkers in St Stephen Coleman Parish, 1612', *London Topographical Record*, **24**, 61–80

Welch, C., 1902, *History of the Worshipful Company of Pewterers of the City of London* (2 vols.)

Welch, C., 1916, *History of the Cutlers' Company of London* (2 vols.)

Westman, A., 1987, 'The Church of St Alphege', *Archaeology Today*, **8** (**11**), 23–5

Wheatley, H. B., 1916, 'Original Plan of Durham House . . . 1612', *London Topographical Record*, x, 150–62

Whinney, M., 1964, *Sculpture in Britain 1530–1830*

Williams, G. A., 1963, *Medieval London: From Commune to Capital* (repr. 1970)

Williams, J. H., 1979, *St Peter's Street, Northampton*, Northampton Archaeological Monograph

Williams, T., 1982, 'St Peter's Hill', *Popular Archaeology*, **4** (July 1982), 24–30

Wilson, C., 1976, 'The Original Design of the City of London Guildhall', *JBAA*, **129**, 1–14

Woods, D., Rhodes, M., & Dyson, T., 1975, 'Africa House Sections, London 1973', *Trans. LAMAS*, **26**, 252–66

Wood, M., 1965, *The English Medieval House*

Yule, B., in prep. 'Winchester Palace'

Zagorin, P., 1969, *The Court and the Country*

Index

musketry, 91
mustardstones, 27

Nantes (France), cushions from, 132
Nayler, Bryan, 8
Nedeham, James, carpenter and surveyor of the king's works, 86, 114, 178
Needlers Lane, 145
Nettlestead Place (Kent), 37
Neville, Ralph, bishop of Chichester and chancellor, 35, 47
　Ralph, of Raby, 153
　Richard, Earl of Warwick, 185
Neville's Inn, 2, 62, 153, Fig. 242
New Conduit (Aldersgate), 3
New Fresh Wharf, 27, 31, 52, 137, 174, Figs. 28, 92, 153, 157, 254
New Street (later Converts' Lane and Chaunceler's Lane), 47
New Temple, 14, 23, 78
Newgate, 10–11, 141; plan of gate in 1676, Fig. 4; see also 134; gaol in, Fig. 4
Newington, parish of, 196
Newington Butts, 5
[St] Nicholas Lane, 61, 67, 81, 85, 92, 142, Figs. 50, 100a
Nicholl, Richard, and Mary his wife, 142
Noah, in wall painting, 128, Fig. 145
noble residences, 25, 35–44
Noble Street, 153
noise, 7
Norden, John, 4, 23
Norfolk, 41
　Duke of, see Howard
　Earls of (Bigods), 165
Norman, prior of Holy Trinity, 10
　son of Alfred Horeh, 10
North, Sir Edward (later Lord), 102, 48, 143
Northampton (Northants.), 27
Northampton, John de, mayor, 167
　Marquess of, 193; see also 28
Northampton Inn, 167
Northerne, Stephen le, ironmonger, 128, 131–2
Northolt (Middx), manor-house, 151
Northumberland, Earls of, 71, 134; see also Percy
Northumberland Alley, 71, 101
Northumberland Inn (Fenchurch St), 43, 71
Northumberland Inn (or Place, Aldersgate St), 134
Norwich (Norfolk), 26, 31, 60, 88; Bridewell, 60; King Street, 32; St Martin at Palace Plain, 32
Norwich, bishop of, 35; Inn of the bishop of (Norwich Place), 160; see also 195
nunneries, 14, 250

oak, 129, 131, 140–1; heart of, or seasoned, 89, 175, 196; trees, 89
offal, dumping of, 7
Ogilby and Morgan, map, 2, 44, 8, 12, 22, 25, 27, 53, 60, 64–5, 68, 71, 79, 82, 84, 88, 99, 103, 107–8, 110, 112, 114, 117–18, 121, 126, 128, 130–1, 136, 143, 149, 153, 157, 166, 170, 185, Figs. 52, 73, 195
Okebourne (Ogbourne, Wilts.), Inn of the prior of, 38
Old Bailey, 9, 88–9, 140, 143, Fig. 48
Old East India House, supposed, 115, Fig. 230
Old Fish Street Hill, 144; see also Fish Street Hill (Lambeth Hill)
Old Fishmongers' Hall, 144, Fig. 240
Old Ford, 8
Old Fountain (Minories), Fig. 165
Old Jewry (Vicus Judaiorum), 31, 149; see also 46
Old Soar, Plaxtol (Kent), 37
Old Swan Lane, 171
Oldbourne Hall, 152
Olyver, John, draper, 128–32
　John, shearman, 190
Or San Michele, Florence, 21
oratory, 106
orchards, 89, 39, 157, 195
Orgar the Rich, 34, 193
oriels and oriel windows, 41, 102–3; on Bishopsgate, 10; on a door, 191; see also bay windows
Ormond Place, 182
Ormston, Thomas, clothworker, 179
Ottery St Mary (Devon), College of, property, 113
Our Lady, tenement name, 172
outhouses, 88–9
ovens, 59, 116, 233, 69, 76, 88, 164–5, 175, 189; on London Bridge, 8; in shops, Fig. 62a–b
oxen, 89
Oxford (Oxon.), 7, 60, 177; corn from, 21; stone from 159
　Inn of the Earl of, 43
Oxford Place, see 34
Oxfordshire, traffic from, 21

Paesschen, Hendrick van, 25
Page, John, carpenter, 55, 89
Paget, William, 156
Paget's Place, 156
paint and paintings, 47, 128, Figs. 143–6; on plaster, 74;

red lead, 128; on internal walls, 54, 120–5
painters and painter-stainers, 123, 3
Painter-Stainers' Company, Hall, 47
Pakemann's Wharf, 52, 175, Figs. 18, 255, 257
Palmer, Andrew, goldsmith, 181
Pancras Lane, 92, 145, Fig. 70; access pattern through house, Fig. 100c
panelling, 120, 96, 107, 149; see also wainscot
panels, carved, 105
pantries, 71, 107, 53, 85, 103, 112, 128, 139, 149, 152, 162, 166, 170, 178; at Guildhall, 17
Papey, Brotherhood of, hall, see 121
parclos (screen), 32
parells (fireplace surrounds), 115
Paris (France), 5, 38, 84; Ste Chapelle, 35
Paris, Matthew, chronicler, 38
Paris Garden Manor, 8
Parish Clerks' Company (Fraternity), Hall I, 47, 23; Hall II, see 23; almshouses, 56, 23
parishes, formation of, 12; records, 3
Parker, Richard, parson, 44
parks, 195
parlours (interloquitorium, parlorium), 2–3, 5, 41, 44, 47, 49, 66–8, 81–2, 86, 89, 107–8, 111, 113, 130–2; ground-floor or probably so, 3, 10, 15, 22–3, 26, 30, 40, 45, 48, 52, 55–6, 59, 66, 69–70, 72, 76, 85, 98, 112, 115, 121, 128, 139, 142–5, 149, 151, 154–5, 162, 166, 173, 175, 178–9, 184, 193, 197; first-floor, 2, 8, 96, 169; Long Parlour, 128; summer, 66, 111, 131, 98; used for dining, 85; winter, 98; Figs. 48–51, 54, 57, 59b, 61, 62a, 66, 70, 75a–b, 76, 191–2, 194, 198, 209, 213–14, 226, 233, 240, 255
parmentarius (robe-trimmer), 138
partitions, 73, 81
passages, 86
pasternosterer, 146
Paston, John, 185
　Sir William, 25, 43
Paulshede tavern, 131
Pavedhalle, le, 113
Paycocke, Thomas, clothier of Coggeshall, 96, 126
Payn, Rober, joiner, 2
pear trees, 89
Peasants' Revolt, see 98
Peele, Robert, vicar, 76
Pekker, John, carpenter of Cambridge, 102, 1
Pembridge Inn, see 115
Pembroke, Earl and Countess of, 11, 140; see also Valence
　Margaret, Countess of, 129
Pembroke's Inn, 11
Penshurst Place (Kent), 17, 37, 71, 130; see also 114
Pentecost, robe-trimmer (parmentarius), 138
pentices, 76, 111, 150
Pepper Alley (Southwark), Fig. 108
pepperers, 13, 20, 145, 174
Pepysian collection (Magdalen College, Cambridge), 4
Percy, Henry, 2nd Lord, 134
　Henry, 1st Earl of Northumberland, 134
　his son Henry (Hotspur), 134
　Henry, 2nd Earl of Northumberland, 71
　Henry, 4th Earl of Northumberland, 71, 134
Perrers, Alice, 41, 170
Perry, Sir John, 72
Peter, of Kingston, 174
Peter and Paul tavern (Paternoster Row), 54, 65, 79, 103, 115, 135, 146
[St] Peter's Hill, 48–9, 56, 140, 147, Fig. 65a
Petersham (Surrey), 140
Peverell, Richard, 142
pewter, cleaning of, 70
pewterers, 121
Pewterers' Company, 54; Hall, 47, 96, 106, 123, 130, 121; inventories, 128; bowling alley, 91; cistern, 118; kitchen, 118; parlour, 106
Pheasant Court (Cow Lane), 189, Fig. 59a
Philpot Lane, 2, 80, 116, 140, 69, 148, Fig. 91
physicians, 142
Pie (Pye) Corner (Giltspur St), 116, 88, Fig. 62a
pigeons, 235
pigs, 88–9; pigsties, 88; obstructing Walbrook, 6
Pikeman, Adam, fishmonger, 174
pikes and halberds, racks for, 233–4
Pilgrim Street, 11
Pindar, Sir Paul, 102, 111, 119, 149, 28, Figs. 98–9, 115, 125; ceilings, Figs. 137b, 138–9
　Ralph, 28
Pinelli, Caetano, merchant of Genoa, 22
Pinners' Company, Hall, 49
pipe boards, 150
Pistoia (Italy), 38
pits, 31, 138; areas devoid of indicating buildings, 28; for rubbish, 140, Fig. 162; see also cesspits
Plaisterers' Company, Hall, 49
plan, of a building (un patron), 87
planch boards, 142, 150
planks, 142; double-cladding, 143
plans of houses, surviving in documents, 4–5; courtyard-based (Type 4), 34–51; medium-sized houses (Type 3),

51; narrow properties (Type 2), 51–3; small houses (Type 1), 53
plaster, 14, 115, 90, 106, 186; decorated panels, 149, Fig. 99b; see also ceilings
plaster of Paris, 120, 11
Plasterer, Adam le, 11
plasterers, 7
plate, storage of, 49, 74, 139
Plowman, Richard, 26
pointmaker, 50
Pole, Michael de la, 1st Earl of Suffolk, 124, 165
　Michael de la, 2nd Earl of Suffolk, 124
　Sir William de la, merchant, 124
Ponder, Lawrence, and Anne his widow, 109
Pope, John, 196
　Sir Thomas, 25, 105, 144
Pope's Head Alley, 124
Pope's Head tavern (Lombard St), 38, 54, 124
population, of London, estimates, 26
Popyngaye, 81
porches, 61–2, 76, 102, 39, 47, 56, 79, 91, 106, 108, 115, 131, 157, Figs. 44, 255; at Guildhall, 14, 17, 19, Fig. 14
Port of London, 23
portals, 111, 128, 234–5, 145
portcullis, 233, 115; of Bishopsgate, 10
Porter, John, 166
porters, 108, 128; see also lodges, porters'
Porth, John, king's servant, 87, 128–30, 132
portico, 25
portifory, 69
Portland (Dorset), stone from, 135
post-mill, 8
postern gates, 8–9, 11, 30, 41
pots, rack to hang on, 234
potters and pottery making, 7, 87, 108, 8, 10
poultry, 43
Poultry, 62, 149, Fig. 53
Pountney Lane, 90
Poydras, John, clerk, 142
Poyntel, Thomas, goldsmith, 27
Prague (Czech Rep.), 31–2
prentissechaumbre, 66, 71
presses, 129–33, 234–5
priests, 131, 32
Prince Arthur (son of Henry VII), 41
Prince Henry (son of James I), 77
Prince Henry's Room (Fleet St), 1, 119, 77, Fig. 140
Prince of Wales, 41; emblem of feathers, 149, 77; image in tapestry, 129
Prince's Arms, 77
Principal Place, 117
principal posts, 142, 2, 90
printing-house, 134
prior's chamber, 200
prisons, 14; in gates, 11, Fig. 4; for men and women, 193
privacy, 59, 93
privies, 3, 5, 59, 70, 86–7, 234, 2, 35, 40, 62, 76, 85, 87, 89, 110, 141, 143, 146, 149, 152, 162, 164, 173, 175, 177, 181, 183, 191; double, 90; obstructing Walbrook, 6; public, 87; Figs. 48–50, 54, 57–62, 65–6, 70, 75–6, 80, 97, 186–8, 191–3, 199, 202–5, 212–14, 216–18, 220, 236, 238–9, 242, 248–9, 256–7, 259–60, 263; see also cesspits
Privy Council, 59
properties, early development of, 27–31; accretion of, 59; subdivision of, 59, 31, 111; see also boundaries
Prussia, 141
public amenities, buildings and works, 1–2, 14–22, 59
Pudding Lane, 3, 108, 150, Fig. 241
Puddledock, 38
pulley, 235
Pullison, Sir Thomas, mayor, 67
Pulteney, Sir John (de), 71, 90, 138, 114, 169
　Inn of (Pulteney's Inn), 43, 69, 114, Figs. 38, 85a–b, 229
Pump Court (Middle Temple), 78
pumps, 117, 234–5, 115, 128, 145, 166, Figs. 118, 218
puncheons, see studs
Punchon, Richard, carpenter, 128
Purbeck (Dorset) stone/marble, 17, 61, 111, 135, 234, 115; floors, 13, 22; paving, 233–5; walks in garden, 234
purlins, 96; see also roofs, side-purlin
Pykenham, John de, paternosterer, 146

quarries, 7
quarters (timbers), 142, 146; quarter board, 150
Quatremayne, Richard, 142
quays, 160, 193; on Fleet, 80; of stone, 23; see also wharves
Queen Joan's Wardrobe, see Northumberland Inn
Queen Victoria Street, 19, 147
Queenhithe, 12, 14, 21, 87; Saxon, 27; Fig. 17
Querceto, Robert de, see Chesney, Robert de
Quoney, Robard, carpenter, 120, 128

racks, for armour, 234; for buckets, 233; for pikes, 233–4; for saddles, 235; to hang pots on, 234
rafters, 142
ragstone, see stone
rails (balustrade), 234
rainwater, 4, 233, 235